lonely planet

Bhutan

Stan Armington

Bhutan

1st edition

Published by
  Lonely Planet Publications
  Head Office: PO Box 617, Hawthorn, Vic 3122, Australia
  Branches: 150 Linden Street, Oakland, CA 94607, USA
                    10a Spring Place, London NW5 3BH, UK
                    71 bis rue du Cardinal Lemoine, 75005 Paris, France

Printed by
SNP Printing Pte Ltd, Singapore

Photographs by
All of the images in this guide are available for licensing from Lonely Planet Images,
email: lpi@lonelyplanet.com.au

Stan Armington	Richard I'Anson	Nicholas Reuss
Tony Wheeler	Julia Wilkinson	

Front cover: Window shopping in Trongsa, Central Bhutan (Richard I'Anson, Lonely Planet Images)

This Edition
November 1998

**Although the authors and publisher have tried to make the information as
accurate as possible, they accept no responsibility for any loss, injury or
inconvenience sustained by any person using this book.**

National Library of Australia Cataloguing in Publication Data

Armington, Stan.
Bhutan.

Includes index.
ISBN 0 86442 483 3.

1. Bhutan – Guidebooks. I. Title.

915.49804

Stan Armington

Stan Armington started his career as a civil engineer, but after going on a trek in Nepal in 1969 with Tenzing Norgay, his life changed. He worked as a mountain and river guide, first with adventure companies in the United States and later in Nepal, where he now owns and operates one of the larger trekking companies. He has lived for more than 20 years in Nepal, making numerous trips to its remotest areas, and is an authority both on trekking and the Himalaya.

He was one of Lonely Planet's first authors. His guide *Trekking in the Nepal Himalaya* was first published in 1975, and is now in its 7th edition. Stan is a director of the American Himalayan Foundation; fellow of the Royal Geographical Society; and member of the Explorers' Club, American Alpine Club, and the Alpine Stomach Club. He still lives in Kathmandu.

From the Author

I received an enormous amount of assistance with research for this book from both Bhutanese and expatriates in Bhutan. Everyone was eager to help make this book accurate, not to attract more tourists to Bhutan, but to help those who do come to understand this tiny, little known and often misunderstood Buddhist Himalayan kingdom. The biggest thank you is to Tshering Phuntsho, Thuji D Nadik and Sonam Tobgay of the Tourism Authority of Bhutan (TAB) who allowed me to travel throughout the country and provided extensive background information and advice. Lyonpo Om Pradhan, Minister for Trade and Industry, kindly clarified many government policies, as did Lyonpo C Dorji, Planning Minister, and Lyonpo Dawa Tsering, Minister of Foreign Affairs.

Sonam Wangmo and Rinzin Ongdra Wangchuk of Yu-Druk Travels arranged travel facilities and answered an incredible number of questions. Susan Fallon provided much of the original background and reference material. Bob Peirce scoured libraries for out-of-print books and joined Nicholas Reuss and I on the long trek across Bhutan. Cultural background was provided by Sangye Wangchuk of the Special Commission for Cultural Affairs; Dasho Dawa Dem of NWAB; Kunzang Thinley, principal of the National School of Arts and Crafts; Kinley Dorji of Kuensel; Khendum Dorji of Chhundu Travels; Jigme Tsering of Druk Hotel; Yonten Dagye of the National Library; Dago Bena of Etho Metho Tours and Dorji Gyaltshen of the Dzongkha Development Commission.

Environmental and natural history advice was provided by Sangay Wangchuk and Durga Devi Sharma of the Nature Conservation Section; Deki Yonten and Tashi Wangchuk from the Department of National Parks; Hishey Tshering and Mincha Wangdi of RSPN; and Mingma Norbu Sherpa and Kay Kirby of WWF Bhutan.

Additional help was provided by Nima Chhodup Sherpa, Central Statistical Organisation; Sonam Penjor of the Land Use Planning Section; Nado Rinchhen of Kuensel; Dr Paolo Morisco and Dragana Vilinac from the Institute for Indigenous Medicine; and Peter Schmidt. Background of the unusual customs of eastern Bhutan was provided by Lam Kezang of the Rigney Institute in Trashi Yangtse and by Kaka Tshering, Sonam Gyaltshen and Mindup Tshering of Tangmachu high school. Anne Meldgaard, Peter Janssen and Erkki Heinonen of UNHCR and Kanak Dixit of Himal helped with the section on recent history.

Numerous monks and caretakers shared their knowledge of the temples under their charge. Gangte Trulku was especially helpful and Kesang Dorji opened many hidden doors in Bumthang.

Special thanks to Kunzang D Dorji of TAB and Karma Ura of the National Planning Commission for their insightful writings on Bhutanese culture.

Ugyen Rinzin and Jurmin Wangdi of Yangphel Travels, Captain George DeSerres,

Julia Wilkinson, Di McNab, Jim Williams, William Ma and Adam Pain helped with information on trekking routes and Adam also wrote the section on birds. Tandin Tshering and Dorji Wangdi organised some spectacular treks and several drivers transported me back and forth across the country.

Dr David Shlim wrote the medical section to reflect the special needs of travellers and trekkers in Bhutan. Prof. Gerald Clarke at the University of New Brunswick kindly made his geographical research available. The town maps and accurate trek elevations were produced with differentially corrected GPS data thanks to equipment and software provided by Trimble Navigation.

Gerry Moffatt of Equator Expeditions, Peter Knowles and David Alardice of Ultimate Descents provided information about river running. Mike Westmacott searched the Alpine Club database for peak elevations and Ken Hudnut of Cal Tech found the information about the 1897 earthquake. Jungly John reviewed the section on Himalayan Buddhism. Barbara Adams provided material on textiles and Leonard Nadybal helped with information about postage stamps. Brent Olson, Charles Samuelson, Don Messerschmidt, Bob Morgenthaller, Lily Leonard and many more people provided assistance and advice. Michael Slaughter reviewed the text and helped clarify many points.

Thanks to Roger Williams of Snow Lion Graphics for permission to reproduce several quotations from *Lands of the Thunderbolt: Sikhim, Chumbi & Bhutan* by the Earl of Ronaldshay.

From the Publisher

This 1st edition was edited by Martin Hughes of Lonely Planet's Melbourne office. Paul Piaia put the book through mapping, design and layout with boundless joie de vivre. Together, they had a hoot.

Sally Dillon assisted with editing, and Diana Saad provided the proofing filter before moving on to bigger and better things. Mark Germanchis helped out with mapping, Simon Bracken designed the cover and Sarah Jolly provided the scratch-style illustrations.

Thanks to Leonie for being generally great and making everyone's job at Lonely Planet a whole phew! easier. Thanks to Andrew for technical patience, Andy for pocket money, Stan for his enthusiasm, SBS for the World Cup coverage, and Cal for being in the right place all the time.

Warning & Request

Bhutan is in a process of change and modernisation and many of these changes will affect rules and facilities for travellers. A new airport terminal is under construction; Druk Air is looking for ways to enhance its international service; the government is actively developing new towns to reduce migration to the capital and Taktshang monastery will soon be rebuilt in the same style as its previous incarnation. Thimphu and Mongar are to undergo major changes as part of a town planning process and new restaurants and hotels will open and existing facilities will be renovated. It's even possible that there will be a domestic air service.

So, if you find things better or worse, recently opened or long since closed, please tell us and help make the next edition even more accurate and useful.

We value all of the feedback we receive from travellers. Julie Young coordinates a small team who read and acknowledge every letter, postcard and email, and ensure that every morsel of information finds its way to the appropriate authors, editors and Lonely Planet publishers.

Everyone who writes to us will find their name in the next edition of the appropriate guide and will also receive a free subscription to our quarterly newsletter, Planet Talk. The very best contributions will be rewarded with a free Lonely Planet guide.

Excerpts from your correspondence may appear in new editions of this guide; in our newsletter, Planet Talk; or in updates on our Web site – so please let us know if you don't want your letter published or your name acknowledged.

Contents

Map Legend

BOUNDARIES

▪—▪—▪—▪—▪	.... International Boundary
—·—·—·—·—	.... Administrative Boundary

ROUTES

——————	.... Major Road
——————	.... Minor Road
– – – – –	.... Minor Road - Unsealed
==================	.... Town Road
==================	.... Town Street
==================	.... Town Lane
– – – – –	.... Walking Track
==========	.... Specified Trekking Route
▪+▪+▪+▪+▪+▪	.... Ropeway

AREA FEATURES

▓▓▓▓▓	.... Building
░░░░░	.... Market
✿	.... Park, Gardens
▓▓▓▓▓	.... Urban Area

HYDROGRAPHIC FEATURES

~~	.... Coastline
~~	.... Creek, River
◯ ◯	.... Lake, Intermittent Lake
»»))− ⊂	.... Rapids, Waterfalls
◯	.... Salt Lake

SYMBOLS

✪ **CAPITAL**	.... National Capital	✈	.... Airport	🏛	.... Museum
◉ **Capital**	Administrative Capital	∿	... Ancient or City Wall	♟	.... National Park
● **Town**	.... Large Town	⸫	...... Archeological Site	←	.... One Way Street
● Town	.... Town or Village	❸	.... Bank	🏛	.... Palace
		⌒	.... Cave	🅿	.... Parking
		⚲	.... Chorten	)(	.... Pass
■	.... Place to Stay	🈁	.... Church	⛽	.... Petrol Station
🅰	.... Camping Area	⌢	... Cliff or Escarpment	○	.... Point of Interest
		🏯	.... Dzong	★	.... Police Station
▼	.... Place to Eat	◔	.... Embassy	✉	.... Post Office
🍺	.... Bar	⌦	Goemba or Lhakhang		.... Ridge
		⚑	.... Golf Course	❖	.... Shopping Centre
		⊕	.... Hospital	◎	.... Spring
		🈂	.... Lookout	☎	.... Telephone
		⚣	.... Monument	❶	.... Tourist Information
		▲	.... Mountain or Hill	⊖	.... Transport

Note: not all symbols displayed above appear in this book

Introduction

'With our passage through the bridge, behold a curious transformation. For just as Alice, when she walked through the looking-glass, found herself in a new and whimsical world, so we, when we crossed the Pa-chhu, found ourselves, as though caught up on some magic time machine fitted fantastically with a reverse, flung back across the centuries into the feudalism of a mediaeval age.'

**The Earl of Ronaldshay, 1921,
describing his arrival in Bhutan**

Bhutan is not an ordinary place. It has one foot in the past and one in the future. Its far-sighted leaders recognise the necessity of being part of the modern world, but they realise that once their forests and culture are destroyed, they can never be recovered. They have maintained a very traditional culture, yet they have adapted what they need from modern technology. Thus you'll find monks transcribing ancient Buddhist texts into computers and traditionally dressed archers using the most modern high-tech bows and arrows.

It is a country of rolling hills and towering crags, with only small patches of cultivation and very little deforestation. There are no massive landslides as there are in other parts of the Himalaya. Bhutan is often compared to Switzerland, not only because their sizes are similar, but also because many parts of Bhutan look like the Swiss Alps, with green hills, houses that look like chalets and snow peaks sticking out of nowhere.

Bhutan has many surprises and a visit to the country is a splendid adventure. The standard of English is excellent, and you can

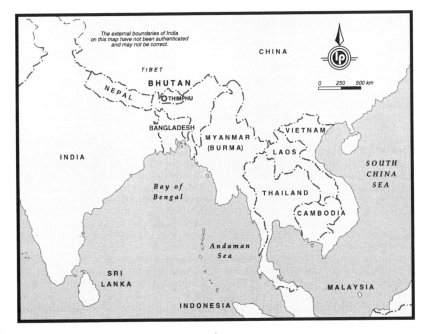

easily converse with schoolchildren and educated people. The Bhutanese are very curious about life outside of their mountain kingdom and are eager to hear stories about your country and how you live.

There are western-style hotels and food throughout the country, but the best facilities are in Thimphu, the capital, and the town of Paro where the airport is. If you travel to eastern Bhutan, be prepared for some rougher hotels and less westernised meals. To see the best of Bhutan, you should spend a week or more on foot, trekking through the great forested wilderness that covers most of the country.

Facts & Myths

Bhutan is a land replete with myths and legends, and many tales contribute to its reputation of being an impossible place to visit. While certainly isolated and remote, it is not a difficult place to travel to, and you do not need any special influence or 'pull'. Subject to some well-defined restrictions, it is actually easy and comfortable to arrange a trip to Bhutan. You can even arrange a journey as an independent traveller; you do not have to travel in a group. It takes time to arrange a visa, but if you fax the information to Bhutan, you can set up a trip with as little as 10 days advance planning.

There is no quota or limit on the number of tourists allowed to visit Bhutan; as long as the government is not overwhelmed with visitors, you will be welcomed as an honoured guest.

It's a little-known country, and not much information is available. Sometimes it is inaccurately described as a 'living museum'. It does visibly maintain its traditions, but its temples, monasteries and cultural centres are active and viable institutions that are very much a part of the modern world. It is not a nation of saintly, ascetic, other-worldly monks; you will find Bhutan to be full of active, well-educated, fun-loving and vibrant people.

There are numerous contradictions in the various sources that describe Bhutan's history. Facts and figures are often missing or

Say What?

Before you arrive in Bhutan we recommend you read the pronunciation guide in the Language chapter. There are some unusual sounds in Dzongkha and it's worth taking a few minutes to learn how to pronounce such seeming tongue-twisters as *ngultrum* (the unit of currency) and Trashigang (the town). A basic knowledge will help you read this book and understand your guide better.

confused. There is no authoritative list of place names, no list of mountain peaks, and population figures are based on estimates. The statistics and description of historical events presented here are based on the most authoritative and credible reference materials, but many of these 'facts' are open to interpretation. Much of the information about temples, monuments and local history was provided by monks, caretakers and school teachers who do not always agree with each other – or with the history books – about events, dates and other information.

Many issues and historical events are described from a Bhutanese perspective. Most of these are religious beliefs and folk tales, but there are also a few controversial political and social issues. Other governments and international organisations have very different opinions about some of these subjects. There is no need to belabour these differences or to argue either viewpoint. The Bhutanese are quite open, and they point out that you are most welcome to come to Bhutan and see things for yourself. If you do so, you will find that people are willing to discuss their culture and problems, and you can then draw your own conclusions.

This book provides an insight into the underlying cultural identity of the Bhutanese people that will, hopefully, help you to understand the reasons why they have developed their opinions and have formulated their unusual rules for foreign visitors.

A basic understanding of Bhutan's Bhuddism is essential to understanding the Bhutanese. Our description of religion is presented in lay terms, and is not intended as a scholarly treatise. Buddhist scholars and practitioners should look to the reference works in the book list for a complete explanation though the definitive sources are published only in Dzongkha.

Finally, travel within Bhutan can be difficult and frustrating. It is always an adventure, because the unexpected continually happens. Sometimes this utter fortuitousness causes problems. Other times the surprises are the joy of friendship, understanding or unsurpassed beauty that will bring you back again and again. If you visit Bhutan, you will become one of the few who have experienced the charm and magic of the country and may become a proponent of the kingdom's tourism policy and its efforts to maintain its identity.

Facts about Bhutan

HISTORY

Bhutan's early history is steeped in Buddhist tradition and mythology. It's said that a saint who had the ability to appear in eight different forms visited Bhutan and left the imprint of his body and his hat on rocks. Bhutanese schoolbooks describe demons that threatened villages and destroyed temples until they were captured through magic and converted to Buddhism. Tales abound of ghosts who destroyed temples, and angels who rebuilt them. Another story tells of a saint who flew on the back of a tiger and turned into a garuda, a bird that is a distant relative of the griffin.

The kingdom's more recent history is no less amazing, with intrigue, treachery, fierce battles and extraordinary pageantry all playing an important part.

Researchers have attached dates to many mythological historic events, though these often do not seem to fit together into a credible and accurate chronology. When reading Bhutanese history, it's easier to let your imagination flow: try visualising the spirit of the happenings rather than rationalising events as historical truth. This will, in part, help prepare you for a visit to Bhutan, where spirits, ghosts, yetis, medicine men, and lamas reincarnated in three different bodies are accepted as a part of daily life.

Bhutan's medieval and modern history is better documented than its ancient history, but no less exotic. This is a time of warlords, feuds, giant fortresses and castles. The country's recent history begins with a hereditary monarchy that was founded in the 20th century and continued the country's policy of isolationism. It was under the leadership of the third king that Bhutan emerged from its medieval past of serfdom and reclusion. Until the 1960s the country had no national currency, and no telephones, schools, hospitals, postal service or tourists. Development efforts have now produced all these – plus a

national assembly, airport, roads and a national system of health care. Despite the speed of modernisation, Bhutan has maintained a policy of careful, controlled growth in an effort to preserve its national identity. The government has also limited its acceptance of tourism, television and satellite dishes.

Early History

Many of the important events in the country's early history involved saints and religious leaders and were therefore chronicled only in scriptures. Most of these original documents were destroyed in fires in the printing works of Sonagatsel in 1828 and in Punakha Dzong in 1832. Much of what was left in the old capital of Punakha was lost in an earthquake in 1897 and more records were lost when Paro Dzong burned in 1907. Therefore much of the early history of Bhutan relies on reports from British explorers, on legend and folklore, and on a

Origin of the Name 'Bhutan'

Few agree on the origin of the name Bhutan. It may have evolved from the Sanskrit 'Bhotant', meaning 'the end of Tibet', or from 'Bhu-uttan' meaning 'high land'. Early British explorers called it Bootan or Bhotan, and they believed the name derived from 'Bhotsthan', meaning 'land of the Bhotias' (Bhotia is Sanskrit for people from Tibet). Whatever the origin, the name evolved into the current form of Bhutan, and the people are known as Bhutanese.

Though known as Bhutan to the outside world, the country has been known as Druk Yul, 'land of the thunder dragon', to its inhabitants since the 13th century. The people call themselves Drukpa, and their religion is the Drukpa Kagyupa lineage of Mahayana Buddhism.

few manuscripts which were safely preserved in monasteries.

Archeological evidence suggests Bhutan was inhabited as early as 1500 BC, or possibly even 2000 BC. Its first inhabitants were nomadic herders who lived in low-lying valleys in winter and moved their animals to high pastures in summer; many Bhutanese still live this way today. The river valleys of Bhutan provided relatively easy access across the Himalaya, and it is believed that the Manas River Valley was used as a migration route from India to Tibet.

India influenced Bhutan from the early days: particularly the kingdom of Cooch Behar in what is now the Indian state of West Bengal. Indian rulers established themselves in Bhutan, but their influence faded in the 7th century as the influence of Tibet grew after the introduction of Buddhism.

Some of the early inhabitants of Bhutan were followers of Bon, an animistic tradition that was the main religion throughout the Himalayan region before the advent of Buddhism. It is believed that the Bon religion was introduced in Bhutan in the 6th century.

Buddhism was probably introduced to Bhutan as early as the 2nd century, although historians say the first Buddhist temples were built only in the 7th century. The story of the construction of these temples is an interesting one.

The Tibetan king, Songtsen Gampo, who ruled from 627 to 649, declared Buddhism the state religion of Tibet. But a demoness lay across the whole land, preventing the spread of the religion and interfering with the construction of the Jokhang cathedral in Lhasa. The king decided to construct 108 temples throughout the Himalayan region in a single day to pin down the demoness and pacify the region. In that flurry of construction several temples were built in Bhutan. Of these, two are believed to pin down important parts of the demoness: Jambey Lhakhang in Bumthang pins her left knee and Kyichu Lhakhang in Paro holds her left foot. These temples still exist and are im-

portant pilgrimage sites. (See the boxed text 'The Ogress in Tibet' in the Western Bhutan chapter.)

Visits of Padmasambhava
In 746 Sendha Gyab, the king of Bumthang, had a conflict with another Indian king in the south of Bhutan. As a result of this dispute, Sendha Gyab became possessed by a demon, and it required a powerful tantric master to exorcise it. The greatest master was the teacher Padmasambhava, better known as Guru Rimpoche (precious master). Sendha Gyab's secretary eventually found Padmasambhava meditating in the cave of Ugyen Dag in Bhutan's southern region of Khyeng and invited him to Bumthang.

After an extended process involving trickery and magic dances, the Guru captured the demon and converted it to Buddhism. For good measure, he also converted the king and his rival, restoring the country to peace. (For a complete description of Padmasambhava's exploits, see the boxed text 'The Story of Kurjey Lhakhang' in the Central Bhutan chapter.)

The first visit of Guru Rimpoche to Bumthang is recognised as the true introduction of Buddhism to Bhutan.

He left an impression of his body on the rock upon which he meditated near the head of the Choskhor valley in Bumthang. On this site the temple of Kurjey Lhakhang was built, and Guru Rimpoche's body print can still be seen.

On the Guru's second trip to Bhutan he visited the districts of Bumthang, Mongar and Lhuentse. At Gom Kora, in eastern Bhutan, he left another body print and an impression of his head with a hat. After establishing the monastery of Singye Dzong in Lhuentse, he flew in the form of Dorji Droloe (one of his eight manifestations) to Taktshang in Paro on a flaming tigress, giving the famous Taktshang monastery the name 'Tiger's Nest' (see Taktshang Monastery in the Around Paro section of the Western Bhutan chapter).

It is believed that Guru Rimpoche also made a third visit to Bhutan during the reign

Guru Rimpoche

Guru Rimpoche is also known by the names Padmasambhava, Precious Master and Ugyen Rimpoche. *Padma* is a Sanskrit word meaning lotus flower and is the origin of the Tibetan and Bhutanese name Pema; *sambhava* means 'born from'. He is a historical figure of the eighth century, and his birth was predicted by the Buddha Sakyamuni. He is regarded as the second Buddha and had miraculous powers, including the ability to subdue demons and evil spirits.

Guru Rimpoche is credited with many other magical deeds and is regarded as the founder of Nyingma Buddhism. He is one of the most important of Bhutan's religious figures and his visit to Bumthang is recognised as the true introduction of Buddhism to Bhutan. He left an impression of his body on the rock upon which he meditated near the head of the Choskhor Valley in Bumthang. On this site the temple of Kurjey Lhakhang was built, and Guru Rimpoche's body print may still be seen there. His statue appears in almost all temples built after his visit to Bhutan in 746 AD.

His birthplace is Uddiyana in the Swat Valley of what is now Pakistan. Uddiyana is known in Dzongkha as Ugyen, and some texts refer to him as Ugyen Rimpoche. He travelled in various manifestations throughout Tibet, Nepal and Bhutan, meditating in numerous caves, which are regarded as important power places. He preserved his teachings and wisdom by concealing them in the form of *terma* (hidden treasures) to be found by enlightened treasure discoverers called *tertons*. His biographer urges us not to regard Guru Rimpoche as a normal human being, because by doing so we will fail to perceive even a fraction of his enlightened qualities.

Bhutanese and Tibetans differ over a few aspects of his life; the following description reflects the Bhutanese tradition.

Eight Manifestations The Guru is depicted in eight forms (*Guru Tshen-gay*). These are not really different incarnations, but representations of his eight main initiations, in which he assumed a new personality that was symbolised by a new name and appearance. Because initiation is equivalent to entering a new life, it is a form of rebirth. The eight forms follow the chronology of Guru Rimpoche's life.

He was born as an 8-year-old, from a blue lotus on the Lake Danakosha in Uddiyana, and was invited to become the son of King Indrabodhi. Then he was called *Tshokye Dorji* (diamond thunderbolt born from a lake). He later renounced his kingdom and went to receive teachings and ordination from the master Prabhahasti in the cave of Maratrika (near the village of Harishe in eastern Nepal), becoming *Shakya Senge* (lion of the Shakya clan). In this form Padmasambhava is identified with Sakyamuni, the historical Buddha.

After studying the teachings of the Vajrayana and mastering the sciences of all Indian Pandits, he obtained full realisation and was able to see all the gods and deities. Then he was called *Loden*

of the Tibetan king, Muthri Tsenpo, the son of Trisong Detsen.

Medieval Period

The grandson of Trisong Detsen, Langdarma, ruled Tibet from 836 to 842. He banned Buddhism, destroyed religious institutions and banished his brother, prince Tsangma, to Bhutan. It is believed that many monks fled from Tibet and took refuge in Bhutan during this period. Despite the assasination of Langdarma and the re-introduction of Buddhism, Tibet remained in political turmoil and many Tibetans migrated to Bhutan and settled in the western part of the country.

Between the 9th and 17th centuries numerous ruling clans and noble families emerged in different valleys throughout Bhutan. The various local chieftains spent their energy quarrelling among themselves

Chogsey (possessor of supreme knowledge). He took as his consort Mandarava, the daughter of the king of Zahor (in the Mandi district of Himachal Pradesh, India). This enraged the king, who condemned them both to be burned, but through his powers the Guru turned the pyre into a lake and converted the kingdom to Buddhism. Then he was called *Padmasambhava*.

He returned to Uddiyana to convert it to Buddhism, but was recognised as the prince who had renounced his kingdom and was again burned, along with his consort. He was not consumed by the fire and appeared sitting upon a lotus in a lake. This lake is Rewalsar, also called *Tsho Pema* (the lotus lake), in Himachal Pradesh and is an important pilgrimage spot. His father, King Indrabodhi, offered him the kingdom and he became *Padma Gyalpo* (the lotus king), remaining for 13 years and establishing Buddhism.

When he was preaching in the eight cremation grounds to the *khandroma* (female celestial beings), he caught the life force of the evil deities and he turned them into protectors of Buddhism. Then he was called *Nyima Yeozer* (sunbeam of enlightenment). Later, 500 heretic masters tried to destroy the doctrine of Buddha, but he vanquished them through the power of his words and brought down a thunderbolt destroying the non-Buddhists in a flash of hail and lightning. He was then called *Sengye Dradrok* (roaring lion).

When he came to Bhutan the second time and visited Singye Dzong in Kurtoe and Taktshang in Paro, he was in the form of *Dorji Drakpo* (fierce thunderbolt). He subdued all the evil spirits who hindered Buddhism and blessed them as guardians of the doctrine. In this form, Guru Rimpoche rides a tigress.

Statues of Guru Rimpoche Most statues of Guru Rimpoche are in his manifestation as Padmasambhava, wearing his royal robes and holding the insignia of spiritual realisation. His hat is known as the 'lotus cap' and is adorned with a crescent moon, the sun, and a small flame-like protuberance that signifies the union of lunar and solar forces. The hat is surmounted by a *dorji* (thunderbolt) and also an eagle's feather, which represents the Guru's soaring mind, penetrating the highest realms of reality.

Most statues of Padmasambhava are flanked by statues of two female devotees. These are the Indian princess *Mandarava*, the lady of wisdom, and the Tibetan khandroma *Yeshe Tsogyal*, who is regarded as an incarnation of Sarasvati, the goddess of knowledge. She was gifted with such a perfect memory that she was able to remember the Guru's every word and became Padmasambhava's sole biographer. She is depicted as a white heavenly being with traditional ornaments and flying scarves; Mandarava is usually depicted as an Indian hill princess.

Guru Rimpoche's celestial abode or heaven is named *Zangto Pelri*. The four gates are guarded by the four guardian kings, and in the centre is a three-roofed pagoda, with Guru Rimpoche enthroned on the ground level, flanked by his two consorts.

and with Tibet, and no important nationally recognised political figure emerged during this period.

The Bhutanese Form of Buddhism
Back in Tibet, Lama Tsangpa Gyare Yeshe Dorji founded a monastery in the town of Ralung, just east of Gyantse, in 1180. He named the monastery Druk (Dragon), after the thunder dragons that he heard in the sky as he searched for an appropriate site upon which to build a monastery. The lineage followed here was named after the monastery and became known as Drukpa Kagyu.

In the 11th and 12th centuries there was a further large influx of Tibetans into Bhutan. Many Drukpa lamas left Tibet because of persecution at the hands of the rival Gelugpas. Most of these lamas settled in the western part of Bhutan and established branches of Drukpa monastic orders. Western Bhutan became loosely united through the weight of their teachings. Charismatic lamas emerged as de facto leaders of large portions of the west, while the isolated valleys of eastern and central Bhutan remained separate feudal states.

One of the most important of these lamas was Gyelwa Lhanangpa, who founded the Lhapa Kagyu lineage. He established Tango monastery on a hill above the northern end of the Thimphu valley and established a system of forts in Bhutan similar to that found in Tibet. These forts were called *dzongs*, but they were strictly defensive structures and were different from the present-day Bhutanese dzongs, which serve as monasteries and government offices as well as being forts.

Lama Phajo Drukgom Shigpo (1184-1251), a disciple of Lama Tsangpa Gyare, came to Bhutan from Ralung and defeated Lama Lhanangpa. He and his companions established a small dzong named Dohon Dzong on the west bank of the Wang Chhu and took control of Tango monastery. Lama Phajo is credited with establishing the Bhutanese form of Buddhism by converting many people to the practice of the Drukpa Kagyu school. His presence and success was resented by other lamas and they tried to kill him through magic spells. Phajo turned the spells back on the lamas, destroying several of their monasteries.

Many Bhutanese nobles are descended from Lama Phajo. Between the 13th and 16th centuries, the Drukpa Kagyu lineage flourished and Bhutan adopted a separate religious identity. Many more lamas from Ralung were invited to Bhutan to teach and build monasteries.

Among the visitors to Bhutan during this period was a lama named Ngawang Choegyal. He made several trips and was often accompanied by his sons, who established several *goembas* (Buddhist monasteries). They are credited with building the temple of Druk Choeding in Paro and Pangri Zampa and Hongtsho goembas near Thimphu. Another visitor was Lama Drukpa Kunley, the divine madman, who lived from 1455 to 1529 and established Chime Lhakhang near Punakha.

Between the 11th and 16th centuries numerous *terma* (sacred treasures) hidden by Guru Rimpoche in caves, rocks and lakes were discovered, as he had prophesied, by tantric lamas called *tertons*. The tertons were important religious figures: the best known of these was Pema Lingpa, who recovered his first treasure from the lake of Membartsho near Bumthang in 1475. Pema Lingpa constructed several monasteries in Bumthang and is one of the most important figures in Bhutanese history. (For more information see the boxed text 'Terton Pema Lingpa' in the Central Bhutan chapter.)

The Unification of Bhutan

By the 16th century the political arena was still fragmented between many local chiefs, each controlling his own territory and engaging in petty feuds with the others. There were numerous monasteries competing for superiority, and the lamas of western Bhutan were working to extend their influence to the east of the country.

The whole scene changed in 1616 when another monk from Ralung, the original home of the Drukpa Kagyu in Tibet, came to Bhutan. This was Ngawang Namgyal, who lived from 1594 to 1651. In his early years he studied religion and art and is said to have been a skilled painter. He was a descendent of Yeshe Dorji, the founder of Ralung. At age 12 he was recognised as the reincarnation of Pema Karpo, the prince-abbot of Ralung monastery. This recognition was challenged by the ruler of another principality in Tibet, and Ngawang Namgyal found his position at Ralung very difficult. When he was 23, the deity Yeshey Goenpo (Mahakala) appeared to him in the form of a raven and directed him south to Bhutan.

As Ngawang Namgyal travelled throughout western Bhutan teaching, his political strength increased. Soon he established himself as the religious ruler of Bhutan with the title Shabdrung Rimpoche (Precious Jewel at Whose Feet One Prostrates), thus becoming the first in the line of Shabdrungs. He

Light and shade in Bhutan
Clockwise from top: awaiting inspiration; a family stroll; school's out in Thimphu; and a holy man divines wisdom.

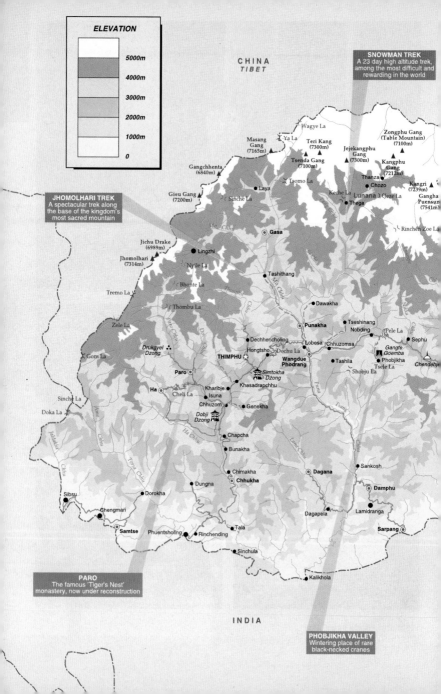

ELEVATION

5000m
4000m
3000m
2000m
1000m
0

CHINA
TIBET

SNOWMAN TREK
A 23 day high altitude trek, among the most difficult and rewarding in the world

Wagye La

Masang Gang (7165m)

Ya La

Teri Kang (7300m)

Zongphu Gang (Table Mountain) (7100m)

Jejekangphu Gang (7300m)

Kangphu Gang (7212m)

Gangchhenta (6840m)

Tsenda Gang (7100m)

Tsomo La

Thanza

Chozo

Kangri (7239m)

Gieu Gang (7200m)

Sinche La

Laya

Keche La

Lunana

Jeze La

Gangha Puensum (7541m)

JHOMOLHARI TREK
A spectacular trek along the base of the kingdom's most sacred mountain

Thega

Rinchen Zoe La

Jichu Drake (6989m)

Lingzhi

Gasa

Mo Chhu

Jhomolhari (7314m)

Nyile La

Tremo La

Bhonte La

Tashithang

Mo Chhu

Thombu La

Dawakha

Zele La

Tseshinang

Nobding

Pele La

Gom La

Drukgyel Dzong

Dechhencholing

Punakha

Lobesa

Chhuzomsa

Sephu

Hongtsho

Dochu La

Wangdue Phodrang

Gangte Goemba

Chendebji

Paro

THIMPHU

Simtokha Dzong

Tashila

Phobjikha

Tsele La

Ha

Cheli La

Kharibje

Khasadrapchhu

Shobju La

Isuna

Sinche La

Chhuzom

Genekha

Doka La

Dobji Dzong

Chapcha

Bunakha

Sankosh

Chimakha

Dagana

Damphu

Sibsu

Dungna

Chhukha

Dorokha

Chengmari

Dagapela

Lamidranga

Samtse

Phuentsholing

Rinchending

Tala

Sarpang

Sinchula

Kalikhola

PARO
The famous 'Tiger's Nest' monastery, now under reconstruction

INDIA

PHOBJIKHA VALLEY
Wintering place of rare black-necked cranes

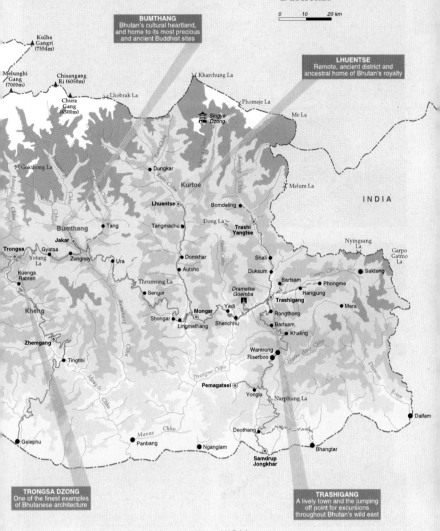

CHINA
TIBET

Bhutan

0   10   20 km

BUMTHANG
Bhutan's cultural heartland,
and home to its most precious
and ancient Buddhist sites

LHUENTSE
Remote, ancient district and
ancestral home of Bhutan's royalty

Kulha
Gang
(7554m)

Melunghi
Gang
(7000m)

Chisangang
Ri (6050m)

Lhobrak La

Chura
Gang
(6500m)

Kharchung La

Phomeje La

Me La

Singye
Dzong

Gokthong La

Dungkar

Kurtoe

Melum La

INDIA

Mangde Chhu

Kuri Chhu

Kulong Chhu

Lhuentse

Bomdeling

Nyingsang
La

Garpo
Gatmo
La

Bumthang

Tang

Tangmachu

Dong La

Trashi
Yangtse

Jakar

Gyatsa

Trongsa

Yotang
La

Zungney

Ura

Domkhar

Shali

Sakteng

Kuenga
Rabten

Thrumsing La

Autsho

Duksum

Bartsam

Phongme

Drametse
Goemba

Rangjung

Sengor

Yadi

Trashigang

Mera

Kheng

Shongar

Mongar

Sherichhu

Rongthong

Lingmethang

Bartsam

Zhemgang

Khaling

Tingtibi

Wamrong

Riserboo

Drangme Chhu

Nyera Amy Chhu

Dhansiri
River

Pemagatsel

Yongla

Narphung La

Mangde Chhu

Manas Chhu

Deothang

Daifam

Gelephu

Panbang

Nganglam

Bhangtar

Samdrup
Jongkhar

INDIA

TRONGSA DZONG
One of the finest examples
of Bhutanese architecture

TRASHIGANG
A lively town and the jumping
off point for excursions
throughout Bhutan's wild east

TONY WHEELER

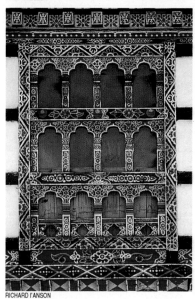

RICHARD I'ANSON

NICHOLAS REUSS

Ornamental decoration complements all Bhutanese architecture. Wooden surfaces are painted with various shapes including swastikas, floral patterns representing the lotus, cloud whirls and the eight auspicious symbols.

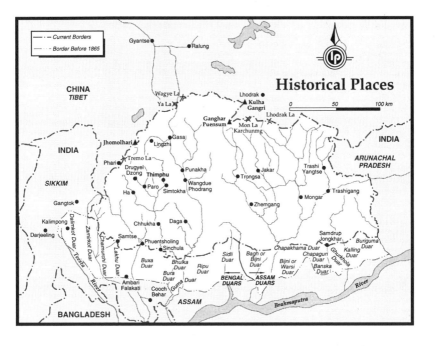

built the first system of dzongs at Simtokha, just south of present-day Thimphu. While the primary function of earlier Bhutanese dzongs was to serve as an invincible fortress, the Simtokha Dzong also housed a monastic body and administrative facilities as well as fulfiling its defensive function. This combination of civil, religious and defensive functions became the model for all of Bhutan's later dzongs.

The Shabdrung's rule was opposed by the leaders of rival Buddhist lineages within Bhutan. They formed a coalition of five lamas under the leadership of Lama Palden and attacked Simtokha Dzong in 1629. This attack was repelled, but the five-lama coalition then aligned themselves with a group of Tibetans and continued their opposition. The Shabdrung's militia defeated the Tibetans on several occasions, and the influence of the rival lineages diminished. Finally, after forging an alliance with the brother of King Singye Namgyal of Ladakh, the Shabdrung's forces defeated the Tibetans and their five-lama allies. In 1639 an agreement was reached with the Tsang Desi in Tibet recognising Shabdrung Ngawang Namgyal as the supreme authority in Bhutan.

The Shabdrung further enhanced his power by establishing relations with neighbouring kings, including Rama Shah, the king of Nepal, and Raja Padmanarayan of Cooch Behar. It was at this time that the king of Ladakh granted the Shabdrung a number of villages in western Tibet for the purpose of meditation and worship. These included Darchen, Nyanri and Zuthulphuk goembas on the slopes of the holy Mount Kailas. The Bhutanese administration of these goembas continued until the Chinese takeover of Tibet in 1959. Other goembas that came under Bhutanese administration were Rimpung, Doba, Khochag, and De Dzong, all near Gartok. A Bhutanese lama was sent as representative to Nepal, and Bhutanese monasteries were established at Boudhanath (Chorten Jaro Khasho) and Swayambunath in Kathmandu. Bhutan administered Swayambunath until after the Nepal-Tibet war of 1854-56, when it was seized back by Nepal, on the suspicion that Bhutan had helped the Tibetans.

During his reign, Shabdrung Ngawang Namgyal ordered the construction of many monasteries and dzongs throughout Bhutan. Of these, the dzongs at Simtokha, Paro, Punakha and Trongsa are still standing. He established the first *sangha* (community of monks) at Chari Goemba near Thimphu. When Punakha Dzong was completed in 1635, the sangha was moved there and became the central monk body, headed by a supreme abbot called the *Je Khenpo*.

Invasions From Tibet

In the meantime, strife continued in Tibet, between the Nyingma (known as red hat) group of Buddhists and the Gelugpas (yellow hat), who are now headed by the Dalai Lama. The Mongol chief Gushri Khan, a patron of the Dalai Lama, led his army in an attack on Tibet's Tsang province, where he overthrew the Rinpong dynasty and established the supremacy of the Gelugpas in the region.

In 1644 the Mongols and Tibetans, who were used to the extremely high plains of Tibet, launched an assault from Lhodrok into Bumthang, but found themselves overpowered by the forests and relative heat of Bhutan. Shabdrung Ngawang Namgyal personally led the successful resistance and several Tibetan officers and a large number of horses were captured. Much of the armour and many weapons that were taken during this battle are on display in Punakha Dzong. Drukgyel Dzong was built at the head of Paro valley in 1647 to commemorate the victory and to preclude any further Tibetan infiltration.

One of the strongest of Tibet's Dalai Lamas was the 'Great Fifth'. During his administration, he became jealous of the growing influence of the rival Drukpas on

his southern border and mounted further invasions into Bhutan in 1648 and 1649. Each attempt was launched via Phari in Tibet, from where the Great Fifth's forces crossed the 5000m high Tremo La pass into Paro valley. They were repelled, and again the Bhutanese captured large amounts of armour, weapons and other spoils. Some of this booty may still be seen in the National Museum (Ta Dzong) in Paro. Legend relates that the Shabdrung built a *thos*, a heap of stones representing the kings of the four directions, to subdue the Tibetan army. You may not find this one, but similar thos can still be seen in the courtyards of many of Bhutan's goembas.

Shabdrung Ngawang Namgyal's success in repelling the Tibetan attacks further consolidated his position as ruler. The large militia that he raised for the purpose also gave him effective control of the country. Mingyur Tenpa, who was appointed by the Shabdrung as *penlop* (governor) of Trongsa, undertook a campaign to unite all the valleys of the central and eastern parts of the country under the Shabdrung's rule, which he accomplished by about 1655. At this time the great dzongs of Jakar, Lhuentse, Trashi Yangtse, Shongar (now Mongar), Trashigang and Zhemgang were constructed.

In 1668 Mingyur Tenpa was enthroned as the third *desi* (secular ruler). He ruled for 12 years, during which time he extended the boundaries of Bhutan westward to Kalimpong, which is now part of India.

A Bhutanese Identity Emerges

The Shabdrung realised that Bhutan needed to differentiate itself from Tibet in order to preserve its religion and cultural identity. He devised many of Bhutan's customs, traditions and ceremonies in a deliberate effort to develop a unique cultural identity for the country.

As a revered Buddhist scholar, he had both the astuteness and authority to codify the Kagyu religious teachings into a system that was distinctively Bhutanese. He also defined the national dress and instituted the festival of *tsechu*.

The Shabdrung created a code of laws that defined the relationship between the lay people and the monastic community. A system of taxes was developed; these were paid in kind in the form of wheat, buckwheat, rice, yak meat, butter, paper, timber and clothing. The people were subject to a system of compulsory labour for the construction of trails, dzongs, temples and bridges. These practices lasted almost unchanged until the third king eliminated the practice in 1956.

In the 1640s the Shabdrung created the system of Choesi, the separation of the administration of the country into two offices. The religious and spiritual aspects of the country were handled by the Shabdrung. The political, administrative, and foreign affairs aspects of the government were to be handled by the desi, who was elected to the post. The office of the Shabdrung theoretically had greater power, including the authority to sign documents relating to an important matter within the government. Under the system at that time, the Shabdrung was the spiritual ruler and the Je Khenpo was the chief abbot and official head of the monastic establishment. The Je Khenpo had a status equal to the desi and sometimes held that office.

The first desi was Tenzin Drugyey (1591-1656), one of the monks who came with Ngawang Namgyal from Ralung monastery. He established a system of administration throughout the country, formalising the position of penlop as that of provincial governor. There were initially three districts: Trongsa in the centre, Paro in the west and Dagana in the south. The penlops became the representatives of the central government, which was then in Punakha. There were three officers called *dzongpen* (lord of the dzong) who looked after the affairs of the sub districts of Punakha, Thimphu and Wangdue Phodrang.

Shabdrung Ngawang Namgyal went into retreat in Punakha Dzong in 1651. He didn't emerge again, and although it is likely that he passed away very early in the period of retreat, his death remained concealed until

1705. It is believed that the four successive desis who ruled during this period felt that the continued presence of the Shabdrung was necessary to keep the country unified and to keep Tibet at bay. Nonetheless, Tibet mounted seven attacks on Bhutan between 1656 and 1730.

Civil Wars

When the abbot of the monastic body, the Je Khenpo, finally announced the death of the Shabdrung in 1705, he said that three rays of light emanated from the Shabdrung's body, representing the *ku sung thug* (body, speech and mind) of Ngawang Namgyal. This indicated that the Shabdrung would be reincarnated in these three forms, though only the reincarnation of the Shabdrung's mind was considered to be the head of state. Because the position of Shabdrung was a continuing one, it was necessary for the mind incarnation to be reborn after the death of the previous incarnation.

This structure resulted in long periods when the Shabdrung was too young to rule and the desi often became the de facto ruler. Because the desi was an elected position, there was considerable rivalry among various factions for the office. These factions also took advantage of uncertainty over which of the three incarnations of the Shabdrung was the 'true' incarnation. None of the successive incarnations had the personal charisma or political astuteness of Ngawang Namgyal.

The next 200 years were a time of civil war, internal conflicts and political infighting. While there were only six mind incarnations of Shabdrung during this period, there were 55 desis. The longest-serving desi was the 13th incumbent, Sherab Wangchuk, who ruled for 20 years. Few of the rulers finished their term; 22 desis were assassinated or deposed by rivals.

Things got so far out of control that some of the rival factions appealed to the Tibetans for assistance. In 1729 and 1730 Tibet took advantage of Bhutan's instability and invaded the country three times. The Tibetans eventually ended hostilities through a truce initiated by the lamas. The rival Bhutanese factions submitted their case to the Chinese emperor in Beijing for mediation. But the issue was only finally resolved when several of the Bhutanese protagonists died, leaving the currently recognised mental incarnation of the Shabdrung as the ruler. At the same time, formal diplomatic relations were established between Bhutan and Tibet, which noted Bhutan historian Michael Aris says 'helped to guarantee the fact of Bhutanese independence'.

Bhutan & Cooch Behar

In 1730 the 10th desi assisted Gya Chila, the ruler of Cooch Behar, to defeat invaders and to settle a family feud; Bhutan was then allowed to station a force in that southern kingdom. In 1768 the desi tried to suppress the influence of the religious establishment in Bhutan and to strengthen his own influence outside of the country. He established alliances with the Panchen Lama in Tibet and with King Prithvi Narayan Shah of Nepal. In 1772 the Bhutanese invaded Cooch Behar to help settle a feud over succession. They won, and kidnapped the crown prince and the queen of Cooch Behar. The Bhutanese also captured Raja Dhairjendra Narayan in the same year.

Involvement of the British

In his book, *Lands of the Thunderbolt*, the Earl of Ronaldshay wrote:

'... it was not until 1772 that the East India Company became conscious of the existence, across its northern frontier, of a meddlesome neighbour.'

The first contact the British had with Bhutan was when the claimants to the throne of Cooch Behar appealed to the East India Company to help drive the Bhutanese out of their kingdom.

Because the East India Company was a strictly commercial enterprise, its officers agreed to help when the deposed ruler of Cooch Behar offered to pay half of the revenues of the state in return for assistance. In December 1772 the British governor-general, Warren Hastings, sent Indian troops and guns to Cooch Behar and, despite suffering heavy losses, routed the Bhutanese and restored the king to the throne. However, Cooch Behar paid a very high price for this assistance. Not only did its rulers pay 50,000 rupees, but in 1773 they also signed a treaty ceding the kingdom to the East India Company.

The British pushed the Bhutanese back into the hills and followed them into Bhutan. The British won another major battle in January 1773 at the garrison of Chichacotta (now Khithokha) in the Wang Chhu valley, east of what is now Phuentsholing. A second battle was fought near Kalimpong in April 1773. The Bhutanese troops were personally led by the 16th desi but, after the second defeat, he was deposed by a *coup d'état*.

First Treaty with the British

The new desi wanted to make an agreement with the British and appealed to the Panchen Lama in Tibet for assistance. The Panchen Lama then wrote what the British described as 'a very friendly and intelligent letter' that was carried to Calcutta by an Indian pilgrim. The British, more eager to establish relations with Tibet than to solve the issue of Bhutan, agreed to comply with the Tibetan request. The result was a peace treaty between Bhutan and the British signed in Calcutta on 25 April 1774. In this treaty the desi agreed to respect the territory of the East India Company and to allow the company to cut timber in the forests of Bhutan. The British returned all the territory they had captured.

The East India Company wasted no time in sending a trade mission to Tibet. In May 1774 George Bogle led a party through Bhutan to Tibet. The group spent a few weeks in Thimphu waiting for permission to go to Tibet, and eventually reached the seat of the Panchen Lama in Tashilhunpo in October. The written account of this mission provides the first western view into the isolated kingdom of Bhutan and is described in the Exploration by Western Travellers section later in this chapter.

The British in India attached their own names, derived from Sanskrit, to the titles used by the Bhutanese. They called the Shabdrung the Dharma Raja, and the desi Deb Raja. Raja is Sanskrit for 'king'; therefore the Dharma Raja was the king who ruled by religious law and the Deb Raja was the king who delivered wellbeing or material gifts. Deb is a corruption of the Sanskrit word *deva* or *devata* (the giver).

The Problem of the Duars

The political intrigue and civil wars continued in Bhutan, and there were numerous skirmishes over boundaries and trading rights. The British were engaged in the Burmese war of 1825-26. As a result of this war, the British gained control of Assam, the territory that forms the eastern half of Bhutan's southern border.

The area of plains between the Brahmaputra River up to and including the lowest of the hills of Bhutan was known as the *duars*, which means doors or gates (see the boxed text 'The Duars' later in this chapter). The western part of this area, known as the Bengal Duars, had been annexed by the third desi, Mingyur Tenpa, and the Bhutanese considered it their territory. The eastern part, the Assam Duars, had long been administered in a complex rental agreement between Bhutan and Assam.

In 1826 the British and Bhutanese came into conflict over the ownership of the duars. Other than the area's strategic importance, the British were attracted to the duars because they were excellent tea-growing country. They were also a malarial jungle, and the British had a very difficult time keeping the troops stationed there healthy.

After the Burmese war, the British took over the peculiar land rental arrangement for the Assam Duars, along with what were described as 'very unsatisfactory relations of the Assamese with the Bhutanese'. Major disagreements between the British and Bhutan resulted. The agreement with the Assamese allowed the British to occupy the region from July to November, and the Bhutanese to occupy it the remainder of the year in return for payment in horses, gold, knives, blankets, musk and other articles. The new arrangement meant that Bhutan sent the payment to the British, who accused the Bhutanese of delivering piebald horses and other defective goods. The Bhutanese insisted that inferior goods had been substituted by middlemen working for the British.

The 1897 Earthquake

One of the most devastating natural disasters in Bhutan was the great Assam earthquake that occurred at 5.06 pm on 12 June 1897. The epicentre was about 80km south of Bhutan and had a magnitude of 8.7 on the Richter scale, which seismologists categorise as 'catastrophic'. Of course, there were no seismometers to measure the event and the magnitude was estimated from its devastating effects. By comparison, the 1975 Kobe quake measured 7.2, the San Francisco earthquake of 1906 measured 8.3, and the Prince William Sound earthquake in 1964 had a magnitude of 9.2.

The earthquake destroyed the dzongs in Punakha and Lingzhi. It severely damaged the dzongs of Wangdue Phodrang, Trongsa, Jakar and the utse of Trashi Chhoe. Paro Dzong escaped largely unharmed.

This earthquake is famous, not only because of its size, but because it was the first documentation of a quake producing vertical accelerations greater than 1 G. Large boulders were actually lifted from their location and moved to a new spot without touching the ground.

Disagreements over payments and administration escalated between the British and the Bhutanese. The British annexed Buringma Duar in the far west, then returned it when Bhutan paid a compensation of 2000 rupees. In 1836 the British mounted an attack on Deothang (then known as Dewangiri), in the east, to force the surrender of fugitives who had committed crimes in British territory. The dzongpen refused to comply and attacked the British detachment. The British won that battle and annexed Deothang and the entire Banska Duar. The following year, however, at the request of the desi, they agreed to return control of the duar to the Bhutanese.

The British annexed the two easternmost duars in 1840 and the rest of the Assam duars in September 1841, agreeing to pay Bhutan an annual compensation of 10,000 rupees. Lord Auckland wrote to the deb and dharma rajas that the British were:

'...compelled by an imperative sense of duty to occupy the whole of the duars without any reference to your Highnesses' wishes, as I feel assured that it is the only course which is likely to hold out a prospect of restoring peace and prosperity to that tract of country.'

Perhaps more revealing is a letter from Colonel Jenkins, the Governor General's agent, outlining the need for taking over the Assam duars. He wrote:

'Had we possession of the Dooars, the Bhootan Government would necessarily in a short time become entirely dependent upon us, as holding in our hands the source of all their subsistence.'

This was the time of the Afghan War and the Anglo-Sikh wars. The British Indian administration had little time to worry about Bhutan, and major and minor conflicts and cross-border incursions continued. Although there were making plans to annex the Bengal duars, they were not able to follow through. Their troops were kept busy trying to suppress the Indian revolt of 1857, which was a movement against British rule in India.

Bhutan took advantage of the instability in the region and mounted numerous raids in the Bengal duars. To compensate for their losses, the British deducted large sums from payments they owed the Bhutanese. In 1861 the Bhutanese retaliated by raiding Cooch Behar, capturing a number of elephants and kidnapping several residents, including some British subjects.

The Trongsa Penlop Gains Control

At this time the Shabdrung was a youth of 18, and the affairs of state were handled by the Lhengye Tshog (Council of Ministers) which consisted of the Trongsa and Paro penlops, several dzongpens and other officials. There was constant infighting and intrigue between the Paro and Trongsa penlops, both of whom were vying for power through attacks, conspiracy and kidnapping. When one gained control, he appointed a desi and enthroned him; soon the other penlop gained control, ejected the opposing desi and placed his own representative on the throne.

Through a series of shrewd alliances the Trongsa penlop, Jigme Namgyal, gained the upper hand and established effective control of the country. This was the first time peace had prevailed since the time of the first Shabdrung. Jigme Namgyal was working to strengthen his power and that of the central government when he had an inconvenient visitor.

The Humiliation of Ashley Eden

The British had managed to extend their influence into Sikkim, making it a British protectorate. They decided to send a mission to Bhutan to, among other things, establish a resident British representative promoting better communications with the rulers. According to the official account, the mission was designed:

'...on a scale calculated to impress the Court with the importance which the British Government attaches to the establishment of clear and decisive relations with the Government of Bhootan, and the adoption of some means whereby the present unsatisfactory state of affairs on the Frontier may be put a stop to, and that the mutual rendition of persons charged with the commission of heinous crimes may be secured.'

Despite reports of political chaos in Bhutan, Ashley Eden, the secretary of the government of Bengal, set out from Darjeeling in November 1864 to meet the desi, or deb raja. Ignoring numerous messages from the Bhutanese that the British mission was not welcome, Eden pushed on past Kalimpong, through Daling, Ha and Paro, reaching Punakha on 15 March.

It's not clear whether it was more by accident or by design, but Eden's party was jeered, pelted with rocks, made to wait long hours in the sun and subjected to other humiliations. Both Bhutanese and British pride suffered badly. As Eden describes it:

'The Penlow (the penlop) took up a large piece of wet dough and began rubbing my face with it; he pulled my hair, and slapped me on the back, and generally conducted himself with great insolence. On my showing signs of impatience or remonstrating, he smiled and deprecated my anger, pretending that it was the familiarity of friendship, much to the amusement of the large assemblage of bystanders.'

Eden exacerbated the situation by sending the Lhengye Tshog a copy of a draft treaty with terms that he had been instructed to negotiate. His actions implied that this was the final version of the treaty that the Bhutanese were to sign without any discussion. The Bhutanese took immediate exception to Eden's perceived high-handedness and soon presented him with an alternative treaty that returned all the duars to Bhutan. One clause in the treaty stated:

'We have written about that the settlement is permanent; but who knows, perhaps this settlement is made with one word in the mouth and two in the heart. If, therefore, this settlement is false, the Dharma Raja's demons will, after deciding who is true or false, take his life, and take out his liver and scatter it to the winds like ashes.'

Reading this, it's little wonder that Eden feared for the safety of his party. He signed the treaty, but under his signature added the English words 'under compulsion', which, naturally, the Bhutanese could not read.

The Duar War of 1865
Although the British considered Eden's mission a failure, and reprimanded him for his conduct, they continued the dispute with Bhutan over payment for the Bengal Duars. The Bhutanese, in turn, were furious the British had renounced the treaty Eden had signed. In November 1864 the British summarily annexed the Bengal Duars, and proceeded to occupy them, gaining effective control of the entire south of Bhutan. The Trongsa penlop mounted a carefully planned counter-attack. His troops, protected by shields of rhinoceros hide, captured two British guns and drove the British forces out of Bhutan in January 1865.

The British regrouped and recaptured various towns, including Samtse (then called Chamurchi). A fierce battle at Deothang (Dewangiri) on 2 April essentially ended the war, with the British destroying all the buildings and slaughtering their captives. Negotiations continued through the summer. Eventually the Bhutanese returned the captured guns and accepted a treaty. The treaty of Sinchula was signed, under duress, by the Bhutanese on 11 November 1865. In it the Bhutanese ceded the duars to Britain forever and agreed to allow free trade between the two countries.

Through this treaty, Bhutan lost a major tract of valuable farmland and a large portion of its wealth. Its borders became the foot of the hills bordering the plain of India. Among the important landmarks the Bhutanese lost were the town of Ambari Falakati, north of Cooch Behar, the town of Deothang in the east and the territory on the east bank of the Teesta River, including what is now the town of Kalimpong.

Back in Bhutan's heartland there were continuing civil wars, but Trongsa penlop Jigme Namgyal retained his power and in 1870 was enthroned as the 50th desi. The next 10 years were again a time of intrigue, treachery, power-brokering and continual strife. The penlops of Paro, Punakha and Wangdue Phodrang all challenged the position of Desi Jigme Namgyal and his successor, who was his half-brother. After he retired as desi, Jigme Namgyal remained in firm control of the country and in 1879 appointed his 17-year-old son, Ugyen Wangchuck, as Paro penlop. Michael Aris' book, *The Raven Crown,* gives a detailed description of this extraordinary period.

After Jigme Namgyal died in 1881, his son consolidated his own position following a feud over the post of Trongsa penlop. At age 20, Ugyen Wangchuck marched on Bumthang and Trongsa and in 1882 was appointed penlop of Trongsa, while still retaining the post of Paro penlop. Because his father had enhanced the powers of the office of Trongsa penlop, this gave him much more influence than the desi. When a battle broke out between the dzongpens of Punakha and Thimphu, Ugyen Wangchuck tried to mediate the dispute.

He sent in his troops after unsuccessful negotiations and his forces defeated the troops loyal to both dzongpens and seized control of Simtokha dzong. The monk body and the penlop of Paro tried to settle the conflict and in 1885 arranged a meeting at Changlimithang. During the meeting a fight broke out and the representative of the Thimphu Dzongpen was killed and the dzongpen fled to Tibet. Following the battle, Ugyen Wangchuck emerged as the most powerful person in the country, assumed full authority, installed his own nominee as desi, and reduced the post to a ceremonial one.

Bhutan's First King
In order to re-establish Bhutan's sovereignty and help consolidate his position, Ugyen Wangchuck developed closer relations with the British. He accompanied Francis Younghusband during his invasion of Tibet in 1904 and assisted with the negotiations that resulted in a treaty between Tibet and Britain. The British rewarded the penlop by granting him the title of Knight Commander

of the Indian Empire. In 1906 Sir Ugyen Wangchuck was invited to Calcutta to attend the reception for the Prince of Wales and returned to Bhutan with a better appreciation of the world that lay beyond the country's borders.

In 1907 the desi died and Ugyen Wangchuck was elected by a unanimous vote of the Bhutan chiefs and principal lamas as hereditary ruler of Bhutan. He was crowned on 17 December 1907 and installed as head of state with the title *Druk Gyalpo* (Dragon King). He continued to maintain excellent relations with the British, partly in an effort to gain some security from the increasing Chinese influence in Tibet.

The Treaty of Punakha, 1910
British-Bhutanese relations were enhanced in the treaty of Punakha, which was signed in 1910. This treaty stated that the British government would 'exercise no interference in the internal administration of Bhutan'. It was agreed that Bhutan would 'be guided by the advice of the British Government in regard to its external relations'. The compensation for the duars was doubled to Rs 100,000 per year and Bhutan agreed to refer disputes with Cooch Behar and Sikkim to the British for settlement.

Bhutan still refused to allow the appointment of a British resident, and continued to maintain a policy of isolation aimed at preserving its own sovereignty in an era of colonisation. In 1911 King Ugyen Wangchuck attended the great durbar held by the King Emperor of Britain at Delhi and was given the additional decoration of Knight Commander of the Order of the Star of India.

The Second King, Jigme Wangchuck
Ugyen Wangchuck died in 1926 and was succeeded by his 24-year-old son, Jigme Wangchuck, who became the second hereditary king of Bhutan. He ruled during the time of the Great Depression and WW II, but these catastrophic world events did not affect Bhutan because of its barter economy and isolation.

His Majesty King Jigme Wangchuck refined the administrative and taxation systems and brought the entire country under his direct control. He made Wangdichholing Palace in Bumthang his summer palace, and moved the entire court to Kuenga Rabten, south of Trongsa, in the winter. Karma Ura's book, *The Hero With a Thousand Eyes,* gives a wonderful insight into the protocol and workings of the Bhutanese court in those days.

After India gained independence from Britain on 15 August 1947, the new Indian government recognised Bhutan as an independent country. In 1949 Bhutan signed a treaty with independent India that was very similar to their earlier treaty with the British. The treaty reinforced Bhutan's position as a sovereign state. India agreed not to interfere in the internal affairs of Bhutan, while Bhutan agreed to be guided by the government of India in its external relations. The treaty also returned to Bhutan about 82 sq km of the Duars in the southeast of the country, including Deothang, that had been annexed by the British.

King Jigme Dorji Wangchuck Modernises Bhutan

King Jigme Wangchuck died in 1952. He was succeeded by his son, Jigme Dorji Wangchuck, who had been educated in India and England and spoke fluent Tibetan, English and Hindi. He constituted the National Assembly in 1953 and abolished serfdom in 1956. To improve relations with India he invited Pandit Jawaharlal Nehru and his daughter, Indira Gandhi, to visit Bhutan in 1958.

When the Chinese took control of Tibet, it became obvious that a policy of isolationism was not appropriate in the modern world. King Jigme Dorji Wangchuck knew that in order to preserve Bhutan's independence, the kingdom had to become a member of the world community. In 1961 Bhutan emerged from centuries of self-imposed isolation and embarked on a process of planned development.

The country joined the Colombo Plan in 1962. This gave Bhutan access to technical assistance and training from member countries in South-East Asia. The first 'five-year plan' for development was implemented in 1961 and India agreed to help finance and construct the large Chhukha hydroelectric project. Not all Bhutanese approved of the pace of change. There were clashes between rival power groups; the prime minister, Jigme Palden Dorji, who was a leading proponent of change, was assassinated on 5 April 1964. After a period of confusion, the king assumed the duties of that post; the Council of Ministers still does not include the office of Prime Minister.

Bhutan joined the Universal Postal Union in 1969 and became a member of the United Nations in 1971. In the same year, Bhutan and India established formal diplomatic relations and exchanged ambassadors.

King Jigme Dorji Wangchuck's domestic accomplishments were also impressive. In 1953, early in his reign, he established the *Tshogdu* (National Assembly) and drew up a 12-volume code of law. He abolished serfdom, reorganised land holdings, created the Royal Bhutan Army (RBA) and police force, and established the High Court. However, as he led Bhutan into the modern world, he emphasised the need to preserve Bhutanese culture and tradition.

The King of Bhutan

King Jigme Dorji Wangchuck died in 1972 at age 44. He was succeeded by his 16-year-old son, Jigme Singye Wangchuck. Like his father, he was educated in India and England, but he also received a Bhutanese education at the Ugyen Wangchuck Academy in Paro. He pledged to continue his father's programme of modernisation and announced a plan for the country to achieve economic self-reliance. This plan took advantage of Bhutan's special circumstances: a small population, abundant land and rich natural resources. Among the development goals set by His Majesty was the ideal of economic self-reliance and what he nicknamed 'gross national happiness'.

The coronation of King Jigme Singye

Wangchuck as the fourth Druk Gyalpo on 2 June, 1974 was a major turning point in the opening of Bhutan, and was the first time that the international press was allowed to enter the country. A total of 287 invited guests travelled to Thimphu for the event, and several new hotels having been built to accommodate them. These hotels later provided the basis for the development of tourism in Bhutan.

The King has emphasised modernisation of education, health services, rural development and communications. He was the architect of Bhutan's policy of environmental conservation, which gives precedence to ecological considerations over commercial interests. He continued the reforms begun by his father in the areas of administration, labour and justice, including the introduction of a secret ballot and the abolishment of compulsory labour. He promotes national identity, traditional values and the concept of 'One Nation, One People'.

In 1988 the Royal Wedding solemnised His Majesty's marriage to the sisters Ashi Dorji Wangmo, Ashi Tshering Pem, Ashi Tshering Yangdon and Ashi Sangay Choedon. The King and his Queens have five princes and five princesses, including the Crown Prince, His Royal Highness Dasho Jigme Khesar Namgyal Wangchuck.

Problems in the South
Several political problems in the south of the country have affected Bhutan's relations with its neighbours.

Nepali-Speakers In the late 19th and the early 20th centuries many Nepalis migrated to Bhutan and settled in the south of the country. They now comprise much of the population in that region, to the extent that the term Lhotshampa (southern Bhutanese) is synonymous with Nepali-speaker.

Though the Nepali-speakers are from many ethnic groups, the majority of them are Hindus, with traditions that are different from the Drukpas who live in the north of the country. Some Nepalis asserted that they faced discrimination from the Drukpas

and demanded political changes as long ago as the 1950s, when the now-defunct Bhutan State Congress Party was formed.

From the 1950s the Bhutanese government took steps to integrate the ethnic Nepalis. For the first time they were granted citizenship, represented in the National Assembly and admitted into the bureaucracy. Nepali was taught as a third language in primary schools in southern Bhutan and was made the second official language of the country. Also, recognition was given to the festivals, customs, dress and traditions of the Lhotshampas. The Nepalis remained culturally distinct from the Bhutanese of the northern valleys. However, up until the 1980s, there seemed to be little or no conflict between the Drukpas and the Lhotshampas.

Major problems didn't really emerge until the late 1980s. At that time, the government began to focus on preserving what it saw as Bhutan's threatened national identity. It introduced a policy of *driglam namzha* (traditional values and etiquette) under which all citizens had to wear the national dress of *gho* and *kira* at schools, government offices and official functions. At the same time, changes were made in the education system: the Nepali language was eliminated from the primary school curriculum and the change justified as reducing the burden on students. Resentment began to stir among some Nepalis in the south, exacerbated by what the government now concedes was overzealous enforcement of the policies by some district officials.

Mindful of the country's extremely porous border – and Bhutan's attractiveness because of its fertile land, low population and free health and education facilities – the government in 1988 conducted a nationwide census. This was aimed partly at identifying illegal immigrants, defined as those who could not prove family residence before 1958. Thousands of ethnic Nepalis lacked proper documentation. A series of violent acts in the south, including robberies, assaults, rapes and murders – primarily against legitimate Bhutanese citizens of Nepali descent – created a sense of fear and insecurity that led to an exodus of Nepali-speakers from Bhutan. How much of the migration was voluntary and to what extent it was involuntary remains a matter of fierce debate, but tens of thousands of Nepali-speakers left Bhutan between 1988 and 1993.

At the very same time, a set of dissident leaders emerged charging human rights abuses in the treatment of Nepalis inside Bhutan and demanding full democracy and other political changes in the kingdom. This movement received some international attention.

By the end of 1992, some 80,000 Nepali-speakers who said they were from Bhutan were housed in several camps in the Jhapa district of south-eastern Nepal, organised by the UN High Commissioner for Refugees (UNHCR). By early 1993 the exodus had virtually stopped. Initially, all those who arrived were accepted into the camps as a group; in June 1993 the UNHCR established a screening centre at Kakarbhitta on the Nepal-India border. At the end of 1997 there were 93,674 people in the camps, 10% to 11% of whom were born there.

Bhutan and Nepal agreed that they would settle the problem on a bilateral basis. They have held several rounds of talks to try to identify which residents of the camps are legitimate citizens of Bhutan and to find an appropriate solution to this very complex problem. Unfortunately, not much progress had been made at the time of research. The Royal Government of Bhutan has, on occasion, allowed delegations from agencies such as Amnesty International and the International Committee for the Red Cross to come to study the situation with regard to human rights, political prisoners, jail conditions and so on, and is heeding many of their recommendations.

The status of the people in the camps of Jhapa is protected by the UNHCR, which uses donor support to provide the survival rations and shelter. It is likely that if the support disappears, and if the two countries continue in deadlock in how to resolve the crisis, those in the camps, most of them

former farmers, would enter the larger diaspora of Nepali-speakers in South Asia.

ULFA & Bodo The north-eastern region of India has suffered years of separatist violence carried out by three major factions which are believed to have bases in the jungles of southern Bhutan from which they mount assaults. It's estimated the actions of these groups have claimed the lives of more than 20,000 people.

The Bodos are Mechey tribal people that have two militant groups, the Bodo Liberation Tiger Force and the Bodo Security Force, both of which are fighting for a Bodo homeland. The United Liberation Front of Assam, more commonly known as ULFA, is a separatist group formed in 1979 with a goal of an independent Assamese nation. They have staged numerous attacks, including derailing a train with a bomb.

The Indian Army has stationed 50,000 troops in the region to try to deal with these groups. However, Bhutan does not have enough soldiers to aggressively patrol its long and open border with India; in any case, their limited supply of weapons is no match for the high-tech weaponry that the rebels possess. The situation becomes even more complicated because, by treaty, nationals of Bhutan and India are allowed to cross freely into each other's country.

Exploration by Western Travellers

Some of the most interesting stories of Bhutan, and much of Bhutan's recorded history, came from the descriptions provided by the early explorers. These records provide an insight into what they observed and reveal the extraordinary attitudes of some of the envoys Britain sent to negotiate with Bhutan.

Portuguese Priests The first western visitors to Bhutan were two Portuguese Jesuit priests. In early 1627 Father Cacella and Father Cabral travelled from Calcutta to Bhutan en route to Shigatse in Tibet. They stayed for a few months in Chari Goemba with the Shabdrung. There is no complete written account of their journey, but one of their letters provides an interesting insight into the first Shabdrung's character:

'He received us with a demonstration of great benevolence, signifying this in the joy which he showed on seeing us and on knowing where we had come from, where we were from, that is from what country or nation, and he asked the other questions normal at a first meeting.

[He] is at the same time the chief lama ... He is proud of his gentleness for which he is highly reputed, but less feared ... He is also very celebrated for his abstinence in never eating rice or meat or fish maintaining himself only with fruit and milk ... He occupied himself, as he told us, in praying and in his spare time he made various objects and he showed us one of them, which was the best, being an image of the face of God in white sandalwood, small but very well made and this is an art of which he is very proud, as also that of painter at which he is good ... [He] also has a great reputation as a man of letters ...

[The Shabdrung] has a long beard and some of its hairs reach his waist ...'

George Bogle's Mission The first British expedition to Bhutan was in 1774, just after the first British treaties with Bhutan and Tibet were signed. The Court of Directors of the East India Company sent a mission to Tibet via Bhutan to find out about goods, 'especially such as are of great value and easy transportation'. The expedition team, led by George Bogle, planted potatoes wherever they went, providing a new food crop for Bhutan and a lasting legacy of Bogle's mission.

The party spent five months in Thimphu, then travelled on to Shigatse in Tibet. Bogle found the Bhutanese 'good-humoured, downright, and so far as I can judge, thoroughly trustworthy'. He did, however, note that the practice of celibacy by large numbers of monks led to 'many irregularities' and the cold resulted in 'an excessive use of spirituous liquors'.

Turner's 1783 Expedition In the next few years two small expeditions travelled to Bhutan. Alexander Hamilton led a group to Punakha and Thimphu in 1776, and another in 1777, to discuss the Bhutanese claims to Ambari Falakati and to consolidate the transit rights through Bhutan to Tibet that had been negotiated by Bogle's mission.

The next major venture into Bhutan was in 1783, when Samuel Turner led a grand expedition with all the accoutrements of the British Raj. They travelled through the duars in *palanquins* (sedan chairs) and followed Bogle's route to Thimphu. They also visited Punakha and Wangdue Phodrang before crossing to Tibet. Among the members of the 1783 expedition was Samuel Davis, who was a draftsman and surveyor. His journal and outstanding paintings provide one of the earliest views of Bhutan. Much of Davis' material is presented in *Views of Mediaeval Bhutan* by Michael Aris.

Ashley Eden's Mission of 1863 Minor British expeditions to Bhutan were made in 1810 and 1812 and again in 1815 when the British sent an Indian officer, Kishen Kant Bose, to try to settle frontier disputes with the desi. RB Pemberton led a mission in 1837 from eastern Bhutan via Deothang and Trongsa to Punakha, where he tried, unsuccessfully, to resolve the conflict over the duars.

The Ashley Eden mission of 1863 was the next attempt to resolve the issue of the duars. Among the members of this expedition was Capt HH Godwin-Austen of the Indian Topographical Survey. Godwin-Austen had explored Pakistan's Baltoro Glacier in 1861 and on some maps K2, the second highest peak in the world, is named after him.

Contradicting Bogle's impression, Eden said of the Bhutanese: 'They are totally untrustworthy, more faithless indeed than the worst savages on our Frontier'. In his journal he ridiculed Buddhist practices and described the ex-penlop of Paro as 'physically worn out with debauchery of every description'.

Eden's party crossed the Cheli La from Ha into Paro valley in February and had an extremely difficult time in the deep snow.

Some years later, John Claude White suggested that Eden may have been given incorrect directions, perhaps on purpose. It is astounding that, even when he had admitted failure, Eden still viewed his as a 'friendly mission'. His report certainly was a major factor in the British annexation of the duars. He advocated a punitive policy to teach the Bhutanese that they would not be allowed to 'treat our power with contempt'.

White's 1905 Mission There were no formal British expeditions to Bhutan for more than 40 years after Eden's, but the Survey of India sent several agents disguised as lamas and pilgrims to explore Bhutan and Tibet in 1883 and 1886.

By 1905 the Bhutanese and British were friends because of the assistance the Trongsa penlop, Ugyen Wangchuck, had provided to the 1904 Younghusband expedition to Lhasa. John Claude White, a British political officer, travelled to Bhutan to present the insignia of Knight Commander of the Indian Empire to the penlop. White had been a member of the 1904 expedition and was an old friend of Ugyen Wangchuck.

White and his large party travelled from the city of Gangtok, in Sikkim, into Ha and Paro, en route to the investiture ceremony in Punakha. Later, White and his party were guests of Ugyen Wangchuck at his new palace of Wangdichholing in Bumthang. The expedition later returned with the first photographs of dzongs and the court of Bhutan.

In 1906 White made a reconnaissance through eastern Bhutan to southern Tibet. He made a third trip, in 1907, when he was invited as the British representative to the coronation of Ugyen Wangchuck as the first king of Bhutan. As the party neared Punakha, his own contingent of British officers and their band of pipes and drums was met by a Bhutanese delegation. The Bhutanese escorted them to the dzong on muleback, accompanied by a marching band playing trumpets, drums and gongs. As they approached the dzong, they were greeted by a salute of guns and the procession was joined by dancers who twirled down the path in front of the British contingent.

A summary of White's account appeared in the April 1914 issue of the *National Geographic* magazine and made Bhutan known to the world for the first time.

British Political Officers Between 1909 and 1947 the British government dealt with Bhutan in the same way as it did with other Indian princely states, but it never specifically defined its relationship with Bhutan. Starting with CA Bell in 1909, numerous British political officers visited Bhutan and presented the king with decorations.

In 1921 the Earl of Ronaldshay, who was described as a 'closet Buddhist', travelled to Bhutan as a guest of King Ugyen Wangchuck. He travelled from Gangtok to Paro, where he was met with great fanfare. He described the procession: trumpeters led and:

'... behind them tripped the dancers, who brought the whole procession to a halt whenever they came to a piece of ground which they deemed suitable for the treading of a measure.'

The party visited Taktshang and witnessed the Paro tsechu festival, but never met the king, who was in Punakha, ill with influenza.

In 1927 Lt Col FM Bailey attended the coronation of the second king. Lt Col JLR Weir travelled to Bumthang in 1931 to present the king with the insignia of Knight Commander of the Indian Empire.

History of Tourism
Until the beginning of King Jigme Dorji Wangchuck's modernisation efforts in 1960, most of the non-Indian foreigners who entered Bhutan were the explorers listed earlier. A few foreigners were permitted into the country during the 1960s, but only the royal family had the authority to invite foreigners to Bhutan, so almost all visitors were royal guests.

The First Trekkers Early trekkers included Desmond Doig, a friend of the royal family who trekked in 1961 on assignment for *National Geographic*. In 1963 Professor Augusto Gansser travelled throughout the country studying geology, and in 1964 a group of British physicians, Michael Ward, F Jackson and R Turner, mounted an expedition to the remote Lunana region.

Pioneering Tourists The coronation of the present king in 1974 was the first time that a large number of foreign visitors had entered the kingdom. After the coronation, in another experiment with modernisation, small groups of tourists were allowed into the country and given permission to visit the dzongs and goembas in Thimphu and Paro. From these beginnings, the pattern for Bhutan's tourism industry evolved.

The first group of paying tourists arrived in 1974, organised and led by Lars Eric Lindblad. Lindblad encouraged the government to limit tourism and to charge high fees. The government soon established a quota of 200 tourists a year, who had to travel in a group of six or more. The cost was set at US$130 per day – a lot of money at that time. Because there was no airport, entry was via road from India, through the southern border town of Phuentsholing. At that time, travellers needed a special 'inner line' permit to cross the northern part of India, and this took six weeks to arrange through the Indian Embassy in Delhi. At first, tourists were restricted to Phuentsholing, Paro and Thimphu. Visits to Punakha and Wangdue Phodrang were allowed in 1978, and in 1982 Trongsa and Bumthang were added. Trekking in Western Bhutan was started in 1978, and by 1982 it was possible to trek in Central Bhutan.

Paro airport was opened in 1983 and the newly formed national airline, Druk Air, operated flights from Calcutta using small turbo-prop Dornier aircraft. This meant travellers could avoid the long drive and time-consuming permit restrictions in India and be deposited in the heartland of Bhutan. The airport runway was extended in 1990 and Druk Air began operating a 72-passenger BAe-146 jet aircraft, with direct international connections.

Until 1991, all tourists were only handled by the Bhutan Tourism Corporation, a government agency. Tourism was privatised in that year and soon numerous agencies were established, most are run by ex-employees of the now-disbanded government tourist company. Though they have to abide by government rates and standards, the tour operators are free to operate as independent profit-making concerns. The Tourism Authority of Bhutan (TAB), a government agency under the Ministry of Trade & Industry, is responsible for all aspects of tourism.

Mountaineering Bhutan opened its mountains to climbers for a short period from 1983 to 1994, and the country's mountaineering history is correspondingly brief. Jhomolhari was climbed from Tibet in 1937 by F Spencer Chapman and a Sherpa and again in 1970 by a joint Indian-Bhutanese team. A Bhutanese expedition scaled 4900m Thurigang, north of Thimphu, in 1983. Jichu Drake was attempted three times before it was successfully climbed in 1988 by an expedition led by Doug Scott. Masang Gang was climbed by a Japanese expedition in 1985, and Gangkhar Puensum (7541m) remains the highest unclimbed peak in the world after unsuccessful attempts by Japanese and British teams in the 1980s.

GEOGRAPHY
Bhutan is a landlocked country about 300km long and 150km wide, encompassing 46,500 sq km. It is bounded on the north-west and north by Tibet. The rest of the country is surrounded by India: on the east by the state of Arunachal Pradesh, on the south by Assam and West Bengal and on the west by Sikkim. Tibet's Chumbi valley, the old trade and expedition route from India to Lhasa, lies between the northern parts of Bhutan and Sikkim. Beginning in 1921, British Everest expeditions travelled to the mountain via the Chumbi valley and remarked on the beauty of the sacred Bhutanese mountain of Jhomolhari, which towers over the valley.

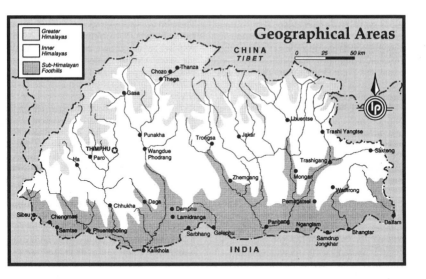

Virtually the entire country is mountainous, and ranges in elevation from 100m to the 7554m Kulha Gangri peak on the Tibetan border. It can be divided into three major geographic regions, from north to south: the high Himalaya of the north, the hills and valleys of the centre, and the foothills and plains of the south.

The Great Himalaya

A range of high Himalayan peaks divides Bhutan and Tibet and forms part of the northern and western borders of the country. These giant peaks are the thrones of the gods; almost none have been climbed, many are virtually unexplored and some are not even named. There are four high mountain passes that cross the Himalaya. For the most part it remains an impenetrable snow-clad barrier (20% of the country is under perpetual snow). The Himalayan range extends from Jhomolhari (7314m) in the west to Kulha Gangri, near the centre point of the northern border. A chain of lower peaks extends eastward from Kulha Gangri to the Indian state of Arunachal Pradesh.

The Lunana region, just south of the mid-

point of Bhutan's border with Tibet, is an area of glacial peaks and high valleys which are snowbound during the winter. A range of high peaks forms the southern boundary of Lunana and isolates it from the rest of the country.

The Inner Himalaya

South of the high peaks lies a maze of broad valleys and forested hillsides from 1100m to 3000m in elevation. This is the largest region of Bhutan and all the major towns, including Thimphu, are here. This part of Bhutan is cut by deep ravines formed by fast-flowing rivers that have their source in the high Himalaya. The hillsides are generally too steep for farming; most have remained covered in virgin forest. Significant differences exist in this region between the western and eastern parts of the country.

The West The greater part of Bhutan's western border is formed by the Himalayan range, including the peaks of Jhomolhari and Jichu Drake. Several forested ridges extend eastward from this range, and these define the large valleys of Thimphu, Paro, Ha and Samtse. Between Punakha and Thimphu lies a well-defined ridge that forms the watershed between Thimphu's Wang Chhu river and Punakha's Puna Tsang Chhu. The east-west road crosses this ridge through a 3050m pass, the Dochu La.

The Black Mountain range lies to the east of the Puna Tsang Chhu watershed, forming the major barrier between eastern and western Bhutan. Pele La (3500m) is the most important pass across the Black Mountains and was an important mule track before the road was constructed.

Central Bhutan A north-south range of hills separates the Trongsa and Bumthang valley systems. The road crosses this ridge via Yotong La (3425m). The southern part of central Bhutan is the ancient kingdom of Khyeng. Further east, the Donga range of hills separates Bumthang from Lhuentse, with Thrumshing La (3780m) as the crossing point for the road. Eastern Bhutan, which encompasses most of the Manas Chhu watershed, lies to the east of this range.

The East Thrumshing La provides the only road access across the Donga range, which drops precipitously on its eastern side to the Kuri Chhu. The steep Rodang La crosses the northern part of this range and there are few lower passes in the south that are still used by herders. The northern region just east of the Donga range is known as Kurtoe.

In the far east, another range of hills runs south from the Himalayan slopes to separate the Lhuentse and Trashi Yangtse valleys.

The Southern Foothills
The plains in the south of the country are part of the region known as the Terai, which extends from Kashmir, through Nepal, to Bhutan. The foothills rise swiftly from the plains, and except for a very narrow band of flat land, this part of the country is either forest or terraced farmland.

The Duars At the south of Bhutan the hills end abruptly and the Indian plain begins.

The fertile valleys that extend 15-30km from the hills to the Indian states of Assam and Bengal are known as the *duars*, as are the lower portion of Bhutan's foothills (see boxed text).

Rivers
Rivers play an important role in Bhutan's geography and their enormous potential for hydroelectric power has helped shape the economy. Flowing south, they have created deep valleys, making all east-west travel a tedious process of climbing over hills, descending to a river and climbing again to the next ridge. There are four major river systems in Bhutan, most known by several names as they flow through the country. A few rivers retain their names when they are joined by a large tributary, but more often when two rivers join the larger river is known by a completely different name, such as the Manas, which is formed by the Kuri Chhu and the Drangme Chhu. Many rivers are known by entirely different names once they flow into India.

Most of the rivers have their headwaters in the high mountains of Bhutan, but the Himalaya is not a continental divide, and there are three rivers that actually flow through the mountains into the country. The Amo Chhu flows from Tibet's Chumbi valley across the south-western corner of Bhutan, where it becomes the Torsa Chhu, and exits at Phuentsholing. Two tributaries of the Manas, in eastern Bhutan, originate outside the country. The Kuri Chhu has its headwaters in Tibet (where it is known as the Lhobrak Chhu) and crosses into Bhutan at an elevation of only 2600m; the other tributary, the Gemri Chhu, rises in India's Arunachal Pradesh.

The Thimphu Chhu, known in its lower reaches as the Wang Chhu, powers the Chhukha hydroelectric project and eventually becomes the Raidak River in India. The Pho Chhu and Mo Chhu join at Punakha to form the Puna Tsang Chhu, which drains the area between the Dochu La and the Black Mountains. This river is known as the Sankosh when it reaches India. The Manas

In many ways Bhutan seems to have one foot in the future and one in the past. Clockwise from top: an arresting billboard and a very modern scourge (top); Thimphu remains the only world capital without traffic lights because residents don't want to replace popular traffic cops (right); and there are no television channels but video rental shops are big business (left).

NICHOLAS REUSS

DANIEL J. MILLER/COURTESY OF

NICHOLAS REUSS

WWF/COURTESY OF

Flora & Fauna
Clockwise from top: *Prunus cerosoides*; the rare and endangered black-necked crane; the takin, Bhutan's national animal, unkindly dubbed the 'beestung moose'; and the rarely seen blue poppy, national flower of the kingdom.

The Duars

Duar is a Sanskrit word meaning 'passes' or 'gates', and is the origin of the English 'door'. Before the British annexed Bhutan's southern regions, known as the duars in 1865, each was under the control of a Bhutanese dzongpen. As the duars were covered in malaria-infested jungle, they were unoccupied by the Bhutanese, who stayed in the northern hills.

Each duar is named for a river valley that leads out of Bhutan, though the duar itself is actually the land between two rivers. The land ranges from an elevation of about 100m to almost sea level at the Brahmaputra River, though the slope is barely perceptible. The fertile land supports tea gardens, huge rice paddies and a few protected forest areas like the Buxa Tiger Reserve.

Seven of the duars abut the border of Assam between the Dhansiri (Durlah) and Manas rivers. The remaining 11, from the Manas River to the Teesta River in the east, border on the state of Bengal. (See map on page 17.)

Their names, east to west:

The Bengal Duars	The Assam Duars
Dalimkot Duar (which includes Kalimpong)	Bijni (also known as Warsi) Duar
Zamirkot Duar	Chapakhama Duar
Chamurchi Duar	Chapaguri Duar
Lakhu Duar	Banska Duar
Buxa Duar	Ghurkhola Duar
Bura Duar	Kalling Duar
Bhulka Duar	Buriguma Duar
Guma Duar	
Ripu Duar	
Sidli Duar	
Bagh (also known as Bijni) Duar	

is Bhutan's largest river, draining about two-thirds of the country; in its upper reaches it is known as the Drangme Chhu. The Mangde Chhu flows from Trongsa and joins the Manas Chhu just before it flows into India. Unlike most other rivers that flow from Bhutan into India, the Manas retains its original name when it crosses the border. All of Bhutan's rivers eventually flow through the duars to become part of the Brahmaputra, which is known in Tibet as the Yarlung Tsampo, with a source near Mt Kailas in the far west.

Because the central Himalaya of Bhutan receives the full brunt of the monsoon, Bhutan's rivers are larger and have created much broader valleys than rivers further to the west in Nepal and India. In their upper reaches, most Bhutanese rivers have created large fertile valleys such as those of Paro, Punakha, Thimphu, Ha and Bumthang. As the rivers pass through the centre of Bhutan, the valleys become steeper and narrower, and roads have to climb high on the hillside. In eastern Bhutan the Manas valley is generally broader, and some roads run alongside the river itself.

When they reach the plains, the rivers drop much of the glacial silt they have collected and follow a meandering course over gravel stream beds. There are several oxbow lakes in the plains where rivers have changed their course over the years.

GEOLOGY

Millions of years ago the space Bhutan occupies was an open expanse of water, part of the shallow Tethys Sea, and the Tibetan plateau, or 'roof of the world', was beach-front property. Some 60 million years ago, however, the Indo-Australian plate collided with the Eurasian continent and was pushed under Eurasia. The Earth's crust buckled and folded, and mountain building began. Ancient crystalline and sedimentary rocks were pushed upward, and then folded into great ridges.

The new mountains blocked off rivers that once flowed unimpeded from Eurasia to the sea. However, on the southern slopes of the young mountains, new rivers formed as moist winds off the tropical sea were forced upward until they cooled and shed their moisture. As the mountains continued to rise and the gradient became steeper, these rivers cut deeply into the terrain. The continual crunching of the two plates, augmented by phases of crustal uplifting, created additional new mountain ranges; once again the rivers' courses were interrupted and a few east-west valleys evolved.

The mountains are changing even today, not only through erosion and displacement of material downstream, but through plate movement pushing the ranges higher still. The geology of Bhutan is complex, but may be roughly categorised into the same three regions that are used to define the geography.

Great Himalaya
From north of Paro through the Thimphu valley to Trongsa is what Augusto Gansser, the authority on Bhutan's geology, defines as the 'main central thrust fault'. North of this fault is a crystalline mass of gneiss (coarse grained metamorphic rock) that Gansser labelled Taktshang gneiss. A large intrusion of tourmaline granite, which Gansser named Jhomolhari granite, forms the peak of Jho-molhari and the western portion of the Paro valley. Just north of this deposit is the Lingzhi valley, which is composed of a wide deposit of sedimentary rocks. Along Bhutan's north-ern border, a large granite mass forms the high Himalaya.

North of Bhutan is the plateau of Tibet, which is largely composed of uplifted sedi-mentary deposits.

Inner Himalaya
Gansser has mapped a 'main boundary fault', which is the line at which the Indian plate pushed under the Eurasian plate. The fault extends across part of the far south of Bhutan, passing south of Phuentsholing: it enters Bhutan near Gelephu, passes north of Deothang and then continues east, back into India. Just north of the main boundary fault are several sedimentary deposits which have sheared, faulted and metamorphosed into a complex structure. The central region has layers of quartziferous sandstone, and Eastern Bhutan has thin layers of coal. Other deposits found in the Inner Himalaya are quartzite, shale and dolomite.

South of the main central thrust fault the land is composed of a wide band of gneiss. South of the band of gneiss is the Paro metamorphic belt, a band which includes marble and quartzite. Iron is found in Paro and Punakha, and British explorers re-counted how a magnet would pick up bits of iron from the soil.

Southern Foothills
The region south of the boundary fault is mostly sandstone and ancient sedimentary deposits.

CLIMATE
Bhutan is at the same latitude as Miami and Cairo. The climate varies widely depending on the elevation. In the southern border areas it is tropical; at the other extreme, in the high Himalayan regions, there is perpetual snow. Temperatures in the far south range from 15°C in winter to 30°C in summer. In Paro the range is from -5°C in January to 30°C in July, with 800mm of rain. In the high moun-tain regions the average temperature is 0°C in winter and may reach 10°C in summer, with an average of 350mm of rain.

Only in the high Himalayan regions does the snow remain year-round – in the form of glaciers. Some snow falls in northern and central Bhutan but does not remain on the ground for long. As a general rule, snow melts immediately below 2400m, stays a short while (longer in shaded areas) between

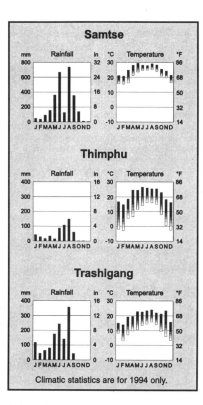

Climatic statistics are for 1994 only.

During the monsoon heavy rain falls almost every night; in the day there may be long periods without rain. Low clouds hang on the hills, obscuring views and, if they are too low, forcing the cancellation of flights at Paro airport.

Very little rain falls during the autumn, from October through December, making this the ideal season for trekking and mountain viewing.

ECOLOGY & ENVIRONMENT

Thanks to its early isolationism, small population and difficult terrain, Bhutan emerged into the 20th century with much of its forest and ecosystem intact. But now, with an increasing population, improved roads and communication and limited farming land, a major effort is required to protect the country's natural resources.

Government Policy

The government policy is influenced by Buddhist belief in the sanctity of life, the preservation of nature and giving back to the earth what you have taken. Protecting nature and culture is part of the Bhutanese value system and is an important aspect of the traditional way of life. In addition to its own efforts, the government works with conservation organisations to protect the environment, to ensure a better quality of life for its people and preserve the country's heritage for future generations. Just as it is striving to protect its culture, Bhutan is trying to learn from its neighbours and to adopt practices that will preserve its natural environment.

As it does with every aspect of modernisation and development, the Royal Government of Bhutan is proceeding cautiously in an effort to integrate environmental concerns into all its programmes. An environmental impact assessment is performed for all new public or private investment projects. The country's commitment to conservation is reflected in the 1995 ruling of the National Assembly that at least 60% of the country must be maintained as forest for all time.

2400 and 3000m, and remains on the ground until early March above 3000m.

Rain occurs primarily during the southwest monsoon season from June to September. Bhutan bears the brunt of the monsoon, receiving more rainfall than other Himalayan regions – up to 5.5m a year. Only 150km south of Bhutan, Cherrapunji in Assam has recorded the highest rainfall in the world, averaging 9.5m annually with a record of 19.7m, the height of a six-storey building.

Precipitation varies significantly with the elevation. The average rainfall is:

- Himalayan regions – less than 500mm per year
- Inner central valleys – 500-1000mm per year
- Southern foothills – 200-2000mm per year
- Southern border area – 3000-5000mm per year

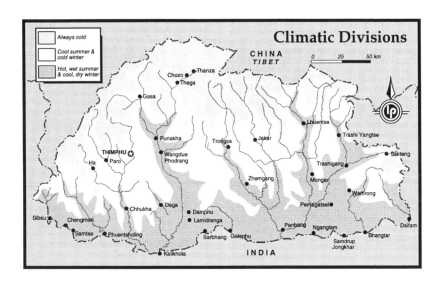

Conservation Trust Fund In 1991 a trust fund was established as a mechanism to help Bhutan finance its conservation activities. Donors include the Global Environment Facility, WWF (see Conservation Organisations later in this chapter) and the governments of Switzerland, Netherlands, Norway and Finland. The fund has more than US$25 million in assets, and the income supports many of Bhutan's conservation activities throughout the country.

The trust fund has paid to revise and expand the system of national parks and protected areas and has allowed a management plan to be developed for Royal Manas National Park, in the country's south. Income from the fund has paid for an increase in staffing of the Nature Conservation Section of the Forestry Services Division, has upgraded the curriculum of the Bhutan Forestry Institute and developed a biodiversity information system.

Environmental Issues
Conservation policy is established by the National Environment Commission and is monitored and administered by the Nature

Conservation Section of the Forestry Services Division.

Firewood Wood is used as fuel in rural areas, and it was only Bhutan's low population that spared the forests before a conservation plan was introduced in the 1960s. Managing firewood harvesting is a major problem. At 1.92 cubic metres per person, Bhutan's annual consumption of wood is one of the highest in the world. Wood accounts for 80% of Bhutan's energy consumption, and there are efforts to develop alternative sources wherever possible and to adopt practices that will ensure a sustainable supply of firewood.

Grazing & Farming Practices The high grazing lands often infringe on the habitat of protected species. There are programmes under way to try to balance the needs of herders with protecting wildlife.

A significant amount of shifting cultivation ('slash and burn', called *tseri* in Dzongkha) occurs in Bhutan, particularly in the east of the country. Villagers clear forests, grow corn and other crops for a few years, then abandon the fields and move on. Several methods, including education and fertiliser supply, are being implemented to change this practice.

Poaching Both wildlife and trees are poached. Many of Bhutan's species of wildlife are sought after for body parts that are supposed to have medicinal or other valuable properties. Though killing and poaching are unacceptable in Buddhist tradition, the high prices that wildlife products such as rhino horn, tiger bone and musk command make the practise difficult to control. Two organisations, the Convention on International Trade in Endangered Species of Wild Fauna and Flora (CITES) and Trade Record Analysis of Flora and Fauna (TRAFFIC), are helping to reduce poaching.

Bhutan's Forestry Services Division operates an anti-poaching programme designed to protect endangered plants and animals, and to enforce forestry rules, and control trade in wildlife parts and products.

A system of forest guards tries to stop trees being illegally felled throughout the country. Road checkpoints have been established throughout the country to monitor the transportation of wood and other forest products.

Logging Historically, forest products, including firewood and timber, have been exported to India. This movement has been controlled and reduced because of the government's concern over maintaining a sustainable forest resource. Some timber is still sold to India, but both the harvesting and sale are closely controlled through a government auction process. A plywood factory was established in 1990 at Gedu, north of Phuentsholing, but the Forestry Services Division closed it in 1996 because it was consuming too much wood.

Urban Growth The central business districts of all the major towns are relatively new, with most of the construction and growth having occurred after 1970. Despite their newness, most were constructed without ex-tensive town planning. It's estimated that the urban population will increase fourfold by 2020; plans have been instituted for proper city planning, sewage and water treatment and other related facilities.

Biodiversity
Because of the great variety of plants and animals within Bhutan, the country is included in Conservation International's list of global 'hotspots' for the conservation of biological diversity. Ecologists consider the eastern Himalaya to be an area critically important to the global efforts to preserve biological diversity.

The hotspot list identifies the high biodiversity ecosystems under the greatest threat of destruction as well as wilderness ecosystems that still remain virtually intact. The list, first compiled in 1990 and reviewed and updated in 1996, identifies 19 priority biodiversity hotspots, based on two criteria: the number of endemic species an ecosystem contains and the degree of threat it faces.

These hotspots occupy less than 2% of the Earth's land surface and contain a disproportionately large percentage of unique biodiversity. Of all the plants and animals that are found in these areas, almost 40% are not found anywhere else. The hotspots contain more than 50% of Earth's terrestrial biodiversity and two-thirds to three-quarters of the most endangered species of plants and animals.

Conservation Organisations
Royal Society for the Protection of Nature (RSPN) This NGO was established in 1986 and is actively involved in conservation education and has established nature clubs in many schools throughout the country. Among the innovative programmes it has developed is a study course called 'Follow that Stream'. Under the guidance of RSPN-trained teachers, students observe the transformation in water quality and life forms as a stream passes through their village. RSPN performs an annual census of the endangered black-necked cranes in the

Phobjikha valley and in Bomdeling, near Trashi Yangtse, and has also produced two documentary videos on the cranes.

WWF The WWF is known in the US and Canada as the World Wildlife Fund, and elsewhere as the Worldwide Fund for Nature. The WWF Bhutan programme began in 1977 with a series of training opportunities for Bhutanese conservationists. WWF established a programme office in Thimphu in 1992 and works with the government to manage protected areas and promote conservation awareness.

Important WWF projects include surveys that helped establish Bhutan's system of protected areas, and the creation of Bhutan's first nature study centre in Black Mountain National Park. Another project helps and supports the conservation activities of the National Women's Association of Bhutan (NWAB) and the RSPN. WWF has worked closely with the government to formulate and implement a management plan for the fragile environment of Royal Manas National Park and has developed a project to reduce poaching and illegal wildlife trade. To learn more about how you can support WWF's activities in Bhutan, write to them at PO Box 210, Thimphu (☎ 975-2-23528; fax 23518).

FLORA & FAUNA
Flora
Bhutan supports a great variety of plants, ranging from tropical species in the south to alpine tundra in the Himalayan regions in the north. Though the government policy is to maintain at least 60% of the land as forest, the present ratio is higher, with a remarkable 72% of the country covered in forests of fir, mixed conifers, temperate and broadleaf species.

An astonishing array of plants grow in Bhutan: over 5000 species, including 300 species of medicinal plants and over 50 species of rhododendron. Of the more than 600 species of orchid, most are commonly found up to 2100m, although some hardy species thrive even above 3700m.

Bhutan's heavy rain encourages tree growth. Forests are found up to 4500m and serve not only as a source of fuel, timber and herbs, but also as a cultural resource, as they form the basis of many folk songs and ritual offerings to the gods in the form of wood, flowers and leaves. The trees of the far eastern Himalaya are very different from those of the western Himalaya of India and Nepal.

Because glaciation had no impact on the lower reaches of the Himalaya, these foothills remain repositories of plants whose origins can be traced back before the ice age. That makes this area home to some of the most ancient species of vegetation on earth.

In Bhutan the vegetation profile falls into five general classes:

- Tropical – up to 1000m
- Subtropical – 900m to 1800m
- Temperate – 1800m to 3500m
- Subalpine – 3500 to 4500m
- Alpine – 4500 to 5500m

Tropical & Subtropical Tropical evergreen forests growing below 800m are repositories of unique biodiversity, but much of the rich vegetation at these lower elevations has been cleared for pasture and terraced farmland. In the next vegetation zone are the subtropical grasslands and forests, found between 900m and 1800m. The tree rhododendron is found in this zone, along with forests of oak, walnut and sal, and numerous varieties of orchid.

Forests of sal, a hardwood used for building construction and railroad ties (for export to India), are found in the south. Sal grows at elevations as high as 1250m, and is the dominant species wherever it occurs. The evergreen Indian laburnum, which bears vivid yellow flowers between April and June, is also found here. The distinctive flame of the forest bears vivid orange flowers between February and May.

The easily identifiable hemp, with its five-pointed leaves, grows on the perimeters of cultivated land and along road edges, even in Thimphu. Hemp has, of course, many uses other than the obvious one, and has been traditionally woven into rope and cloth. In Bhutan hemp is considered a weed and is fed to the pigs – imagine a pig with the 'munchies'!

The chir pine is a tall, straight conifer that appears on sunny slopes in the subtropical zone. It has long, often bright green, needles and medium-sized, oval cones. You can easily distinguish it from its relative, the blue pine, by counting the number of needles in a bundle. The needles of the chir pine are in groups of three and those of the blue pine are shorter and in groups of five. The wood is used for rough furniture and boxes. The chir can be harvested for its resin, which is used to make rosin and turpentine.

Temperate The temperate zone is a region of great diversity, largely influenced by the elevation. The tropical vegetation of the lower zones gives way to dark forests of oak, birch, maple, magnolia and laurel. On most hills, the sunny south side is forested with broadleaf species such as oak, and the damp, shady north side with rhododendron and conifers.

Above 2400m is the spruce, yew and weeping cypress, and higher still, growing up to the tree line, is the east Himalayan fir. A high-altitude variety of oak is found between 2250m to 2850m and above this are substantial forests of birch.

Throughout this zone you'll find rhododendron, poplar, willow, walnut, ash, aspen and magnolia. Conifers include blue pine, hemlock, larch and fir. In the autumn you will see the mauve or pinkish flowers of the Himalayan wild cherry blooming in the hills between 1200m and 3000m.

Between March and May the hillsides are ablaze with the deep red flowers of the etho metho. This used to be Bhutan's national flower, and is the country's most famous rhododendron. The Bhutanese commonly call white rhododendron species *takpa* and red rhododendrons *takma*.

The blue pine is found at altitudes up to 4000m and is often mixed with juniper and birch trees. The wood of the blue pine is

often used for roofing shingles and the bark of the tree is often cut to collect resin.

Subalpine & Alpine Between the tree line and the snow line at about 5500m are low shrubs, rhododendron, Himalayan grasses and flowering herbs. Junipers are found in a dwarfed form at altitudes over 4000m. Their distinctive foliage, short prickly needles and reddish-brown bark that peels off in long strips, should be unmistakable. Look for their fleshy, berry-like fruit as well. Also in this region are lichens, mosses and alpine flowers such as the tiny rhododendron nivale, edelweiss, and varieties of primula.

As the snows begin to melt at the end of the long winter, the high-altitude grazing lands are carpeted with a multitude of wildflowers, which remain in bloom until early summer. After the onset of the monsoon, in July, a second and even more vibrant flowering occurs, which extends until the end of the monsoon, in late August or early September. Some of the varieties found at these higher elevations include anemones, forget-me-nots, dwarf irises, dwarf rhododendrons, primulas, delphiniums and ranunculus, among others.

Blue Poppy The blue poppy, Bhutan's national flower, is a delicate blue or purple-tinged bloom with a white filament. In Dzongkha it is known by the name *euitgel metog hoem*. It grows to nearly 1m tall, on the rocky mountain terrain found above the tree line (3500-4500m elevation). The flowering season occurs during the early monsoon, from late May to July, and the seeds yield oil. It is a monocarpic plant, which means that it blooms only once. It grows for several years, then flowers, produces seeds and dies. Poppies can be found atop some high passes from the far eastern parts of the country all the way across to the west.

At one time the blue poppy was considered to be myth, along with the yeti, because its existence was not confirmed. In 1933 a British Botanist, George Sherriff, who was in Bhutan studying Himalayan flora, found the plant in the remote mountain region of Sakten in eastern Bhutan. Despite this proof that the flower exists, few people have seen one; a mystique surrounds the species in the same way it does the snow leopard.

Useful Trees & Shrubs As well as sal and the other trees just mentioned, several other forest species in Bhutan are important for commercial, medicinal and domestic purposes. The east Himalayan fir is used for roofing shingles and its leaves have medicinal properties. The wooden bowls that are used in Bhutan are made from maple. Birch is used for the carved wooden blocks used to print Buddhist texts. The national tree is the weeping cypress, which is valued as timber and for producing incense. Oak is used extensively for firewood.

Lemongrass is harvested for essential oil production. Bhutanese handmade paper is made from the daphne plant, which grows at higher elevations, or from a lowland plant known as edgeworthia. Both of these plants are known as *dhey shing* or *dheykap* in Dzongkha.

In deciduous forests in the duars grows sissoo, used in furniture, and semal, which is used for matches, plywood and paper. The two plants that produce the ingredients in *doma* (betel nut) are also found here. The nut comes from the khair, a palm-like tree, and the leaf used to wrap it comes from the betel leaf vine.

Fauna

Bhutan has 165 species of mammals. The region near Royal Manas National Park is home to a large variety of well-known south Asian game species.

Takin The takin, (see boxed text), resembles a cross between a gnu and a musk deer. It has an immense face and a tremendously thick neck. Short, thick legs support its heavy body, which rises to more than 1m at the shoulder. They live in north-western and

---

The Takin – Bhutan's National Animal

The reason for selecting the takin as the national animal is based both on its uniqueness and its strong association with the country's religious history and mythology. When the great saint Lama Drukpa Kunley, the Divine Madman, visited Bhutan in the 15th century, a large congregation of devotees gathered from around the country to witness his magical powers. The people urged the lama to perform a miracle.

However, the saint, in his usual unorthodox and outrageous way (see the boxed text 'The Divine Madman' in the Western Bhutan chapter), demanded that he first be served a whole cow and a goat for lunch. He devoured these with relish and left only the bones. After letting out a large and satisfied burp, he took the goat's head and stuck it onto the bones of the cow. And then with a snap of his finger he commanded the strange beast to rise up and graze on the mountainside. To the astonishment of the people the animal arose and ran up to the meadows to graze. This animal came to be known as the *dong gyem tsey* (takin) and to this day these rather clumsy animals can be seen grazing on the mountainsides of Bhutan.

The takin continues to befuddle taxonomists, who cannot quite relate it to any other animal. The famous biologist George Schaller called it a 'beestung moose', referring to its humped nose and similarity in size to the North American moose. Taxonomists have now put it into a class by itself, *budorcas taxicolor*.

The takin's grazing and browsing behaviour further befuddles their taxonomic status. In the open meadows they behave like herd animals such as the wildebeest of the Serengeti plains of Africa. They stay in a herd and are physically large, and have horns to defend themselves in the open and exposed meadows. In the forest they behave like animals adapted to dense forests

far north-eastern Bhutan, although the likeliest place to see one is in the mini-zoo in Thimphu.

Monkey Three species of monkey are found in Bhutan. The rhesus monkeys, earth-coloured with short tails, travel on the ground in large, structured troops, and are unafraid of humans. The langur are arboreal, and have black faces, grey fur and long limbs and tails. The rhesus habitat ranges from the duars up to 2400m, while the langur's goes higher, up to 3600m.

Golden Langur Bhutan is the only place in the world where the golden langur is found; the small primate's existence was not even known to the scientific community until the 20th century. Not surprisingly, its distinctive feature is its golden coat, which varies in lightness from season to season, as well as by region. Even within Bhutan, its range is only from the Puna Tsang Chhu in the west to the Manas river system in the east. The northern limit is the Black Mountains. If you are fortunate enough to see a golden langur, it will undoubtedly be in the trees, probably in open forest. The animal has a specially adapted stomach that allows it to digest leaves.

Elephant The Asian elephant roams in and around the Royal Manas National Park and in the rainy season may travel far into the hills to the north. This elephant is starkly different from its African relative, and belongs to a separate genus. Elephants are also known to maintain matriarchal societies, and females up to 60 years of age bear calves. Though able to reach 80 years of age, elephants' life spans are determined by their teeth: their molars are replaced as they wear down, but only up to six times. When the final set is worn, the elephant dies of starvation.

Snow Leopard The snow leopard's extraordinarily beautiful coat – soft grey with black or dark grey spots – has, unfortunately, been its downfall worldwide. It has been

---

and the herd scatters and most animals remain solitary, much like deer.

In summer, takins migrate to subalpine forests and alpine meadows above 3700m and graze on the luxuriant grasses, herbs, and shrubs found there. By migrating they escape the leeches, mosquitoes, horseflies, and other parasites of the monsoon-swept lower valleys. This is also the time when the vegetation in the alpine region is richest in nutrients. Thus, takins can gain several kilograms of storable energy: some males become massive, weighing as much as 1000kg or more. Summer is also the time when takins mate. The gestation period is between seven and eight months, and young – usually a single calf – are born between December and February. These are black, in contrast to the golden yellow and brownish coat of the adults. Sometimes the Himalayan black bear follows pregnant female takins and immediately after she has given birth, chases her away and eats the calf.

In late August takins start their slow descent to the lower valleys. They do this in stages, grazing as they descend lower. They arrive at the winter grazing grounds in temperate broadleaf forests between 2000m and 3000m by late October.

Hunting is banned by law, and poaching is limited since there is no high economic value placed on the body parts of the takin. In traditional medicine, however, the horn of the takin, consumed in minute amounts, is supposed to help women during a difficult childbirth.

The major threats the takin face are competition with domestic yaks for food in the alpine regions and loss of habitat in the temperate regions. In the temperate zones, logging may have detrimental effects on the takin's survival.

Tashi Wangchuk

hunted relentlessly and is now in danger of extinction. Elusive and elegant, the big cat is almost entirely solitary, largely because a single animal's hunting territory is so vast (about 10,000 sq km) and prey is scarce throughout the very high-altitude areas in which it lives. However, when its favourite prey, the blue sheep, migrates to lower valleys in winter, the snow leopard follows. It is then that the sexes might meet, although the females are only receptive to mating for one week.

Tiger Of the world's large predators, the tiger is perhaps the most spectacular. Tigers are strongly territorial, like domestic cats, and basically solitary. Each male's territorial range is up to 100 sq km, and a female's range is only a little smaller. Though they are mostly concentrated in and around Royal Manas National Park, tigers may be found throughout Bhutan, even at higher altitudes, and as far north as Jigme Dorji National Park.

Several tiger conservation measures already have been implemented in Bhutan and, coupled with the strong protected areas system, has provided a favourable environment for the animal. The protected regions of Bhutan and India provide sufficient habitat to sustain viable breeding populations.

Other Cats Several species of cat share the tiger's habitat; these include the Asiatic golden cat, fishing cat, clouded leopard, common leopard and marbled cat.

Rhino The greater one-horned rhino is the largest of the three Asian species of rhino and belongs to a totally different genus to that of the two-horned African varieties. It has poor eyesight and, though weighing up to two tonnes, is amazingly quick. Rhinos are not to be trifled with.

Bear & Panda The Himalayan black bear is omnivorous and a bane to farmers growing corn in the temperate forests. Bears do occasionally attack humans, probably because their poor eyesight lead them to interpret

that a standing person is making a threatening gesture. If a bear approaches to attack, the best defence is not to run, but to lie face down on the ground.

Black bears are known to roam in winter instead of hibernating. The common black bear is found at elevations below 2000m.

The sloth bear is a medium-sized bear with a shaggy black coat and a white U or V-shaped mark on its chest. It eats mostly termites.

The red panda, or cat bear, is known in Bhutan as *aamchu donkha* and is most commonly found near Pele La, Thrumshing La, and parts of the Gasa district. It is about 50cm tall, bright chestnut-coloured, and has a white face. It is largely herbivorous: it eats leaves, roots and grasses. The red panda is nocturnal, sleeping in trees during the day and coming to the ground to forage at night.

Wild Dogs Jackals and wild dogs can be found both inside and outside of the protected regions.

Deer The sambar, with its large, imposing horns, is the largest deer in Bhutan. The barking deer, or muntjac, usually makes its presence known by its sharp, one-note alarm call. Both are found in forested areas up to 2400m.

The unusual musk deer, with antelope-like features, is only 50cm high at the shoulder and is taxonomically stranded between deer and antelopes. The male is not only hornless, but also has oversized canine teeth that protrude from its mouth. The males also have a musk gland in their abdomens, and the high value of musk as an ingredient in perfume has accelerated the demise of the species. This diminutive deer is very secretive and prefers forest cover near the tree line.

Goat & Antelope The blue sheep, or bharal, is genetically defined somewhere between goats and sheep. It turns a bluish-grey in winter and is found in the Himalayan region from 1800m to 4300m.

You will see large herds of blue sheep on many trek routes.

The Himalayan tahr is difficult to classify, though its niche is that of a 'mountain-goat'. Except during the winter rutting season, these animals are found in two different kinds of herds, male and female. The males are sometimes seen alone and have long flowing manes and coats and short, curved horns.

The Tibetan gazelle is found at elevations above 5000m in a few of the higher valleys opening into Tibet.

The brown goral is found only in the eastern Himalaya. It has small, backward-facing horns and lives at elevations between 900m and 2400m, though it occasionally moves higher.

The serow is a large, thick-set animal whose coat ranges in colour from almost black to red. Its preferred habitat is wooded areas between 1800m and 3000m elevation.

Other Mammals Other large mammals include the wolf, yak, wild water buffalo, gaur and wild pig. Fat marmots whistle as you pass their burrows in the high alpine pastures.

Birds Each year Bhutan's extensive bird list grows longer, a consequence of both Bhutan's biodiversity and the small amount of systematic birding that has been done in the kingdom.

So far, 675 species have been recorded in Bhutan. This reflects the kingdom's wide range of agro-ecological environments – from subtropical to alpine – and its location at the northern edge of the zoogeographical Indomalayan (Oriental) region and the

The Black-Necked Crane

The rare and endangered black-necked crane occupies a special place in Bhutanese hearts and folklore. Its arrival every autumn from Tibet inspires songs and dances; it usually heralds the end of the harvesting season and also the time when farm families start migrating to warmer climates.

Many legends and myths exist about the bird, which the Bhutanese call *thrung thrung*. The high mountain valleys of Phobjikha, Bumdeling and Gyetsa serve as the winter habitat for about 360 birds. Like other cranes, these have an elaborate mating ritual, a dance in which pairs bow, leap into the air and toss vegetation about while uttering loud bugling calls. It can be difficult to distinguish the sexes because the coloration is so similar, but the females are slightly smaller. Preferred delicacies include fallen grain, tubers and insects.

The world's entire population of 5600-6000 black-necked cranes breed in Tibet and Ladakh. They winter in south-central Tibet and north-eastern Yunan province in China, as well as in Bhutan.

The plumage of the male Himalayan monal is a shimmering array of iridescent green, gold, blue and purple.

permeable and fluid (for birds) border with China.

The variety of birds can be highly variable over a short distance and is also very seasonal. Bhutan is famous for its overwintering populations (about 350 birds) of the vulnerable black-necked crane in the valleys of Phobjikha, Bomdeling and Gyetsa (in Bumthang). Less well-known are the overwintering populations, mainly as solitary individuals, of the endangered white-bellied heron, for which there are about five records in the last five years, including one on the Mo Chhu above Punakha.

Some bird species are even more transient, migrating through Bhutan between Tibet and northern India in autumn and spring. Pailas' fish eagle, which is considered rare, is regularly seen migrating up the Punak Chhu near Wangdi in spring. It is often in the company of ospreys, a wide range of ducks, waders such as the pied avocet, and other species that breed in Tibet.

As well as the seasonal migrants, there is widespread internal migration. Winter brings numerous species down to lower altitudes, including accentors, rosefinches, grosbeaks, snow pigeons and pheasants such as the satyr tragopan, the Himalayan monal and the blood pheasant. Observant early-morning walkers can often find these on the mountains and passes around Thimphu. In the east of Bhutan, the rare Blyth's tragopan has been recorded. The Khalij pheasant is relatively common throughout the year. In summer many lowland species move to higher altitudes to breed: these species include the exotic-looking hoopoe, various species of minivets, cuckoos (one can commonly hear at least five different species calling), barbets, warblers, sunbirds, fulvettas and yuhinas.

Given the density of forest cover and the steep vertical descents, the road is often the best place from which to watch birds, as the traffic volume is very low. Recommended stretches include the road down from Dochu La to Wangdue Phodrang (the adventurous can take the old trail, which is even better), from Wangdue Phodrang to Nobding (on the way to Pele La), and before Trongsa. For those who go east, the 2000m descent between Sengor and Limithang is spectacular: Ward's trogon and the Rufous-necked hornbill have been recorded in this area. Trekking will provide you with a greater chance of seeing high-altitude birds, including the lammergeier, the Himalayan griffon, the raven, the unique high-altitude wader – the ibisbill – and pheasants.

Even the casual observer can be sure to see the blue whistling-thrush (usually diving into a culvert), yellow-billed blue magpies, the wallcreeper (in jerky, crimson-streaked flight), white capped water redstarts, plumbeous water redstarts and spotted nutcrackers in pine forest, and red-billed choughs on the roofs of dzongs.

There are no specific bird guides for Bhutan, but Salim Ali's *Field Guide to the Birds of the Eastern Himalayas* and *Pictorial Guide to the Birds of the Indian Subcontinent* (both Oxford University Press, India) are recommended. However, many species names that he uses are outdated and a current listing can be found in T Inskipp, N Lindsey and W Duckworth's *An Annotated Checklist of the Birds of the Oriental Region* (available through the Oriental Bird Club c/o The

Winter brings the blood pheasant down
to lower elevations.

Lodge, Sandy, Bedfordshire SG19 2DL, UK).
If you wish to know the calls – and this is
often the only way of identifying reclusive or
hidden species – then Scott Connop's tape
Birds Songs of the Himalaya covers the calls ·
of 70 species.

Endangered Species All animals in
Bhutan are protected by the Buddhist ethic
that prohibits killing. As further protection,
the 1995 Forest & Nature Conservation Act
defines several species as totally protected.
These are the Asian elephant, clouded leopard, golden langur, musk deer, pangolin,
pygmy hog, snow leopard, takin, tiger, wild
buffalo, black-necked crane, monal pheasant,
peacock pheasant, raven, Rufous-necked
hornbill, golden mahseer, spotted deer, gaur,
leopard, leopard cat, Himalayan black bear,
red panda and serow.

NATIONAL PARKS & PROTECTED AREAS

A total of 26% of the country is in protected
areas. All of these protected areas encompass
regions in which there is a resident human
population. Bhutan's Nature Conservation
Section, with assistance from the WWF, has
developed an Integrated Conservation and
Development Programme to allow people
living within a protected area to graze
animals, farm, collect plants and cut firewood in harmony with park management
and protection programmes. Preserving the
culture and fostering local traditions is part
of the mandate of Bhutan's national park
system.

In 1993 the existing protected area
system was revised and an extra 1500 sq km
added, including the Black Mountains and
Thrumshing La national parks. These areas
were set aside for their potential importance
and to preserve the biodiversity of the
country. The Nature Conservation Section
has done research in the Black Mountains,
Royal Manas and Jigme Dorji national
parks, but most of the other protected areas
have not yet been fully studied and the indigenous species have not as yet been
catalogued.

Bhutan established its national park
system to protect important ecosystems,
and they have not been developed as tourist
attractions. You will not find the kind of facilities you may normally associate with
national parks such as entrance stations,
campgrounds and visitor centres (or even
signs). In many cases you won't even be
aware that you are entering or leaving a national park.

Jigme Dorji National Park

This is the largest protected area in the
country, encompassing an area of 4349 sq
km. It protects the western parts of Paro,
Thimphu and Punakha dzongkhags and
almost the entire area of Gasa Dzongkhag.
Habitats in the park range from subtropical
areas at 1400m to alpine heights at 7000m.
The park management has to cope with the
needs of both lowland farmers and semi-
nomadic yak herders. Villagers are also
allowed to harvest indigenous plants such
as juniper, fir and rhododendron to manufacture incense.

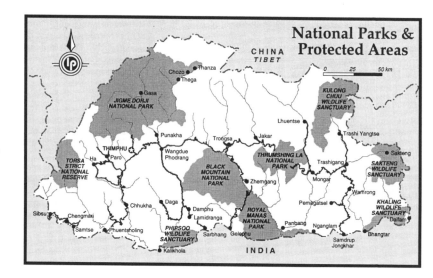

The park is the habitat of several endangered species, including the takin, snow leopard, blue sheep, musk deer, red panda and serow. Other mammals to be found are leopards, wild dogs, sambar, barking deer, goral, marmot and pika. More than 300 species of birds have been catalogued within the park.

Three of the country's major trekking routes pass through the park. Ecotourism guidelines are being established to prevent environmental damage.

In consultation with the local people, an Integrated Conservation and Development Project was developed for the area by the Bhutanese government and the WWF Bhutan Programme. The project seeks to encourage the park's residents to participate in the conservation, development and management of the park at all stages, from planning to implementation, monitoring and evaluation.

The project focuses on overgrazing, overharvesting of medicinal plants, firewood consumption, ecotourism and community development. A management plan that is currently being prepared for the park will ensure this rich reserve is protected in the long term. The park headquarters is at Gasa and there are several outposts throughout the area.

Royal Manas National Park
This 1023 sq km park in south Central Bhutan adjoins the Black Mountain National Park to the north and India's Manas National Park and Manas Tiger Reserve to the south. Together they form a 5000 sq km protected area that runs from the plains to the Himalayan peaks.

The area has been protected as a wildlife sanctuary since 1966 and was upgraded to a national park in 1988. It is the home of rhinoceros, buffalo, tiger, leopard, gaur, bear, elephant and several species of deer. It is also home to several rare species, including the golden langur and capped langur. An amazing 362 species of birds have been catalogued here.

Black Mountain National Park
The Black Mountain reserve (1723 sq km) protects the range of hills that separates eastern and western Bhutan. It is an important area because it includes virgin forests

in an area that is generally known as the middle hills. This band of hills extends across the entire Himalayan foothills of Nepal and India and has largely been cleared of forests.

The Black Mountains represent the only significant area in the entire middle hills that is still in its natural state. Its plant life includes a wide range of broadleaf species, conifers and alpine pastures. Animals found in the park include tiger, Himalayan black bear, leopard, red panda, goral, serow, sambar, wild pig and golden langur. The Phobjikha valley, wintering place of black-necked cranes, is included in the park.

The park's southern boundary adjoins Royal Manas National Park and it adjoins the Phobjikha conservation area. WWF helped to develop the park management plan and has established a nature study centre at Khebethang at the southern end of the Phobjikha valley.

Phipsoo Wildlife Sanctuary

This 278 sq km area was set aside in 1974 as a wildlife reserve and upgraded to a wildlife sanctuary in 1993. On the southern border of Bhutan, about 50km east of Phuentsholing, it was established to protect the only remaining natural sal forest in Bhutan. Several protected species thrive in the sanctuary, including axis deer, chital, elephant, gaur, tiger, golden langur and hornbill. The WWF is working with the Bhutan government to develop and maintain a suitable protection and management system for the Phipsoo sanctuary.

Thrumshing La National Park

The 768 sq km Thrumshing La National Park lies between Bumthang and Mongar. It was set aside to protect temperate forests of fir and chir pine. It is also home to red panda.

Kulong Chhu Wildlife Sanctuary

The Kulong Chhu Wildlife Sanctuary protects most of Yangtse Dzongkhag. Within the 1300 sq km reserve is a large area of alpine tundra. The sanctuary protects the sambar and adjoins the Bomdeling conservation area, which is an important roosting place of black-necked cranes. Kulong Chhu Sanctuary lies on the eastern border of Bhutan, adjoining a planned reserve in the Indian state of Arunachal Pradesh.

Sakteng Wildlife Sanctuary

This sanctuary is unique because it is the only reserve in the world created specifically to protect the habitat of the yeti. It's in the easternmost part of the country, where 650 sq km of temperate forests of eastern blue pine and rhododendron are protected. This sanctuary lies on the Indian border and adjoins a planned national park in India.

Migoi – The Bhutanese Yeti

Naturally, Bhutanese yetis have different characteristics from yetis (or not found) in Tibet and other Himalayan regions. The Bhutanese name for a yeti is *migoi* (strong man) and they are believed to exist throughout the northern part of the country. The Sakteng Wildlife Sanctuary in eastern Bhutan has been set aside to protect a likely migoi habitat.

The migoi is covered in hair that may be anything from reddish-brown to almost black, but its face is hairless, almost human. It is similar to the yetis of Nepal and Tibet in that the breasts of the female are large and sagging and both sexes have an extremely unpleasant smell. But Bhutanese migoi are special because they have the power to become invisible, which accounts for the fact that so few people have seen them. Another feature that helps them escape detection is that on many yetis their feet face backwards, confusing people who try to follow them.

The book *Bhutanese Tales of the Yeti* by Kunzang Choden (White Lotus Press, Bangkok) is a wonderful collection of tales told by village people in Bhutan who have seen, or have met people who have seen, a migoi.

Khaling/Neoli Wildlife Sanctuary
In far south-eastern Bhutan, 273 sq km have been set aside as the Khaling/Neoli Wildlife Sanctuary. Wild elephant, gaur, pygmy hog, hispid hare and other tropical wildlife are protected here. This sanctuary adjoins India's proposed Khaling reserve.

Torsa Strict Nature Reserve
The Torsa reserve is in the western part of the Ha district, where the Torsa river enters from Tibet. The 644 sq km reserve was set aside to protect the temperate forests of far west Bhutan.

GOVERNMENT & POLITICS
The present form of the legislative, judicial and administrative systems in Bhutan was established in 1968 as part of the late King Jigme Dorji Wangchuck's modernisation programme.

In many ways, the government has assum-ed a very protective role. This is possible because of the small population and compact size of the country. The King and senior government officials are very concerned about issues of development, education and health care, and environmental and cultural preservation.

This protectiveness also extends to various aspects of tourism. While many aspects of the tourism policy are designed to protect Bhutan's culture, economy and environment from excessive influence from tourists, some controls are intended to safe-guard tourists themselves from harm. Most of the southern part of Bhutan is off-limits because of the danger of attacks from mili-tant Indian separatist groups that have sought refuge inside Bhutan.

The government makes an effort to explain the reasoning behind the many rules and regulations it implements and people generally comply with established proce-

Bhutanese Symbols
The National Flag
The upper half of the flag is yellow, signifying the secular authority of the king. It is the colour of fruitful action, both in the affairs of religion and of the state.

The lower half of the flag is orange, representing the religious practice and spiritual power of Buddhism as it is manifested in the Kagyu and Nyingma lineages.

The *druk* (dragon) honours the thunder dragon after which the country is named. White represents purity and expresses the loyalty of the country's various ethnic and linguistic groups. The snarling mouth of the druk expresses the stern strength of the male and female deities protecting Bhutan. In the druk's claws are jewels representing the country's wealth and perfection.

The National Anthem
In the Thunder Dragon Kingdom adorned with sandalwood,
The protector who guards the teachings of the dual system,
He, the precious and glorious ruler, causes dominion to spread,
While his unchanging person abides in consistency,
As the doctrine of the Lord Buddha flourishes,
May the sun and peace of happiness shine on the people.

The Raven Crown
The crown of Bhutan is known as Usa Jaro Jongchen. Its brim is embroidered with a motif called Jachung and on the top is the head of a raven. This symbol is in recognition of Mahakala, the protective deity of the first Shabdrung. On the head of the raven are a sun and moon, together a symbol of longevity, steadfastness and enlightenment, and the Norbu, a sacred gem symbolising the fulfilment of right endeavour.

---

dures for taxes, licensing and social standards. Even drivers follow the rules, though this is the only way to survive when driving on Bhutan's narrow roads.

Bhutan's six development goals, as expressed by King Jigme Singye Wangchuck, are:

- Self-reliance
- Sustainability
- Efficiency and development of the private sector
- People's participation and decentralisation
- Human resource development
- Regionally balanced development

The National Assembly
The Tshogdu, or National Assembly, has 154 members, who fall into three categories. The largest group, with 105 members, are the *chimis*, representatives of Bhutan's 20 *dzongkhags* (districts), who are elected for three-year terms. The regional monk bodies elect 12 monastic representatives who also serve three-year terms. Another 37 representatives are senior civil servants nominated by the king. They include the 20 *dzongdas* (district officers), ministers, secretaries of various government departments and other high-ranking officials.

The Tshogdu elects a speaker who presides over the twice-yearly meetings. The speaker may also call special sessions when the need arises. The Tshogdu enacts legislation and advises the government on all matters of national importance. Decisions are passed by a simple majority, though a secret ballot is sometimes used for certain issues. Any Bhutanese over the age of 25 can be a candidate for election as a chimi. At the insistence of the third king, the Tshogdu has the power to replace the monarch by a two-thirds vote. In June 1998 the king instituted major political reforms and instructed the Tshogdu to endorse a mechanism for a vote of confidence in the Druk Gyalpo.

The Royal Advisory Council

A body known as the Lodoi Tsokde, or Royal Advisory Council, was formally established in 1965 to advise the king and government ministers on important questions and to supervise the implementation of programmes and policies laid down by the Tshogdu. The chairman is appointed by the king. There are six representatives of the people and two from the monk bodies. The Lodoi Tsokde is always in session.

The Council of Ministers

The *Lhengyal Shungtshog* is composed of the *lyonpos* (ministers) of the government departments and nine Royal Advisory Councillors. The eight ministries are Home Affairs, Trade and Industry, Health and Education, Finance, Foreign Affairs, Planning, Agriculture and Communication. Until 1998 lyonpos were appointed by the king, and many served for extended periods, including Lyonpo Dawa Tsering, who holds a place in the *Guinness Book of Records* as the world's longest-serving Foreign Minister (1972-1998). Since political reforms in 1998, lyonpos are elected by the National Assembly, with the chairmanship of the Lhengyal Shungtshog held in rotation among them.

The Monastic Order

Religious institutions gain important patronage from the government. The state supports about 5000 monks in various monk bodies collectively known as the *sangha*. The Je Khenpo is the chief abbot of Bhutan and the head of the monastic establishment. The office is an elected one and the present incumbent is the 70th in an unbroken succession of Je Khenpos since the office was created by the Shabdrung in 1637. The Je Khenpo is chosen by members of the *dratshang* (central monk body), who send the nomination to the king for his consent.

The dratshang is presided over by the Je Khenpo, who is the spiritual head of Bhutan.

The Je Khenpo is the only person besides the King who wears the saffron scarf, an honour denoting his authority over all religious institutions.

The Judiciary

Bhutan's legal code, both civil and criminal, is based on that laid down by Ngawang Namgyal, the first Shabdrung. While a number of modifications have been made, the code preserves the spirit and substance of traditional Buddhist precepts. The present laws, called the Thrimshung Chenmo (Supreme Laws), were enacted by the National Assembly in 1957 under the leadership of the third king.

Minor litigation is practically a national pastime in Bhutan. Most disputes are settled at the local level by *gups* (village heads) or the chimi. The legal system encourages compromise and arbitration to avoid the expense of going to court. The Bhutanese legal system does not have a formal system of solicitors and lawyers, but it does permit those accused in criminal cases to appoint a trained para-legal counsel, called a *jambi*, to represent them.

Each dzongkhag has its own *dzongkhag thrimkhang* (district court) headed by a *thrimpon* (district magistrate). The *Thrimkhang Gongma* (high court) was established in 1968, with both original and appellate jurisdictions. The high court has eight judges, presided over by a chief justice. All citizens are treated equally in the eyes of the law, and if they feel they have been treated unfairly by the court system, everyone has the right to make an appeal to the king.

Autonomous Bodies

The government includes several other independent institutions, some of which are unique to Bhutan.

Special Commission for Cultural Affairs

This commission, known as the Solzin Lhentshog, was established in 1985 and is responsible for preserving Bhutan's religious and cultural heritage. The council, under the chairmanship of the home minister, administers the National Museum, National Library, Royal Academy of Performing Arts and the School of Arts and Crafts.

National Environment Commission Bhutan has an independent national commission that is charged with making and regulating policies to manage and preserve the country's natural resources. The body is chaired by the planning minister and includes ministers and secretaries from several related government departments.

Council for Ecclesiastical Affairs Known as the Dratshang Lhentshog, this nine-member council is presided over by the Je Khenpo. The council is responsible for preserving the purity of religious teaching, ensuring the well-being of the monk body and administering religious establishments.

Dzongkha Development Commission This independent body advances Dzongkha, the national language, and coordinates all linguistic matters. Its activities include producing school textbooks and establishing standards for transliterating Dzongkha to English.

Royal Civil Service Commission The Department of Manpower, which was established in 1973, was renamed the Royal Civil Service Commission in 1992 and is responsible for developing and implementing the civil service's personnel policies.

Royal Audit Authority This independent commission is responsible for auditing the accounts of all ministries, divisions, dzong-khag administrations and projects.

Royal Monetary Authority The functions of Bhutan's central bank are performed by the Royal Monetary Authority. It issues banknotes and coins and supervises Bhutan's two commercial banks.

Royal Institute of Management Training and development of the country's public administration system is performed by the Royal Institute of Management, based in Simtokha.

Local Government
The dzongs are the focal points of every district's administration, as well as its economic, social and religious affairs. The country is divided into 20 administrative districts called dzongkhags, each with a district administrator, called a dzongda, who is responsible to the home minister. *Rabdeys* (district monk bodies) are based in dzongs and are presided over by an abbot.

Larger dzongkhags are divided into smaller sub-districts called *dungkhags*, which are presided over by a *dungpa*.

The lowest administrative level is the *gewog* (block), headed by an elected official known as a gup. A gup is elected by the people of the community for a three-year term. Because of regional linguistic differences, these officials are called *mandals* in the south. Village or block councils are called Gewog Yargay Tshokchung, commonly referred to by the initials GYT.

The next level of community forum is the dzongkhag development council, Dzongkhag Yargay Tshokchung, or DYT. These are citizen groups that can make recommendations to the Tshogdu through their representative, the local chimi. Because Bhutan is such a small country, many issues that in other places would be strictly local matters are dealt with at the national level.

ECONOMY
The per-capita income in 1995 was US$470. One reason for the low figure is that 85% of the population is engaged in subsistence farming and has minimal cash income. Subsistence farming means just that; if the farmer doesn't take care of the crops, or there is some natural disaster, the family has no food.

Only 7.8% of the land is used for agriculture. Most of this is in the south. Cash crops are maize, rice, millet, wheat, buckwheat, barley, mustard, potato, vegetables, orange, apple and cardamom. Most people raise cattle or, in the high country, yaks.

Though the vast majority of the population still farms, the agricultural sector's share of gross domestic product has dropped to less than 50% since the sale of hydroelectric power started contributing to the national income.

The Department of Mines enforces the government's conservation policies that control mining and quarrying. Small mines, mostly in the south, produce gypsum, limestone, dolomite, coal, talc, marble and slate.

Hydroelectric Power

The export of power already provides 25% of government revenue. Bhutanese officials see the export of electricity as the key to gaining economic independence from foreign donors. The government's policy is that the future backbone of the economy will be power. Hydroelectric power is Bhutan's largest resource and is sustainable, renewable and environmentally friendly. The government wants to eventually fund the country's entire budget by selling power.

Bhutan's other resources include forests and minerals, but it has so far chosen not to exploit them in a big way. Its strategy gives priority to conservation, and its hydroelectric projects are based mainly on river power rather than large dams, which damage the environment.

Power engineers estimate that the country has the potential to generate as much as 30,000MW. The Chhukha project is already generating 336MW, 78% of which is exported. The Tala project, also on the Wang Chhu, was started in 1996 and is planned to come on line in 2006 with a capacity of 1,020MW. Others include the 60MW project on the Kuri Chhu near Mongar and the 60.8MW Basochhu project near Wangdue Phodrang.

Despite the abundance of hydroelectric power in Bhutan, many rural homes are without electricity. Because it is expensive to construct power transmission lines to small villages in the hills, a portion of the income from the sale of hydroelectric power goes to develop local sources of energy.

Micro hydroelectric facilities are being constructed to serve rural communities throughout the country. The country has also embarked on a programme of introducing solar power into remote areas. The government's rural energy unit has a goal of electrifying all schools and monasteries where hydroelectric power is infeasible. Tshungmed, the country's first private solar energy company, is actively promoting solar energy and is working on a pilot project to bring electric lighting to the remote valley of Gasa.

Exports

As well as electricity, Bhutan exports calcium carbide, wood products and cement. Its other major export is agricultural products, including apples, canned fruit and jam. A new cash crop being successfully exported is mushrooms. More than 457 varieties of mushrooms are grown in Bhutan, of which 137 varieties are edible. The matsutake mushroom, known in Bhutan as *sangay shamu*, is exported to Japan, Singapore, Thailand and India. These mushrooms are found in Thimphu, Bumthang, Ha and Paro. With the help of the National Mushroom Project, farmers are also cultivating shiitake mushrooms in Thimphu and the east.

Other exports include ferrosilicon and cement. The Dungsam cement factory is planned with a capacity of 1500 tonnes a day. Bhutan Board Company is producing high-quality furniture from chipboard. Large trading partners are India and Bangladesh.

Stamps One of Bhutan's more unusual exports is postage stamps. The post office has produced an extensive collection of exotic stamps, including some made of metal or silk, others three-dimensional images and even stamps that are miniphonograph records. Many of the stamps have Bhutanese themes: dzongs, flowers and animals are commonly portrayed. Other, peculiar collections portray things like Roman emperors or Mickey Mouse and other Disney characters (see the colour section 'Collecting Bhutanese Stamps' between pages 96 and 97).

Essential Oil Production Oil is extracted from lemongrass, a fast-growing plant found throughout eastern Bhutan. It is distilled in local factories using large stainless steel boilers. The resulting oil is exported for use in perfume and as a deodorising agent in detergent and phenol. (For more information see the boxed text 'Essential Oil' in the Eastern Bhutan chapter.)

Development Policy

The government's policy is to restrain development to try to prevent failures, rather than allowing uncontrolled development and having to correct problems later.

Overall, Bhutan remains cautious about foreign influences. Although it allowed American soft drink manufacturer Pepsi to build a manufacturing plant in 1997, it still does not allow satellite television in an attempt to protect what the monarchy describes as a fragile culture.

Efforts are being made to develop growth centres in rural areas to discourage migration to the cities. The decision to locate the country's only college in the rural community of Kanglung in eastern Bhutan is an example of this strategy. Other schools and government facilities have been built in rural areas to encourage shopkeepers to look towards smaller markets rather than concentrating only on larger towns.

An ambitious eighth five-year plan was launched in 1997, and emphasised developing health, education, communication, roads and hydroelectric power. The king visited every district in the country and held meetings, at which every household was represented, to explain the plan to the people and to discuss their needs and problems.

Foreign Aid

In 1994 (the most recent statistics available at the time of research) Bhutan received US$77.7 million in foreign aid, most of it from India, Japan and Western Europe. Its total 1995-96 budget is Nu 5.15 billion (about US$145 million), with most going towards major construction efforts such as hydroelectric projects.

The government is quite concerned that socio-economic development should not lead to deterioration of either the people's way of life or their traditional values. Each project is scrutinised and may be slowed or stopped if it affronts religious faith or adversely affects the environment.

Development agencies working in Bhutan include several UN agencies under the overall umbrella of the UN Development Project (UNDP). Other important agencies are the Asian Development Bank, World Bank, WWF and several development agencies of the European Union. In addition to the large assistance provided by India, Bhutan has development ties with Japan, Switzerland, Denmark, Austria, the Netherlands, Canada, Australia and New Zealand.

The government wants to reduce its dependence on foreign aid and to become totally self-sufficient within 10 to 15 years. It has projected that the sale of hydroelectric power will meet the entire national budget within that period.

POPULATION & PEOPLE
Population

In 1994 the estimated population of Bhutan was 600,000, with 43% of the population aged under 15. The population growth rate is 3.1% per year, which is one of the highest in the world. As in many non-industrialised countries, the high infant mortality rate in the past induced people to have more children in the hope that at least some of them would survive. With the introduction of better medical facilities, many more children now survive, but it takes time for people to adjust their habits.

The government is keenly aware that an increased population will strain the country's resources. At present, Bhutan has a ratio of resources to population that provides adequate housing and food as well as an unspoiled environment. The government is working to introduce measures which will reduce the growth rate. They include birth control, provision of better education and increased employment opportunities for women.

The country is still predominantly rural. An estimated 80% of the population lives more than a one hour walk from a road and as much as 50% lives more than one day of walking from a motorable road.

There is some confusion over the discrepancy between a population figure of 1.2 million that was published by the UN and the current estimate of 600,000.

In 1971, when Bhutan applied for UN membership, the population was estimated at just less than 1 million. No census data existed and government officials estimated the population as best they could, choosing to err on the high side in order to help gain world recognition. Over the years, this nearly-a-million figure was adjusted upward in accordance with estimates of Bhutan's population growth figures, finally reaching the 1.2 million figure. In some publications this total was even listed at 1.5 million!

The 600,000 estimate is based on the census of 1988 and is now the accepted figure.

Ethnic Groups
The population can be categorised into three main ethnic groups.

Sharchops The Sharchops, who live in the east of the country, are recognised as the original inhabitants of Bhutan. They are Indo-Mongoloid; it is still unclear exactly where they migrated from and when they arrived in Bhutan. Their name, Sharchop, is translated 'people of the east'.

Ngalong The Ngalong are descendants of Tibetan immigrants who arrived in Bhutan from the 9th century. These immigrants settled in the west of the country; Ngalongs dominate the region west of the Black Mountains.

Lhotshampa The third group is the Nepalis, who began settling in the south of Bhutan in the late 19th century. The Lhotshampa represent numerous Nepal-speaking ethnic groups – primarily Brahman, Chettri, Gurung, Rai and Limbu.

Minority Groups Several smaller groups, many with their own language, form about 1% of the population. Many of these groups comprise fewer than 1000 people. The most important of these groups are the *Bumthap* in Bumthang, the *Mandhep* in Trongsa, the *Kheng* in the central region of Zhemgang, and the *Layap* in the north-west. Other smaller groups are the *Brokpa* in the far eastern villages of Mera and Sakteng, the *Doya* and *Lhopu* in the southern district of Samtse, the *Dagpa* in the east, *Tibetans* in the central-west and north and the *Lepcha* in the west.

Health
Once ranked as having one of the world's poorest health standards, Bhutan has made great efforts to improve health facilities and now provides free health care to all its citizens. It has achieved a child immunisation rate of nearly 100%, iodine deficiency has been eliminated and 50% of the population has access to clean water.

Life expectancy has increased from 47.4 years in 1984 to 66 years in 1994. Infant mortality was once the highest in the world, at 142 per thousand births; by 1995 it had been halved to 70.7 per thousand births.

Health care in Bhutan is provided on a four-tiered network consisting of the National Referral Hospital in Thimphu, two regional referral hospitals and smaller hospitals in the headquarters of each district. Rural health care is provided through a network of Basic Health Units (BHUs) staffed by a health assistant, nurse midwife and a basic health worker. These medical practitioners also serve a role similar to 'walking doctors' and provide services to more distant villages through a system of outreach clinics that they visit on a regular schedule.

EDUCATION
Until the 1950s, the only education available in Bhutan was from the monasteries. To obtain a secular education, students travelled to schools in Darjeeling. While monastic education continues to play an important role in Bhutan, western-style education has been

The First Rule
In a mountain village named Laya, I was standing in a schoolhouse and staring at a document entitled *Manual for Teachers of Mathematics*. What caught my eye is something that is offered as a 'first rule'.

'Always remember that you are a human being as well as a teacher, that your students are also human beings, and that you are here because you have something important to give them that they need'.

It is not what one would expect as a first rule for math teachers anywhere else in the world. But this is Bhutan, and in Bhutan, I am learning, people are not the abstract ciphers they can come to be in a more urban environment. They are human beings who, even in official matters, tend to deal with each other as human beings. 'I am not as much concerned about the Gross National Product' the king is supposed to have said, 'as I am about the Gross National Happiness.'

Robert Peirce

expanded and is now available throughout the country. Literacy has increased from 28% in 1984 to 54% in 1996 and this is being further enhanced through adult education programmes.

Primary & Secondary Education
In 1996, 72% of the primary school-aged population was enrolled in a total of 312 schools. The government's goal is to have 95% of the school-age population attending school. School time is 8.30 am to 3.30 pm and the annual holiday is in winter, from 17 December to 9 March.

Since 1961 the medium of instruction has been English. Dzongkha, the national language, is taught as a second language. One reason for this arrangement was the shortage of Bhutanese teachers when the educational system was established. It has proved to be a wise decision and enables Bhutanese students to gain an excellent, international-standard education. Many of Bhutan's teachers are hired from India, particularly the state of Kerala, and they are fluent in English.

Nepali was taught as a third language up to grade 5 in schools in southern Bhutan, but this was discontinued in 1988 when, on the advice of foreign consultants, the govern-ment adopted the 'New Approach to Primary Education'.

The educational structure provides for 11 years of basic schooling: one year of pre-primary schooling, six years of primary, two years of junior high and two years of high school. Students have to undergo an examination to move from primary school to junior high, and another to graduate from junior high to high school.

Education is aimed at providing basic literacy skills and a knowledge of Bhutan's history, geography and traditions. It is a very interesting reflection on Bhutan's value system to discover that the other important subjects are agriculture, environment, health, hygiene, population and moral science. The schools employ a contemporary system of activity-based learning to teach these subjects. There is even an emphasis on the use of computers in high schools.

Most villages in Bhutan have community or primary schools. There are 19 junior high schools, ten high schools, one college and six specialised training institutes. Under the eight five-year plan many of these facilities are to be upgraded and many new primary schools will be established. Four of the high schools also provide junior college facilities. Free education and textbooks are provided to all students until they reach tertiary level. Morning prayers and the national anthem start the day for all students throughout the kingdom. It is quite a spectacle to see several hundred children in national dress lined up and singing in the morning sunshine.

One of the major issues facing Bhutan's education system – and perhaps the entire country – is described in the documents of the eighth five-year plan under the heading *Students' Expectations*:

'One of the growing concerns facing the development of education in Bhutan is the increasing expectation among students for 'white-collar' employment in government. Related to this is the general reluctance to undertake any manual work and the preference, instead, for office-related jobs no matter how unproductive and lowly paid these may be. This has led to the disproportionate demand for academic education compared to training in technical and agricultural skills, which has further contributed to the emerging problems related to youth and rural-urban migration. While these problems are a reflection of wider social and economic influences, education is perceived as playing a pivotal role and, therefore, there is an increasing call from public and private sector institutions, as well as from parents, for the education system to tackle them.'

College & Vocational Education
A key aspect of Bhutan's development plan involves training doctors, engineers and other professionals. With only one college, the country relies heavily on donor assistance to send young graduates to foreign universities.

The country's only college is Sherubtse College at Kanglung in Eastern Bhutan. Tertiary education involves two years of junior college and a three-year undergraduate programme.

Other facilities are the two vocational schools: the Royal Bhutan Polytechnic at Deothang and the Royal Technical Institute at Kharbandi, north of Phuentsholing.

There are two teacher training institutes: the National Institute for Education in Samtse and the Teacher Training College in Paro.

Monastic education is important, taking place in *shedras* (Buddhist colleges) and *drubdras* (meditation centres) inside dzongs and goembas.

A particularly interesting form of education is the *rigney* curriculum where modern education and technology are blended with Buddhist values. Rigney is a Choekey (classical Tibetan) term derived from *rig* (science or craft) and *ney* (domain or place), but it is commonly used loosely to refer to the study of Buddhist literature. The Rigney Institute at Simtokha provides training in Dzongkha grammar, Buddhism and traditional arts. A similar facility in Trashi Yangtse places more emphasis on the arts as a tool for craftsmen.

Environmental Education
Environmental and nature conservation studies are part of the school curriculum from primary school all the way through to college. The RSPN works to enhance this study through its programme of nature clubs.

WWF has been helping Sherubtse College develop an environmental studies programme, and the college conducts environmental workshops and training programmes on campus and at the Khebethang Nature Study Centre in Black Mountain National Park.

The Royal Institute of Management (RIM) was established in 1968 to train government administrators. It also has an innovative programme that teaches accounting, typing and the use of computers to school dropouts. It offers 11 one-year or two-year training programmes in fields like accounting, auditing and administrative management. It also runs special courses such as an Environmental Education and Awareness programme for chimis. The institute also conducts two four-week orientation courses per year for newly arrived international volunteers. RIM also provides a refresher course in *driglam namzha* (traditional values and etiquette) for university graduates who return from courses abroad.

ARTS

Bhutanese tradition defines *zorig chusum* (thirteen arts) which are practised in Bhutan. Kunzang Thinley, principal of the National School of Arts and Crafts, kindly provided much of the following material to explain this complex and fascinating tradition.

All Bhutanese art, dance, drama and music has its roots in the Buddhist religion. Paintings are not done for tourists, but for specific purposes. Festivals are not quaint revivals, but are living manifestations of a long tradition and national faith. Almost all representation in art, music and dance is a dramatisation of the struggle between good and evil.

Bhutanese arts and crafts have been undergoing a period of revival, in recent years, largely as a result of the government's emphasis on the preserving and promoting the nation's rich cultural heritage.

The Purpose of Buddhist Art

Buddhist art has a much different purpose from other contemporary art, being more subjective, symbolic and impersonal. Buddhism teaches that things are created by the mind, rather than the mind just perceiving things that exist. Therefore, Buddhist arts are concerned with interpreting values rather than describing facts. The artist is trying to transmit in symbols, shapes or signs something that contains a spark of that eternal stream of life or consciousness which abides when material forms decay. An artist's basic aim is to teach, by the symbolic value of their art, the way to the spiritual experience of which their work is the outward and visible sign. The issue of whether Buddhist art is 'beautiful' or not is irrelevant to its intended purpose.

The Artistic Tradition in Bhutan

Inspired by their close relationship with nature and their gods, and by the extraordinary scenery of their country, Bhutanese craftsmen have preserved the ancient skills of their ancestors through work in bronze, iron, silver, clay and wood.

The development of a high order of Buddhist arts and crafts in Bhutan may be traced to the great 15th century terton Pema Lingpa, who was an accomplished painter, sculptor and architect. The country's artistic tradition received a further boost when, in 1680, under instructions from the Shabdrung (himself an artist), Desi Tenzin Rabgye opened the School of Bhutanese Arts and Crafts.

Traditional Bhutanese artistry is maintained through the support of all levels of society. The royal family, nobility and clergy have provided continued zealous patronage. Meanwhile, the common people support the arts because they depend on artisans to provide the wide variety of wooden and metal objects indispensable to typical Bhutanese households.

Bhutanese art has two main characteristics: it is religious and anonymous. The Bhutanese consider commissioning paintings and statues as pious acts, which gain merit for the *jinda* (patron). The name of the jinda is sometimes written on the work so that their pious act may be remembered. Often the artist is a religious man who also gains merit from creating the work. However, the artist's name is almost never mentioned.

Because the iconographical conventions in Bhutanese art are very strict, the first responsibility of the Bhutanese artist is to observe them scrupulously. However, artists can also express their own personality in minor details or scenes.

Paintings and sculptures are executed by monks or laymen who work in special workshops. The disciples of a master do all the preliminary work, while the fine work is executed by the master himself.

Thirteen Arts & Crafts of Bhutan

Even such seemingly mundane activities as carpentry, blacksmithing and weaving are part of Bhutan's heritage of Zorig Chusum, and are therefore integral elements of Buddhist artistic tradition.

Painting This tradition is called *lhazo*, and encompasses all types of painting, including *thangkas* (religious scroll paintings), wall paintings and decorative paintings. Proficiency in lhazo is basic to all other arts. The geometric proportions and iconography that are essential to Buddhist art are important parts of the school of painting.

Carpentry Woodworking for the construction of dzongs, monasteries, houses and household goods is called *shingzo* (wood art).

Carvings *Parzo* is the art of carving in wood, slate and stone. Parzo plays an important part in the Tibetan Buddhist tradition because most religious texts are printed from wooden blocks on which monks have laboriously carved a mirror image of the text.

Sculpture *Jinzo* (mud work) includes the making of clay statues and ritual objects such as drum stands, ritual cakes (*torma*) and masks. Most large statues are made by forming plaster or mud on a hollow frame and are part of this tradition. Jinzo is understood specifically as the making of statues and ritual objects, but may also be applied to construction works using mortar, plaster and rammed earth.

Casting *Lugzo* applies to two types of casting: sand casting and the lost wax method. Lugzo craftsmen produce statues, bells and ritual instruments. The term is also used for jewellery and less exotic items such as kitchen goods.

Blacksmith The *garzo* tradition is the manufacture of iron goods such as swords, knives, chisels, axes, spades, shovels, darts, helmets, chains and plough blades.

Bamboo Works *Tshazo* is the art of working with cane and bamboo. These craftsmen produce bows and arrows, baskets (*bangchung*) to carry food, *zem* and *palang* for storing and carrying the local drinks (*arra* and *chang*), bamboo hats (*belo*), bamboo mats (*redi*), *lachu* and *bohm* for storing grains and bamboo thatch (*balep*).

Goldsmithing & Silversmithing The art of working with gold and silver is called *serzo ngulzo*. These craftsmen produce objects ranging from household goods to jewellery to ritual objects. Some of these objects include *koma japtha* (brooches and chains), *thingkhap* (rings), *chaka timi* and *batha* (cases for carrying doma), *dung* (ritual trumpets), *dorji* (thunderbolt symbols) and *gau* (Buddhist amulets).

Weaving *Thagzo* involves the entire process of weaving, from preparation of yarn, to dyeing and eventually to the final weaving.

Embroidery *Tshemzo* is the art of working with needle and thread, specifically embroidering. There are two categories of tshemzo. *Tshendrup* is embroidery, and includes traditional boot making. The second is *lhendrup* (appliqué), the technique of sewing pieces of cloth onto a background to produce a picture. This process is used in thondrols (huge thangkas) such as the ones displayed at Paro and Punakha dzongs during festivals.

Masonry The art of cutting and stacking stone walls is called *dozo*. This term is especially applied to the construction of the huge stone outer walls of dzongs, monasteries and other buildings.

Leather Works *Kozo* is the art of working with leather. These craftsmen produce such items as *gayu*, the leather bags for carrying grains, and *shadha*, leather ropes and belts for swords.

Paper Works The art of making paper is *dezo*. The word *de* refers to the daphne plant, from which the traditional paper is made.

The Special Role of Painting
Other than its spectacular architecture, the most visible manifestation of Bhutanese art is painting. Bhutanese tradition defines three forms of painting: thangkas, wall paintings and statues. A painting may

depict a deity, a legend or religious story, a meditational object or an array of auspicious symbols, but it is always religious in nature. Despite the religious aspect of the painting, many artists are laymen, not monks.

A monastery may sponsor paintings, but most are commissioned by a lay person, often a noble or member of the Royal Family, as an act of merit making. The jinda often specifies the central figure, which is usually a favourite deity important to the achievement of certain personal goals. The main figure may be surrounded by other related deities or by prescribed designs that include clouds, flowers, trees, scrolls and geometric borders.

Paintings, in particular the portrayal of human figures, are subject to strict rules of iconography. The proportions and features must be precise, and there is no latitude for artistic license in these works.

The initial layout is constructed with a series of geometrical patterns using straight lines to lay out the proportions of the figure. These proportions are well defined in religious documents called *zuri pata*. In other cases the initial sketch is made with a stencil providing the basic outline of the figures. The outline is transferred to the canvas by patting the stencil with a bag filled with chalk dust.

For many paintings a master artist makes the initial sketch and apprentices or lessskilled artisans do the remainder of the work. The master artist is usually responsible for the final intricate details of the all-important face and hands. The artist rarely signs the work, though the name of the jinda may appear.

Thangkas are painted on canvas that is stretched and lashed to a wooden frame. When the work is completed it is removed from the frame and surrounded by a border of colourful brocade, with wooden sticks at the top and bottom to use for hanging. Though some thangkas are hung permanently, most are rolled up and stored until they are exhibited at special events. This applies particularly to the huge thondrols which are displayed for a short time in the early morning from the front of dzongs during a tsechu.

Thondrols are often classified as paintings because they follow the normal rules of iconography, but they are usually always appliqué.

The inner walls of dzongs and *lhakhangs* (temples) are usually covered with paintings. In Bhutan most wall murals are painted on a thin layer of cloth applied to the wall using a special paste. Old paintings are treasured because of their historic and artistic value, but this was not always the case in the past. Many old wall paintings were repainted because the act of painting gives merit to both the jinda and the artist.

Most statues are finely painted to sharply define the facial features. Many religious statues in lhakhangs, especially the larger statues, are made from clay. In addition to the face, the entire surface of these large figures is painted, often in a gold colour, giving them a bronze aspect. On bronze statues, some of which are quite small, only the face is painted. The amount of a particular statue that has been painted is a good aid to determine from a distance whether a particular statue is made of clay or bronze.

Even after the 15th century, Bhutanese paintings tended to favour a central composition with adjacent figures. Examples of these paintings are found in the monasteries of Taktshang (17th century) Tango (17th century), and Phajoding (18th century).

Other artists used the entire space and the interest is not focused on one main figure. Sometimes, the artist would freely illustrate scenes of a famous person's life around a central figure. An example is the illustration of Milarepa's life in Paro Dzong.

Over the centuries, Bhutanese style has become more and more ornate, with increasingly lavish use of gold paint and landscape elements treated in the Chinese manner. Chinese influences, mixed with earlier influences into a harmonious Bhutanese blend, can be seen from the 17th century onward.

Many of the paintings are inscribed with the names of the figures represented, which help to date the works.

Paints are traditionally made from earth, minerals and vegetables, though in recent times chemical colours are also used. The material is first reduced into powder and then mixed with water, glue, and chalk. The brushes are made from twigs and animal hair. The colours are applied in a particular order with symbolic meaning.

Dance

The primary dance form is the classical lama dancing (*chham*) at the tsechu and other festivals. The form of these dances was established by the terton Pema Lingpa in the 15th century and further enhanced by the Shabdrung in the 17th century. All of the dances are religious and symbolise the destruction of evil spirits. Tsechus take place outdoors, in the courtyards of the great dzongs. The festivals celebrate the faith, legends, myths, and history of Bhutan and are important religious and social gatherings. (See the section 'Dances of the Tsechu' on pages 111-13.)

Folk dances are performed in schools and villages, and also by professional dancers as interludes during the tsechus. The dancers form a line or circle and move in an intricate series of forward and backward walking steps accompanied by graceful arm movements. Each song has different dance steps, and, while the songs sound monotonous to the western ear, they are actually quite varied. Most of the dancers are women who sing the accompanying songs, but men frequently join the line.

Music

Bhutanese popular music is beginning to evolve, and a few local bands occasionally play in Thimphu. Cassette tapes of this music are available at several outlets in Thimphu and in shops in Bumthang and Trashigang.

The music is an interesting blend of Tibetan and Bhutanese tunes, with some influence from popular Hindi film music. The Bhutanese music scene has numerous popular male and female singers.

Architecture

The style of Bhutanese houses varies depending on the location and, particularly, elevation. Thatched bamboo houses predominate in the southern foothills and the duars. At high altitudes, most homes are simple stone structures or even yak-hair tents. Though the design varies from place to place, homes in the Inner Himalayan zone are built in a Bhutanese style oddly similar to that of Swiss chalets.

Dzongs Bhutan's massive dzongs are outstanding examples of grand design and construction. Each dzong has a unique design, yet each follows the same general layout. Dzong architects don't prepare any plans or drawings. They rely only on a mental concept of what is to be built. This tradition continues to the present day; the reconstruction of Thimphu's Trashi Chhoe Dzong in 1966 was carried out without any blueprints or sketches. The Bhutanese proclaim proudly that no nails are used even to construct dzongs.

Bhutanese architecture tends to be in straight lines and there are few curved lines in any buildings except in watchtowers. Most dzongs have an inward-sloping wall, which helps to make the building look even larger than it is. They usually have only one massive door, which leads into a small passage that makes two right-angle turns before it enters the main courtyard. This is a design feature to keep invaders from storming the dzong.

The main courtyard of the dzong is the *dochey* which is paved with large flagstones. Along the outer walls of the dzong are several storeys of rooms and galleries overlooking the paved courtyard. All of these rooms are the monks' quarters and classrooms. Because the monastic portion of the dzong is separated from the secular portion, many dzongs have two dochhen, the second being surrounded by administrative offices.

The extensive use of wood means houses and dzongs are highly susceptible to fire. Most dzongs have been damaged by severe fires at least once, many several times. Many of these were caused by butter lamps being overturned and setting wall hangings or paintings on fire.

Monasteries & Temples Bhutan has an enormous number of religious buildings. According to one count, 525 lhakhangs are owned by the state in the custody of the dratshang and another 144 lhakhangs are in the care of reincarnate lamas. In addition, there are another 800 village lhakhangs and an estimated 500 privately-owned temples. Each was designed for a different purpose to suit the wishes of the founders, architects or sponsors.

A primary criterion for selecting the location of a monastery is to have a remote location where the monks may find peace and solitude. This is particularly evident in Bhutan where monasteries are built atop rocky crags or on remote hillsides. In Dzongkha, a monastery is called a goemba, and the word is pronounced quite differently from the corresponding Tibetan word *gompa*.

Several monasteries in Bhutan were built at sacred caves that had previously been places of meditation. Taktshang in Paro and Kurjey in Bumthang are two famous examples built around caves yywhere Guru Rimpoche is believed to have meditated for extended periods.

All Bhutanese goembas are different, but they all possess certain common features. They are self-contained communities, with a central lhakhang and separate quarters for sleeping. The lhakhang is at the centre of a dochey, similar to that of the dzongs. The dochey is used as a dancing area by the monks during festivals.

The term lhakhang is a bit confusing, because it may be used to refer both to the building itself and to the room inside the building that is the primary chapel. Some goembas have several lhakhangs within the central building. To avoid further confusion,

Dzoe – Bhutanese Spirit Catcher

Sometimes you will come across a strange construction of twigs, straw and rainbow-coloured thread woven into a spider web shape. You may see one near a building or by a roadside with flower and food offerings. This is a *dzoe* (also known as a *tendo*), a sort of spirit catcher used to exorcise something evil which has been pestering a household. The malevolent spirits are drawn to the dzoe. After prayers, the dzoe is cast away, often on a trail or road, to send away the evil spirits it has trapped.

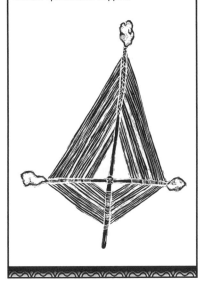

The central structure is a tower-like building called the *utse*. In most dzongs, the utse has a series of chapels, one on each floor. On the ground floor of the utse is the lhakhang. See the description of temples in the boxed text 'Inside a Lhakhang' later in this chapter.

On dzongs and all religious buildings in Bhutan a painted red band called a *khemar* runs just below the roof. One or more circular brass plates or mirrors representing the sun (*nima*) are often placed on the khemar.

Houses

A typical Bhutanese house is two storeys high with an attic. In rural areas the ground floor is always used as a cattle barn. The upper floor is the living quarters and usually contains an elaborately decorated room that serves as a chapel.

The foundation is made from stones placed in a trench and built up to a height of about 50cm above the ground. In central and eastern Bhutan the walls are usually made of stone. In the west the walls are 80cm to 100cm thick and made of compacted mud, which provides an extremely strong and durable structure. To build these walls, a wooden frame is constructed and filled with damp mud. The mud is compacted by pounding it with wooden poles to which a flat ram is attached. When the wall reaches the top of the frame, the frame is shifted upwards and the process begins again.

The pounders are usually teams of women, who sing and dance as they beat the walls. Though Bhutanese women are usually shy and modest with outsiders, they traditionally loosen their inhibitions and exchange ribald comments with men as they perform the pounding, which can take several weeks for a large house. Once the mud wall is finished, it is left in its natural colour or whitewashed.

Openings for a door and perhaps some windows are left in the mud walls which form the front of the house, which traditionally faces south. The upper floor is supported by oversized wooden beams that fit into holes in the mud wall. Central pillars are used to support the beams, because it is difficult to find a single piece of timber to span the entire width of the house. The earthen walls for the upper floor form only the back of the house and the back half of the two side walls. The front portion of the residential area is always built of wood, which is sometimes elaborately decorated, with large divided windows facing south. The wooden portion of the house extends out over the front and side mud walls.

Following tradition, the windows on the lower floor are small; larger windows are built on upper floors. In older houses the windows are sliding wooden panels, not glass. Above all windows in Bhutan is a cut-out of a curved trefoil motif, called a *horzhing*. In Bhutan there are often several explanations for everything, and this motif is said to be either a Persian influence or simply a practical design which allows a person to look out of the window while the smoke blows out through the opening above their head.

An elaborate wooden cornice is built around the top of the house. Traditional roofs are made from wooden shingles held in place with large stones to prevent them from blowing off during the strong windstorms that occur in early spring. The roof is built on a slope of about 15°, because the shingles would slide off if it were steeper. Because of the minimal slope, rain runs off quite slowly, and you may find that most roofs tend to leak in heavy rainstorms. The feature missing in all Bhutanese architecture is a gutter – expect to get wet when you enter or leave a house during a rainstorm.

The inside walls, and often parts of the outside walls, are built with a timber frame that is filled in with woven bamboo and plastered with mud. This construction is called *shaddam* (weave-mud). Heavy wooden doors are made from several planks held firmly together using a tongue-and-groove technique. This technique is used to fit together all the woodwork, and not a single nail is used in the entire structure. The door hinge is a pair of wooden pegs which fit into round holes above and below the door frame.

A large space is left below the roof. This serves as an attic and a place for storing hay or for drying animal skins and chillies. In winter the hay helps insulate the house. Sometimes woven bamboo mats are placed around the attic, but often it is simply left open.

The stairway to the upper floor is a ladder made by carving steps into a whole tree trunk. If you find yourself climbing one of these ladders, reach around behind the right edge and you may find a groove cut there to serve as a handrail.

Exterior Decoration After a house is built, the all-important decoration begins. Wooden surfaces are painted with various designs, each with a special significance. Swastikas, floral patterns representing the lotus, cloud whirls and the eight auspicious symbols are the most common. Beside the front door are larger paintings, often of mythical animals such as the garuda, or large red phalluses. The phallus is not a fertility symbol; it is supposed to ward away evil. Many houses are decorated with carved wooden phalluses, often crossed by a sword: which are hung at the four corners or over the door. A prayer flag is erected on the centre of the roof of all Buddhist homes.

Features of a Bhutanese House:

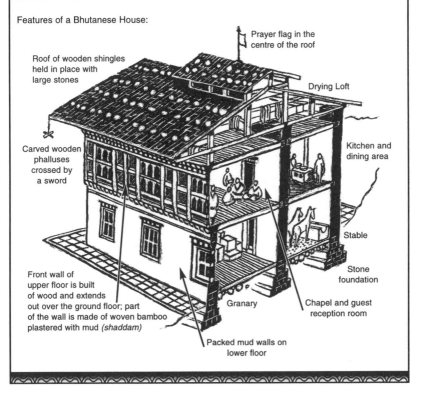

Prayer flag in the centre of the roof

Roof of wooden shingles held in place with large stones

Drying Loft

Carved wooden phalluses crossed by a sword

Kitchen and dining area

Stable

Stone foundation

Front wall of upper floor is built of wood and extends out over the ground floor; part of the wall is made of woven bamboo plastered with mud *(shaddam)*

Granary

Chapel and guest reception room

Packed mud walls on lower floor

in the rest of this book, 'lhakhang' will be used to refer to the building, and the room will be called a 'chapel'.

A typical lhakhang has a cupola and a gold-coloured ball-shaped ornament called a *tserto* on the roof. Most have a paved path around the circumference of the building. On the outside wall are racks of prayer wheels which monks and devotees spin as they circumambulate the building.

On a typical lhakhang the door opens out to a raised veranda called a *gorikha*,

Chortens

A chorten is literally a receptacle for offerings, and in Bhutan all chortens contain religious relics. The classical chorten shape is based on the ancient Indian form of a stupa. Each of its five elements has a symbolic meaning. The square or rectangular base symbolises earth. The half-spherical dome symbolises water. The conical or pyramidal spire symbolises fire. The main structure's 13 step-like segments symbolise the 13 steps leading to Buddhahood. On top is a crescent moon and a sun, symbolising air, and a vertical spike symbolising ether or the sacred light of Buddha. Inside is placed a carved wooden pole called a *sokshing* which is the life-spirit of the chorten.

Some chortens, such as the Memorial Chorten in Thimphu, are built in memory of an individual. Others commemorate the visit of a saint or contain sacred books or the bodies of saints or great lamas. Bhutan has three basic styles of chorten, usually characterised as Bhutanese, Tibetan and Nepali.

The Nepali style chorten is based on the classical stupa. On Nepali chortens the four sides of the tower are painted with a pair of eyes, the all-seeing eyes of Buddha. What appears to be a nose is actually the Sanskrit character for the number one, symbolising the absoluteness of Buddha. The prototypes for the Nepali chortens in Bhutan are Swayambhunath and Boudhanath in Kathmandu. The large Chorten Kora in Trashi Yangtse and Chendebji chorten near Mongar are two examples of the Nepali style of chorten.

The Tibetan style has a shape similar to the stupa, but the rounded part flares outward instead of being a dome shape. The memorial chorten in Thimphu is an excellent example of this style.

The Bhutanese chorten design is a square stone pillar with a *khemar* (red band) near the top. The exact origin of this style is not known, but is believed to be a reduced form of the classical stupa, with only the pinnacle and square base. Some Bhutanese chortens have a ball and crescent representing the moon and sun on top.

Several other types of chorten are found in Bhutan. The chorten *khonying* (two legs) is an archway which forms a gate over a trail. Travellers earn merit by passing through the structure, which is decorated inside with paintings on the walls and a mandala on the roof. The *mani chukor* is shaped like a Bhutanese chorten but is hollow and contains a large prayer wheel. It is built over or near a stream so that the water may turn a wooden turbine below the structure, which then turns the prayer wheel.

Another structure common in Bhutan is the mani wall. As its name implies, this is a wall with carved *mani* (prayer) stones placed in it. Bhutanese mani walls are usually quite short, but long mani walls can be found in Bumthang. Always walk to the left of a chorten or mani wall.

Dzongs

Bhutan's dzongs are perhaps the most visibly exotic aspect of the kingdom. These huge white citadels dominate the major towns and serve as the administrative headquarters of all 20 of the country's dzongkhags and the focus of secular and religious authority in each district. As well as the large active district dzongs, a few dzongs have been destroyed or abandoned, or are now used for other purposes, such as Simtokha Dzong and Dobji dzong south of Chhuzom. Not all dzongs are ancient monuments; a new dzong was built in Trashi Yangtse in 1998.

The word dzong is of Tibetan origin and translates as 'fortress'. Tibetan dzongs were large castle-like structures perched on hilltops overlooking broad river valleys. The dzongs were both military fortresses and administrative centres. Often the entire population of the valley sought refuge in the dzong for protection during a war.

The dzong system is said to have been introduced into Bhutan in 1153 by Gyelwa Lhanangpa, a monk from Desung in Tibet. In those early days many Bhutanese dzongs were administered by clans based in Tibet. The Shabdrung Ngawang Namgyal established the Bhutanese system where dzongs are dual-purpose facilities housing monasteries and administrative offices as well as protective structures.

Trashichhoe Dzong in Thimphu, built as the symbol of the capital.

RICHARD I'ANSON

Dzongs were primarily fortresses, strategically built with high walls, as at Paro (below) and often protected with cantilever bridges, as at Punakha (bottom).

Because dzongs were usually placed on ridges, a tunnel was often constructed to the nearest water supply so that the dzong could survive a long siege. Many dzongs had a watch tower (ta dzong) which was either part of the building, as in Jakar, or separated as in Paro and Trongsa. This structure was also used as an ammunition store and dungeon. Many dzongs were protected by cantilever bridges as an additional defensive measure.

During the time of the Shabdrung, the dzongs served their primary function as fortresses well and each was the stronghold of a penlop. Many of the feuds and battles for control during the 17th to 20th centuries were waged by penlops whose troops attacked neighbouring dzongs. The key to success in these battles was to capture the dzong of the opposing penlop, thereby gaining control of that district.

Bhutan's dzongs were built of stones or beaten mud and a considerable amount of timber, including shingle roofs. This, combined with the large number of butter lamps used in temples, has caused fires in almost all dzongs. Most of

RICHARD I'ANSON

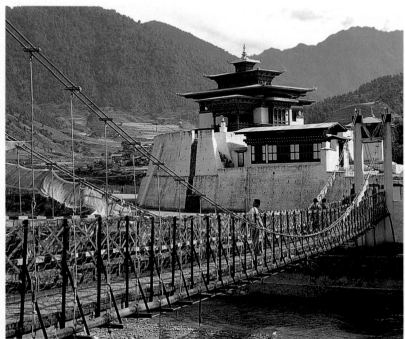

NICHOLAS REUSS

Bhutan's dzongs suffered severe damage during the 1897 earthquake and were repaired or rebuilt in their original style. All important dzongs have been (or are being) rebuilt using ancient construction methods, though in many places corrugated metal roofs have replaced the traditional wooden shingles.

Dzongs are divided between an ecclesiastical wing where the monks' quarters and the lhakhang are, and a temporal wing for government offices. The monastic wing of many dzongs actually serves as a monastery, with a resident monk body called a rabdey. In early days, most dzongs had a rabdey, but today only the dzongs of Thimphu, Punakha, Paro, Mongar, Trongsa, Jakar and Trashigang serve as monasteries. The drathshang maintains monastic schools in the dzongs of Punakha, Trongsa and Paro. The Punakha dzong is the seat of the supreme abbot, His Holiness the Je Khenpo.

Entry to dzongs is through a single gate controlled by a policeman who restricts entry and enforces dzong protocol. Bhutanese are required to wear formal dress (gho or kira) and scarf (kabney

The inner walls of most dzongs are covered with paintings which only reveal their significance upon closer inspection.

RICHARD I'ANSON

NICHOLAS REUSS

RICHARD I'ANSON

for men and rachu for women) at all times within the dzong.

According to tradition, no lady may be in a dzong between sunset and sunrise. This tradition was only broken once, when Indian Prime Minister Indira Gandhi stayed in Trashi Chhoe Dzong in Thimphu after receiving special permission from the Je Khenpo (see also under Architecture).

NICHOLAS REUSS

The vast dzongs are perched upon ridges and are visual symbols of strength, authority and spiritual unity as at Trashigang (right) and Trashichhoe (below).

NICHOLAS REUSS

which is covered with murals, usually depicting the guardians of the four directions or a wheel of life. The main entrance is a large painted wooden door that is often protected by a heavy cloth or yak-hair curtain. The interior may have an anteroom which is called a *tshokhang* (prayer hall), though the entrance of many lhakhangs leads directly into the elaborately-decorated main chapel which is dominated by a large statue of a deity. (See the colour section 'Important Figures of Drukpa Kagyu Buddhism' between pages 176 and 177 for the names of some of these deities.)

In the lhakhang of all goembas there is a room called a *dukhang* that is the gathering place for the monks for ceremonies and communal meals. The dukhang often has an altar with statues and elaborate paintings that describe the life of Buddha on the walls.

In most lhakhangs, often on the upper floor, is a room called a *goenkhang*, which is devoted to the protective and terrifying deities. The statues in these rooms are usually covered except when rituals are performed. Weapons are stored in this room and may include old muskets, armour and round shields made from rhinoceros hide. Teams of archers sometimes sleep in the goenkhang before a major match. Women are never allowed to enter the goenkhang, and the monks are reluctant to allow any visitors into these chapels.

SOCIETY & CONDUCT
Names
The system of names in Bhutan differs between the north and south of the country. In the north, with the exception of the royal family, there are no family names. Two names are given to children by monks a few weeks after birth. These are traditional names of Tibetan origin and are chosen because of their auspicious influence or religious meaning. Two names are always given, though a few people have three names. It is often impossible to tell the sex of a Bhutanese person based on their name. A few names are given only to boys, and

others apply only to girls, but most names may apply to either.

People may be called by both names, or simply by the first name, but it's not correct to use only the second name. It does become complicated, however, because many names, particularly Dorji, are commonly used as both first and second names. For example, Kunzang Dorji helped with this book and Dorji Wangdi is a trekking cook. You would not call Kunzang 'Dorji', and should not call the cook simply 'Wangdi'.

In the south of the country, where there is more Hindu influence, a system resembling family names exists. Brahmans and Newars retain their caste name, such as Sharma or Pradhan, and others retain the name of their ethnic group, such as Rai or Gurung.

Titles & Forms of Address
Titles are extremely important in Bhutan. All persons of rank should be addressed by the appropriate title followed by their first or full name. Members of the royal family are addressed as Dasho if they are male, and Ashi if female. A minister has the title Lyonpo (pronounced 'lonpo').

The title Dasho designates those persons who have been honoured by the king with the title and the accompanying red scarf. In common practice, many senior government officals are addressed as Dasho even if they have not received the title, but officially this is incorrect.

You would address a senior monk or teacher with the title *lopon* or, if he has been given the title, as *lam*. A *trulku* (reincarnate lama) is addressed as Rimpoche and a nun as *anim*.

A man is addressed as *aap* and a boy as *busu*; an older woman is addressed as *am* and a girl as *bum*. If you are calling someone whose name you do not know, you may use *ama* for ladies and *aapa* for men. In the same situation, girls are *bumo* and boys *alou*. When Bhutanese talk about a foreigner whose name they don't know, they use the word *chilip*.

At night, do not shout a person's name, as it's believed this may attract a ghost.

Visiting Temples

Himalayan Buddhism has a generally relaxed approach to religious sites, but you should observe a few important rules if you are invited to enter a lhakhang or goemba. It is customary to remove one's shoes upon entering the important rooms of a temple. You will most likely be escorted by a caretaker monk, and you can follow his example in removing your shoes at the appropriate doorway. Leave cameras, umbrellas and hats outside. Always move in a clockwise direction and do not speak loudly.

Followers of Himalayan Buddhism will prostrate themselves three times before the primary altar and occasionally before secondary shrines to important saints. You may approach the central altar, and in Bhutanese goembas you will often find a cup containing three dice. Bhutanese roll these dice and the monk interprets the auspiciousness of the result. It is customary to leave a small offering of money on the altar. When you make this offering, the monk accompanying you will pour a small amount of holy water, from a sacred vessel called a *bumpa*, into your hand. You should make the gesture of drinking a sip of this water and then spread the rest on your head.

Dress

The traditional dress of Bhutan is one of the most distinctive and visible aspects of the country. It is compulsory for all Bhutanese to wear national dress in schools, government offices and formal occasions. Men, women and children wear traditional clothing made from Bhutanese textiles in a variety of colourful patterns. The men wear a gho, a long robe similar to the Tibetan *chuba*. The Bhutanese hoist the gho to knee length and hold it in place with a woven cloth belt called a kera. The kera is would tightly around the waist, and the large pouch formed above it is traditionally used to carry a bowl, money and the makings of doma. One man suggested that the best part of the day was when he was able to loosen the uncomfortably tight belt.

To be perfectly correct, men should carry a small knife called a *dozum* at the waist. Traditional footwear is high embroidered leather boots, but these are now worn only at festivals, and most Bhutanese men wear leather shoes or show off with fancy trainers, running shoes or trekking boots.

Ghos come in a wide variety of patterns, though often they have plaid or striped designs reminiscent of Scottish tartans. Flowered patterns are taboo, and solid reds and yellows are avoided because these are colours worn by monks; otherwise patterns have no special significance. Historically, Bhutanese wore the same thing under their gho that a true Scotsman wears under his kilt, but today it's usually a pair of shorts. In winter it's correct to wear a pair of tights or thermal underwear, but it's more often a pair of jeans or a track suit, which gives the costume a peculiar look that some people liken to a dressing gown. Formality in Thimphu dictates that legs may not be covered until winter has arrived, which is defined as the time that the monks move to Punakha.

Formal occasions, including a visit to the dzong, require a scarf called a kabney (see boxed text) that identifies a person's rank. The kabney has to be put on correctly so it hangs in exactly the right way. In dzongs, and on formal occasions, a Dasho or someone in authority carries a long sword called a *patang*.

Women wear a long floor-length dress called a *kira*. This is a rectangular piece of brightly-coloured cloth that wraps around the body over a Tibetan-style silk blouse called a *wonju*. The kira is fastened at the shoulders with elaborate silver hooks called *koma* and at the waist with a belt that may be of either silver or cloth. Over the top is worn a short, open jacket-like garment called a *toego*. Women often wear large amounts of jewellery in the Tibetan manner.

The kira may be made from cotton or silk and may have a pattern on one or both sides. For everyday wear women wear a kira made from striped cloth with a double-sided design, and on more formal occasions they wear a kira with an embellished pattern woven into it. The most expensive kira are *kushutara* (brocade dress), which are made of hand-spun, hand-woven Bhutanese cotton, embroidered with various colours and designs in raw silk or cotton thread. The Kurtoe region is known for its kushutara designs.

When visiting dzongs, women wear a cloth sash called a *rachu* over their left shoulder in the same manner as men wear a kabney.

White silk scarves are exchanged as customary greetings among ranking officials and are offered to high lamas as a sign of respect.

For guidelines on how to wear traditional Bhutanese dress, see the boxed text 'Donning a Gho' and 'Wearing a Kira' in the Thimphu chapter.

Hair Style
Unlike most women in regions of Tibetan influence, Bhutanese women wear their hair short.

TRADITIONAL CULTURE
In accordance with Buddhist tradition, there is a strict taboo on killing in Bhutan. This prohibition applies to the act of killing, but a practising Buddhist may eat meat that is slaughtered by someone else. Hindus and some Tibetans handle the local meat production in Bhutan.

Fishing also violates this precept, and it

Kabney – Ceremonial Scarves
Bhutanese men wear a scarf called a *kabney* (covering) as part of the protocol on formal occasions and when visiting dzongs and monasteries. The kabney, about 90cm wide and 3m long, is usually made of raw silk with long fringes at the ends. Wearing the kabney is an important part of Bhutanese etiquette, and must be put on in a particular manner so that it drapes in the correct way and can be ceremonially 'unfurled' for the traditional respectful bow to the king, the Je Khenpo or other high officials. It is always worn over the left shoulder and the colour denotes a person's rank. Historically, the kabney is derived from the shawl or shoulder scarf worn by Tibetan monks.

The kabney is not an item of everyday wear, and is usually carried over the arm or on the dashboard of a vehicle until the wearer enters a dzong. Despite its ceremonial importance, the kabney may also be used for lesser purposes such as carrying luggage.

Citizens wear a kabney of unbleached white silk and each level of officials wears different coloured scarves:

- Saffron for the King and Je Khenpo
- Blue for the Royal Advisory Council
- Red for those with the title Dasho and senior officials whom the king has recognised
- Orange for *lyonpos*
- White with red stripes on the outside for *gups*
- White with blue stripes for *chimis*
- Small white cloth scarf with a red border for members of the army

Women wear a coloured shoulder cloth called a *rachu* (small cloth). These are smaller than the kabney – about 90cm by 2m. Women use it unfolded to carry children on their backs. For formal occasions it is folded in thirds lengthwise and once to bring the two ends together, forming a narrow scarf which is draped over the left shoulder. A more convenient modern version of the rachu – a small pre-folded cloth – is frequently worn by women working in government offices.

The rachu is traditionally woven in silk or raw silk in festive shades of red, maroon or orange, and is embellished at the fringed ends with fine embroidery.

Protecting a Unique Identity
Desmond Doig, writing in the *National Geographic* in 1961, said:

'When the first bales of Indian cotton find their way into Bhutan's market places, when the first real tourist arrives, the old Bhutan will begin to shrink into the far corners of its beautiful valleys, and its living culture will be on its way to the museum.

Or worse still, that precious culture may disintegrate under attack from alert and ruthless enemies. Either way, the country I have been privileged to see will die a little or completely. And only a few who have seen the virgin Bhutan – Bhutan the contented, the uncluttered and untouched – will know what the world has lost.'

Though they welcome tourism and modernisation, the Bhutanese still feel that their independence and culture are threatened by the exact changes that Desmond Doig described. Many of their attitudes towards tourism, politics and the environment are based on the vulnerability they feel as their country expands its contacts with the modern world.

The desire of Bhutan's first Shabdrung to create and maintain a distinct cultural identity for his country continues today. Bhutanese realise their country can easily be swallowed by either of its huge neighbours. However, rather than feel inferior because of the country's size and insecure geographical position, Bhutan defines its strength in terms of its identity and cultural uniqueness.

Numerous factors threaten this identity, and many Bhutanese feel they are almost an endangered species. You will often hear a Bhutanese person say 'it is our very survival that is at stake'. Most people sincerely feel that cultural and environmental preservation is the only way to ensure the survival of Bhutan as an independent country.

---

is not allowed in many streams in Bhutan, though it is possible to obtain a fishing licence. You can fish in lakes and some rivers in the countryside, but you are not allowed to fish in the cities. There is no commercial fishing in Bhutan; all the fish sold in the market is from India.

Various foreign-sponsored projects have tried to set up small scale industries in Bhutan and have found that the activities violate Buddhist principals. There are plenty of mulberry trees in the country, and silkworms thrive at altitudes of about 1000m, but pious Bhutanese refuse to throw the cocoons into boiling water as is required for quality silk. Instead, they let the worms chew their way out, which results in a poor grade of silk. Beekeeping projects have limited success because Bhutanese are reluctant to kill the bees in order to extract the honey.

Efforts to control the proliferation of stray dogs in Thimphu and other towns causes conflicts with Bhutanese tradition. There was an outcry when dogs were poisoned, and another when local officials put dogs in jute bags and threw them in the river. There is now a campaign to sterilise dogs in order to reduce the population; and sterilised dogs are marked by cutting off their tails.

Archery
Datse (archery) is Bhutan's national sport (see the boxed text 'Archery' in the Facts for the Visitor chapter).

Traditional Games
Daygo Monks are forbidden to participate in archery, so often play a stone-throwing game called daygo. A round, flat stone is tossed at a target and the winner is the one that gets the closest.

Pungdo The Bhutanese version of shot put is called pungdo, and is played with large heavy stones.

A (Bhutanese) Dog's Life
'If merit is to be earned, be good and kind to dogs.'

– Popular Bhutanese aphorism

Dogs are more than man's best friend in Bhutan and there are several reasons why a Bhutanese dog's life isn't actually so bad.

Unlike Darwinian theory which points to the ape family as the next closest to humans, Bhutanese believe that, from among sentient beings, dogs have the best opportunity to be reborn as humans.

Folklore also refers to a time when the gods were displeased with excessive human greed and decided to withhold the natural bounty of this earth. The dogs are said to have interceded with the gods and pleaded with them to at least leave something for all beings to share. It is said that the food left behind for the dogs is what we survive on today.

Dogs are also said to be helpful in our afterlife: when we're lost in the darkness of the hereafter, dogs are believed to lead us with a light glowing on their tails to a better place.

Many of the Himalayan Buddhist saints, such as the irrepressible Drukpa Kunley, had dogs as their closest companions.

Kunzang Dorji

Khuru This is a darts game played on a field about 20m long with small targets similar to those used by archers. The darts are usually home-made from a block of wood, and a nail and some chicken feathers for fins. If a chicken can't be found, bits of plastic make a good substitute. Teams compete with a lot of shouting and arm waving designed to put the thrower off his aim. The game is a favourite of kids; beware of dangerous flying objects if you are near a khuru target.

Dos & Don'ts
Despite the deep religious sentiment and the pervasiveness of traditional culture, the Bhutanese people are quite open and liberal. They have a reputation for being the least complicated Asian people to communicate with. There are many complex customs and traditions in Bhutan, but you are not expected to follow all of these.

If you adhere to western standards of common courtesy and are respectful of religious sentiment, you are unlikely to cause offence. Using the word *la* at the end of a sentence in either Dzongkha or English is a sign of respect, as in *kuzo zangpo la* (hello).

You should also follow the normal Asian standards of courtesy and behaviour in Bhutan. These include respect for religion and the monarchy, modest dress and no public displays of affection. Use the right hand or, better yet, both hands to give or receive an object. Don't use your finger to point, especially at deities or religious objects; use an open hand with the palm up. When waving someone towards you, keep your palm pointing down.

Shoes In most monasteries and temples it is customary to remove your shoes before entering. Many people follow a similar practice in their homes. In some temples and homes it is not necessary to remove your shoes; just follow the example of your guide. A pile of shoes outside a doorway is your cue to remove your footwear.

Feet & Face As in all Asian countries, you should never point your feet at someone. If you are sitting on the floor, cross your legs or kneel so that your feet are pointed behind you. If you happen to sleep in a room where there is an altar or statue, ensure your feet do not point towards it.

The Asian concept of face also applies in

Bhutan. Try to suggest instead of insisting. When things go wrong, as they are certain to do at some stage, be patient while your guide figures out a solution. Remember, Asian people dislike saying 'no'. If your request to visit a certain landmark, order a particular dish in a restaurant or depart at a specified time is met with an obviously lame excuse, this probably means that it is impossible.

Photography A camera is still a curiosity in most of Bhutan, particularly in remote villages, and your camera may draw a curious crowd. See Photography & Video in the Facts for the Visitor chapter for advice on photographing people. Photography is not allowed inside any temples; don't embarrass your guide by asking. If you are attending a festival, do not let your picture-taking interfere with the dancers or block the view of the spectators.

Dress Here again, Asian standards of modesty apply. Both men and women should avoid wearing revealing clothing, including short-shorts, halter neck tops and tank tops. Nudity is completely unacceptable.

Resident expatriates in Thimphu are adamant that visitors should dress up when attending a tsechu or other festival. Bhutanese are too polite to suggest it, and would not openly criticise those who did not dress correctly, but they do appreciate the gesture. If you have an appointment with a government official, correct dress is required. Bhutanese are flattered if foreigners wear traditional dress, and are more than happy to help you buy, and put on, a gho or kira – which is not an easy process (see the boxed text 'Wearing a Kira' and 'Donning a Gho' in the Thimphu chapter).

Social Occasions If you are invited to a Bhutanese home, it's appropriate to bring a small gift, perhaps a bottle of wine or box of sweets. Social occasions tend to start late and involve extended rounds of drinks before dinner, often with several visitors dropping by for a short time. The evening is quickly concluded once dinner is finished.

RELIGION

Buddhism is practised throughout the country though, in the south, most Bhutanese people of Nepali and Indian descent practice Hinduism. Minority groups practice various forms of ancient animistic religions including Bon, which predates Himalayan Buddhism.

Monks are held in great respect and play an active part in community life. It is a custom for one son from each family to enter the monastic order at about age 10. The custom is less prevalent today because boys are now free to decide for themselves whether they wish to enter a monastery or not.

Bhutan's official religion is Drukpa Kagyu, a school of tantric Mahayana Buddhism. It is similar to the Buddhism of Tibet, but has unique beliefs and practices. To place Bhutan's religion in the full context of Buddhism, it's necessary to go back nearly 2500 years and trace the points at which the Drukpa Kagyu lineage and its antecedents diverged from other schools of Buddhism.

The Origins of Buddhism

Strictly speaking, Buddhism is not a religion, since it is not centred on a god, but a system of philosophy and a code of morality.

Buddhism was founded in northern India in about 500 BC when Siddhartha Gautama, born a prince, achieved enlightenment. Many schools of Buddhism believe that there were previous Buddhas, and most believe that Gautama Buddha is not expected to be the last 'enlightened one'. Buddhists believe that the achievement of enlightenment should be the goal of every being, and eventually we could all reach Buddhahood.

The Buddha renounced his material life to search for enlightenment but, unlike other prophets, found that starvation did not lead to discovery. Therefore, he developed his rule of the 'middle way' – moderation in everything. The Buddha taught that all life is suffering, but that suffering comes from our sensual desires and the illusion that they are important. By following the 'eight-fold path', these desires will eventually be extinguished and a state of nirvana, where we

Inside a Lhakhang

The focal point of the main chapel of all lhakhangs is a two-tiered *chhoesham* (altar) and a large gilded statue. Depending on when and why the lhakhang was built, this statue may be of Sakyamuni, Guru Rimpoche or another figure. Jampa is the central figure in many older lhakhangs built before Guru Rimpoche's visits, particularly those attributed to Songtsen Gampo. The central statue is usually flanked by two smaller figures, sometimes the consorts of Guru Rimpoche, and otherwise deities related to the central image.

On the upper level of the chhoesham are torma and various objects used in worship such as a *dorji*, conch shells, trumpets made of thigh-bone, small drums and bells. On the lower tier are butter lamps and offerings of rice, flowers, water and money. Often a silk parasol hangs over the altar.

Often just a single butter lamp burns on the altar, unlike temples in Tibet, where there may be hundreds of lamps burning. On auspicious occasions in Bhutan, however, 108 or even 1000 butter lamps are lit. To prevent fires, arrays of butter lamps are often burned in a separate small building.

Another way that lhakhangs in Bhutan differ from those in Tibet is that they feature a pair of elephant tusks alongside the altar to symbolise good. Buddhists revere the elephant because when Buddha was born, his mother had a vision of a white elephant.

If the lhakhang is in a monastery, then opposite the altar, facing the central image, is a throne upon which the abbot, or *khenpo*, sits during ceremonies. Between the khenpo's throne and the altar are rows of cushions that monks sit on during prayers and ceremonies.

The golden deer above a goemba are symbols of the deer park at Varanasi where the Buddha did his earliest teachings.

are free from all delusions, will be reached. Following this process requires going through a series of rebirths until the goal is reached and no more rebirths into the world of suffering are necessary. The path that takes you through this cycle of births is *karma* – but this is not simply fate. Karma is a law of cause and effect; your actions in one life determine the role you will play and what you will have to go through in your next life.

The Buddha is known to the Mahayana Buddhists as Sakyamuni. He never wrote down his *dharma* (teachings), and a schism developed so that today there are two major Buddhist schools.

Theravada Buddhism

The Theravada, 'doctrine of the elders', holds that the path to nirvana, the eventual aim of all Buddhists, is an individual pursuit. Practitioners believe that an individual can work towards an end to the endless cycle of rebirths by practising monastic discipline in accordance with the *sutras* (teachings of the Buddha) and meditating on the impermanent nature of reality; the worship of deities is secondary. The Theravada school is followed in Sri Lanka, Burma (Myanmar) and Thailand, and by the Buddhist Newars in the Kathmandu valley.

Mahayana Buddhism

In contrast, the Mahayana, or 'great vehicle', school holds that the combined belief of its followers will eventually be great enough to encompass all of humanity and bear it to salvation. Today, various forms of Mahayana Buddhism are practised in Vietnam, Japan, Nepal and China.

Mahayana Buddhists believe in the existence of holy beings, or saints, who have sacrificed their own release from suffering in order to aid in the salvation of all living things. Such a person is called a *bodhisattva*, one who has attained enlightenment, but delays their entry into nirvana in order to lead others to enlightenment. The bodhisattva remains in the world as a teacher or guru, suffering and toiling for the salvation of all beings. Thus, in the Mahayana tradition, bodhisattvas are worshipped as Buddhas. The historical Buddha, Sakyamuni, is viewed as one of a succession of Buddhas.

Mahayana Buddhism developed into a more metaphysical form than Theravada Buddhism, with elaborate rituals and symbolism. It emphasises mental development and service to humanity.

Vajrayana Vajrayana Buddhism, the diamond vehicle, evolved from Mahayana traditions, probably in India during the 2nd to 4th centuries. Often called Tantric Buddhism, it focuses on existential problems and emphasises the use of meditation under the direction of an initiated teacher as a means to achieve enlightenment. Unlike the pure Mahayana tradition, which attaches most importance to theoretical aspects of Buddhism, the Vajrayana tradition portrays Buddhism as part of the individual. Yogic and meditative methods are used to bring about a complete transformation of the practitioner. Female energies and goddesses are worshipped and demonesses exert a powerful influence.

Vajrayana students must be accepted by a recognised teacher and must undergo a long process of initiation and training (tantra means 'practice'). The emphasis is to understand compassion through a process of meditation. Eventually, the student learns yogic or contemplative practices and uses *mudras* (gestures and postures) and *mantras* (sacred syllables and phrases). Vajrayana Buddhism has a collection of texts known as the *tantras*, which supplement the initial teachings of the Buddha.

Though Buddhism had been practised in Tibet since the reign of King Songtsen Gampo (618-649), it was not the dominant force in the country until much later. Tibet was plagued by demons, and King Trisong Detsen (755-797) invited Guru Rimpoche to visit Tibet to try to subdue the negative forces that were interfering with the construction of Samye monastery. Every night the demons destroyed all the previous day's work. The Guru subdued the demons, not by destroying them, but by bringing them under his control. The converted demons helped to build the monastery, accomplishing more at night than the workers did during the day, thus establishing Tibet's first Buddhist monastery.

Guru Rimpoche's primary weapon to control the demons was the dorji (see illu-

---

Reincarnation

Followers of Himalayan Buddhism believe that our consciousness persists in an unbroken stream from lifetime to lifetime. This mindstream is reborn into a new body under circumstances dictated by the good and bad actions we've accumulated in our current and past lifetimes. Meditation is a method of stabilising our minds so all negative emotions (attachment, anger, and indifference), and thus all suffering, are eliminated. The mind, thus stabilised, is able to consciously choose to be reborn in order to help teach other people how to reach this state.

Great lamas almost always choose to be reborn in order to continue to benefit other beings. People who are recognised as the reincarnation of a previous great teacher are called *trulkus*. Each time a great Buddhist master dies students or close acquaintances will eventually search out his reincarnation, based on various clues that may have been left by the previous master.

The idea that Buddhist lamas can consciously reincarnate for the benefit of other beings is difficult for non-Buddhists to comprehend. It is worth noting that the great spiritual leaders of Tibet and Bhutan were all identified when they were young children.

and sponsoring the recitation of sacred texts all contribute to one's karma. It is also a merit-making exercise to witness dances and ritual performances by lamas, but no real understanding or active participation is necessary. The Earl of Ronaldshay described Himalayan Buddhism as:

'...a perfectly bewildering medley of gods and goddesses, Buddhas and bodhisattvas, guardian deities and canonised saints, ghouls, goblins and demons, deified kings and spirits of every conceivable description, paradises, earths and hells.'

Lineages of Himalayan Buddhism
Himalayan Buddhism was influenced by the ancient indigenous Bon tradition of Tibet, and a few pockets of Bon remain in the Himalayan regions. Many of the demons and shamanistic traditions of Tibetan Buddhism evolved from its interaction with Bon. These demons, by the way, were very real to the people of Tibet.

stration). This symbol is an important icon, and it is from this that the name Vajrayana evolved (*vajra* is the Sanskrit name for dorji).

This branch of Buddhism is sometimes referred to (incorrectly) in the west as Lama Buddhism or Lamaism. The word lama means 'extraordinary master' and is a title used for the heads of monasteries and monks of superior learning. A more descriptive and accurate name is Himalayan Buddhism.

Himalayan Buddhism is different in practise from many western religions. Although it has a strict moral code, including the prohibition of killing, it does not require the layman to undertake sophisticated study. The monks memorise texts and recite them on important occasions. Those laymen who do understand the texts and rituals are respected, but most people don't fathom the intricacies of the liturgy. People gain merit by hearing the texts, and it is not necessary for them to understand the deeper meaning of the recitations.

Similarly, merit may be achieved by spinning a prayer wheel, the inside of which contains thousands, or millions, of prayers written on paper. Contributing to the construction of a goemba, supporting the monastic community, erecting prayer flags

Many stories tell of Tibetan saints, or bodhisattvas, subduing these demons and spirits and converting them to Buddhism. These saints had great appeal to ordinary Tibetans, and a shamanistic tradition evolved as the popular form of Tibetan Buddhism. While the monks studied texts and followed strict rules, the religious practices of lay people included the worship of favourite saints and calling on sorcerers to solve particular problems such as health, financial difficulty or possession by demons.

Each monastery maintained its own leadership and a number of charismatic teachers became recognised, each with an individual interpretation of certain aspects of the scriptures. This difference in interpretation of the scriptures, combined with the influence of worship of the more popular saints, resulted in the evolution of various lineages or schools within Tibetan Buddhism, each with its distinctive style and traditions.

Nyingma Early western students of Tibetan Buddhism labelled this the 'red hat' school and assumed it was the earliest form of Tibetan Buddhism because its name,

Tashi Tagye

Many homes and temples are decorated with *tashi tagye*, the eight auspicious signs of Himalayan Buddhism. Each has a deep symbolic meaning and represents an object used in religious observances.

Precious Umbrella
The *duk* symbolises the activity of preserving beings from illness and negative forces.

Victory Banner
The *gyeltshen* represents the victory of the Buddhist doctrine over harmful forces.

White Conch
The *dungkar* winds to the right and is a symbol of the deep and melodious sound of the Dharma teachings.

Endless Knot
The noose of eternity, *pelgibeu*, represents the mind and the union of wisdom and compassion.

Golden Fish
The *sernga* represents the auspiciousness of all beings in a state of fearlessness without drowning in the ocean of suffering.

Lotus Flower
The *pema* is a symbol of the purification of the body, speech and mind.

Vase of Treasure
The *bumpa* represents long life, wealth and prosperity.

Golden Wheel
The *khorlo* is the precious wheel of Buddha's doctrine.

Nyingma, means 'old'. It was the practice of Nyingma Buddhism that Guru Rimpoche introduced to Tibet and Bhutan. Nyingma monasteries never became great seats of power because most of their practitioners were local shaman-like teachers in rural villages. Nyingmapa monks may marry and often work individually in small village lhakhangs and remote cave retreats.

Nyingma tradition places a special emphasis on tertons. These are Nyingma lamas who were the rediscoverers of Guru Rimpoche's hidden terma. The terma consisted mostly of sacred texts and teachings, often written in secret languages, as well as statues and ritual objects. The concept of termas is a living tradition, and new termas continue to be revealed to this day.

Gelug Known as the 'yellow hat' school, Gelug is a reformed lineage begun in the 14th century. Its founder, Tsong Khapa, studied Sakya, Kadam and Kagyu teachings, and eventually his teachings led to a new tradition of Tibetan Buddhism, which he named *Gelug* (virtuous ones).

Tsong Khapa instigated a system of examinations, of which the highest degree granted was *geshe*. In 1409 he founded Ganden, west of Lhasa, one of Tibet's greatest and most important monasteries. Gelug followers later established several important monasteries in Tibet, including Drepung, Sera and Tashilhunpo. From Tsong Khapa's disciples came the line of the Dalai Lama, who is believed to be the incarnation of Avalokiteshvara (known in Tibet as Chenrezig), the bodhisattva of compassion.

Sakya The Sakya school was named after its principal monastery in Tibet. Its systematically organised teachings are called *lamdre*. They integrate the precepts of sutra and tantra into a discipline designed to bring about Buddhahood in a single lifetime.

Kadam The patriarch of the Kadam (Bound by Precept) school was Atisha, whose teachings stressed the need for austere monastic discipline and devotion to a teacher before

the start of tantric practice. Students observed four fundamental rules: celibacy, abstinence from intoxicants, and prohibition of travel and money-handling. The Gelug lineage absorbed the Kadampas in the 15th century.

Kagyu The name Kagyu translates as 'whispered transmission'. It places fundamental emphasis on the oral transmission of esoteric teachings directly from master to pupil. The tradition evolved with the early Indian masters, and its most important teacher was the tantric guru Marpa (1012-1093). Among Marpa's disciples was Milarepa, Tibet's greatest poet. Milarepa eschewed the study of classical Tibetan text and wandered throughout Tibet meditating in high mountain caves and composing songs.

One of Milarepa's disciples was Gampopa, who authored important Kagyu texts and passed his teachings on to several gifted students. These students, in turn, founded the monasteries of Drigung, Taklung and Ralung (from which the first Shabdrung, Ngawang Namgyal, came).

The Kagyu system emphasises certain aspects of practical mysticism, including yogic practices of breathing techniques and postures. It is possible to achieve enlightenment within a lifetime, or at the moment of death, by relying on the Six Yogas of Naropa. These are self-produced heat, illusory body, dreams, the experience of light, the intermediate state between death and rebirth and the passing from one existence into another. Following the example of the married priest Marpa, Kagyu tradition does not demand celibacy or association with a religious institution.

There are numerous sub-orders of Kagyu, including Karmapa, Drikungpa and Drukpa. The Karmapa lineage is one of the important schools in present-day Tibet and Sikkim, and the Drukpa lineage is the pre-eminent religion of Bhutan.

Bhutan's Drukpa Kagyu Lineage
The Drukpa Kagyu lineage was established by Tsangpa Jarey Yeshey Dorji (1161-1211)

Buddhism in Bhutan: A Tantric Legacy

The Drukpa Kagyu religion of Bhutan has its roots in the profound philosophical system and practice of Tantric Buddhism. Though I am not a Buddhist scholar, I will attempt a brief explanation of Tantricism and its philosophical relevance.

While mainstream and traditional Buddhism is appreciated by many people because of its universal truths, there is an ambiguous, and sometimes even hostile, feeling towards Tantric Buddhism. Some outsiders see Tantric Buddhism as a degeneration of Buddhism, and a few early scholars even described esoteric Tantric rituals as demon worship and sorcery. These misperceptions are quite understandable given the ostensibly violent, gory and sexual imagery and symbols of Tantric practice. To the uninitiated they appear to be a far cry from the peace, equanimity and sobriety of Theravada and other forms of Mahayana Buddhism. But these misperceptions are based on wrong assumptions and lack of information because, in the past, Tantric practitioners did not divulge their knowledge and skills freely.

Despite the contrary outward appearances, Tantric Buddhist schools – including the Drukpa Kagyupa – are firmly rooted in the basic Buddhist principles and teachings, such as the Four Noble truths, the Eightfold Path, the Triple Gem and the importance of wisdom and compassion. However, Tantric Buddhism does differ from traditional Buddhist outlook in some important ways.

Buddhism emphasises that the path to nirvana is a process of purifying our minds of negativities and obscurations and replacing these with perfected qualities of generosity, concentration, insight etc in order to attain a perfected state at some time in the future. The Tantric premise is that we already possess the nature of enlightened and perfected beings, and we need only recognise it and enact our true roles as deities.

To the Tantric practitioner the end, or goal, is therefore actually the starting point of transformation. This transformation or transcendence of one's normal self in Tantric Buddhist practice is achieved primarily through the process of meditation visualisation using an incredibly rich array of meditative tools such as mantras, mudras, mandalas, masked dances and a host of complex and symbolically complex rituals and practices. The heart-essence of the practice would be to generate and enact in this very moment a perfected being in a perfected environment.

Tantric philosophy also advocates that nothing really needs to be suppressed or annihilated. Indeed, the energy of our desires can be channelised and used effectively to achieve the desired transformation. But an important qualification in this regard is the purity of one's motivation. Given this freedom to use even the desires that we wish to transcend, there are dangerous pitfalls, because this freedom could well be used to justify one's own indulgence. Therefore, critically important in this spiritual process is the role of the master or lama who initiates the disciple into these esoteric practices and the inner meaning of the images, ideas and rituals. In Tantric Buddhism, the important role that the lama plays can be seen from the fact that in addition to taking refuge in the Buddha, the Dharma and the Sangha, one also seeks refuge in the lama who is seen as the living personification of all the Buddhist ideals.

Given the importance of visioning in Tantric Buddhism, it is not surprising that the many fundamental truths of Buddhism have been expressed symbolically, but in a radically different but impressionistic manner. Such complex symbolism abounds and can be confusing and misleading for those unaware of the deeper meanings. For instance, the union of qualities of perfect wisdom and perfect skills/techniques which generates the bliss of enlightenment is graphically symbolised in Tantric Buddhism with a male and female deity entwined in a sexual embrace. Dietrick Seckel says this about the function and validity of such cultural symbols:

'They take something that in its essence is beyond form but reveals itself in visionary forms adapted to our earthly ability for visualisation and conceptualisation'.

This rich and extensive use in Tantric Buddhism of symbolism has found a natural expression in the arts and literature. For instance the Tantric influence is discernible in nearly every aspect of the thirteen traditional skills or crafts (*Zorig Chusum*), and is omnipresent in paintings and carvings, metal, clay and stone artwork. Traditional religious motifs and colours too are very evident in the Bhutanese textiles. The festivals of Bhutan with their masked dances and morality plays are also an expression of many of the ideals and values of Tantric Buddhism.

The influence of Tantric Buddhism since the mid 8th century, has irrevocably shaped Bhutan's history and destiny, and has had an indelible and enlightening impact on the Bhutanese way of life. It affects almost everything: from arts and crafts to the system of government, from folk dances to architectural style. To this day, the importance and relevance of Buddhism has not waned and Buddhist values and traditions still permeate every aspect of the Bhutanese culture and ethos.

Kunzang Dorji

at Ralung Monastery in central Tibet. In the first half of the 13th century, a lama from Ralung, Phajo Drukgom Shigpo, came to Bhutan and established the Drukpa Kagyu school. In the 17th century the Drukpa school was established as the de facto official state religion by Shabdrung Ngawang Namgyal. To this day Drukpa Kagyu remains the state religion and continues to be the dominant Buddhist lineage, though the Nyingma lineage also commands great respect and has a significant following.

Bhutan's religious practices rely heavily on tantric tradition and retain the Kagyu emphasis on solitary meditation in the Milarepa style. The country's main protective deity is Yeshey Goenpo, or Mahakala, who often appears in the form of a raven and is a Tantric Buddhist form of the Hindu god Shiva.

Every house has a *choesham* (altar or shrine room). Each altar usually features statues of the three great lamas: Sakyamuni Buddha, Guru Rimpoche and Shabdrung Rimpoche. In most homes and temples, devotees place bowls filled with water on altars. This simple offering is important because it can be given without greed or attachment. On special occasions monks prepare torma, white and pink sculptures made from *tsampa* (barley flour) and butter, as symbolic offerings to deities. A special shape of torma is associated with each deity.

As all Himalayan Buddhists do, Bhutanese devotees prostrate themselves in front of altars and deities, first clasping hands above the head, again at throat level and then at the chest. This is a representation of the mind, speech and body.

Facts for the Visitor

The previous chapter describes many traditions and customs unique to Bhutan, and you may have found some of the more peculiar aspects of Bhutan's culture and history somewhat implausible. Bhutan has more complications in store; in order to visit you will have to conform to its very unusual rules for tourism.

The Royal Government of Bhutan insists that foreign visitors travel as package tourists with a pre-planned itinerary. If you are used to travelling this way, you will find Bhutan's system convenient, efficient and generally comfortable. You can buy a space on a group tour and have everything arranged for you, or you may travel with your own chosen companions – or even alone.

If you usually travel independently, you have to accept a certain degree of planning and regimentation, but within this framework there are still ways to retain your freedom and avoid many of the drawbacks associated with an organised tour. If you wish, you can design your own itinerary according to dates that are convenient for you. Other restrictions, however, make it difficult to go anywhere you wish, to change your programme as you choose, and to visit most temples and monuments.

Bhutan is a fascinating and rewarding place to travel, but it has an established set of rules that are not going to change. Unless you are a project volunteer (or related to one), an Indian citizen or a friend of the Royal family, you will probably have to accept the Bhutanese way of travel and make the most of it.

PLANNING

Throughout its history Bhutan has never actively encouraged visitors. There were so few foreign visitors before 1974 that most can be chronicled, as they are in the history section of the Facts about Bhutan chapter. When the third king, Jigme Dorji Wangchuck, decided to make Bhutan a part of the international community, his policy was to take a series of small, careful steps, and tourism was not a part of his modernisation programme.

When the government decided to allow foreign visitors, the programme of care and conservatism continued and became a major facet of Bhutan's unique tourism policy. In keeping with its centralised system of management and cautious approach to development, tourism is strictly controlled.

As Bhutan slowly began to admit foreign tourists in the 1970s, foreign tour operators encouraged the government to place limits on the number of visitors. The Bhutanese, horrified at the prospects of a situation similar to Kathmandu's 'freak street' developing in Bhutan, wisely took the advice. Though initially controlled by a government monopoly on tourism facilities and a quota of 2000 foreign visitors a year, the numbers are now controlled through a system of high prices that automatically limits the number of tourists and the length of their stay.

The policy has achieved the goal of keeping numbers low. In 1997 only 5365 tourists visited Bhutan, and this was the highest annual count on record. The largest number were Japanese, American and German. Other major nationalities were British, French and Italian.

Bhutan's Tourism Policy

Tourism is administered by the Tourism Authority of Bhutan (TAB), a department of the Ministry of Trade & Industry. Their rules are simple, yet are carefully thought out and strictly enforced. There are very few loopholes.

The basic policy is that foreign tourists pay US$200 for each night in Bhutan. This, at least, is an all-inclusive rate that covers all your food, accommodation, transport and guide services. A portion of the fee, currently 35%, goes directly to the government as a sort of tourist tax, and the rest

Highlights

Anywhere you travel in Bhutan you will find spectacular scenery, deep forests, high Himalayan peaks and a traditional Buddhist culture with amazing architecture and massive dzongs that dominate the countryside. Almost everything in Bhutan is different from the rest of Asia, and probably unlike anything you have imagined.

The Countryside The first thing that strikes a visitor to Bhutan is the great expanse of green, forested hillsides. There is a great variety of trees, vegetation and wildlife as you drive from subtropical forests over high alpine passes and back down to broad valleys with houses that look remarkably like Swiss chalets scattered across the landscape.

Dzongs Bhutan's extraordinary architecture is best represented by the massive white fortress-monasteries that dominate the major valleys. It's sometimes possible to enter the dzongs and get a close view of the impressive artwork and traditional construction techniques. Even at a distance, the dzongs offer one of the unique and most photogenic highlights in the country (see the colour section 'Dzongs' between pages 64 and 65).

Festivals There are festivals throughout the year, and crowds of Bhutanese and foreign tourists descend on monasteries and dzongs to witness the ceremonies and lama dances that continue for several days. The *tsechu* festivals are colourful pageants and important social occasions, with all comers dressed in their finest traditional dress.

Trekking Bhutan offers a true wilderness experience while still retaining the comforts of a traditional Himalayan trek. On Bhutan's trek routes there are no hotels, few villages and even fewer trekkers.

Bhutanese Hospitality The Bhutanese are extraordinarily friendly and hospitable. In towns almost everyone speaks English, and you will easily make friends during your travels. All Bhutanese you come into contact with, whether a government official, driver, guide or policeman, will treat you with a politeness that is almost embarrassing. Service in hotels, while abundant and enthusiastic, is occasionally amateurish, but the broad smile of the server smoothes over any shortcomings.

Textiles The traditional handloom weaving is so exotic and varied that several museums in the west have permanent exhibitions of Bhutanese textiles. Although it is traditionally used for clothing, you can purchase lengths of the colourful material for use as curtains or bedspreads.

goes to the private tour operator providing the services.

The tourism rules are in keeping with the government's policies of proceeding slowly in all aspects of development and modernisation. The 35% royalty that goes into the national treasury has helped with development and, among other things, providing free medical care and education for everyone in the country.

While the current rate of US$200 per person per day seems excessively high by the standards of a budget traveller, it's actually less than what an international business traveller would expect to pay for an all-inclusive package in any major Asian city. Even the venerable Imperial Hotel in Delhi, which was a backpackers' hotel in the 1970s, now starts at US$160 a night.

The basic Bhutanese policy of low volume

Shangri La

Many travel brochures describe Bhutan as 'the last Shangri La.' This is a name invented by James Hilton in the 1930s classic, *Lost Horizon*. Shangri La is a secluded Himalayan valley where people never age. The high lama of Hilton's Shangri La ensured that the valley was well hidden to protect its people and culture from the influences of the modern world and to preserve its traditions and teachings for a time when the world is free from strife and discord. In the lama's words:

'We may expect no mercy, but we may faintly hope for neglect. Here we shall stay with our books and our music and our meditations, conserving the frail elegancies of a dying age, and seeking such wisdom as men will need when their passions are all spent. We have a heritage to cherish and bequeath. Let us take what pleasure we may until that time comes.'

The high lama seems to be echoing the traditions established by Shabdrung Ngawang Namgyal which have been carried into the 1990s. Hilton's story is based on the Tibetan tradition of 'hidden valleys', or *bey-yuls*. It is believed that when wars or calamities threaten humanity, these special places will serve as refuges for the followers of Buddhism.

There are several valleys within Bhutan that are believed to be bey-yuls preserved in a state of timelessness as a repository for the culture of humans. These include the valley of Ha and also Thowada in the north of Bumthang's Tang valley, which was hidden by Guru Rimpoche's consort Yeshe Chogyal.

and high prices was created by a concerned, culturally sensitive, well-educated and well-travelled government, one that truly feels that this is the best approach for Bhutan. The sensitive and socially conscious traveller will accept these restrictions. The only likely change in Bhutan's tourism policy is an increase in prices when the government feels that the volume of tourists is beginning to overpower the traditional culture.

Special Rules for Indian Citizens Indian tourists are categorised differently from other international tourists. Indian nationals do not require a visa and are not subject to the fixed daily tariff. They may travel independently throughout most of Bhutan, though a special permit is required. Tourism Authority of Bhutan (TAB) recommends that Indian visitors use the services of a Bhutanese tour operator to arrange such permits and to expedite hotel and transport bookings.

What Kind of Trip?

Though you are required to pre-book and pre-pay for your travel in Bhutan, it is not necessary to join a packaged tour group. Booking onto a tour is, however, the easiest and most hassle-free way to visit the kingdom. That's one way.

In the rest of this chapter you'll learn how you can arrange an independent programme to do pretty much what you want. You can design your own itinerary and then contact an agent in Bhutan to arrange your visa and handle the trip.

Bhutan originally classified tourism into two categories, cultural tours and treks, with a lower rate for trekking. Because tour operators abused the system, there is now a single rate for all travel in Bhutan, whether it is in a hotel or under canvas. The term 'cultural tour' has persisted, and most tour operators still use this term to differentiate hotel trips from trekking.

A Fully Inclusive Package Unless you have a special visa provided as part of your employment contract with an embassy or a non-government organisation (NGO), you must arrange your visa through TAB and use a Bhutan tour operator to arrange your

Bhutanese Textiles

Weaving

Weaving is such an integral part of Bhutan's cultural identity that it is sometimes described as a cloth-based culture. Bhutan's weavers, almost all of whom are women, are renowned for producing a range of interesting and beautiful textiles in vibrant colours and patterns. These fabrics, which until recently were largely unknown outside of Bhutan, are so exceptional that they are featured in several private collections and museums in Europe and America.

Until the 1970s the only Bhutanese textiles to reach the outside world were gifts from the royal family or high officials to prominent visitors. The first exhibition of Bhutanese textiles was in 1958 at the Crafts Museum in New York and featured fabrics that were lent and presented by the Queen of Bhutan. There is also a small museum in Neuchâtel, Switzerland, which has a collection of Bhutanese textiles presented by the late king on the condition that it is kept on permanent exhibition. The most recent exhibition was in 1994 at the Peabody Essex Museum in Massachusetts, which was extensively documented in the book *From the Land of the Thunder Dragon; Textile Arts of Bhutan.*

Bhutanese weaving has developed, with new designs and colours, but weavers still produce the same items their ancestors did centuries ago.

NICHOLAS REUSS

In former times taxes were paid in cloth and a person's wealth was measured by the number and – more importantly – quality of gho or kira they owned. Fabrics are considered assets and may be traded in the same manner as gold and stocks. Even today, traditional Bhutanese gifts are pieces of cloth, presented in uneven numbers from one to seven depending on the rank of the beneficiary. Bhutanese still treasure hand-woven fabrics over machine-woven material and no Bhutanese would consider wearing anything but a handmade gho or kira to an important occasion such as a tsechu.

Most Bhutanese textiles are woven from cotton, though silk thread is sometimes used to produce pieces of exceptional quality and value. The traditional centres of sophisticated weaving are in eastern Bhutan, especially Dungkhar and Khoma in Kurtoe, Khaling and Radi in Trashigang and Duksum in Trashi Yangtse. Zungney village in Bumthang is the centre for the weaving of wool into strips called *yathra*.

The exceptional craftsmanship of Bhutanese weavers has been exhibited around the world.

NICHOLAS REUSS

Weaving is, however, a part-time occupation throughout Bhutan. Hired weavers weave cloth for noble households, peasants weave for their own household needs and many others weave at home both for their own use and also for sale in local shops and larger centres such as the NWAB shop in Khaling and the Cottage Industry shop in Thimphu.

The high quality of work has its roots in the feudal system when officials had their own weavers amongst their retainers. These people were not paid by the piece, and were not obliged to work according to strict schedules – or even to work if the spirit did not move them. Consequently when they did weave, they put their heart and souls into what they did and produced pieces of splendid individuality and excellent finish. Though most weavers use the same basic motifs, they produce them in varying patterns so that no two pieces are ever quite alike, and each weaver leaves her own impress on her work.

Bhutanese weavers have perfected the technique of working supplementary warps or wefts into their highly prized fabrics. These labour-intensive techniques create intricate and delicate patterns that seem to float on the cloth like embroidery but are, in fact, woven into the fabric. The most striking use of supplementary wefts is in the weaving of *kushutara*, or 'brocaded dress'. This most colourful and intricate Bhutanese textile is distinguished by a white field patterned with dozens of diamond and half-diamond shaped motifs. Dating from the 17th century, kushutara fabrics are used exclusively for kira and their intricate and contrasting designs have been passed down from mother to daughter for generations in the Kurtoe region.

The Loom

Though there are some horizontal frame looms with treadles, most weaving of cotton in Bhutan is performed on a very basic type of 'back-strap' loom. This is an easily transportable frame which can be attached to any fixed surface such as a wall or a tree. The weaver sits on the ground or floor, leans back against a wide leather strap that holds the threads taut and deftly manoeuvres a bewildering array of seemingly extraneous threads into the background cloth as it is being woven. The design of the loom limits the width of the cloth to about 65cm, and three loom lengths are sewn together to make a single gho or kira.

STAN ARMINGTON

Some or the most elaborate textiles are woven using a portable backstrap loom (left). Other textiles include intricate religious works such as this thangka (below) depicting Guru Rimpoche.

Dyes

Though artificially dyed cotton from India is occasionally used, most weavers prefer indigenous natural dyes. Red is produced from lac, the resinous secretion of an insect, and also from madder. Blue dye is made by an intricate process from the leaves of the indigo shrub, and yellow comes from the symplocos plant (which has no common English name) or from turmeric.

Other Textiles

Bhutan also produces extraordinary appliqués and embroideries. Most of these are produced by men, often by monks, and are pictorial depictions of religious themes and deities that are hung in lhakhangs and dzongs. These range from smallish works, bordered and hung like painted thangkas to the huge *thondrol* banners that you'll see exhibited during tsechus.

NICHOLAS REUSS

The Four Friends

One of Bhutan's favourite fables is that of the four friends. In Dzongkha the name of the story is *Thuenpa puen shi* (cooperation, relation, four) and illustrates the concept of teamwork; you will see paintings illustrating this story on homes and shops throughout the country.

The story tells how the elephant, monkey, peacock and rabbit combined forces to obtain a continual supply of fruit. The peacock found a seed and planted it, the rabbit watered it, the monkey fertilised it and the elephant guarded it. When the fruit was ripe the tree was so high that they could not reach the top. The animals made a tower by climbing on one another's backs and plucked the fruit from the high branches.

School of Arts & Crafts, Thimphu

trip. Out of the US$200 per day that you pay to TAB, US$130 makes it way back to the tour operator, which then provides all meals, accommodation and transportation and will assign you a guide-escort who will accompany you throughout your visit.

Before you arrive, you must pre-arrange a programme with a complete day-by-day itinerary. Once you have finalised the itinerary and paid for the tour, no alteration, except cancellation of the entire trip, is normally allowed. This pre-planning takes a lot of the spontaneity out of travel in Bhutan, but that's part of the plan. You are not supposed to extend your stay or change your destination. You may, however, be *forced* to change your itinerary because of road closure, hotel booking problems or other factors. Such situations can be quite trying, but usually turn out for the best, and if you take things in your stride, you can have a lot of fun.

Group Travel When you apply for your visa – whether you travel as an individual, as a small group of two or three, or as a larger group organised by an adventure travel company – you become a 'group' in the eyes of TAB.

Your group should arrive, travel and depart together, and no other people are supposed to be added to it. A licensed guide will accompany your group throughout Bhutan and ensure that your transportation, hotel, meals and sightseeing are provided in accordance with the itinerary you have arranged.

If you are on your own, or in a small group, you can take a few liberties, such as eating in local restaurants, making short side trips or visiting homes. If you are in a larger group, things become much more formalised, and you will probably eat all your meals at your hotel and have hotel-prepared packed lunches as picnics when you are on long road journeys.

Trekking If you have the time and ability, the best way to experience Bhutan is to take a trek. Treks can last from three to more

than 25 days. Most trekking trails are extremely steep and many treks cross high passes of 4500m or more. In Bhutan most treks offer many days of true wilderness experience that is completely different from typical treks in the Nepal or Indian Himalaya. It may be hard to contemplate paying US$200 a day to sleep in a tent, but the Bhutanese trek operators do a good job and you will be well fed and cared for.

Remaining Independent Historically, tourists to Bhutan have travelled in large organised groups arranged by a travel agent or tour operator and escorted by a leader. Bhutanese tour operators have developed good systems to handle these groups, keeping them in large, quiet hotels away from the noise of towns. The hotels provide buffet meals with a variety of western food and an occasional Bhutanese dish. Sightseeing is well organised and follows established patterns, with a return to the hotel for lunch, followed by a time for rest.

Though this kind of trip is exactly what many people want, for others it creates a feeling of isolation from the culture and people of the country. If you are alone, or in a small group of two to five, it's possible to break out of this pattern.

Be warned, however, that in doing so you will totally confuse your guide. Guides have been trained in the well-established procedures and will normally arrange your meals in the hotel, deposit you there at 5 pm and arrange to meet you the following morning. Be gentle and understanding if you try to subvert the traditional system. It also would be appropriate to convey your desires to the tour operator well in advance so they can be prepared to cope with the changes.

In the early days of Bhutan's tourism, guide-escorts were responsible for controlling every move that their charges made. These days, however, you are allowed considerable freedom, and guides are more than happy to take a day off when one is offered.

Bhutan has no caste system, and there is no social stigma attached to most jobs. You can enhance your Bhutan experience by socialising with your guide and driver in hotels and restaurants – if you can entice them away from their beloved card games!

If you stay in a hotel near the centre of town instead of a resort-type hotel on a hilltop, you can wander into the local market rather than confining yourself to the hotel gift shop. You can choose to have meals in one of the many local restaurants or stop in a bar or food stall for a pre-dinner drink. You can turn your two half-day sightseeing excursions into one full-day outing by carrying a packed lunch or eating in a local restaurant.

Many of the smaller *goembas* (monasteries), palaces and temples mentioned in this book are not on the standard sightseeing programmes. Some of these do welcome *small* groups of visitors who are properly dressed and do not intrude on the surroundings. The Bhutanese are very polite, calm people, and if you present yourself well, they will try to accommodate your wishes as much as possible.

Features of Bhutanese Travel

Value for Money Hotels and meals are generally good but not outstanding, and you don't really get US$200 per day in value. However, much of the value you receive is provided in transport, which is expensive, and you get all your meals and a full-time guide throughout your stay. Even if you don't want all these services, you have paid for them and will get them regardless.

If you subtract the 35% government royalty and pretend that you are paying US$130 per day, then you do actually receive pretty good value.

A Complex Buddhist Culture If you have read the description of the culture and religion of Bhutan, you will probably find the country fascinating. If you have never been to Tibet or any other Himalayan kingdom, and don't have a basic grasp of Mahayana Buddhist architecture and iconography, you may find the culture of Bhutan a bit overpowering. In this case you might consider travelling first to Nepal, Tibet or the Indian

Himalaya before undertaking a visit to Bhutan.

Restricted Entrance to Temples The Bhutanese view their temples and monasteries as living institutions and since 1988 have not allowed tourists to enter them without special permission – which is generally reserved for bona fide practising Buddhists.

Monks have considerable influence and resist the intrusion of tourists; they also quietly resist efforts to modernise monastic life. They express concern that a large number of visitors disturbs the sanctity of holy places and may cause the disappearance of temple treasures.

Long Drives on Winding Roads If you confine yourself to the Paro, Thimphu and Punakha circuit, you'll be in good hotels and your road travel will be in chunks of two or three hours. If you travel to eastern Bhutan, be prepared for full-day drives on winding, bumpy, sometimes frightening, roads that are only 1½ lanes wide. There are great views from high passes, and the white houses scattered across vast expanses of cultivated valleys provide welcome variety on the lengthy drives. There are, however, many long stretches of wooded hillsides, which tend to make long drives seem endless.

Despite the wild country that the roads traverse, they are extraordinarily well maintained. Dantak, the Indian Border Roads Task Force, employs an army of labourers from India who live in shacks alongside the road and perform constant repairs.

You rarely have sight of the great snow peaks of the Bhutan Himalaya because, typically, the views are blocked either by clouds or forested ridges.

Overbooking & Mix-Ups During the high season in October and November and also during festival times, hotels are fully booked, and it is difficult for tour operators to get vacancies. Even if you have confirmation, the hotels may be double (or even triple)

booked, or some unexpected VIP may arrive and demand the last room. You must be prepared to take such problems in your stride if you come to Bhutan. Tour operators, guides and hotels all do their best to provide everything that you have paid for, but it's not always possible. More than once, travellers who have had confirmed hotel bookings have been accommodated in private homes – or in tents. If you view this mix-up as a cultural experience, you can turn it into fun, but if you pout and demand what has been promised, you'll just embarrass everyone – and probably still end up in a tent.

The reservation problem also works in reverse. Everything is arranged in advance, and if you decide you would like to stay an extra day somewhere, this whim will usually cause a major complication.

When to Go

The high season for visiting Bhutan is October and November and during major festivals (see the boxed text 'Future Festival Dates' later in this chapter).

Weather is the most important consideration in timing your visit, but no matter when you go there is likely to be rain. The climate is best in autumn, from late September to late November, when skies are generally clear and the high mountain peaks are visible early in the morning from passes and other vantage points. This is the ideal time for trekking and for travelling throughout the country. Late autumn is also the time when the black-necked cranes arrive at their wintering grounds in central and eastern Bhutan.

The winter can be a good time for touring in western Bhutan, but you will need warm clothing. From December to February, there is often snow in the higher regions and occasional snow in Thimphu. The road from Thimphu to Bumthang and the east may be closed because of snow for several days at a time. You would be safest not to plan a visit to these regions. The days are usually sunny, but it's quite cold once the sun disappears behind the hills at about 4 pm. Even

the Thimphu monk body moves to the warmer climate of Punakha for the winter.

Springtime, March to May, is recognised as the second-best time to visit Bhutan. Though there are more clouds and rain than in the autumn, the flowers are in bloom and birdlife is abundant. You can get occasional glimpses of the high peaks, but these are not the dramatic unobstructed views possible in autumn.

Summer, from June to August, is the monsoon season. And what a monsoon! During these three months 500mm of rain falls in Thimphu and up to a metre falls in the eastern hills. The mountains are hidden, the valleys are shrouded in clouds, and roads disappear in heavy downpours and floods.

Summer is still a great time to visit Paro, Thimphu and other parts of western Bhutan. The intense green of the rice fields contrasts with the darker greens of the forested hillsides in sunlight that is diffused by monsoon clouds. Meat is in short supply because of the lack of refrigeration available, but there is ample fresh fruit and vegetables.

A second factor in choosing a time to visit Bhutan, and one that may override considerations of weather patterns, is the schedule of festivals. These colourful events offer a firsthand glimpse of Bhutanese life and, for most people, provide the only opportunity to see the inside of the great dzongs. It's possible, if you work out dates carefully, to work at least one festival into a tour or trek programme.

The largest festivals – at Paro and Thimphu – take place during the time of the best weather and flights become hopelessly overbooked. You stand a better chance of getting the dates you want if you schedule your trip around one of the less popular festivals.

Maps

There is a dearth of maps of Bhutan. See the trekking chapter for details of topographical maps, but most of these maps are not available to the public. The Survey of Bhutan has published a large 1:250,000 map that is a

Spelling

Dzongkha is written in a script very similar to Tibetan, though the Bhutanese believe theirs is a more elegant version. In 1997 a government agency established a system of transliteration called 'Romanised Dzongkha'. This changed the spelling of several names into forms that are difficult to recognise from the spellings that appear in older books and maps.

Some of the more confusing changes are:

Old	New
Chirang	Tsirang
Gantey	Gangte
Kula Kangri	Kulha Gangri
Lingshi	Lingzhi
Samchi	Samtse
Shemgang	Zhemgang
Tashi Yangtse	Trashi Yangtse
Tashichho Dzong	Trashi Chhoe Dzong
Tashigang	Trashigang
Tongsa	Trongsa
Wangdi Phodrang	Wangdue Phodrang

Bhutan shares India's fascination for official abbreviations and acronyms, and these are used throughout the book and defined in the glossary.

composite of Landsat images overlaid with roads, major towns and district boundaries. It is hard to interpret because the rivers look like ridges, but it's a magic Bhutanese map – if you turn it upside down, everything looks as it should. The survey department also produces several specialised maps that are sold in bookshops. Various sheets show historical places, tourist spots, health centres and farming facilities. Colour maps of Thimphu and Paro valleys with detailed town plans are also available in bookshops and some hotel gift shops.

There is a 1:100,000 series of maps and an atlas produced by the Land Use Planning Section with the assistance of the Danish agency Danida. This series includes a large sheet map of each *dzongkhag* (district) with 200m contour intervals.

There is a handy plastic-laminated folding map by Berndtson & Berndtson in Germany with a road map on one side and maps of Thimphu and Paro on the reverse.

What to Bring

The following list will cover your needs for a vehicle-based cultural tour. If you are going trekking, see the appendix in the Trekking chapter for additional suggestions on specialised trekking clothing and equipment.

Since you will be travelling in a private vehicle, there is less concern about bulk and weight than if you were schlepping your own luggage on and off various forms of public transport. There is a strictly enforced 20kg weight limit (30kg in business class) on Druk Air. You should hold yourself to this allowance; even if you pay for excess baggage, it still travels standby and may be offloaded. Plus, as with all travel, the less you carry, the easier it is to move about and the less there is to misplace.

Clothing Casual clothes are fine, but you would do well to have a set of dress-up clothes (jacket and tie for men, dresses for women). Dress clothing is appropriate for visiting government offices, festivals, and for social occasions in Thimphu homes. Bhutan has a small-town atmosphere, and you might easily find yourself in the company of a high government official. If you have scheduled your trip around a festival, you definitely should carry a set of dressy clothing. Bhutanese people dress quite formally, and your dirty jeans don't fit in on such occasions. Remember, this is a country with a national dress code.

Even in the summer, it can be cool in Paro and Thimphu, and it's downright cold in winter. Days can be quite warm, especially in the lower regions such as Punakha and Phuentsholing, and you could start off driving in the cold of dawn be uncomfortably warm by mid-morning. Use a layering system, starting with thermal underwear and adding a shirt, pile jacket and windbreaker or parka as necessary. If you are not trekking, you will need:

- thermal underwear for cold weather
- swimming costume (for the hotel swimming pool in Punakha)
- cotton trousers
- cotton skirt for women
- pile jacket or sweater – even in summer
- down jacket – in winter; not needed in summer
- T-shirts or short sleeved (not sleeveless) cotton shirts
- sneakers or walking shoes and socks
- sandals or flip flops
- rain jacket – Gore-Tex if you can afford it, otherwise a poncho or nylon jacket
- dress-up clothes for festivals
- sun hat
- warm hat and gloves in winter

Both men and women should avoid wearing shorts in towns. Women will probably feel most comfortable in a skirt, but it's also OK to wear pants.

Bedding All hotels provide sheets, blankets or quilt, and a pillow. Unless you are trekking, you won't need to carry bedding or a sleeping bag. Most hotels also provide some sort of heating in winter, either an electric heater or a wood stove. The heating, plus the pile of blankets on your bed, should keep you warm. Hotel pillows tend to be hard. A small inflatable pillow is a useful addition; it's also good to have during long drives.

Toiletries Hotels provide soap and toilet paper, but don't expect a fancy collection of shampoo and cosmetics laid out in the bathroom. Indian brands of shampoo, toothpaste, shaving lather and other toiletries are available in larger towns. You can find old-fashioned razor blades and Indian brands of double blades that fit most shavers. A roll of toilet paper in your luggage is useful if you are doing any extensive road travel.

Tampons are not readily available – bring your own supply. Indian sanitary pads are available with some searching.

You will be outside a lot, and much of the time at altitudes above 2500m, so there is plenty of sun and wind. Bring a supply of sun cream and some lip protection, such as Blistex; these are not available in Bhutan.

Another item that's hard to find is dental floss. Bring some along to clean out the remains of a meal of tough and stringy Bhutanese chicken or yak meat. The quality of Indian brands of nail clippers, contact lens solution and deodorant is poor. Bring these items along with you.

Essential Extras There are several things that you should carry to make a trip to Bhutan more comfortable. All of the following items are essential.

Pack a folding **umbrella**. Rain is possible any time, but is almost certain from May to September.

Bring a **water bottle** and iodine for water purification (see boxed text 'Water Purification' in the Trekking chapter). Although you can get mineral water in most places, it comes in plastic bottles that cannot be recycled.

Be sure to carry **ear plugs** to reduce the noise from the barking dogs that scavenge through the streets at night. These are one of the most important items you can bring to Bhutan. If you are travelling to eastern Bhutan, you will be spending many hours on winding roads; bring a remedy for motion sickness. Insect repellent is useful during spring and summer.

There are occasional electric cuts throughout the country; so you should always keep a **torch** (flashlight) beside your bed.

Miscellaneous Items It will be difficult to get your laundry done as you will often only stay one night at a particular hotel. Bring some laundry soap and a length of clothesline to do your own washing. You can buy Indian laundry soap in bars which is more convenient than powdered or liquid soap on a rough trip. A large flat sink stopper is a useful addition to your personal laundry kit, and a small sewing kit is always handy.

Carry a pair of sunglasses (as protection

from high-altitude glare). A Swiss army knife has many uses, such as cutting cheese and opening bottles. Bring a small clock with an alarm to help you wake up because not all hotel rooms have telephones. All hotels have locks on the door, and theft is rare. A padlock is not necessary in Bhutan, but is a useful item if you are travelling on to India or Nepal. If you are travelling in winter, you might pack a hot water bottle to warm up your bed at night.

Most Indian batteries are old-fashioned dry cells. You can easily find large 'D' cells, and can often find smaller 'AA' cells, but other sizes are rare. If you are using a camera or tape recorder that uses alkaline or other special batteries, bring your own supply.

Packing If you are on a cultural tour, it's OK to bring a suitcase, though a soft bag is more versatile and easier to pack into the luggage space of a vehicle. You will also want a small rucksack or waist pack to carry your camera, water bottle and other essentials in the vehicle and when you are walking around town or visiting monuments.

SUGGESTED ITINERARIES
In planning your trip, try to arrange to be in Thimphu on a Saturday or Sunday to see the weekend market, and avoid Thimphu on Tuesday when all the shops are closed. Avoid Paro on Monday, the day that the National Museum is closed. If you value sleep, you would do well to schedule your last night in Bhutan at Paro. All flights leave in the early morning; if you spend your last night in Thimphu, you must wake up at 4 am and drive two hours to the airport.

If you have limited time (or money), you can get a good impression of Bhutan with only a three-night stay in the country, visiting Thimphu and Paro. Use the scheduling suggestions above to decide which nights to stay in Thimphu and which in Paro.

For a more comprehensive look at Bhutan, spend a week and add a trip over the mountains to Punakha, staying in Punakha or Wangdue Phodrang. Schedule an extra day

in Paro so you can climb to the point overlooking Taktshang, the remains of the famous 'tiger's nest' monastery, destroyed by fire in 1998.

A longer programme of nine days will allow you a full day in Bumthang with overnight stops in Paro, Thimphu and Trongsa and short stops in Punakha and Wangdue Phodrang as you drive through. A night in the Phobjikha valley will give you a chance to see Gangte goemba and also, during the late autumn, to view the rare and endangered black-necked cranes (see the boxed text 'The Black-Necked Crane' in the Facts about Bhutan chapter).

It takes two weeks to make a trip to the east, visiting Trongsa, Bumthang, Mongar and Trashigang. There is much to see on the way, but the trip involves a lot of driving. You need to arrange a permit in advance and be careful of problems in India, but you can save yourself the long (546km) drive back over the mountains by exiting Bhutan via Samdrup Jongkhar to India. From there you can drive back to Paro or on to Darjeeling, Sikkim or Nepal. You can also fly to Delhi or Calcutta from the Indian airports of Guwahati or Bagdogra.

Treks
You'll need to allow at least three days, and preferably a week, if you want to trek in Bhutan. The Druk Path, which goes from Paro to Thimphu, is a short and relatively simple trek. The Jhomolhari Trek offers some of the best high mountain scenery in Bhutan, but it crosses two high (4500m) passes. An excellent alternative is to do only the first three days of this trek to Jhomolhari Base Camp, spend a day exploring, then return to Paro via a variation of the upward route. This avoids the high passes and still provides spectacular mountain views and visits to highland villages and yak pastures.

TOURIST OFFICES
Local Tourist Offices
TAB, in Thimphu, has a very limited amount of literature available but can refer

you to tour operators who can assist with arrangements to visit Bhutan. Contact TAB directly at:

Tourism Authority of Bhutan
(☎ 975-2-23251, 23252; fax 23695), PO Box 126, Thimphu, Bhutan.

Tour Operators in Bhutan

Most visitors to Bhutan arrange their trip through an agent or adventure travel company in their own country. If you decide to make your own arrangements in Bhutan, you must deal with one of the country's 33 licensed tour operators.

When tourism was privatised in 1991, the state-run Bhutan Tourism Corporation was disbanded. Many of the ex-employees used their expertise to set up their own tour operations.

The companies range from one-person operations to large and professional organisations such as Etho Metho and Bhutan Tourism Corporation Limited (BTCL), which have fleets of vehicles and, in many places, their own hotel facilities.

Remember, the country code for Bhutan is 975, and Thimphu's area code is 02.

Bae-Yul Excursions
(☎ 24335; fax 23728), PO Box 437, Thimphu
Bhutan Adventure
(☎ 23459; fax 23460), PO Box 213, Thimphu
Bhutan Cultural Tours and Treks
(☎ 23372; fax 23777), PO Box 615, Thimphu
Bhutan Mandala Tours and Treks
(☎ 23676; fax 23675), PO Box 397, Thimphu
Bhutan Tourism Corporation Limited
(☎ 24045, 22647; fax 23292, 22479), PO Box 159, Thimphu
Bhutan Tours & Travels
(☎ 23461; fax 23515), PO Box 224, Thimphu
Bhutan Travel Bureau
(☎ 24241, 24092; fax 25100), PO Box 187, Thimphu
Bhutan Treks and Tours Co
(☎ 22387; fax 22036), PO Box 415, Thimphu
Chhundu Travels and Tours
(☎ 22592, 23586, 22547; fax 22645), PO Box 149, Thimphu
Dragon Trekkers and Tours
(☎ 23599; fax 23314), PO Box 452, Thimphu

Etho Metho Tours and Treks
(☎ 23162, 23693; fax 22884, 23883), PO Box 360, Thimphu
Gangri Tours and Trekking
(☎ 23556; fax 23322), PO Box 607, Thimphu
International Treks and Tours
(☎ 29100, ext 318; fax 23675), Lango, Paro
Khorlo Tours and Treks
(☎ 23682; fax 23213), PO Box 557, Thimphu
Kinga Tours, Travels and Treks
(☎ 23468, 23388; fax 22088, 23796), PO Box 635, Thimphu
Kubera Tours & Treks
(☎ 23651; fax 23651), PO Box 695, Thimphu
Lama Treks and Tours
(☎ 24158, 24388; fax 23944), PO Box 704, Thimphu
Lhomen Tours and Trekking
(☎ 24148; fax 23243, 23108), PO Box 341, Thimphu
Masagang Tours and Travels
(☎ 23206; fax 23718), PO Box 363, Thimphu
Namsey Adventures
(☎ 25616; fax 24297), PO Box 549, Thimphu
Rabsel Tours and Treks
(☎ 24165; fax 24918), PO Box 535, Thimphu
Reekor Tours and Travels
(☎ 22733; fax 23541), PO Box 304, Thimphu
Rinchen Tours and Treks
(☎ 24552; fax 23767), PO Box 550, Thimphu
Sakten Tours and Treks
(☎ 23899, 23903; fax 23545), PO Box 532, Thimphu
Singey Travel Service
(☎ 22183; fax 24152), PO Box 289, Thimphu
Takin Travels and Trekking
(☎ 23129, 23853; fax 23130), PO Box 454, Thimphu
Taktshang Tours and Travels
(☎ 22102; fax 22546), PO Box 199, Thimphu
Tashi Tours and Travels
(☎ 23361, 23027; fax 23666), PO Box 423, Thimphu
Thoesam Tours and Treks
(☎/fax 23593), PO Box 629, Thimphu
Yangphel Tours and Travels
(☎ 23293, 23294, 23323, 24509; fax 22897; email yangphel@overseas.net), PO Box 236, Thimphu
Yeti Tours and Trekking
(☎ 23941; fax 23508), PO Box 456, Thimphu
Yod-Sel Tours
(☎ 23912; fax 23589), PO Box 574, Thimphu
Yu-Druk Tours and Travels
(☎ 23461; fax 22116; email yu-druk@overseas.net), PO Box 140, Thimphu

Choosing an Operator in Bhutan

All operators in Bhutan are subject to government regulations that specify services, standards and rates. You are quite safe no matter which company you choose, though the large companies do have more clout to obtain reservations in hotels and on Druk Air.

In addition to Etho Metho and BTCL, the other large operators in Bhutan are Yangphel, Bhutan Mandala and International Treks and Tours.

There are both advantages and disadvantages to dealing with the largest companies. One Bhutanese hotelier suggested that perhaps the fifth to tenth-largest companies would be large enough to handle overseas queries, but still small enough that the owner would pay personal attention to your programme. The operators in this category are Gangri, Takin, Chhundu, Bey-Yul and Kinga.

Chhundu is renowned for its high quality personal service and it's responsible for looking after many VIP clients.Other companies known for their personal attention and quality are Lhomen, Namsey, Yu-Druk and Bhutan Travel Bureau.

If you are planning to go trekking, you might consider one of the companies that specialise in this area. The biggest operators of treks are Yangphel, Lama, International, Yu-Druk, Tashi and Namsey.

Tourist Offices Abroad

There is no official government tourist office outside Bhutan. Bhutan Travel Service in New York was originally set up to represent the state-run travel company. When tourism was privatised, this company became the US representative for Etho Metho Tours and Treks. It arranges both individual and group tours and can arrange Druk Air tickets.

Bhutan Travel Service
(☎ 212-838 6382, 800-950 9908; fax 212-750 1269; email 5195426@mcimail.com), 120 East 56th St, Suite 1130, New York, NY 10022

VISAS & DOCUMENTS
Passport

You need a passport to enter Bhutan and its neighbouring countries. You should ensure that it has lots of empty pages for stamps, especially if you are travelling via India or Nepal. If your passport has less than six months of validity left, it is worth getting a new one, because many countries in this region will not issue visas to persons whose passports are about to expire.

Get your passport well in advance and send the correct number and your name, exactly as written in your passport, to the agent or tour operator who is arranging your trip to Bhutan.

Keep your passport safe. No country other than India has the facility for issuing a replacement passport in Bhutan. If you lose your passport, you must travel 'stateless' to another country to get it replaced. You should carry some additional form of identification and a photocopy of your passport to help in the event of such a disaster.

Visas

Most countries issue visas from their embassies abroad and stamp it in your passport, but not Bhutan. The Bhutan visa process may appear complicated but is actually quite straightforward once you understand it. Visas are issued only when you arrive in the country, either at Paro airport or (if entering by road) at Phuentsholing. You must apply in advance through a tour operator and receive approval before you travel to Bhutan.

There is no point in applying for a visa through a Bhutanese embassy abroad unless you are on some sort of government or official project. All applications for tourist visas must be initialised by a Bhutan tour operator. The operator submits the visa application to the Tourism Authority in Thimphu. TAB, in turn, checks that you have completely paid for the trip and then issues an approval letter to the tour operator. With this approval in hand, the tour operator then makes a final application to the Ministry of Foreign Affairs, which takes a week to process the visa. All applications for tourist visas and extensions must be channelled through TAB and no tour operator is allowed to entertain any visitor whose visa has been processed through other channels.

It's not necessary to fill in a special visa application form. Just provide the following information to the operator in Bhutan: your name, permanent address, occupation, nationality, date and place of birth, passport number and its date and place of issue and date of expiration. If any item is missing the whole process is delayed. Also double check that the information you send is correct; if there are any discrepancies when you arrive in Bhutan, there'll be further delays and complications in issuing the visa.

When the visa clearance is issued by the Ministry of Foreign Affairs, it sends a visa confirmation number to the tour operator and to Druk Air. Druk Air will not issue your tickets to Paro until it receives this confirmation number.

The actual visa endorsement is stamped in your passport when you arrive at one of the two ports of entry for tourists. When the visa is issued, you need to pay US$20 and present two passport photos with your passport number written on the back. You will then receive a visa for the exact period you have arranged to be in Bhutan, up to a maximum of 15 days. If you need a visa extension, your tour operator will arrange it.

It's an amazingly efficient system considering all the time, distance and various levels of bureaucracy. When you arrive in Bhutan, the visa officer will invariably be able to produce your approval form from the file and the visa will be issued on the spot.

Visas for Indian Citizens Upon arrival, Indian visitors are issued a 14-day permit, which may be extended in Thimphu. No passport or visa is required, but some form of identification such as a driving licence or voters registration card is necessary.

Visa Extensions A visa extension for a period not exceeding six months costs Nu 510. Tour operators obtain this as a matter of course for those who need it, though they usually charge extra. You will probably need a visa extension only if you have arranged an extended trekking itinerary.

Restricted Area Permits All of Bhutan outside of the Paro and Thimphu valleys is classified as a restricted area. Tour operators obtain a permit for the places on your itinerary, and this permit is checked and endorsed by the police at immigration checkpoints strategically located at important road junctions. The tour operator must return the permit to the government at the completion of the tour, and it is scrutinised for major deviations from the authorised programme.

There are immigration checkposts in Hongtsho (east of Thimphu), Chhuzom (south of Thimphu), Chhukha (between Chhuzom and Phuentsholing), Phuentsholing, Wangdue Phodrang, Chazam (near Trashigang), Wamrong (between Trashigang and Samdrup Jongkhar), and in Samdrup Jongkhar.

Permits to Enter Temples TAB rules state:

For security reasons, and in view of the fact that many temples and monasteries in Bhutan are living institutions, visitors are not permitted to visit/enter certain places and religious establishments.

This condition precludes entrance to the major *lhakhangs* (temples) and goembas. Visits to dzongs are allowed under special circumstances. The rules vary from *dzong* (fort-monastery) to dzong, but it's sometimes possible to enter the courtyard of a dzong either before or after office hours. Because dzongs are open to all during the time of a *tsechu* (festival), you may visit the courtyard, but not the temples, if your trip coincides with a festival.

Bhutanese citizens may enter dzongs and goembas, but they are required to wear Bhutanese dress, including a *kabney* (formal scarf). If you are a practising Buddhist, you may apply for a permit to visit specific dzongs and religious institutions. This is issued by the Special Commission for Cultural Affairs, and application should be made in advance through a tour operator. The credibility of your application will be enhanced if you include a letter of reference from a recognised Buddhist organisation in your home country.

Visas for Neighbouring Countries
Bangladesh Most visitors need a visa to visit Bangladesh. The Bangladesh embassy in Bhutan can issue tourist visas.

India Nationals of most countries need a visa to visit India. If you are travelling overland to or from Bhutan via the border post in Phuentsholing or Samdrup Jongkhar, you will need an Indian visa.

There is no longer any special permit required to visit the northern regions of West Bengal or Assam, though there is a degree of risk associated with travel in Assam because of the activities of militant separatist groups (see Problems in the South under History in the Facts about Bhutan chapter). If you are travelling to eastern Bhutan, it might be prudent to have an Indian visa in case of road closure.

If possible, get your Indian visa before you leave home. The government of India strongly prefers that you obtain your Indian visa in the country that issued your passport. It is possible to obtain a seven-day transit visa if you have confirmed flights in and out of India, and can produce the appropriate air tickets. Otherwise, you must pay a fee to the embassy to send a fax to the Indian embassy in your own country and wait up to a week for a reply.

The Indian embassy in Thimphu can issue Indian visas. There are also embassies at all the gateway cities to Bhutan, which are Kathmandu, Bangkok, Yangon and Dhaka.

Tourist visas are issued for six months, are multiple entry, and are valid from the date of issue of the visa, not the date you enter India. This means that if you first enter India five months after the visa was issued, it will be valid for one month.

One year visas are only available to businesspeople or students. Tourist visas are not extendable. If you want to stay longer than six months you will have to go to a neighbouring country and get a six month visa.

Six month multiple entry tourist visas cost A\$55 for Australians, UK£19 for Britons, US\$50 for Americans, and FF 200 for French passport holders.

Nepal Visas for Nepal are available at Kathmandu airport or at land border crossings, including Kakarbhitta, the road crossing nearest to Bhutan. Nepal has a complex menu of visas: a single-entry 15-day visa costs US\$15; a 30-day visa is US\$25 for a single entry and US\$40 for a double entry. The double-entry visa is useful if you are making a side trip to Bhutan from Kathmandu, but remember to get the double-entry visa the first time you arrive in Nepal. There's also a 60-day multiple-entry visa for US\$60.

You can obtain a Nepal visa in advance from embassies abroad or from the Nepal embassy or consulate in the gateway cities of Bangkok, Delhi, Yangon, Dhaka or Calcutta.

Myanmar (Burma) If you are travelling to Myanmar you will need a visa. Four-week visas are available from the Myanmar embassy in Kathmandu, Delhi, Dhaka and Bangkok with a minimum of fuss.

Thailand Nationals of most western countries may enter Thailand without a visa for 30 days, whether they arrive by air or road. Most other nationalities can obtain a 15-day transit visa on arrival. Citizens of a few countries must obtain a visa in advance. Check with a Thai embassy before you leave home.

Photocopies
Make a photocopy of the important pages of your passport (the one with your name and photograph). If you have a visa for India, you would do well to photocopy this at the same time. Carry the copies separately from

your travel documents so that you will have some form of identification in case you lose the passport. It's also a good idea to photocopy your airline ticket and list of travellers cheques.

Travel Insurance

A travel insurance policy to cover theft, loss and medical problems is always a good idea. The cancellation rules for Bhutan are severe and quite inflexible. Trip cancellation insurance is almost essential.

Most policies will cover costs if you are forced to cancel your trip because of flight cancellation, illness, injury or the death of a close relative. If you have such a problem, travel insurance can help protect you from major losses due to Bhutan's prepayment conditions and hefty cancellation charges.

Some policies specifically exclude 'dangerous activities', and these can include motorcycling and even trekking. Be sure to read your policy carefully. Ensure that the policy also covers ambulances or an emergency helicopter airlift out of a remote region, or an emergency flight home. If you have to stretch out you will need two seats and somebody has to pay for them. Many travel insurance policies include repatriation and evacuation through the worldwide network of International SOS Assistance.

You may prefer a policy that pays doctors or hospitals directly rather than your having to pay on the spot and filing a claim later. If you have to claim later make sure you keep all documentation. Some policies ask you to call back (they suggest reversing the charges, an impossibility from Bhutan) to a centre in your home country where an immediate assessment of your problem is made.

It's a good idea to photocopy your policy in case the original is lost. If you are planning to travel for a long time, the insurance may seem very expensive – but if you can't afford it, you certainly won't be able to afford to deal with a medical emergency overseas.

Driving Licence & Permits

Driving is a harrowing experience. Roads are narrow, and trucks roar around hairpin bends, appearing suddenly and forcing oncoming vehicles to the side. Because roads are only about 3.5m wide, passing any oncoming vehicle involves one, or both, moving off the pavement onto the verge.

Since all transportation is provided by tour operators, you normally do not have to concern yourself with driving. If for some reason you are arranging your own transportation, you are still far better off using the services of a hired car or taxi. If you insist on driving in Bhutan, you must obtain a driving licence issued by the Surface Transport Authority. Bhutan licences are also valid for the states of Assam and West Bengal in India.

An Indian driving licence is valid in Bhutan, and it's possible for Indian citizens to drive in Bhutan, but unless you are an accomplished rally driver or from a hill station such as Darjeeling and have experience in motoring in the mountains, you are far better off with a professional driver.

International Driving Permit An international driving permit is not valid in Bhutan.

Vehicle Documents If you drive a vehicle into Bhutan, you can get a 14-day permit at the Phuentsholing border. You will need the help of a tour operator to handle the paperwork. If you are driving a vehicle that is registered overseas, you will need a *carnet de passage en douane* in order to get through India.

Indian visitors may travel throughout most of Bhutan in their own vehicle, but need a permit from the Bhutanese police authorities at the border. Traffic regulations are the same as in India and are strictly enforced.

You can recognise how and where Bhutanese vehicles are registered by their licence plates. Any beginning with BP is private, BG is government, BT is taxi, RBA is the Royal Bhutan Army and BHT is the Royal family. The first number indicates where the vehicle is registered: 1 for Thimphu, Punakha and Paro; 2 for Phuentsholing; 3 for Bumthang and Trongsa; and 4 for eastern Bhutan.

Documents

Student & Youth Cards There is a 25% student discount on the Bhutan tourist rate (see Costs in the Money section later in this chapter). If you are a student aged 25 or under and have applied for the discount, carry your student ID card to prove that you are indeed a full-time student.

Seniors' Cards There is no advantage to carrying any sort of senior identification in Bhutan.

International Health Card The only immunisation that is required for Bhutan and neighbouring countries is yellow fever. A health card is unnecessary unless you are travelling directly from a yellow fever area.

EMBASSIES

As already mentioned, unless you are working for an NGO, United Nations or official government project, it is pointless to apply for a Bhutan visa through a Bhutanese embassy. All tourist visas must be channelled through TAB in Thimphu, and from there through the Ministry of Foreign Affairs.

Bhutan Embassies Abroad

Bhutan has chosen not to have a wide network of resident embassies abroad, largely because of the expense involved.

Bangladesh
   Royal Bhutanese Embassy (☎ 880-2-605 840, 886 939; fax 883 553), House No F5 (SE), Gulshan Ave, Dhaka 1212
India
   Royal Bhutanese Embassy (☎ 91-11-688 9807, 688 9230; fax 688 6710), Chandragupta Marg, Chanakyapuri, New Delhi 100 021
Kuwait
   Royal Bhutanese Embassy (☎ 965-256 0932; fax 256 0974), PO Box 1510, Safat 13016
Thailand
   Royal Bhutanese Embassy (☎ 66-2-267 1722; fax 267 7541), 1907 Jewellery Trade Centre Building, 919 Silom Rd, Bangkok 10500
Switzerland
   Permanent Bhutanese Mission to the UN in Geneva (☎ 41-22-798 7971; fax 788 2593), Palais des Nations, 17-19 Champ d'Avier, CH-1209 Geneva
USA
   Permanent Bhutanese Mission to the UN in New York (☎ 1-212-826 1919; fax 826 2998), 2 UN Plaza, 27th Floor, New York, NY 10017

Foreign Embassies in Bhutan

There are only two foreign embassies in Bhutan. Bhutan's relations with other countries are handled through its embassies in Delhi and Dhaka.

Bangladesh Embassy
   (☎ 22539; fax 22629), Thori Lam, Thimphu
Indian Embassy
   (☎ 22162; fax 23195), India House, Thimphu

CUSTOMS

Customs officials are generally lenient with tourists and rarely open their baggage. They do, however, carefully check the baggage of returning residents, both Bhutanese and expatriate.

Arrival

You will receive a baggage declaration form to complete when you arrive in Bhutan. For tourists, the main purpose of this form is to ensure that you re-export anything you bring into the country. List any expensive equipment that you are carrying, such as cameras and portable computers. Customs officials usually want to see the items that you list, then they endorse the form and return it to you. Don't lose it. You must return the form, and may be asked to show the items listed when you leave the country.

There are no restrictions on other personal effects, including trekking gear, that you bring into the country. Duty-free allowances are generous, including two litres of liquor and 400 cigarettes. You can utilise these allowances to bring much-appreciated gifts to your tour operator and guide.

Departure

Departure formalities are straightforward, but you must produce the form that you completed on arrival and show the items listed on it. A lost form means complications and delays. If you lose the form, let your guide know as soon as possible so that special arrangements can be made to avoid inconvenience.

The export of antiques and wildlife products is prohibited. If you purchase a souvenir that looks old, have your guide clear it as a non-antique item with the Division of Cultural Properties in Thimphu (☎ 22284, 24751; fax 23286). Customs authorities pay special attention to religious statues. It would be prudent to have any such statue cleared, old or not.

MONEY
Prices and payment procedures are a bit complicated. If you are dealing through an overseas agent, you can avoid many of the complications, but if you are working directly with a Bhutanese tour operator, you'll spend considerable time sending faxes, and may have to learn more than you want to about making international bank transfers.

Costs
The daily tariff for tourists visiting in a group of four people or more is US$200 per day, whether you stay in hotels (a 'cultural tour') or go trekking.

The rate is applicable per person per night halt in Bhutan. On the day of departure, the tour operator's only obligation is breakfast, and any extra requirements are payable based on the actual cost.

The payment includes all your accommodation, food, land transport within Bhutan, services of guides and porters, supply of pack animals and riding ponies (for emergency use on treks) and cultural programmes as appropriate.

The tour rate applies uniformly irrespective of location, season and the type of accommodation asked for or provided. This clause means that if you have arranged to stay in a fancy hotel and get bumped, you have no recourse.

Small Groups
Individual tourists and smaller groups of fewer than four people are subject to a surcharge, over and above the daily rate, as follows:

One person	US$40 per night
Group of two	US$30 per night per person
Group of three	US$20 per night per person

Visitors qualifying for any kind of discount are not exempt from the small group surcharge.

Extras
Most tour operators expect you to pay separately for all drinks, including liquor, beer, mineral water and bottled soft drinks. Other charges are for laundry, riding horses, and cultural splurges such as a Bhutanese hot stone bath.

Discounts & Special Categories
The following categories of visitors are eligible for discounts on the daily rate:

Diplomats Diplomats from foreign embassies or missions accredited to Bhutan receive a 25% discount on the rates.

Children Children up to the age of six are exempt from the rates. Kids from six to 12 accompanied by parents or guardians receive a 50% discount on the daily rates.

Students Full-time students 25 years and younger with valid identity cards from their academic institutions are allowed a 25% discount, resulting in a rate of US$150 per night (plus small group surcharges, if applicable). It's possible to obtain this student discount even if the other people in your group do not qualify. You should deal directly with a Bhutan tour operator rather than through a travel agent or tour company at home if you plan to utilise this facility.

Group Leaders A discount of 50% on the rates is given to one person in a group of 11 to 15 people. A free trip is allowed for one member per group exceeding 15 people.

Indian Citizens Citizens of India are not subject to the same rules, and may have to pay local rates for food, transportation and accommodation. These rates may vary, however, as service providers sometimes ask you for what they think you can afford instead of giving you the local rate. To avoid paying over the odds, speak to a travel agent in Thimphu about standard rates.

The initial permit is for 14 days, and Indian citizens still need a travel permit to go beyond Paro and Thimphu. Indians may also wander freely into all the border towns of Bhutan, though they must leave by 10 pm unless staying in a hotel.

Volunteers & Project Employees If you are working in Bhutan, you are not subject to the normal rules for tourists, and the agency employing you will arrange your visa. Soon after you arrive in Bhutan, you will be enrolled in a cultural orientation course for new volunteers given by the Royal Institute of Management. Volunteers are allowed two visitors (who must be close relatives) a year that are not subject to the tourist tariff.

Travel Agents Tour companies intending to put Bhutan into their programmes may apply for a discounted familiarisation tour. It's unlikely that you can manage this arrangement unless you are already a serious player in the travel industry. TAB has an excellent network of connections worldwide and will check your bona fides beforehand. They also require both a pre-trip and a post-trip briefing.

Agent Commissions Travel agents receive a 10% commission on the basic tour rate, but not on the small-group surcharge. Some tour operators will deduct the agent commission from payments by independent travellers. There used to be a racket in which tour operators would kick back even more commission in contravention of the TAB rules, but there is a major effort to eliminate this practice. The government takes cases of undercutting seriously because it undermines their entire tourism policy. TAB has threatened to increase the government royalty if operators continue to violate the

rules, in which case visitors would receive even less value for their money.

Payment Procedure
If you have arranged your trip directly with a tour operator in Bhutan and are not using an overseas agent, you must make payment directly to the Royal Monetary Authority (RMA) of Bhutan. This is not a trivial process. You must deposit the full cost of the tour in convertible currency with RMA with instructions for it to be credited to TAB's account with the Bank of Bhutan, Thimphu, in ngultrums (the local currency). The payment rules established by TAB are as follows:

- All tour payments must be made in convertible currencies acceptable to RMA. The exchange rates shall be based on the rates published by the RMA from time to time.
- As far as possible, all payments shall be made either by demand draft drawn in favour of TAB or telegraphic transfer through RMA's accounts abroad, payable into the accounts of TAB with Bank of Bhutan, Thimphu. In both cases, the name of the tour operator should be stated as the 'beneficiary'.
- All tour payments should be made in advance. Except in cases where it is unavoidable, tour operators in Bhutan are to insist on receiving payments in advance from visitors/agents abroad.
- When advance payments are not possible, full payment will be made positively before the end of the tour programme and the final account of the tour submitted within one week of the departure of the tourists.
- TAB monitors all payments and will not process tourist visa applications of those tour operators who have outstanding accounts with TAB.
- Manipulation of approved daily package rates and offering tour programmes at reduced rates to clients is strictly prohibited. This is in view of serious negative implications which could undermine the policy of the Royal Government to promote quality tourism in the Kingdom. Hence, tour operators are strongly advised to refrain from such practices.
- Any other modes of payments other than those mentioned above, especially in cash, are illegal and are discouraged by TAB. However, under circumstances where payments are received in such forms, tour operators shall declare them to TAB along with proper documentary testi-

monials supporting the mode of payments and the amount. Any such payments without the supporting documents shall be considered illegal and shall be liable to confiscation as per foreign exchange rules.

Payment to TAB Payment to TAB on behalf of tour operators may be made to any of the following accounts of the RMA. The payment should state that the beneficiary is the tour operator you have chosen to handle your trip. Once you make the payment, fax a copy of the deposit details to the tour operator in Bhutan so that they can present this documentation to TAB to start the visa process.

Germany
    Deutsche Bundesbank Postfach 100602, D-60006 Frankfurt am Main; DM account No 40825
Hong Kong
    Republic National Bank of New York 606 Connaught Centre, Hong Kong; HK$ account No 11400261
Japan
    Bank of Tokyo-Mitsubishi Ltd Nihonbashi, PO Box 191, Tokyo 100-91; JYen account No 653-0436933
    Bank of Japan CPO Box 203, Tokyo 100-91; JYen account No 0707009
Singapore
    Chase Manhattan Bank 50 Raffles Place, Shell Tower, Singapore 1014; US$ account No 01-51-850197
Switzerland
    Union Bank of Switzerland Bahnhofstrasse 45, CH-8021 Zurich; SFr account No 97.500.05
UK
    Bank of England Threadneedle St, London EC2R 8AH; UK£ account No 4040050
USA
    Citibank NA 111 Wall St, 9th Floor, Zone 6, New York, NY 10005; account No 36021815
    Chase Manhattan Bank United Nations Plaza, New York, NY 10081; account No 001-1-404373

Bhutan's banking system is being modernised, and efforts are under way to simplify the payment process. New procedures may allow direct transfers into the TAB account in Thimphu, or even directly to the Bhutanese tour operators themselves, but at present the preferred method is via the RMA. In exceptional circumstances it is possible to pay in travellers cheques (but not cash) upon arrival in Bhutan.

Refunds Once you have made payment to the tour operator through TAB, any refunds for cancellation or delays will be made in ngultrums or Indian rupees, but not foreign exchange. This is a reasonably serious complication, and you should be certain of your plans before you pay.

Cancellation Charges
Tour programmes booked and subsequently cancelled are subject to cancellation charges. Most travel insurance policies will cover these charges if you are forced to cancel because of illness, accident or other calamity. Such a policy is an extremely worthwhile investment when you must make full payment up front, as with Bhutan. The fee depends on how many days before the start of the tour programme you cancel:

More than 30 days	No charge
Within 21 days	10%
Within 14 days	15%
Within 7 days	30%
Fewer than 7 days or without notice	50%

Cost of Delays
There is no charge for the number of days of delay in your arrival or departure due to weather conditions, Druk Air problems or road blocks. In cases of delayed departure, tour operators are allowed to charge the actual expenses for accommodation, food, transport and any other services required.

The above rules are controlled by requiring tour operators to notify TAB in writing about any change in the programme as a result of delays and to account for any extra services they provide.

Carrying Money
You can use a money belt or a pouch that hangs around your neck to carry money and important documents such as your passport. Because theft is rare, this is probably not

necessary in Bhutan, but such protection is essential in adjoining countries.

Few Bhutanese hotels have safes for guests' valuables, probably because nobody can recall the last time a hotel employee stole anything from a guest.

Banks

Bhutan has two banks, each with branches throughout the country. The Bank of Bhutan, a joint venture between the Bhutan government and the State Bank of India, was established in 1968. A new bank, Bhutan National Bank, was established in 1997 and is a public corporation, though the government retains 51% of its shares.

While the Bank of Bhutan still uses an antiquated hand-written ledger system, the Bhutan National Bank is a modernised operation, with a computer system and relationships with major overseas banks.

The Bank of Bhutan's main branches are open from 9 am to 1 pm Monday to Friday, 9 to 11 am Saturday, closed Sunday. They also have branches in Phuentsholing and Thimphu that operate as 'evening banks' for the convenience of office workers (and travellers). In addition to normal hours, these branches are open from 1 to 5 pm Wednesday to Sunday, 1 to 3 pm Monday, closed Tuesday. You can cash travellers cheques at either bank, though there is a fair amount of paperwork involved.

The Royal Monetary Authority is the central bank. It issues banknotes and processes inter-bank transfers, but does not change money or engage in any banking transactions for the public.

Travellers Cheques

Chhundu tours on Norzin Lam in Thimphu is the American Express agent and can provide US dollar travellers cheques if you have a personal cheque and an American Express card. If you carry American Express travellers cheques, you can also obtain replacements here if they're lost or stolen. There is no replacement facility for any other travellers cheques anywhere in Bhutan.

You can cash travellers cheques at any bank, most hotels and the foreign exchange counter at the airport. There are bank charges of 1% for cheque encashment. You should carry only well-known brands such as American Express, Visa, Thomas Cook, Citibank or Barclays.

Credit Cards & ATMs

You should not plan to use a credit card in Bhutan. American Express cards are accepted at the Government Handicrafts Emporium, a few other handicraft shops and some of the larger hotels in Thimphu, but these transactions take extra time. The only other card honoured in Bhutan is a local one issued by the Royal Insurance Corporation, but Visa and MasterCard may be accepted before long. There are no ATMs in the country.

International Transfers

You are not likely to be in Bhutan long enough to need to have money transferred to you. If, however, you do need to make an international transfer, check with the Bhutan National Bank for their list of overseas correspondent banks and try to initiate the transaction through one of those.

Currency

The unit of currency is the *ngultrum* (Nu), which is equivalent to one Indian rupee. The ngultrum is further divided into 100 *chetrum*. There are notes of 1, 5, 10, 20, 50, 100 and 500 Nu, each depicting a different dzong. There is a handsome Nu 1 coin that depicts the eight auspicious symbols (see the boxed text 'Tashi Tagye' in the Facts about Bhutan chapter). Indian rupees may be used freely anywhere in Bhutan, but ngultrums are not at all welcome in India.

It is OK with the Bhutanese if you bring a reasonable amount of Indian currency into Bhutan, though Indian regulations prohibit currency export.

Currency Exchange

Since your trip is fully prepaid, theoretically you could manage in Bhutan without any

Collecting Bhutanese Stamps

You probably won't strike it rich by buying postage stamps from Bhutan, but they make a colourful addition to any collection. Some items are issued specifically for sale to collectors by an agency in New York, and others are locally produced by the government itself. There is not much demand for Bhutanese stamps, and the value is generally low. However, the number of stamps issued in each series is generally so small that any increase in demand sends prices skyrocketing.

The price of 3D mushroom stamps shot up to US$25 a set when topical collectors of mushroom stamps discovered them and exhausted the supply. The issue of playable record stamps sold out quickly in Bhutan, and only a few thousand were produced because of the expense. These are now worth US$300 a set. Some surcharged provisional issues from the late 1960s fetch US$60 to US$70 at auction and some of the Disney issues are becoming hard to find, with imperforate souvenir sheets selling for US$100 each. Most however, are available in adequate quantities at a reasonable mark-up over face value.

Some shops sell older issues and souvenir sheets, but the philatelic counter in the Thimpu post office has the largest selection.

For more information on Bhutanese stamps check the Internet at www.bhutan.org.

Mickey, Goofy, Buddhist deities and 3D demons – anything goes with Bhutanese stamps.

Guardians of the Four Directions

Paintings or statues of the guardians, or kings, of the four directions appear on the *gorikha* (verandah) to guard the entrance to most lhakhangs. They have an origin in ancient Mongol tradition and each one holds a different object. They are warriors who guard the world against demons and earthly threats.

Chenmizang, the red king of the west, holds a chorten and a snake, and is the lord of the *nagas* (serpents) (main picture).

Yulkhorsung, the white king of the east, plays the lute and is the lord of celestial musicians (top left).

Namthose, the gold king of the north, holds a mongoose and a banner of victory. He is also a god of wealth and prosperity (centre left).

Phagchepo (bottom left), the blue king of the south, holds a sword in his right hand.

ALL PHOTOS BY NICHOLAS REUSS

local money at all, though you'll probably want some to pay for laundry, drinks, souvenirs and tips.

The exchange counters at the airport, larger hotels and the banks in Thimphu, Paro and Phuentsholing can change all the currencies listed below, and sometimes also Netherlands guilders and Scandinavian currencies. If you are headed to eastern Bhutan, you will do better with more common currencies such as US dollars or pounds sterling.

Exchange rates for cash are as follows:

Australia	A$1	=	Nu 25.90
Canada	C$1	=	Nu 27.45
France	FFr1	=	Nu 6.65
Germany	DM1	=	Nu 22.45
Hong Kong	HK$	=	Nu 5.10
India	Rs1	=	Nu 1.00
Japan	¥100	=	Nu 29.75
Netherlands	NG1	=	Nu 19.70
Singapore	S$	=	Nu 23.60
Switzerland	Sfr1	=	Nu 26.60
UK	UK£1	=	Nu 67.95
USA	US$	=	Nu 40.90

In smaller towns foreign currency exchange is an unusual transaction; be prepared for delays while they find the person who knows how to do it.

If you plan to make a major purchase, for example textiles or art, consider bringing US dollars in cash. Most shops will accept this, and it can save you the hassle of exchanging a large quantity of money in advance and then changing it back if you don't find the exact piece you were looking for.

You may change your unused ngultrums back to foreign currency (though usually only into US dollars) on departure if you can produce your original exchange receipts. Hang on to those bits of paper when you exchange money. Ngultrums are useless outside of Bhutan (except as a curiosity).

Black Market

There is no black market in Bhutan. The Indian rupee is a convertible currency, and the rate is set by market conditions, not by the Indian government. Subject to some restrictions, Indians and Bhutanese can buy dollars officially to purchase goods from abroad. Therefore, there is not much difference between the market rate and the official rate for the Indian rupee, and thus, the ngultrum.

It's sometimes possible to buy Indian rupees at a slightly better rate in Bangkok or Hong Kong and then bring them to Bhutan, but the small gain is hardly worth the hassle.

Tipping & Bargaining

Tipping is not common in hotels or restaurants, but it's OK to do so if you want to reward good service. Servers and hotel staff will act embarrassed when they receive a tip, but they do appreciate the gesture.

You will usually be accompanied throughout your visit to Bhutan by the same tour guide and probably the same driver. These people appreciate a tip at the end of the trip. If you are in a group, take up a collection at the end of the tour and hand it over in one packet. A guideline is to allocate the equivalent of US$2 to US$3 per day for the guide and less for the driver. Trekking guides expect considerably more, at least twice this amount.

Bargaining is not a Bhutanese tradition, and you won't get very far with your haggling skills here, except possibly in the local handicrafts section of the Thimphu weekend market. Shops, restaurants and hotels all have fixed price.

Gifts

It is customary to bring a gift when you visit a Bhutanese home. If you expect to be invited to a home, you might purchase one of the premium brands of duty-free whiskey or cigarettes before you board your Druk Air flight.

Strange as it may sound, another gift that is appreciated by men is a fancy pair of long argyle socks. Cloth, whether a length of fabric or a ready-made item, is the most traditional gift in Bhutan.

POST & COMMUNICATIONS
Postal Rates
Airmail postage rates are:

To Europe	Nu 15
To Asia	Nu 14
To America	Nu 16
To India & Nepal	Nu 4
Postcards (to anywhere)	Nu 9

Sending Mail
You can send mail from hotels and post offices. The mail service from Bhutan is quite reliable, and no special procedures are necessary. It would be better, however, to avoid sending important letters, money or film through the mail.

If you mail cards or letters from the Thimphu post office, you can buy exotic Bhutan postage stamps from the philatelic bureau and use them on your letters and postcards.

Bhutan Post offers outgoing EMS (Expedited Mail Service), which is a reliable and fast international mail delivery facility that is cheaper than courier services. It also has a LUM (Local Urgent Mail) service for delivery within Thimphu.

Sending Parcels
If you have made a purchase and want to send it home, it's best to have the shop make all the arrangements for you. Keep the receipt, and let your guide know what you are doing so they can follow up in case the package does not arrive. Send all parcels by air; sea mail, via Calcutta, takes several months.

Receiving Mail
The best way to receive mail is to have it sent to the post office box of the Bhutan tour operator that is handling your trip. Unless you are on a long trek, you will probably not be in Bhutan long enough for a letter to reach you.

Courier
DHL (☎ 02-24729) and OCS provide efficient international courier service to and from Bhutan. There are other several smaller courier companies that specialise in service to India.

Telephone
Telephones were first introduced in Bhutan in 1963. The satellite earth station in Thimphu was installed in 1990 along with a sophisticated international telephone service. Direct dial calls go through quickly and clearly. Domestic telephone service is through a network of microwave links, and most of the country's major towns now have both domestic and international direct dial facilities.

Some telephones in Punakha, Ha, Chhukha and Wangdue Phodrang have three-digit numbers. Calls to or from these numbers must be placed through an operator.

The country code for Bhutan is 975. Local dialling codes are:

Thimphu	02
Paro	02
Bumthang	03
Trongsa	03
Mongar	04
Samdrup Jongkhar	04
Trashigang	04
Phuentsholing	05

International numbers are reached by dialling 00, then the country code and local number. There is no facility for collect calls or home country direct.

There are numerous public call offices (PCO) throughout the country from which you can make STD (long-distance) calls within Bhutan or to India. Some PCOs also offer ISD (international subscriber dialling) calls overseas. In many PCOs the length of your call is likely to be measured by the proprietor's watch, not by a fancy meter. Most hotels can arrange both local and international calls, though only a few have in-room direct dial facilities.

There is a 15% discount on international telephone rates from 5 to 8 am and 6 to 11 pm; between 11 pm and 5 am the discount is 30%. Domestic direct dial calls cost Nu 4 to Nu 8 per minute depending on the time of day.

Fax, Telegraph & Email

Nearly all hotels and some PCOs have facilities to send and receive faxes. Tour operators in Bhutan rely on fax for most of their communications.

There is no Internet service in Bhutan. If you want to send email, you must make an international call to an Internet service provider (ISP). Bhutan's satellite telephone system connects directly to the UK which, in turn, has a fibre-optic connection to the US. If you must send an email, it's best to call an ISP in either the UK or US.

Modems often fail to connect successfully on calls that are routed via satellite – as all international calls from Bhutan are. You have a better, though still not guaranteed, chance of a connection if you set the speed of your modem to a speed of 9600 baud and allow it to drop back as low as 2400 baud if necessary.

One reason that there is no email service in Bhutan is that there are not enough potential subscribers to justify the cost of a full-time leased line to an Internet backbone. A few Bhutan tour operators and NGOs now use email. They must make an expensive overseas call to send and retrieve mail and are therefore also paying to receive messages. If you are corresponding with Bhutan via email, don't include the entire original message in your reply.

BOOKS

There are two bookshops in Thimphu but only one in Phuentsholing. There are also books available in some gift and handicraft shops around Bhutan. Most of the books available locally are published in India. These include books on Bhutan and inexpensive Indian editions of English novels and textbooks. There is a serious lack of variety. If you want a page-turner to while away the time at airports, bring it with you. Both of Thimphu's bookshops have a good collection of children's books and paperback classics.

As you would expect, the selection of books on Bhutan available in Thimphu is more extensive than anywhere else in the world. Some of the books listed below, particularly the history books, are published in India and are available only in Bhutan and esoteric bookshops in Nepal and India. Most of the books that are still in print can be ordered on the Internet through www. amazon.com or www.altbookstore.com. Pilgrims Book House in Kathmandu (☎ 977-1-424942; fax 424943) also stocks most of these titles. You can contact them at PO Box 3872, Kathmandu, Nepal, or order direct from www.gfas.com/pilgrims.

Books are published in different editions by different publishers in different countries. As a result, a book might be a hardcover-only rarity in one country and readily available in paperback in another. Fortunately, bookshops and libraries search by title or author; so your local bookshop or library can advise you on the availability of the following recommendations.

Lonely Planet

Lonely Planet's *India* and *Indian Himalaya* books will help you if you are visiting India before or after visiting Bhutan. Similarly, the *Nepal* book is essential if you are passing through Kathmandu or travelling by road to or from Bhutan.

Travel

So Close to Heaven, The Vanishing Buddhist Kingdoms of the Himalayas by Barbara Crossette is an excellent account of Bhutan's history and culture. The author is a *New York Times* correspondent who has spent considerable time in Bhutan and other Himalayan regions. Published in 1995, the book discusses some of the current development and political problems facing Bhutan.

Dreams of the Peaceful Dragon is a traveller's account of a walk across Bhutan in the 1970s, before the road between Bumthang and Mongar was completed. It gives a good picture of trekking in Bhutan.

In The Himalayas by Jeremy Bernstein describes the author's journeys through Nepal, Tibet and Bhutan. The Bhutan chapter in this travelogue is not extensive, but Bernstein makes many interesting comparisons to the experiences and conditions during his time in Nepal.

Joanna Lumley in the Kingdom of the Thunder Dragon is by Joanna Lumley, the co-star of the BBC programme *Absolutely Fabulous*. Her grandfather was a political officer in Sikkim; the book is based on a TV programme that traced his trek through the country in the 1930s.

History & Politics

The Raven Crown by Michael Aris is the definitive history of Bhutan's monarchy. Aris, who lived in Bhutan from 1967 to 1972, is the leading western authority on Bhutan's history. The book is lavishly illustrated with rare photographs of the early days of Bhutan that help show what a unique civilisation existed in the early 20th century.

Bhutan, the Early History of a Himalayan Kingdom, also by Michael Aris, is the most authoritative history of Bhutan available in English. It is difficult to get through, largely because of the complex transliteration system of Bhutanese and Tibetan terms that is used in the book.

A History of Bhutan is a school textbook published by the Bhutan Ministry of Health and Education. The book comes in two versions: pre-history to 1865 for class 9 and history of the 19th and 20th century for class 10. Both rely on the work of Bhutanese and western scholars and are excellent resources.

Sikhim and Bhutan, Twenty-one Years on the North-east Frontier by J Claude White describes White's 1905 expedition to Bhutan to present the insignia of Knight Commander of the Indian Empire to Sir Ugyen Wangchuck. Originally published in 1909, there is an Indian reprint edition available.

Political Missions to Bootan by Ashley Eden contains a wonderfully Victorian account of the history of Bhutan. Eden disliked the people and their habits intensely, and after reading a few pages, you'll have a better idea of why Eden was treated so badly by the Trongsa *penlop* (governor) when he arrived in Punakha. The original edition is long out of print, but an Indian reprint was issued in 1972.

Bhutan and the British by Peter Collister is a comprehensive and even-handed account of the interaction between Britain and Bhutan from 1771 to 1987.

Lands of the Thunderbolt by the Earl of Ronaldshay is one of the most readable accounts of a British expedition to Bhutan. The earl's full name was Lawrence John Lumley Dundas, Marquis of Zetland. He was president of the Royal Geographic Society from 1922 to 1925.

Bhutan, A Kingdom in the Himalayas by Narendra Singh is a study of the land, people and government of Bhutan. The author is an Indian lawyer who served as the constitutional advisor to the Royal Government of Bhutan in the early 1970s. His description of the history is quite thorough and the appendix includes copies of Bhutan's treaties with Britain and India. The book is out of print; it was published in India and is hard to find.

India and Bhutan; A Study in Frontier Political Relations 1772-1885 by Arbinda Deb is yet another Indian thesis that documents, rather well, the early relations between Bhutan and Britain.

Sources for the History of Bhutan by Michael Aris is a scholarly work that translates several historically important texts.

A Political and Religious History of Bhutan by Dr CT Dorji lists the major personalities in both the religious and political history of the country. The companion volume is *History of Bhutan Based on Buddhism*.

The Jesuit and the Dragon by Howard Solverson is a biography of the late Father William Mackey. It describes his contributions to the establishment of a modern educational system in Bhutan.

Bayonets to Lhasa by Sir Francis Younghusband is a description of the first British expedition to Lhasa, and is relevant because there is an interesting discussion about King Ugyen Wangchuck, who accompanied the expedition when he was still the penlop of Trongsa.

Religion

The Divine Madman by Keith Dowman is a wonderful translation of the poems and works of Lama Drukpa Kunley.

The Treasure Revealer of Bhutan by Padma Tshewang, Khenpo Phuntshok Tashi, Chris Butters and Sigmund K Sætreng is a recent study of Pema Lingpa and the tradition of *tertons* (treasure discoverers).

The Lotus Born, translated by Erik Pema Kunsang, is a complex account of the life of Padmasambhava. It is a translation of the biography written by his foremost Tibetan disciple, the *dakini* (angel) Yeshi Tshoyal. It's very heavy going.

The Power Places of Central Tibet by Keith Dowman has considerable background on Tibetan saints and lamas, many of whom travelled to Bhutan. More detailed information is available in Dowman's *The Sacred Life of Tibet*.

The Tibetan Book of Living and Dying by Sogyal Rimpoche is a translation of Guru Rimpoche's *Tibetan Book of the Dead*. It's a sophisticated Himalayan Buddhist text, but worth a look if you are especially interested in learning about some of Bhutan's religious foundations.

General

The Dragon Country by Nirmala Das was published in 1974 and is out of print, though there are a few copies in Thimphu bookshops. It is an excellent introduction to the history of the country and its dzongs and temples written by the wife of the first Indian representative stationed in Bhutan.

The Hero with a Thousand Eyes by Karma Ura is an historical novel. It is based on the life of Shingkhar Lam, a retainer who served in the court of the second, third and fourth kings of Bhutan. It offers extraordinary insight into social conditions in the early days of the 20th century and the reforms and modernisations that the third king, Jigme Dorji Wangchuck, effected.

The Ballad of Pemi Tshewang Tashi by Karma Ura is a translation of a Bhutanese folk tale with a lot of cultural and historical background notes.

Bhutanese Tales of the Yeti by Kunzang Choden describes the Bhutanese beliefs of where and how this creature may live.

The Thunder Dragon Kingdom by Steven K Berry is one of the few accounts of a mountaineering expedition to Bhutan. It chronicles a 1986 British attempt on Gangkhar Puensum.

Memoirs of a Mountaineer by F Spencer Chapman chronicles the first ascent of Jhomolhari in 1973 from Phari in Tibet, which was described as the dirtiest town on earth.

Conservation & Environment

Bhutan: Environment, Culture and Development Strategy by PP Karan is an Indian publication written by an American professor of geography and is based on several years of research in Bhutan. It chronicles major developments in the country up to 1985.

Geology of the Bhutan Himalaya by Augusto Gansser is a large format book with everything you could possibly want to know about Bhutan's geology.

Bhutan and its Natural Resources is a collection of essays on the environment published by Sherubtse College in Bhutan.

An Introduction to Birdwatching in Bhutan by Carol & Tim Inskipp is a small WWF publication that provides descriptions and drawings of important species of birds found in Bhutan. It also has an introductory section on basic bird-watching practise.

Birds of Bhutan by Salim Ali, B Biswas & S Dillon Ripley was published by the Zoological Survey of India and is available only in India and Bhutan. It does not have illustrations, but has some good descriptions and an extensive list compiled by the recognised authorities on Himalayan birds. Salim Ali's other books, including *Birds of the Eastern Himalayas*, are the best field guides available.

Trees and Shrubs of Nepal and the Himalayas by Adrian & Jimmie Storrs is the best field book on the forests of Bhutan. It was published in Kathmandu but printed in

Thailand; so those are the most likely places to find a copy.

Art & Architecture

Bhutan – Mountain Fortress of the Gods, a coffee-table book, provides the documentation for a 1998 Bhutanese exhibition in Vienna. Edited by Christian Schicklgruber & Françoise Pommaret, it has extensive illustrations and excellent information.

From the Land of the Thunder Dragon; Textile Arts of Bhutan by Diana K Myers is a detailed study of traditional Bhutanese textiles – their uses, design and weaving methods. Based on an exhibition of textiles from Bhutan at the Peabody Essex Museum in Massachusetts, it has colour photographs of many designs and finished items of clothing.

Traditional Bhutanese Textiles by Barbara Adams is the first published study of Bhutanese textiles. There are numerous colour photos of textiles that she collected from Bhutanese who travelled to Nepal in the late 1970s.

An Introduction to Traditional Architecture of Bhutan is a publication of the Bhutan Department of Works, Housing and Roads. It has chapters on iconography and on the design of dzongs, monasteries, chortens and temples. There are detailed descriptions of traditional design and construction methods for houses.

Views of Mediaeval Bhutan by Michael Aris is a coffee-table book that presents the diary and drawings of Samuel Davis, an excellent artist who was a member of George Bogel's expedition to Bhutan in 1783.

Tibetan Thangka Painting, Methods and Materials by Davis & Janice Jackson is a fascinating guide to how artists lay out the intricate designs of Mahayana Buddhist art.

Language

Dzongkha Handbook is a small book published in Bhutan that provides a glossary of English words and phrases with their Dzongkha and Sharchop equivalents.

Dzongkha-English Dictionary by Rinch-

hen Khandu has translations in both Dzongkha script and Roman Dzongkha. All the words are organised by topic and not alphabetically.

ONLINE SERVICES

There are no Internet providers in Bhutan, but several Bhutanese organisations have established web site servers outside of the country. In addition to the commercial sites of travel agencies, Druk Air and *Kuensel* (the national newspaper) there are numerous sites established by people, including many Japanese, with an interest in things Bhutanese.

There is an official government site at www.bhutan-info.org. Other starting points for browsing, with plenty of links, are www .bhutan.org, www.bootan.com and www .tashidelek.com.

Lonely Planet's web page (http:www .lonelyplanet.com) has advice, photographs, travel tales and general information on travelling through the region, with links to other relevant sites. Visit Destination Bhutan for all the latest news and views.

FILMS

There are a few documentary films about Bhutan, the most recent being the BBC TV special *Joanna Lumley in the Kingdom of the Thunder Dragon*, which is described in Books, earlier. The Royal Society for the Protection of Nature (RSPN) has produced a video about the black-necked cranes, but it is not easily available. Much of the film *Little Buddha* was shot in Bhutan, and Bhutanese boys played the role of the Dalai Lama at various ages in the 1997 movie *Seven Years in Tibet*.

Nomad films in Australia produced several half-hour award-winning documentaries on Bhutan that may be ordered through their Internet site at www.ekidna .com/nomad or from Nomad Films International (☎ 61-3-9819 3350; fax 9819 3395), PO Box 176, Prahran, Melbourne, Vic 3181, Australia. The films are *Tiger's Nest, Mountain of the Goddess*, *Man of the People* and *Man of the Forest*.

NEWSPAPERS & MAGAZINES

Kuensel is the weekly national newspaper of Bhutan. The name translates as 'enlightenment', and it is available on Saturday morning in English, Dzongkha and Nepali editions. It is well edited, articulate and informative. Each edition contains local news, cultural titbits, a summary of the week's international news, a children's page and numerous government announcements. It is available from bookshops in Thimphu and at many agencies throughout the country.

If you want to stay in touch with current events in Bhutan, you can subscribe to *Kuensel* or visit their web site at www .kuensel.com. A one-year subscription, delivered by airmail, costs US$76 to America, US$66 to Europe, US$56 to Asia, Africa and Australia and US$14 to India, Nepal and Bangladesh. For more information contact Kuensel Corporation (☎ 22483; fax 22975), GPO Box 204, Thimphu.

Indian newspapers and magazines are available in Phuentsholing and Thimphu. They arrive one or two days after publication. Look for the Indian news magazines *India Today* and the *Illustrated Weekly of India*. A few copies of international news magazines appear on newsstands about 10 days after publication.

RADIO & TV

Bhutan Broadcasting Service is on the air from 4 to 8 pm on the 60m band (5030 kHz) and FM 96 on weekdays. On Sunday it broadcasts from 10 am to 4 pm on the 49m band (6035 kHz) and FM 96. Programmes are in Dzongkha, English, Nepali and Sharchop. The English news is at 7.15 pm on weekdays and Saturday, and at 3 pm on Sunday.

There are no TV stations or satellite dishes in Bhutan. Thus, no hotel has television, though many homes have TVs that are used to watch videos.

VIDEO SYSTEMS

There is an enormous number of video rental shops throughout the country. All video tapes use the PAL format. Many of the videos are second or third-generation copies of Hindi song and dance epics. There is also a large collection of English films. You won't find videos with sexual content but, surprisingly, some portray extreme violence.

One Bhutanese company has produced an MTV-style music video of Bhutanese popular songs called *Joge Joge* (Let's Go, Let's Go).

PHOTOGRAPHY & VIDEO
Film & Equipment

Bring as much film as you think you will need, and then add several more rolls. You will be unhappy if you run out of film in Bhutan.

Some colour print film makes its way into the country and is sold in shops throughout the country. The major brand available is Konica ASA 100 colour print film, and it costs more than it does overseas. If you are shooting transparencies, bring all your film with you, because slide film is not available.

There are colour-printing facilities in Thimphu and Phuentsholing. Kuenphen Colour Lab (☎ 24058) on Thimphu's Norzin Lam has an automatic machine. The quality of processing sometimes suffers because the labs don't have enough business to change the chemicals as frequently as they should. Unless you are processing snapshots that you want to give to people in Bhutan, it's best to wait until you get home, or to a place like Bangkok or Hong Kong, to have your film developed.

Fit a UV filter to your lens to cut down ultraviolet light and to protect your lens from scratches. You will probably find a telephoto, or better yet, zoom lens useful for photographing people without having to stick a camera in their faces.

Many of the dzongs and mountain peaks are best photographed at a distance with a long lens. Bear in mind that there will be little or no opportunity for photography inside buildings, therefore you don't need to organise a flash attachment and tripod for that purpose. A polarising filter will help make your mountain pictures more dramatic by increasing the contrast between the sky and the white peaks and clouds. Be sure to carry extra batteries, as these are hard to find in Bhutan. If you are going trekking, buy a good camera bag to protect your camera and lens from dust and rain.

Photography
It has been said that it's impossible to take a poor photograph in Bhutan. Indeed, the landscape, buildings and people are some of the most photogenic in the world.

Be careful with exposure settings. The extreme light intensity in the mountains and at higher elevations can overexpose your pictures. Most good photographs are taken during the first or last few hours of the day when the light is softer and shadows more pronounced.

Many areas of Bhutan are forested, and it's cloudy for much of the year. You will need film with a rating of at least 100 ASA for these conditions. If you are using a telephoto lens, you may find ASA 200 or faster film useful.

Video
Properly used, a video camera can give a fascinating record of your holiday. As well as videoing the obvious things – sunsets, spectacular views – remember to record some of the ordinary everyday details of life in the country. Often the most interesting things occur when you're actually intent on filming something else. Remember too that, unlike still photography, video 'flows' – so, for example, you can shoot scenes of the winding road from the front window of a vehicle, to give an overall impression that isn't possible with ordinary photos.

If your camera has a stabiliser, you can use it to obtain good footage while travelling on bumpy roads.

Make sure you have the necessary charger, plugs and transformer to handle Bhutan's 230V power supply. Don't count on finding video cartridges in Bhutan, but you might find them in duty free shops en route.

Remember to follow the same rules regarding people's sensitivities as for a still photography – having a video camera shoved in your face is probably even more annoying and offensive than a still camera. Always ask permission first.

Restrictions
Bhutan is generally liberal about photography by tourists. There are a few places with signs prohibiting photography such as the radio tower complex above Thimphu. It would also be prudent to refrain from taking pictures of military installations.

There are no restrictions on photographing the outside of dzongs and goembas. Photography is strictly prohibited inside goembas and the lhakhangs within dzongs. There are several reasons for this. One is that tourists in the past have completely disrupted holy places with their picture taking. Another is the fear that photos of treasured statues will become a catalogue of items for art thieves to steal. And thirdly, some early tourists made photographs of religious statues into postcards that were then sold, which is unacceptable to the Bhutanese religious community.

During festivals you may enter the dzong courtyard where the dances take place. This provides an excellent opportunity to photograph the dzongs, people and local colour.

Remember, however, that this is a religious observance and that you should behave accordingly. Use a telephoto lens without a flash. Don't intrude on the dance ground or on the space occupied by local people seated at the edge of the dance area. If you do end up in the front row, remain seated.

Commercial Filming There is an extensive set of rules and restrictions, including payment of royalties, for commercial movie making in Bhutan. TAB publishes a booklet that details all these rules.

Photographing People
Bhutanese people are naturally shy but will usually allow you to take a photograph, especially if you ask them first. Many people,

especially children, will pose for you, and a smile or joke will help to make the pose a little less formal. Remember that almost everyone understands English, even if they are too embarrassed to try to speak it.

After you take a picture, many people will write down their address so that you may send them a copy. This seems a simple request. Don't take pictures of people unless you are prepared to honour it (many people leave their best intentions at Paro airport on their way home). Don't photograph a member of the royal family, even if you happen to be at a festival or gathering where they are present.

Airport Security
You could consider a lead-lined bag as protection from X-ray inspection of your luggage. There is an X-ray machine for hand luggage at Paro airport and stringent X-ray inspection at all airports that are served by Druk Air. Most of these airports will, reluctantly, agree to hand-inspect film, though they will insist that their machines will not damage your film. If you are worried about X-ray damage, take your film out of the box and canisters and keep it in a separate clear plastic bag so it's obvious what it is.

Avoid placing film in your checked baggage because it may be zapped with powerful X-rays on check-in or before it is delivered to you at your destination.

TIME
Bhutan time is GMT/UTC plus six hours; there is only one time zone throughout the country. The time in Bhutan is 30 minutes later than India, 15 minutes later than Nepal, and one hour earlier than Thailand. When it is noon in Bhutan, standard time is 6 am in London, 4 pm in Sydney, 1 am in New York and 10 pm the previous day in San Francisco.

ELECTRICITY
Voltage & Cycle
The voltage in Bhutan is the same as India: 230V, 50 cycles AC. The Chhukha hydroelectric project provides a reliable, well-regulated power supply throughout western Bhutan. If you are planning to use sensitive electronic equipment, you should still be prepared for possible outages and fluctuations, especially power surges. Electricity in the rest of Bhutan is generated by small hydroelectric projects near major towns. Floods and landslides often disrupt the generating stations or the distribution lines. In central and eastern Bhutan there are occasional short and long-term power failures and voltage instability.

Plugs & Sockets
Bhutan uses the standard Indian round pin sockets. These come in a variety of sizes, and there's no assurance that a particular plug will fit the socket in your hotel. Most European round-pin plugs work, but their pins are usually smaller than the Indian variety, and they fit loosely and provide an unreliable connection. There are plenty of electrical shops in Thimphu that can make up an adapter if you have trouble plugging in an appliance.

WEIGHTS & MEASURES
The metric system is used throughout the country. In villages, rice is sometimes measured in a round measure called a *gasekhorlo*. There is a scale called a *sang* that is used for butter and meat.

LAUNDRY
Hotels can do laundry but few hotels have dryers. Same-day service is possible but it depends on the amount of sunshine available. The only dry cleaning shops are in Thimphu and Phuentsholing. Dry cleaning will take longer than you're used to so plan accordingly.

TOILETS
There are few public toilets except near the town vegetable market in Thimpu. Existing public toilets are of the Asian squatting variety and toilet paper is never available, though there may be a container of water to use. Most hotels and guesthouses provide western toilets and loo paper, though there

are some exceptions, particularly in eastern Bhutan.

In older goembas and palaces you may find an old-fashioned Bhutanese toilet. This is a strange hobbyhorse commode built in a little room that extends out from the side of the building, featuring a large pipe leading straight down into a pit.

WOMEN TRAVELLERS
Attitudes to Women

Bhutan prides itself on its lack of a class system and an absence of sexual discrimination. Bhutanese women have the same rights as men, including the right of education, voting and holding positions in the government.

The family system is basically matriarchal, with the daughters inheriting the family estate. Upon marriage the husband moves into the wife's house and becomes part of her family. Women are free to decide whom to marry and either the husband or wife has the right to initiate a divorce – which is a frequent occurrence in Bhutan. Society does not look down on a divorcee or unwed mother. In such cases the father is required to pay 20% of his salary as support until the child reaches age 18.

Bhutanese women are proud of their position in society. Many women own shops and run family businesses while their husbands work in government offices. Several large travel agencies are run by women. Rural women are active in farming and the growing of cash crops and their sale in the market.

There are few women in high government positions. Until the 1950s, women had limited opportunities for education; the problem today is a lack of educated women, not discrimination.

However, women are catching up in this department and many women have taken exams and become gazetted government officers, and some women are rising to high government positions. Women in government compete equally with men according to their own capability, not on any system of quotas.

In spite of the generally liberated position of women, a few ancient discriminatory traditions still exist. In archery, Bhutan's national sport, women are not allowed to touch an archer's bow and arrow, and archers refrain from sleeping with a woman the night before a match.

In most temples there is a room called the *goenkhang* that contains statues of warlords and other deities that women must not view. Women are not allowed to sleep in dzongs or enter rooms where weapons are stored.

Promiscuousness on the part of Bhutanese males is accepted and common, but women are expected to remain faithful to a single partner.

Safety Precautions

Women, both foreign and Bhutanese, are not subject to harassment and do not need to take any special precautions, other than following sensible practices of behaviour and dress. Bhutanese are more likely to help a woman in distress than a man.

Young men have a reasonably liberated attitude towards their relations with women. There are several opportunities for misunderstanding if you don't make your intentions clear from the very outset. Female travellers should be aware that romantic liaisons between tourists and Bhutanese guides are quite common. You might also be invited to a 'party' at the home of a Bhutanese male, and discover too late that you are the only guest.

Organisations

The only women's organisation in the country is the National Women's Association of Bhutan (NWAB; ☎ 22910), established in 1981 and now headed by Dasho Dawa Dem, one of two women who have received the honorific title of Dasho from the king.

NWAB operates and manages many projects for rural women, including non-formal education, credit schemes and training centres and sales outlets for handicraft production. NWAB has also been active in the installation of fuel-efficient smokeless stoves in rural homes.

GAY & LESBIAN TRAVELLERS

Like most Asians, the Bhutanese believe that what one does in private is strictly a personal matter, and they would prefer not to discuss such issues. Public displays of affection are not appreciated and everyone, regardless of orientation, should exercise discretion.

DISABLED TRAVELLERS

A cultural tour in Bhutan is a challenge for a traveller who cannot walk, but possible with some planning. The Bhutanese are eager to help, and one could arrange a strong companion to assist with moving about and getting in and out of vehicles. The roads are rough and sidewalks, where they exist, often have holes and sometimes steps. Hotels and public buildings do not have wheelchair access, and there are no toilets designed to accommodate wheelchairs.

For further general information there is a World Wide Web site for and by disabled travellers at http://www.travelhealth.com/disab.htm.

SENIOR TRAVELLERS

Because of the high cost of travelling in Bhutan, many visitors are seniors travelling in organised groups. Hotels, guides and tour operators are all familiar with the needs of seniors and treat them with the traditional respect that the Bhutanese have for their elders. The primary precaution one should take is to have an ample supply of any special medicines, since these probably will not be available in Bhutan.

TRAVEL WITH CHILDREN

As there are discounts for children travelling in Bhutan, it won't totally break the bank if you bring kids along. They may become bored, however, because there are long, monotonous drives and there is no TV and not much other 'entertainment' available. On the other hand, children will be immediately accepted by Bhutanese kids and their families, and they will probably make many new friends. Lonely Planet's *Travel with Children* by Maureen Wheeler has lots of useful advice and suggestions. Peter Steele's book *Two and Two Halves in Bhutan* describes the joys of travelling with children here.

DANGERS & ANNOYANCES

Fortunately, travel in Bhutan is still largely immune to the major banes of travel in Asia – theft and begging. It does, however, have some irritations of its own.

Altitude

The maximum elevation that you can reach on a Bhutanese road (3150m in the west and 3750m in the east) is lower than that which causes altitude problems for most people. There are rare individuals who can suffer from altitude problems even at elevations as low as Thimphu (2300m); if you have had previous altitude problems at these elevations avoid travelling to Bhutan.

Most treks go to extremely high elevations. If you are planning a trek, you should follow the advice about acclimatisation in the Trekking chapter.

Winding Roads & Breakdowns

If you venture east of Thimphu, you will spend hours driving on rough, winding roads. Even those who have never been carsick before can get squeamish with the constant bouncing and motion, especially in the back seat of a van or bus. Vehicles do break down, no matter how well maintained they are, and there is no emergency road service. It's unlikely, but not impossible, for you to be forced to spend a night sleeping in a vehicle at the side of the road, or hitch a ride in a crowded bus to the next town.

Dogs

Those same cute dogs that wag their tails for you during the day turn into barking monsters at night. Don't forget to bring the earplugs recommended earlier. There is little danger of dog bites, but if you are going trekking, be wary of big dogs if you enter what looks like someone's front yard.

Weather

You are close to nature in Bhutan, and often this proximity affects your travel plans. Even on a cultural tour you will be windblown in towns like Paro, Wangdue Phodrang and Jakar. Clouds often obscure the mountain views that you made such an effort to see. Rain can turn trails and footpaths into a sea of mud, and flights are frequently delayed by bad weather. Leeches inhabit the lower valleys, and can be a real irritation in the monsoon season. A rainstorm can turn small streams into torrents, moving huge boulders and smashing bridges.

Hotel Service

Food in hotels and restaurants can sometimes take a frustratingly long time to prepare, but there is no hint of this when you order. Be patient, or choose a meal from the buffet.

Just when you are used to everyone speaking fluent English, you will ask someone for something and they will nod knowingly even though they haven't the faintest idea what you are talking about. You will then receive something totally unexpected, or – more likely – nothing at all because they were too embarrassed to ask you to repeat your request.

BUSINESS HOURS

Government offices open at 9 am and close at 5 pm in the summer and 4 pm in the winter, Monday to Friday.

Banks are open from 9 am to 3 pm on weekdays 9 am till noon Saturday. Shops are usually open from 8 am until 8 or 9 pm. In Thimphu and Phuentsholing, shops are open weekends, but closed Tuesday. In other towns, most shops are open every day. Some bars and restaurants in Thimphu stay open as late as 10 pm, but many close earlier.

The idea of appointments is a relatively new one in Bhutan. Unless you are meeting a very high-level official, you will probably be given a vague appointment time – usually anytime during the morning (or afternoon). When you arrive, the person will often be out, or in another meeting. Be patient and wait, or come back later.

HOLIDAYS & SPECIAL EVENTS

Bhutan's national day is 17 December, the date of the establishment of the monarchy in 1907. Other important holidays are the king's birthday on 11 November and Coronation Day on 2 June.

The new year is called *Losar*, and is celebrated according to the highly complicated Bhutanese calendar. Losar usually falls between mid-January and mid-March. To complicate matters further, there are different dates for the new year in various parts of the country.

Festivals are scheduled according to the Bhutanese calendar. Dates can be predicted in advance to within one or two weeks, but determining the precise date requires a consultation with an astrologer. TAB prepares a list, usually in June, of the correct festival dates for the following year and distributes it to all tour operators.

Bhutanese Calendar

The Bhutanese calendar is based on the Tibetan calendar, which evolved from the Chinese. In the 17th century the Bhutanese scholar Pema Karpo developed a new way of computing the days of the week. This caused a divergence between the Tibetan and Bhutanese calendars, and dates do not agree between the two systems.

In the Bhutanese system, months have 30 days, with the full moon falling on the 15th. The eighth, 15th and 30th days of the month are auspicious. The fourth is also auspicious, because Buddha first preached his religious principles on the fourth day of the sixth month.

Years are named according to the Tibetan system of five elements and 12 animals, producing a 60-year cycle. The year 1998 is Earth Tiger year, and 1974, the year of King Jigme Singye Wangchuck's coronation, is the Wood Tiger year.

The calendar operates according to a very flexible system that allows bad days to be avoided. Astrologers sometimes add a day if it's going to be an auspicious one or lose a day if it's not. They can even change months. In some years, for example, there may be no

Future Festival Dates

Festival dates are determined according to the Bhutanese calendar, which can change significantly from year to year. Every June, TAB supplies tour operators with festival dates for the coming year. The following are the dates for 1999. Dates for later years will usually be within two weeks of those shown here, but they are sometimes adjusted by a month or more to conform to auspicious dates. Before you schedule a trip around a specific festival, check with a tour operator for the correct dates for the year in which you plan to travel.

Festival Name	Place	Dates
Punakha Dromche	Punakha	20 to 24 February
Punakha Serda	Punakha	24 February
Chorten Kora Tsechu	Trashi Yangtse	16 & 17 March
Gom Kora Tsechu	Trashi Yangtse	25 & 26 March
Chhukha Tsechu	Chhukha	25 & 26 March
Paro Tsechu	Paro	27 to 31 March
Ura Yakchoe	Bumthang	25 April to 1 May
Nyimalung Tsechu	Bumthang	21 to 23 June
Kurjey Tsechu	Bumthang	23 June
Thimphu Domche	Thimphu	16 & 17 September
Wangdue Tsechu	Wangdue	17 to 20 September
Tamshing Phala Chodpa	Bumthang	19 to 21 September
Thimphu Tsechu	Thimphu	20 to 22 September
Thangbi Mani	Bumthang	24 to 26 September
Jambey Lhakhang Drup	Bumthang	24 to 28 October
Prakhar Tsechu	Jakar	25 to 28 October
Mongar Tsechu	Mongar	15 to 18 November
Trashigang Tsechu	Trashigang	16 to 19 November
Trongsa Tsechu	Trongsa	17 to 20 November
Lhuentse Tsechu	Lhuentse	17 to 19 December

October because it has been deemed an inauspicious month, or it might have two Augusts because that happens to be a good month.

Bhutanese include the nine months in the womb in the calculation of their age. Everyone considers themselves a year older on Losar, the day of the winter solstice, and thus people can be nearly two years younger than they say they are.

Cultural Events

Most dzongs and many monasteries have an annual festival, the largest of which is the tsechu (see the section 'Dances of the Tsechu' on pages 111-15). This is a festival in honour of Guru Rimpoche. The biography of the Guru is highlighted by 12 episodes on the model of the Buddha Sakyamuni's life. The dates and the duration of the festivals vary from one district to another but they always take place on or around the 10th day of the month in the Bhutanese calendar.

The dances of the tsechu are performed by monks as well as lay people. Many of the dances were composed by the Shabdrung Ngawang Namgyal and Pema Lingpa. The dancers take on the aspects of wrathful and compassionate deities, heroes, demons, and animals. The dances, known as *cham*, bring blessings upon the onlookers, to instruct

The Bhutanese Calendar

The Bhutanese calendar was adapted from Tibetan astronomical traditions, which in turn were influenced by the Chinese and Indian calendars. The calendar is based on the lunar system. A year has 360 days, with some days omitted to make it correspond with the waxing and waning of the moon. An extra short month is added to the twelve months every third year to adjust it to the solar calendar.

The year begins with *Losar*, which normally falls in the Gregorian calendar month of February with the rise of the new moon. The months (*dawa*) do not have names, and are simply called first, second, third and so on. A week is divided into seven days (*zal*). Years are named by combining the 12 animals of the zodiac with the five elements of fire, earth, iron, water and wood to produce a 60-year cycle.

The complete list of 60 years is as follows:

Years in Bhutanese Sexagenary Cycle

1952	Water-Dragon	1972	Water-Mouse	1992	Water-Monkey
1953	Water-Serpent	1973	Water-Ox	1993	Water-Hen
1954	Wood-Horse	1974	Wood-Tiger	1994	Wood-Dog
1955	Wood-Sheep	1975	Wood-Hare	1995	Wood-Pig
1956	Fire-Monkey	1976	Fire-Dragon	1996	Fire-Mouse
1957	Fire-Hen	1977	Fire-Serpent	1997	Fire-Ox
1958	Earth-Dog	1978	Earth-Horse	1998	Earth-Tiger
1959	Earth-Pig	1979	Earth-Sheep	1999	Earth-Hare
1960	Iron-Mouse	1980	Iron-Monkey	2000	Iron-Dragon
1961	Iron-Ox	1981	Iron-Hen	2001	Iron-Serpent
1962	Water-Tiger	1982	Water-Dog	2002	Water-Horse
1963	Water-Hare	1983	Water-Pig	2003	Water-Sheep
1964	Wood-Dragon	1984	Wood-Mouse	2004	Wood-Monkey
1965	Wood-Serpent	1985	Wood-Ox	2005	Wood-Hen
1966	Fire-Horse	1986	Fire-Tiger	2006	Fire-Dog
1967	Fire-Sheep	1987	Fire-Hare	2007	Fire-Pig
1968	Earth-Monkey	1988	Earth-Dragon	2008	Earth-Mouse
1969	Earth-Hen	1989	Earth-Serpent	2009	Earth-Ox
1970	Iron-Dog	1990	Iron-Horse	2010	Iron-Tiger
1971	Iron-Pig	1991	Iron-Sheep	2011	Iron-Hare

them in the teachings of the Buddhist dharma, to protect them from misfortune, and to exorcise evil influences. It is a religious festival and it is believed one gains merit by attending it. Deities are invoked during the dances; through their power and benediction, misfortunes may be annihilated, luck increased and wishes realised. It is also a yearly social gathering where the people rejoice together, dressed in their finest clothing and jewellery.

During the dances *atsara* (clowns) mimic the dancers and perform comic routines wearing masks with long red noses. The name is a corruption of the Sanskrit *acharya* (master). While entertaining the onlookers, they also help to keep order and have developed the habit of harassing tourists for money. Take it as a good-natured game; if you contribute you may even receive a blessing from the wooden phallus they carry.

continued on page 116

The Dances of the Tsechu

The following is the sequence of dances at the Thimphu tsechu. Most dances are the same at other tsechus, but the sequence varies.

Day One

The Dance of the Four Stags *(Shacham)* This shows how Guru Rimpoche subdued the God of the Wind, who created much unhappiness in this world, and rode the stag which was the god's mount. The dancers in the role of stags wear yellow knee-length skirts and masks of horned deer.

Dance of the Three Kinds of Ging *(Pelage Gingsum)* This is the visual representation of Zangto Pelri, the heavenly paradise of Guru Rimpoche, as seen by Pema Lingpa. The dances show how to subdue the demons that are creating obstacles to religion. Although the demons are fleeing throughout the three worlds, the *ging* (beings that are emanations of Guru Rimpoche) with the sticks can find them thanks to their foreknowledge. They catch them with the hook of compassion, beat them with the stick of wisdom and tie them with the noose of compassion.

The Lords of the cremation grounds bring a box that contains the mind and the body of these demons. Then the ging with the swords purify the atmosphere from evil deeds that are caused by the demons. After the demons have been vanquished, the ging with the drums dance with happiness. For the dance with the sticks the ging wear animal masks, and for the dance with the swords and the drums, they wear terrifying masks.

Dance of the Heroes *(Pacham)* When Pema Lingpa arrived at Zangto Pelri he saw Guru Rimpoche sitting among his assistants in the centre of a limitless mandala (mystic geocentric figure) which was made of lines of rainbow beams. This dance is to lead the believers of the human world into the presence of Guru Rimpoche. The dancers wear yellow skirts and golden crowns without a mask. They carry a small bell (*dri-lbu*) and a small drum (*damaru*).

Dance of the Stag and the Hounds *(Shawo Shachi)* This dance represents the conversion to Buddhism of the hunter Gonpo Dorji by the saint Milarepa. It is performed like a play in two parts. The first part takes place the first day, and the second part is on the second day of the Thimphu Tsechu. The first part is quite comical: the hunter's servant appears and jokes with the clowns. Then comes the hunter, crowned with leaves, carrying a bow and arrows and accompanied by his two dogs. The servant jokes very irreverently with his master who, before going hunting, must perform some good-luck rituals. The priest who is called performs the ritual in ways contrary to the Buddhist tradition, while the *atsaras* (clowns) and the servant go on with their jokes.

Dance with Guitar *(Dranyeo Cham)* This is a cheerful dance to celebrate the diffusion of the Drukpa lineage in Bhutan by Shabdrung Ngawang Namgyal. The dancers carry swords and are dressed in a circular headdress and heavy woollen clothes with felt boots, a long black skirt, yellow shirt and brown coat. One dancer carries a guitar called a *dranyen*.

Day Two

Black Hat Dance *(Shana)* The dancers wear brocade dresses, wide-brimmed black hats and black aprons with an image representing the protecting deities whose images are kept in the *goenkhang* (chapel). The black-hat dancers assume the appearance of yogis who have the power of killing and recreating life. It is believed that the gestures of the dancers' hands are transformed into *mudras* (sacred mystic gestures) and their feet, which pound the earth, form a mandala. The dancers first build a mandala and then cut the demons into pieces. Thus they take possession of the earth in order to protect it and they dance the special thunderbolt step to impress their power on it.

Because of its importance, the Shabdrung himself used to perform this ritual. This is a ground purification rite also performed for the construction of dzongs, temples and chortens. Its aim is to conciliate the malevolent beings of the ground in order to take possession of the site from them.

Dance of the 21 Black Hats with Drums *(Shaa Nga Cham)* In honour of the victory of religion over the enemies, the black hats beat the great drums of Buddhism. The sound of the drums represents the religion itself, which cannot be represented in any other way because it has no visible form. The dancers wear large black hats, felt boots and a long, colourful, brocade dress.

Kyecham An accompanying dance is performed by dancers carrying swords and wearing knee-length yellow skirts, bare-feet and animal masks.

Dance of the Noblemen and the Ladies *(Pholeg Moleg)* This dance depicts events in the life of King Norzang. It is a comical and very crude play rather than a dance.

The actors are two princes, two princesses, an old couple and the clowns. The princes go to war and leave the princesses in the care of the old couple. As soon as they depart the clowns frolic with the princesses and corrupt the old woman who is also misbehaving. When the princes return, they are scandalised by the behaviour and cut off the noses of the princesses and the old lady as punishment. Then a doctor is called to put the nose back, but the old woman smells so much that the doctor has to use a stick because he does not want to approach her. Finally the princes marry the princesses and everybody is reconciled.

Dance of the Drums from Drametse *(Drametse Nga Cham)* The learned lama Kuenga Gyeltshen, son of Pema Lingpa, had a vision of Guru Rimpoche and his paradise Zangto Pelri during his meditation. The attendants of Guru Rimpoche were transformed into one 100

NICHOLAS REUSS

STAN ARMINGTON

Previous page: tsechus are a riot of colour and pageantry with an irresistible Bhutanese flavour.

Tsechus take place in the enchanting courtyards of the great dzongs, as this one at Gangte, Western Bhutan.

NICHOLAS REUSS

JULIA WILKINSON

The dances are performed by monks and lay people, who take on the aspects of wrathful and compassionate deities, demons, and animals. The dances, known as cham, bring blessings upon the onlookers.

NICHOLAS REUSS

JULIA WILKINSON

NICHOLAS REUSS

A huge thondrol is unfurled briefly during each tsechu, this one depicting Guru Rimpoche and his manifestations (right). As well as providing a spectacular backdrop for the dances, it is believed that one's sins are washed away by simply viewing the relic. Its name means 'liberation on sight'. Masks and drums (below) are essential props in the dramatisation of the allegories.

NICHOLAS REUSS

NICHOLAS REUSS

kinds of peaceful and terrifying deities. They took in their left hand a big drum and in their right hand a drumstick and they performed a dance. Kuenga Gyeltshen came to Drametse Goemba in eastern Bhutan and established the tradition of this dance, which depicts his vision. The players hold big drums and wear knee-length yellow skirts and animal mask.

Dance of the Stag and the Hounds *(Shawo Shachi)* This is the conclusion of the dance staged on the first day and is more serious and religious. Milarepa appears, wearing a long white dress and a white hat, holding a pilgrim's staff. He holds his right hand near his ear and sings in a soft voice. The dogs, the stag and the hunter arrive and Milarepa converts them with his song. The conversion is symbolised by a rope that the dogs and the hunter have to jump.

Day Three

Dance of the Lords of the Cremation Grounds *(Durdag)* This dance was composed by the Shabdrung, Ngawang Namgyal. The dancers represent the protectors of the religion who live in the eight cremation grounds on the external edges of the symbolic Mount Sumeru. They wear short white skirts, white boots and white skull masks.

Dance of the Terrifying Deities *(Tungam)* This dance is performed with the aim of delivering the beings by showing them Zangto Pelri. The costumes are beautiful brocade dresses, boots and terrifying masks. This dramatic dance has a very deep symbolic meaning, namely that a sacrificial murder is performed. First the dancers representing the gods try to enclose the bad spirits in a circle and in a box. Once this is done, Guru Rimpoche, in the form of Dorji Drakpo (fierce thunderbolt), kills them with a *phorbu* (ritual dagger). He thus saves the world from them and delivers them into salvation at the same time.

Dance of the Rakshas and the Judgement of the Dead *(Raksha Mangcham)* This is based on the *Bardo Thoedrol* (Book of the Dead), a text hidden by Guru Rimpoche and rediscovered by Karma Lingpa in the 14th century. This is one of the most important dances of the tsechu and is watched carefully by many old people in preparation for their own death.

When all beings die, they wander in the *Bardo* (intermediate state) waiting to be led by the love of the Buddhas into the pure fields where no suffering exists. However, the Buddhas assume both peaceful and terrifying forms. Those who didn't adore the Buddhist doctrine do not recognise the Buddhas in their terrifying form and are frightened and cannot be led into the paradises.

Shinje Chhogyel, Lord of Death, estimates the value of the white and black deeds during the judgement. Also present are the White God and Black Demon who live with every being from birth, and all the helpers who emanate under numerous forms. These include: the ox-headed justice minister; the wild hog-headed helper who takes account of the black and white deeds; the khyung-headed bird, who holds a small sword to cut the root of the three poisons (ignorance, envy, anger) and a big hammer to destroy the rocky mountains of sins;

a lion-headed helper holds a lasso representing love and an iron chain representing compassion; the fierce bear-headed helper holds the magical noose binding the means and wisdom together and a saw to cut selfishness; a serpent-headed helper holds a mirror reflecting all actions; and the monkey-headed helper weighs them on a scale.

All these helpers are called *rakshas* and they separate the black actions from the white actions of all beings. The frightening Court of Justice cannot be avoided by the damned beings. But after enduring certain sufferings, their sins are washed away and they are purified. This dance shows everyone that if they devote themselves to virtuous actions, they will be sent immediately to the pure fields and paradises. Then after life, when they have to cross the Bardo and meet the helpers and the assembly of peaceful and terrifying deities, they recognise them as incarnations of Buddha and are delivered from the frightening Bardo.

The dance is like a play and lasts over two hours. First is the long dance of all the rakshas, the helpers of Shinje. Then Shinje himself appears, symbolised by a huge puppet holding a mirror. The White God and the Black Demon enter with him. The judgement begins. The Black Demon and his helpers perform a dance. The sinner, dressed in black and wearing a red hat, is frightened and tries to escape but is recaptured each time. From his basket a freshly severed cow's head is taken, implying that the sinner was responsible for killing it. As the judge weighs his actions the White God sings of the merits of the man and the Black Demon expounds the sins. Finally a black strip of cloth symbolising the road to hell is spread and the sinner is sent to hell.

After a general dance everyone sits again. Another man arrives, clad in white and holding a prayer flag and a ceremonial scarf. The same scene is re-enacted and at the conclusion a white strip of cloth, symbolising the road to heaven, is deployed. Fairies elaborately dressed in brocade and bone-ornaments come to fetch him. At the last moment, the Black Demon, furious at having lost a being, tries to grasp the virtuous man but the White God protects him.

Day Four

Dance of Tamshing in Bumthang *(Bumthang Ter Cham)* On the occasion of the consecration of the Tamshing Monastery in Bumthang, Pema Lingpa had a dream and composed this dance to depict what he saw. The dance is performed in white, peaceful-looking, masks and knee-length yellow skirts and the dancers carry a little bell and drum. When this miraculously discovered dance is performed, all the earth demons in the country are appeased and the Gods rejoice.

Dance of the Lords of Cremation Grounds *(Durdag)* The same as the dance performed on day three.

Dance of Ging and Tsholing *(Ging dang Tsholing)* On the occasion of the consecration of the Samye Monastery in Tibet, Guru Rimpoche initiated this dance to show the people Zangto Pelri. When the ging and tsholing perform this miraculous dance, they demonstrate their magical powers in order to discourage the demons.

The ging wear orange skirts which hang like a skin, terrifying black and orange masks with a flag on top, and hold a big drum. They represent the assembly of heroes, deities and fairies (*khandroma*) as well as the various male and female terrifying deities. On the outside dance the tsholing, who represent the protectors of religion, wearing long colourful dresses and terrifying masks.

The dance is a ceremony of purification before the arrival of Guru Rimpoche. People whistle to chase away bad spirits and the ging hit everybody on the head with their drumsticks to chase impurity out of the body. After having destroyed the evil spirits (symbolised by an effigy in a black box), the tsholing are chased away by the ging who then stay alone to beat their drums and perform a victory dance.

Dance of the Eight Manifestations of Guru Rimpoche *(Gere Tshen Gyed)* The eight different forms of Guru Rimpoche are represented in this dance. With Guru Rimpoche are his two consorts, Mandarava on the right and Yeshey Tshogyal on the left.

This dance is a play and a dance at the same time. People believe in the manifestations of Guru Rimpoche during the dance. Guru Dorji Drakpo enters first, dressed in a colourful brocade dress and wearing a terrifying red mask.

The eight manifestations enter as follows: *Tshokye Dorji* in a brocade dress, a peaceful-looking, blue-green mask and carrying a small thunderbolt; *Loden Chogsey* in a red brocade dress, peaceful whitish mask, carrying a small drum and a bowl; *Padmasambhava*, wearing a red and yellow monk dress, white mask and tall red hat; *Guru Rimpoche*, himself, under a canopy, wearing a golden mask (he has khandroma as attendants, symbolised by small children with white masks); *Shakya Senge* wearing a red and yellow monk dress, Buddha-like mask with blue hair, and carrying a bowl; *Padma Gyalpo* in a red brocade dress, orange bearded mask with white tufts of hair, carrying a small drum and a mirror; *Nyima Yoezer* wearing a golden brocade dress, yellow bearded-mask with blue tufts of hair, and carrying a trident; and *Sengye Dradrok* in a blue brocade dress and terrifying blue mask, followed by his retinue who also wear frightening blue masks.

Guru Rimpoche sits under a canopy, followed by Shakya Senge, while all the other manifestations dance turn by turn as people rush to be blessed by Guru Rimpoche. When a manifestation finishes his dance, he joins the others sitting with the Guru.

Then appear 16 fairies who sing and perform two dances in front of the Guru and his manifestations. They dance, first holding drums, then small bells and small drums. They have brocade dresses and carved bone-ornaments. After these dances, everybody goes out in a long procession.

Religious Song *(Chhoeshey)* This dance is performed to commemorate the opening of the gateway to the pilgrimage site of Tsari in eastern Tibet by Tsangpa Jarey, founder of the Drukpa School. The costumes are similar to those in the Guitar Dance: elaborate and heavy woollen clothes, long black skirt, yellow shirt, folded brown coat, felt boots, a circular head-dress and a sword.

Courtesy of the Royal Government of Bhutan

continued from page 110

During many tsechus a large *thangka* (religious picture) is unfurled from the building overlooking the dance area before sunrise. Large thangkas of this sort are called *thondrol*, and are usually embroidered rather than painted. The word means 'liberation on sight', and it is believed that one's sins are washed away simply by viewing one of these large relics. When the thondrol is rolled up again, old people chant to ensure that they will see it the following year.

During the intervals between the masked dances a team of elegantly dressed ladies sing and perform traditional dances. During some tsechus a small fair is erected outside the dzong or goemba. Some of the stalls offer various kinds of gambling for astonishingly high stakes.

ACTIVITIES

There are lots of things to do in Bhutan after you have had your fill of dzongs and temples. Tour operators are developing new activities in an effort to convince visitors to stay longer, and some of these offer some unusual opportunities.

Being a landlocked country, Bhutan has no aquatic sports except for the covered swimming pool in Thimphu. You might find an Indian-made bicycle for rent in the flats of Phuentsholing, but they are not available in any other towns. Mountain biking is being introduced in a limited way (see Mountain Biking).

There are many possible day hikes, particularly in Thimphu, Paro and Bumthang. These are described in the related sections. For serious treks ranging from three to 25 days, see the Trekking chapter. Mountaineering in Bhutan has been closed since 1994. There are riding horses available in Paro and on some treks, but remember the Bhutanese adage:

It is not a horse that cannot carry a man uphill, and it is not a man that cannot walk downhill.

Fishing is possible in many lakes and a few rivers, though it is frowned upon by the Bhutanese. A license is required, and fishing is prohibited in many rivers, including the Mo Chhu in Punakha.

Game viewing is generally confined to Royal Manas National Park in the south of the country, currently off-limits because of the dangers posed by separatist groups in India.

Rafting & Kayaking

Equator Expeditions did a survey of rivers in Bhutan and rated the suitable rivers as follows:

Paro Chhu	Class 3-4
Mo Chhu	Class 4
Mangde Chhu	Class 4-5
Gamre Chhu	Class 4+
Dangme Chhu	Class 4-5
Kuri Chhu	Class 5

TAB is promoting rafting as a way to give tourists access to beautiful undeveloped areas of Bhutan without unduly affecting the local population. Though rafting in Bhutan is in its infancy those who have scouted the rivers feel that it has the potential for some of the best rafting on earth.

The fees for river rafting are the same as cultural tours and trekking. Several operators are offering river programmes in Bhutan (see Specialised Tours in the Getting There & Away chapter).

Mountain Biking

There are no mountain bikes for rent in Bhutan, but some adventure travel companies have organised trips that allow bikers to bring their own cycles and travel throughout Bhutan accompanied by a 'sag wagon' for support. Long journeys are problematic because there's a lot of uphill peddling and approaching vehicles roar around corners, not expecting cyclists. Local cycling excursions in the Paro, Thimphu and Bumthang valleys offer a safer and less strenuous mountain biking experience.

Golf

There's an international standard golf course in Thimphu and there are small courses in

Rafting & Kayaking in Bhutan

Peter Knowles, author of *White Water Nepal*, is an authority on Himalayan rivers and writes:

We made two reconnaissance visits to Bhutan in 1997 with teams of expert kayakers at the invitation of the tourism authorities.

The rivers in Bhutan are generally very steep and powerful; valley sides are usually precipitous and jungle clad; road access is limited – these factors mean that only relatively short sections of the main rivers are suitable for kayaking and rafting. Unlike neighbouring countries there are no obvious multi-day rafting trips.

But, on the positive side, Bhutan offers a unique destination for the recreational kayaker, with incredible rivers that are both challenging and some of the most beautiful in the world. The rivers are clean and pristine with crystal-clear turquoise coloured water. Wildlife is phenomenal. I can't think of another river where I have rolled up at the bottom of a rapid to find a family of otters grinning at me! We kayaked about 12 different rivers – mainly class 4. The outstanding ones were the Mo Chhu upstream of Punakha and the 'Ema Datse Canyon' on the Mangde Chhu.

The lower section of the Mo Chhu flowing down past Punakha Dzong would make an easy, safe, and highly photogenic float trip. It is probable that this will be offered as a commercial rafting option in the near future and I highly recommend it as a pleasant, relaxed change from trekking and sightseeing.

Peter Knowles, Rivers Publishing, UK.

Ha and Deothang. The Thimphu course is used mainly by Bhutanese and expatriate residents, though a few Japanese tourists play there both for the experience and because it's very inexpensive compared with green fees in Japan.

COURSES

There are no formal courses offered in Bhutan but, if given advance notice, your tour operator may be able to arrange programmes to meet your particular interest. Given sufficient notice, the Dzongkha Development Commission can arrange brief courses and lectures on language and music.

The Royal Institute of Management and the Royal Civil Service Commission team up twice a year to provide a two-week long orientation course on Bhutanese religion and culture for international volunteers working in Bhutan.

WWF (☎ 23528; fax 23518) and RSPN (☎ 23189) can arrange lectures and discussion groups on wildlife and environmental issues.

VOLUNTEER WORK

Bhutan is quite selective about the type of projects it wants in the country and disdains indiscriminate assistance. Each donor or charitable agency is limited to specified projects or activities and is allowed only a certain number of volunteers. The opportunities for volunteer work in Bhutan are therefore limited. Since 1980, only 647 volunteers from various organisations have served in Bhutan, and in 1997 there were 82 working in the country.

Overseas Aid Agencies

If you want to do volunteer work in Bhutan, the following agencies may be able to help. Americans will find it difficult to get a position, because the US Peace Corps does not have a Bhutan programme.

The United Nations has numerous programmes in Bhutan, all co-ordinated through the UN Development Programme (UNDP). Among the agencies are the UN Children's Fund (UNICEF), UN Capital Development Fund (UNCDF), United Nations Volunteers

(ENV) and the UN Educational, Scientific & Cultural Organisation (UNESCO).

Australian Volunteers Abroad
(☎ 61-303-9279 1788; fax 9416 1619),
Overseas Service Bureau Programme,
PO Box 350, Fitzroy, Vic 3065, Australia
Coordinating Committee for International
Voluntary Service (☎ 33-1-45 68 27 31), c/o
UNESCO, 1 rue Miollis, 75015 Paris,
France
Voluntary Service Overseas (VSO)
(☎ 44-0181-780 2266; fax 780 1326), 317
Putney Bridge Rd, London SW15 2PN, UK

Other agencies that operate programmes in Bhutan include the European Community, Save the Children, DDC (Austrian), SNV (Dutch), VSA (New Zealand), JOCV (Japan), Danida (Danish) and Helvetas (Swiss).

ACCOMMODATION
Tour operators are supposed to book you into TAB-approved hotels. Since you pay the same rate whether you stay in a noisy local guesthouse or in the best place in town, it makes sense to ask for the top of the line when you make your travel arrangements. During the high season, particularly at tsechu time, you may not get the hotel you have asked for, and you might even be accommodated in a hotel that caters primarily to Indian and Bhutanese travellers. Still, these can be comfortable, though the toilet facilities may not be ideal or, at least, what you're used to, and there may be more noise than you'd wish.

Hotels
There is a variety of hotels in Bhutan, ranging from simple huts that cater to Bhutanese yak herders to Paro's fancy Olathang Hotel, which was built for royal guests. There are no international chain hotels and not much imported hotel equipment; what you get is a Bhutanese version of what they think western tourists expect. In most cases, the facilities and service are pretty good, but still only about the standards of India and Nepal 20 years ago.

All rooms in the TAB-approved hotels in

Thimphu, Paro and Phuentsholing have electricity, telephones that sometimes work, private baths and (at certain times of day) hot water. Most have a restaurant that serves buffet meals and à la carte dining. Bars, when they exist, are usually just a few stools in a corner of the dining room.

There's a strange system when you discuss hotel rates, because Indians and project people can book a hotel directly (without a Bhutanese travel agent). All the hotels publish their room rates and many have various standards of rooms, including normal and deluxe rooms, as well as suites, though the difference between these facilities in most hotels is often minimal. When you book a trip, you may be able to specify which hotel you wish, but unless you are particularly charming to the agent, you'll probably get a standard room. If you want fancy accommodation or a single room, you may be asked to pay for this in addition to the standard tourist fee. Most hotels charge government tax at 10% and often levy a 10% or 15% service charge, but this is absorbed by the tour operator.

In Bhutan, as in many parts of the Indian subcontinent, the word 'hotel' is often used to identify a place to eat. Many small establishments in Bhutan that have signs saying 'hotel' are, in fact, restaurants and have no accommodation available.

No matter how simple the accommodation is, the room is likely to be elegantly decorated in Bhutanese style, and at first glance you may think you are being shown into a monastery, not a hotel room. Lavish use of wood for floors and panelling is the norm. Bedspreads and curtains are often made of colourful handloom material, the bedside table is of brightly painted carved wood, and there are usually paintings ranging from mediocre to exquisite.

In Thimphu and Paro there are electric heaters, and in Bumthang many hotel rooms are heated by a wood stove called a *bukhari*, which often has a pile of rocks on the top to retain the heat.

Many of the older hotels, especially those run by BTCL, have old-fashioned British

Raj-style metal teapots that burn your fingers – use a napkin when you pick them up. In several hotels the hot and cold water taps are mislabelled; check both taps before you give up and wash with cold water. In many hotels the water heaters, including those of most solar heating systems, are placed far from the rooms. You may have to run the water for a long time before hot water reaches you. If there is an electric heater (called a *geyser*) in the room, check whether it is turned on when you arrive.

Be sure that there is drinking water in your room. The flasks in hotel rooms are not always filled, and there is no assurance that the water they contain is boiled. (For details on purifying water see the boxed text 'Water Purification' in the Trekking chapter.)

Reservations
Your tour operator will arrange bookings, ideally at the hotels you desire. A confirmed hotel reservation, however, does not carry much weight in hotels as small as those in Bhutan. A large tour group can exert a powerful influence, and you may discover that there is an extended negotiation taking place between your guide and the desk clerk when you check in. Don't worry; *something* will be arranged.

Many hotels are owned and operated by tour companies. When space is tight, you might get bumped in favour of clients on a tour arranged by the company owning the hotel. The biggest chain of hotels is operated by BTCL; in many towns theirs are the only facilities approved by TAB. The listings in this book mention when a travel agency owns a particular hotel.

Stone Baths
A traditional Bhutanese stone bath is said to have health benefits in addition to its cleansing properties. The bathtub is either a wooden structure or simply a hole dug into the ground. A fire is built nearby to heat large stones, which are eventually rolled down a metal chute into the tub. A wooden grill inside the tub separates you from the heated rocks as they splash and sizzle into

the water. It's an amusing experience, and one bather commented that she came out only a little bit dirtier than when she went in.

It takes time to heat the rocks – typically two hours or more. Hotels charge extra for this luxury. At the Eye of the Tiger in Paro, the rate is Nu 800 for one person, Nu 600 per person if there are two of you and Nu 300 per person for four.

FOOD
Since travel in Bhutan is an all-inclusive package, you can expect to eat most of your meals in hotels. Most hotels cater to groups and have developed the habit of providing meals buffet-style. Even if you are alone and the only guest in a hotel, you may find a mini-buffet set up just for you. There is usually a continental dish, and sometimes an Indian, Chinese or Bhutanese dish. There is almost always rice, either white or the local red variety, and *daal* (a lentil soup). If you are in a small group, or have booked your tour directly, you can specify that you want to order from the menu, though sometimes the buffet meals offer a wider selection.

The food in hotels is often the best in town, but if you want to sample local restaurants, your guide can arrange it so that the tour operator pays for your restaurant meals. Restaurant food in Bhutan is not particularly special, and beware of local dishes with chillies. Drinks, including mineral water, are usually charged as extras and payment is collected at the end of the meal or the following morning when you check out of the hotel. If you are ordering from a menu, don't be surprised if two-thirds of the offerings are not available. In eastern Bhutan you may find that there is no meat, bread or other key item of food available in the whole town.

Meat is frequently dry and stringy. There are no slaughterhouses, and only a few cold storage facilities. Beef and fish come from India, often travelling long distances in unrefrigerated trucks. Don't eat beef during the monsoon season, and be very wary of pork at any time. During the summer you are usually limited to a chicken, or vegetarian, diet. Yak meat is sometimes available, but only in the winter.

One dish that is frequently available is *daal bhat* (rice and lentils), the traditional mainstay of Nepali meals. Hotel and trekking cooks make some excellent non-spicy dishes, such as *kewa datse* (potatoes with cheese sauce) and *shamu datse* (mushrooms with cheese sauce).

Packed Lunches

On long drives or hikes you will not return to your hotel for lunch, and most tour operators arrange packed lunches from the hotel. These tend to be an uninspired collection of sandwiches, boiled potatoes, eggs, fruit and inevitably a small carton of mango juice. You could consider a visit to a bakery for some bread or rolls and perhaps also buy some cheese or Indian biscuits to make your picnic more interesting.

There's another way to liven up the lunch, but this will also confuse everyone who is used to the standard system of handling tour groups. Since the driver and guide will probably want to stop for lunch at a place where they can eat rice, you could discuss the possibility of foregoing a packed lunch and eating in a local roadside restaurant. This is really a hit-or-miss situation; some of these are fine, and in some places they are nonexistent or dreadful. Check the road descriptions in this book to see what facilities there are on the route you plan to travel and try to avoid the restaurant in Yadi, between Mongar and Trashigang.

Local Food

All large towns have restaurants, but in smaller villages there is often no public eating facility at all. In many smaller restaurants the fare is likely to be tea and biscuits or a bowl of instant noodles.

Traditional Bhutanese food always features spicy red or green chillies. The traditional dish *ema datse* comprises large green (hot) chillies, prepared as a vegetable, not as a seasoning, in a cheese sauce. The second most popular dish is *phak sha laphu* (stewed pork with radish). Other typical dishes are *no sha huentseu* (stewed beef with spinach), *phak sha phin tshoem* (pork with rice noodles) and *bja sha maroo* (chicken in garlic and butter sauce).

Pork fat is a popular dish in the wilds because of its high energy content. Western visitors find it almost inedible because it is usually quite stale or is just fat with lumps of hairy skin attached – no meat.

Several Tibetan-style dishes are common in Bhutan. Small steamed dumplings called *momos* may be filled with meat or cheese. Fried cheese momos are a speciality of several Thimphu restaurants. Another Tibetan dish is *thukpa* (noodles), which may be fried or served in soup. Both of these are available in many small restaurants and are good to order when you want a quick meal. Village people also eat *tsampa*, the Tibetan-style dish of barley flour mixed with salt and butter tea and kneaded into a paste.

Though there is plenty of white rice, the Bhutanese prefer a locally-produced red variety, which has a slightly nutty flavour. At high altitudes where rice is not available, wheat and buckwheat are the staples. *Zow* is rice that is boiled and then fried. It's commonly carried in a *bangchung* (covered basket). In Bumthang *khule* (buckwheat pancakes) and *utta* (buckwheat noodles) replace rice as the foundation of many meals. A common snack food in the east is *gesasip*, corn (maize) that has been fried and beaten.

Be careful of Bhutanese chillies. If you bite into a bunch of hot chillies, a few mouthfuls of plain rice will often help ease the pain. Thai people have a trick of eating a spoonful of sugar, which seems to absorb some of the fiery oil.

Vegetarian

There is a good variety of vegetarian food available throughout Bhutan, although much of it is made using chillies as the primary vegetable.

Even if you are a keen carnivore, you might temporarily go vegetarian during the monsoon season because of the lack of reliable refrigeration for meat.

Paan

One of the great Bhutanese vices is *doma*, also known by its Indian name, *paan*. The centrepiece is a hard nut that is chewed as a digestive. Though the nut is called the 'betel' nut, it is actually from the *areca catechu* palm. Indians use dried nuts for their paan, but the Bhutanese prefer the nuts fresh.

The nut is mixed with lime powder (the ash, not the fruit) and the whole collection is rolled up in a heart-shaped betel leaf and chewed slowly. It's a bittersweet tasting, mildly intoxicating concoction and it stains the mouth bright red. When the remains are spat out, they leave a characteristic stain on the pavement.

There is an array of accoutrements associated with the chewing of doma that many men carry in the pouch of their gho. The ingredients are carried in ornate boxes and there are special knives designed to slice the nuts.

Worryingly however, studies in India and the US have found a direct link between the consumption of paan and submucous fibrosis (SMF), a painful disease of the mouth, for which there is no cure. Sufferers of SMF are 400 times more likely to contract oral cancer than nonsufferers. Trying paan occasionally may not cause any harm, but don't make a habit of it.

The government is trying to convince people not to chew paan but the great incidence of stained teeth you'll see in Bhutan indicates a singular lack of success.

DRINKS
Nonalcoholic Drinks

Tea & Coffee Coffee is invariably instant Nescafe. Often you will simply be presented with a cup of water, a jar of instant coffee and a spoon. Tea may be served in a pot, but more often it appears as a cup filled with hot water, with a tea bag on the saucer.

Sweet tea is called *ngad-ja* in Dzongkha. Bhutanese frequently drink *sud-ja*, tea with salt and butter in the Tibetan style, though they do not churn the tea the way the Tibetans and Sherpas do.

Water Don't drink water from a tap or flask anywhere in Bhutan. The only exception is the tap water at the Swiss Guest House in Bumthang, which has its own safety-tested spring. The flasks in hotel rooms, if they are filled at all, are sometimes filled with untreated water.

Ideally, you should drink water that has been boiled to kill the various germs in it, but few restaurants boil the drinking water they serve. You can confine yourself to hot drinks or, better yet, treat the water yourself using iodine (see the boxed text 'Water Purification' in the Trekking chapter). Water filters do not protect against some water-borne diseases, most importantly hepatitis.

Mineral Water Bottles of 'mineral water' are available in Bhutan. There's a Bhutanese brand of mineral water that is available only in Thimphu. In other towns you can find Indian water that is packaged in non-recyclable plastic bottles.

Besides the obvious absurdity of sitting alongside one of Bhutan's wild, fast-flowing rivers drinking water from Calcutta, the other reason to spurn mineral water is the disposing of huge numbers of plastic bottles throughout Bhutan's landscape.

It's also pretty well documented that many brands of Indian 'mineral water' are simply tap water that has been 'purified' by passing it through a filter and ultraviolet light system. You are far better off carrying your own water bottle and treating the contents with iodine.

Soft Drinks Indian brands of soft drinks are available throughout Bhutan. Pepsi is the most easily available, thanks to an aggressive marketing and distribution system to support their bottling plant in Phuentsholing. You can usually find colas, lemon drinks and soda water.

Excellent Bhutanese apple juice is served in hotels and restaurants. Large cans of Druk brand orange, mango, tomato and pineapple juice are available, but outside of hotels, you might have to buy the whole can. Small cartons of sweet mango juice are available throughout the country and will invariably appear in your picnic lunch.

Alcoholic Drinks

There is no beer brewed in Bhutan except for a few bottles of home-made beer in Bumthang. Other than the odd can of imported beer, you will find mostly large (650ml) bottles of Indian beer. The most popular brands in Bhutan are Black Label and Dansberg from Sikkim. There's also Danube, Golden Eagle and canned Strohs, which is produced by a US-Indian joint venture. If you want a cheap high, try one of the brands with 8% alcohol content: Strohs extra strong, Hoffstein, Black Knight or Volcano. Beer is inexpensive thanks to a strange loophole in the taxation system. In shops a 650ml bottle of Dansberg costs Nu 22, and Black Label Nu 25. Prices are higher, of course, in bars and hotels. At altitudes even as low as Thimphu beer may have a more potent effect than you are used to.

Army welfare projects have a monopoly on Bhutanese alcohol production. There are several brands of whiskey, including Special Courier, Black Mountain (which was previously known as Bhutan Mist), Royal Supreme and Changta, the cheapest. The better brands compare favourably with good Scotch whiskey. There are two local rums: XXX Bhutan Rum is the stronger, and Dragon Deluxe the next. There are also the local Crystal and Pacham gins. Most hotels also have a stock of international brands.

Whatever wine ends up for sale in Bhutan has probably had a hard journey. A bottle of wine in Bhutan is likely to be both expensive and disappointing. If you want wine with your meals, stock up at a duty free shop en route to Bhutan.

The most common local brew is *bang chhang*, a warm beer-like drink made from wheat. The favourite hard drinks are *arra*, a spirit distilled from rice, and *sinchhang*, which is made from millet, wheat or rice. *Chhang kuy* is a soupy drink made from fermented rice; it is usually regarded as a 'woman's' drink.

ENTERTAINMENT
Cinemas

There are only five cinemas in the country. Two are in Phuentsholing and one is in Thimphu. The others are in Samtse (which is an unlikely destination for tourists) and the last is a rough facility with wooden benches in Samdrup Jongkhar. All show three-hour-long Hindi films with extravagant sets and rampant singing and dancing. In Thimphu they also show one old English film daily. Cinema tickets are at a premium, with long queues, pushing and crowding involved in purchasing one.

Nightclubs

Saturday is disco night, and well-heeled Bhutanese of all ages frequent the few establishments in Thimphu and Paro that have loud music.

Pubs/Bars

The bar scene consists mostly of tiny shops with a few tables and a supply of beer and local spirits. If you poke your head into any small establishment that advertises itself as a bar, you will probably be welcomed. In towns virtually everyone speaks English and it's easy to strike up a conversation and often very rewarding.

Many bars are also carom parlours. This is a game played on a board like a small pool table with a pocket in each corner. Instead of stroking balls, the players flick checkers into the pockets. Carom is a highly competitive game, usually played with beer or money as the stakes. Cards are another common diversion; the most common card game is a very complicated one called 'marriage'.

SPECTATOR SPORT
Archery

Datse (archery) is Bhutan's national sport. See the boxed text.

Football

Football tournaments are held most summer evenings in large towns. During the national school tournament in August, Thimphu's Changlimithang Stadium is crammed with

Archery

Since time immemorial Bhutanese have been passionate about their national sport of *datse* (archery). Nearly all villages in the kingdom boast an archery range and each dzong has a space set aside nearby for a *bha cho* (field of target).

Competitions are a riot of colour and excitement, with two teams in traditional Bhutanese dress shooting at small wooden targets placed 140m apart (Olympic standard is 50m). The distance is so great that team members gather dangerously close to the target to yell back to the archer how good his aim was. This feedback is often accompanied by howls, chanting, encouragement and jokes. Members of the opposing team may shout back and tell the archer how terrible his aim is and make ribald remarks. When an arrow hits the target, the archer's team-mates perform a celebratory slow-motion dance and sing the praise of the shooter who tucks a coloured scarf into his belt.

For major tournaments each team brings its own cheerleading section of girls decked out in their finest clothes. They perform dances in between play, and during the shooting, they do brief routines and shout lewd and disparaging comments about the opposing archer's parentage or sexual prowess.

Tradition has it that women are not allowed to touch an archer's bow, and it is believed to decrease performance if an archer sleeps with a woman the night before a contest.

The traditional Bhutanese archery equipment is a long bamboo bow. Most archers nowadays use state-of-the-art carbonite Hoyt brand bows with a complicated-looking pulley system that releases the arrows with tremendous speed.

The use of imported equipment hasn't diluted the rich traditions of the game although Bhutanese archers are now encouraged to train for the Olympics. International coaches who have trained Bhutan's Olympic archers have been impressed with the natural talent and think that, with expert coaching, Bhutan could possibly win an Olympic medal one day. As *Kuensel*, the national newspaper, urges young archers, including women, 'It is time to shoot beyond participation'.

The Bhutan National Archery Federation organises two national archery tournaments a year, one with traditional bamboo bows and one open to archers using modern imported equipment. The traditional bow tournament takes place in Dechenchoeling in May.

Archery matches are among the most picturesque and colourful events you'll find here and well worth a visit. There are formal competitions on many weekends, and archers practice most afternoons and weekends when there is no competition. It's easy to find a session to watch.

spectators as teams battle it out to the cheers of hordes of schoolgirls. The season continues through the summer, from May to October – even in the heaviest downpours.

THINGS TO BUY

Bhutan boasts a variety of high-quality handicrafts. Until recently, nothing in Bhutan was made especially for sale to tourists and it was possible to find high-quality arts and crafts almost everywhere. Now there is a fair amount of tourist schlock on offer; one of the worst places for this is alongside the trail to Taktshang goemba. A few creative souvenir items, such as Dragon Kingdom T-shirts, bangchung coin purses and Bhutan flags are also available.

There are many handicraft shops in Thimphu and Paro, and most hotels have a shop selling Bhutanese crafts. As you shop, remember that it is illegal (and immoral) to export antiques. Don't get carried away. Try to visualise how an ethnic Bhutanese mask or ritual object will look in your living room at home.

Some of the items sold in Bhutan are actually made in Nepal or India; if in doubt, ask. Most shopkeepers will be honest with you, and your guide can probably offer some independent advice. There does not seem to be a racket of shops paying commissions, and you can rely on the guide for an objective opinion.

Thangkas

Thangkas are Buddhist paintings, usually on canvas. Traditionally, they are mounted on a background of brocade and hung by a stick sewn across the top. You can also buy an unmounted painting and roll it up to take home. If you buy an expensive one and don't want it damaged in your luggage, stop at a hardware shop and get a short length of plastic pipe to protect it.

Prices vary tremendously, with small paintings selling for Nu 300 to Nu 500 and large mounted mandalas starting from Nu 30,000. The price depends on size, quality of work and detail. One excellent place to buy paintings is the school of arts and crafts

in Thimphu (for an example of its craft see the colour section 'Important Figures of Drukpa Kagyu Buddhism' between pages 176 and 177). The money you pay here goes to the students to help support their training. You can be confident that any painting you buy in Bhutan was made by a local artist.

Textiles

Hand-woven cotton fabric is the most traditional and useful item you can buy in Bhutan. The quality is almost always good, but the price will vary depending on the intricacy of the design and whether any expensive imported silk is used in the weaving. Hand-woven fabric is sold in 'loom lengths' that are 30 to 45cm wide and 2.5m to 3m long. Bhutanese sew three of these lengths together to make a *gho* or *kira*. You can find handmade cloth in handicraft shops or in the Khaling handloom project in eastern Bhutan, but it may be more fun to search in ordinary fabric shops.

Indian machine-made cloth, in a variety of Bhutanese designs, is also sold at a price far lower than handmade cloth. Handwoven woollen cloth is also available.

Yathra are lengths of rough woollen cloth that can be sewn together to make sweaters, scarves or blankets. A length costs Nu 700 to Nu 1000, depending on the tightness of the weave and whether wool or cotton threads are used for the weft. Prices for a loom length vary from Nu 600 to Nu 1000. The best place to shop for yathra is in Zungney in Bumthang's Chhume valley.

Other Items

Brass statues and Buddhist ritual items, such as bells, cymbals, trumpets and *dorjis* are available from specialist shops, and you can also find ritual items at the north end of the weekend market in Thimphu.

Jewellery and other silver items are best purchased from a reputable shop or from the artisans themselves. Much of the low-priced silver work sold in Bhutan is actually made in Nepal from white metal.

If you have lots of space in your luggage, you can buy excellent carved wooden pieces.

Useful items, such as picture frames and furniture are available, as are wooden masks similar to those used in the tsechu dances. Prices vary considerably, and shipping can be a problem. Wooden bowls, either plain or lined with silver, are a speciality of eastern Bhutan.

Bamboo work is available in most of the handicraft shops and sometimes at roadside stalls. The round bangchung baskets, which some people have nicknamed Bhutanese Tupperware, are a typical Bhutanese item and you can easily stuff them into a bag or suitcase. The large baskets called *zhim* that are fastened on horses to carry gear on treks are hard to find, but a smaller version is available in many shops. Another unusual item are the large bamboo pipes covered with weaving that are used for carrying local liquor.

Handmade paper is available in large sheets and sometimes is packaged into handy packets of letter-writing size. Several local artists sell their paintings in small art galleries in Thimphu and sometimes in hotel shops.

Carpet manufacturing is a recent innovation in Bhutan. There is now a large factory in Phuentsholing and a small carpet workshop in the Phobjikha valley, but traditionally most carpets in Bhutan were imported from Tibet or Nepal. Carpets are available in most handicraft shops, and a limited supply is on hand at the workshop behind the Phunsho Chholing Guest House in Phobjikha.

Some of Bhutan's minority groups wear peculiar-looking hats, any of which make curious gifts for your friends at home. If you look carefully, you can find bamboo hats from Laya, and Brokpa yak hair and conical bamboo Bumthang hats in shops throughout Bhutan.

Traditional Bhutanese songs can be haunting, though they are monotonous. The popular songs are an interesting combination of Bhutanese, Tibetan and Indian influences, and you can find cassette tapes with recordings of classical and popular Bhutanese songs in most towns. The tapes are not high quality, but for Nu 35 to Nu 40, they provide a lingering reminder of the spirit of Bhutan.

Health & Safety

This chapter was written by Dr David R Shlim, Medical Director of the CIWEC Clinic Travel Medicine Centre, Kathmandu, Nepal. Because many people using this book will be trekking, it provides extensive advice on self-treatment.

There are no private health clinics or physicians in Bhutan. If you are ill, you must go to the hospital for treatment. In most large towns there are shops that sell medicines, and the shopkeeper may be able to give some advice, but they are not trained pharmacists. Most of the medical supplies mentioned in this chapter are available in Bhutanese pharmacies without a prescription.

Your tour operator will be able to arrange a visit to a hospital if you are in need of medical attention. There are no intensive care units in any of Bhutan's hospitals; if you are seriously ill or injured you should consider evacuation to the excellent medical facilities in Bangkok.

The best facility is the National Referral Hospital in Thimphu. It has general physicians and several specialists, labs and operating rooms. Treatment is free, even for tourists.

All district headquarters towns have a hospital, and will accept travellers in need of medical attention.

In rural Bhutan medical care is provided by Basic Health Units (BHUs) in larger villages. In more remote regions there are outreach clinics that walking health workers visit once a month to provide immunisations and distribute medicine.

Because Bhutan is a relatively uninhabited, naturally beautiful country, it can temporarily lull the visitor into thinking that it is not a developing country. The main health concerns in Bhutan are similar to those in other South Asian destinations: the relatively high risk of acquiring travellers' diarrhoea, a respiratory infection or a more exotic tropical infection. If you go trekking, there are also risks associated with accidents and altitude illness. The infectious diseases can interrupt your trip and

Everyday Health
Normal body temperature is 37°C or 98.6°F; more than 2°C (4°F) higher indicates a high fever. The normal adult pulse rate is 60 to 100 per minute (children 80 to 100, babies 100 to 140). As a general rule the pulse increases about 20 beats per minute for each 1°C (2°F) rise in fever.

Respiration (breathing) rate is also an indicator of illness. Count the number of breaths per minute: between 12 and 20 is normal for adults and older children (up to 30 for younger children, 40 for babies). People with a high fever or serious respiratory illness breathe more quickly than normal. More than 40 shallow breaths a minute may indicate pneumonia.

make you feel miserable, but they are rarely fatal. Falling off trails, or having a rock fall on you as you trek, is rare, but can happen.

The advice in this chapter reflects the fac that the various health risks in the Himalayan regions have been well defined. The risk o becoming ill, or the length of time that you trek is interrupted, can be significantly reduced by obtaining the proper immunisa tions, following preventive advice, and using this chapter to help diagnose and treat your self in the event that you become ill in the absence of medical care.

PREDEPARTURE PLANNING
Immunisations
The government of Bhutan does not check vaccination records when you enter the country. However, there are several major dis eases that can be prevented, or whose risks can be significantly decreased, by immunisations

Your doctor can refer you to a good trave medicine clinic if they do not stock the vac cines that you require. Specialised trave medicine clinics make it easier for travellers to achieve their goal of receiving all the appropriate vaccines and prophylaxis, and not receiving any that are not appropriate to their current travel objective. The following section discusses the individual products in detail, helping you to make an informed choice as to which vaccines and prophylaxis are right for you on this particular trip. Bring this chapter with you when you go to consult about your immunisations for Bhutan.

Hepatitis A Hepatitis A is a miserable disease that can be fatal on rare occasions. It almost always ends one's trip, and can lead to months of recuperation. New vaccines against hepatitis A have made it extremely easy to avoid this disease. There are currently two regimens, which are equally effective. The original regimen consists of three shots of the single-strength vaccine at zero, one month, and six months. The second regimen consists of one double-strength injection, followed by one booster between six and 12 months later. With the single-strength regimen, you need to have the second shot before you travel. With the double-strength regimen, you should have the first shot at least three weeks before you travel. Side effects are minimal, and the protection lasts for at least 10 years, and maybe longer.

Hepatitis B Hepatitis B can be a much worse infection than hepatitis A, leading to chronic liver disease, cirrhosis and death in some cases. It is acquired through contact with blood or through sexual contact. Thus there is little chance of casually acquiring this infection without exposure to contaminated needles, receiving a transfusion, or having unprotected sex. The hepatitis B vaccine is recommended for long-term travellers visiting many different countries, or for expatriates who plan to be abroad for several years. It is safe and effective with few side effects. If you anticipate doing medical work, or being sexually active with local people, this vaccine is highly recommended. The regimen for hepatitis B immunisation is a series of three shots over a six month period.

Typhoid Fever Although almost never fatal in travellers, typhoid fever makes people severely ill, and recovery may take several weeks. Three typhoid vaccines are available. The original vaccine, consisting of killed bacteria, offers a very high level of protection, but the shot itself can make people feel mildly to moderately ill for 24 to 48 hours, and two shots a month apart are necessary for complete protection. A new oral typhoid vaccine (Vivotif) has become popular owing to its lack of side effects, but it may not be as protective as the injectable vaccine. It is available in capsule form (one pill taken every other day for three or four doses). A third vaccine, called the capsular polysaccharide typhoid vaccine (Typhim Vi), is marketed by Merieux. Good protection is offered by a single injection, which has very few side effects. None of these vaccines offer 100% protection but you should feel reasonably safe using any of these products.

Polio The current generation in the west is no longer afraid of polio because vaccination has made it rare there. However, polio has not been eradicated entirely from Bhutan, and a booster for people who have been previously immunised is recommended before travelling here. Childhood polio immunisations wear off over time because there is no longer any boosting effect from exposure to wild polio virus. If you have been immunised in childhood, one booster as an adult (either oral or injectable) should be obtained before you travel to Asia. If you somehow grew up without getting immunised, you should have the injectable vaccine before you head out to Asia. Do not use the oral polio vaccine as an adult if you have never had polio vaccine in any form. You can use the oral vaccine as a booster if you have been previously immunised by either method.

Rabies This is a severe brain infection caused by a virus transmitted by animal bites, mainly from dogs. The disease is uniformly fatal once the symptoms have appeared. Therefore, every effort must be made to avoid getting the disease once you have been exposed. Modern rabies vaccine is now a highly purified substance with high effectiveness and few side effects. The drawback is that it is relatively expensive.

There are two strategies employed with the rabies vaccine. One is called pre-exposure immunisation and consists of three shots spaced over one month. These injections prime your immune system against rabies, and if you are bitten by an animal, you need two more shots, three days apart, as a booster. If you don't take the pre-exposure immunisation, and you are bitten by a potentially rabid animal, you will need the full post-exposure immunoprophylaxis, which consists of five injections spaced over one month and a single injection of rabies antibodies called human rabies immune globulin (HRIG). HRIG is often very hard to obtain, and is not available in Bhutan. If you were bitten in Bhutan and required HRIG, you would have to fly to either Bangkok or Nepal to obtain this product.

Tetanus & Diphtheria The vast majority of people from western countries receive these vaccines in childhood. The tetanus and diphtheria germs occur worldwide. You should have a booster if it has been longer than 10 years since your last one. It is especially important to ask for a tetanus booster if you are over 50 years old, as studies have shown that this population is more likely to have let their tetanus boosters lapse.

Cholera Although cholera vaccination is no longer required to enter any country in Asia, the recent spread of cholera to South America, and the emergence of new strains in Asia, have kept that disease in the limelight. Although the disease can be devastating to local populations at times, the risk of acquiring cholera as a traveller is close to zero, and the few cases have been indistinguishable from ordinary travellers' diarrhoea. Therefore, cholera vaccine, whether the old injectable vaccine or the new oral vaccine, is not necessary in Bhutan.

Japanese B Encephalitis (JE) This disease is caused by a virus transmitted by mosquitoes, with a maximum risk during the monsoon and just afterwards. The risk to travellers in Bhutan is unknown, but the location and geography of the lower areas suggest that the risk may be similar to southern Nepal and northern India. Consider vaccination against JE if you will be staying a month or more in southern lowland areas from July to December. There is no need to have the JE vaccine in order to visit the main tourist areas of Bhutan.

Yellow Fever It is a legal requirement in many countries, including Bhutan, to have this vaccination if you are coming from an infected area, eg Africa or South America, even though vaccination records are not checked. The disease does not exist in Bhutan.

Tuberculosis This disease is endemic in Bhutan. However, because infection requires continuous close contact with an infected person, tuberculosis cases are extremely rare among travellers to Bhutan. Those who are concerned about acquiring TB while travelling should have a skin test before travel; if the test is negative they can be tested after they return to see if they have been exposed to TB. Although a vaccine exists that offers some protection against TB, it gives incomplete protection, and changes the skin test to positive, making it difficult to tell if a person has actually been exposed to TB or not. We do not recommend TB vaccine for travellers to Bhutan.

Malaria Medication

There is currently no vaccine against malaria. Travellers to areas where malaria is a risk must rely on trying to prevent mosquito bites and taking prophylactic medication to try to avoid malaria infections.

In Bhutan, malaria transmission is limited to the lowland area adjoining India (the Duars) and the low valley of Punakha. Resistance to chloroquine is confirmed. There is no risk of malaria in Paro, Thimphu, or any of the main trekking areas. To my knowledge, no one has ever acquired malaria while trekking in Bhutan, but treks have been ruined by adverse reactions to antimalarial drugs not needed in the first place.

If you will be spending time in these lowland districts, you should consider taking either mefloquine (Lariam) 250mg weekly or doxycycline 100mg daily during your stay and for four weeks afterwards.

Malaria is increasing in many areas in India, including areas adjoining Bhutan. Resistant malaria has become a serious problem in certain parts of India that did not have a problem only a few years ago. If you are planning to travel to India, make sure you take malaria prophylaxis that covers resistant *Plasmodium falciparum*. India is no longer a low-key malaria risk.

Health Insurance

Make sure that you have adequate health insurance. See Travel Insurance in the Visas & Documents section of the Facts for the Visitor chapter.

Travel Health Guides

If you are planning to be away or travelling in remote areas for a long time, you should consider taking a more detailed health guide.

Staying Healthy in Asia, Africa & Latin America, Dirk Schroeder, Moon Publications, 1994. Probably the best all-round guide to carry; it's compact, detailed and well organised.

Travellers' Health, Dr Richard Dawood, Oxford University Press, 1995. Comprehensive, easy to read, authoritative and highly recommended, although it's rather large to lug around.

Where There is No Doctor, David Werner, Macmillan, 1994. This is a very detailed guide intended for someone, such as a Peace Corps worker, going to work in an underdeveloped country.

Travel with Children, Maureen Wheeler, Lonely Planet Publications, 1995. Includes advice on travel health for younger children.

There are also a number of excellent travel health sites on the Internet. From the Lonely Planet home page there are links at http://www.lonelyplanet.com/weblinks/wlp rep.htm to the World Health Organization and the US Center for Disease Control & Prevention.

If you have specific questions while preparing for your trip that are not answered in this chapter, you may find the answer at the CIWEC web site at http://www.bena. com/ciwec. The web site offers more in-depth discussion of certain health risks, and will provide updates on recent health concerns. If your question is still unanswered, you can contact CIWEC via email at advice@ciwecpc.mos.com.np for a personal answer.

Other Preparations
Make sure you're healthy before you start travelling. If you are going on a long trip make sure your teeth are OK. If you wear glasses take a spare pair and your prescription.

If you require a particular medication take an adequate supply, as it may not be available locally. Take part of the packaging showing the generic name, rather than the brand, which will make getting replacements easier. It's a good idea to have a legible prescription or letter from your doctor to show that you legally use the medication to avoid any problems.

BASIC RULES
Food
Just treating your water carefully will not eliminate the chances of eating harmful bacteria. Lapses in kitchen hygiene, such as the preparation of raw meat on the same counters as other foods, failure to wash kitchen surfaces regularly, and cooks who do not wash their hands after going to the toilet, contribute to the risk of gastrointestinal illness. Vegetables and fruits can also be contaminated from the soil they are grown in, or from handling along the way.

The general rule is to not eat any vegetables that cannot be peeled or freshly cooked unless you are certain of the methods that have been used to soak them. Many restaurants soak their vegetables in an acceptable

Nutrition
If you're travelling hard and fast and therefore missing meals, or if you simply lose your appetite, you can soon start to lose weight and place your health at risk.

Make sure your diet is well balanced. Cooked eggs, tofu, beans, lentils (daal in Bhutan) and nuts are all safe ways to get protein. Fruit you can peel (bananas, oranges or mandarins for example) is usually safe (melons can harbour bacteria in their flesh and are best avoided) and a good source of vitamins. Try to eat plenty of grains (including rice) and bread. Remember that although food is generally safer if it is cooked well, overcooked food loses much of its nutritional value. If your diet isn't well balanced or if your food intake is insufficient, it's a good idea to take vitamin and iron pills.

In hot climates make sure you drink enough – don't rely on feeling thirsty to indicate when you should drink. Not needing to urinate or small amounts of very dark yellow urine is a danger sign. Always carry a water bottle with you on long trips. Excessive sweating can lead to loss of salt and therefore muscle cramping. Salt tablets are not a good idea as a preventative, but in places where salt is not used much adding salt to food can help.

Medical Kit Check List

Consider taking a basic medical kit including:

☐ **Aspirin** or paracetamol (acetaminophen in the USA) – for pain or fever.

☐ **Antihistamine** (such as Benadryl) – useful as a decongestant for colds and allergies, to ease the itch from insect bites or stings, and to help prevent motion sickness. Antihistamines may cause sedation and interact with alcohol so care should be taken when using them; take one you know and have used before, if possible.

☐ **Antibiotics** – useful if you're travelling well off the beaten track, but they must be prescribed; carry the prescription with you.

☐ **Loperamide** (eg Imodium) or diphenoxylate (eg Lomotil) for diarrhoea; prochlorperazine (eg Stemetil) or metaclopramide (eg Maxalon) for nausea and vomiting.

☐ **Rehydration** mixture – for treatment of severe diarrhoea; particularly important for travelling with children.

☐ **Antiseptic** such as povidone-iodine (eg Betadine) – for cuts and grazes.

☐ **Multivitamins** – especially for long trips when dietary vitamin intake may be inadequate.

☐ **Calamine** lotion or aluminium sulphate spray (eg Stingose) – to ease irritation from bites or stings.

☐ **Bandages** and Band-Aids

☐ **Scissors, tweezers** and a **thermometer** (note that mercury thermometers are prohibited by airlines).

☐ **Cold** and **flu tablets** and throat lozenges. Pseudoephedrine hydrochloride (Sudafed) may be useful if flying with a cold to avoid ear damage.

☐ **Insect repellent, sunscreen, lip salve** and **water purification tablets.**

☐ **A couple of syringes,** in case you need injections in a country with medical hygiene problems. Ask your doctor for a note explaining why they have been prescribed.

manner to make them safe, but if you are not sure, don't eat them. Avoid salads.

Ice cream is available in hotels and shops in many towns. In general, it's probably best to avoid it.

It's a good idea to avoid cream-filled pastries except at the Swiss Bakery in Thimphu.

Much of Bhutan's meat (particularly beef and pork) and fish comes from India and is transported to the interior in unrefrigerated trucks, and you should avoid these products during the warm season. Most chicken served in restaurants is freshly killed and therefore safe. If you like meat, you can at least be assured that cooking meat that doesn't actually appear spoiled will kill all the harmful bacteria.

Water

Tap water is not safe to drink in Bhutan (see Water in the Drinks section in the Facts for the Visitor chapter). If you are staying in hotels, the most environmentally friendly solution is to carry a water bottle and treat water yourself with iodine. You can also ask your tour company to provide you with bottled water at meals and in your hotel room. Local Bhutan mineral water is available in Thimphu. In other towns, only Indian mineral water in non-recyclable plastic bottles is available.

Water Purification

See the boxed text 'Water Purification' in the Trekking chapter for a detailed description of the options available for purifying water, including chemical solutions and filters.

Personal Hygiene

Making a point of washing your hands frequently can also help prevent illness. The tiny amounts of water that might cling to dishes and glasses washed in untreated water are not likely to make you sick, and drying the dishes can eliminate this problem. In general, the likelihood of getting sick is related to the amount of contaminated material you ingest. You should always do your best to avoid known sources of contamination, but don't worry excessively about those areas over which you have no control.

ENVIRONMENTAL HAZARDS
Altitude Sickness
Lack of oxygen at high altitudes (over 2500m) affects most people to some extent. The effect may be mild or severe and occurs because less oxygen reaches the muscles and the brain at high altitude, requiring the heart and lungs to compensate by working harder.

Treat mild symptoms by resting at the same altitude until recovery, usually a day or two. Paracetamol or aspirin can be taken for headaches.

For detailed information see the boxed text 'Acclimatisation & Altitude Illness' in the Trekking chapter.

Fungal Infections
Fungal infections occur more commonly in hot weather and are usually found on the scalp, between the toes or fingers, in the groin and on the body (ringworm). You get ringworm (which is a fungal infection, not a worm) from infected animals or other people. Moisture encourages these infections.

To prevent fungal infections wear loose, comfortable clothes, avoid artificial fibres, wash frequently and dry carefully. If you do get an infection, wash the infected area at least daily with a disinfectant or medicated soap and water, and rinse and dry well. Apply an antifungal cream or powder like tolnaftate (Tinaderm). Try to expose the infected area to air or sunlight as much as possible and wash all towels and underwear in hot water, change them often and let them dry in the sun.

Frostbite
Frostbite refers to the freezing of extremities, including fingers, toes and nose. Signs and symptoms of frostbite include a whitish or waxy cast to the skin, or even crystals on the surface, plus itching, numbness and pain. Warm the affected areas by immersion in warm (not hot) water or with blankets or clothes, only until the skin becomes flushed. Frostbitten parts should not be rubbed. Pain and swelling are inevitable. Blisters should not be broken. Get medical attention right away.

Hypothermia
Too much cold can be just as dangerous as too much heat. If you are trekking at high altitudes or simply taking a long bus trip over mountains, particularly at night, be prepared. In Bhutan you should always be prepared for cold, wet or windy conditions even if you're just out walking or hitching.

Sunburn
In the tropics, the desert or at high altitude you can get sunburnt surprisingly quickly, even through cloud. Use a sunscreen, hat, and barrier cream for your nose and lips. Calamine lotion or Stingose are good for mild sunburn. Protect your eyes with good quality sunglasses, particularly if you will be near water, sand or snow.

MEDICAL PROBLEMS & TREATMENT
Diarrhoea
Diarrhoea is the most common illness acquired by travellers in Bhutan. Travellers' diarrhoea is simply infectious diarrhoea, acquired while travelling, usually because standards of public health and hygiene in developing countries are minimal to nonexistent. The organisms that cause diarrhoea are passed in faeces, and are acquired from eating or drinking contaminated food or water. See the earlier Basic Rules section for advice on how to avoid contaminated food and water.

Travellers' diarrhoea is often described in travel books as a mild, self-limiting disorder, for which no specific treatment is required. However, antibiotic treatment for travellers' diarrhoea has been shown to be highly effective at shortening the illness, sometimes ending it within several hours. Since travellers' diarrhoea can vary in intensity from a few loose bowel movements to severe fever, cramps, vomiting and watery diarrhoea, the decision to treat should be based on the severity of illness and the need to carry on with your travel plans. Dehydration is the main danger with any diarrhoea, particularly in children or the elderly, and fluid replacement is the most important thing to remember. The following section discusses when and how to treat your own diarrhoeal illness.

Causes The vast majority of cases of travellers' diarrhoea in Bhutan are caused by some form of bacteria. This fact makes it easier to guess what might be causing your particular case of diarrhoea. Bacteria are all susceptible to antibiotics, and thus a bacterial diarrhoea can easily be shortened by antibiotic treatment.

Bacteria causing diarrhoea include *Escherichia coli*, *Shigella*, *Campylobacter* and *Salmonella*, in decreasing order of frequency.

There are several other organisms, known collectively as protozoa, that can also cause diarrhoeal disease. The most common protozoan is *Giardia lamblia*, which accounts for about 12% of diarrhoea cases. Amoebiasis is caused by the protozoan *Entamoeba histolytica*. It accounts for only about 1% of diarrhoea in travellers although local laboratories tend to overdiagnose it. From late spring to midsummer, another protozoan called *Cyclospora* is a significant risk of diarrhoea, but this is outside the main tourist seasons.

Diarrhoea can also be caused by toxins or viruses. The toxins are waste products of certain bacteria that can grow on food and, once ingested, can cause severe intestinal symptoms, such as vomiting and diarrhoea, for six to 12 hours. This is what is known as food poisoning; no infection takes place in the intestine and treatment can only be supportive. Viruses can cause vomiting and diarrhoea, or either one alone, but only account for an estimated 5% to 10% of diarrhoea cases in Bhutan. Once again, treatment can only be supportive.

Diagnosis The most common variety of diarrhoea, bacterial diarrhoea, is characterised by the sudden onset of relatively uncomfort-able diarrhoea. Protozoal diarrhoea is characterised by the gradual onset of tolerable diarrhoea. Although these two syndromes can overlap to some extent, this is a useful way of distinguishing between the two. 'Sudden onset' means that you can usually recall the precise time of day your illness began. Patients will also report that the diarrhoea and associated symptoms were quite troublesome right from the start. In contrast, protozoal diarrhoea usually begins with just a few loose stools, making people wonder if they are getting sick. The symptoms might be two to five loose stools per day, with mild cramping and urgency as the usual accompanying symptoms. People often wait one to two weeks before seeking treatment, whereas those with bacterial diarrhoea will seek help within one to two days.

Bacterial Diarrhoea Fever, vomiting or blood in the stool can all be present, and are much more often associated with bacterial diarrhoea than with protozoal diarrhoea. Sulphurous-smelling farts and burps, thought by many to be an indication of a *Giardia* infection, are also common with bacterial infections.

Food poisoning can appear exactly like bacterial diarrhoea. However, food poisoning is usually of shorter duration (six to 12 hours), after which recovery is complete. People with bacterial diarrhoea may have vomiting and fever in the first 12 hours of their illness, but these symptoms usually subside spontaneously, leaving diarrhoea and cramps as the only persistent symptoms. The distinction between food poisoning and bacterial diarrhoea is not critical to make in the first 12 hours, since the patient can't take an antibiotic until the vomiting has stopped anyway. If all symptoms go away rapidly, no therapy is needed; if diarrhoea persists, it is likely to be a form of bacterial diarrhoea.

Bacterial diarrhoea is almost always self-limiting, varying from a few hours to over two weeks. Currently, all pathogenic bacteria that can cause diarrhoea are susceptible to a group of antibiotics known as fluoroquinolones. The two most commonly used are norfloxacin and ciprofloxacin. Treatment with a fluoroquinolone can shorten the illness to one day, and side effects are extremely rare.

The treatment doses for bacterial diarrhoea are either norfloxacin 400mg twice a day for two days, or ciprofloxacin 500mg twice a day for two days. Longer treatment is not necessary. Some studies have shown that a single dose of ciprofloxacin or norfloxacin can cure a bacterial diarrhoea. There is little difference between norfloxacin and ciprofloxacin; we prefer norfloxacin since it works very well, is less expensive, and may have slightly fewer side effects than ciprofloxacin.

Children can be treated with a liquid form of nalidixic acid (an antibiotic distantly related to the fluoroquinolones, but safe for children). The dose is 50mg, per kg of body weight, per day in three divided doses. The course should be given for three days. Children with a seizure disorder should not take this drug. An alternative is liquid azithromycin, in a single daily dose of 10mg per kg of body weight. This can also be given for just two days. Mild cases of bacterial diarrhoea do not require treatment, but if the child is obviously uncomfortable, or racing through your entire trip's supply of nappies, treatment can dramatically shorten the illness. Dehydration can occur more rapidly and more severely in children, so this issue should always be addressed.

Other antibiotics, such as sulfamethoxasole-trimethoprim (Bactrim), ampicillin, tetracycline and doxycycline are much less effective against bacterial diarrhoea in Bhutan. Bacterial resistance to these antibiotics ranges from 30% to 95%.

Protozoal Diarrhoea Protozoa are single-celled animals which inhabit the upper intestine, just beyond the stomach. When they decide it's time to move to another host, they secrete a sturdy outer coating and become a nonactive cyst. These cysts are strong enough to survive in mountain streams, in dust, and to pass through the intense stomach acid of a new host. They can be killed in water by boiling or by adding iodine.

Giardiasis *Giardia* accounts for an estimated 10% to 15% of diarrhoeal episodes in Bhutan. Once Giardia protozoa have been ingested, they begin causing symptoms after one or two weeks (not the day after a suspect meal). Upper abdominal discomfort, 'churning intestines', foul-smelling burps and farts, and on-and-off diarrhoea are the main characteristics of Giardia infections. Vomiting is rare. There is often a daily pattern of several loose stools in the morning, followed by a relatively normal day except for the occasional urgent bowel movement. Often people have symptoms for weeks or months or more before deciding to seek treatment because it is not very severe each day, and they hope it will go away.

The best treatment for giardiasis is tinidazole, which is available in Bhutan without prescription. The dose is 2g as a single dose each day for two consecutive days. Side effects of tinidazole include mild nausea, fatigue and a metallic taste in the mouth. Tinidazole cannot be taken with alcohol. An alternative is albenazole (400mg) once a day for seven days. This drug has very few side effects.

Amoebiasis The term amoebiasis refers to an infection with a specific type of amoeba known as *Entamoeba histolytica*. A person with amoebiasis will commonly have several weeks of low-grade diarrhoea, alternating every few days with either normal stool or constipation. Very rarely, a person with *E histolytica* infection will have the symptoms of classic amoebic dysentery: frequent passage of small amounts of bloody, mucoid stool, associated with cramps and painful bowel movements.

E histolytica infection is treated easily with 2g of tinidazole per day for three consecutive days, followed by 500mg of diloxanide furoate (furamide) three times a day for 10 days. However, diloxanide furoate may not be readily available in Bhutan. This follow-up treatment does not have to be taken immediately after the tinidazole, but should be obtained within two to three weeks of initial treatment, if possible. This regimen is highly effective and well tolerated. In the USA, tinidazole is not available, and metronidazole is used at a dose of 750mg three times a day for 10 days.

Cyclospora This organism infects the upper intestine, causing diarrhoea, fatigue and loss of appetite. The illness lasts from two to 12 weeks, averaging six weeks. The risk of Cyclospora in Bhutan is unknown, but in neighbouring Nepal, Cyclospora is a risk mainly from May to September, which is outside the main trekking seasons, so most trekkers are not at risk. It has been shown to be water borne; iodine does not kill it but it is easily killed by boiling and can be filtered by most water filters. The treatment for Cyclospora diarrhoea is trimethoprim-sulfamethoxazole (Bactrim DS) taken twice a day for seven days. This is a sulphur drug, and cannot be taken by people allergic to sulphur.

Treatment See under the individual entries earlier for details of antibiotic treatment for diarrhoeal diseases.

Supportive Care Diarrhoea can result in the loss of a great deal of fluid from the body, and much of the ill feeling associated with diarrhoea (weakness, dizziness) occurs as a result of dehydration. Under all circumstances *fluid replacement* (at least equal to the volume being lost) is the most important thing to remember. Weak black tea with a little sugar, soda water, or soft drinks allowed to go flat and diluted 50% with clean water are all good. Oral rehydration solution (ORS), a mixture of sugars and salt that is easily absorbed by the intestines, is important when vomiting is present, limiting the amount of fluid intake, and for severe diarrhoea. ORS is also very important in the care of diarrhoea in infants, who can lose proportionally more water in a shorter period of time than adults. In an emergency you can make up a solution of six teaspoons of sugar and a half-teaspoon of salt to a litre of clean water. In adults, allow the person to drink whatever fluids seem palatable at the time. ORS solutions often taste salty, and may actually limit the amount of fluid taken in if this is the only liquid allowed. Urine is the best guide to the adequacy of replacement: if you have small amounts of concentrated urine, you need to drink more. The best approach to rehydration is to take frequent small sips of fluid.

Much has been written about specific dietary approaches to diarrhoea, but there is no scientific evidence to support any one view. Some people believe that not eating for a while will improve diarrhoea, while others suggest specific foods such as bananas, dry toast or yoghurt. However, none of these ideas have been tested. If you are not hungry, you should not force yourself to eat, but should continue to drink fluids. If you're hungry, it is OK to eat foods that appeal to you as long as you initially avoid greasy or spicy foods.

When you have diarrhoea there is an exaggeration of the gastro-colic reflex, which means that when you put food in your stomach, it immediately causes your intestines to contract, resulting in cramps and more diarrhoea. This reflex is not harmful, nor will it make whatever caused your diarrhoea worse. Once the initial cramps or diarrhoeal episode pass, it is often possible to finish eating your meal.

Antimotility Drugs Antimotility drugs, such as diphenoxylate hydrochloride (Lomotil) or loperamide (Imodium) can be used to control the symptoms of diarrhoea until the self-limited infection runs its course. However, care should be taken with these drugs as prolongation of symptoms in people who have invasive bacterial diarrhoea is a major risk. Also, use of these drugs may cause distended bowel, increased discomfort and prolonged constipation. CIWEC Clinic Travel Medicine Centre recommends that diarrhoea severe enough to make you think about an antimotility agent should be treated with an antibiotic. An antimotility drug should be used when travel is required before the antibiotic can bring the infection under control. What else can you do when you wake up at 5 am with severe diarrhoea and have to ride a bus for the next 12 hours?

Vomiting

Vomiting associated with bacterial diarrhoea is a potentially serious problem, since it adds to dehydration and hinders efforts at rehydration. We have never seen severe dehydration in adults who had diarrhoea without vomiting. Vomiting almost always occurs at the beginning of bacterial diarrhoea, and usually lasts six to 12 hours. Rarely, vomiting and diarrhoea persist together for four or five days, resulting in individuals who are dehydrated. In this situation, they often have to be helicoptered out of the Himalaya in this condition.

Vomiting also means you can't take an oral antibiotic to shorten the infection. There are currently no injectable drugs known to shorten the course of bacterial diarrhoea. The only option is to try treatment with an anti-vomiting drug until the person can take an oral antibiotic, such as norfloxacin. In our experience, however, it is almost impossible to stop the vomiting associated with bacterial diarrhoea by injecting an anti-vomiting agent. Anti-vomiting therapy appears to work most effectively if given just as the repeated, spontaneous vomiting is stopping. An injection of promethazine, or prochlorperazine, or a suppository of either drug, can eliminate the threat of further vomiting, allowing norfloxacin to be taken, which will then shorten the diarrhoeal illness dramatically. You could also try an oral anti-vomiting agent at this point.

Upper Respiratory Tract Infections

Colds Upper respiratory tract infection almost always begins as a virus (the common cold). The symptoms consist of some combination of runny nose, congestion, sore throat and cough. The viruses can be picked up on aeroplanes, crowded buses and trains, in restaurants, or any place where you might encounter people with colds. Under normal circumstances the cold should last three to seven days and go away by itself. However, under the stress of travel, and particularly trekking, colds can be complicated by bacterial infection. The viruses break down the defensive barriers in the lining of your nose, throat and lungs, allowing the normal bacteria that are living there to become invasive. This can result in ear infections, sinus infections or bronchitis (chest infection). Severe colds can result in missed treks and missed goals on a trek. Knowing how to recognise and treat the complications of a cold appropriately can save you many days of misery, and help preserve your long-established trekking plans.

Sinus Infection Sinus infection (Sinusitis) is the most common complication of a cold. The sinuses are hollow spaces in the bones of the face that connect to little holes in the back of the nose. Viruses can travel from the nose to the sinuses, causing inflammation which can allow bacteria to invade. Symptoms of sinusitis include pressure or pain around the sinuses, and thick yellow and green mucus from your nose. Finding small amounts of blood when you blow your nose is also common. As the infection goes on, you may lose your appetite and feel much more tired than usual.

There may be no clear-cut division between your initial cold symptoms and the sinus infection. Many people come to us with a 'cold' that simply hasn't gone away after two or three weeks. This is how sinus infections most commonly present. Any cold that is either not getting better, or getting worse, after seven to 10 days should be considered a possible sinus infection, and you should think about taking an appropriate antibiotic. Some of these prolonged infections will eventually clear up on their own, but an antibiotic will make them better within days. A new antibiotic, azithromycin 250mg, has the advantage of once a day dosing for five days. A good alternative is cephalexin 500mg four times a day for 10 days (if you are not allergic to penicillin).

Bronchitis & Pneumonia Bronchitis is the second-most common complication of a cold. Bronchitis is an infection of the breathing tubes in the lungs. The symptoms are a progressively worse cough, accompanied by the production of greenish or yellowish mucus when you cough. Bronchitis is similar to sinusitis in that there may not be a clear point in time at which your viral cold becomes a bacterial bronchitis. Seven to 10 days is long enough to wait before thinking of treating a cough that is not getting any better on its own. The same drugs recommended for sinusitis are good treatment for bronchitis as well, and the two infections often occur at the same time.

A deep cough accompanied by high fever may represent pneumonia (an infection of the lung tissue itself). The same antibiotics can be used, but you may be quite sick with pneumonia and should seek professional medical attention.

Inner Ear Infection The third common complication of a cold is an inner ear infection (otitis media). This type of infection is very common in young children. The infection is uncommon in adults, but seems to be more common in adult travellers. A cold is almost always present for several days, followed by the sudden onset of severe ear pain, usually in only one ear. If medical care is not available, you can treat yourself with any of the antibiotics used to treat sinusitis or bronchitis (see previous sections).

Fever
Fever means an elevation in body temperature. Normal body temperature is usually 37°C (98.6°F). Fever almost always means that you have acquired some kind of infectious disease. By itself, it does not tell you the cause, but by evaluating the associated symptoms and the travel history, you can often make a good guess, even while trekking in a remote area. Some fever-related illnesses go away without treatment (eg the flu), while others require treatment (eg typhoid fever). The purpose of trying to guess the cause of a fever is to determine

whether specific treatment will be of benefit, and whether the trek should be abandoned.

If specific symptoms are associated with a fever, the cause can usually be determined. If it is associated with the onset of severe diarrhoea and fever, a bacterial dysentery can be suspected. If you have fever together with a thick or colourful nasal discharge and sinus pain, sinusitis may be present. Fever with a severe cough may be bronchitis or pneumonia. A large abscess in the skin can also cause a fever.

Sometimes a fever occurs with only a vague feeling of being unwell, such as headache, fatigue, loss of appetite, or nausea. In the first few days of such an illness it is difficult to determine the cause of the fever. In South Asia, however, there are six main diseases which account for almost all the presentations of fever with headache and malaise. By taking a careful history and noticing key aspects of the fever and headache, a presumptive diagnosis can often be made. The six diseases are as follows:

Viral Syndromes The circumstances of travel bring exposure to many more viruses than one would encounter at home. Influenza viruses can be passed through respiratory droplets, which means they can be inhaled in aeroplanes, buses and crowded restaurants. The disease usually has an abrupt onset of fever, often very high (40°C) on the first day. A headache is often present, and is typically very motion-sensitive, which means it hurts to turn the head suddenly or to step down hard. The illness usually lasts two to four days and goes away without specific treatment. It usually ends abruptly, the fever and headache staying for the duration of the illness. The pointers to a viral infection are the abrupt onset, the characteristic motion-sensitive headache, and the fact that it goes away just about the time that you are getting worried that it might not.

Enteric Fever Enteric fever is an infection with one of two specific bacteria, *Salmonella typhi* (typhoid fever) or *Salmonella paratyphi* (paratyphoid fever). The bacteria are passed in the stools of infected people. The same precautions that one follows to prevent diarrhoea will help to prevent enteric fever. Any of the three typhoid vaccines (see Immunisations earlier) can significantly reduce, but not eliminate, your chances of getting enteric fever. So don't think that because you took a typhoid vaccine that you can't get enteric fever.

The illness begins with the gradual onset of fever, headache and fatigue. For the first few days the fever is often low, and it is hard to tell if you are really getting sick or not. After three or four days, the fever rises to 40°C or more, and fatigue begins to be profound, although some people have milder cases. The headache is typically dull and not motion-sensitive. Loss of appetite, nausea, and even vomiting can develop as well as poor concentration. Overall, after four or five days, the patient feels very weak, moves slowly, and doesn't want to eat. The disease can be distinguished from the viral illnesses by its gradual onset, the dull character of the headache, and the fact that the person is getting worse at a time when the viral patient should be getting better.

Enteric fever is one of the treatable causes of prolonged fever. If suspected, treatment should be started while trekking, since the person will remain sick for up to a month without treatment, and complications can result. The treatment for adults is ciprofloxacin (500mg) every 12 hours for 10 days. In children under 18, the drug of choice is amoxicillin in high doses: 50mg per kg per day in three divided doses. For a 40kg child, this would be 50 x 40 = 2000mg per day divided by three, or 667mg every eight hours. This can safely be rounded down to 500mg every eight hours. Some cases of enteric fever will be resistant to amoxicillin, in which case the only alternative would be ciprofloxacin. This should be given to a child only under the guidance of a physician, as the safety of ciprofloxacin in children is not fully established.

The response to treatment is slow but steady, with the fever persisting for another two to five days. You can tell that the treatment is working because the patient starts to feel better, and the height of the fever is a little bit lower each day until it is gone. The infected person is only contagious through his or her stool, and does not need to be isolated from the group. Since the disease produces such profound fatigue and malaise, the person almost always has to abandon their trek.

Hepatitis A Hepatitis A is a viral infection of the liver which is acquired by eating something contaminated with stool from an infected person. There are three main viruses which can cause hepatitis in Bhutan: hepatitis A and hepatitis E are passed in stool, while hepatitis B is only spread by blood or sexual contact. Hepatitis A can be prevented by vaccination (see Immunisations earlier). If you get sick with fever, headache and nausea, and you have been immunised against hepatitis A, you can basically rule it out as the cause. Hepatitis E is an illness very similar to hepatitis A, and there is currently no way to immunise against this virus. Very few travellers, however, get hepatitis E.

The incubation period of hepatitis is usually four weeks. Shorter periods have been noticed, but they are unusual. If you have travelled for a few months, and have not taken any protection against hepatitis A, then you must consider the diagnosis. Hepatitis A starts with the gradual onset of fever, headache, nausea and loss of appetite. The nausea and loss of appetite are often more pronounced than in the other illnesses. The headache is slightly motion-sensitive, but is usually dull. These symptoms go on for four or five days. At this point the urine turns a dark tea colour, and the whites of the eyes appear yellow (this colour change is called jaundice). The fever ends at this point; nausea, fatigue and loss of appetite are now the main symptoms and can go on for two weeks to a month.

There is no specific treatment to shorten the illness, and the trek (and usually the whole trip) is finished at this point. The person should be encouraged to drink to prevent dehydration, and to eat and drink whatever they can stomach (except alcohol) to avoid profound weight loss. The bright side is that illness with hepatitis A does confer lifelong immunity to the disease.

The main clues to hepatitis A infection are at least a month of travel in developing countries; no history of immunisation or prophylaxis against hepatitis A; relatively gradual onset of fever, nausea and loss of appetite; and the abrupt end of fever when the jaundice becomes apparent.

Malaria Malaria is a disease caused by a protozoan parasite which is transmitted between humans by certain species of mosquito. There are four types of malaria, but two types, *Plasmodium falciparum* malaria and *P vivax* malaria account for 90% of all cases worldwide. *P falciparum* malaria is the most severe form of malaria, and can occasionally be rapidly fatal. It also tends to rapidly become resistant to drugs. Malaria can be prevented in most cases by taking appropriate prophylactic drugs and trying to avoid mosquito bites in endemic areas; see the section on Malaria Medication earlier. The risk of malaria in the normal tourist areas in Bhutan is nonexistent. However, the lowland districts of Bhutan have a known malaria risk throughout the year. If you have been travelling in a malaria endemic area before you trek, then malaria could begin while you are in a remote mountain area. This has happened a number of times among trekkers.

The clues to a malaria infection are travel in an endemic area without prophylaxis (or in a *Plasmodium falciparum* area that might be resistant), and the abrupt onset of chills followed by high fever and sweats. The initial bout resolves in several hours, leaving the person feeling remarkably well between episodes of illness. A return bout of the symptoms in one to two days is the clue that malaria might be present. Steady fever can also occasionally be a symptom of malaria, and a blood test might eventually be necessary to make the diagnosis. Only self treat if you do not have access to medical services.

The incubation period is usually a minimum of two weeks, but it can stretch to several months or a year or more in the case of *P vivax* malaria, so if someone has malaria symptoms, check their travel history.

The treatment of malaria is complicated by the fact that *P falciparum* can be highly resistant to the usual drugs, and it is difficult to tell which form of malaria you might have without a blood test by a highly experienced technician. If you suspect malaria, try to have a smear done at a local health post before treatment. Then begin treatment with fansidar by taking three pills all at once. If it is available, also start taking doxycycline (100mg) twice a day for seven days; if not, fansidar alone should be sufficient. Bring your blood smear back with you to a reliable medical centre to see if the diagnosis can be confirmed. If you have *P vivax* malaria, you will need a follow-up course of primaquine as well.

Dengue Fever Dengue fever is caused by a virus carried by a mosquito which tends to favour urban environments. It is endemic in northern India, particularly during the month of October. The disease is not known to exist in the upper parts of Bhutan. Whether there is a risk of dengue fever in the lowlands is not known.

The disease has a very predictable incubation period, from three to 10 days. Thus, if the person has not been in an endemic area within the past 10 days, the disease is not possible. Exposure in transit in Delhi or Bangkok, however, can be a risk for the disease.

Dengue fever has very typical symptoms which can allow the diagnosis to be made presumptively in most cases. The onset is very abrupt, with high fever on the first day. Headache is almost always present, centred behind the eyes, and movement of the eyes exacerbates the pain. Muscle aches and backaches are more prominent than in the other diseases discussed here. The nickname for the disease is 'breakbone fever'. Nausea and vomiting can be present. A characteristic rash is almost always present, but is not seen unless looked for. The rash is a continuous faint reddening of the skin on the trunk, which resembles a light sunburn. If you press your hand flat against the stomach or back for a few seconds, and then remove it, the skin will blanch white from the pressure and preserve the imprint of the hand for a few seconds. This blanching effect lasts only a half-second or so on normal skin.

There is no treatment for the disease, but making the diagnosis allows you not to start treatment for some other disease, or to panic. Note that aspirin should be avoided. The fever lasts from three to six days, then goes away suddenly, along with all the other symptoms. Most people feel weak for an additional one to two weeks, but some recover quite quickly.

Dengue fever can progress to a more severe form, dengue haemorrhagic fever, which has a high mortality, but it is rare among travellers.

Other Diseases

Rabies All mammals are thought to be capable of carrying and passing on rabies. Dogs are the most common transmitter of rabies virus to humans, but the virus has been passed by cats, monkeys, cows, horses, raccoons, foxes, bats and skunks among others. Although rodents are generally thought not to become rabid, it is not certain that they cannot transmit rabies. Bhutan is considered to be highly endemic for rabies, mainly in the dog population. Although rodent bites are thought to be low risk, we recommend rabies treatment for rodent bites acquired in Bhutan.

Dogs infected with rabies may not show any signs of illness at the time you are bitten. However, all infected dogs who had rabies virus in their saliva at the time they bit you will go on to show signs of brain infection within seven to 10 days. The bottom line is that if you receive a bite or a scratch from an animal in Bhutan, and the animal is not a closely observable pet, you will need to seek post-exposure rabies immunoprophylaxis. You should try to obtain these shots as soon as possible after the incident, but it is not necessary to try to find a doctor in the middle of the night.

There are many acceptable rabies vaccines available in Asia. The two most common are purified vero cell rabies vaccine (Verorab), and purified check embryo cell vaccine (Rabipur). These can be interchanged during a series of injections. Human rabies immune globulin is required to treat an animal bite in someone who is not pre-immunised for rabies (see Immunisations earlier). This product is not available in Bhutan, but is available in Bangkok, and in Kathmandu (from the CIWEC Clinic Travel Medicine Centre).

Conjunctivitis Conjunctivitis is a bacterial or viral infection of the pink lining around the eye (the conjunctivae). Signs of conjunctivitis include a slightly swollen eye with increased redness in the pink areas, and occasionally some redness in the white part of the eye. Usually there is some sticky material around the eye that you can wash away in the morning. Although it can be painful, it is more of a nuisance than anything else. Antibiotic eye drops can clear up bacterial infections within a day or so. Viral infections will clear themselves in a few days as well. Most of the infections seem to be bacterial, so using antibiotic eye drops makes sense. The infection almost always starts in one eye, but can spread to the other eye. Use the drops frequently on the first day, every two to three hours. As the infection improves, you can use the drops less often, and then stop as soon as the eye seems normal (usually two to three days).

If the eye is severely painful, or the white part of the eye is very red, or your vision is impaired, seek medical help from an eye specialist. There are a few eye conditions which travellers occasionally get that require specialised diagnosis and treatment, such as uveitis, or herpes virus infections of the cornea.

Gastritis The stomach and upper intestine are usually reasonably resistant to the normal stomach acid that aids in digestion.

However, raw areas in the stomach lining or intestinal lining can develop, and these raw areas are very sensitive to acid, much as an abrasion on your skin would be more sensitive to acid than your intact skin would be. If these raw areas are in your stomach, we call the illness 'gastritis'. If the raw area is in the intestine beyond the stomach we more often call it an 'ulcer'. The main symptoms of gastritis or an ulcer are burning pain in the upper part of the stomach. In the beginning it can be intermittent, either when your stomach is quite empty, or sometimes right after you eat. If you develop a consistent pattern of burning upper abdominal pain while trekking, you can treat it either with antacid pills or liquid, which soak up the acid in your stomach, or more effectively, with an acid-blocking medication which stops the stomach from making acid. The two most commonly used acid-blocking medications are cimetidine and ranitidine. If you have any history of ulcer or gastritis, it would be a good idea to carry some of these medicines with you on a trek, just in case your symptoms are stirred up by the combination of new organisms, stress and diet.

Skin Diseases Skin problems are common in travellers. Travellers generally are bothered by one of four major problems: allergic reactions, bacterial skin infections, fungal infections and skin mites (scabies).

A generalised rash due to an allergic reaction consists of raised red spots in a variety of locations, often symmetrical on both sides of the body. You can also get slightly raised flat red lesions called urticaria (hives) that come and go relatively rapidly over a period of time. These rashes are usually caused by a new medicine, a new vaccine, or a new food. However, in many instances, it is impossible to figure out just what triggered the rash. Travellers are often taking new medications for the first time and may discover that they have an allergy to one of these new drugs. In general, a rash scattered over most of the body is due to something taken internally, and not to something that you touched with your skin. The rash can be treated with

antihistamines in mild cases, or corticosteroids in more severe cases.

A painful, red swelling that worsens is probably a bacterial skin infection. Staphylococcal infections that cause boils are common in travellers and account for about two-thirds of the skin problems in our clinic. If the boil is tense and painful, it may need to be opened and drained by a physician. Antibiotics are necessary to get rid of the infection. Cephalexin (dose: 500mg 4 times daily for 10 days) is the best choice (if you are not allergic to penicillin).

A round red patch, clearing in the centre and advancing at its edges, is usually a fungus and can be treated with an antifungal cream. These lesions can also occur in the groin and in the armpits. They are not painful, and do not cause swelling of the skin around the lesion.

Small, very itchy red spots, usually seen in clusters or in small straight lines, suggest an infestation with a tiny skin mite, causing a disease called 'scabies'. This is relatively common in travellers, and is treated by a skin cream rubbed onto the whole body and left on for one day.

Many other skin conditions can arise, but we can't list them all here. Just remember that skin conditions (such as psoriasis, eczema and allergic dermatitis) that could have occurred at home can coincidentally occur while travelling. You need to consider whether it's travel-related or not.

Sexually Transmitted Diseases

Most of the STDs that we used to worry about have become minor concerns in the face of the very real threat of acquiring HIV infections (AIDS) from casual sexual contact.

Travellers often behave as if the time that they spend travelling is not part of their 'real' life. Those looking for adventure may be looser with their sexual behaviour than when they are at home. They may be lonely after prolonged travel, or just in search of new thrills. The new sexual partner might be another traveller, a local man or woman, or a prostitute. Any of these people could be a source of an STD. Apart from abstinence, the only sure way of minimising the chances of contracting STDs is to use condoms.

Sores, blisters or rashes around the genitals, discharges or pain when urinating are common symptoms of gonorrhoea, herpes and syphilis. In some STDs, such as genital warts and chlamydia, symptoms may be less marked or not observed at all in women. Syphilis symptoms eventually disappear completely but the disease continues and can cause severe problems in later years.

HIV & AIDS

HIV, the Human Immunodeficiency Virus, develops into AIDS, Acquired Immune Deficiency Syndrome, which is a fatal disease. HIV is a major problem in many countries. Any exposure to blood, blood products or body fluids may put the individual at risk. The disease is often transmitted through sexual contact or dirty needles – vaccinations, acupuncture, tattooing and body piercing can be potentially as dangerous as intravenous drug use.

AIDS can also be spread by infected needles and by blood transfusion. Insist on brand-new disposable needles and syringes for injections. These can be purchased from local pharmacies. Blood screening for AIDS has been introduced in most Asian countries, but can't always be done in an emergency.

Fear of HIV infection should never preclude treatment for a serious medical condition.

WOMEN'S HEALTH
Vaginitis

Yeast vaginitis, often known as thrush, is an uncomfortable irritation and itching of the vagina due to an overgrowth of yeast. There is often an increased vaginal discharge. Taking antibiotics can sometimes initiate a yeast infection. The risk of developing vaginitis while trekking is large enough that all women should carry with them an appropriate treatment. Definitive treatment is with an antifungal cream or pessary, such as miconazole or clotrimazole. A new oral medication, taken as a single dose, is also available, but can have side effects. If the symptoms don't clear up promptly you should try to see a doctor if you can.

Amenorrhoea

Some women travellers note that their periods stop for a while, or become irregular. This may be associated somehow with the stress of travel. Your periods will return to normal after a while. Pregnancy is the other main reason that travellers might stop having periods, so be sure to check for this possibility if you have been sexually active.

Urinary Tract Infection

The urinary tract is usually free from bacteria. In women, the short tube from the bladder to the outside (the urethra) can allow bacteria to invade from the vagina. An infection called cystitis (inflammation of the bladder) can result. The symptoms are burning on urination and having to urinate frequently and urgently. Blood can sometimes be seen in the urine. There is usually no fever unless the infection has spread to the kidneys. Sexual activity with a new partner, or with an old partner who has been away for a while, can trigger an infection, probably from the trauma of sexual intercourse. Symptoms of cystitis should be treated with an antibiotic because a simple infection can spread to the kidneys, causing a more severe illness. The best choice of antibiotic is either norfloxacin (400mg) or ciprofloxacin (500mg), taken twice a day for three days. Commonly used antibiotics for urinary tract infections, such as Bactrim and amoxicillin, are not as effective in South Asia due to widespread resistance to these two antibiotics, but are better than nothing.

Pregnancy

Although not much is known about the possible adverse effects of altitude on a developing foetus, almost all authorities recommend not travelling above 3650m while pregnant. In addition to altitude, there is the constant risk of getting ill, and not being free to take most medications to relieve either the symptoms or the disease. There's no evidence that travel increases the risk of miscarriage, but one in five pregnancies ends in miscarriage in any case, sometimes accompanied by profound bleeding which might require emergency treatment and could put you at risk of requiring a blood transfusion.

Most vaccinations can be given safely during pregnancy, but the actual effects of all immunisations during pregnancy are not known.

There are certainly examples of successful travel while pregnant. But since the outcome of pregnancy is always in doubt, you should be careful about exposures to altitude, infectious diseases or trauma while pregnant.

Getting There & Away

There are only two entry points to Bhutan open to foreigners. Most travellers arrive by air at Bhutan's only international airport in Paro. The alternative is to travel through the Indian state of West Bengal and enter Bhutan by road at Phuentsholing on the southern border of Bhutan. If you make special arrangements you may be allowed to exit (but not enter) Bhutan via Samdrup Jongkhar in the east of the country. In any event, you are required to fly in one direction using Druk Air, the national carrier.

AIR

Druk Air operates a fleet of two BAe 146-100 four-engine jet aircraft with 72 (10 business class and 62 economy class) seats each. The schedule changes frequently, but normally there are two flights per week from New Delhi (via Kathmandu) and four flights a week from Bangkok via Dhaka, Calcutta or Yangon, depending on the day of the week. To accommodate extra visitors to the Thimphu tsechu festival in October and the Paro tsechu in April the airline adds extra flights and schedules are shuffled.

Double-check the Druk Air schedule with your tour operator a few weeks before departure to ensure that the schedule has not changed, and reconfirm your flight time the day before your departure. Druk Air is quite good about announcing schedule changes at least a week in advance in *Kuensel,* the local newspaper. However, you should check in early for a Druk Air flight as they occasionally depart before the scheduled time.

Druk Air schedules are very different during summer and winter. In summer, flights depart earlier, while it is still cool. High temperatures reduce engine power, so in hot weather, the aircraft can take less weight and scheduled passengers must be offloaded. Between mid-February and mid-May high afternoon winds in the Paro valley make landing difficult, and schedules are rearranged (particularly from Kathmandu).

Because of the elevation of Paro airport (2235m), the range of the aircraft is severely limited when carrying a full load. Therefore all flights to and from Bangkok make an intermediate stop to take on enough fuel to return in case cloud cover prevents a landing in Paro. When this happens (about 10 times a year) there is no charge for the unscheduled tour of Bagdogra or Calcutta. Druk Air flights are all no-smoking.

Visitors, or your tour operator, must obtain a 'visa clearance' from the Ministry of Foreign Affairs in Thimphu before Druk Air is allowed to issue tickets. When the visa is authorised, the information is entered into the computer record for your reservation. Druk Air will issue your ticket once it receives this number. For this reason, tickets for a flight to Paro cannot be issued along with your other international air tickets.

Connections

Druk Air has no interline agreements with other carriers. Because you have a separate ticket for your Druk Air flight, you cannot check your baggage via a connecting flight. When travelling to Paro, you will need to reclaim your baggage and re-check it at the Druk Air counter. Similarly, when you depart from Bhutan, you can only check baggage as far as you are travelling with Druk Air, not all the way through to your final destination.

Paro Airport

All landings and takeoffs in Paro are by visual flight rules (VFR), which means the pilot must be able to see the runway before landing, and the surrounding hills before takeoff. No flights can be operated at night or in poor visibility. When Paro valley is socked-in, flights are delayed, sometimes for a few days. The record is three days waiting for weather to clear. When this happens, your tour programme will have to be changed and everything rebooked. The upside of such a delay is that you can probably put some spontaneity into your schedule in Bhutan and make a few modifications as you go, depending on what you find interesting.

A large new terminal complex should be open sometime in 1999.

On Arrival

Be sure you have US$20 and two photos with your passport number written on the back. The first task when you arrive is to queue at the visa counter where the clerk will miraculously find your clearance and issue your visa. It's then like any normal airport arrival. You get your passport stamped, change money, and clear customs. On the customs form you should list any expensive items like cameras. Don't lose the form; you'll need it when you leave.

Druk Air Fares

Because there is no competition with other airlines for flights to Paro, Druk Air fares are expensive. There are no discounts or student fares except for citizens of Bhutan. The Druk Air rules say that if fares are increased after the ticket is issued, they may collect the difference when you check in. This is an unlikely scenario given the close controls on the issuance of tickets. One-way fares to Paro in US dollars are:

From	Economy	Business
Bangkok	$329	$395
Calcutta	$165	$200
Dhaka	$175	$210
Delhi	$286	$345
Kathmandu	$175	$210
Yangon	$286	$345

Druk Air Offices & Agents

Bangladesh
Vantage Tours & Travels (☎ 2-811641 – ext 4946, 326920, 323986, airport 891066), L-270 Office Arcade, Sonargaon Hotel, Dhaka

India
Indo-Japan Air Services (☎ 11-331 0990, 332 3174, airport 565 3207; fax 332 0586), Chandralok 36, Janpath, New Delhi 110 001
Druk Air Corporation (☎ 33-240 2419, airport 569976; fax 247 0050), 51 Tivoli Court, 1A Ballygunge Circular Rd, Calcutta

Nepal
Shambala Travels & Tours (☎ 1-225166, 239810; fax 227229), Durbar Marg, PO Box 4794, Kathmandu

Thailand
Druk Air Corporation (☎ 2-535 1960; fax 535 3661), Room 3232, Central Block, Bangkok International Airport
Oriole Travel & Tours (☎ 02-237 9201; 237 9200), Skulthai Surawong Tower, 141 Surawong Rd, Bangkrak, Bangkok 10500

Thai International has the ability to issue tickets on Druk Air; their Bangkok offices know how to do this, but most of their overseas offices are not familiar with the procedures. Druk's computer system in Thimphu is not linked to the international airline network, so reservations must be confirmed manually. Once your Bhutan agent has confirmed the flight and the visa authority has been issued, allow another week for the reservation information to make its way to Thai's computers. You'll probably still have to communicate several times with your agent in Thimphu to get Druk Air to send a confirmation message to Thai International.

You can check Druk Air's schedules on their Web site at www.drukair.com. The airline also has a relationship with Aviation & Tourism International, a worldwide network of travel agents.

Many overseas agents that arrange groups to Bhutan have the tickets issued in Bangkok or Delhi. A local representative waits at the Druk Air counter to deliver the tickets and check you in for your flight. If you are not on a group package, you may have to spend a day in Bangkok or Delhi in order to purchase a Druk Air ticket. If you have booked directly with a Bhutan tour operator, you can avoid this delay by sending payment for the airfare directly to the agent in Thimphu as a separate bank transfer, not as part of the payment you make for the tour. The agent can then issue the Paro ticket and mail it to you.

The Flight from Kathmandu to Paro

The Druk Air flight from Kathmandu to Paro provides the most dramatic view of Himalayan scenery of any scheduled flight (get a window seat on the left if you can). After the plane climbs out of the Kathmandu valley a continual chain of peaks appears just off the left wing. The captain usually points out Everest (a black pyramid), Makalu (a grey chair-shaped peak) and Kanchenjunga (a huge massif), but if you have trekked in Nepal and are familiar with the mountains you can pick out many more. The elusive Shishapangma (8013m) is visible inside Tibet. Other easily recognisable peaks are the notched shape of Gauri Shankar (7185m), Cho Oyu (8153m), the long ridge of Nuptse (7906m), Lhotse (8501m) and the huge mass of Chamlang (7319m). With a sharp eye, you can even spot Lukla airstrip and the town of Namche Bazaar at the foot of Khumbila (5761m).

As you pass Kanchenjunga, look for the dome-shaped peak on the western skyline. That is Jannu (7710m), which the French called 'the peak of terror'; the Nepalis have renamed it Khumbakarna. Once past Kanchenjunga, the peaks are further away. This is the Sikkim Himalaya and the major peaks, west to east, are Chomoyummo (6829m), Pauhunri (7125m) and Shudu Tsenpa (7032m).

As the plane approaches Paro you may be able to spot the beautiful snow peak of Jhomolhari (7315m) and the grey ridge-shaped peak of Jichu Drake (6974m). The plane then descends, often through clouds, into the wooded valleys of Bhutan.

If you are flying with Captain Datta, he will announce that you are about to see the mountains closer than you have ever seen them before. He's not joking. Depending on the approach pattern that day, you may drop into the Paro valley and weave through the hills, with goembas and prayer flags on the hillsides above. If you are on the left side of the plane, look for Taktshang monastery and Paro Dzong as you descend towards the airport, finally using almost the entire 1830m of the runway to stop. On other occasions, you may overfly the airport, then bank, skim over a few tree-covered ridges and housetops and make a gut-wrenching plunge into the valley before turning for the final approach.

Connecting to Druk Air

You will need to buy a ticket to and from whatever place you choose to connect to Druk Air. Bangkok is the best place to connect if you are coming from North America, Australia or Asia. Delhi is the best, though tedious, place to connect if you are coming from Europe or the Middle East. A connection via Kathmandu will give you a taste of the Himalaya and of Tibetan Buddhism before you fly to Bhutan. Other connections via Calcutta, Yangon and Dhaka are possible, but these are off the routes of direct flights for major airlines, and few discounted airfares are available to these places.

Buying Tickets

Planning your international itinerary and buying a plane ticket can be an intimidating business. It is worth putting aside a few hours to research the current state of the market. Start early: some of the cheapest tickets have to be bought months in advance, and some popular flights sell out early. Look at the ads in newspapers and magazines, consult reference books and watch for special offers. Phone around travel agents for bargains, especially those that specialise in India and Thailand. Don't neglect Internet travel sites like www.expedia.com and www.travelocity.com as well as the sites of large international carriers.

Airlines can supply information on routes and timetables; however, except at times of inter-airline war they do not supply the cheapest tickets. Find out the fare, the route, the duration of the journey and any restrictions on the ticket. (See Restrictions in the boxed text 'Air Travel Glossary'.) Then sit back and decide which is best for you.

Use the fares quoted in this book as a guide only. They are approximate and based on the rates advertised by travel agents at the time of going to press. Quoted airfares do not necessarily constitute a recommendation for the carrier. If you find a cheap flight

Air Travel Glossary

Apex Apex, or 'advance purchase excursion' is a discounted ticket, which must be paid for in advance. There are penalties if you wish to change it.

Baggage Allowance This will be written on your ticket: usually one 20kg item to go in the hold, plus one item of hand luggage.

Bucket Shop An unbonded travel agency specialising in discounted airline tickets.

Bumped Having a confirmed seat doesn't mean you're going to get on the plane – see Overbooking.

Cancellation Penalties If you have to cancel or change an Apex ticket there are often heavy penalties involved; insurance can sometimes be taken out against these penalties. Some airlines impose penalties on regular tickets as well, particularly against 'no-show' passengers.

Check-In Airlines ask you to check in a certain time ahead of the flight departure (usually 1½ hours on international flights). If you fail to check in on time and the flight is overbooked the airline can cancel your booking and give your seat to somebody else.

Confirmation Having a ticket written out with the flight and date you want doesn't mean you have a seat until the agent has checked with the airline that your status is 'OK' or confirmed. Meanwhile you could just be 'on request'.

Discounted Tickets There are two types of discounted fares – officially discounted (see Promotional Fares) and unofficially discounted. The lowest prices often impose drawbacks like flying with unpopular airlines, inconvenient schedules, or unpleasant routes and connections. A discounted ticket can save you other things than money – you may be able to pay Apex prices without the associated Apex advance booking and other requirements. Discounted tickets only exist where there is fierce competition.

Full Fares Airlines traditionally offer first class (coded F), business class (coded J) and economy class (coded Y) tickets. These days there are so many promotional and discounted fares available from the regular economy class that few passengers pay full economy fare.

Lost Tickets If you lose your ticket an airline will usually treat it like a travellers cheque and, after inquiries, issue you with another one. Legally, however, an airline is entitled to treat it like cash and if you lose it then it's gone forever. Take good care of your tickets.

No-Shows No-shows are passengers who fail to show up for their flight. Full-fare passengers who fail to turn up are sometimes entitled to travel on a later flight. The rest of us are penalised – see Cancellation Penalties.

On Request An unconfirmed booking for a flight – see Confirmation.

Open Jaws A return ticket where you fly out to one place but return from another. If available this can save you backtracking to your arrival point.

being advertised by an obscure bucket shop and feel suspicious about a firm, don't give them all the money at once – leave a deposit of 20% or so and pay the balance when you get the ticket. If they insist on cash in advance, go somewhere else. Once you have the ticket, ring the airline to confirm that you are actually booked onto the flight.

Overbooking Airlines hate to fly empty seats and since every flight has some passengers who fail to show up airlines often book more passengers than they have seats. Usually the excess passengers balance those who fail to show up but occasionally somebody gets bumped, most likely passengers who check in late.

Promotional Fares Officially discounted fares like Apex fares, which are available from travel agents or direct from the airline.

Reconfirmation At least 72 hours prior to departure time of an onward or return flight you must contact the airline and 'reconfirm' that you intend to be on the flight. If you don't do this the airline can delete your name from the passenger list and you could lose your seat. You don't have to reconfirm the first flight on your itinerary or if your stopover is less than 72 hours. It doesn't hurt to reconfirm more than once.

Restrictions Discounted tickets often have various restrictions on them – advance purchase is the most usual one (see Apex). Others are restrictions on the minimum and maximum period you must be away, such as a minimum of 14 days or a maximum of one year – see Cancellation Penalties.

Stand-by A discounted ticket where you only fly if there is a seat free at the last moment. Stand-by fares are usually only available on domestic routes.

Tickets Out An entry requirement for many countries is that you have an onward or return ticket, in other words, a ticket out of the country. If you're not sure what you intend to do next, the easiest solution is to buy the cheapest onward ticket to a neighbouring country or a ticket from a reliable airline which can later be refunded if you do not use it.

Transferred Tickets Airline tickets cannot be transferred from one person to another. Travellers sometimes try to sell the return half of their ticket, but officials can ask you to prove that you are the person named on the ticket. This is unlikely to happen on domestic flights but, on international flights, tickets may be compared with passports.

Travel Agencies Travel agencies vary widely and you should ensure you use one that suits your needs. Some simply handle tours while full-service agencies handle everything from tours and tickets to car rental and hotel bookings. A good one will do all these things and can save you a lot of money but if all you want is a ticket at the lowest possible price, then you really need an agency specialising in discounted tickets. A discounted ticket agency, however, may not be useful for other things, like hotel bookings.

Travel Periods Some officially discounted fares, Apex fares in particular, vary with the time of year. There is often a low (off-peak) season and a high (peak) season. Sometimes there's an intermediate, or shoulder, season as well. At peak times, when everyone wants to fly, not only will the officially discounted fares be higher but so will unofficially discounted fares or there may simply be no discounted tickets available. Usually the fare depends on your outward flight – if you depart in the high season and return in the low season, you pay the high-season fare.

You may decide to pay more than the rock-bottom fare by opting for the safety of a better-known travel agent. Firms such as STA, which have offices world-wide, Council Travel in the USA or Travel CUTS in Canada are not going to disappear overnight, leaving you clutching a receipt for a non-existent ticket, but they do offer good prices to most destinations.

Once you have your ticket, write its number down, together with the flight number and other details, and keep the information somewhere separate. If the ticket is lost or stolen, this will help you get a replacement. It's sensible to buy travel insurance as early as possible. If you buy it the week before you fly, you may find, for example, that you're not covered for delays to your flight caused by industrial action.

Round-the-World (RTW) Tickets & Circle Pacific Fares

RTW tickets can get you to both Delhi and Bangkok, but you still have to purchase an extra ticket to Paro. RTW tickets are often real bargains, and can work out even cheaper than an ordinary return ticket. Prices start at about UK£850, A$1800 or US$1300 and are subject to numerous restrictions.

Circle Pacific tickets use a combination of airlines to circle the Pacific – combining Australia, New Zealand, North America and Asia. As with RTW tickets there are advance purchase restrictions and limits to how many stopovers you can take. Circle Pacific tickets are likely to be around 15% cheaper than RTW tickets.

Travellers with Special Needs

If you have special needs of any sort – you've broken a leg, you're vegetarian, travelling in a wheelchair, taking the baby, terrified of flying – you should let the airline know as soon as possible so they can make arrangements accordingly. You should remind them when you reconfirm your booking (at least 72 hours before departure) and again when you check in at the airport. It may also be worth ringing round the airlines before you make your booking to find out how they can handle your particular needs.

Airports and airlines can sometimes be surprisingly helpful, but they do need advance warning. Most international airports will provide escorts from check-in desk to plane where needed, and there should be ramps, lifts, accessible toilets and reachable phones. Unfortunately, none of these facilities exist at Paro but, with advance notice, a tour operator could arrange for someone to assist with special arrangements.

Aircraft toilets are likely to present a problem for disabled travellers and you should discuss this with the airline at an early stage and, if necessary, with your doctor.

Guide dogs for the blind will often have to travel in a specially pressurised baggage compartment with other animals, away from their owner, though smaller guide dogs may be admitted to the cabin. All guide dogs will be subject to the same quarantine laws (six months in isolation etc) as any other animal when entering or returning to countries currently free of rabies such as Britain or Australia.

Children under two travel for 10% of the standard fare (or free, on some airlines), as long as they don't occupy a seat. They don't get a baggage allowance either. 'Skycots' should be provided by the airline if requested in advance; these will take a child weighing up to about 10kg. Children between two and 12 can usually occupy a seat for half to two-thirds of the full fare, and do get a baggage allowance. Push chairs can often be taken as hand luggage.

The USA & Canada

The best connections and cheapest fares to make a connection to Bhutan from the US west coast are to Bangkok at US$750/1110 one way/return. From the east coast you also travel to Bangkok or you can find a return ticket to Delhi for around US$1330. The cheapest one-way tickets will be around US$865. An alternative way of getting to Delhi from New York is to fly to London and buy a cheap fare from there.

The *New York Times*, the *LA Times*, the

Chicago Tribune and the *San Francisco Examiner* all produce weekly travel sections in which you'll find any number of travel agents' ads. Council Travel and STA Travel have offices in major cities nationwide. The magazine *Travel Unlimited* (PO Box 1058, Allston, Mass 02134) publishes details of the cheapest airfares and courier possibilities for destinations all over the world.

A reliable US agent that specialises in tickets to Thailand, India and Nepal is Himalayan Treasures and Travels (☎ 510-222 5307, 800-223 1813; email govindsh@him trek.com), 3596 Ponderosa Trail, Pinole, CA 94564.

CUTS has offices in all major Canadian cities. The *Toronto Globe & Mail* and the *Vancouver Sun* carry travel agents' ads.

Australia & New Zealand

Advance-purchase return fares from the east coast of Australia to Delhi are A$1350 to A$1700 depending on the season. Fares are slightly cheaper from Darwin and Perth. Tickets from Australia to London or other European capitals with a Bangkok or Delhi stopover range from A$900 to A$1500 one way and A$1775 to A$2300 return, again depending on the season.

Return advance-purchase fares from New Zealand to India and Thailand range from NZ$2285 to NZ$2350 depending on the season. STA Travel (☎ 1300-360 960 in Australia, 0800-100 677 in New Zealand) and Flight Centres International (☎ 131 600, Australia only) are major dealers in cheap airfares in both Australia and New Zealand. Check the travel agents' ads in the *Yellow Pages*, local newspapers and travel magazines, and ring around.

The UK

Various excursion fares are available from London to both India and Thailand, but you can get better prices through London's many cheap-ticket specialists. Check the travel page ads in the *Times, Business Traveller* and the weekly entertainment guides such as *Time Out*; or check freebies like *TNT*. Two reliable London specialists are Trailfinders, with

offices at 194 High St Kensington, London W8 7RG (☎ 0171-938 3939) and 42-50 Earls Court Rd, London W8 (☎ 0171-938 3366); and STA Travel, with offices at 86 Old Brompton Rd, London SW7 (☎ 0171-581 4132) and 117 Euston Rd, London NW1 (☎ 0171-465 0484). Also worth trying are Quest Worldwide (☎ 0181-547 3322) at Quebec House, 4-10 Richmond Rd, Kingston upon Thames, Surrey KT2 5HL, and Bridge the World (☎ 0171-911 0900) at 1-3 Ferdinand St, Camden Town, London NW1.

From London to Delhi, fares range from around UK£199/325 one way/return. The cheapest fares are usually with Middle Eastern or Eastern European airlines. Thai International always seems to have competitive fares despite its high standards.

Most British travel agents are registered with the Association of British Travel Agents (ABTA). If you have paid for your flight to an ABTA-registered agent who then goes out of business, ABTA will guarantee a refund or an alternative. Unregistered bucket shops are riskier but also sometimes cheaper.

Continental Europe

Fares from continental Europe are mostly far more expensive than from London, although Amsterdam is edging in on the cheap airfare market.

Middle Eastern airlines have good deals from Amsterdam to Delhi with return excursion fares around DFL1060 (UK£322). From Paris to Delhi, return excursion fares range upwards from FF3550 (UK£362; about one-third the standard return economy fare). From Frankfurt to Mumbai (Bombay) or Delhi, return excursion fares are around DM1060 (UK£364). In Amsterdam, NBBS is a popular travel agent.

Africa

There are plenty of flights between East Africa and Mumbai due to the large Indian population in Kenya. From Mumbai you can make your way to Delhi or Kathmandu to connect to Paro. Typical fares from Mumbai to Nairobi are around US$653 return with either Ethiopian Airlines, Kenya

Airways, Air India or Pakistan International Airlines (PIA, via Karachi).

Asia

Bangkok has replaced Hong Kong as the discount-ticket capital of the region. Its bucket shops are at least as unreliable as those of other cities. Ask the advice of other travellers before buying a ticket. STA, which is reliable, has branches in Hong Kong, Tokyo, Singapore, Bangkok and Kuala Lumpur.

LAND

Unless you are an Indian national, you are required to either enter or exit Bhutan on a Druk Air flight, limiting the options for road travel. The best way to plan a trip via road is to start in Kathmandu and travel one direction by air and the other by land, perhaps visiting Darjeeling and Sikkim en route. You could also enter Bhutan by road and then exit by air to Yangon or Bangkok.

To/From Phuentsholing

If you are travelling to or from Bhutan by land, all roads lead through Siliguri, the major transport hub in north-east India. Here you have the option of a train or bus connection to Calcutta or Delhi, a road trip to Nepal, or a flight from nearby Bagdogra to Delhi or Calcutta. From Siliguri you can also travel on to Sikkim or the hill stations of Darjeeling and Kalimpong.

The easiest way to travel the 169km between Phuentsholing and Siliguri is to arrange for your Bhutan tour operator to provide a vehicle. There are also taxis and shared hire cars available in both Phuentsholing and Siliguri. If you are given a choice, opt for the less crowded route via the 'coronation bridge' to Mainaguri, then on to Hasimara, Jaigaon and finally Phuentsholing.

A Bhutanese transport company (the name changes every year) operates a direct bus service twice a day between Siliguri and Phuentsholing; buses leave at 8 am and 2 pm and cost Rs 35 for the 3½ hour journey. In Siliguri the booking office is on Tenzing Norgay Rd (also known as Hill Cart Rd), opposite the Shree Punjab Hotel.

You can also find Bhutanese taxis (yellow-roofed minivans with license numbers beginning with BT) looking for a return fare and can buy a seat for Rs 100 or charter the whole taxi for about Rs 400. Indian bus companies also operate services between Siliguri and Jaigaon on the Indian side of the Bhutan border.

Arrival Formalities Don't forget to get yourself stamped out of India. The Indian immigration office in Jaigaon is in a compound about 400m south of the Bhutan entrance gate. If your transport has already deposited you in Bhutan, you can simply walk back across the border to complete the paperwork.

Foreigners need to present their passport, two photos and a US$20 fee to the visa officer in the *drungkhag* (sub-district) office near the east end of town. The arrival details will be stamped in your passport when you pass the immigration post at Rinchending, 5km away.

Indian nationals need to fill in two copies of a form and present two photocopies of an identification document such as a drivers license or voter card to the Indian embassy liaison office in Phuentsholing. You then receive a request form that is to be presented to the Rinchending immigration officer along with two photographs. The 14-day permit, with your photograph attached, is then returned to you.

Nepal

Panitanki, in northern West Bengal, is opposite the eastern Nepal border town of Kakarbhitta. A long bridge separates the two towns across the Mechi river. Bhutanese tour operators are able to pick you up or drop you at Panitanki, but their vehicle is not allowed to enter Nepal.

Panitanki is only one hour (35km) from Siliguri. Buses run regularly on this route (Rs 6) and taxis are easy to arrange for Rs 250. A cycle-rickshaw across the border to Kakarbhitta costs Rs 5. Buses depart Kakarbhitta daily at 5 pm for Kathmandu (17 hours, Nepal Rs 250), a long rough drive via

Narayanghat, Mugling and the Trisuli River valley. Lonely Planet's *Nepal* book has details of what to see and do along this route.

A better option is to take a four-hour bus or taxi ride to Biratnagar and take a domestic flight to Kathmandu. There is a closer airport at Bhadrapur, but there are only two flights a week and these tend to be booked far in advance. Fares to Kathmandu are US$77 from Biratnagar and US$99 from Bhadrapur. Royal Nepal has offices in Bhadrapur (☎ 023-20362) and Biratnagar (☎ 021-25576, 25335). Necon Air (☎ 021-25987, 23838) operates four flights a day from Biratnagar to Kathmandu. Jhapa Travels Agency (☎ 023-29006) in Kakarbhitta may be able to book a flight for you.

India
Delhi & Calcutta The nearest mainline Indian railway station to Phuentsholing is in New Jalpaiguri. It's a 12 hour rail journey to Calcutta and a 33 hour trip to Delhi. You can travel by road direct to New Jalpaiguri or connect via local train from Siliguri.

Darjeeling & Sikkim From Siliguri it's easy to arrange a shared taxi or bus to Darjeeling (77km) or to Gangtok in Sikkim. If you are travelling to Sikkim, be sure to arrange a permit in Siliguri at the Sikkim Tourism office.

From Samdrup Jongkhar
Foreign tourists are not allowed to enter Bhutan at Samdrup Jongkhar, only to depart. Indian nationals may, however, enter via Samdrup Jongkhar. Check with Bhutanese or Indian authorities on the current status of Assamese separatist groups before you decide to travel by land through Assam.

The primary reason you would want to exit this way is to avoid the long drive back over the mountains to Thimphu after visiting eastern Bhutan. The easiest connection from Samdrup Jongkhar is to fly to Calcutta from Guwahati airport in Assam. It is an 80km, 2½ hour drive from the Bhutan border to Guwahati, on the south bank of the Brahmaputra River. It is then a further 20km from Guwahati to the airport. Fares are US$60 to Calcutta, US$190 to Delhi and US$43 to Bagdogra.

The alternative is a 400km drive through the Indian Duars to Siliguri. You could also visit Kaziranga National Park, famous for its rhino population, 233km east of Guwahati.

DEPARTURE TAXES
The airport tax on departure from Paro is Nu 300, which must be paid in Bhutanese or Indian currency. Other airport taxes in the region are:

Bangkok	Baht 500
Dhaka	Taka 300
Kathmandu	NR 600 to SAARC countries
	NR 700 to other destinations
Calcutta	INR 150
Delhi	INR 150 to SAARC countries
	Rs 750 to other destinations
Yangon	US$6

ORGANISED TOURS
There are a few travel agents and adventure travel companies that specialise in Bhutan, but most operate one or two Bhutan trips only as part of a series of programmes. In addition to removing the hassle of faxing Thimphu and transferring money, they will also arrange your tickets on Druk Air.

Most group tours to Bhutan fly to Paro together. A representative of the tour agent waits at the check-in counter in Bangkok, Delhi or Kathmandu with the tickets in hand. The agent should also be able to either recommend a group flight or arrange air transportation, hopefully at a reasonable rate, on flights that they have pre-booked to the connecting point for the flight on to Paro.

Many adventure travel companies organise treks in Bhutan in addition to cultural tours. They normally operate group treks that are escorted by a leader, though many can also organise private trips.

Australia
Peregrine Adventures
(☎ 03-9663 8611; fax 9663 8618), 258 Lonsdale St, Melbourne, Vic 3000

World Expeditions
(☎ 02-9264 3366; fax 9261 1974; email enquiries@worldexpeditions.com.au), 3rd floor, 441 Kent St, Sydney, NSW 2000

USA & Canada
Adventure Center
(☎ 800-227 8747; fax 654 4200; email tripinfo@adventure-center.com), 1311 63rd St, Suite 200, Emeryville, CA 94608
Asian Pacific Adventures
(☎ 213-935 3156, 800-825 1680; fax 935-2691; email travelasia@earthlink.net), 826 South Sierra Bonita Ave, Los Angeles, CA 90036
Bhutan Travel
(☎ 212-838 6382, 800-950 9908; fax 212-750 1269; email 195426@mcimail.com), 120 East 56th St, Suite 1130, New York, NY 10022
Far Fung Places
(☎ 415-386 8306; fax 386 8104; email jdkez@hooked.net), 1914 Fell St, San Francisco, CA 94117
Geographic Expeditions
(☎ 415-922 0448; fax 346 5535; email info@geoex.com), 2627 Lombard St, San Francisco, CA 94123
Himalayan Travel
(☎ 800-225 2380; fax 203-359 3669), 110 Prospect St, Stamford, CT 06901
Ibex Expeditions
(☎ 541-345 1289; fax 343 9002), 2657 West 28th Ave, Eugene, OR 97405
Journeys International
(☎ 313-665 4407; fax 665 2945; email info@journeys-intl.com), 4011 Jackson Rd, Ann Arbor, MI 48103
Mountain Travel Sobek
(☎ 510-527 8100; fax 525 7710; email info@mtsobek.com), 6420 Fairmount Ave, El Cerrito, CA 94530
Wilderness Travel
(☎ 510-558 2488; fax 548 0347; email info@wildernesstravel.com), 1102 Ninth St, Berkeley CA 94710

UK
Abercombie & Kent
(☎ 0171-730 9600; email info@abercrombiekent.co.uk), Sloane Square House, Holbein Place, London SW 1W 8NS
Exodus Travels
(☎ 0181-675 5550), 9 Weir Rd, Balham, London SW12 OLT

Explore Worldwide
(☎ 01252-344161; fax 343170; email info@explore.co.uk), 1 Frederick St, Aldershot, Hants GU11 1LQ
Himalayan Kingdoms
(☎ 0117-923 7163; fax 974 4993; email 101460.2022@compuserve.com), 20 The Mall, Clifton, Bristol BS8 4DR
KE Adventure Travel
(☎ 017687-73966; fax 74693; email keadventure@enterprise.net), 32 Lake Road, Keswick, Cumbria CA12 5DQ
Steppes East Ltd
(☎ 01285-810267; fax 810693; email sales@steppeseast.co.uk), Castle Eaton, Cricklade, Wilts SN6 6JU
WEXAS International
(fax 0171-589 8418), 45 Brompton Rd, Knightsbridge, London SW3 1DE
World Expeditions
(☎ 0181-870 2600; fax 870 2615; email worldex@dircon.co.uk), 4 Northfields Prospect, Putney Bridge Rd, London SW18 1PE

Germany
Dav Berg-und-Skischule
(☎ 089-651 0720; fax 651 07272), Am Perlacher Forst 186, D-81545 München
Hauser Exkursionen
(☎ 089-235 0060; fax 291 3714), Marienstrasse -17, D-80331 München

Other European Countries
ARTOU
(☎ 022-818 0220; fax 818 0229; email info@artou.ch), 8 Rue de Rive, CH-1204 Geneva, Switzerland
France Explorator
(☎ 01-53 45 85 85; fax 42 60 80 00; email explorator@explo.com), 16 Rue de la Banque, 75002 Paris
Horizons Nouveaux
(☎ 027-771 7171; fax 771 7175; email voyage@horizonsnoveaux.com), Centre de l'Etoile, Case postale 196, 1936 Verbier, Switzerland
Rotas do Vento
(☎ 01-364 9852; fax 364 9843; email i-rotas@rotasdovento.pt), R Lusiadas 5 4-K, PO Box 3010, 1300 Lisboa, Portugal

Asia
Oriole Travel & Tours
(☎ 66-2-237 9201; fax 2-237-9200; email oriole@samart.co.th), Skulthai Surawong Tower, 141 Surawong Road, Bangkrak, Bangkok 10500, Thailand

Specialised Tours

Motorcycle Trips Motorcycle trips can be arranged through:

Himalayan Road Runners
(☎ 908-236 8970; fax 236 8972; email roadrunr@ridehigh.com), PO Box 538, Lebanon, New Jersey 08833

Kayaking & River Rafting These trips can be booked with:

Equator USA
(☎ 208-726 7427; fax 726 7458; email info@equatorusa.com, homepage: www.equatorusa.com), PO Box 6070, Ketchum ID 83340

Ultimate Descents
(☎/fax 977-1-411933; email rivers@ ultimate.wlink.com.np.), PO Box 6720, Kathmandu, Nepal

WARNING

The information in this chapter is particularly vulnerable to change: prices for international travel are volatile, routes are introduced and cancelled, schedules change, special deals come and go, and rules and visa requirements are amended. Airlines and governments seem to take a perverse pleasure in making price structures and regulations as complicated as possible. Check directly with the airline or a travel agent to make sure you understand how a fare (and the ticket you buy) works. In addition, the travel industry is highly competitive and there are many lurks and perks.

The upshot of this is that you should get opinions, quotes and advice from as many airlines and travel agents as possible before parting with your cash. The details given here are pointers and not a substitute for your own careful, up-to-date research.

Getting Around

Because Bhutan has no domestic air service, doesn't possess any helicopters, and does not include an inch of railway track, the only way to see the country is either by foot or by road.

There is one main road; the National Highway, a 2.5m-wide stretch of tarmac which winds its way up and down mountains, across clattering bridges, along the side of rock cliffs, and over high mountain passes. Rivers, mud flows and rockfalls present continual hazards, especially in the rainy season. The road can easily become blocked due to landslides and can take anywhere from an hour to several days to clear. Take plenty of reading material.

Unless you want to walk, the only way to travel between towns in the south of Bhutan is via India. This is impractical for foreigners since the only road entry point is Phuentsholing, though foreigners are allowed to exit via Samdrup Jongkhar.

If you are on a tourist visa, the tour operator will arrange all your travel once you arrive in Bhutan. The cost of all local transportation is included in the price of your trip. If you are an Indian national or working with a project, you are allowed to use public transportation. If you are not on a tourist visa you will not have a vehicle at your disposal and may have to rely on public transportation.

BUS

Public buses are crowded and rough, and the winding roads make them doubly uncomfortable. The government's Bhutan Post Express, Barma Travels and other companies operate Indian minibuses. Some private corporations, including the new Leksol Bus service, use more comfortable Toyota Coasters at about double the normal fare. You also might arrive at the bus terminal to discover that your bus is actually a truck with seats in the back.

There are three or four buses a day between Thimphu and the major centres of Phuentsholing, Paro and Punakha. Fares and schedules are all monitored by the Surface Transport Authority.

Tour Buses

Tour operators use Japanese buses, minivans and cars, depending on the size of the group. These vehicles can take you almost anywhere in the country, but for trips to central and eastern Bhutan during winter or the monsoon a 4WD vehicle is an advantage, and often a necessity.

CAR, JEEP & MOTORCYCLE

There are taxis in Phuentsholing and Thimphu, but they are expensive. It is also possible to hire a vehicle with a driver. If you don't already have a vehicle at your disposal, the best way to hire one is through a travel agency (for a list of travel agents see Tourist Offices in the Facts for the Visitor chapter).

Most two-wheelers are Indian scooters that are used in towns and also for long distance journeys across mountain passes. It's

---

Bailey Bridges

Many rivers are spanned by rattling girder bridges known as Bailey bridges. These are structures composed of rectangular panels about 3m long that are pinned together to produce spans of up to 64m. The bridge is named after its inventor, Sir Donald Coleman Bailey (1901-1985), a British engineer. The Bailey bridge was used extensively during and after WWII and, though it was designed as a portable, temporary structure, many early bridges still survive 50 years later.

They are excellent for spanning Bhutan's rivers because they are easily transportable along the country's narrow roads, are easy to assemble, and do not need any specialised design.

unlikely that you'll find one for rent. Himalayan Roadrunners in Delhi operates motorcycle tours in Bhutan, but they are hair-raising adventures because it's necessary to dodge lots of oncoming trucks.

Road Rules

Traffic moves on the left, and is much more orderly than most other South Asian countries. Speeds are low in towns and on rural roads; you will be lucky to average 40km/hr on the hairpin bends of roads in the hills.

As is the case throughout Asia, it is important that the police establish who was at fault in any traffic accident. This means that the police must arrive and make the decision before any of the vehicles can be moved, even if the vehicles are blocking the narrow road. A relatively minor fender-bender can block the road for hours while everyone waits patiently for the police to arrive from the nearest town.

BICYCLE

Some travellers have ridden mountain bikes in Bhutan, and TAB is interested in promoting this kind of travel. As with motorcycles, it is sometimes frightening to turn around a sharp curve into the path of a large, roaring, oncoming truck. It doesn't take a cycling expert to work out that roads without much traffic make for better biking territory. Good routes include the upper parts of the Paro and Thimphu valleys. For a wild ride, how about getting dropped off at the top of the Cheli La above Paro and riding 35km non-stop downhill?

Rental

You might find a clunky Indian bike for rent in the flats of Phuentsholing, but there are no bikes for rent in Thimphu. Several entrepreneurs are interested in opening mountain bike rental shops in Thimphu and Paro, and these might be in operation before long.

HITCHING

Most people pay for a ride, either in a bus or cab or back of a truck. But bus service is limited, especially in the east, and it's not unusual to see someone flagging down a vehicle asking for a ride. It is silly to hitch if you have paid for a vehicle unless that vehicle has broken down and you are stranded on a mountain road. Hitching is never entirely safe in any country in the world, and we don't recommend it, but if you do have to hitch because of a breakdown, Bhutan is about as safe a place as you could find.

LOCAL TRANSPORT
Taxi

There is a plan to introduce taxi meters, but currently taxis operate on a flat rate that is very much open to negotiation.

You should expect to pay Nu 30 for a local trip, Nu 500 for a full day and Nu 1000 from Thimphu to Phuentsholing. If you are travelling between Thimphu and Phuentsholing, look for a taxi that is from the place you want to go (BT-2 license plates are from Phuentsholing and BT-1 are from Thimphu or Paro), and you may be able to negotiate a lower price.

Thimphu

There were *goembas* and a small population in the Thimphu valley even before the time of the Shabdrung, but Thimphu didn't really exist as a town until it became the capital in 1961. The first vehicles appeared in Thimphu in 1962 and the town remained very rural until the late 1970s. The population has grown dramatically since 1990, and is now estimated to be about 40,000.

It is often said that Thimphu is the only world capital without traffic lights. One was installed several years ago, but the residents complained about its impersonalness and ugliness and it was removed within days. Traffic continues to be directed by policemen stationed at two traffic circles, one at the north end and another near the south end of Norzin Lam, Thimphu's wide, tree-lined main street. They keep Thimphu's traffic flowing throughout the day using elegant, exaggerated gestures. They disappear at night and leave drivers to sort things out among themselves.

At an elevation of 2320m, don't be surprised if you become short of breath or have trouble sleeping your first few nights here.

ORIENTATION

Thimphu lies in a wooded valley, sprawling up a hillside on the west bank of the Thimphu Chhu. Several north-south streets run through the town, and numerous smaller streets weave their way uphill to government offices and the posh suburb of Motithang at the top of the town.

In the central district, numerous lanes and alleys lead off the north-south streets to provide access to the shops, bars and small restaurants.

The road from Chhuzom passes the suburb of Lungtenphug and enters Thimphu from the south. The bus station is beneath the east end of Lungten Zampa, the bridge that leads across the Thimphu Chhu into town. Just across the bridge is a petrol pump which demarcates the southern end of the

HIGHLIGHTS
• A visit to Trashi Chhoe Dzong, built as the symbol of the capital
• Spectacular views of Thimpu valley from the Telecoms Tower
• Exploring the shops along Norzin Lam, Thimpu's main street
• A hike up to either Tango or Chari Goemba
• The atmosphere of the weekend market
• An evening cultural show with the Tashi Nencha dance company

central business district. The following right turn leads onto Norzin Lam, Thimphu's main street, which leads through the town centre to the northern traffic circle. From here Desi Lam leads north to the *dzong*, golf course and government offices. North of the dzong is the large India House compound, and beyond that is Dechencholing Palace.

Doebum Lam leads south, making a loop to the west of the central business district and passing the Ministry of Trade and Industry and the large swimming pool and sports complex before reaching the Memorial Chorten. Here you have a choice of three roads: Zogchen Lam winds its way downhill to the foot of Norzin Lam; Chorten Lam loops back to the southern traffic circle, and Gongphel Lam leads south past the hospital and motor workshops, then loops back north, passing under the bridge to become Chhogyal Lam.

Most shops and hotels are centred around Thimphu's main intersection at the southern traffic circle. Shops are numbered, but in no apparent sequence. Part of Norzin Lam is one way north; a parallel street, Wogzin Lam, provides southbound access, passing a square that is dominated by a small clock tower and surrounded by travel agency offices. North of the traffic circle are shops, the Bank of Bhutan, the cinema and the government

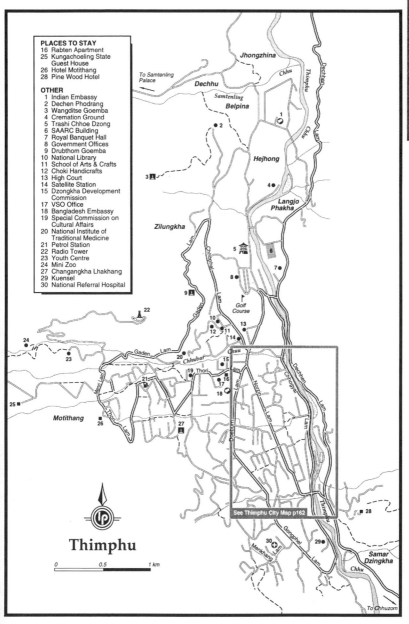

PLACES TO STAY
16 Rabten Apartment
25 Kungachoeling State
    Guest House
26 Hotel Motithang
28 Pine Wood Hotel

OTHER
1 Indian Embassy
2 Dechen Phodrang
3 Wangditse Goemba
4 Cremation Ground
5 Trashi Chhoe Dzong
6 SAARC Building
7 Royal Banquet Hall
8 Government Offices
9 Drubthom Goemba
10 National Library
11 School of Arts & Crafts
12 Choki Handicrafts
13 High Court
14 Satellite Station
15 Dzongkha Development
    Commission
17 VSO Office
18 Bangladesh Embassy
19 Special Commission on
    Cultural Affairs
20 National Institute of
    Traditional Medicine
21 Petrol Station
22 Radio Tower
23 Youth Centre
24 Mini Zoo
27 Changangkha Lhakhang
29 Kuensel
30 National Referral Hospital

Thimphu

0   0.5   1 km

THIMPHU

handicraft emporium. Changlimithang Stadium and a few shops and hotels are along Chang Lam, between Norzin Lam and the river.

Maps
The survey department of Bhutan publishes a colour map of Thimphu that is available in bookshops and in the Etho Metho handicraft shop near the cinema. A similar map of Thimphu city is reproduced on the reverse side of the Bhutan road map published by Berndtson & Berndtson. These maps have all the government offices marked, though the maps are out of date and many offices have since moved.

It's hard to get lost in Thimphu; the town really has only one main street, and most local people are amazed that a tourist might need a map. Though all streets have names and are well marked by signposts, most Bhutanese do not bother with the street name and give directions by referring only to well-known shops and landmarks.

INFORMATION
Shops are open daily, except Tuesday, from 8 or 9 am until 8 or 9 pm, depending on the owners. All shops in Thimphu are required to close on Tuesday; be sure to work out your itinerary with this in mind. Government offices and travel agencies are open Tuesday. Government offices close for the weekend and travel agencies close on Sunday.

There are three petrol stations, all with electric pumps, unlike those in the hinterland. The Bhutanese architecture of the petrol station at the south end of town, at the western end of the bridge, makes it a minor tourist attraction.

Thimphu has undergone a lot of recent development but still retains its charm because buildings are not allowed to exceed a certain height and must be designed in traditional Bhutanese style. There is a new town plan being implemented to improve the infrastructure of roads, electricity, water and sewage. This has resulted in a considerable amount of construction work, particularly at the southern end of town.

Foreign Consulates
The only diplomatic representatives in Bhutan are in Thimphu. India House is in a large compound north of the dzong. The Bangladesh embassy is on the hill above the town and South Korea has an honorary consul with an office in the Tashi Tours & Travel office near the clock tower.

Money
Most hotels can change money at the normal government rates, though they usually have a limited supply of cash on hand. The computerised office of Bhutan National Bank, in the same building as the post office, provides efficient service.

Money changing is such an uncommon service that you are led into a back office and invited to relax in a chair while the staff do the paperwork.

The Bank of Bhutan's main branch tends to be crowded, but its smaller city branch on Wogzin Lam is only two blocks away and is open late on weekdays as well as Saturday and Sunday.

Credit Cards A few places advertise that they accept American Express cards, but credit card transactions are so rare that you may have to wait for the one person in the shop who knows how to write up the charge slip. This all may change when Bhutan National Bank's application to act as agent for Visa and MasterCard is finalised.

Post
The central post office is on most tour itineraries, but the philatelic counter is not a particularly inspired facility. Many hotels and shops have stamps for sale, and you can buy postcards and stamps at a small shop on the ground floor of the Tandin Hotel. Unlike many Asian countries, it is safe to simply drop cards and letters into post boxes here.

Telephone & Fax
The country code for Bhutan is 975 and Thimphu's area code is 02.

Directory inquiries is ☎118 for Bhutan and ☎116 for international numbers. Many hotels and Public Call Offices (PCOs) have direct international dialling. Trunk calls may be booked through the operator at 117 for international and 119 for domestic numbers.

Travel Agencies & Airline Offices

Travel agency offices are clustered around the clock tower and the cinema. Since it is likely that you will already be in the hands of a travel agent by the time you reach Thimphu, and it's almost impossible to change agencies in the middle of a trip, there's not much point in chasing down other agents, unless you want to plan a return trip to Bhutan with a different company.

The Druk Air office (☎ 22215, 22825; fax 22775) is on Doebum Lam, just west of the northern traffic circle. It's far more efficient to buy your ticket and reconfirm reservations with a tour operator than trying to make arrangements directly with the airline.

No other airlines have offices in Bhutan. Most of the travel tour operators can arrange reservations and tickets for international connecting flights, but most have to do it through their associates abroad. Only two agents, Bhutan Travel Bureau (☎ 24241, 24092; fax 25100) and Tashi Tours & Travel (☎ 23027, 23361; fax 23666), have airline computers and can confirm flights immediately. The offices of both agencies are in front of the clock tower. Other agents that specialise in international ticketing are Takin Travels (☎ 23124) on Wogzin Lam and Chhundu Travel near the northern end of Norzin Lam (for contact details see Tourist Offices in the Facts for the Visitor chapter).

Bookshops

Both of Thimphu's bookshops carry *Kuensel*, Indian newspapers and periodicals and a moderately extensive selection of books on Bhutan, Tibet and Buddhism. You can also find children's books, text books and English novels to read while you wait for a flight. Prices are quite reasonable, especially for Indian editions. Pekhang Enterprises (☎ 24777) is next to the cinema and DBS Books Enterprises (☎ 23123) is opposite the clock tower.

Libraries

The small Thimphu public library is at the northern end of Norzin Lam. For books about Bhutan, the National Library may be a better resource, though the selection of books in English is small.

Laundry

Most hotels offer laundry and dry cleaning services. If your hotel does not offer laundry facilities, try Kunzang Dry Cleaners on Norzin Lam. Remember that there are few clothes dryers in Bhutan, and in bad weather same-day service may result in laundry that is either returned damp, or else the following day.

Medical Services

The Jigme Dorji Wangchuck National Referral Hospital (☎ 22496, 22497) in Thimphu is the best in Bhutan, but there is no intensive care unit. The India Bhutan Friendship Hospital is a second alternative.

Because medical services are free to Bhutanese citizens, there are only a few shops selling medical supplies. Norbu Rabten is on Wogzin Lam, upstairs in the back of the shopping arcade below the Central Hotel. Druk Medical House and Norling Medical are on Wogzin Lam, opposite the Tandin Hotel.

Emergency

For an ambulance call ☎ 22596, 22497 or 112. The Thimphu police number is ☎ 22470 or 113, and the fire department is on ☎ 22555 or 110.

Dangers & Annoyances

There's almost nothing in Thimphu to cause concern. The dogs roam at night and bark across town at each other, but earplugs solve that problem quite easily. Beware of steep steps and open drains on the sidewalk along the west side of the main street, Norzin Lam.

WALKING TOUR

The best way to see Thimphu is to wander along the main street, diverting into lanes and following your nose to see where it leads you. It's impossible to get lost; if you get confused in the maze of streets, just head downhill and you will soon come across something you recognise.

For a slightly more strenuous excursion, start from the southern traffic circle and walk uphill to the Memorial Chorten, then turn north along Doebum Lam for a short distance. The first turn to the left leads uphill and loops around until it passes Changangkha Lhakhang, perched on a ridge like a fortress. Climb to the courtyard for a view, then just follow your instincts. Either head straight downhill back to the town centre, or continue north for a while before turning east and walking downhill. Any of these roads will take you past houses and tiny shops and restaurants as you make your way back to the main street.

TRASHI CHHOE DZONG

In 1216 the lama Gyalwa Lhanangpa built Dohon (Blue Stone) Dzong on the hill above Thimphu where Dechen Phodrang now stands. A few years later Lama Phajo Drugom Shigpo, who brought the Drukpa Kagyu lineage to Bhutan, took over Dohon Dzong. In 1641 the Shabdrung acquired the dzong from the descendants of Lama Phajo and renamed it Trashi Chhoe Dzong (Fortress of the Glorious Religion). He then arranged to house both the monks and civil officials in the same dzong, which soon was found to be too small for both bodies. The Shabdrung then built another dzong, known as the lower dzong, for the civil officials and used the original building for the monks. The 13th

Druk Desi, Chhogyel Sherab Wangchuck (1744-1763), later enlarged Trashi Chhoe Dzong so that it could again accommodate both civil officials and monks.

The original dzong burned in 1771 and was abandoned in favour of the lower dzong, which was expanded. That dzong burned in 1866 and twice more after that.

The five-storey *utse* (central tower) was damaged in the 1897 earthquake and rebuilt in 1902. Between 1962 and 1969 King Jigme Dorji Wangchuck completely renovated and enlarged the dzong to become the symbol of the new capital of Thimphu. The royal architect performed the repairs without touching the utse, Lhakhang Sarpa or any other of its chapels at the centre. Other than this structure, the entire dzong was rebuilt in traditional fashion, without nails or written plans.

The dzong housed the original National Assembly and now houses the secretariat, the throne room and the offices of the king. The northern portion is the summer residence of the Central Monk Body.

The outer structure is two storeys high with three-storey towers at the four corners projecting out over the walls. The outer walls are built of trimmed and fitted granite blocks, unlike other dzongs, which were made of roughly dressed stones. Similarly, the *dochey* (courtyard) is paved with rectangular stone slabs, in contrast to other dzongs, which use only rough, irregularly shaped stones as paving.

Unlike most other dzongs, Trashi Chhoe has two main entrances. One leads to the

NICHOLAS REUSS

RICHARD I'ANSON

STAN ARMINGTON

JULIA WILKINSON

Thimphu
Despite recent development, Thimphu remains a bastion of traditional architecture. Clockwise from top: Trashichhoe Dzong dominates this panoramic view; the National Library; detail on a Bhutanese home; and Memorial Chorten, the focus of daily worship for many in the capital.

Weekend Market, Thimphu
Well-heeled Thimphu residents mingle with villagers in a unique rural and urban blend at the colourful weekend market.

administrative section at the south and a separate entrance at the north leads to the monastic quarter where the dances of the annual tsechu festival are performed.

Below the dzong is an excellent example of a traditional **cantilever bridge**. To the south of the dzong are a set of low buildings that house additional administrative offices.

SAARC BUILDING

The large traditional Bhutanese-style building across the river from Trashi Chhoe Dzong was built in the early 1990s to provide a venue for a meeting of the heads of state and government from the South Asia Association for Regional Co-operation (SAARC). There are seven members of SAARC: Bangladesh, Bhutan, India, Maldives, Nepal, Pakistan and Sri Lanka. The meeting was never held in Bhutan and the structure now houses the Planning and Foreign ministries. The National Assembly was relocated to this building in 1993. Nearby is the Royal Banquet Hall.

MEMORIAL CHORTEN

This large Tibetan-style chorten was built in 1974 to honour the memory of the third king, Jigme Dorji Wangchuck. There are numerous religious paintings and complex tantric statues inside reflecting both peaceful and wrathful aspects of Buddhist deities.

The memorial chorten is one of the most visible religious structures in Thimphu, and for many people it is the focus of their daily worship. Throughout the day people circumambulate the chorten and worship at a small shrine just inside the gate.

NEAR TRASHI CHHOE DZONG
National Library

The National Library is just in front of the golf course. It was established in 1967 to preserve many ancient Dzongkha and Tibetan texts.

The traditional books are kept on the upper floor. These books are Tibetan-style, printed or written on long strips of handmade paper stacked between pieces of wood and wrapped in silken cloth. In another section are some wooden blocks that are used for printing books and prayer flags. The library has a branch at Kuenga Rabten palace south of Trongsa.

There is a collection of English-language books and a small collection of modern academic texts on the ground floor. Most of these are about Buddhism and Himalayan history. There are also a few travel books about India and Tibet. They have a collection of bound volumes of *Kuensel* in all three languages and another collection that includes many of the reports produced by various agencies that undertook development or research projects. There is a small collection of books about Bhutan on a shelf behind the checkout desk.

Sometimes you will see people circumambulating the National Library building and chanting mantras. This is because the building houses many holy books. An altar on the ground floor, with statues of Bhutan's most important historic figures, Shabdrung Ngawang Namgyal, Pema Lingpa and Guru Rimpoche, also contributes to the building's sacred importance.

School of Arts and Crafts

The School of Arts and Crafts, commonly known as the painting school, is under the administration of the Special Commission for Cultural Affairs. It offers an eight year course which provides instruction in many of Bhutan's traditional arts to boys from throughout the country whose aptitude is more artistic than academic. The images of the Buddhist deities in the colour section 'Important Figures of Drukpa Kagyu Buddhism' between pages 176 and 177, were painted by senior students of the school.

Most tour operators can arrange a visit to the school, and offer a look into various classrooms where the students follow a comprehensive course that starts with drawing and progresses through painting, wood carving and statue-making.

There is a small shop at the school that sells some of the students' works at reasonable prices, about Nu 500 for a medium-sized painting.

THIMPHU

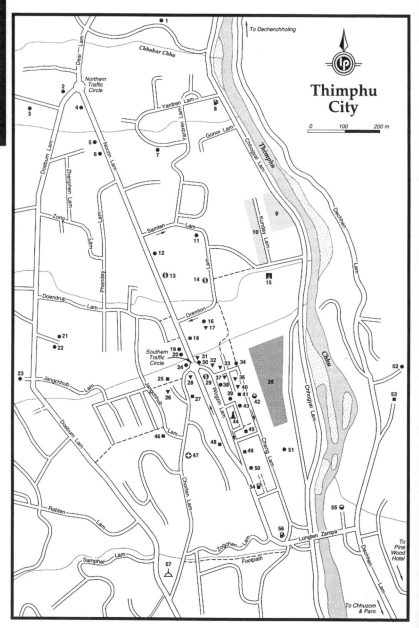

Thimphu City

0   100   200 m

PLACES TO STAY
18 Hotel Tandin
25 Taktsang Hotel
27 Hotel 89
41 Hotel Wangchuk
45 Hotel Druk
46 Yeedzin Guest House;
    Jichu Drakey Bakery
48 Kelwang Hotel
49 Hotel Jhomolhari
50 Druk Sherig Guest
    House
53 Hotel Riverview

PLACES TO EAT
17 Pekhang Restaurant;
    Etho Metho
    Handicrafts
26 Swiss Bakery
28 Lhanam Restaurant;
    Plums Cafe
31 Wangdi Restaurant
32 Hasty Tasty
33 Benez
36 Hotel UK
37 Sambara
40 Cottage Industry
    Shop

OTHER
1 Royal Academy of
   Performing Arts
2 Druk Air
3 Archery Shop
4 National Women's
   Association (NWAB)
5 Royal Society for the
   Protection of Nature
   (RSPN)
6 Public Library
7 World Wildlife Fund
   (WWF)
8 Petrol Station
9 Weekend Market
10 Lower Market
11 UN Development
   Programme (UNDP)
12 Handicraft Emporium
13 Bank of Bhutan
14 Bhutan National Bank;
   Post Office
15 Zangto Pelri Lhakhang
16 Cinema; Pekhang
   Bookshop
19 Tshering Dolkar
   Handicrafts
20 Norling Tshonkhang

21 Ministry of Trade
   & Industry
22 Tourism Authority of
   Bhutan (TAB)
23 Sports Complex
24 Pekhang Handicraft
29 Bank of Bhutan
   (City Branch)
30 Kuenphen Colour Lab
34 Druktrin Rural
   Handicrafts
35 Changlimithang
   Stadium
38 Norbu Rabten
   Medical Shop
39 Art Gallery
42 Taxi Stand
43 DBS Books
   Enterprises
44 Clock Tower
47 India Bhutan
   Friendship Hospital
51 Archery Field
52 Paper Makers
54 Club X
55 Bus Terminal
56 Petrol Station
57 Memorial Chorten

There is a plan to build five new buildings to replace the crowded wooden structure. A large cultural centre is planned as a further expansion of the school just below the present facility. This is projected to be completed about 2005.

Behind the school, a narrow lane leads through a garden to a small house where a traditional craftsman makes drums and Tibetan violins. If the artisan is home, and you have space in your luggage for a large fragile object, they make an unusual and interesting souvenir.

Royal Academy of Performing Arts
The Royal Academy was established in 1967 to provide formal training for masked dancers and to preserve the folk dancing heritage. Unless there's a practice session on there's little to see here. The professional dancers from this school perform several of the dances at the Thimphu tsechu. With advance notice they will provide a one-hour performance for tour groups.

National Institute of Traditional Medicine
One of the more interesting facilities in Thimphu is the National Institute of Traditional Medicine, which was established in 1988. The European Union (EU) now provides funding for this project which prepares and dispenses traditional herbal and other medicines. There is an impressive, large new laboratory and production facility ensuring the quality of the products, the components of which may include plants, minerals, animal parts, precious metals and gems.

The production of medicines is directed entirely towards the needs of the Bhutanese, though there is a plan to eventually export traditional medicines. There is a day-care facility and clinic where traditional doctors

Traditional Medicine

The Himalayan Buddhist system of medicine is called *So-ba Rig-pa* and is practised in many countries today. Because it originally developed in ancient Tibet, it is commonly known as Tibetan Medicine.

It is believed that at the beginning of time, the art of healing was a prerogative of the gods. It wasn't until Kashiraja Dewadas, an ancient Indian king, went to heaven to learn medicine that medicine could be offered to humans as a means to fight suffering. He taught the principles and the practice of healing, and this knowledge was spread as part of early Buddhist sacred writings. Some of the fundamental beliefs of this system are the basis of Buddhism itself.

When Buddhism was first brought to Tibet some of these medicinal texts were translated into Tibetan and the rulers became interested in the subject. From that time, So-ba Rig-pa was considered a single system of medicine although some differences are found in the different lineages based on the discovery of *terma*, which occasionally include medicinal teachings.

When Shabdrung Ngawang Namgyal came to Bhutan, his Minister of Religion, Tenzin Drukey, an esteemed physician, spread the teaching of So-ba Rig-pa. Though the basic texts are the same, the Bhutanese tradition of So-ba Rig-pa has developed independently from its Tibetan origins. Today, the Himalayan Buddhist tradition is the most common type of medicine practised in Bhutan and has been recognised by the Royal Government as the official medical tradition of the country and has been included in the national health system since 1967.

Therapeutic Practices Several forms of treatment are applied in Bhutanese traditional medicine. Hundreds of medicinal plants, minerals and animal parts form the basic drugs used by the practitioners. These basic ingredients are processed and mixed in different combinations to make about 300 medicines in the form of pills, tablets, syrups, powders and lotions. Other treatments include dietary and behavioural advice.

There are also so-called surgical procedures that include *gtar* (blood letting), *bsregs* (cauterisation by herbal compounds), *gser bcos* (acupuncture by a golden needle), *tshug* (cauterisation with instruments of different materials), *dugs* (applying heat or cold to parts of the body), *byugs-pa* (medicated oil massage), *sman-chu* (stone-heated bath), *tsha-chu* (bath at a hot spring) and *lum* (vapour treatment).

Diagnostic Techniques The decision about what kind of treatment to use for a particular condition is made by the physician mainly through the reading of the pulses. In modern medicine, pulse reading is only used to detect anomalies of the heart and of the circulatory system. Using the So-ba Rig-pa method, it is possible to detect diseases of any organ through the pulses. The eyes, tongue and urine are also examined for signs that will help with the diagnosis, and sometimes the physician will record the patient's medical history.

diagnose patients and prescribe appropriate traditional medicines or treatments.

The institute also researches the use of medicinal herbs and plants and operates a trial plot on the premises. It has field units which collect medicinal plants from far away places such as Lingzhi in west Bhutan, where a number of important medicinal species grow in abundance.

CENTRE OF THIMPHU
Weekend Market

The weekend market is in a permanent set of stalls north of Changlimithang stadium. Vendors from throughout the region arrive on Friday afternoon and remain until Sunday night. It's an interesting place to visit, where village people jostle with well-heeled Thimphu residents for the best – and cheapest –

vegetables and foodstuffs. This is the only time that fresh produce is easily available and the shopping is enhanced by the opportunity to catch up on the week's gossip.

Among the food items on display weekly are potatoes, onions, numerous varieties of chillies, red and white rice, buckwheat, flour, cauliflower, cabbage, lettuce, eggplant, asparagus, peas, squash, yams, several kinds of mushrooms and ferns, strange spices and herbs. Fruits come from local orchards and from the south of the country. You'll find oranges, apples, pineapples, bananas, mangoes, apricots, peaches and plums. If you wander off into one corner of the market, you'll find an odiferous collection of dried fish, beef and balls of *datse*, home-made soft cheese that is used to make sauces. During the height of winter you can even pick up a leg of yak.

At the northern end of the market is a collection of stalls called the indigenous goods and handicrafts section. Here you will find locally produced goods, including religious objects, cloth, baskets and strange hats from various minority groups. They are more than happy to sell these to tourists, but it's really intended for local consumption. If you shop here, you may find a Bhutanese housewife or a monk from a nearby monastery to advise you on the quality of your purchase.

Zangto Pelri Lhakhang

This private chapel, built in the 1990s by Dasho Aku Tongmi, a musician who composed Bhutan's national anthem, is just south of the weekend market. It's beside the older Yigja Dungkhar (prayer wheel) Lhakhang and is a replica of Guru Rimpoche's celestial abode. It is Bhutan's tallest lhakhang and houses many large statues, including a 4m-high image of Guru Rimpoche.

Changlimithang Stadium

The national stadium occupies the field where, in 1885, a battle took place that helped establish the supremacy of Ugyen Wangchuck, Bhutan's first king. It is now the site of the national archery ground, a large football stadium cum parade ground,

basketball, tennis and squash courts, as well as the headquarters of the Bhutan Olympic committee. It's always worth checking what event is taking place when you are in town.

UNDP Office

A fancy Bhutanese-style building next to the post office houses the various United Nations agencies that operate in Bhutan.

MOTITHANG

Motithang is the region above the town. The original Motithang hotel was built to accommodate visitors to the 1972 coronation of King Jigme Singye Wangchuck in 1974. Along with the Olathang in Paro, it was one of the first hotels in the country. Tour groups stayed here until the mid-1990s when it became too expensive to maintain and was turned into a youth centre. The Druk path trek to Paro starts from here.

Above the old Motithang hotel is the **Kungachoeling State Guest House**, a place where you are unlikely to stay if you are reading this book.

Mini Zoo

Above the Motithang is a large fenced area that was originally established as a mini zoo. The king decided that such a facility was not in keeping with Bhutan's environmental and religious convictions, and it was disbanded some time ago. The animals were released into the wild but the takin were so tame (some people say they are simply stupid) that they wandered around the streets of Thimphu looking for food, and the only solution was to put them back into captivity. It's worthwhile taking the time to see these strange, quite ugly animals, though they are behind a mesh fence that makes photography almost impossible. (For more on this curious creature see the boxed text 'The Takin – Bhutan's National Animal' in the Facts about Bhutan chapter.)

Changangkha Lhakhang

Changangkha Lhakhang is a fortress-like temple and monastic school perched on a ridge above Thimphu, south of Motithang. It was established in the 12th century on a site chosen by Lama Phajo Drugom Shigpo, who came from Ralung in Tibet. The central statue is Chenrezig in a manifestation with 11 heads, and the books in the temple are larger in size than usual Tibetan texts. There is an excellent view of Thimphu from the courtyard.

Telecoms Tower

There's a wonderful view of Thimphu valley from the telecommunications tower (elevation 2685m) high above the town. Don't photograph the telecommunications installation, but the valley is worth a few snaps. The area is known as Sangaygang and it becomes a lover's lane late at night.

Drubthob Goemba

As you leave the Telecoms Tower, turn north and you will find yourself on Gaden Lam, the road that runs high above the golf course. There are some great views of the town, and of Trashi Chhoe Dzong along this road, and above you can see Drubthob Goemba, which now houses the Zilukha nunnery.

Dechen Phodrang

At the end of Gaden Lam is Dechen Phodrang, the site of Thimphu's original Trashi Chhoe Dzong. It is now the state monastic school, and a long procession of monks often travels between here and the dzong. The 12th century paintings in the goemba's Guru Lhakhang are being restored by a UNESCO project. The upper floor features a large figure of Shabdrung Ngawang Namgyal as well as the goenkhang. The central figure in the downstairs chapel is the Buddha Sakyamuni.

ACTIVITIES

It hardly seems worth spending US$200 a day to swim, play tennis or go to a cinema, but these activities are available if you want them. Japanese visitors find the prices of the Thimphu Golf Club reasonable, even considering the government tourist rate, compared to playing golf in Japan.

There are two tennis courts, squash courts and a basketball court at the north end of the Changlimithang Stadium.

Golf

The Royal Thimphu Golf Club (☎ 25429) has a nine-hole course beautifully situated above Trashi Chhoe Dzong. Indian Brigadier Gen TV Jaganathan, posted in Bhutan between 1968 and 1973, got permission from King Jigme Dorji Wangchuck to construct a few holes. The king later granted permission to expand the course to nine holes, recognising that it would provide a green area to preserve the beauty of Trashi Chhoe Dzong. It was formally inaugurated in 1971 as the Thimphu Golf Club and was renovated in 1992 as part of a Japanese project.

The green fee for foreigners is US$25 for a whole day, or US$500 for a full year membership. You can hire a set of clubs for Nu 600, and you can buy lost balls from kids who retrieve them from the course and sell them for Nu 20 to Nu 30. Caddies are available, but since they are mostly schoolboys, they are not on site until late afternoon. You don't need to make an appointment to play, but weekends are busy, and you may have to wait for a turn to tee off. There is a bar and restaurant in the clubhouse.

Swimming

It costs Nu 50 for a one-hour swim at the indoor pool in the Thimphu's sports complex (☎ 22064). The pool is open weekdays from 4 to 8 pm and weekends from 1 to 6 pm. The pool closes in December and January when it's too cold to heat it. The sports complex also has a basketball court and gym. The whole facility is particularly busy and noisy in the afternoon when schoolchildren take tae kwon do classes.

PLACES TO STAY

If you are on a normal tourist visa, you will probably be booked into one of the top-end hotels unless you have scheduled your trip in the autumn during the Thimphu tsechu. All hotels are completely full at tsechu time, and you may find yourself in a smaller guesthouse, a private home, or even a tent. If you end up as a house guest, you will certainly have a chance to make new friends, and will have found the perfect recipient for the bottle of duty free liquor you bought en route to Paro.

If you are an Indian national or are working in Bhutan on a project, you may want to choose a more moderate hotel. The mid-range hotels listed here are not as fancy as the tourist hotels, but they're all quite adequate, though they can be noisy once the dogs start howling.

Places to Stay – top end
Many people consider the *Hotel Druk* (☎ 22966; fax 22677) to be the best in Thimphu. It's in the centre of town and boasts, among its facilities, a bar, a restaurant noted for its Indian food, a hair salon and a health club with a gym, sauna and steam bath. Rates for its 34 rooms are Nu 1500/1800/4000 for a single/double/suite.

BTCL's *Hotel Motithang* (☎ 22435; fax 23392) was previously known as the Zangto Pelri. It is in the Motithang area, quite a distance above the business district. It has 15 large wood-panelled rooms that cost Nu 850/1075 for a single/double.

The *Hotel Riverview* (☎ 25030; fax 23496) is a large concrete structure in pseudo-Bhutanese style above the east bank of the Thimphu Chhu. All 50 of the well-appointed rooms have IDD phones and a balcony with a view of the town. There's a restaurant, bar, business centre, conference room and gift shop. It usually hosts a disco on Saturday nights and special occasions. Rates are Nu 1200/1500/3600 for a single/double/suite. Riverview and the Motithang are inconvenient if you want to wander around town.

The *Hotel Jumolhari* (☎ 22747; fax 24412) has been extensively renovated and has now regained its position as one of Thimphu's better hostelries. It is on Wagzin Lam, just south of the clock tower, and has 27 rooms that rent for Nu 900/1050 single/double. There's a good restaurant with continental, Indian, Chinese and Bhutanese dishes. If you're into karaoke, try the small room just off the lobby.

Managed by the same team as the Jumolhari, the *Hotel Wangchuk* (☎ 23532; fax 25174) is a new place overlooking the stadium. The 20 rooms are simple with carpets and wood panelling and cost Nu 650/900. The Wangchuck is a favourite of many project staff and expatriates, and you may find an interesting collection of knowledgeable Bhutan hands in the dining room.

Opposite the Swiss Bakery is the 34-room *Hotel Taktsang* (☎ 22102; fax 23284), with rooms· at Nu 1100/1300. The Taktsang has some interesting features such as a proper bar, a sun deck on the roof, and rooms with a fascinating view over the centre of town. The restaurant has one of the most extensive menus in town though, like all the others, they suffer from a lack of ingredients.

The *Yeedzin Guest House* (☎ 22932; fax 24995) is a pleasant 16-room establishment on Jangchhub Lam, in the same building as the Jichu Drakey bakery. Singles/doubles cost Nu 500/700. For long-staying guests they have three deluxe suites equipped with their own kitchen. There's a good restaurant in the hotel (Prince Charles ate here), and you can gorge on fresh pastries from the bakery downstairs.

The newest hotel in Thimphu is the homestyle *Pine Wood Hotel* (☎ 25924; fax 25507), on a hill above the eastern end of Lungten Zampa. All the nine rooms and suites are of different sizes. The mid-range rooms cost Nu 2000/2500; to stay in a suite here as Richard Gere did, you would probably have to pay a surcharge to the tour operator.

Places to Stay – middle
The centrally located *Hotel 89* (☎ 22931) has 24 rooms priced at Nu 375/550 and is a favourite with Indian tourists. It also has one of the most consistently good and popular restaurants in Thimphu.

The *Druk Sherig Guest House* (☎ 22598), with only 10 rooms at Nu 800, is often used by WWF guests and expatriates. There is no restaurant, but the staff can arrange meals if you order in advance.

Less expensive options include the *Kelwang Hotel* (☎ 23458; fax 23692), above the restaurant of the same name. The hotel reception desk is at the restaurant cashier counter. The *Hotel Tandin* (☎ 22380) is right in the centre of the city, near the cinema. Across the street, the *Dragon Inn* (☎ 24651) and *Hotel Norling* (☎ 22997, 23997) have smaller rooms with basic facilities. Many people working on long contracts stay at the *Rabten Apartments* (☎ 23587).

PLACES TO EAT

Hotel restaurants add 10% tax and 10% or 15% service charge (usually identified as such on the bill). There is no tax or service charge in small restaurants.

Restaurants

There are plenty of restaurants in Thimphu, but it's hardly a gourmet paradise. You can escape the tourist buffets that hotels provide, but all restaurants produce pretty much the same dishes.

Menus tend to be a fantasy of what the hotel would like to serve, and don't reflect what is actually in the kitchen. Be sure to ask what meat is available before you get your heart set on a beef or pork dish. There are few cold storage facilities in town. Except in the dead of winter the only meat that is usually available is chicken. Bhutanese food is available in most restaurants, but beware of the hot chillies that are an essential ingredient in many dishes.

In most restaurants you can expect to pay about Nu 100 for a complete meal, though in larger hotels prices may go up to Nu 200. In smaller snack places you can eat for Nu 30 to Nu 50.

The most reliable restaurants for health, variety and consistent quality are in hotels. The *89 Restaurant*, a wood-panelled room in the hotel of the same name, serves both western and Indian food and is a favourite of expatriates. The speciality here is fried cheese momos and Indian Tandoori food. Drinks are accompanied by a complimentary plate of the best chips (French fries) in Bhutan. The restaurant at *Hotel Tandin* has friendly staff and serves excellent Indian food. It caters to a largely Indian clientele and does not serve beef. The restaurants in the *Wangchuk, Jumolhari* and *Druk* hotels are all good.

It's a bit hard to find the entrance to *Plums Cafe*. There's a small sign above a door that leads upstairs to the Plums bakery. Climb another flight of stairs to reach the restaurant, which has tablecloths, cloth napkins and a buffet table which swings into action for groups. They offer a small range of continental food, including a chicken sizzler plate and an extensive menu of both Chinese and Bhutanese dishes. It's open daily except Sunday from 11 am until 9.30 or 10 pm, and also provides catering services for local functions. *Lhanam Restaurant* is upstairs in the back of the same building. It's a good place for a quick lunch of curry or momos and is packed with Bhutanese office workers.

The *Swiss Bakery* is on a hill just above the southern traffic circle and is the closest thing to a fast-food joint that you'll find in Thimphu. It serves great cheese omelettes or you can order from a display of plastic-wrapped sandwiches and hamburgers. At the far end of the counter is a selection of rum balls, cakes, pastries, 'moon rocks' and potato crisps. Despite its rustic appearance, it's a high-tech operation; they microwave the hamburgers and have several electronic gadgets including an electronic lock on the toilet door, and a fancy phone system.

This is a favourite lunch spot for expatriates and Bhutanese office workers, and can become quite crowded during the traditional 1 to 2 pm lunch hour. It's open daily except Sunday from 8 am to 6.30 pm.

Benez is a small restaurant in the centre of town. With a tiny bar in the back that is very popular with locals, it tends to be more lively than other restaurants in Thimphu. The menu is basic rice, curry, chow mien and momos at extremely reasonable prices. *Sambara* is opposite Benez and is more of a drinking place than a restaurant, though it does have an extensive western menu. It sometimes runs short of beer but there's lots of Bhutanese whisky available.

Jichu Drakey Bakery used to have a restaurant, but now prepares its cakes, pies and pastries only for take away from 7 am to 7.30 pm. Most items are Nu 10, including cream rolls, eclairs and tarts. It also produces apple pie, strudel and several varieties of bread. The owner, Ugyen Dorji, hails from the Lhuentse district and learned his trade as an apprentice pastry chef in Austria.

Indian Food Indian cooking in Thimphu suffers from a lack of ingredients and good chefs. The best Indian food is at the *Druk, 89* and *Tandin* hotels. The *Pekhang Restaurant* in the Etho Metho building serves Indian vegetarian snacks. The restaurant upstairs in *Hotel Kelwang* has mediocre Indian food.

ENTERTAINMENT
Entertainment is sparse in Thimphu unless it's tsechu time. There are occasional concerts and video shows at the sports complex, and these are all well advertised with posters and in *Kuensel*.

Cultural Programmes
If you are in a group of more than four, your tour operator can arrange a dance performance at the *Royal Academy of Performing Arts*. A more relaxed atmosphere prevails at *Tashi Nencha Music Studio* near the Zangto Pelri Lhakhang, which can provide a Bhutanese meal and an evening of classical and folk music around a bonfire.

Cinema
The cinema in the centre of town screens two Hindi movies and one ancient English movie daily. It's a crowded, uncomfortable facility and the ticket window is inside a metal cage designed to keep the queue orderly.

Nightclubs
Club X, on the lane behind the Druk Sherig Guest House and Hotel Jumolhari, is open only on Saturday. It has no sign. It opens at 9 pm, but becomes lively from about 11 pm until its 2 am closing time. You could also try the disco in the *Riverside Hotel*, but only

on Saturday. There is a karaoke parlour in the *Hotel Jumolhari*.

Pubs & Bars
There are numerous small bars throughout the town. The most likely places to find a few drinking companions are the *Sambara* and *Benez* restaurants. Another possibility is *Yeedzin Guest House*, which has a happy hour from 5 to 7 pm.

SPECTATOR SPORT
Archery
Archers practise at the target field at the south end of Changlimithang stadium on most weekends (see the boxed text 'Archery' in the Facts for the Visitor chapter).

Football
The national football tournament takes place in August with teams from schools throughout the country competing. At major matches the Royal Bhutan Army (RBA) band provides the half-time entertainment.

THINGS TO BUY
Most shops in Thimphu contain a hodgepodge selection of items. Many shops advertise themselves as 'general' shops, and even a tiny shop may sell diverse items like light bulbs, stationery, farm implements, shampoo, computer disks and canned fish. To provide even more variety, they may sell drinks by the glass and their sign may read 'shop cum bar' or the all-encompassing 'general cum bar shop'.

Many of the items on sale are made in India but there are lots of interesting Bhutanese products, especially textiles, baskets, jewellery, books and religious items. Thimphu is especially known for the fine metal work that local artisans produce.

There is a Duty Free Shop in Thimphu, but it's for diplomats and senior government officials only.

Handicrafts
High-quality handicrafts are available from the Tshering Dolkar shop near the southern traffic circle.

Further north on Norzin Lam is the large government Handicraft Emporium. Be sure to visit the upper floor, as it's not obvious that it's part of the sales area. The Cottage Industry Development Project (☎ 24469; fax 24470), opposite the stadium on Chang Lam, is another source of quality goods at reasonable prices. They have a display of vegetable dyes and have some weavers working in the back room.

Opposite the Swiss Bakery is the new Bhutan Arts & Crafts Centre that has a large supply of Indian goods in addition to Bhutanese handicrafts. Druktrin Rural Handicrafts (☎ 24500) is on the 3rd floor above the Sakten Health Club on Chang Lam and offers great variety.

Choki Handicrafts (☎ 24728; fax 23731) near the School of Arts and Crafts, manufactures and sells high-quality masks, thangkas, paintings and painted lama tables called *choektse*. They accept American Express cards.

Don't neglect the handicraft section at the weekend market and also look in the Druk shopping complex on the lower floors of the Hotel Tandin. Other places to shop are the Danida woodcraft project and the incense factory on the road to Bangladesh embassy.

The Archery Shop

A new shop in Thimphu caters to the large community of Bhutanese archers. It's rare to find a foreigner in the Archery Shop (☎ 23323; fax 22897), Thori Lam. It specialises in American-made Hoyt brand bows that range in price from Nu 6000 for a fibreglass version to Nu 30,000 for the top-of-the-line carbonite variety. The bows can be set for pulls of 35 to 80 pounds. Arrows are steel-tipped Easton brand that sell for Nu 280 to Nu 500. It's a relatively expensive sport.

The archery shop sponsors several tournaments with prestigious prizes such as free bows and trips to Bangkok.

Music Cassettes

Cassette tapes of Hindi and Bhutanese songs are available for Nu 35 in a shop inside the

---

Donning a Gho

The gho, when first put on, should reach almost to the ground. Fold the sleeves of the *tego* (shirt) back to form cuffs. Tuck the right front panel into the left and bring the left panel over to the right. Grasp the gho at the sides and fold towards the back. Gather the material at your waist until the hemline is above the knee (the king wears his below the knee).

The gho is secured with a *kera* (narrow woven belt) which forms a pouch. You need shoes and knee-high socks to complete the outfit. Pants are worn under the gho in winter and tucked into the long socks.

Norling Tshonkhang shopping centre on Norzin Lam and from a kiosk in the weekend market.

Jewellery
Norling Handicrafts, also in Norling Tshonkhang shopping centre, is a reliable dealer in jewellery and semi-precious stones.

Gho & Kira
If you want to try wearing Bhutanese dress (see the boxed texts for practical guidelines), you have many shops to choose from in Thimphu. Gyeltsen Dorji Shop, just north of Tshering Dolkar's handicraft shop, has ready-made gho and kira in a variety of patterns and qualities, including children's sizes.

Gho range from Nu 800 for machine-woven cloth and Nu 1900 for hand-woven cloth to Nu 5000 for a silk gho. A handmade kira costs about Nu 1200, and a silk kira sells for Nu 6000 or more. You can find all the necessary accessories there to complete your Bhutanese outfit.

Postage Stamps
Bhutan Post occupies the northern half of a large building on Dremton Lam, a back road just north of the cinema. The Philatelic Bureau (☎ 22296) has a counter near the front door and sells sheets and souvenir packets of exotic Bhutanese stamps (see the colour section 'Collecting Bhutanese Stamps' between pages 96 and 97).

Contemporary Paintings & Handmade Paper
There are two paper makers across the river above the Riverview Hotel. The Jungshi Handmade Paper Factory produces paper as well as cards, envelopes, calendars and other items from traditional Bhutanese paper. A short, but rough, gravel road leads to the Mangala Paper House (☎ 22898) which produces high-quality paper in unusual designs.

The Art Gallery near the clock tower has Bhutanese paper and paintings, and another art gallery next door to Yu-Druk Travels sells watercolours of dzongs and lhakhangs among other subjects.

Wearing a Kira
The kira is first draped around the back under the right arm. Wrap it around the front and fasten on your left shoulder with a *koma* (silver hook). Fold it left to right across your front and then right to left. The remaining cloth is gathered under the left arm and wrapped around the back to the right shoulder, and fastened with a second koma. A *kera* is wrapped around the waist to form a pouch.

The *kaymeto* (widthways border) is always worn at the back.

A *toego* (jacket) is often worn with the kira, and the sleeves of the *wonju* (blouse) can be folded back over the toego to form cuffs.

GETTING THERE & AWAY
Paro Airport
Druk Air operates a vehicle, usually a six-passenger jeep, between Paro airport and Thimphu. It leaves the Druk Air office in Thimphu about 4 am to connect to departing flights, and returns to Thimphu after a flight arrives. There is no facility for pre-booking a space on this vehicle, and you are far better off using the vehicle that your tour operator provides or, if you are on your own, a public taxi.

Paro to Thimphu
It is 53km from Paro airport to Thimphu; the journey takes less than two hours.

Paro Airport to Chhuzom
18km, ½ hour
Just outside of the airport is the settlement of Bondey, where there are some lovely old traditional Bhutanese houses. From Bondey the road follows the north bank of the Paro Chhu downstream to Shaba, where there is an army camp and the pleasantly situated Pegyel Hotel. At Isuna, 12km from the airport, the road crosses back to the south bank again and travels through mostly uninhabited country to Chhuzom. The monastery above Isuna is **Draka**, and the temple on the north side of the river is **Tamchhog Lhakhang**, built by Thangtong Gyalpo of Tibet, who was responsible for numerous iron bridges throughout Bhutan.

Chhuzom, better known as the 'Confluence' is at the juncture of the Paro Chhu and Thimphu Chhu, which join to form the Wang Chhu. Sometimes this confluence is considered a union of a mother and father river similar to that of the Pho Chhu and Mo Chhu at Punakha. The Paro Chhu represents the father, and is sometimes called the 'Pho Chhu', and the Wang Chhu is the 'Mo Chhu', or mother river. English maps and road signs use the name 'Confluence' as the translation of Chhuzom (*Chhu* means river, *zom* is to join).

Because Bhutanese tradition regards such a joining of rivers as inauspicious, there are three chortens here to ward away the evil

spells of the area. Each chorten is in a different style: Bhutanese, Tibetan and Nepali.

Chhuzom is also a major road junction. One road leads along the west bank of the Wang Chhu, climbing 79km to the Ha valley. Another road leads south along the eastern bank of the Wang Chhu and travels 141km to the border town of Phuentsholing. The third road leads north up the east bank of the Thimphu Chhu.

A check post here verifies that your permit is in order and controls access to the restricted region of Ha. Dantak, the Indian road construction organisation, operates an ice cream parlour and espresso coffee shop just north of the check post. People from nearby villages often sit by the side of the road just south of the check post selling vegetables, apples and dried cheese.

Chhuzom to Thimphu
31km, 1 hour
The countryside is almost barren and you may wonder about the stories of Bhutan's extensive forest cover as you drive through this area. Foresters believe that this valley, as well as the lower part of the Paro valley, were never forested because of the lack of groundwater on these slopes. They cite the absence of landslides as evidence of this. Despite this, you can see the afforestation efforts on the lower hillsides.

A kilometre past Chhuzom is a rough, unpaved side road that leads to Genika and the start of the Dagala trek. The road passes **Kharibje**, a village in a valley on the opposite side of the river. This village is inhabited by *bja-wap* (goldsmiths) who make jewellery and brass trumpets, butter lamps and other items used in goembas. A small bridge across the Thimphu Chhu provides road access to the village.

Khasadrapchhu is a small settlement with a few shops and restaurants. On the opposite side of the river is the hydro plant that served Thimphu before the large Chhukha hydroelectric project came on line in 1988. The road up the side valley to the west follows the Bemang Rong Chhu to a marble factory, a leprosy hospital, and eventually Bjimena and

Tshelungnang villages. A new industrial park is being developed in this valley.

The valley widens near the small village of Namseling. Below the road are extensive rice paddies. Rice is planted in mid-June and harvested in October. Terraces are barren during the winter. Above the road are numerous apple orchards. Much of the fruit is exported, especially to Bangladesh. In the autumn people sell apples and mushrooms from informal stalls at the side of the road. After rounding a sharp bend, the road passes large statues of the guardians of the east and north.

At several places along the road you will see what looks like **ancient ruins**. These are the remains of houses that either burned or were replaced. It is considered unlucky to move into the house of a family whose members have died out or that a family has abandoned, therefore there are numerous derelict houses scattered around the country. The packed mud walls are so tough that they survive for years after the rest of the structure has disappeared.

The large ponds by the side of the river as you near Simtokha are part of Thimphu's new sewage treatment plant, which was funded by Danida. The project uses a microbiological system to treat urban waste from Thimphu so that no polluted water flows to communities downstream. Just beyond the headquarters of the Dantak construction project the road rounds a corner and enters **Simtokha** (see Around Thimphu).

The road crosses a bridge and turns a switchback. As the road climbs, you can look back and see Simtokha Dzong on the hill to the south. Vehicles detour around a large prayer wheel in the middle of the road, then go under a road overpass at the junction of the road that leads to Punakha and the east of the country.

Soon you can see Thimphu, and at the suburb of Lungtenphug you arrive at the outskirts of the town. The headquarters of the RBA is above the road and there is a new suburban housing development below. The road passes the bus station, crosses the bridge over the Thimphu Chhu and enters the city from the south.

To/From Phuentsholing
This journey took up to 10 days before the road was completed. See the description of the six hour road journey from Thimphu to Phuentsholing in the Chhukha Dzongkhag section of the Western Bhutan chapter.

GETTING AROUND
If you are on a normal tourist visa, you will have a car, driver and guide available throughout your stay in Bhutan, and you'll have little trouble getting around. Most shops and points of interest are within easy walking distance of Thimphu's major hotels; it's easy to pop out for a drink or a round of shopping on foot.

Bus
There is no public bus service within the town. At the new bus station below the east end of the bridge at the southern end of town you can find crowded buses to Phuentsholing and other destinations throughout the country.

Taxi
Most of the taxis are Indian Maruti brand minivans, though there are still some old Indian Mahindra jeeps which the government is trying to phase out. The taxi stand is on Chang Lam, next to the Changlimithang Stadium, though you can sometimes flag down an empty taxi in the street. There are no taxi meters, although they may be introduced soon, and prices are very much negotiable. Taxi drivers have a habit of charging foreigners, including Indians, as much as they can – one of Bhutan's few flagrant rip-offs. You should be able to hire a taxi for the whole day for about Nu 300, and local trips should cost between Nu 30 and Nu 60, though locals pay as little as Nu 10 for a ride in a shared taxi.

Bicycle
At the time of research there were no bicycles for rent in Thimphu. Several tour companies are planning to import mountain bikes, and these may be available for rent in the future. A mountain bike would provide an excellent way to tour the area.

Around Thimphu

As you travel up the east side of the Thimphu Chhu north of Lungten Zampa, make a right turn just beyond the Riverview Hotel to two small traditional paper factories. Return to the main road and continue past the SAARC building, which overlooks the dzong, and on the opposite side of the river you may catch a glimpse of Samtenling Palace, the cottage that is the king's residence. A short distance north is the suburb of Taga where the Forestry Institute has its offices.

DECHENCHOELING PALACE
The large Dechenchoeling Palace is some distance north of the dzong. It was built in 1952 and is the official residence of the Queen Mother. North of the palace is the Royal Body Guard (RBG) facility.

PANGRI ZAMPA TEMPLE
Just north of Dechenchoeling is Pangri Zampa, two imposing white buildings in a grove of giant cypress trees. The Shabdrung Ngawang Namgyal lived here after he arrived in 1616 because this temple appeared in the vision that directed him from Tibet to Bhutan. A well-respected astrologer now lives on the upper storey.

TANGO GOEMBA
Continuing up the valley the road crosses to the east side of the Thimphu Chhu at Begana, near a training facility operated by the electricity department. A few kilometres beyond this, 12km from Thimphu, a road leads east and climbs a short distance to a parking lot. The trail to Tango is a climb of 280m and takes about half an hour if you follow the steeper shortcut, or about an hour if you take the longer, more gradual trail.

Lama Gyalwa Lhanampa founded the goemba in the 12th century. The present building was built in the 15th century by the 'divine madman', Lama Drukpa Kunley (see the boxed text 'The Divine Madman' in the

Western Bhutan chapter). In 1616 the Shabdrung Ngawang Namgyal visited Tango and meditated in a cave near the goemba. His meditations helped ensure the defeat of an invading Tibetan army. The head lama, a descendent of Lama Drukpa Kunley, presented the goemba to the Shabdrung, who carved a sandalwood statue of Chenrezig which he installed in the monastery.

The picturesque three-storey tower and several surrounding buildings were built in the 18th century by the eighth desi, Druk Rabgye. The Shabdrung Jigme Chhogyel added the golden roof in the 19th century.

There are no restaurants or shops around here so if you plan a full-day excursion to either Tango Goemba or Chari Goemba bring a water bottle and a packed lunch.

CHARI GOEMBA
A short distance beyond the turnoff to Tango Goemba the road ends at Dodina (elevation

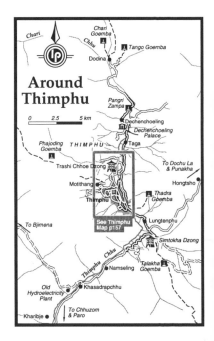

2600m). A walk of about 1½ hours leads to Chari Goemba. The trail starts by crossing a lovely covered bridge that spans the Thimphu Chhu, then climbs steeply to the monastery.

The monastery's full name is Chari Dorji Dhen. The Shabdrung, Ngawang Namgyal, built this goemba in 1620 and established the first monk body here. A silver chorten inside the goemba holds the ashes of the Shabdrung's father.

SIMTOKHA

Simtokha is about 5km south of Thimphu on the road to Paro and Phuentsholing. The junction with the road to eastern Bhutan is just before Simtokha.

In the valley below the road are the EU-funded plant and soil protection project, the National Mushroom Centre and the large, red-roofed Royal Institute of Management.

Simtokha Dzong

Officially known as Sangak Zabdhon Phodrang (Palace of the Profound Meaning of Secret Mantras), Simtokha Dzong was built in 1629 by Shabdrung Ngawang Namgyal. It is often said to be the first dzong built in Bhutan. In fact, there were dzongs in Bhutan as early as 1153, but this is the first dzong built by the Shabdrung, is the oldest dzong that has survived as a complete structure, and is the first structure that incorporated both monastic and administrative facilities. Since 1961 it has been the home of a *rigney* (religious and classical studies) school; its students are both monks and lay people.

The site is said to have been chosen to guard over a demon that had vanished into the rock nearby, hence the name Simtokha, from *simmo* (demoness), *do* (stone). Conveniently, the site is also an excellent location

from which to protect the Thimphu valley and the valley leading to the Dochu La and eastern Bhutan. The dzong is about 60m square and the only gate is on the east side, overlooking the valley.

The utse is three storeys high and behind the usual prayer wheels around the outside there is a line of more than 300 fine slate carvings depicting saints and philosophers. The central figure in the lhakhang is of Sakyamuni; he is flanked by images of eight Bodhisattvas: Jampelyang, Channa Dorji, Chenrezig, Jhampa, and the less familiar Sai Hingpo (Shritigarva), Dupa Nampasel, Namkhe Hingpo (Akash Garva) and Kuentu Zangpo. The paintings inside the lhakhang are said to be some of the oldest and most beautiful in Bhutan. One of the lhakhangs, Gen Khang, may be visited only by the lamas.

Expansion and restoration of the dzong was performed by the third Druk Desi, Mingyur Tenpa, in the 1670s after Tibetan invaders attacked it in 1630. It has been enlarged and restored many times since.

During its construction Simtokha Dzong was attacked by a coalition of Tibetans and five Bhutanese lamas who were opposed to the Shabdrung's rule. The attack was repelled and the leader of the coalition, Palden Lama, was killed. In 1630 the Tibetans again attacked and took control of the dzong. The Shabdrung regained control when the main building caught fire and the roof collapsed, killing the invaders. Descriptions of the original Simtokha Dzong were provided by the two Portuguese Jesuit priests who visited here in 1629 on their way to Tibet.

DAY WALKS

In addition to Tango and Chari (described earlier) there are good walks to several monasteries on hillsides above Thimphu. You cannot go into the monasteries, but most are architecturally interesting and command good views of the valley.

Hikes to Nearby Monasteries

You can walk uphill from Simtokha Dzong to the 15th century **Talakha Goemba**

(3050m) or save your legs by driving up the gravel road before setting out on foot.

It is a 5km walk uphill from the old Motithang hotel to **Phajoding Goemba** (3700m). Shagcha Rinchen built this monastery in the 15th century. You can continue further to Thugjedra and Jimilangtsho lakes. This is the last day of the Druk Path Trek in reverse. See the trekking chapter for details.

Another strenuous two hour uphill hike leads to **Thadra Goemba** (3270m). You can drive through the gate of the RBA headquarters and then through the camp to the start of the trail.

It's two hours from the hillside above Hongtsho to the **Tashigang Goemba** (3200m).

A one hour walk uphill from the Central Monastic School at Dechen Phodrang takes you to **Wangditse Goemba**, which was founded in the 18th century by the eighth desi.

Dechenphug Monastery is a 30 minute walk from Dechenchoeling village in a side valley.

Important Figures of Drukpa Kagyu Buddhism

This brief guide to some of the gods and goddesses of the Drukpa Kagyu pantheon may help you to recognise a few of the figures in paintings and as statues in Bhutan's goembas. They are known in Bhutan by their Tibetan names, but many also have Sanskrit names which are shown in brackets.

Guru Rimpoche (Padmasambhava)

The 'lotus-born' Buddha – an 8th century missionary and saint who visited Bhutan in 746AD. He is worshipped in Bhutan as the second Buddha and may appear in eight forms or manifestations. Most lhakhangs in Bhutan built after Guru Rimpoche's visit have a statue of the Guru as the central figure.

Jampa (Maitreya)

The 'Buddha of the future'. He is passing the life of a Bodhisattva and will return to earth in human form 4000 years after the disappearance of the Buddha Sakyamuni. Statues of Jampa are the focal point in most older lhakhangs built before Guru Rimpoche visited Bhutan. Jampa is easily recognised because he is either standing or seated in a western style. Statues of all other deities are seated in a cross-legged posture.

Chenrezig (Avalokitesvara)
'Glorious gentle one' – one of the four great Bodhisattvas and the special guardian of the Bhutanese religion. He is the Bodhisattva of compassion and is pictured sitting in a lotus position, with the lower two of his four arms in a gesture of prayer. He may also appear with 11 heads and 1000 arms arranged in a circle about him.

Jampelyang (Manjushree)
'Princely lord of wisdom' – the embodiment of wisdom and knowledge. He carries a sword in his right hand to destroy the darkness of ignorance. He is the patron of learning and the arts.

Channa Dorji (Vajrapani)
'Thunderbolt in hand' – the God of power and victory. The thunderbolt represents power and is a fundamental symbol of Tantric faith; it is called a *dorji* in Tibetan and *vajra* in Sanskrit. He is pictured in a wrathful form with an angry face and one leg outstretched.

Sakyamuni

The 'historical Buddha' – born in Lumbini in southern Nepal in the 5th century BC, he attained enlightenment under a pipal (Bo) tree and his teachings set in motion the Buddhist faith. In Tibetan-style representations he is always pictured sitting cross-legged on a lotus flower throne.

Milarepa

A great Tibetan magician (1040-1123) and poet of the Kagyu lineage who is believed to have attained the supreme enlightenment of Buddhahood in the course of one life. He travelled extensively throughout the Himalayan border lands and is said to have meditated at Taktshang in Bhutan where he composed a song. Most images of Milarepa picture him smiling and holding his hand to his ear as he sings.

Tara

'The saviouress' has 21 different manifestations or aspects. She symbolises fertility and is believed to be able to fulfil wishes. Statues of Tara usually represent Green Tara, who is associated with night, or White Tara, who is associated with day. In Bhutan, Tara is known as Dem.

Tara is said to represent the two wives of the Tibetan king Songtsen Gampo. The Nepali wife is Green Tara and the Chinese wife is White Tara. You can recognise statues of White Tara because she has seven eyes, including ones on her forehead, each palm and the sole of each foot.

Shabdrung Rimpoche

Ngawang Namgyal (1594-1651) is revered in Bhutan as Shabdrung Rimpoche (precious jewel at whose feet one prostrates). He is an important Bhutanese saint and his statue appears in many lhakhangs throughout the country. He is depicted in a seated position and has a long grey beard.

Western Bhutan

Whether you arrive by air at Paro or by road at Phuentsholing, your first impression of Bhutan is one of stepping into a world that you thought existed only in storybooks or your imagination. Western Bhutan is the heartland of the Drukpa people and you are confronted with the largest, oldest and most spectacular dzongs in the kingdom. You will soon realise you are off the beaten path of world tourism and far away from the culture you call home.

HISTORY

The history of western Bhutan is reflected in the history of Bhutan as a whole. Punakha was the capital of a unified Bhutan from the 17th to the 19th century. The seat of government was later moved to Paro, which became the commercial, cultural and political centre of the country. Before the construction of roads, most of Bhutan's trade came through Paro, either from Tibet via the Tremo La or from the south via Ha and the Cheli La.

GEOGRAPHY

The rugged Black Mountain range forms a barrier that separates western Bhutan from the rest of the country.

There are three major river systems in western Bhutan: the Torsa in the south-west, the Wang Chhu in the west and the Puna Tsang Chhu to the east. The Wang Chhu and Puna Tsang Chhu are separated by a range of hills that extends from the Tibetan border in the north to the Indian border in the south. The only road across this range traverses the Dochu La at 3150m, between Thimphu and Punakha.

Two major rivers flow into the Wang Chhu, each in its own large valley. The Paro valley extends from Jhomolhari on the Tibetan border all the way to Chhuzom, the confluence of the Paro Chhu and Thimphu Chhu. A side valley leads to the Tremo La, the 5000m pass that was an important trade route to Tibet and also the route of several

---

Tibetan invasions. The Ha Chhu flows from the head of the steep, isolated Ha valley to join the Wang Chhu as it flows through a deep gorge below Chapcha.

The Puna Tsang Chhu is formed by the Pho Chhu and the much larger Mo Chhu, which join at Punakha. The river then flows south, passing below Wangdue Phodrang and exiting Bhutan at the small border town of Kalikhola.

The Torsa Chhu cuts across the far southwest of the country, flowing from Tibet into Bhutan, forming a valley south of Ha, then flowing out of Bhutan near Phuentsholing.

Paro Dzongkhag

Willow trees line many of the roads, contrasting with the bright green of the rice terraces and the brilliant white of the dzongs and temples to give the valley a fresh look and pleasant atmosphere. As the broad Paro valley is excellent agricultural land, the people of Paro are better off than many in Bhutan. One indication of their affluence is the preponderance of metal roofs throughout the valley, replacing the traditional wooden shingles.

There is quite a large Japanese-assisted

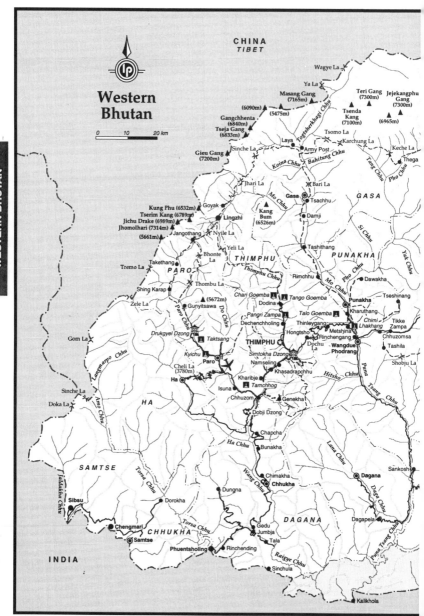

Western Bhutan

0   10   20 km

CHINA
TIBET

Wagye La

Ya La

Masang Gang
(7165m)

Teri Gang
(7300m)

Jejekangphu
Gang
(7300m)

(6090m)▲
(5475m)

Tsenda
Kang
(7100m)

(6965m)▲

Gangchhenta
(6840m)
Tseja Gang
(6833m)

Tsomo La

Karchung La

Keche La

Thega

Gieu Gang
(7200m)

Sinche La

Laya

Army Post

Koina Chhu

Bahitung Chhu

Togtsherkhug Chhu

Tang Chhu

Pho Chhu

Jhari La

Bari La

Gasa

Tsachhu

GASA

Kung Phu (6532m)
Tserim Kang (6789m)
Jichu Drake (6989m)
Jhomolhari (7314m)
(5661m)▲

Goyak

Lingzhi

Jangothang

Nyile La

Mo Chhu

Kang
Bum
(6526m)

Damji

Si Chhu

Yak Chhu

Yeli La

Tashithang

PUNAKHA

Bhonte
La

Takethang

THIMPHU

Rimchhu

Mo Chhu

Dawakha

Tremo La

PARO

Thimphu Chhu

Pho Chhu

Tseshinang

Shing Karap

Thombu La

Chari Goemba

Tango Goemba

Punakha

Kharuthang

Zele La

▲(5672m)
Gunyitsawa

Dodina

Do Chhu

Pangri Zampa

Talo Goemba

Thinleygang

Chimi
Lhakhang

Tikke
Zampa

Gom La

Drukgyel Dzong

Taktsang

Dechencholing

THIMPHU

Hongtsho

Rinchengang

Metshina

Chhuzomsa

Tashila

Kyichu

Paro

Simtokha Dzong

Dochu
La

**Wangdue
Phodrang**

Cheli La
(3780m)

Namseling

Shobju La

Ha

Khasadrapchhu

Hitsho Chhu

Langgharpo Chhu

Amo Chhu

Kharibje

Isuna

Tamchhog

HA

Chhuzom

Genekha

Puna Tsang Chhu

Sinche La

Doka La

Dobji Dzong

Chapcha

Ha Chhu

Bunakha

Lanu Chhu

SAMTSE

Torsa Chhu

Chimakha

Chhukha

Dagana

Sankosh

Jaldaka Chhu

Sibsu

Dorokha

Dungna

Wang Chhu

Dagapela

Daga Chhu

DAGANA

Chengmari

CHHUKHA

Torsa Chhu

Gedu
Jumbja
Tala

Puna Tsang Chhu

Samtse

Phuentsholing

Rinchending

Raigye Chhu

Sinchula

INDIA

Kalikhola

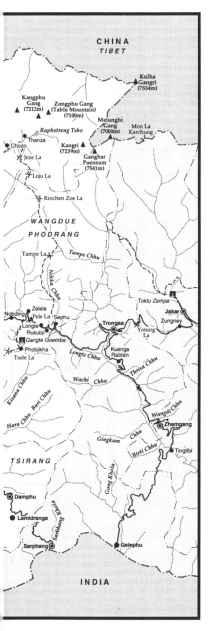

agricultural project in the valley. One of their projects was to line much of the area between the airport and Paro town with a new embankment that protects the valley from flooding and damage by the Paro Chhu. Another was the construction of an unpaved road along the upper portion of the valley. This was designed to allow farmers to move tractors into their fields. Among the important crops here, in addition to both red and white rice, are apples, strawberries and asparagus.

A high ridge separates the Paro valley from the Ha valley to the south. A road crosses this ridge via the 3780m Cheli La; tourists are allowed to travel as far as the pass, but not to Ha itself. To the north of Paro is another valley formed by the Do Chhu. A gravel road follows this side valley north from Paro town. On the eastern side of the Do Chhu valley several passes lead across the hills into the Thimphu valley. The Druk Path trek follows one of these routes, crossing the Dungtsho La.

PARO TOWN
The town of Paro (2280m) lies in the centre of the valley just south of the Paro Chhu and a short distance north-west of Paro Dzong.

Orientation
The new town centre, built in 1985, is aligned along a wide street about 500m long which parallels the river in a roughly north-west to south-east direction. The road from Chhuzom and the airport enters the town from the south, then makes a left turn at a T-junction into the main street near the archery practice field.

Central Paro is littered with shops and video stalls as well as eating and drinking places of varying standards. There's a grass area that forms a town square. Along the square are more shops and a few hotels, handicraft shops and restaurants. Many of the shops have doors at the back and a strange ladder system provides access through the front window. At the south-east end of the square is a large white chorten. The petrol station, bus station and police post mark the western limits of the town proper. If you follow the main street south-east instead of turning south towards the airport, you'll reach the archery practice field, Ugyen Pelri Palace and the covered bridge to the massive structure of Paro Dzong.

Downstream from the dzong is a large complex housing the Teachers Training Centre, one of two teacher training institutes in the country. The other is in Samtse, in the south-west of Bhutan.

Information
Post & Communications Paro's post office is on the south-eastern corner of the town square. There are also several shops with signs offering services as public telephone booths.

Medical Services A new hospital is on a hill to the west of town, and will accept visitors in cases of extreme emergency.

Paro Dzong
Paro Dzong is one of Bhutan's most impressive and well-known dzongs, and the finest example of Bhutanese architecture you'll see. The inward-sloping walls form a massive structure that towers over the town and is visible as a great white monolith from vantage points throughout the valley.

The dzong's correct name is Rinchen Pung Dzong, which means 'fortress on a heap of jewels'. This is usually contracted into a shorter version: Rinpung Dzong. In 1646 Shabdrung Ngawang Namgyal ordered its construction on the old foundation of a monastery built by Guru Rimpoche. It has always been one of Bhutan's strongest and most important fortresses and on numerous occasions was used to defend the Paro valley

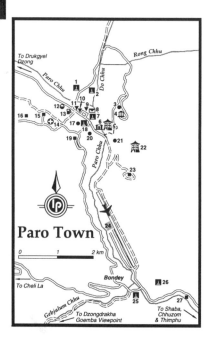

PLACES TO STAY
15 Dechen Cottages
16 Olathang Hotel
19 Gantey Palace
23 Hotel Druk
27 Pegyel Hotel

PLACES TO EAT
 9 Rendez Vous Inn
10 Sonam Trophel
11 Snow View Restaurant & Bar

OTHER
 1 Dumtse Lhakhang
 2 Pana Lhakhang
 3 High School
 4 National Museum (Ta Dzong)
 5 Paro Dzong
 6 Ugyen Pelri Palace
 7 Chhoeten Lhakhang
 8 Post Office
12 Bus Stand
13 Petrol Station
14 Hospital
17 Sunday Market
18 Druk Choeding
20 Archery Ground
21 Teacher Training Centre
22 Zuri Dzong
24 Airport Terminal
25 Bondey Lhakhang
26 Pelri Goemba

Paro Town

from invasions by Tibet. John Claude White reported that in 1905 there were old catapults for throwing great stones stored in the rafters of the dzong's verandah.

The dzong survived the 1897 earthquake and caught fire only once, in 1907. The fire severely damaged the dzong, and it was rebuilt the following year. Large statues of Sakyamuni, Guru Rimpoche and Shabdrung Ngawang Namgyal were installed during the reconstruction. The dzong was formerly the meeting hall for the National Assembly and now houses the Paro monastic school and government offices.

The dzong is built on a steep hillside, and the courtyard of the administrative section is 6m higher than the courtyard of the monastic portion. Though a bridge leads to the foot of the dzong, the only entrance is from the hillside on the north wall. A motor road climbs the hill to the dzong's entrance, which leads into the *dochey* (courtyard) on the 3rd storey. The *utse* (central tower) inside the dochey is five storeys tall and was built in the time of the first Paro Penlop in 1649. There are two *lhakhangs* (temples) on the utse's top storey which have excellent wood carvings on the beams. To the east of the utse is another small lhakhang dedicated to Chuchizhey, an 11-headed manifestation of Chenrezig.

A stairway leads down to the monastic quarter, which houses about 200 monks. In the south-east corner is the Kunre, which is where the monks eat their communal meals. Numerous paintings adorn the walls in front of this structure, including an unusual Bhutanese mystic spiral interpretation of a *mandala* (cosmic diagram). On the opposite side of the monastic dochey is the large *dukhang* (ceremonial room). The paintings

on the porch of this building depict the life of Milarepa.

Outside the dzong, to the north-east of the entrance, is the archery competition field and a stone-paved area where the dancers perform the Paro tsechu each spring. A *thondrol* (huge thangka) more than 18m square is unfurled early in the morning on the final day of the tsechu. The Paro thondrol depicts Guru Rimpoche as the central figure. It was commissioned in the 18th century by the eighth desi, Chhogyal Sherub Wangchuck, and survived the 1907 fire.

Many scenes from the 1995 film *Little Buddha* were filmed in Paro Dzong. You may recall that at the end of this film they discovered three incarnations of the same bodhisattva; a phenomenon similar to the body, speech and mind incarnations of both Shabdrung Ngawang Namgyal and Pema Lingpa.

West of the dzong a traditional wooden covered bridge called **Nyamai Zam** spans the Paro Chhu. This is a reconstruction of the original bridge, which was washed away in a flood in 1969. Earlier versions of this bridge were removed in time of war to protect the dzong. You can walk from the parking area near Ugyen Pelri Palace across the bridge to the outside walls of the dzong. The most famous pictures of Paro Dzong are taken from the west bank of the river, just downstream from the bridge.

National Museum (Ta Dzong)

At the top of the hill above the dzong is an old structure that was renovated in 1968 to house the National Museum. This unusual round building is said to be in the shape of a conch shell; it was completed in 1656 and was originally the watch tower (*ta dzong*) of Paro Dzong. The museum is open from 9 am to 4 pm Tuesday to Saturday, 11 am to 4 pm Sunday, and closed Monday and national holidays. There is a specific route to follow through the entire building that ensures that you walk clockwise around important images. Cameras are not allowed inside the museum. The museum is a local, as well as a tourist, attraction. When you visit you may

be accompanied by Bhutanese from remote villages or groups of schoolchildren on an outing.

The museum is managed by the Special Commission for Cultural Affairs, which has recently rearranged its exhibitions with help from UNESCO and other sources. There are six floors of galleries, each with a special emphasis.

Among the exhibits are a spectacular collection of thangkas, both ancient and recent. Of particular importance are thangkas depicting Shabdrung Ngawang Namgyal, the first Je Khenpo and the first Druk Desi. Other thangkas portray all of Bhutan's important saints and teachers.

There is a display of Bhutan's extensive philatelic collection on the top floor. At the end of the gallery a doorway leads to the **Tshogshing Lhakhang**, the Temple of the Tree of Wisdom, which was built between 1965 and 1968.

The centrepiece of this temple is a complex four-sided carving depicting the history of Buddhism and its propagation. On one side is Sakyamuni and the great teacher Atisha, representing the Sakya school. On the next is Geylup, a disciple of the Dalai Lama, and Dagpo Lhaje, representing the Geylup lineage. Another side represents the Nyingma lineage, with Guru Rimpoche as the centrepiece, and the final side is Drukpa Kagyu with figures of Vajra Dhara, Marpa, Milarepa and the Indian teachers Naropa and Tilopa.

Be sure to remove your shoes before entering the temple and walk clockwise around the room.

Other galleries include ancient bronze and stone objects, an exquisite collection of bronze statues and a display of ancient weapons and shields, many captured during various Tibetan invasions. There are stuffed animals, old and new household objects, jewellery and decorative arts on the lower floors.

There is said to be an underground tunnel that leads from the watch tower to the water supply below. You can walk down a path from the museum to the dzong and back to the town, allowing good views of the valley and of Ugyen Pelri Palace.

Ugyen Pelri Palace

Ugyen Pelri Palace is in a secluded wooded compound on the south side of the river just west of the dzong. This palace was built by Paro penlop Tshering Penjor in the early 1900s and is now a residence of the queen mother. It is designed after Guru Rimpoche's celestial paradise, Zangto Pelri, and is one of the most beautiful examples of Bhutanese architecture.

On the road beside Ugyen Pelri Palace are five square chortens that were built in memory of the first king, Ugyen Wangchuck. Remember, walk to the left of these chortens.

Chhoeten Lhakhang

This lhakhang, shaped like a large Bhutanese-style chorten, in the centre of town. The caretaker is an elderly woman who lives on the ground floor and may allow you to visit the upstairs chapel.

Druk Choeding

Also known as Tshongdoe Naktshang, this is the town temple. It was built in 1525 by Ngawang Chhogyel (1465-1540), one of the prince-abbots of Ralung in Tibet and an ancestor of the Shabdrung Ngawang Namgyal.

Dumtse Lhakhang

To the west of the road is Dumtse Lhakhang, a chorten-like temple that is closed to tourists. This unusual building was built in 1433 by the iron bridge builder Thangtong Gyalpo (see the boxed text 'The Iron Bridge Builder' later in this chapter). It has three floors representing hell, earth and heaven and the paintings inside are said to be some of the best in Bhutan.

Just beyond Dumtse Lhakhang, to the east of the road, the tiny **Pana Lhakhang** is quite old and believed to have been built at the same time as Kyichu Lhakhang (see Kyichu Lhakhang in the Around Paro section).

Places to Stay

Paro is one of the most scenic valleys in Bhutan, and many hotels are placed to offer spectacular views. The town itself was only developed in the mid-1980s, after many of the hotels were built. Much of the accommodation is in resort-style hotels throughout the valley, not in the town itself.

Resort Hotels The large *Hotel Druk* (☎ 29120, 71258) is on a forested hill with a spectacular view of the Paro valley and the airport. It's built in the style of a dzong and dominates the top of a hillock to the east of the airport. It has the requisite bar, restaurant, gift shop and a conference hall that is sometimes used by Indian groups. It is part of the Druk Hotel chain; singles/doubles cost Nu 1500/1800.

On the opposite side of valley is BTCL's *Olathang Hotel* (☎ 29115, 71304; fax 29114), another dzong-like stone structure where you are greeted by a stuffed tiger and yak. There are 24 rooms in the main building at Nu 1020/1270, and a suite with elaborate Victorian furniture for Nu 2600/ 2800. This hotel has abundant Bhutanese decor and was built in 1974 for guests invited to the coronation of the present king. The best accommodation in Paro is in one of the Olathang's 32 well-appointed wooden cottages. Each cottage has an electric heater and a balcony overlooking the Paro valley; the rate for cottages is Nu 1260/1510.

About 3km up the valley from Paro town is the *Kyichu Resort* (☎ 29135, 71318), a collection of stone buildings on the banks of the Paro Chhu. The central building houses a restaurant, bar, gift shop and conference hall. This hotel is also popular with Indian tourists as well as Bhutanese and expatriates from Thimphu looking for a weekend getaway. It's owned by International Trekkers, which is building other hotels in Wangdue Phodrang and Bumthang. There is a disco here on Saturday night.

Tiger Nest Resort, also called the *Eye of the Tiger* (☎ 71391), is beyond Satsam Chorten, just past the trail to Taktshang. It offers a view to what is now, sadly, the ruins of Taktshang Monastery (see Taktshang Monastery in the Around Paro section and the boxed text 'The Fire at Taktshang Monastery') and, on clear days, Jhomolhari. It has 11 rooms, all with private facilities, in four cottages and also a stone bath. Yotsel Tours operates it and charges Nu 650/750 for a room, but a stone bath costs extra.

Smaller Hotels & Cottages *Dechen Cottages* (☎ 71392) is in a secluded area below the road, before it reaches the Olathang Hotel. The hotel is owned by Thoesam Tours and rooms are Nu 650/750. There is a good view of the dzong and the lower part of the valley.

Pemaling Villa (☎ 29143) is just below Olathang Hotel and has six double rooms in Bhutanese style, all with attached bath.

Gantey Palace (☎ 29113, 71301) is housed in a 19th century traditional palace-style building that was once the residence of the Paro Penlop. It has 19 double rooms, each with attached bath (or, if you prefer, you can arrange for a stone bath) that rent for Nu 850/950. It is on a low hill overlooking Paro town and was renovated during summer 1997. Just outside the gate is the small Gangten Lhakhang.

Pegyel Hotel (☎ 29142) is in Shaba, 9km from Paro town in a rural setting among rice fields. It has 16 double rooms.

Central Hotels *Hotel Blue Heaven* (☎ 71347) has a few very basic rooms on the main street in Paro town as does the smaller *Rendez Vous Inn*. There are several smaller guesthouses along the town square including the *Hotel Highland* (☎ 71365), *Hotel Riwang* (☎ 71367) and *Hotel Yangzom* (☎ 71366). There are lots of barking dogs in Paro; expect to pay Nu 250/350 for a noisy room in any of these places.

Places to Eat

In addition to the hotels, Paro has some good restaurants and bars. The *Sonam Trophel* is upstairs over a shop, has excellent food and is popular with Japanese volunteers working in Paro. Momos (dumplings) are a speciality.

WESTERN BHUTAN

Unfortunately the only beer it stocks is expensive imported brews or extra-strong Indian brands like Black Knight.

The *Rendez Vous Inn*, in the square near the post office, has a pleasant atmosphere and staff. It boasts an extensive western menu and caters for tour groups with an evening buffet.

Next to the post office is the *Zamling Hotel* which offers basic rice and curry. At the western end of town, near the petrol station, is the *Jachung Milk Backery* (jachung means garuda), where you can load up on bread and pastries. The *Snow View Restaurant & Bar* at the north end of town offers fried chillies and other Bhutanese versions of fast food. It's a favourite eating spot for the monks from the dzong, and it's a good place to visit for a drink, but we thought twice about ordering a meal – and didn't.

Getting There & Away

Paro airport is 7km from Paro town and 53km from Thimphu. Taxis are rare and you should ensure that there is a vehicle meeting your flight.

AROUND PARO

Though the valley extends west all the way to the peaks on the Tibetan border, the road only goes 11km beyond Paro town as far as Drukgyel Dzong. There is an unpaved road that leads north from the centre of Paro up the Do Chhu valley to the village of Atshochhubar. A third road leads south from Bondey and climbs over the 3780m Cheli La to the Ha valley.

A rough unpaved road leads west from Bondey to some houses and fields and the small recently-constructed Changchi Lhakhang. A walk or drive up this road affords a view of the four sets of buildings hanging on the side of a cliff.

Several treks begin in the Paro valley. The Jhomolhari, Laya-Gasa and Snowman treks all lead west from Drukgyel Dzong to Jhomolhari base camp and then wind their way through Lingzhi and beyond. The Druk Path trek is a short trek that begins near Ta Dzong and crosses a pass between Paro and Thimphu (see the Trekking chapter for details).

West of Paro

The road leads north-west out of town past the Sonam Pelkhil sawmill, then turns generally west, following quite close to the river on a route lined with willow trees. There are rice fields and many houses to the south of the road.

Kyichu Lhakhang A short distance south of the road is Kyichu Lhakhang. This temple is said to have been built in 659 by King Songtsen Gampo of Tibet. It holds down the left foot of an ogress that is so large that it covers Bhutan and most of eastern Tibet (see boxed text opposite).

The original building burned once and was rebuilt with a large statue of Sakyamuni as the central figure. Additional buildings were constructed in 1839 by the Paro penlop and the 25th Je Khenpo. A large statue of Chenrezig with 11 heads and 1000 hands were added at that time, as well as a golden roof. A new temple was constructed in 1968 by the Queen Mother Ashi Kesang. In the new temple is a 5m-high statue of Guru Rimpoche and another of Tara, who represents one of the wives of King Songtsen Gampo. There is also a statue of the iron bridge builder Thangtong Gyalpo (see the boxed text 'The Iron Bridge Builder' later in this chapter), and another of Dilgo Khyentse Rimpoche, a revered Nyingma Buddhist master who passed away in 1992.

The road passes **Satsam Chorten**. On a side road is **Drongja Goemba**, where Dilgo Khyentse Rimpoche was cremated, and a royal guesthouse. The unpaved Japanese-funded road that traverses the edge of the valley ends here. High on the hill on the opposite side of the valley Tsacho Chuko monastery is visible; below it is a small private goemba.

Taktshang Monastery Taktshang is the most famous of Bhutan's monasteries, perched on the side of a cliff 900m above the floor of Paro valley where the only sounds are the murmurs of wind and water and the chanting of monks. The name means 'tiger's nest'; it was named because

---

The Ogress in Tibet

The Tibetan king Songtsen Gampo married the Chinese princess Wencheng in 641. A part of the dowry was a statue called Jowo, which was an Indian image of the Buddha Sakyamuni as a small boy. As the statue was being transported through Lhasa, it became stuck in the mud and could not be moved. The princess divined that the problem was being caused by a huge supine demoness lying on her back with her navel in the place that Lhasa's cathedral, the Jokhang, now stands.

In 659 the king decided to build 108 temples in a single day to pin the ogress to the earth forever and, at the same time, convert the Tibetan people to Buddhism. The head of the ogress was to the east, and her legs were to the west, so temples were constructed at the shoulders and hips, which corresponded to the four districts of central Tibet. The knees and elbows of the demoness were in the provinces, which were also duly pinned and the people converted. The arms and legs lay in the borderlands of Tibet, and several temples were built in Bhutan to pin down the left leg.

The best known of these temples are Kyichu Lhakhang in Paro, which holds the left foot, and Jambey Lhakhang in Bumthang, which pins the left knee. Other lesser-known temples were also built throughout Tibet and Bhutan. Many of these have been destroyed, but it is believed that, among others, Kanchosum Lhakhang in Bumthang, Khaini Lhakhang south of Lhuentse, and two temples in Ha may have been part of this ambitious project.

Guru Rimpoche is said to have flown to the site of the monastery on the back of a tigress. He then meditated in a cave here for three months.

On 19 April 1998 a fire, cause still unknown, destroyed the main structure of Taktshang and all its contents. It had already suffered a previous fire and was repaired in 1951. There are plans to rebuild the monastery in its original style, and construction will start when an auspicious date has been determined.

The site has long been recognised as a holy place and was visited by Shabdrung Ngawang Namgyal in 1646 and is now visited by pilgrims from all over Bhutan. Milarepa is also said to have meditated here and Thangtong Gyalpo revealed a treasure text at Taktshang. The primary lhakhang was built in 1684 around Guru Rimpoche's meditation cave by the penlop of Paro, Gese Tenzi Rabgye. There are several other buildings in the complex. The **Temple of Phorbu** contains a *phorbu*, the three-bladed ritual dagger used to stab demons. Above the main temple complex is **Ugyen Tshemo Lhakhang**, and higher still is another goemba,

named **Zangto Pelri** after Guru Rimpoche's heavenly abode.

The monastery itself is closed to tourists except by special permit. However, the two-hour walk to a viewpoint where there is a small tea house, improbably named a cafeteria, provides a close-up view of the monastery. Allow about four hours for the round trip, including a rest stop at the viewpoint. If you have the energy, it's worth walking another hour up from the cafeteria for an even closer view. This hike was a major part of any tourist itinerary before the 1998 fire and is still worthwhile for the spectacular view and historical interest, and as a good warm-up hike if you are going trekking.

To get to the viewpoint, take a conspicuous trail that begins 8km north of Paro town. If you arrange horses a day in advance, you can ride them to the viewpoint instead of making the strenuous hike. The trail descends to the Paro Chhu, crosses on a footbridge and starts gently uphill through blue pine forests to the settlement of **Shari**. People from nearby villages sit alongside the lower part of the trail with displays of

WESTERN BHUTAN

The Fire at Taktshang Monastery

The *Dubkhang*, the most sacred sanctum of the Taktshang Monastery in Paro, has been found to be safe and a number of the most precious relics and treasures have been retrieved from the ruins of the main monastery, which was severely damaged by fire on Sunday, April 19, 1998.

The Tshennyi Lopon (Master of Dialectical Studies) of the Dratshang (Central Monk Body) explained that the sacred essence of Taktshang was the Dubkhang (also called the *Pelphug*), the holy cave in which Guru Rimpoche meditated in the 8th century (as did many other renowned saints), and the *kudung* (relics) of his disciple, Langchen Pelkyi Singye, which had been placed deep in the rocks under the site of the kudung chorten.

'The sanctity of Taktshang cannot be destroyed by the natural elements, be it fire or water,' the Tshennyi Lopon told *Kuensel*. On April 23, His Majesty the King visited Taktshang and saw the Dubkhang and the religious artefacts that had been recovered. His Majesty commanded the Dratshang, Rabdeys, Shedras and Drubdas, Gomdeys, and all the other religious institutions in the country to offer the Guru Soendoep Dungjor (the offering of 100 million prayers to Guru Rimpoche).

The Chairman of the Special Commission for Cultural Affairs, Lyonpo Dago Tshering said that, as commanded by His Majesty the King, the government would reconstruct the monastery with its original aura, authenticity and architectural splendour.

The sacred essence of Taktshang, one of the most revered Buddhist *nyes* (sacred sites) in the world, was established in the 8th century by Guru Rimpoche. The Guru, in the wrathful form of Guru Dorji Drolley, subdued the evil spirits and then meditated in the Pelphug in Taktshang.

Other saints who meditated in the cave include Milarepa, Phadampa Sangye, Machi Labdoenma, Thangtong Gyalpo and Shabdrung Ngawang Namgyal.

The main monastery around the Pelphug in Taktshang was constructed in 1692 by the great fourth Desi, Tenzing Rabgye. Between 1961 and 1965 it was renovated by Je Sheldrup Yoezer. The latest additions were made in 1982.

The Dubkhang is opened once a year during an annual ceremony. The Tshennyi Lopon explained that 71 members of the monk body performed the annual Guru prayers for 21 days in the fifth Bhutanese month. As in the past, the prayers will be performed this year as usual in the Dubkhang.

The Tshennyi Lopon said that if the destruction of the Taktshang Monastery was a deliberate evil deed then it was a reflection of the decline of the dharma. But if the monastery was destroyed by natural causes then it is natural for people to perceive it as an inauspicious sign.

'However, what is most important is that the people should avoid superstition and doubt and place their faith in Guru Rimpoche and the Triple Gem,' said Tshennyi Lopon. 'We can only safeguard our nation and spiritual heritage with genuine faith in the dharma.'

Kuensel editorial, reprinted with kind permission

KUENSEL

Taktshang Monastery will be rebuilt in its original style (as above) once an auspicious date has been chosen.

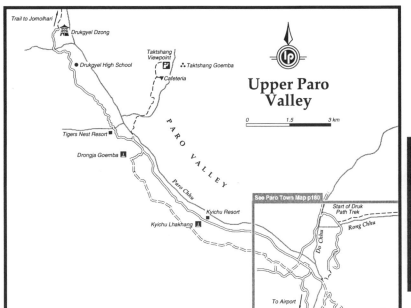

Upper Paro
Valley

Trail to Jomolhari

Drukgyel Dzong

Taktshang Viewpoint

• *Drukgyel High School*

⁘ *Taktshang Goemba*

▼ *Cafeteria*

Tigers Nest Resort ■

Drongja Goemba ▲

P A R O   V A L L E Y

Paro Chhu

See Paro Town Map p180

Start of Druk Path Trek

Rong Chhu

Kyichu Resort

Kyichu Lhakhang ▲

Do Chhu

To Airport

0   1.5   3 km

WESTERN BHUTAN

handicrafts, encouraging you to buy with cries of 'shopping, shopping'. Most of the goods are of mediocre quality, and bargaining is very much in order. Above Shari the trail crosses a stream, passes some water-driven prayer wheels and follows the stream for a very short distance. As the steep part of the climb begins, you can look down and see the small Sasum Goemba in the trees beside the stream.

The trail then switchbacks steeply up the ridge. Be sure to wear a hat; there is little shade on the ridge, and the sun is intense. If you have just flown in to Paro walk slowly, because the elevation is above 2500m and you are likely to become breathless because of the altitude. There are excellent views across the valley. The village to the south-west is Drukgyel; you can see the large school below the village and the army camp above it. After a climb of about two hours and a gain of 500m from the bottom of the

hill you should reach a small chorten and some prayer flags on the ridge. It's then a short, level walk to the cafeteria, which consists of a few buildings with wood-shingle roofs. You can sit in front of the building and admire the monastery as you drink the tea that your guide will arrange. The cafeteria also serves full meals; if you arrange your schedule correctly, you can have breakfast or lunch here. Soft drinks are available, and so is beer, but it is expensive at Nu 60 per bottle.

Most visitors return downhill from this viewpoint, making the downhill trip in just over an hour. The trail to Taktshang itself continues up from the chorten on the ridge. If you have time and are feeling fit, continue for another hour uphill through the trees, bearing right at all obvious trail junctions. This will bring you to a spectacular lookout that is at the same level as the monastery. From this vantage point Taktshang looks like it is growing out of the rocks. It seems almost close enough to touch, but it's on the far side of a deep chasm, about 150m away. If you descend a bit from the first point at which you can see the monastery you will come to a second viewpoint where a cable crosses the deep chasm in front of the monastery. The cable is used to carry heavy goods across the chasm because the trail between here and the goemba is very narrow and exposed. If you don't have a permit to visit Taktshang, this is as far as you should go.

Drukgyel Village Beyond Taktshang, 11km from Paro, is the farming village of Drukgyel. Below the road is a large school that was built as part of a British aid project. Above the road is a Royal Bhutan Army (RBA) facility.

Beyond Drukgyel village there are army training camps scattered in the bushes and pine forests. Farther on are the houses of Tshentop village, which is inhabited by people from the valley of Ha.

Drukgyel Dzong At the end of the road, 14km from Paro, stands the ruins of Drukgyel Dzong. This dzong was built in 1649 by Shabdrung Ngawang Namgyal in a location chosen for its control of the route to Tibet. The dzong was named *Druk* (Bhutan) *gyel* (victory) to commemorate the victory of Bhutan over Tibetan invaders in 1644. One of the features of the dzong was a false entrance that was designed to lure invaders into an enclosed courtyard. This is said to have worked successfully during the second attack by Tibetan invaders in 1648.

The dzong sits at the point where the trail from Tibet via the Tremo La enters the Paro valley. Once the Tibetan invasions ceased, this became a major trade route between Bhutan and the Tibetan town of Phari. A small amount of informal trade continues to the present day. On a clear day there is a spectacular view of Jhomolhari from the area near the dzong.

Drukgyel Dzong was featured on the cover of the US *National Geographic* magazine when an article was published about

Bhutan by John Claude White in 1914. The building was used as an administrative centre until 1951, when a fire caused by a butter lamp destroyed it.

Now the dzong is in ruins and is closed to all visitors. There have been a few attempts at renovation, but all that has been accomplished is the installation of some props to keep the roof of the five-storey main structure from collapsing. You can walk up a short path into the front courtyard of the dzong. On the way up you can see the remains of the large towers and the tunnel that was used to obtain water from the stream below during a long siege.

North of Paro
Passing Dumtse Lhakhang, the wide new bridge built by the Japanese in 1995 leads to the Do Chhu valley. A paved road leads uphill to the junior high school, the entrance to the dzong and the national museum.

South-East of Paro
The road that leads south-east from Paro is the main exit from the valley and leads to the confluence at Chhuzom, 24km from Paro and 17km from Bondey.

Paro to Bondey Just south of Paro town is the settlement of Taju, which has a bank and telephone exchange. The road passes above the airport and then past **Kahangkhu Lhakhang** to Bondey.

In Bondey is the 400-year-old **Bondey Lhakhang** and the intersection of the road to Cheli La and Ha.

Bondey to Chhuzom Bondey is at the eastern end of the airport. Here the road crosses to the north side of the Paro Chhu and follows the valley south-west to Chhuzom. Above the north side of the bridge is the small Pelri Goemba and in the village is an unusual round chorten-shaped temple.

About 3km from Bondey is **Shaba**, a small settlement with an army camp and also the *Pegyel Hotel* (☎ 29142, 29100), which looks after Druk Air's flight catering.

At Isuna, 8km from Chhuzom, the road crosses a bridge to the south bank of the Paro Chhu. There are a few houses here and **Dzongdrakha**, a meditation place of Guru Rimpoche, clings to the rocks above.

On the opposite side of the river is **Tamchhog Lhakhang**, a private temple owned by the descendants of Thangtong Gyalpo, the great iron bridge builder. The red soil around the temple contains low-grade ore that once supplied the raw material for iron works.

Cheli La Tourists are allowed on this road as far as the Cheli La. It makes an interesting road excursion and is an excellent jumping off point for day walks. From the pass at 3780m there are views of Jhomolhari as well as down to the Ha valley. One of Bhutan's designated treks is a walk from Bondey to the Cheli La, a 1500m elevation gain, followed by a trek downhill to Drukgyel Dzong.

Punakha Dzongkhag

THIMPHU TO PUNAKHA
The 77km, 2¾-hour drive from Thimphu to Punakha, on the National Highway via Dochu La, leads from the cold of Thimphu to the hot, almost-tropical country of the Punakha valley.

Thimphu to Dochu La
23km, ¾ hour
From Thimphu the road goes south to Simtokha (2250m). The route to the east leaves the road to Paro and Phuentsholing and loops back over itself to meet the east-west National Highway, which was constructed in 1984. About a kilometre past the turnoff there is a good view of Simtokha Dzong (see Around Thimphu in the Thimphu chapter). The route climbs through apple orchards and

WESTERN BHUTAN

The Iron Bridge Builder
Thangtong Gyalpo (1385-1464) was a wonder-working Tibetan saint who is believed to have originated the design of using heavy iron chains to build suspension bridges and built 108 bridges throughout Tibet and Bhutan.

He was also known as *Lama Chazampa* (Lama Iron-bridge). In 1433 he came to Bhutan in search of iron ore and built eight bridges in places as far removed as Paro and Trashigang. His

only surviving bridge is believed to be at Duksum on the road to Trashi Yangtse in eastern Bhutan, and his most famous one crossed the Tsangpo at Chaksam, 50km southwest of Lhasa in Tibet.

He cast images of Buddhist saints and built the chorten-shaped Dumtse Lhakhang in Paro. His descendants still maintain Tamchhog Goemba at the eastern end of the Paro valley. Among his other achievements was the composition of many occupational songs, still sung today by people as they thresh wheat or pound the mud for house construction.

He was an important terton of the Nyingma lineage and attained the title *Drubthob* (Great Magician). Statues of Thangtong Gyalpo depict him as a stocky shirtless figure with a beard, curly hair and a topknot.

forests of blue pine. On a hill above the road is **Hongtsho Goemba** and some monks' meditation cells. Ngawang Choegyal founded this goemba in the 15th century; he was a cousin of Lama Drukpa Kunley and also founded Druk Choeding in Paro. At the village of Hongtsho (2800m) is an immigration check post that controls all access to eastern Bhutan. You must have a restricted-area travel permit to proceed; this is arranged as a matter of course by all tour operators.

High on a ridge across the valley to the south is **Tashigang Goemba**, which was built in 1786 by the 12th Je Khenpo. It is an important meditation centre, and there are numerous small houses for pilgrims near the goemba. In addition to about 16 monks, there are a few *anims* (nuns). Inside the lhakhang there are statues of several Je Khenpos who meditated here.

The road climbs to **Dochu La** (3150m), marked by a large array of prayer flags and a chorten. On the hill just above the pass is a *cafeteria* (☎ 31610) that affords (on a clear day) a close-up view of the Bhutan Himalaya. Such days are rare in Bhutan. You will have the best chance of a view in the early morning between October and February.

There is a powerful binocular telescope in the cafeteria. This was a gift from the Kyoto University Alpine Club after they made the first ascent of 7200m Mt Masang Gang in 1985. A photograph on the wall above the telescope has the peaks labelled (with different spellings and elevations than those shown here). From west to east they are:

Gangchhenta	(6840m)
Gangkhar Puensum	(7541m)
Jejekangphu Gang	(7100m)
Kang Bum	(6526m)
Kangphu Gang	(7212m)
Masang Gang	(7165m)
Teri Gang	(7300m)
Tsenda Gang	(7100m)
Zongophu Gang	
'Table Mountain'	(7100m)

Gangkhar Puensum is the highest peak that is completely inside Bhutan; Kulha Gangri (7554m) is higher, but it is on the border with Tibet. Using the telescope, it's also possible to see the distinctive shape of Gasa Dzong, a small white speck almost 50km to the north.

The cafeteria serves tea and snacks and can prepare meals if you're willing to wait. There's also a gift shop with paintings, old and new weavings, masks and other souvenirs. Each item is labelled with a very stiff price quoted in US dollars – and some in hundreds of dollars.

The area near the pass is believed to be inhabited by numerous spirits, including a cannibal demoness. Lama Drukpa Kunley, the 'divine madman', (see the boxed text 'The Divine Madman' opposite) built Chimi Lhakhang (see under Metshina to Punakha later in this section) to subdue these spirits and demons.

Dochu La to Metshina
42km, 1½ hours

The vegetation changes dramatically at the pass from maple and blue pine to a moist mountain forest of rhododendron, magnolia, cypress, hemlock and fir. There is also a large growth of daphne, a bush that is harvested for making traditional paper. The road makes a long descent past **Thinleygang** (1888m), where the vegetation becomes more tropical with cactus, oranges and bamboo. There is a large spring beside the road that flows with holy water that has its source in a lake far above. Along the winding route are several Bhutanese roadside versions of *mani* walls. Instead of being carved, as is traditional in the hills, mantras are painted on rocks and cliffs. Some invoke the traditional *om mani peme hum* and others display the Guru Rimpoche mantra, *om ah hum vajra Guru Pema siddhi hum*, a sacred chant.

High on the opposite hill is **Dalay Goemba**, and just to the east is **Talo Goemba**, founded by the Shabdrung and affiliated with the Nalanda University in India.

Just below Mendigang there is a small resort, *Dechen Cottages* (☎ 23504), operated by Yangphel Travels. It's a steep 15 minute drive on an unpaved road up to a grove of rhododendron, orchids and chir pine. Here you'll find a pleasant collection of cottages with 18 rooms renting for Nu 650/750. The rooms have attached toilets, but for a bath you have to rely on the hot stone one in a small building above the cottages.

The road continues its descent, making a switchback along the side of valley, to a road junction at **Metshina**. This is a small bazaar where a road to Punakha branches off from the National Highway. The small *Passang Restaurant cum Samol Bar* offers snacks and drinks, but not real meals.

Metshina to Punakha
12km, ½ hour
The road makes a switchback down past Sopsokha into a small valley. It then follows a stream before climbing over a ridge into

the valley of the Punak Chhu. The road drops to the river and then follows it upstream.

Above the road at **Kharuthang** is a large construction site. The Punakha bazaar is being relocated here in order to keep the dzong and bazaar areas separate. The large complex just west of Kharuthang is a junior high school. It's then a short distance to the high school and an excellent view of the Punakha Dzong at 1250m. North of the high school is the small bazaar and a foot bridge leading across the Mo Chhu to the dzong.

Chimi Lhakhang On a hillock in the centre of the valley below Metshina is Chimi Lhakhang, built by Lama Drukpa Kunley.

The Divine Madman
Lama Drukpa Kunley (1455-1529) is one of Bhutan's favourite saints. He was born in Tibet, was trained at Ralung monastery and was a contemporary and a disciple of Pema Lingpa. He travelled throughout Bhutan and Tibet as a *neljorpa* (yogi) using songs, humour and outrageous behaviour to dramatise his teachings. He felt that the stiffness of the clergy and social conventions were keeping people from learning the true Buddhist teachings. His teaching was through conduct that was shocking, insulting or obscene.

His outrageous actions and sexual antics were a deliberate method of provoking people to discard their preconceptions. He is also credited with having created Bhutan's strange animal, the takin, by combining the body of a cow with the head of a goat. On one occasion when he received a blessing thread to hang around his neck, he wound it around his penis instead, saying he hoped it would bring him luck with many more ladies.

He spoke the following verse on one occasion when he met Pema Lingpa:

I, the madman from Kyishodruk,
Wander around from place to place;
I believe in lamas when it suits me,
I practise the Dharma in my own way.
I choose any qualities, they are all illusions,
Any gods, they are all the Emptiness of the Mind.
I use fair and foul words for Mantras; it's all the same,
My meditation practise is girls and wine;
I do whatever I feel like, strolling around in the Void,
Last time, I saw you with the Bumthang trulku;
With my great karmic background, I could approach.
Indeed it was auspicious, to meet you on my pilgrim's round!

His sexual exploits are legendary, and the flying phalluses that you see painted on houses and hanging from rooftops are his.

He subdued the demoness of the Dochu La with his 'Magic Thunderbolt of Wisdom'. A wooden effigy of the lama's thunderbolt is preserved in the lhakhang, and childless women go to the temple to receive a *wang* (blessing) from the saint.

It's a 20 minute walk across fields from the road at Sopsokha to the temple. The trail leads across rice fields to the tiny settlement of Pana, which means field. It then follows a tiny stream downhill to **Yoaka** ('in the drain') and across more fields before making a short climb to Chimi Lhakhang. During the wet season, this is an especially muddy and slippery walk.

There are a few monks at the temple, which is surrounded by a row of prayer wheels and some very beautiful slate carvings. No permit is required for entrance to the temple, so you may visit and see the statues of the lama and his dog as well as statues of the Shabdrung, Sakyamuni and Chenrezig. The small chorten on the altar is said to have been crafted by Drukpa Kunley himself.

PUNAKHA

The low altitude of the Punakha valley allows two rice crops a year. The climate is also good for growing fruit, and oranges and bananas are in abundance.

Orientation & Information

The road enters Punakha proper near the high school. From the roadside opposite the school is an excellent view of Punakha Dzong. The Mo Chhu (mother river) and Pho Chhu (father river) join here to form the Punak Chhu. In the south of Bhutan this river is known as the Sankosh.

Beyond the high school the road enters the small Punakha bazaar, which is just opposite the dzong. Upstream from the bazaar is a large new hospital housed in a series of traditional Bhutanese-style buildings.

A road leads up the west side of the Mo Chhu past Puntsho Pelri Palace to Tashithang, 18km from the dzong. The first 5km is paved, and the rest is gravel. Tashithang is the jumping-off point for treks to Gasa

and the hot springs below it; it's also the ending point of the Laya-Gasa trek (see the Trekking chapter for details).

Post & Communications The post office is just behind the bazaar. There is no Public Call Office (PCO), but some shops have telephones.

Punakha Dzong

Punakha Dzong was the second of Bhutan's dzongs. For many years, until the time of the second king, it served as the seat of the government. The construction of Punakha Dzong was foretold by Guru Rimpoche, who predicted that '... a person named Namgyal will arrive at a hill that looks like an elephant'. The Shabdrung visited Punakha and chose the tip of the trunk of the sleeping elephant at the confluence of the Mo Chhu and Pho Chhu as the place to build a dzong. It's not obvious, but with a

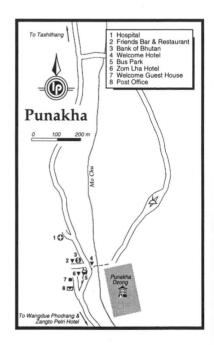

To Tashithang

Punakha

0   100   200 m

1 Hospital
2 Friends Bar & Restaurant
3 Bank of Bhutan
4 Welcome Hotel
5 Bus Park
6 Zom Lha Hotel
7 Welcome Guest House
8 Post Office

Mo Chhu

Punakha Dzong

To Wangdue Phodrang & Zangto Pelri Hotel

Western Bhutan
Man and nature coexist harmoniously in Bhutan and traditional architecture complements the landscape. Clockwise from top: the dzong in Gasa; a hotel in the Phobjhika valley, a water-driven prayer wheel, and a typical residential settlement.

NICHOLAS REUSS

JULIA WILKINSON

Paro
On your approach to Paro airport (top), this could be your first glimpse of the kingdom. Meanwhile, there's harvesting to be done in front of Paro Dzong (bottom).

NICHOLAS REUSS

RICHARD I'ANSON

RICHARD I'ANSON

Central Bhutan
The prayer flags in front of Kurjey Lhakang (top) mark the ashes of former kings. Meanwhile, the bus is late but locals take it in their stride (left) and collecting firewood is a big job for little hands (right).

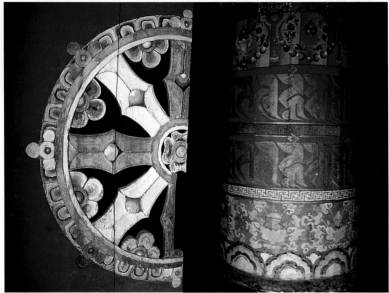

RICHARD I'ANSON

TONY WHEELER

JULIA WILKINSON

Central Bhutan

Buddhist symbols are ubiquitous throughout Bhutan. Some include: deities and lotus flowers as seen on this prayer wheel and door detail from Jakar Dzong, Bumthang (top); the less common kalacakra symbolising occult knowledge (right); and the flying phallus which is often painted on houses to distract and thereby ward off evil spirits (left).

bit of imagination you may be able to visualise the hill as an elephant.

There was a smaller building here called Dzong Chu (small dzong) which housed a statue of Buddha. It is said that the Shabdrung ordered the architect, Zowe Palep, to sleep in front of the statue. While Palep was sleeping, the Shabdrung took him in his dreams to Zangto Pelri and showed him the palace of Guru Rimpoche. From his vision, the architect conceived the design for the new dzong, which, in keeping with tradition, was never committed to paper.

Construction started in 1637 and was completed the following year. It was named **Druk Pungthang Dechhen Phodrang** (Palace of Great Happiness). Later embellishments included the construction of a chapel to commemorate the victory over the Tibetans in 1639. The war material captured during the battle is preserved in the dzong.

The Shabdrung established the Central Monastic Body here with 600 monks that were brought from Chari Goemba in the upper Thimphu valley. Punakha is still the winter residence of the Central Monk Body. The dzong was the seat of government when Punakha was capital, and King Jigme Dorji Wangchuck convened the new National Assembly here in 1952.

Punakha Dzong is 180m long and 72m wide and the utse is six storeys high. The gold dome on the utse was built in 1676 by the Punakha Dzongpen Gyaltsen Tenzin Rabgye. Cantilever bridges across the Mo Chhu and Pho Chhu were constructed between 1720 and 1730. They have both been destroyed, however, and the Mo Chhu is now spanned by a cable suspension bridge

that stands next to the remains of the original cantilever bridge.

In addition to its strategic position, the dzong has several features to protect it against invasion. The steep wooden stairs at the front are designed to be pulled up, and there is a heavy wooden door that is still closed at night. The dzong is unique because it has three dochey instead of the usual two. The front gate leads first to the northern courtyard, which houses the administrative functions. The second courtyard is in the monastic quarter and the utse is here. In this courtyard are two halls, one of which was used when King Ugyen Wangchuck was presented the Order of Knight Commander of the Indian Empire by Sir John Claude White in 1905.

In the southernmost courtyard is the temple where the remains of the treasure discoverer Pema Lingpa and Shabdrung Ngawang Namgyal are preserved. The Shabdrung died in Punakha Dzong, and his body is still preserved in **Machey Lhakhang** (*machey* means 'sacred embalmed body'). The casket is sealed and may not be opened. There are two lamas, Machin Zimpon and Machin Simpon, who are assigned to look after the room where the casket is kept. Other than these lamas, only the king and the Je Khenpo may enter this room. Both come to take blessings before they take up their offices.

There is also the 'hundred pillar' congregation hall, which actually has only 54 pillars. The paintings in this hall, which was commissioned by the second Druk Desi, are said to be exceptional.

Another temple, **Nag Yul Bum**, is closely associated with the Je Khenpo. Inside the dzong is a set of the 108 volumes of the *Kanjur*, the holy book of the Drukpa Kagyu lineage, written in gold.

Fires, Floods & an Earthquake The dzong burned in 1750 and again in 1798. During the reconstruction after the second fire, several new temples were added. Lama Lhakhang was built to house a statue of Shabdrung Ngawang Namgyal. Also added were Genkhang Chhenpo (temple of Mahakali and Mahakala) and Nange Tseum (receptacles for the relics of the saints). Many of the dzong's features were added between 1744 and 1763 during the reign of the 13th desi, Sherab Wangchuk. He was also responsible for the gold statues of Buddha, Guru Rimpoche and the Shabdrung that are in the main assembly hall. Another item he donated was the thondrol named *Chenmo*, a large thangka depicting the Shabdrung that is exhibited to the public once a year during the tsechu festival. A brass roof for the dzong was a gift of the seventh Dalai Lama, Kelzang Gyatso.

There was another fire, which was believed to have been deliberate, in 1802. The dzong again burned in 1831 and 1849, then suffered more damage in the severe 1897 earthquake. A flood damaged the dzong in 1960, and in October 1994 a glacial lake burst on the Pho Chhu, causing further damage that has since been repaired. Outside of the dzong is a memorial to the 23 people killed in that flood.

The latest fire, in 1986, damaged the residence of the Je Khenpo in the south-west corner of the dzong. It is now being repaired using traditional methods. The workshop of the craftspeople performing the repairs is just to the south of the dzong. A visit to this workshop is an interesting view into the techniques of traditional crafts making. The Je Khenpo's residence is now in the northeast corner of the dzong.

Beyond the dzong is the cremation ground, which is marked by a large chorten.

Places to Stay
The accommodation in Punakha is very limited, and many people opt to stay in the Dechen Cottages in nearby Mendigang or in one of the hotels in Wangdue Phodrang.

The *Zangto Pelri Hotel* (☎ 84125), named after the heaven of Guru Rimpoche, is 8km south of Punakha. It stands on a hill high above the Punakha valley. There are rooms in the central building, and several cottages offer additional facilities. The hotel has a total of 30 rooms for Nu 1000/1200. A

swimming pool is on the grounds just below the hotel. If you stay here, get up very early and drive 6km up the paved road to Laptshaka (1900m) for a beautiful view of the mountains.

The *Welcome Guest House* (☎ 84106), on a side road just above the bazaar, opposite the dzong, is a smaller and less expensive option.

Places to Eat
There are a few small restaurants next to the bus stand in the centre of the sleepy town centre. The *Welcome Hotel, Friends Bar & Restaurant* and the *Zom Lha Hotel* cater primarily to locals.

Wangdue Phodrang Dzongkhag

Legends relate that the Shabdrung Ngawang Namgyal met a small boy named Wangdi playing in the sand on the banks of the Punak Chhu and was moved to name the new dzong *Wangdi Phodrang* (Wangdi's Palace).

PUNAKHA TO WANGDUE PHODRANG
It's 21km from Punakha to Wangdue Phodrang. Follow the road back to Metshina and drive a kilometre to Lobesa. The large campus of the Natural Resources Training Institute and the *Lobesa Guest House* (☎ 29331) are a short distance above the road. The road traverses high along the south bank of the Pho Chhu (known here as the Punak Chhu) as the valley widens, with rice terraces below and forests above. The long buildings on the hill opposite are the barracks of the army training centre.

Soon the dramatic Wangdue Phodrang Dzong comes into view, draped along the end of a ridge above the river. The cacti that cover the hillside below the dzong were planted long ago as protection against any invaders.

There is a police and immigration check

post just before the bridge across the Punak Chhu. A road leads from the bridge to the southern region of Tsirang and the Basochhu hydroelectric project. Tourists are discouraged from visiting this area because of the lack of suitable accommodation and the security problems in the south (see Problems in the South under History in the Facts about Bhutan chapter).

The original bridge over the Punak Chhu is said to have been built in 1685. Old photos show this as a wooden cantilever structure with massive turrets. Floods washed it away in 1968, and now a steel Bailey bridge spans the river next to the remains of the original structure.

As the road climbs you can look back to **Rinchengang** on the opposite side of the river. Many of the people who live in this compact village work as stone masons. It's then a short climb to the main bazaar.

WANGDUE PHODRANG (WANGDI)

The old spelling of this town was Wangdi Phodrang, and it is still known colloquially as Wangdi. Because it is on an exposed promontory overlooking the river, Wangdi

is usually windy and dusty, particularly in the afternoon.

Many houses in town have roofs made from slate that was mined at slate mines in Tashichholing and Tseshinang, on the hills above Wangdi.

The town is spotlessly clean thanks to the district *dzongda* (administrator), Pem Dorji, who is strict about cleanliness and makes periodic inspections. He was previously posted in Bumthang, and the result of his efforts may still be seen in Jakar town.

Orientation & Information

The road loops around a large paved parking lot that also serves as the bus station and petrol pump. The bazaar is lined with a row of 87 whitewashed shops and small restaurants.

The town's only hotel and the dzong are down a side road to the south-west of the bazaar. Nearby is the 17th century **Radak Naktshang**, the town temple, which is dedicated to an ancient warlord. The main statue is of Sakyamuni, and there is also a statue of a mermaid who lived in the river and was an obstacle to the construction of this building.

At the eastern end of town is the bank and junior high school. The main vegetable market and high school are far below the bazaar on a side road. A large army training centre sprawls on the hill to the east of the bazaar.

Post & Communications The post office is in a compound just behind the bazaar, and the telephone exchange is on the road to the dzong. You would probably be better off waiting for a larger town from which to post your letters. Shops will let you make telephone calls, but Wangdi still has a manual telephone system. Calls go through an operator and you must wait for the connection to be made.

Wangdue Phodrang Dzong

Wangdue Phodrang Dzong was founded by the Shabdrung in 1638. It sits atop a high ridge between the Punak Chhu and Dang

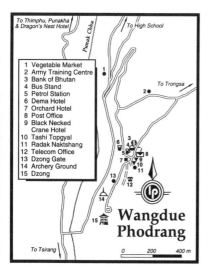

1 Vegetable Market
2 Army Training Centre
3 Bank of Bhutan
4 Bus Stand
5 Petrol Station
6 Dema Hotel
7 Orchard Hotel
8 Post Office
9 Black Necked Crane Hotel
10 Tashi Topgyal
11 Radak Naktshang
12 Telecom Office
13 Dzong Gate
14 Archery Ground
15 Dzong

To Thimphu, Punakha & Dragon's Nest Hotel
To High School
Punak Chhu
To Trongsa
To Tsirang

Wangdue Phodrang

0   200   400 m

Chhu. It is obvious that the site was selected for its commanding view of the valleys below. Legend relates another reason for choosing this spot: as people searched for a site for the dzong, four ravens were seen flying away in four directions. This was considered an auspicious sign, representing the spreading of religion to the four points of the compass.

Wangdi is important in the history of Bhutan because in the early days it was the country's secondary capital. After Trongsa Dzong was established in 1644 the Wangdue Phodrang penlop became the third most powerful ruler, after the penlops of Paro and Trongsa. The dzong's position gave the penlop control of the routes to Trongsa, Punakha, Dagana and Thimphu. It is a complex shape, and is actually three separate narrow structures that follow the contours of the hill. There is only one entrance, a large door flanked by huge prayer wheels, which is reached by a road that leads downhill from the bazaar.

The administrative portion surrounds a large flagstone-paved dochey at the north end of the dzong. The utse divides the two portions of the dzong. A thondrol depicting Guru Rimpoche is unfurled from this each year in the early hours of the final day of the autumn tsechu festival. Inside the main prayer hall at the far south of the dzong are statues of Sakyamuni, Guru Rimpoche and Shabdrung Ngawang Namgyal. As in most temples, the walls are covered with paintings depicting the lives of the Buddha. The dzong was repaired after a fire in 1837 and

again after it was severely damaged in the 1897 earthquake.

Places to Stay
There's not a lot of demand for hotel rooms in Wangdi. Most travellers stay in Punakha and then drive straight through to Gangte, Trongsa or Bumthang. At tsechu time, however, the town is packed and rooms are at a premium. The *Orchard Hotel* (☎ 297) is just below the bazaar on the road to the dzong. The restaurant and three rooms with private baths at Nu 750 are in the main building. Six more rooms with a common bath are in a separate facility on the opposite side of the road and cost Nu 500, whether used as a single or double. They operate a restaurant in a tent during the Wangdi tsechu.

The *Dragon's Nest Hotel* (☎ 274) is on the west side of the river quite a distance below Wangdi. Built in 1997 by the owners of Rinchen Tours & Travel, it has 17 rooms, all with attached bath. There's also a new facility under construction in Chhuzomsa, 11km from town on the road to the Pele La.

Places to Eat
The *Black Necked Crane Hotel* is a good place for lunch; try their Nepali-style daal bhat (rice and lentils). The restaurant in the Orchard Hotel also serves good food. There are numerous small restaurants where you can get a quick meal of noodles or momos. The *Tashi Topgyal* is run by a friendly family and the *Dema Hotel* has overstuffed chairs and a sofa so you can relax with a beer and watch the world pass by the front window.

PHOBJIKHA VALLEY
Phobjikha is a glacial valley on the western slopes of the Black Mountains. The valley is a designated conservation area and borders on the Black Mountain National Park. Because of the large flock of black-necked cranes that winter here, it is one of the most important wildlife preserves in the country. In addition to the cranes there are also muntjak (barking deer), wild boar, sambar, Himalayan black bear, leopard and

red fox in the valley and surrounding hills. The Nakey Chhu drains the valley, flowing south-west and into the lower reaches of the Punak Chhu.

Some people refer to this entire region as Gangte after the goemba that sits on a ridge above the valley.

Gangte Goemba

Gangte Goemba is on a ridge overlooking the large green expanse of the Phobjikha valley. The extensive complex consists of the goemba itself and several other buildings which include monks' quarters, meditation centres, schools and a small hotel. In front of the yellow-roofed goemba is a Tibetan-style chorten with a wooden cover.

During a visit to the Phobjikha valley, Pema Lingpa prophesised that a goemba named *gang-teng* (hill-top) would be built on this site and that his teachings would be spread from there. A temple was founded here in 1613 by Gyalse Pema Thinley, the grandson and mind reincarnation of Pema Lingpa, and the goemba was built by Tenzing Legpai Dhendup, the second reincarnation.

The current abbot, Kunzang Pema Namgyal, is the ninth reincarnation. Overseas friends of Gangte Goemba publish a newsletter available from Yeshe Khorlo (☎ 562-429 1331; email yeshekhorlo@yahoo.com), c/o Charles Samuelson, 4615 Hazelbrook Ave, Long Beach CA 90808 USA.

It is a Nyingma goemba and is affiliated with other Nyingma goembas in Bhutan including Tamshing in Bumthang, the home of Pema Lingpa (see boxed text 'Pema Lingpa' in the Central Bhutan chapter). The *tshokhang* (prayer hall) is built in the Tibetan style and is one of the largest in Bhutan. Inside the lhakhang are statues of the eight manifestations of Guru Rimpoche. The *shedra* (Buddhist college) was built in 1986 with government funds. The long white building on the hill to the north of the goemba is Kuenzang Chholing, a *drubda* (retreat and meditation centre for monks) that was started in 1990 by the Je Khenpo. The normal period of meditation is three years, during which time the monks remain

inside and eat food that is passed in to them only by another monk.

Around the Valley

There are no telephones, and because of concerns about wildlife, there is no electricity in this sparsely-populated valley. The valley is snowbound during the height of the winter and everyone, even the monks, shifts to winter residences in Wangdue Phodrang during December and January.

The road from Gangte Goemba descends to the valley floor, then traverses the edge of the valley past fields and scattered houses. The extensive fields of potatoes that are the region's primary cash crop enhance the rich green of the valley. Gangte potatoes are sold throughout Bhutan and are one of Bhutan's important exports to India.

In the small settlement of **Phobjikha**, near the foot of the valley, is a primary school and the picturesque Phunsho Chholing Guest House. The road continues another 3km past the hotel, then it's a one hour walk to the **Khebethang Nature Study Centre**, a Royal Government of Bhutan project with WWF assistance that was completed in 1996. The facility has housing and research facilities for scientists to help determine conservation needs and management methods. It has exhibits and is the site of workshops and interpretation courses for farmers, park staff and students.

The centre of the valley is swampy and is the winter residence of a flock of 200 to 300 rare and endangered **black-necked cranes** (see boxed text in the Flora & Fauna section of the Facts about Bhutan chapter) that migrate from Tibet to Bhutan in late autumn, typically between the 23rd and 26th of October. The Bhutanese have great respect for these magnificent birds, and songs about the cranes are popular among village folk. In mid-February, the cranes fly back across the Himalaya to their summer homes in Tibet. One of the most popular folk songs of the people of Phobjikha is about the cranes, and laments the time when the cranes leave the valley to return to Tibet. If you get permission from the Nature Conservation section

WESTERN BHUTAN

in Thimphu (☎ 02-23161) you can view the roosting place of the cranes from a wooden blind. The trail starts just before the bridge where the road reaches the valley floor. It's about a 20 minute walk to the blind on a trail that crosses the swamp on rough wooden slabs. The best time is at dawn and dusk when all the birds in the valley congregate for the night.

Just behind the Phunsho Chholing Guest House is the small **Norsang Carpet Factory**. Established in 1992 by a local woman, Dorji Wangmo, it has a small hall with eight weavers who produce about 90 carpets a year. Most of the carpets are bed-sized and sell for Nu 3000 to Nu 3500; they also produce smaller carpets designed to be used on the seats of chairs or cars.

Places to Stay

The *Tashiling Guest House* is pretty basic. It's on the road just as you reach the valley floor and is often closed, though it's usually open at festival time in late autumn.

The *Phuntsho Chholing Guest House*, at the far end of the valley, is a very large Bhutanese-style house that was converted to a hotel in 1995. It has lovely polished wood floors, shared bath (one western and one Asian toilet on each floor). It has 10 rooms at Nu 200/400; each has wall paintings that are characteristic of well-to-do homes, and there is a chapel on the 2nd floor. The hotel is run by a friendly family, and a stay provides a good opportunity to experience firsthand the traditional architecture and rural life of Bhutan. Most tour guides arrange a 'cultural show', which features the weavers from the carpet factory dancing and singing folk songs in the hotel dining room. They usually don't have a supply of drinks, but you can pick up a bottle of local spirits at the very rustic Black Neck Crane Hotel just down the road. There's no telephone in the hotel, but you can leave a message at the nearby BHU (☎ 29370).

The *Goemba Hotel* is on the ridge above the valley, opposite the Gangte Goemba. It's a concrete structure, which makes it quite cold. All eight rooms have attached bath-

rooms. The dining-cum-sitting room has big overstuffed chairs, which look strangely out of place in the rustic setting.

Getting There & Away

The road to Phobjikha diverges from the main road 47km from Wangdi, just east of Nobding. It's a 13km, 45 minute drive on a dirt road that climbs through forests to a pass at 3140m, where you may encounter a few stray yaks. There are also barking deer and serow in this area. The lichen hanging down from the trees is *usnea*, commonly called 'old man's beard'. The road descends into the picturesque Phobjikha valley, passing scattered houses until it reaches the turnoff to Gangte Goemba. From the goemba junction, the road switchbacks steeply down to the green expanse of the valley floor.

Gasa Dzongkhag

Gasa is in the far north of the country. Previously a subdistrict of Punakha, it was upgraded to a Dzongkhag in 1995.

GASA

The village of Gasa is north of Punakha. No road extends up the valley yet and the only way to get here is on foot. There is a road from Punakha to the southern border of the district at Tashithang, and there is a plan to build a road as far as Damji, a day's walk away. The Laya-Gasa and Gasa Hot Spring treks pass through this region (see the Trekking chapter).

Many houses and offices in Gasa are powered by a solar electricity system, and the headquarters of Jigme Dorji National Park is just north of the village centre.

Trashi Thongmoen Dzong

The Trashi Thongmoen Dzong in Gasa lies on the old trade route to Tibet. The Shabdrung built it in 1646 after his victories over the Tibetans. Originally called Drukgyel (Victorious) Dzong, it saw a lot of activity defending the country against Tibetan invasions in the 17th and 18th centuries. It lay in ruins after being destroyed by fire, but has now been renovated and serves as the dzongkhag administrative headquarters.

LAYA

Laya is a large, isolated region in the far north-west of the Gasa district. The roughly 800 people of this area are from a group called Layap, who have their own language, customs and distinct dress. Laya language is similar to Dzongkha but if people speak fast, Dzongkha speakers cannot understand them. The Layap language uses a very respectful form of speech.

The women keep their hair long and wear peculiar conical bamboo hats with a bamboo spike at the top, held on by a beaded band that reaches to the back of the head. They dress in a black woollen jacket with silver trim and a long woollen skirt with a few stripes in natural earth colours like orange and brown. They wear lots of silver jewellery on their backs; on many women this display includes an array of teaspoons.

Spread out over a hillside near the Tibetan border, Laya is one of the highest villages in the country at 3700m. The peak of the daunting **Masagang** (7165m) towers over the village. The villagers raise turnips and mustard and produce one wheat or barley crop a year, then the region is snowed in for the winter.

This is Bhutan's primary yak breeding area; during the summer, people move to the high pastures and live in black tents woven from yak hair.

The village women are easily encouraged to stage an evening 'cultural show', which consists of Bhutanese circle dancing accompanied by traditional Bhutanese and Layap songs.

Women often offer to sell their bamboo hats for Nu 150 or so. It's fine to buy these because they are made locally from native materials, but don't buy ones with beads as these are often family heirlooms and, once sold, cannot be replaced except with cheap plastic beads. Layap women also sometimes come around to trekking camps selling jewellery; most of this is made in Nepal and you'll probably get less value than what you pay for.

The Shabdrung Ngawang Namgyal passed through Laya and in a small meadow below the village is a chorten with the footprints of the Shabdrung and his horse.

The region is believed to be a *Bey-yul* (hidden land) protected by an ancient gate that leads to Laya village. The Layaps perform a ceremony each year in honour of the protective forces that turned all the stones and trees around the gate into soldiers to repel Tibetan invaders.

Getting There & Away

Without a helicopter, the only way to get to Laya and Gasa is on foot. The Laya-Gasa

Laya women are easily recognised by their distinctive dress.

WESTERN BHUTAN

and the Snowman treks pass through Laya village (see the Trekking chapter).

LINGZHI

Lingzhi is actually a *drungkhag* (subdistrict) within Thimphu Dzongkhag, and is placed here only for geographical convenience.

It is in the far north-western corner of the country and may be visited on either the Jhomolhari or Laya-Gasa treks. It is a very isolated region and, from whatever direction you approach it, it's necessary to cross a pass more than 4500m high to reach it. There are several settlements near Lingzhi dzong at an elevation of about 4000m.

The Lingzhi region has a wide variety of herbs, many of which have medicinal value. The Institute of Traditional Medicine in Thimphu has a large herb collecting and drying project here. Because of the high elevation, the only other major crop that grows well is barley.

The Lingzhi La at the head of the valley was a trade route between Punakha and Gyantse and was also used by Tibetan armies during various attacks on Bhutan.

Yugyel Dzong

The third Druk Desi, Minjur Tenpa, who ruled from 1667 to 1680, built the dzong in Lingzhi. It is on a hill about 200m above Lingzhi village and is quite close to the Tibetan border. The dzong was destroyed in the 1897 earthquake, but was rebuilt in the 1950s to serve as an administrative headquarters.

It is quite small, with a few offices along the outside wall and a two-storey utse in the centre. Some years ago the basement was used as a jail to house murderers and temple robbers, but the facilities were quite primitive and the dzong is no longer used for this purpose. There are only a few monks that stay in the dzong.

Getting There & Away

The only way to reach Lingzhi is to trek for several days over high passes. See the Trekking chapter for details.

Chhukha Dzongkhag

The Chhukha district, in the south, extends from Chhuzom to the Indian border. Phuentsholing, the primary land crossing to Bhutan, is here. This dzongkhag is also the location of the large Chhukha hydroelectric project that produces electricity for all of western Bhutan with enough surplus to export to India.

THIMPHU TO PHUENTSHOLING

The trip by car from Thimphu to Phuentsholing takes about six hours to cover 174km. The route follows the first road in Bhutan, which was built in 1962 by Dantak, the Indian Border Roads Organisation.

Thimphu to Chhuzom
31km, 1 hour

See Chhuzom to Thimphu in the Getting There & Away section of the Thimphu chapter for details.

Chhuzom to Chapcha
23km, ¾ hour

The road follows the Wang Chhu south from Chhuzom, passing beneath the remains of **Dobji Dzong**, which sits atop a promontory high above the river. Staying near the banks of the river, the road passes the settlements of Hebji Damcho (2020m) where the *Dechen Hotel* offers simple meals for Nu 30. About 4km further is the *Hotel Damcho* which caters primarily to truckers – hence the large parking lot. The road starts slowly climbing away from the river, becoming steeper as it makes its way out of the valley. You can see the road to Ha high on the opposite side of the Wang Chhu valley. There are said to be many bears roaming the western slopes of this valley.

Finally the road crests a ridge and passes the **Chapcha Bjha** (Chapcha rocks), a vertical rock face to the left, and an equally vertical drop to the right of the road. Cross the Chapcha La to reach the Dantak road construction camp at Chapcha (2490m).

High above the village are the ruins of **Chapcha Dzong** and a few small temples surrounded by prayer flags.

Chapcha to Chhukha
34km, 1 hour
There are farms and houses scattered on the hillside beyond the Dantak camp; on a cliff far above is a goemba built into the side of a rock face. The road descends to a large new bridge that the Dantak engineers named **Tachhong Zam** (Most Excellent High Bridge). It then climbs the side of a steep forested slope to Bunakha (2300m) where the *Hotel White Lake View* restaurant caters to travellers. The restaurant looks like a country-style log cabin and has an extensive menu (though not everything is available) and also clean restrooms. The valley is quite picturesque, with big Bhutanese-style houses below the road and across the valley.

From Bunakha the road climbs again to a petrol station and the goemba of Chhukha Rabdi. There is a large monk body here which performs the Chhukha tsechu each April. In **Chimakha** (its old name was Chimakothi) at 2130m are several local-style restaurants, including the *K.S. Restaurant* and the *Hotel Sonam*. If you get stuck here, the only accommodation available is at the *Karma Hotel* (☎ 221) for Nu 150. A small side road leads 2km uphill from here to Tshilakha and the offices of the Chukkha project.

The road switchbacks down to the Chhukha hydroelectric project. Several roads lead down to the dam site and the intake structures that divert the river into seven tunnels bored though the hill. The road descends further to the entrance to the powerhouse and distribution system for the Chhukha project. There is a substantial fast-food restaurant beside the road.

Chhukha to Gedu
38km, 1 hour
Just beyond this restaurant there is an immigration check post and the **Theg Chen Zam** (Strong High Bridge) which takes the road to the west side of the Wang Chhu.

This is the mid-point between Thimphu and Phuentsholing.

The road climbs to a lookout where a sign advertises a 'bird's eye view' of the Chhukha project. Far below are the long buildings that once housed construction workers and have now been converted into the Chukkha high school. The turbines are inside the hillside, but you can see the transformers and the transmission station. Beside the distribution station are the ruins of **Chhukha Dzong**. Just before the lookout is the first of several roads leading to the new 1020MW Tala hydroelectric project. This road leads 8.5km to the intake structure.

The rest of the climb is over the ridge that separates the Wang Chhu valley from the Torsa Chhu drainage. The road climbs to a chorten that is a memorial to an important official who died here in a road accident, then passes Awakha, which is nothing more than a Dantak road construction camp. There's a short bridge over Toktokachhu falls (also known as Takti Chhu), a picturesque cascade; another spectacular high waterfall is also visible to the east on the opposite side of the Wang Chhu valley. Atop the next ridge at 1980m is a Dantak canteen that specialises in Indian-style dosas. It also has public toilets. Beyond another road crew camp at Asinabari lies the small settlement of Chasilakha (*la kha* means grazing field).

Another climb leads to **Gedu**, a fair-sized village with several small restaurants near the road. The Gedu Wood Factory operated here from 1990 until 1996. Large buildings both above and below the road house the equipment used to produce plywood. The government closed the factory because of the environmental damage that the tree harvesting caused. The offices of the plywood factory have been converted into the administrative facility for the construction of the Tala Project. A road leads 18km downhill from Gedu to Mirching and the Tala project. Just past Gedu is a *restaurant* that specialises in expresso coffee.

WESTERN BHUTAN

Gedu to Rinchending
41km, 1¼ hour

A short distance on is a chorten that marks Jumbja village at 2050m. There is a dairy facility here that processes cheese and butter from milk produced in nearby villages. A large road leads 35km from here to Pasakha and the Tala powerhouse; this road will eventually connect to Phuentsholing and provide an alternative route to the border. The old road climbs to Gonglakha and starts winding its way down the final hill to the plains.

At Sorchen there is a road construction camp to house the workers who continually repair damage from huge landslides that occasionally close the road. A diversion was built in 1997 that avoids the area most prone to problems, but the road is still under constant attack from the elements. As you cross the top of the slide there is the first view of Phuentsholing and the plains. From the bottom of the slide area it's a 12km drive through forests to the check post at Rinchending.

Rinchending to Phuentsholing
5km, 10 minutes

Rinchending is the immigration post where your passport is stamped and your departure from (or arrival in) Bhutan is recorded. Below Rinchending is the town of Kharbandi and the Royal Technical Institute. Below the technical school is the Grand Queen Mother's winter residence and the small **Kharbandi Goemba**. There is a small group of resident monks and tourists are allowed to visit the lhakhang. The temple was built in 1967 and houses large statues of Sakyamuni, Shabdrung Ngawang Namgyal and Guru Rimpoche. On the grounds are examples of eight different styles of Tibetan chortens. Below Kharbandi the road switchbacks down to Phuentsholing, which sprawls from the hills onto the edge of the plains.

PHUENTSHOLING

The road from Thimphu enters Phuentsholing from the east, passing the post office and archery ground, then makes a turn onto the main street and the often-photographed Bhutanese-style entrance gate. If you are coming from India, you will travel north through the crowded bazaar of Jaigaon. At the top end of town the road turns east and passes through the gate where you will notice an instantaneous change in the degree of cleanliness and organisation.

To the north of the town a stream, the Dhoti Chhu, flows west to join the Torsa River, which in its upper reaches is known as the Amo Chhu and has its headwaters in Tibet's Chumbi valley. On the opposite side of the Torsa Chhu is the home of the minority group known as the Doya.

Orientation

The main road through town is in an east-west direction. From the gate it passes the Druk Hotel and bus terminal on the south side and several smaller hotels on the north side. About 200m from the gate it reaches a roundabout. The road to the left leads to an industrial and residential area. The road to Thimphu turns right and climbs a hill to the post office, banks and government offices, then starts immediately climbing towards the capital, 174km away.

The bazaar, called the upper market, is to the north of the Thimphu road and is dominated by a park and the Zangto Pelri temple, which is a replica of Guru Rimpoche's celestial paradise. Surrounding the park are shops, a large department store complex and the Namgay Hotel. To the west of the park is Tharpai Lam with the Central Hotel, many shops and small restaurants. At the east end of Tharpai Lam is Thuen Lam; one side of this street is in Bhutan, the other in India.

Information

Tourist Office Bhutan Tourism Corporation, Limited (☎ 52350) has an office on the main road, opposite the bus terminal.

Foreign Consulate There is an office of the Indian embassy (☎ 52635, 52101) near the post office. Indian nationals should report here to obtain the form required for a 14-day entry permit.

Immigration Indian nationals may wander freely into Phuentsholing during the day, but are required to leave by 10 pm unless staying in a hotel. Since the immigration check post is 5km away in Rinchending, foreigners may also cross back and forth across the border – a useful facility in case you neglected to complete Indian departure formalities before you crossed into Bhutan.

Post & Communications The Post Office is next to the headquarters of the Bank of Bhutan and the Royal Insurance Corpora-

tion of Bhutan on a hill above the town. There are numerous PCOs, and several have automated billing systems.

Bookshops Pekhang Enterprises (☎ 52771) is a branch of the largest bookshop in Thimphu and has paperback novels, children's books, Indian newspapers and a few books about Bhutan.

Markets In addition to the weekend market, there is a bazaar in the market area each Wednesday. The vegetable market is separate

WESTERN BHUTAN

Phuentsholing

0   100   200 m

PLACES TO STAY
3 Hotel Penjor
4 Hotel Sinchula
6 Om Hotel
8 Hotel Namgay
12 Central Hotel
16 Hotel Peljorling
17 Kuenga Hotel
18 Local Hotels
20 Druk Hotel

PLACES TO EAT
7 Bhutan Hotel

OTHER
1 Norgay Cinema
2 Weekend Market

5 Vegetable Market
9 Taxi Stand
10 Zangto Perli Temple
11 Tashi Department Store
13 Bank of Bhutan (Bazaar Branch)
14 Mig Cinema
15 Bhutan Gate
19 Petrol Station
21 Bus Stand
22 Football Field
23 India Liaison Office
24 Petrol Station
25 Archery Field
26 Immigration Office
27 Royal Insurance Co
28 Post Office
29 Bhutan National Bank

from the weekend market and is open throughout the week; fresh vegetables are always available.

Places to Stay & Eat
The rates shown here do not include the 10% hotel tax that is levied in Phuentsholing. For meals, stick to the larger hotels or the restaurant in the Hotel Peljorling.

Tourist Standard All the tourist standard hotels have attached bath facilities. The *Hotel Druk* (☎ 52428, 52427; fax 52929) is next to the bus station and has 35 rooms with IDD phones. Standard rooms with fans cost Nu 850/1000. Rooms with air conditioning are Nu 1200. There's a well-managed bar, and the restaurant serves good Indian food.

The *Central Hotel* (☎ 52172, 52173) in the town centre is popular with Indian tourists and charges Nu 250/350. On the main square is the *Hotel Namgay* (☎ 52374) with 14 well-appointed rooms at Nu 385/485. The older *Sinchula Hotel* (☎ 52589, 52772) has 17 rooms for Nu 250/350 and a rooftop terrace bar that looks out on the surrounding hills. The new *Hotel Om* (☎ 52387) has 18 rooms at Nu 140/200.

Local Standard Smaller hotels with singles/doubles in the Nu 100/150 to Nu 150/200 range are the *Hotel Kuenga* (☎ 52293), *Hotel Paradise* (☎ 52145) and *Hotel Peljorling* (☎ 52365, 52833). Others are *Hotel Deki* (☎ 52379), *Hotel Himalaya* (☎ 52828), *Hotel Holiday Inn* (☎ 52819), *Hotel Rignam* (☎ 52810), *Hotel Rigya* (☎ 52370) and *Hotel Saluja* (☎ 52834).

Opposite the bus station there are the *Moon Lite*, *Blue Dragon* and *Rangzen*, which cater to Bhutanese students and bus passengers.

Entertainment
If you like Hindi movies, you are in luck. The *Mig Cinema* in the centre of town and the *Norgay Cinema* near the Dhoti Chhu at the north end of town offer several three-hour performances daily.

For a drink, the favourite local gathering

places are the garden of the *Hotel Peljorling* and the funky bar at the *Hotel Bhutan*.

Getting There & Away
Jaigaon is a large, nondescript Indian village opposite Phuentsholing. You can make road connections from Jaigaon or Phuentsholing to the airport in Bagdogra or the railway station in Siliguri, both in West Bengal (169km, about six hours). There are also convenient connections to the Nepal border at Kakarbhitta or the Indian hill stations of Kalimpong, Gangtok and Darjeeling. Bhutanese vehicles may ply freely in India, and a Bhutan tour operator can easily arrange a vehicle to any of these destinations.

Indian Immigration The office is open 24 hours and is in a compound on the east side of the main road in the centre of Jaigaon.

Jaigaon The gate between Phuentsholing and Jaigaon closes at 8 pm for vehicles, but people can cross on foot until 10 pm.

Ha Dzongkhag

The Ha valley lies at an elevation of 2700m. The valley runs north-east to south-west and lies just south of the Paro valley. One road into Ha diverges from the Phuentsholing-Thimphu road at Chhuzom and travels south, high above the Wang Chhu, before turning into the Ha valley. Another road reaches Ha from Paro, crossing the 3780m Cheli La. The people of the remote Ha region are less sophisticated than those in more accessible regions. Ha is off limits to tourists, partly because of the large Indian army installation here, and partly because there are several routes into Tibet through country that is impossible to patrol.

Ha is the ancestral home of the Dorji family, to which the Queen Mother, Ashi Kesang Wangchuck, belongs.

It is a large fertile valley, and the staple crops are wheat, potatoes, barley and millet. Though there is easy access to Tibet from

Ha, it was never a major trade route because of the remoteness of the valley. Many people from Ha move to Samtse in winter.

Wangchulo Dzong
Ha dzong is one of Bhutan's newest, built in 1915 to replace a smaller structure that was destroyed. It is a large square structure in the traditional style with inward-sloping walls.

Southern Districts

TSIRANG DZONGKHAG
This district (formerly spelt as Chirang) is in the south of the country but separated from the southern border by Sarpang Dzongkhag.

The major town is **Damphu**, reached by a road leading south from Wangdue Phodrang. It passes through Sankosh, said to be the hottest place in the country, then continues south-east from Damphu to the border town of Sarphang.

DAGANA DZONGKHAG
This dzongkhag was previously known as Daga. The headquarters is in **Dagana** and the region is noted for farming and cattle production. It is said that the people of 17th-century Dagana were lawless and out of control, and Shabdrung Ngawang Namgyal sent Donyer Druk Namgyal with soldiers to conquer them. Druk Namgyal built the dzong in 1655 and gave it the name Daga Tashiyangtse Dzong.

SAMTSE DZONGKHAG
Samtse (previously spelled Samchi) is in the far south-west of the country and is closed to tourists. The only access is from India, though a road is under construction from Phuentsholing. The Teachers' Training College is here, as is the factory that produces Druk brand tinned fruit and jams.

Early British expeditions used a route through Samtse to travel to the centre of Bhutan. From Darjeeling they crossed over the hills of Samtse to Ha, then over the Cheli La to Paro.

WESTERN BHUTAN

Central Bhutan

There is a great variety of people, architecture and scenery in central Bhutan, and it is difficult enough to get to for the countryside and hotels to be less crowded. Until he 1970s the only way to reach this part of Bhutan was on foot or atop a sure-footed mule. The route across the high Pele La leads to the large, fertile Mangde Chhu valley, which is protected by the great Dzong at Trongsa. A short drive over the mountains from Trongsa leads to the four valleys of Bumthang, Bhutan's cultural heartland where the landscape is dotted with palaces, ancient temples and monasteries.

HISTORY

Central Bhutan is believed to be the first part of Bhutan to be inhabited, with evidence of prehistoric settlements in the Ura valley of Bumthang and the southern region of Khyeng. These and many other valleys were separate principalities ruled by independent kings. One of the most important of these kings was the 8th century Indian Sindhu Raja of Bumthang, who was eventually converted to Buddhism by Guru Rimpoche. Bumthang continued to be a separate kingdom, ruled from Jakar, until the time of Shabdrung Ngawang Namgyal.

During the rule of the first *desi*, Tenzin Drugyey, all of eastern Bhutan came under the control of the Drukpa government in Punakha. Chhogyel Minjur Tenpa unified central and eastern Bhutan into eight provinces known as Shachho Khorlo Tsegay. He was then promoted to Trongsa *penlop* (governor).

Because of Trongsa dzong's strategic position, the penlop exerted great influence over the entire country. It was from Trongsa that Jigme Namgyal, father of the first king, rose to power.

Bumthang retained its political importance during the rule of the first and second kings, both of whom had their principal residence at Wangdichholing palace.

GEOGRAPHY

Bordered on the west by the Black Mountains and on the east by a chain of near-vertical hills, central Bhutan is drained by two major rivers. The Mangde Chhu flows from the peaks of the Himalaya through a narrow gorge to Trongsa. As the river flows south the valley widens and becomes a collection of fertile rice terraces. To the east the Bumthang Chhu drains four culturally rich valleys before joining the Mangde Chhu. In the south the Royal Manas National Park protects a region of tropical vegetation and jungle wildlife.

Trongsa Dzongkhag

WANGDUE PHODRANG (WANGDI) TO TRONGSA

It takes almost four hours to drive the 129km between the windswept town of Wangdi, in Western Bhutan, and Trongsa. The route crosses the Pele La (3400m) and passes through the Black Mountain National Park (see National Parks & Protected Areas under Flora & Fauna in the Facts about Bhutan chapter) before entering the broad, heavily cultivated Mangde Chhu valley.

Wangdi to Pele La
61km, 1¾ hours

Leaving the town, the road passes the turnoff to the army camp and traverses the valley, high above the Dang Chhu. There are no settlements along the road itself, but there are several villages on the hills both above and on the opposite side of the river from the road. Unlike the dense forests

between Thimphu and Punakha, the hillsides here are relatively bare, with only grass and small bushes covering the slopes. The large building far below the road, alongside the river, is a jail.

Just before Samtengang is the junction of a road leading north to the slate mines at Tashichholing and Tseshinang. By the time the road reaches **Chhuzomsa**, 11km from Wangdi, it is level with the river. A resort hotel is under construction here. When it's complete, it will help alleviate the shortage of hotel facilities in the region.

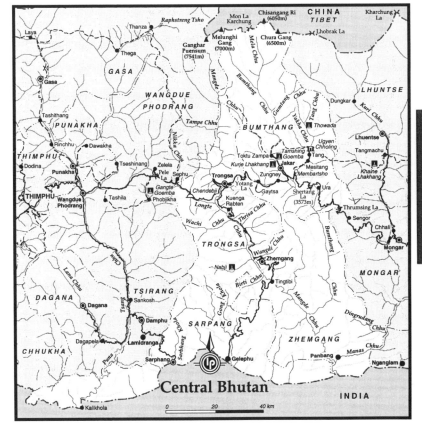

CENTRAL BHUTAN

Just beyond Chhuzomsa is a ropeway that climbs 1300m to **Tashila**. The ropeway is primarily used to carry goods up to the village and to bring logs back down the hill, but it makes two special trips daily to carry people. Passengers sit in an open wooden box and dangle high above the trees for 45 minutes (if there is no breakdown) to the top. Tourists are welcome to ride. The price is negotiable; you can charter the whole contraption for Nu 1000 or so. The Gangte trek ends here, and some trekkers ride the ropeway down from Tashila.

At **Tikke Zampa**, a few kilometres past Chhuzomsa, the road crosses to the south bank of the Tang Chhu and begins a long climb to Pele La. It goes past rice terraces and a few houses scattered on the hillside. The valley gets steeper as the road ascends along the edge of the valley, following a spectacular, and occasionally frightening, route. In many places the way for the road is blasted out of the side of the cliff and hangs high above the deep forests of the valley below.

From **Nobding** (2890m), a small village with little to offer except a refreshing cup of tea at the small *Tashi Delek* hotel, it's another 7km to the turnoff to Gangte Goemba and the Phobjikha valley. Gangte is 13km up a gravel road (see Gangte Goemba under Phobjhika Valley in the Western Bhutan chapter). There are a few basic local-style restaurants at the intersection, which is a cold, damp place in deep forests.

It's a long, hair-raising climb to the top of the pass. In this stretch the road is subject to frequent landslides and is often closed by snow during winter. There's a road construction camp at **Zelela**, just before the final climb to the pass, and crews are on standby here. They can usually reopen the road quickly, but there is always a chance of an extended delay of several hours to several days.

Yaks

We tend to oversimplify the many manifestations of the yak into this single word, yet it is only the full-blooded, long-haired bull of the species *Bos grunniens* that truly has the name yak. In Bhutan the name is pronounced like *yuck* and females of the species are called *jim*. Females are prized for their butterfat-rich milk, used to make butter and cheese.

Large, ponderous and clumsy looking, they have the ability to move very quickly when startled. They are used as pack animals for seasonal migration to alpine pastures in Laya and other high regions of western Bhutan. If you are trekking with yaks, give them a wide berth, and don't put anything fragile in your luggage. If an animal becomes alarmed, it charges up a hill, your baggage falls off and gets trampled as the yak bucks and snorts when its keeper tries to regain control.

Unlike Nepal, yaks in Bhutan are not usually crossbred with local cows, so most are massive animals with thick furry coats and impressive sharp horns.

Much of the hillside is covered with a strange dwarf bamboo called *cham*. This bamboo never gets large enough to harvest for any useful purpose, but when it is small, it is a favourite food of yaks and horses. This stretch of road is the best and easiest place in Bhutan to see yaks. Be alert though as these great shaggy beasts are skittish and likely to run off into the forest when your vehicle approaches.

Pele La is marked by a chorten and an array of prayer flags. A side road leads uphill from the pass to a logging area. You can see Jhomolhari (7219m) and other peaks from the pass, which is recognised as the boundary between western and central Bhutan and also marks the western border of Black Mountain National Park.

Pele La to Chendebji
27km, ¾ hour

From Pele La the road drops into the abundant evergreen forests of the Longte valley. You will pass large piles of roofing shingles stacked alongside the way. These are cut from a tree known in Dzongkha as *bashi* (spruce). The Dzongkha word for shingles is *shing-lep* (wood rectangle).

The first village on the east side of the pass is **Longte**. Here, in the upper part of the valley, people raise sheep and yaks in addition to producing wooden shingles.

Lower down into the valley the vegetation changes to broadleaf species and bamboo. The road passes opposite **Rukubji** village with its big school and goemba. Unusual in Bhutanese architecture, the houses in this village are all clustered closely together. Surrounding the village are extensive fields of mustard, potato, barley and wheat.

The groups of small white houses along the road are quarters for road maintenance crews. Road workers are housed throughout Bhutan near those parts of the road that require frequent repair. Most of the road workers are from India and are employed in Bhutan on contract for a fixed period of time.

The road drops into a side valley to **Sephu** village (2500m), which is beside the bridge that spans the Nikka Chhu. It's worth a brief stop here to examine the bamboo baskets that villagers sell in stalls near the bridge. This is the ending point of the 23 day Snowman Trek that starts from Paro and passes through the remote Lunana district (see the Trekking chapter).

It is a gentle, winding descent through rhododendron and ferns to the village of **Chendebji** (2400m) on the opposite side of the Nikka Chhu. This was a night halt for mule caravans travelling from Trongsa during the reign of the second king.

Just 2km beyond Chendebji village is **Chendebji Chorten**, a large white structure beside a stream. The chorten is patterned after Swayambhunath in Kathmandu and was built in the 19th century by Lama Shida, from Tibet, to cover the remains of an evil spirit that was killed at this spot. The proper name of this structure is Chorten Charo Kasho; it is the westernmost monument in a 'chorten path' that was the route of early Buddhist missionaries. The easternmost monument in this path is Chorten Kora in Trashi Yangtse. The Bhutanese-style chorten nearby was constructed in 1982.

Chendebji to Trongsa
41km, 1¼ hours

From the chorten the road continues down the valley through a deep forest of cedars. After passing a few farms and crossing a side stream it climbs again to a ridge, passing above the village of Tangsibji. The valley widens and the road turns a corner into the broad Mangde Chhu valley. After the road weaves in and out of a few side valleys there is a view of Trongsa and its huge, sprawling white dzong with a distinctive yellow roof. The dzong is perched at the end of a ridge and seems to hang in space at the head of the valley.

On the opposite side of the Mangde Chhu you can see the road that heads south to Zhemgang and Gelephu near the Indian border.

The shrubs along this part of the road are edgeworthia, which is used to make paper, and the brown monkeys you will probably

CENTRAL BHUTAN

see are rhesus macaques. Pass the settlement of Tashiling to another lookout. There is a small chorten here and an excellent view of the dzong, which looks almost close enough to touch even though it's still 14km away.

To reach Trongsa, you switchback into the upper reaches of the Mangde Chhu valley, cross the river on a Bailey bridge, and then climb again above the north bank of the river to finally reach Trongsa at an elevation of (2120m).

TRONGSA

Trongsa is smack in the middle of the country, separated from both the east and the west by high mountain passes. The town has had a large influx of immigrants from Tibet, and Bhutanese of Tibetan descent run most shops here. The Tibetans are so well assimilated into Bhutanese society that there is almost no indication of Tibetan flavour in the town.

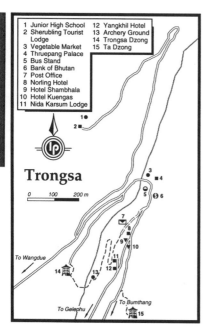

1 Junior High School
2 Sherubling Tourist Lodge
3 Vegetable Market
4 Thruepang Palace
5 Bus Stand
6 Bank of Bhutan
7 Post Office
8 Norling Hotel
9 Hotel Shambhala
10 Hotel Kuengas
11 Nida Karsum Lodge
12 Yangkhil Hotel
13 Archery Ground
14 Trongsa Dzong
15 Ta Dzong

Trongsa

0   100   200 m

To Wangdue

To Gelephu

To Bumthang

Orientation & Information

Just as the road enters the town a turnoff leads uphill to the tourist lodge and the junior high school. The main road stays level, traverses above the dzong and makes a switchback just after it crosses a stream. Just east of the stream is the vegetable market; nearby is the small Thruepang palace where the second king, Jigme Dorji Wangchuck, was born in 1928.

The road climbs to a cluster of shops and hotels that form the bazaar. A traffic circle marks the junction of the road that leads south to Gelephu. This road was completed in 1972. Foreigners are discouraged from travelling on this route south of Kuenga because of the lack of suitable accommodation and the security threat posed by Indian separatist groups (see Problems in the South in the History section of the Facts about Bhutan chapter).

The southern road goes downhill from the traffic circle, passing several hotels and shops, then travels about a kilometre to the town's only petrol pump. There are good views of the dzong from several points along this road. The road towards the east goes uphill from the traffic circle. A short walk on this road leads to a steep, narrow path that will take you to the *ta dzong* (watch tower).

The Bank of Bhutan is open from 9 am to 1 pm weekdays, 9 to 11 am on Saturday, closed Sunday. You can cash travellers cheques here although there is a fair amount of paperwork involved.

There is no formal bus stand in Trongsa. The few buses that ply this route stop on the roadside near the traffic circle.

Trongsa Dzong

Trongsa is the most impressive dzong in the kingdom, and can be seen from a great distance in its strategic position high above the Mangde Chhu. It has been described as being perched so high on a mountain that the clouds float below it. It is one of the most aesthetic and magnificent works of traditional Bhutanese architecture.

The dzong was built in its present form in

How Trongsa Got Its Name

Trongsa Dzong has a rich history going back to the 16th century. The first construction on the site of the dzong was carried out by Lam Ngagi Wangchuk, son of Ngawang Chhojey who established the Pangri Zampa in Thimphu. He came to Trongsa in 1541 and lived in the village of Yueli, which is a few kilometres above the dzong.

One night while meditating at Yueli, he observed a light burning on a ridge below. This was an auspicious omen and he went down to the light and saw the footprints of the horse of Palden Lhamo, Bhutan's guardian deity. Realising that this was a sacred abode of Palden Lhamo, he built a *tshamkhang* (small meditation quarter) and meditated there.

Lam Ngagi Wangchuk attracted many disciples who built other tshamkhangs and temples nearby. The people of Yueli, observing that the place now began to look like a new village, called the area Trong-sar (the people of Yueli pronounce *Dong,* or village, as *Trong*, hence Dong-sar or Trong-sar, meaning new village).

1644 by Chhogyel Minjur Tenpa, the official who was sent by the Shabdrung to unify eastern Bhutan, and enlarged at the end of the 17th century by the desi Tenzin Rabgye. Its official name is Chhoekhor Raptentse Dzong, though it is also known by its short name of Choetse Dzong.

The *utse*, named Chorten Lhakhang, is believed to have existed as an early form of Trongsa Dzong. It was probably built in 1543, before the current surrounding structure. The dzong was severely damaged in the 1897 earthquake. Repairs were carried out by the Trongsa penlop Jigme Namgyal, father of Bhutan's first king. Most of the existing decoration, including a 6m-tall statue of Buddha, was designed during the rule of the first king, Ugyen Wangchuck. The audience hall is still preserved as it was during his reign. There is a painting of the court as

it was then, and other paintings of the guardians of the four directions and the deity Phurpa in the main hall. There is also a 17th century mural depicting Swayambhunath in Nepal.

The dzong is a rambling collection of buildings that trails down the ridge. It has a remarkable succession of street-like corridors, wide stone stairs and beautiful stone courtyards. Its location gave it great power over this part of the country. The only mule and foot trail between eastern and western Bhutan leads through Trongsa and used to run through the dzong itself. Before the construction of the road, this gave the Trongsa penlop complete control over all east-west travel in the country. The interior is described as a series of street-like corridors alternating with wide stone stairs and plazas that give the impression of walking

in a mediaeval village. There are extensive wood carvings that make it the most elaborately decorated dzong after Trashi Chhoe in Thimphu.

Trongsa Dzong is the ancestral home of Bhutan's royal family. The first two hereditary kings ruled from this dzong, and it is still a tradition that the crown prince first serves as Trongsa penlop before acceding to the throne. The monks shift to Trongsa for the summer and Bumthang in the winter, just as they do between Thimphu and Punakha. Major renovation work is under way to repair cracks in the exterior walls.

Ta Dzong

There are three watch towers on the hill to the east of the dzong, and it's worth making the short climb for the view and to take a brief look at the Ta Dzong tower.

A chapel inside the tower is dedicated to the Trongsa penlop Jigme Namgyal. In another small chapel upstairs, there is an interesting representation of a palace, with small statues of horses, yaks and elephants. Two British soldiers are said to have been kept in the dungeon here for several months during the Duar war.

Places to Stay & Eat

There are only two tourist hotels in town. The *Sherubling Tourist Lodge* (☎ 03-21116; fax 21107) is run by BTCL and has 14 rooms renting for Nu 600/750 in the main building and another nine rooms in adjoining cottages for Nu 400/550, all with attached bath. It has a good view of Trongsa Dzong and the Mangde Chhu valley.

The *Norling Hotel* (☎ 03-21135) occupies a new cement building in the centre of town; rooms cost Nu 375/750. All 12 rooms have private bath, and the food in the dining room is quite good.

The *Yangkhil Hotel* (☎ 03-21126) and *Nida Karsum Lodge* (☎ 03-21133) are on a short spur off the main road at the southern end of town. Both are small, friendly places with simple rooms upstairs and Tibetan-style restaurants downstairs. In the Nida Karsum rooms are Nu 170/250 and the proprietor,

Tshering Dolma, will invite you into the kitchen to sit by the fire if it's cold. You can expect to pay about Nu 30 to Nu 50 for a meal of rice and vegetables and Nu 30 for a plate of momos at both.

There are a few other eating places in the bazaar. The *Hotel Shambhala* (☎ 03- 21135), and *Hotel Kuenga* (☎ 03-21139) both really merit the title 'Restaurant cum Bar' as opposed to 'hotel'.

AROUND TRONGSA

Tshangkhar village, a few kilometres from Trongsa, has a large shiitake mushroom farm.

Kuenga Rabten

The winter palace of the second king, Jigme Wangchuck, is 23km (one hour) south of Trongsa. It's an interesting drive, if only to see the beautiful large expanse of rice terraces in the lower Mangde Chhu valley, south of Trongsa. The palace is under the care of the Special Commission for Cultural Affairs, and you don't need a permit to enter. It's a good afternoon side trip from Trongsa and gives an intimate insight into life in the early days of Bhutan's monarchy.

The 1st storey was used to store food; the 2nd was the residence of royal attendants and the army; and the 3rd housed the royal quarters and the king's private chapel. Part of the 3rd storey has been converted into a library and many books from the National Library are stored here. On the top floor is Sangye Lhakhang with statues of Sakyamuni, the Shabdrung and Guru Rimpoche.

Bumthang Dzongkhag

'Many great kings and ministers have graced these valleys,
And many are the magnificent monasteries there.'
From an ancient text

The Bumthang region encompasses four major valleys: Choskhor, Tang, Ura and Chhume. Because the dzongs and the most important temples are in the large Choskhor valley, it is commonly referred to as the Bumthang valley.

There are two versions of the origin of the name Bumthang. The valley is supposed to be shaped like a *bumpa*, the vessel that contains holy water and is usually found on the altar of a lhakhang. *Thang* means field or flat place. The less respectful translation relates to the particularly beautiful women who live here – *bum* means girl.

The sale of tobacco is banned in Bumthang because the valley was of special significance to Guru Rimpoche, who is believed to have been opposed to tobacco. If you smoke, be sure to load up on cigarettes in Trongsa. Though the government discourages smoking, many people do, and you are welcome to smoke in Bumthang except in dzongs, goembas, the hospital and any restaurants and shops that have 'no smoking' signs. (You are not looked down upon because you smoke.)

TRONGSA TO JAKAR

It takes 2½ hours to cover the 68km from Trongsa to Bumthang. It's one of the easier and more interesting drives in Bhutan because it passes numerous villages and goembas in the Chhume valley.

Trongsa to Yotong La
28km, 1 hour

The road switchbacks up the ridge above Trongsa, climbing steeply for 7km to a viewpoint where you can look down on the town and dzong. It's then a long climb past the small Dorjun Goemba to the head of a valley. Finally the road traverses across the top of the valley to Yotong La (3425m).

Yotong La to Zungney
24km, 1 hour

The descent from the pass is through firs, then dwarf bamboo. The road enters the upper part of the **Chhume valley** at Gaytsa. There are numerous monasteries on the north side of the road in the upper part of the valley, though most are some distance from the road. Just before Gaytsa is the **Bula**

Lhakhang, and to the east of Gaytsa **Samtenling Goemba** stands on a forested knoll. The red roofs of **Tharpaling Goemba** are visible on a cliff to the north-east above the town. The Nyingma philosopher and saint Longchen Rabjampa (1308-1364) founded Tharpaling. It has several temples, and houses about 100 monks. Above Tharpaling, at about 3800m, is the large white complex of **Choedrak Goemba**. Pema Lingpa revealed several terma near these monasteries.

From Gaytsa the road follows a stream gently down the valley for 2km to Domkhar. A dirt road leads uphill to the south of this village for about 500m to **Domkhar Tashichhoeling**, the summer palace of King Jigme Wangchuck. It was completed in 1937 and is a replica of Kuenga Rabten, which is south of Trongsa. It served for several years as the residence of the elder queen mother, and is now under the care of the Monk Body of Trongsa Dzong. The large building to the south of Domkhar palace is a monastic school built in 1968 by the previous reincarnation of the Karmapa, but is not currently in use.

Beyond Domkhar village is the settlement of Tume with several shops along more than 500m of straight road, perhaps the longest stretch of its kind in the hills of Bhutan.

The people of this valley have traditionally been sheep herders. The Australian government is helping to upgrade the quality and quantity of the wool produced here. If you are interested in this project, you can visit the Bhutan Australian Sheep and Wool Development project offices, just west of Zungney town.

On the outskirts of **Zungney** village (2750m) is the 1.5MW Chhume mini-hydro plant which supplies electricity to Trongsa and Bumthang.

At the eastern end of Zungney village are two shops selling yathra. These are distinctive strips of woven woollen fabric in numerous colours and patterns. You can buy ready-made woollen jackets or blankets made by sewing three strips together.

CENTRAL BHUTAN

Yathra

Yathra is hand-spun, hand-woven wool with patterns specific to the Bumthang region. They are mostly geometric designs, sometimes with a border. Three strips may be joined to produce a blanket or bed-cover called *charkep*. In earlier days yathra was often used as a shawl or raincoat to protect against the winter cold of Bumthang. Older yathra were made from wool from Tibet; nowadays some of the wool is imported from New Zealand or from recently introduced sheep breeding projects in Bumthang.

Since Bhutan does not have the carpet weaving tradition of the Tibetans, yathra pieces often served the functions that Tibetan rugs would. Today it is fashioned into a *toego*, the short jacket that women often wear over a kira in cold weather.

Zungney Lhakhang is the small building just to the west of the first yathra shop.

Zungney to Jakar
16km, ½ hour

Just east of Zungney is **Prakhar Goemba**, on a promontory on the opposite side of the river. A one hour walk south of Prakhar leads to **Nimalung**, a Nyingma goemba.

The road follows the valley down past the apple orchards of Mangar and into chir pine forests. It's a short climb to Kiki La, a small pass at 2750m marked by a chorten and many prayer flags. The pass leads over a side ridge, and the road descends into the Choskhor valley towards the Bumthang Chhu.

JAKAR

Near the foot of the Choskhor valley, Jakar is the major trading centre of the region. This will probably be your base if you visit the valley as most of the hotels and services are found here. The rest of the valley is covered under the separate heading Choskhor Valley later in this chapter.

Weather

There is a strong wind from the south every afternoon, which makes it extremely cold during the evenings so be sure to dress warmly.

Most guesthouses have *bukharis* (wood stoves) heating the rooms. If you're cold, ask the room attendants to light the stove –

they start it with a dollop of kerosene. The efficient bukharis heat the room quickly, but don't burn very long.

Orientation & Information

The road from Trongsa enters Jakar from the south, passing a football field that doubles as an army helipad. A traffic circle and the 14th century village temple, **Jakar Lhakhang**, mark the centre of the town at 2580m. A wide main street leads east from the traffic circle to a bridge over the Bumthang Chhu. Just before you cross the bridge to leave the town a small pagoda marks the spot where a Tibetan general's head was buried after the defeat of a 17th century Tibetan invasion force.

There are many shops and a few restaurants lining the main street and, as in Trongsa, many are run by people of Tibetan descent. Some Chinese goods make their way over the high passes from Tibet and are for sale here.

There is a T-junction at the eastern end of the bridge; the northbound road leads to the Swiss Guest House and temples on the eastern side of the Bumthang Chhu. The southbound road is the route to Mongar and eastern Bhutan. On the hill above the east side of the bridge is the recently-constructed Namkhe Nyingpo Goemba.

Turning left from the traffic circle, a road leads up the west side of the valley. It makes a short climb past the petrol station and Chhoezom Guest House to an intersection

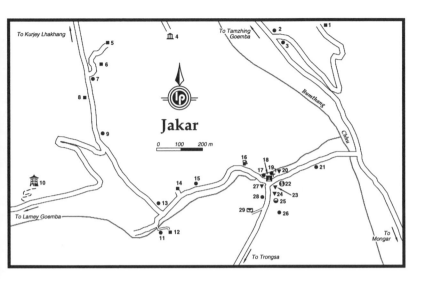

Jakar

0   100   200 m

To Kurjey Lhakhang
To Tamzhing Goemba
Bumthang
Chhu
To Lamey Goemba
To Trongsa
To Mongar

PLACES TO STAY
1 Swiss Guest House
5 Wandichholing Lodge
6 New Tsering Guest House
8 Tsering Guest House
12 Udee Guest House
14 Chozom Guest House

PLACES TO EAT
20 Deki Hotel
23 Thuenpa Puenzhi Bakery

24 Yanchen Restaurant & Bar
27 Tashi Restaurant & Bar

OTHER
2 Swiss Cheese Factory
3 Automobile Workshop
4 Wandichholing Palace
7 Archery Ground
9 Primary School
10 Jakar Dzong
11 Udee Woodcarving

13 Beekeeping Project
15 Veg Dye Project
16 Petrol Station
17 Udee Shopping Complex
18 Jakar Lhakhang
19 Vegetable Market
21 Medicine Shop
22 Bank of Bhutan
25 Bus Stand
26 Football Field
28 Town Gate
29 Post Office

CENTRAL BHUTAN

at the top of the town. A dirt road leads south to the Udee Guest House and a wood-carving factory. Another unpaved road leads west to the Public Works Department camp. The paved road leads north past a bee-keeping project, the primary school and the road to the dzong, then continues past the hospital up the western side of the valley to Kurjey Lhakhang.

If you are having car trouble, you're in luck. The large Tandin Dorje automobile workshop on the east side of the road at the turnoff to the Swiss Guest House is one of the better repair facilities in the country.

Jakar is a compact town and most facilities are within a very short walking distance of the traffic circle. The Bank of Bhutan is open from 9 am to 1 pm weekdays, 9 to 11 am Saturday, closed Sunday, and you can cash travellers cheques here. There are several PCOs throughout the town. If you want fresh vegetables they are available from the vegetable market behind the Jakar Lhakhang.

Jakar Dzong

According to legend, when the lamas assembled in about 1549 to select a site for a monastery, a big white bird rose suddenly in the air and settled on a spur of a hill. This was interpreted as an important omen, and the hill was chosen as the site for a monastery and for Jakar Dzong, which roughly translates as 'castle of the white bird'.

The site chosen for Jakar Dzong is a picturesque location overlooking the Choskhor valley. The current structure was built in 1667 and is said to be the largest dzong in Bhutan, with a circumference of more than 1500m. Its official name is Yuelay Namgyal Dzong in honour of the victory in a battle with troops of the Tibetan ruler Phuntsho Namgyal. The utse is about 50m tall and is located on the outside wall so that there is no way to circumambulate it other than walking around the entire dzong. A covered passage leads from the dzong to a nearby spring so that water could be obtained in the event of a long siege. The dzong was damaged once by fire and was severely damaged in the 1897 earthquake.

The paintings inside the lhakhang include Chana Dorje and several that depict the life of Milarepa. Compared to other dzongs, there are relatively few wood carvings here; most of the timber is decorated with paintings.

The road to the dzong starts just south of the primary school and climbs westward to a parking lot. The final approach to the dzong is made on foot along a stone-paved path. Even if you don't have a permit to enter the dzong it's a worthwhile climb because there is a good view of Choskhor valley from the front courtyard. The road continues past the dzong to the high school and Lamey Goemba.

The entrance to the dzong leads into a very narrow courtyard surrounded by administrative offices. The utse is on the east side of the courtyard, and beyond that is the monks' quarters and the district court. The Monk Body from Trongsa moves here in the winter; there is only a small group of caretaker monks during the summer. When the monks arrive, they perform a ceremony commemorating the defeat of the Tibetan invaders from Lhobrak in 1644. At the west end of the dzong is a slightly larger courtyard with the dzongda's office at the far west end.

Wangdichholing Palace

The extensive palace of Wangdichholing was built in 1857 on the site of a battle camp of Trongsa penlop Jigme Namgyal. His son, King Ugyen Wangchuck, chose it as his principal residence. It was used throughout his reign and also the reign of the second king. Wangdichholing was the early home of the third king, who then moved the court to Punakha.

It was inherited by Ashi Choeki Wangchuck, an aunt of the present king, but is no longer used and is not open to the public. It is reached by turning south on a road that passes behind the eastern side of the hospital. There are five giant water-driven prayer wheels inside square chortens as you approach the gates of the palace.

Lamey Goemba

High on a hill sits Lamey Goemba, a large palace and monastery built in the 18th century by Dasho Phuntsho Wangdi, grandson of King Ugyen Wangchuck. Its design is the palace style of the time, similar to Wangdichholing. It is now being used by a joint Swiss-Bhutan forestry study project. There is a large elaborately decorated courtyard that is being renovated and restored. There are a few houses nearby. A trail leads from Lamey Goemba over the hill to Tharpaling Goemba in the Chhume valley.

Vegetable Dye Project

An interesting project just west of the Chhoezom Guest House is supported by Ideas International, an Australian NGO with additional assistance from a Bangladesh NGO. They are producing traditional vegetable dyes to use in the production of cotton thread and a raw silk. Some of the plants they use to produce various colours are indigo (blue), turmeric (yellow), onion skin (off-white), oak bark (brown), walnut shell (blackish-brown), fern (light yellow), peach bark (cream colour), madder (light red), walnut bark (dark brown and grey) and rhododendron bark (yellow). This project is affiliated with the Cottage Industries Development Project in Thimphu where you can purchase products from this project if you don't get them here.

Places to Stay
The *Chhoezom Guest House* (☎ 03-31219) is the closest hotel to Jakar town. It has eight rooms with private baths at Nu 500/600. All the rooms open onto the parking lot like a motel.

BTCL's *Wangdichholing Lodge* (☎ 03-31107; fax 31130) has 14 rooms in a series of cottages arranged around a central dining hall and bar on the grounds of the old Wangdichholing palace. All the rooms have attached baths and bukharis for heat; the cost is Nu 800/1000.

Nearby is the *Tsering Guest House* (☎ 03-31244), which has two parts: the reception, restaurant and 11 rooms (only two have attached bathrooms) are just opposite the gate to the Wangdichholing Lodge. On the main road is a newer stone building that contains eight rooms with attached toilet facilities.

The *Swiss Guest House* (☎ 03-31145) is in a pleasant setting perched on a hill 60m above the valley floor, surrounded by an apple orchard. The hotel has 13 double rooms; all share common toilet facilities – you have a choice between indoor plumbing and a rustic outhouse. The hotel is decorated with lovely carvings and varnished pine panelling throughout. The water supply is from a rock spring; this is probably the only place in south Asia that advertises that you can safely drink the tap water. Each of the two buildings has its own private dining room that is heated by a bukhari in the winter. Rooms cost Nu 250/400.

The *Udee Guest House* (☎ 03-31139), is a small hotel near the woodcarving factory. All its rooms share toilet facilities. The *Tamzhing Guest House* (☎ 03-31184) is on a hillside 3km north of the main town on the road to Tamshing. It has nine rooms with attached bath and is run by Etho Metho tours.

Places to Eat & Drink
There are plenty of small bars and local restaurants along Jakar's main street, but they only offer snacks and thukpa (noodle soup). The only place that serves something approaching a real meal is *Deki Hotel*, next to the vegetable market. It also has a pot of the local fast food, momos, steaming away in the kitchen. The *Thuenpa Puenzhi Bakery* has a limited selection of bread and pastries.

The local Bumthang Beer is brewed locally in such limited quantities that you are unlikely to find a bottle for sale.

Many of the small bars are carom parlours. Competitions can be intense, with lots of cheering spectators. It costs Nu 5 per game, and the losing team buys a round of beer for the winners. To see a game, take a look in the *Yanchen Restaurant & Bar* or the *Tashi Restaurant & Bar*.

Things to Buy
As in most towns in Bhutan, the shops in Jakar contain a hodgepodge of goods. A typical shop may sell shoes, pens, nails, candy, soap, toy cars, locally made baskets, dried fish and prayer flags. A shop on the corner just south of the traffic circle advertises, 'Fulfil your wishes with all kinds of Bhutanese traditional gift items'. They have a few baskets and strips of yathra as well as chillies, potatoes and stationery.

One item in good supply in Jakar is *chugo*, dried cheese that is good to munch on. Unless you want to break your teeth, let a piece soften for a long time in your mouth before you bite into it.

Udee Woodcarving Factory The town's only furniture factory has a few woodcarvers that turn out traditional items. They sell lama tables and painted wood carvings from a showroom in the back of the Udee Shopping Complex in the centre of Jakar.

Dhe Wang Handmade Paper Factory A short dirt road leads from the paved road near Jambey Lhakhang to a traditional paper factory. They sell large sheets of Bhutanese paper in various colours and thicknesses. They sometimes have a few made-up speciality items like envelopes and folders for sale.

Swiss Farm The outlets for produce from the Swiss project are alongside the road near the junction of the road to the Swiss Guest House. The Yoezer Lhamo shop sells cheese, apple juice, brandy and apple wine. There's soft Gouda cheese at Nu 150 per kg and hard Emmental at Nu 138. This cheese is made for eating, unlike the soft Bhutanese *ema*, which is used only in sauces.

DAY HIKES
There are many opportunities for hikes in the Bumthang region, most involving visits to remote goembas (see Choskhor Valley section, following). If you are on a tourist visa, you will have a vehicle at your disposal, and can arrange for the driver to take you to the start of the walk and then collect you from a different spot at the end. You can walk the 17km to Thankabi Goemba from Kurjey Lhakhang and have a vehicle pick you up. It's a full day excursion if you want to continue up the valley to Ngang Lhakhang.

You can also walk from Lamey Goemba over the ridge to Tharpaling Goemba at 3500m and then down to the road at Domkhar where you can meet your vehicle.

You can also begin or end many walks in the Tang valley, walking from the Swiss Guest House to Petsheling Goemba and Kunzangdrak Goemba, high on a cliff above the valley.

CHOSKHOR VALLEY
To most people the Choskhor valley *is* Bumthang and the Choskhor valley is often called the Bumthang valley or just simply Bumthang.

It is too high to grow rice here. Instead, large fields of buckwheat cover the valley, and buckwheat noodles and pancakes are a Bumthang speciality. The Bumthang Chhu is famous for its large stock of trout, and despite the Buddhist reluctance to take life, fish do mysteriously appear on dinner plates.

A large Swiss development project has been in operation here for many years, and the milk from large Jersey cattle is used in Bhutan's only commercial cheese factory. The Swiss project has also introduced farming machinery and fuel-efficient smokeless wood stoves.

The road which leads up the western side of the valley reaches many of the most interesting features of Bumthang. Most of the temples on this side of the valley are connected in one way or another with the visit of Guru Rimpoche to Bumthang in 746.

Sey Lhakhang
Just beyond the hospital is Lhodrak Seykhar Dratshang, also known as Sey (Gold) Lhakhang. This is a monastic school, established in 1963, and has about 25 monks in study.

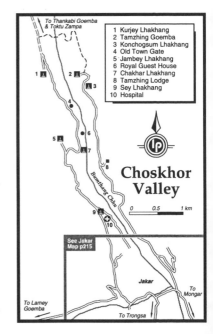

1 Kurjey Lhakhang
2 Tamzhing Goemba
3 Konchogsum Lhakhang
4 Old Town Gate
5 Jambey Lhakhang
6 Royal Guest House
7 Chakhar Lhakhang
8 Tamzhing Lodge
9 Sey Lhakhang
10 Hospital

Choskhor Valley

The central figure in the lhakhang is Marpa Lotsawa, a great teacher of the Kagyu lineage.

Jambey Lhakhang
The temple of Jambey Lhakhang is up a short side road about 1.5km past Sey Lhakhang. It is believed to have been built in the year 659 on the same day as Kyichu Lhakhang in Paro by the Tibetan king Songtsen Gampo (see boxed text 'The Ogress of Tibet' in the Western Bhutan chapter). The central figure in the lhakhang is Jampa, the Buddha of the future, which is protected by an iron chain mail that was made by Pema Lingpa.

The temple was visited by Guru Rimpoche during his visit to Bumthang and was renovated by the Sindhu Raja after the Guru restored his life force. It was repaired several times, and a golden roof built over time by various Trongsa penlops. When Ugyen Wangchuck was penlop of Trongsa, he added the temple of **Dus-Kyi-khorlo**, which is within the enclosed compound, on the northern side of the *dochey*.

Chimmi Dorji, the administrator of Jakar Dzong, added another temple, **Guru Lhakhang**, on the south side of the dochey. In the centre of the courtyard is a chorten in memory of Lama Pentsen Khenpo, spiritual advisor of the first and second Bhutanese kings. There are two large stone chortens behind the temple; one is in memory of the second king's younger brother, Gongsar Dorji.

The pile of carved mani stones in the parking lot in front of the goemba is a *thos*, representing the guardians of the four directions. Tourists are allowed to enter the courtyard, passing four large prayer wheels in front and two more inside. The building in the centre of the courtyard has 1000 butter lamps.

Inside the primary chapel are three stone steps representing ages. The first signifies the past, the age of the Buddha Sakyamuni. This step has descended into the ground and is covered with a wooden plank. The next age is the present, and its step is level with the floor. The top step represents a new age. It is believed that when the step representing the present age sinks to ground level, the gods will become like humans and the world, as it is now, will end.

Under the lhakhang is said to be a lake in which Guru Rimpoche hid several terma. There is an alcove up above the front door, facing the altar, in which sits a statue of the Guru. He sat in this alcove and meditated, leaving behind a footprint.

In October one of the most spectacular festivals in Bhutan, the **Jambey Lhakang Drup**, is staged here. On one evening, after the lama dances, the monastery is lit by a fire dance to bless infertile women so that they may bear children.

Chakhar Lhakhang
Beside the main road, a short distance beyond Jambey Lhakhang, is Chakhar (Iron Castle) Lhakhang. Though it is easy to mistake it for a house and drive right by, this is an interesting temple and is worth a short visit. It is the site of the palace of the Indian king Sendha Gyab, better known as the Sindhu Raja, who invited Guru Rimpoche to Bumthang. The original palace was made of iron, hence the name Chakhar, and was said to have been nine storeys high, holding within it all the treasures of the world. The current building was built in the 14th century by the saint Dorji Lingpa. Its correct name is Dechen Phodrang. The main statue inside the lhakhang is of Guru Rimpoche, and there are numerous masks that are used for a small festival which takes place here in the autumn.

Kurjey Lhakhang
Kurjey Lhakhang is named after the body print of Guru Rimpoche which is preserved in a cave inside the oldest of the three buildings that make up the temple complex. It is at the end of the paved road, 7km from Chamkhar Lhakhang, at an elevation of 2640m.

As you enter the complex, the monks' quarters are on the left. There are three large lhakhangs against a hillside on the right. The

The Story of Kurjey Lhakhang

In 746 the saint Padmasambhava made his first visit to Bhutan. Sendha Gyab, an Indian, established himself as the king of Bumthang, with the title Sindhu Raja. He was feuding with Naochhe (Big Nose), a rival Indian king in the south of Bhutan. Naochhe killed the Sindhu Raja's son and 16 of his attendants. The Raja was so distraught that he desecrated the abode of the chief Bumthang deity, Shelging Karpo, who then angrily took revenge by stealing the king's life force, bringing him near to death.

One of the king's secretaries invited the tantric master Padmasambhava to Bumthang to use his supernatural powers to save the Sindhu Raja. The Guru came to Bumthang and meditated, leaving an imprint *(jey)* of his body *(kur)* in the rock, hence the temple's name. Guru Rimpoche was to be married to the king's daughter, Tashi Khuedon. He sent her to fetch water in a golden ewer. While she was away the Guru transformed into all eight of his manifestations and, together, they started to dance in the field by the temple. Every local deity appeared to watch this spectacle; every local deity, that is, except the stony-faced Shelging Karpo who stayed hidden away in his rocky hideout above the present temple.

Guru Rimpoche was not to be set back by this rejection and when the princess returned he changed her into five separate princesses, each clutching a golden ewer. The sunlight flashing off these ewers finally attracted Shelging Karpo, but before he ventured out to see what was going on he first transformed himself into a white lion. On seeing the creature appear the Guru changed into a garuda, flew up and grabbed the lion and told Shelging Karpo in no uncertain terms to behave himself. He thus recovered Sendha Gyab's life force, and for good measure converted both the rival kings to Buddhism, restoring the country to peace.

Shelging Karpo agreed to become a protective deity of Buddhism (he's still the deity of the Kurjey Lhakhang) and the Guru planted his staff in the ground at the temple where its cypress tree descendants continue to grow. Furthermore Guru Rimpoche made King Sendha and his enemy from the south make peace and a stone pillar at Nabji in the Black Mountains marks the spot where the agreement took place.

first temple is the oldest and was built in 1652 by Minjur Tenpa when he was Trongsa penlop. Protruding just below the roof is a figure of a white lion with a garuda figure above, a representation of the famous struggle between Guru Rimpoche (appearing as the garuda) and the local demon, Shelging Karpo (as the white lion) – see the boxed text. At the entrance to the lower-floor sanctuary is a small crawl-through rock passage; Bhutanese believe that in crawling through a narrow tunnel like this you will leave your sins behind. The lower-floor sanctuary has statues of the past, present and future Buddhas, while the far wall has paintings of gods connected with riches and wealth.

The upper-floor sanctuary is the holiest at the complex, and has an image of Shelging Karpo just inside the door. There are 1000 small statues of Guru Rimpoche all neatly lined up along the same wall, plus three larger statues. The main statue in this sanctuary is again of Guru Rimpoche, flanked by his eight manifestations. Hidden behind this image is the meditation cave where he left his body imprint. The far wall has paintings of Guru Rimpoche, his manifestations, his disciples and various other figures connected with the Guru. The big cypress tree behind the lhakhang is said to have grown from the Guru's walking stick.

Ugyen Wangchuck, the first king of Bhutan, built the second temple in 1900, when he was still Trongsa penlop. On the entrance porch of the temple are paintings of the guardians of the four directions and of various local deities who were converted to Buddhism by Guru Rimpoche at the same time as Shelging Karpo. The white ghostlike figure on the white horse is Shelging Karpo. Inside the temple is a statue of Guru Rimpoche, this one 10m high, flanked again by his eight manifestations. A smaller image of the Guru sits against the opposite wall.

The third building is a new lhakhang built by the Queen Mother, Ashi Kesang Wangchuck, in 1990. She also had the courtyard in front of the three temples paved with stones and built a wall with 108 chortens around the whole complex. On the porch in front of the temple is a large 'wheel of life' depicting various hells and heavens. At the bottom you can see a man being judged to decide which place he's going to be sent. There's a beautiful mystic spiral mandala on the opposite wall and paintings of the kings with the four directions in the hallway. The inside is elaborately decorated, and contains the largest statue of Guru Rimpoche in Bhutan.

Two gigantic *lhadhar* (prayer flags) and a chorten dominate the centre of the courtyard. These mark the cremation sites of the first three kings of Bhutan.

The **Kurjey tsechu** is held in June and include a masked dance that dramatises Guru Rimpoche's defeat of Shelging Karpo. A large *thangka*, called Guru Tshengye Thondrol depicting the eight manifestations of Guru Rimpoche, is unfurled in the early morning before the dances, which are performed by the monks from Trongsa.

Thankabi Goemba
The yellow-roofed Thankabi Goemba was founded in 1470 by Shamar Rimpoche and, after a dispute, was taken over by Pema Lingpa. It's a 17km drive north of Kurjey Lhakhang on an unpaved road to Toktu Zampa. You leave the road here, cross a stream on a small suspension bridge and walk 20 minutes past fields of buckwheat to Thankabi Goemba. This is the same route as the beginning of the Bumthang cultural trek (see the Trekking chapter).

Ngang Lhakhang
Several hours walk up the Bumthang Chhu from Thankabi Goemba is the small region known as **Ngang-yul** (Swan Land). It's a climb of about 100m above the valley to Ngang Lhakhang, the Swan Temple. The site was visited by Guru Rimpoche, but the present temple was built in the 15th century by Lama Namkha Samdup, a contemporary of Pema Lingpa.

Despite the rustic and decrepit exterior, the interior contains numerous statues and paintings that were restored in the 1930s and again in 1971. The primary statue is of Guru Rimpoche, flanked by his two consorts Yeshi Chogyal from Tibet and Mindarawa from India. There is a painting of the Shabdrung on the wall opposite the altar and a picture of Guru Rimpoche with the lotus and the swans.

A three day festival, the **Ngangbi tsechu**, is held here each December with masked dances in honour of the founder.

The upper chapel is the *goenkhang* with statues of Chenrezig, Jampa and Yeshey Goenpo (Mahakala). The masks for the tsechu are stored along the rafters here.

East of the Valley
The best way to visit the eastern side of the Choskhor valley is to walk from Kurjey Lhakhang across a footbridge, then uphill to a trail on the opposite side. Follow the trail south to a small (30kw) hydroelectric plant and on to Tamshing Goemba. The walk takes about 30 minutes, and you can send your vehicle back through Jakar to meet you on the opposite side. Most of the road here is unpaved and is a slow, rough drive. If you want some exercise, walk the 5km from Tamshing Goemba back to Jakar, or save a kilometre of walking and have your vehicle pick you up at the Swiss cheese factory. There are good views from Tamshing back across the river to Kurjey Lhakhang.

As you travel back down this side of the valley you will pass a square white chorten with a Sanskrit inscription. On a nearby rock there are marks made by the claws of a garuda. If you are on foot, be careful as you walk along the road south of the Tamshing Lodge. There's an archery field where the archers shoot *across* the road.

Terton Pema Lingpa

Pema Lingpa (1450-1521) was one of the five great *tertons* (treasure discoverers) of Nyingma Buddhism, and the most important one in Bhutan. The texts and artefacts he found, the dances he composed and the art he produced are important parts of Bhutan's heritage.

Pema Lingpa was born in the hamlet of Chel in Bumthang's Tang valley. As a boy he learned the craft of blacksmithing from his grandfather. It's said that some of the frying pans and knives that he made are still in existence. At age 25 he had a dream in which a monk gave him a scroll in a fairy script that instructed him to take five companions and go to a point at the foot of the Tang valley where he would find a treasure.

His First Terma On the night of the full moon he collected his younger brothers and went to a point where the river forms a large pool that looks like a lake, but could see no one. After a while, standing on a large rock, he saw a temple with many doors, only one of which was open. He plunged naked into the lake, entered a large cave where there was a throne upon which sat a life-sized statue of Lord Buddha and many large boxes. An old woman with one eye handed him one of the chests and he suddenly found himself standing on the rock at the side of the lake holding the treasure.

He and his brothers excitedly took the chest back to their father, who suggested that Pema Lingpa go to a monastery and pray and try to decipher the text. He eventually managed to translate the *khandroma* (angels) script and transcribed it. This was a huge project, because in the fairy script one word stands for 1000 words and each has a deeper meaning. Later, assisted by *dakinis*, he used the text as a basis for teachings. His residence at the time was in Kunzangling, which is on a cliff above the Tang valley and is now the site of the Kunzandrak Goemba.

The Burning Lake His second discovery was the most famous. In the original terma there were instructions to return to the lake and collect more treasure. When Pema Lingpa went back to the lake, many people gathered to watch the event and the sceptical penlop of the district accused him of trickery. Under great pressure to prove himself, Pema Lingpa took a lighted lamp and proclaimed: 'If I am a genuine revealer of your treasures, then may I return with it now, with my lamp still burning; if I am some devil, then may I perish in the water.' He jumped into the lake, was gone long enough that the sceptics thought they were proven right, and then suddenly emerged back on the rock with the lamp still burning holding a statue and a treasure chest. The lake became known as **Membartsho**, or Burning Lake (see Membartsho in the Tang Valley section of this chapter).

The major influence in the temples on this side of the valley was Pema Lingpa, the great *terton* of the 16th century.

Tamshing Goemba is at the northern end of the road, 5km from Jakar. Its correct name is Tamshing Lungrub Chholing (Temple of the Good Message). It was established in 1501 by Pema Lingpa and is the most important Nyingma goemba in the kingdom. Pema Lingpa built the structure himself with the help of *khandroma* (female celestial deities, similar to angels) who made many of the statues. On the inner walls are what are believed to be original unrestored images that were painted by Pema Lingpa, though recent research has uncovered even older paintings beneath them.

In the outer courtyard are monks' quarters. The entrance to the lhakhang is via an inner courtyard, or dochey. On the east side of the dochey is the small **Dunkur Lhakhang**, built in 1914 and looked after by an old nun from Tibet. The lhakhang itself has

More Treasures & Visions During his life he found a total of 34 statues, scrolls and sacred relics in Bhutan and as far away as Samye in Tibet. Many of the statues and relics he discovered are preserved in lhakhangs throughout Bhutan.

In his visions, Pema Lingpa often visited Zangto Pelri, Guru Rimpoche's celestial paradise. During these visions he observed the dances of the *khandroma* and *yidam* (tutelary deities). He taught three of these dances, called Pa-cham, to his disciples and several of these are still performed as part of the tsechu festival.

Pema Lingpa built Tamshing monastery in Bumthang in 1518. He also built Kunzandrak monastery in Bumthang. After his death he was reincarnated in three forms, consisting of *ku* (body), *sung* (speech) and *thug* (mind).

Through his six sons, one daughter and numerous reincarnations, Pema Lingpa left behind a legacy that still influences much of Bhutan. His most important son, Dawa Gyeltshen, was born in 1499 and settled in Chhume, one of Bumthang's valleys. One of his sons, Pema Thinley, was a reincarnation of Pema Lingpa himself. This incarnation founded the Gangte Goemba in the Phobjikha valley and the Gangte Trulku lineage continues, with Kuenzang Pema Namgyal, born in 1955, as the ninth reincarnation.

Another of his sons, Kuenga Wangpo (born 1505) settled in Lhuentse (known then as Kurtoe). His great grandsons founded Dungkhar Dzong, north of Lhuentse Dzong. The royal family of Bhutan, the Wangchuck Dynasty, is descended from this line.

Pema Lingpa is one of the most important figures in Bhutanese history.

an unusual design with the main chapel in the centre of the assembly hall, almost like a separate building. In the front part of the hall are three thrones for the three incarnations (body, mind and speech) of Pema Lingpa. During important ceremonies the reincarnations sit here, though a statue may be substituted if one of the incarnations is not present.

The upper floor is a balcony around the assembly hall. Pema Lingpa was a short man and it is said that he built the low ceiling of the balcony to his exact height. Around the outside are 100,000 old paintings of Sakyamuni. In the upper chapel is a statue of Tshepamey, the Buddha of long life, and a large collection of masks that are used for lama dances. On the walls are paintings of Guru Rimpoche's eight manifestations, four on each side.

In the inner sanctuary the primary statue is of Guru Rimpoche. On his right is Jampa (Maitreya, the Buddha of the future) and on the guru's left is Sakyamuni, the historical

Buddha. The statue of Guru Rimpoche here is a particularly important one because it was sculpted by khandroma. The statue's eyes are looking upward, following the angels in their flight; another unique aspect of the statue is that the Guru is not wearing shoes. Above the altar are two crocodiles and a garuda. On the walls are paintings of the eight manifestations of Guru Rimpoche, four on each side.

A small statue of Pema Lingpa occupies a glass case in front of the upper chapel. On the lower floor is a chain mail armour made by Pema Lingpa. It weighs about 25kg and it is an auspicious act to carry it around the goemba three times.

Konchogsum Lhakhang A short distance below Tamshing is a small rural-looking temple – the source of many interesting stories. It was renovated in 1995 and looks quite fresh, but it is very old, probably dating back to the 6th or 7th century. The current structure, however, dates from the 15th century, when Pema Lingpa restored it.

There is a pedestal in the courtyard upon which a large and ancient bell used to sit. It is said that when this bell was rung, it could be heard all the way to Lhasa in Tibet. A 17th century Tibetan army tried to steal the bell but the weight was too great and they dropped and cracked it. It is now on display in the National Museum in Paro and is said to contain 10% gold, 20% silver, 50% bronze and 20% tin.

It was on the hillside behind this goemba, and also in the lake beneath the temple, that Pema Lingpa and the terton Daktshalpa revealed the terma.

The small statues of the three Buddhas (past, present and future) in the sanctuary are said to have flown here straight from Khaine Lhakhang in Kurtoe. Hence the name of this lhakhang is Konchogsum – *konchog* (divine being), *sum* (three).

The central figure in the lhakhang is Vairocana (also known as Namnang, the Dhyani Buddha of vast space). On Vairocana's left is Avalokitesvara, and to the right is Guru Rimpoche. Other statues are Pema Lingpa and Longchempa, a great Nyingma scholar, on the far right.

TANG VALLEY

Tang is the most remote of Bumthang's valleys. As it is higher than Choskhor and the soil not as rich, there's not much agriculture here. The people of this valley raise sheep and, at higher elevations, yaks.

From Jakar it is a 10km drive past the Dechenpelrithang sheep farm to an unpaved road that leads to the north. The road passes **Chel**, Pema Lingpa's birthplace, where there is a small chorten, but no longer a village. The road continues past the school at Rimochen to Mishitang, 15km from the paved road. The Bumthang Cultural Trek ends nearby; depending on the arrangements, trekkers either walk or drive back down the valley. The road continues further, to Gamling and on to a sheep breeding project at Wobtang, but it gets rougher the further it goes.

On the hillside above the west side of the valley is Kunzandrak Goemba which was founded by Pema Lingpa. If you have a permit you may visit this goemba and see the footprint of Pema Lingpa on a golden rock.

Membartsho

There is a parking spot a short distance up the road leading to the Tang valley. It is then a five minute walk to Membartsho (Burning Lake), which is actually a wide spot in the Tang Chhu.

Pema Lingpa found several of Guru Rimpoche's hidden terma here. A wooden bridge crosses the river and is a good vantage point to look down into the lake. Perhaps you can spot the temple that is said to exist in the depths. The importance of the site is indicated by the extensive array of prayer flags and the small clay offerings called *tse tsa* in rock niches.

There is a large rock with a carving of Pema Lingpa and his two sons. Under the rock with the carvings is a cave that virtuous people, no matter how big they are, can crawl through. Beware; it's quite a small hole, and very dusty.

Central Bhutan
Nowhere is Buddhism more visual than in Central Bhutan, especially in the kingdom's spiritual heartland of Bumthang. Novice monks take a break from their studies at Trongsa Dzong (top); the oft-spun prayer wheels of Jampey Lhakhang, Bumthang (right); and an intricate wheel of life painting at Trongsa Dzong (left).

Eastern Bhutan

Chorten Kora (top) was modelled on the stupa of Boudhanath in Nepal and is a focus of worship for Buddhists from all over Eastern Bhutan. Painstaking attention to detail goes into depicting religious images as on this fresco at Lhuentse Dzong (right) and on the dragon gate in front of the Drametse Goemba near Mongar (left).

Kunzangdrak Goemba

It is a two hour walk above Chel to one of the most important sites related to Pema Lingpa. He began construction of the goemba himself in 1488, and many of his most important sacred relics are kept here, one of which is a gilded stone bearing his footprint.

One of the four buildings is Pema Lingpa's house. Another, the Khandroma Lhakhang, is spectacularly situated against a vertical rock face, which was made possible by the help of khandroma during its construction. Holy water seeps from the rock face above the building.

Ugyen Chholing Palace

From the road at Gamling it's a steep climb to this 16th century palace, built by Deb Tshogey Dorji, a descendant of Pema Lingpa. There are servants' quarters and storage rooms in the buildings that surround the palace. The residence is a massive building in the centre, and the lhakhang is a two storey structure on the right.

The goenkhang is in a small room upstairs and houses a well-preserved armoury of old guns, hats and rhino-hide shields as well as the special deity of the temple.

Outside, just to the left of the temple, is a small chorten with a door. There is said to be a small, boiling lake beneath this chorten.

Thowada Goemba

Thowada Goemba clings to the highest rocks above the north end of the Tang valley.

The monastery is said to have been founded by Mandarava, the Indian mystic consort of Guru Rimpoche, and the Guru is believed to have meditated here. The goemba was built by Dorji Lingpa into the rock with balconies overlooking the valley, and there are numerous small meditation caves on the hillside above.

The region is also said to have been sealed as a *bey-yul* (hidden valley) by Guru Rimpoche's consort Yeshe Chogyal.

URA VALLEY

Ura, south-east of Jakar, is the highest of Bumthang's valleys and is believed by some to have been the home of the earliest inhabitants of Bhutan.

Jakar to Ura
48km, 1½ hours

The road crosses the bridge to the east of Jakar town, then travels south along the east bank of the Bumthang Chhu. It climbs a bit, winds around a ridge and heads east. Pass the turnoff to Tang valley and Membartsho and cross a bridge over the Tang Chhu. The road starts climbing from here past a few small villages and chir pine forests. As the road climbs, you can look back at excellent views up the Tang, Choskhor and Chhume valleys.

The few houses that make up **Tangsibi** village are about 24km from Jakar; there are large fields of potatoes on both sides of the road. The road climbs a fern-covered hillside to 3420m, where there is a monument with a cross in memory of a Christian Indian road supervisor who died here in a 1985 road accident.

The road reaches a false summit and finally crosses the **Shertang La** (3573m), marked with a yellow road department marker and small mani wall. Just before the pass there is a view of the Gangkhar Puensum (7540m) peak to the north.

It's a long descent into the Ura valley and the village of Ura is below the road.

Ura Village

Ura (3100m) is quite a large village. A new lhakhang dominates the town, which is reached by turning off the road to Mongar on a short unpaved road. A 50kw hydroelectric plant provides power for the village.

There are about 40 closely packed houses along cobblestone streets that give the town a mediaeval atmosphere. There is a large lhakhang above the village and a school below it.

It's possible to go into Ura by vehicle on an unpaved road that leads off the main road just east of the village.

A traditional addition to the clothing of Ura women is a sheepskin shawl that serves as both a blanket and cushion.

CENTRAL BHUTAN

Ura Village, Yesterday & Today

An impression of changes in a Bhutanese village

The arresting beauty – most striking in the summer – of this blessed valley contrasts with the meagreness of its land. In earlier times, nothing was plentiful in winter apart from radishes buried under the straw in the attic with their bundled dried leaves. Hens scratched deep into the soil for food and animals foraged hungrily on the dry and cold slopes. In the evening, people huddled around the fire, the men patching clothes and repairing tools and the women spinning wool in the flickering light of resin wood. While the children inched closer to the fire, the old people, almost bandaged with quilts, murmured mantras from·dark corners of the house.

Subsistence farming, which involved each family doing a little of everything, was the main drive of the village. Every household had a few domestic animals, tended by the children who also collected firewood during the day.

At the start of the village day, juniper or spruce smoke billowed above every house while, inside, children recited their alphabets. Early risers chatted on the streets on their way to fetch water from ponds and springs before these could become contaminated by animals. Then they would leave to work in the fields.

People worked in poor soil with backbreaking effort to raise wheat, buckwheat and vegetables. The preparation of fallow land *(amg li ri)* by breaking the frosty sods and burning them through the winter was particularly hard, but it served to increase the temperature of the soil and allow the decomposition of vegetative materials. The figure of a wizened woman or man threshing a clump of pale yellow sod in the chilly wind was an all-too-familiar sight.

Yet even after this grim effort, food shortages were not unknown. Borrowing flour, salt or chillies was part of a dependable relationship among the villagers. Otherwise, locally grown foods were supplemented with chillies, maize, millet and rice, exchanged with people in sub-tropical areas for butter and textiles woven by the women.

Most houses had three floors: the lowest for domestic animals; the middle the family's living and sleeping quarters; and the top the family shrine and accommodations for lamas and guests. Beliefs and faith ruled people as much as law and custom. People turned to lamas to be cured of illness and to parents and local worthies for guidance. Death was not always prevented by rituals, which were the remedies of first choice. But the bereaved took solace in knowing that the best that could have been attempted was done.

For more than a generation, a few enlightened lamas and respected elders provided remarkable leadership for the village. With a moral stature that set them above the others, they together possessed an alchemy of leadership that allowed them to keep peace and order, never betraying the motto that within a village, achievements are collective and misfortune should be shared. No outsider got hints of unsavoury disputes in the village because they were able to contain controversy, and no difference was referred to an external authority. The alluring myth of a civilised village with people of temperate nature spread far and wide; it was widely believed that the people of Ura were more human and sensible than most.

The village was ruled from the fortress of Jakar where the district governor and his small staff – authorities that were held in both fear and respect – lived. People went to the fortress to receive instructions on which temple, fortress, bridge, or mule track they had to repair and maintain, and where official consignments had to be transported. Taxes were heavy and the obligatory contribution of labour was all too frequent.

Most people were small in stature, perhaps because of carrying loads on their backs during childhood, eating mediocre food and suffering parasitic infections. Tattered and patched clothes, readily repaired with thread and needle stuck to the collar, were common. But once a year these were put away during the village festival when the whole population gorged on delicacies and drinks and came out in their raw silk dresses. During the festival, youth awakened to sexuality during riotous moments of celebration late at night. Around the ramparts of the temple, the venue of the festival, the young flirted and

His Majesty Jigme Singye Wangchuck lunching with students of Ura Junior High School.

COURTESY OF THE ROYAL GOVERNMENT OF BHUTAN

teased, sang and danced, and found love and friendship, with dawn breaking before anyone found sleep.

In winter, many villagers migrated to warmer, sub-tropical places where they camped in rice terraces in imitation of their ancestors' lifestyle of transhumance. Every few years, some would go to the border towns of India to get a stock of soaps, salt, pots and clothes. People did not marry outsiders nor did they settle far away. Messages, written or verbal, were sent with travellers passing through the village. An average villager lived and died within the horizon of a few surrounding districts.

That is how life was some 25 years ago. That things would change so much in 25 years was inconceivable to anybody in my village at that time. Most of my friends thought the future would be like the past and saw no reason to continue their studies. They dropped out of the village school, which had difficulty in getting enough students to keep going. Now, with parents realising that education leads to jobs and financial success, enrolment has jumped to more than 80%. In Bhutan, both education and medical care are free.

Many new amenities have come to the village. There is a referral hospital in the next valley and a basic health unit in the village, where contraceptives are available and fearful AIDS posters are displayed. A few shops have sprung up next to the village. Electricity from a mini-hydel provides lighting. Stoves that emit less smoke have been installed, and there is a piped water tap near every house.

Now a motor road passes right around the village and the transporting of goods on back or in caravans is very rare. The valley has a phone line from which it is even possible to call Europe. Many villagers have been on pilgrimages to India, and some have travelled further abroad by air. Tourists – no longer a curiosity – pass by in increasing hordes, encouraging the villagers to suspect that people elsewhere are very rich and life is more enjoyable in the land from which the tourists come. The villagers, like tourists, increasingly wear imported fabrics. Fewer woven textiles are seen. Much-wanted articles like video recorders, radio, Swiss boots and refrigerators have come within some families' reach. A few even own trucks and Toyotas, although they come with mortgages.

The sight of tourists encourages villagers to suspect that life is better elsewhere.

RICHARD I'ANSON

Farming systems have changed. Brown Swiss breeding bulls and halfinger stallions are kept in the village livestock centre for raising the cross-breed cattle that can be seen grazing on clover and alfalfa pastures around the village. Merino sheep from Australia have also been introduced. People no longer keep their livestock in their houses. They are penned outside the perimeter of the village. Less buckwheat and wheat is cultivated because farmers can buy imported rice out of wage income or profits from potato sales, their main cash crop. Yet it is harder for them to protect their crops effectively from the wild boars that have increased with the expanding forest. Thanks to stringent environmental policies, the forest around the village is growing rapidly, but at the same time, the village's open grazing area is shrinking.

A block development committee consisting of elected members meets regularly to consider issues of general interest. There are also special committees concerned with the temple, its calendar rituals and festivals, the school, and the mini-hydel project. But there are some entanglements that are not resolved by any committee. Recently, an ugly squabble broke out, tying everyone in knots. The venality of the villagers, rarely seen earlier, seems to have been triggered by cunning manipulation.

Although the village birth rate has increased, the number of people actually living in the village has decreased. Many people leave to get jobs or join government service. Others marry outside the village. The village then has no real meaning in their lives, nor they in its. They may come to visit, but more as sentimental guests than as villagers.

An acute labour shortage has left a large portion of the fields lying fallow year after year. To make up for this, a few people have bought power tillers that now can be heard shattering the silence of the mountains. The government provides agricultural machinery at a huge subsidy and preferential credit, but not every field is flat enough for machines. The ploughman won't disappear overnight. A pair of draft animals can be grunting under a yoke in the field next to the roaring power tiller.

Despite astounding progress, some younger people expect more amenities to come in the next stage of development and are anticipating an easier future. The older villagers think that enough has been provided and, now that everybody is comfortably above hardship and the subsistence level, the next preoccupation of the village should be culture and faith. However, ambitious and materialistic youth think that the leaders live in the twilight of the past.

The village was honoured by a visit by His Majesty in the autumn of 1997. The people listened with folded hands to His Majesty, who is revered as a bodhisattva, as he gave precious advice to the students and explained his larger vision for the country. In the 25 years of his rule, Ura has gone from a marginal community in a harsh environment to a prosperous valley.

Karma Ura

Karma Ura is the author of the historical novel The Hero with the Thousand Eyes *and works for the National Planning Commission.*

Southern Districts

Two dzongkhags lie on the southern border of central Bhutan. Unfortunately tourists are not permitted to travel in these regions because of the threat posed by separatist groups across the border in Assam. Years ago it was possible to trek here and to visit what is now Royal Manas National Park. If the region reopens, it offers a uniquely natural experience in an area of extreme biodiversity.

ZHEMGANG DZONGKHAG

Zhemgang, along with Mongar, was once a collection of tiny principalities collectively known as Khyeng that was absorbed into Bhutan in the 17th century.

Nabji

A two day walk from Zhemgang leads to Nabji where a stone pillar commemorates the settlement of the dispute between the Sindhu Raja and Naochhe that was mediated by Guru Rimpoche.

SARPANG DZONGKHAG

Sarpang is on the southern border, and a large part of the district is protected within the Royal Manas National Park. **Kalikhola** is a border town that has no road connection with the rest of Bhutan. It is in the far western part of Sarphang Dzongkhag.

Gelephu

The large border town of Gelephu is the gateway to the south and the Manas area. There are a few hotels here including the *Dragon Guest House* (☎ 03-51019), *Hotel Peagadly* (☎ 03-51079), *Hotel Lhaden* (☎ 03-51101), and *Hotel Tashi Paykhel* (☎ 03-51143).

Royal Manas National Park

There are simple lodges at Kanamakra, Rabang and Panbang and, if the area is re-opened, a tented camp can be established at Pantang. A 25km road leads from Gelephu to Kanamakra at the south-western corner of the park. There is also a road from Tingtibi on the Trongsa-Gelephu road. This 40km-long road passes along the northern boundary of the park from Gomphu to Panbang village.

Eastern Bhutan

Even though it is the most densely populated region, eastern Bhutan remains the kingdom's hinterland. Roads reach the major towns, but there are numerous remote and isolated valleys hidden among the hills, some of which are home to minority ethnic groups comprising less than 1000 people.

The dominant language here is Sharchop (language of the east), though there are many local languages and dialects. Sharchop is different enough to Dzongkha that people from eastern and western Bhutan usually have to use English or Nepali to communicate.

People in this part of Bhutan are fond of a tipple. Don't become overly concerned if you see someone sleeping it off by the side of the road. Eastern Bhutanese are also great fans of chillies, and both Lhuentse and Trashigang are known for their excellent large green chillies.

Much of eastern Bhutan is farmed using a slash-and-burn system of shifting cultivation, called *tseri* in Dzongkha. Farmers clear land and grow crops on it for a few years, then abandon the fields and move to another area. Because of the shifting agricultural methods the forest cover at lower elevations is less extensive than in other parts of Bhutan.

Many of the extensive fields of corn here are a result of tseri. The government is making efforts to eliminate the practice by introducing fertiliser and improved farming methods so that a plot of land can remain productive for many years.

The general quality of hotels and food in eastern Bhutan is far lower than it is in Thimphu and Paro. Don't venture into this part of the kingdom unless you are prepared for a few rough spots and are able to take the lack of hot water and western toilets in your stride.

HISTORY

In ancient times eastern Bhutan was a collection of separate petty states, each ruled by a king. The region was an important

trade route between India and Tibet. Goods flowed via Bhutan through what is now Singye Dzong in the Lhuentse district to the Tibetan town of Lhobrak.

The most important figure in this region's history was Chhogyel Mingyur Tenpa. When he was Trongsa penlop he led his armies to eastern Bhutan to quell revolts in Bumthang, Lhuentse, Trashigang, Mongar and Zhemgang. His efforts were responsible for bringing eastern Bhutan under the rule of the *desi* and went a long way towards the ultimate unification of the country. Mingyur Tenpa built the Trongsa Dzong and was responsible for the construction of most of the dzongs in eastern, as well as central, Bhutan. In 1668 he was enthroned as the third desi and ruled until 1680.

GEOGRAPHY

Eastern Bhutan is separated from the rest of the country by a large and extremely steep chain of hills that runs from the Tibetan border almost to the Indian border. The road from Bumthang crosses these hills via Thrumshing La (3750m). Other than trails, this one road is the region's only link to the rest of the country. If the road is closed because of snow or landslides, the only way to reach Thimphu by road is to travel via India.

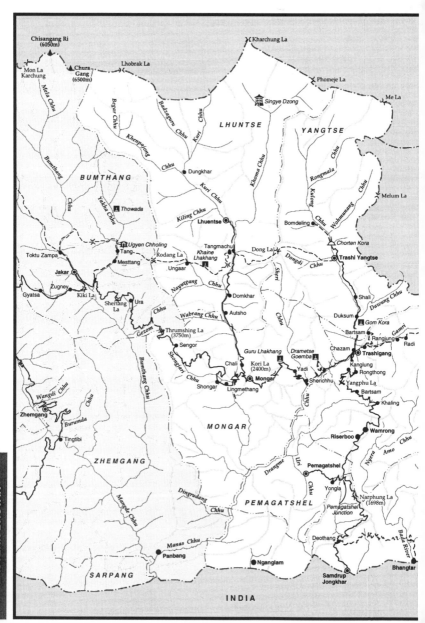

The Manas river system, Bhutan's largest river and a major tributary of the Brahmaputra, drains most of eastern Bhutan. Two tributaries of the Manas extend through the region and form a large system of relatively low valleys. The headwaters of the Kuri Chhu are in Tibet; it crosses into Bhutan at only 1300m elevation where it passes below Lhuentse. The Kuri Chhu flows below Mongar and is tapped by a large hydroelectric project before it joins the Drangme Chhu to become the Manas. One fork of the Drangme Chhu rises to the east of Bhutan, in the Indian state of Arunachal Pradesh. The other major fork drains the Trashi Yangtse valley, then flows south and joins the Indian branch and flows below Trashigang before turning south-west to join the Kuri Chhu. Just before it exits Bhutan, the Manas is joined by the Mangde Chhu, which drains Trongsa and most of central Bhutan.

Mongar Dzongkhag

The Mongar district is the northern portion of the ancient region of Khyeng. Shongar Dzong, Mongar's original dzong, is in ruins and the new dzong in Mongar town is not as architecturally spectacular as others in the region. Drametse Goemba, in the eastern part of the district, is an important Nyingma monastery, but it's difficult to get to. The Manas trek started from the Mongar district; if conditions allow this trek to be reopened it will make Mongar a more important destination for visitors.

JAKAR TO MONGAR
It takes about seven hours to cover the 193km between Jakar and Mongar, crossing two passes and traversing several wild roads that cling to the side of the hills. It is one of the most spectacular drives in the country, descending 3200m in a distance of 84km.

For a description of the road between Jakar and Ura see the Ura Valley section of the Central Bhutan chapter.

EASTERN BHUTAN

Ura to Thrumshing La
36km, 1¼ hours

Beyond an Austrian forestry project and the 50kw Japanese-funded hydroelectric plant, the road crosses the small Lirgang Chhu on a large bridge called Liri Zam. It climbs and winds in and out of side valleys on the north side of the river, passing an area that has been extensively logged. The road also crosses a ridge, drops into another valley, crosses a stream and starts climbing again past a road workers' camp and a small local-style restaurant.

The forest is mostly rhododendron, with several varieties and colours, including large red and pink types and also a small yellow one. Because the soil is very sandy, the road is unstable and has left a large scar on the hillside. You reach a *mani* wall and prayer flags on the pass where a sign proclaims 'You are at the highest point'. This is **Thrumshing La** (3750m), 85km from Jakar and the border of Mongar Dzongkhag; you are now officially in eastern Bhutan.

Thrumshing La to Sengor
22km, 1 hour

The eastern side of the pass is much rockier; the road switchbacks down through a fir forest past a road sign that says 'Life is a journey, complete it'. At about 3000m, 20km from the pass, the route emerges from the trees and enters the pastures of the Sengor valley. There is a settlement at **Sengor** of a few houses near the road, though the main part of the village, about 20 houses, is in the centre of the valley, a few hundred metres away. If you're carrying a picnic lunch and have not already eaten it, this is an excellent place to do so – there is no good place to stop for the next two hours. A large road construction contingent here keeps the pass open. The Dantak public works guesthouse in the back of the compound has been converted into an outreach clinic and school.

Sengor to Kuri Chhu
62km, 1¾ hours

The next stretch of road is one of the wildest in Bhutan, and perhaps the world. After leaving the Sengor valley, the road clings to the side of a rock cliff, with numerous streams and waterfalls leaping out onto it.

There are several chortens here – memorials to the almost 300 Indian and Nepali contract labourers who were killed during the construction of this portion of the road. As you drive along the narrow way that was hacked into the side of a vertical cliff, you may wonder if you will soon join them. A road sign proclaims 'Nature is not to be commended, but to be negotiated'.

There are no settlements here except for a camp at **Namling**, about 20km from Sengor, where a crew works frantically to protect the road from tumbling down the mountainside.

About 17km from Namling, after a long descent that traverses the cliffside, the road reaches safer ground. It emerges into the upper part of a large side valley of the Kuri Chhu, a land of bamboo, ferns and leeches. You pass extensive cornfields and descend to the valley floor on a road that winds around like a pretzel. Rice terraces appear and the vegetation becomes much more tropical.

Near the foot of the valley, where the elevation is quite low, tropical fruits like mango and pineapple flourish.

Atop a hill on the opposite side of the river, just past the 'km 123' marker, is a view of the ruins of **Shongar Dzong**. This was built in 1100 and was the original Mongar dzong. Like Trongsa, Shongar was powerful because the dzong was in an ideal place from which to control movements between eastern and western Bhutan. It was destroyed by fire in the early 19th century and the dzong was rebuilt in Mongar town. There's not much to see – just some stone walls almost hidden by trees on the top of a hillock.

A few kilometres further, in **Lingmethang** (650m), there is an animal husbandry farm where they raise Jersey cows, which are known for their excellent milk. It's not much of a village, just a PWD station, some small rough wooden shops and a big sawmill.

EASTERN BHUTAN

Essential Oil

The rural community of the four eastern dzongkhags received a boon in 1993 when the Essential Oil Development Project was established.

Twenty sets of distillation equipment were distributed to villagers throughout the region in 1995. Eight tonnes of lemongrass oil was produced the following year, generating revenue of Nu 3.2 million. Profits go directly to the villagers distilling the oil while project staff market the product and provide technical back-up and training.

Lemongrass is currently the only commercially processed plant and most of the produce is sold to Germany. There are plans to expand into the production of, possibly, wintergreen, artemisia, silver fir, juniper, rhododendron and pine (oils).

The spin-off effects have also been considerable with grass and firewood cutters also benefiting from the project. The equipment has since been modified, making it cheaper, lighter and more portable, and another 200 units will be distributed from 1998 to 2003.

Kunzang Dorji

The road turns north at a chorten which marks the junction of the main Kuri Chhu valley. After dropping to the river at 550m it crosses a Bailey bridge with lots of prayer flags hanging from it – a total descent of 3200m from the pass. At the bridge is a large chorten that is patterned after Boudhanath in Nepal; it is said to contain relics from the original Shongar Dzong. A secondary road leads downstream 7.5km to the construction site for the 60MW Kuri Chhu power project.

Beside the bridge is a factory that extracts oil from lemongrass and another that makes Bhutanese paper from the extensive stands of edgeworthia in the region.

Kuri Chhu to Mongar
25km, ¾ hour

The road to Mongar climbs up the eastern side of the Kuri Chhu valley. A side road leads to the Mongar hydroelectric plant, which will become redundant when the Kuri Chhu project starts production in 2001.

To the north you can see the road to Lhuentse traversing the side of the valley. This road leaves the Mongar road at Gangola, 12km before Mongar, and travels 65km to Lhuentse (see Mongar to Lhuentse in the Lheuntse Dzongkhag section later in this chapter).

The Mongar road climbs through corn and potato fields toward a cluster of houses on top of the hill. Potatoes are grown in what used to be rice terraces. Years ago wild deer ate all the rice, and many people stopped growing rice and switched to potatoes. A final switchback leads into Mongar at 1600m.

MONGAR

Most towns in the west of Bhutan are in valleys. In the eastern part of the country most towns, including Mongar, are on the top of hills or ridges. A row of large eucalyptus trees protects the town from the wind.

There is little of real interest to see in Mongar, but you will probably have to spend a night here if you are travelling to Trashigang. The drive from Jakar to Mongar is too long to complete in a day unless you decide to drive at night, which is pointless in such an extraordinarily beautiful countryside.

Orientation

Mongar town was redesigned in 1997 when a new bypass road was constructed and a large part of the bazaar razed and rebuilt. At the western end of the town is a turnoff that leads to the petrol pump, football ground and new hospital. There are two hotels in a tiny cul-de-sac that leads off the main street.

EASTERN BHUTAN

The bazaar is in a row of houses along the main road. Most of the town's buildings are three or four storeys high and face toward an unpaved road. The main road is higher, and the shops and hotels on the main road are actually in the back of houses and the entrance is into the third storey. The lane along the front of the houses leads to the lower market where there are some wooden shops and the vegetable market.

There are numerous small local-style hotels here because the Trashigang-Thimphu bus stops in Mongar on the first night of its three-day journey. At the south-eastern end of town, about 1km from the centre, is a road leading to Shonggar Lodge and high school. The dzong is on a ridge above the town.

Information

Money The Bank of Bhutan is open from 9 am to 1 pm weekdays, 9 to 11 am Saturday and closed Sunday. You can change travellers cheques although there is a fair amount of paperwork involved.

Post & Communications The post office is up the hill to the south of the bazaar, on the road to the dzong. There is a public telephone booth in the bazaar next to the Tashiling Hotel.

Medical Services The new hospital in Mongar is a regional referral hospital and has specialist services and more extensive facilities than the smaller district hospitals.

Mongar Dzong

The present Mongar Dzong was rebuilt in 1953 and is quite small. It is two storeys high with the *utse* and *lhakhang* in the middle. The original structure was established here in 1930 to replace the original Shongar Dzong. When Shongar burned, it was decided to rebuild the dzong on the hill

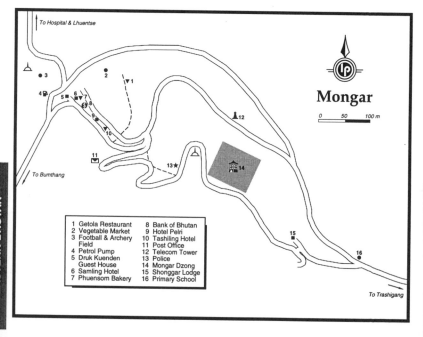

To Hospital & Lhuentse

Mongar

0   50   100 m

To Bumthang

To Trashigang

1 Getola Restaurant	8 Bank of Bhutan
2 Vegetable Market	9 Hotel Pelri
3 Football & Archery Field	10 Tashiling Hotel
4 Petrol Pump	11 Post Office
5 Druk Kuenden Guest House	12 Telecom Tower
6 Samling Hotel	13 Police
7 Phuensom Bakery	14 Mongar Dzong
	15 Shonggar Lodge
	16 Primary School

EASTERN BHUTAN

because of the better climate. There are 50 to 60 monks in the dzong, many of them young boys eight to 10 years old.

The images in the lhakhang are of the Buddha of long life, Tshepamey, as well as Guru Rimpoche and the Shabdrung.

Places to Stay

The *Shonggar Lodge* (☎ 04-41107) is operated by BTCL and housed in a former royal guesthouse. It's a delightful traditional building with extensive Bhutanese decoration on the outside and polished wood floors inside. Only two of the 11 rooms have attached bathrooms; rates are 425/600 or 1200/1400 for a suite with an outrageously large bathroom.

The *Druk Kuenden Guest House* (☎ 04-41121) is in the cul-de-sac at the end of the bazaar overlooking the football field. It's a cement building with four guest rooms; only one has attached bath.

Just opposite is the *Samling Hotel* (☎ 04-41111) with 12 rooms. Rooms with common bath cost Nu 160; they have three rooms with attached toilet facilities at Nu 350, though there is no hot water.

Other smaller and more basic hotels in the bazaar cater to bus passengers. These include the *Lucky Star* (☎ 04-41182) and *Tashiling* which are next door to each other.

Places to Eat

The wooden *Getola Hotel* is good for light meals. It has beer for sale at Nu 30 a bottle and thukpa (noodles with soup) for Nu 25. *Hotel Pelri* offers similar fare.

The *Phuensom Bakery*, at the end of the lane leading to the vegetable market, is the place to load up on bread for the following day's picnic lunch.

There are a few other eating places that cater to bus passengers.

AROUND MONGAR
Drametse Goemba

Though it's in Mongar dzongkhag, Drametse is accessible only from far eastern Bhutan. From Mongar it's 93km to Sherichuu and another 12km from Sherichuu to

Drametse turnoff. It's then a 19km, 1¼ hour drive north to Drametse, a goemba and small village at 2100m. The road is steep (climbing 1350m), unpaved and very rough. In the rainy season there's a lot of mud; at that time the road is suitable only for 4WD vehicles.

There are 90 *gomchens* (married Nyingma monks) here. The monastery was founded by the grand-daughter of Pema Lingpa, Choedroen Zangmo, and her husband, Yeshe Gyalpo.

Inside the outer wall of the goemba is a large flagstone-paved *dochey* (courtyard) and a three-storey lhakhang. The pictures in the front of the lhakhang were painted in the 1950s and repainted in 1982. Drametse's three-day festival is in the middle of the ninth Bhutanese month, September-October (see boxed text 'Future Festival Dates' in the Facts for the Visitor chapter). Visitors may go into the courtyard between 6 am and 7 pm, but not inside the lhakhang.

This is wonderful potato-growing country. In the autumn there are huge piles of potatoes waiting for trucks to carry them down to the market for eventual sale in India and Bangladesh. There are some very basic food stalls in the village. There is also an agricultural extension project office just south of the monastery. In the distance to the south-east you can see the college at Kanglung.

Lhuentse Dzongkhag

Lhuentse is an isolated district although there are many sizeable villages in the hills throughout the region. It is very rural and there are fewer than five vehicles, including the ambulance, and not a single petrol station, in the whole district.

Formerly known as Kurtoe, the region is the ancestral home of Bhutan's royal family. Though geographically in the east, it was culturally identified with central Bhutan, and the high route over Rodang La was a major trade route until the road to Mongar was completed.

EASTERN BHUTAN

Prayer Flags

Prayer flags are ubiquitous in Bhutan, found fluttering on mountain passes, ridges, mountain meadows, rooftops, dzong and temple courtyards and in front of houses.

The prayer flags are in five colours – blue, green, red, yellow and white – symbolising the elements of water, wood, fire, earth and iron respectively. They also stand for the five *dhyani* or meditation Buddhas; the five wisdoms; the five directions; and the five mental attributes or emotions.

They may all look similar, but prayer flags have several important variations. Some prayer flags are hung from strings near holy places, but traditional Bhutanese prayer flags are long strips of printed cloth mounted on vertical poles. The text for the flag is carved into wooden blocks and then printed on the cloth in repeating patterns. Each of the four varieties of prayer flag has a specific function, but they all serve the same basic purpose – they invoke the blessings and protection from the deities for conscious beings, living or dead.

Goendhar The smallest prayer flags are those mounted on the rooftops of Buddhist homes. These white banners have small blue, green, red and yellow ribbons attached to their edges. They invoke the blessings and patronage of Yeshey Goenpo, the main protective deity of the country, to ensure the family's welfare and prosperity. A purification ceremony is performed and the goendhar is erected once a house has been completed. Each year, during a special ceremony celebrated by Bhutanese families honouring their personal local deities, a new banner is unfurled.

Lungdhar The *lungdhar* (wind flag) is erected on hillsides or ridges for a number of purposes. It invokes various gods according to the needs, be they mundane or spiritual, of the person for whom it flutters. It could be for good luck, protection from an illness, the achievement of a personal goal or acquisition of wisdom. These flags are printed with the Wind Horse or *Lungta*, which carries a wish-fulfilling jewel on its back.

The name and age of the person is printed on the flag along with the text pertaining to the exact need. Astrological charts are used to determine the direction, colour and location of the flag, and a consecration ceremony is performed when it is erected.

Manidhar The *manidhar* (prayer flag) is erected on behalf of a deceased person, and features prayers to the Bodhisattva of compassion, Chenrezig. When a family member dies, such flags are commissioned to cleanse the sins of the deceased. The mani prayer banner takes its name from the mantra *om mani peme hum*, which is the special sacred mantra of Chenrezig. These prayer flags are generally erected in batches of 108 and invoke Chenrezig's blessing and immeasurable compassion for the deceased.

Both the Lungdhar and the Manidhar are placed at strategic high points from which a river can be seen. In this way, the belief is that the prayers will waft with the wind to the river, and be carried by the river on its long and winding journey.

Lhadhar The largest flag in the country is the *lhadhar* (god flag). These huge flags can be seen outside dzongs and other important places and represent victory over the forces of evil. There is normally no text on these flags; they are like a giant version of the goendhar. The only difference, apart from size, is at the top, where the lhadhar is capped by a colourful silk parasol. You must be formally dressed to enter any place where a lhadhar stands.

The Pole At the top of the pole is a *redi*, a wood carving of a traditional knife. It is joined to the flagpole by a *khorlo*, a wooden wheel. The redi represents the god of wisdom, Jampelyang, and the khorlo lotus, which is associated with the birth of Guru Rimpoche.

Kunzang Dorji

MONGAR TO LHUENTSE

Lhuentse is 65km from the road junction at Gangola, and 77km (three hours) from Mongar town. The Gangola to Lhuentse road was inaugurated in 1980. There are some rough spots, but the road is well maintained and it's a relatively comfortable drive.

Mongar to Autsho
38km, 1 hour

It is 12km down the hill from Mongar to the junction of the Lhuentse road at Gangola (1050m). The Lhuentse road winds around the hill to Chali then to the few houses of Palangphu. Here it begins a descent towards the Kuri Chhu and the few shops at Rewan. Passing a large Tibetan-style chorten, the road reaches Autsho (800m). Near the river you may be able to spot rhesus monkeys playing on stones and cormorants looking for fish.

This region is famous for its bamboo baskets, which are made only in the winter when the bamboo is dry. You may find baskets for sale in Autsho, or 5km beyond in the pleasant settlement of Phowan.

Autsho to Tangmachu
26km, 1 hour

The road passes beneath some towering cliffs en route to Phowan. Beyond the village there's a stretch where the route was blasted out of the side of a cliff. The road climbs quite a way above the river to the roadside settlement of Gorgan opposite the large valley of the Noyurgang Chhu, which enters from the west. Along this stretch of road, in **Umling**, are said to be the remains of an ancient underground stone castle built by Bangtsho Gyalpo in about 1500 BC.

After a while the Kuri Chhu valley begins to widen. Just beyond a large white chorten the road crosses to the west bank of the river on a Bailey bridge at 1150m. Tangmachu is a large collection of settlements that lies in a bowl-shaped side valley above the road. Oranges grow at the foot of the valley and the hillside is planted with red and white rice, millet and corn. A rough unpaved road leads 10km up through the valley to the isolated Tangmachu high school on a ridge 600m above.

Tangmachu to Lhuentse
13km, ½ hour

The road traverses the foot of the Tangmachu valley for about 6km, passing a road construction camp and a Royal Bhutan Police post at Sumpa. Rounding a corner there's a view of Lhuentse Dzong, which dominates the head of the valley. A small suspension bridge leads across the river here, providing access to the trail to Singye Dzong. The valley narrows and the road begins climbing towards the town. As the road passes the new hospital there is an excellent view of the dzong perched dramatically atop a bluff.

LHUENTSE

There is little to see and do in Lhuentse, but the dzong is one of the most picturesque in Bhutan. There are a few shops and food stalls along the road as it enters the town. The road terminates at a parking lot in front of the dzong; nearby is the telecommunications office and the Bank of Bhutan. Adjoining the parking lot are quarters for government officials working in Lhuentse who have been posted to this remote area where housing is scarce.

The Government Guest House is at the end of a paved road that climbs about a kilometre up a hill south of the dzong.

The Lhuentse region is known for weaving, embroidery, *kushutara* (brocade dress) and basket-making. There is no large factory, but in many homes people weave the round baskets called *bangchung* and *zhim*, larger baskets that are used to transport goods.

Lhuentse Dzong

Correctly known as Lhuentse Rinchentse Phodrang Dzong, it sits high on a rocky outcrop overlooking the Kuri Chhu valley. There are near-vertical drops on all sides of the dzong; the entrance is reached by a flagstone-paved path that switchbacks up the hill from the parking lot on the south-east side. It leads into the administrative portion

EASTERN BHUTAN

of the dzong; the utse and monastic sector are at the north end on a slightly higher level.

Though Pema Lingpa's son Kunga Wangpo established a small goemba on this site early in the 16th century, the dzong itself was built by the Trongsa penlop Mingyur Tenpa in 1654. It has been renovated several times and numerous lhakhangs have been added. It now houses a body of more than 100 monks.

Places to Stay & Eat

Lhuentse's only hotel is the *Government Guest House* (☎ 04-45109), on a hill 100m above the town. It has three rooms renting for Nu 350, single or double. The rooms are cold and damp; they have attached bathrooms, but no hot water.

From the garden of the guesthouse is an excellent view of the dzong and the snow peaks at the head of the Kuri Chhu valley. The peak at the head of the valley to the north-west of the guesthouse is Sheri Nyung.

If you arrive here without a packed lunch, order some rice or noodles at the *Hotel Chukhar Noryang* (☎ 04-45122), which is alongside the road at the north end of town. It used to have a few rooms for rent, but is now only a restaurant and PCO.

AROUND LHUENTSE
Dungkhar

A two day walk up the Kuri Chhu leads to the village of Dungkhar. Kunga Wangpo settled here, and it is through him that Bhutan's royal family, the Wangchucks, trace their ancestry to the Kurtoe region. Jigme Namgyal, father of the first king, was born here in 1825 and left home when he was 15 to eventually become Trongsa penlop and the 48th.

Singye Dzong

Singye Dzong is a great power place of Guru Rimpoche and an important pilgrimage place for Bhutanese. It is possible to trek there, taking three days in each direction. Yeshe Tshogyal, the consort of Guru Rimpoche who concealed many *terma* here, founded the goemba.

It is on the old trade route from Bhutan to Lhobrak in Tibet.

Trashigang Dzongkhag

Trashigang is the heart of eastern Bhutan and was once the centre of important trade with Tibet. There are several goembas and villages that make a visit worthwhile, but it is a remote region and requires a lot of driving to reach.

MONGAR TO TRASHIGANG

The Mongar to Trashigang stretch is easier and shorter than the journey from Jakar to Mongar, but it still requires about 3½ hours to cover the 92km between the two towns. The road crosses one low pass, then follows a river valley before making a final climb to Trashigang.

Mongar to Kori La
17km, ½ hour

Leaving Mongar, the road climbs past fields of corn, then through rhododendron and blue pine forests to the few houses in the scattered settlement of Naling. Soon the road is clinging to the side of a cliff, passing through a deep forest of rhododendron and orchids.

About 3km past a forest nursery is Kori La (2400m), where there is an outreach clinic and a small mani wall. The forest surrounding the pass is under a management plan regulating the harvest of trees and bamboo.

Kori La to Yadi
21km, 1 hour

The road drops from the pass into the upper reaches of the Manas Chhu drainage, switchbacking down through corn fields. In Ngatshang is **Guru Lhakhang**, a small private goemba at 1890m. Alongside the road, just beyond the goemba, are several small buildings used by monks as retreat and meditation centres.

The road continues its descent through corn fields past the two houses of Ningala, finally reaching the substantial village of **Yadi** (1470m). There are a few shops here, and the *Sherubtse Hotel* offers very mediocre food and emergency accommodation.

Yadi to Chazam
45km, 1½ hours

Beyond Yadi a long stretch of prayer flags line the road; below are numerous switchbacks, nicknamed the **Yadi Loops**, that lead down through a forest of chir pine, dropping 350m in 10km. There is a good viewpoint where you can see the road weaving down the hill; pictures taken from here often appear in books and brochures to show how circuitous Bhutan's roads are. The unpaved road, which heads west just before the loops begin, leads to the village of Chaskhar and a 20kW hydroelectric plant.

At the foot of the steepest part of the loops is a stream and the Doejung Essential Oil Distillation Unit. This is a government project which uses big stainless steel boilers to process locally grown lemongrass into oil that can be exported to India.

After more switchbacks, the road finally crosses a Bailey bridge into the nondescript bazaar of **Sherichhu** (600m). There are a few local-style tea shops, a road construction camp and a small rosin and turpentine factory in a grove of eucalyptus trees. A large new bridge is under construction.

Climb a bit out of the Sherichhu valley to a chorten and cross a ridge to meet the large Drangme Chhu, which flows from the eastern border of Bhutan and is a major tributary of the Manas. The road doesn't climb much but traverses grassy hillsides and winds in and out of side valleys. There are a few rice terraces below.

About 12km from Sherichhu is a side road to Drametse monastery, the biggest and most important monastery in eastern Bhutan (see Drametse Goemba under Around Mongar earlier in this chapter).

From several points along the road above the Drangme Chhu, it's possible to see Trashigang Dzong high above the south bank of the river. The hillside beside the road is mostly conglomerate. The big boulders embedded in sand often break loose during rainstorms and fall onto the road, causing delays while road crews scramble to remove them.

After passing the Indian PWD camp at Rolong and some tatty road construction shacks, the road reaches a frail-looking, 73m-long suspension version of a Bailey bridge at **Chazam** (690m). This place was named after the original chain link bridge here, said to have been built by the Tibetan bridge builder Thangtong Gyalpo (see boxed text 'The Iron Bridge Builder' in the Western Bhutan chapter) in the 15th century (*cha* is iron, *zam* means bridge). The remains of the abutments of the old bridge can be seen nearby; the chain is on display in the courtyard of Trashigang Dzong.

An unpaved side road leads steeply uphill from Chazam to Gangthung and Yangnyer. The complex that is visible a short distance up this road is a jail.

Chazam to Trashigang
9km, ¼ hour

On the north side of the bridge is an immigration check post where your road permit is checked. The road that goes north from here follows the Kulong Chhu valley to Trashi Yangtse and Chorten Kora (see Chorten Kora in the Yangtse Dzongkhag section later in this chapter).

The road switchbacks up through cornfields towards Trashigang, passing a turnoff that leads down to the small settlement of Chenary and the old Trashigang hydroelectric plant. There's also a nursery here that produces seeds for subtropical fruit. The Druk Seed Corporation grows olives, pomegranates, passion fruit, almond, fig, citrus and mango.

At the top of the hill is a collection of motor workshops and a road junction. The road to southern Bhutan leads to the right. The left fork leads to the terminus of the

EASTERN BHUTAN

National Highway at Trashigang, 3km away. Go round a bend where there's a good view of Trashigang Dzong, then follow the road into Trashigang, which is well hidden in a wooded valley.

TRASHIGANG

Trashigang is a reasonably large town with lots to explore; it is a good place to use as a base for excursions to Trashi Yangtse, Khaling, Pemagatshel, Phongme and elsewhere in Eastern Bhutan.

The accommodation here is pretty basic, but there is a variety of good restaurants and at least one amusing place to drink. Not many tourists make it to Trashigang, but there used to be many Canadian teachers working here and the people of Trashigang are used to westerners.

Orientation

Trashigang is at the foot of a steep wooded valley with the Mithidang stream running through it. The road enters the town from the north and just as you enter there's a cobbler shop, almost next door to which is the tiny

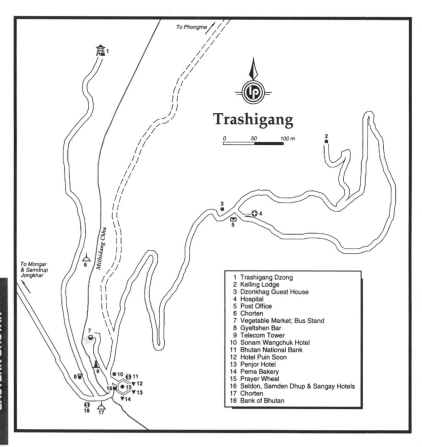

Trashigang

0   50   100 m

1 Trashigang Dzong
2 Kelling Lodge
3 Dzonkhag Guest House
4 Hospital
5 Post Office
6 Chorten
7 Vegetable Market; Bus Stand
8 Gyeltshen Bar
9 Telecom Tower
10 Sonam Wangchuk Hotel
11 Bhutan National Bank
12 Hotel Puin Soon
13 Penjor Hotel
14 Pema Bakery
15 Prayer Wheel
16 Seldon, Samden Dhup & Sangay Hotels
17 Chorten
18 Bank of Bhutan

To Phongme

To Mongar & Samdrup Jongkhar

Mithidang Chhu

shop of Deepak, the only barber in the eastern hills of Bhutan. The road crosses the stream on a substantial bridge just beyond a chorten. Another leads downhill from the chorten past a collection of shops, bars and small restaurants, then through trees and bougainvillaea past a chorten to the dzong.

On the right of the main road, just opposite the large telecommunication tower, is a central plaza and parking area. A large prayer wheel sits in the centre of the square. The pedestal on the covered structure, holding the prayer wheel, is a favourite sleeping place for villagers waiting for buses. People turn this wheel day and night, with a bell signalling each revolution. Surrounding the parking area are several hotels and restaurants, the bakery and the main liquor outlet.

An unpaved road leads downhill from the centre of Trashigang to Rangjung and then to Radi and Phongme. This road begins just as the main road leaves the town and starts to emerge from the valley.

From the bazaar the road climbs the hill, turning two long switchbacks, to a dogleg around the Dzongkhag Guest House. The junior high school and post office are on the right and a short distance beyond the road forks at the hospital. The left fork leads to the Kelling Lodge, a short distance downhill. The road makes a large loop through a residential area and eventually returns back to the hospital.

Information

Money The town boasts two banks. The Bank of Bhutan is next to the bridge, and the Bhutan National Bank is in the town square. Both banks are open from 9 am to 1 pm weekdays, 9 to 11 am Saturday and closed Sunday. If you have the patience you can cash travellers cheques at either one.

Post & Communications The post office is above the town, near the high school. There are numerous PCOs in the bazaar.

Newspapers The only *Kuensel* agent in town is a small unnamed medical shop on the road leading to Radi. The newspaper

arrives here each week on Tuesday or Wednesday.

Electricity The electricity supply in Trashigang is fairly reliable. It comes from the new 2.2MW Rangjung power station, which also serves Pemagatshel and Trashi Yangtse. The new power plant replaces an older, unreliable 0.75MW plant on the Chenary stream.

Medical Supplies The small shop on the road leading to Radi sells medicine.

Being in a remote region, the hospital in Trashigang is small, and some medical supplies might be in short supply. It can handle emergencies but may not be the best choice for long-term treatment.

Trashigang Dzong

The dzong is on a high promontory that overlooks the confluence of the Drangme Chhu and the Gamri Chhu. It was built in 1667 by Mingyur Tenpa, Bhutan's third Desi. The entire eastern region was governed from this dzong from the late 17th century until the beginning of the 20th century. It was destroyed by fire and rebuilt in only three years.

This dzong is different in that both the administrative and monastic sectors face onto a single dochey. Just inside the gate are paintings of the kings of the four directions. Inside the lhakhang is a statue of the deity, *Gasin-re* or *Yama,* the wrathful aspect of Chenrezig. He is a protector of the faith, the god of death and the king of law. He is the one that weighs good and evil at the end of a person's life. Many lama dances are performed in Trashigang to appease Yama. This particular dance is not included in the festival schedule, but if one happens when you are in town, you will be welcomed.

Places to Stay

The *Kelling Lodge* (☎ 04-21145) is the best facility in town. All rooms have attached baths, but the toilets are the Asian squatting variety and hot water is delivered in a bucket, not from the tap. The hotel has 11 rooms in two wings. The dining hall is a separate gazebo-like structure that has an excellent view of the valley and dzong. All the beds are uncomfortably soft. It's run by BTCL, which charges Nu 425/600. The hotel parking lot is a favourite gathering place for kids on bicycles and women chatting in the sun.

The *Sonam Wangchuck Hotel* (☎ 04-21152) is very much a second choice with 18 rooms at Nu 100 a double. It's on the main street, but most of the rooms face to the back. It used to be called the Ugyen. Its restaurant serves good momos.

Places to Eat

Meals are less expensive in eastern Bhutan and you can find momos for Nu 25 and rice and curry for Nu 35. As in most of Bhutan, in Trashigang the word hotel becomes confused with restaurant. The *Hotel Seldon*, *Samden Dhup Hotel* and *Hotel Sangay* (☎ 04-21140) are all restaurants, and are operated by members of the same family sharing a common building. There are some rooms for rent upstairs, but they tend to be noisy because of the continual ringing of the bell on the prayer wheel in the town square.

The *Hotel Puin Soon* (☎ 04-21137) provides reasonably good western food, though you need to order meals well in advance. At Nu 75 to Nu 100, meals here are more expensive than at other restaurants in town. There's a pleasant wood-panelled dining room upstairs, but be careful of the low-hanging ceiling fans. Some people spell the name of this place as Puensum.

The *Pema Bakery* (☎ 21196) on the main square produces the standard fare of rolls, bread and pastries and has a small garden where they serve tea and cakes. They open late and close early; if you are planning an early morning start for a road trip, pick up your supplies the afternoon before.

The *Hotel Sonam* (☎ 21184), on the lower level of the Sangar and Samden hotels, faces the main street and offers basic rice and dal and is a favourite of guides and drivers.

The *Penjor Hotel* has rice and curry and western food, though less variety than the Puin Soon.

Entertainment

There are plenty of small restaurants in the town which serve drinks. You must drink quickly, though, as the entire town closes promptly at 8 pm.

On the lower street leading toward the dzong is the *Gyeltshen Bar* (☎ 21149), open every day. The sign simply says 'bar' and has a picture of a cowboy on one side and a local artist's peculiar adaptation of Donald Duck on the other. The owner, Chozom, is an hospitable hostess, and the bar is a popular gathering place. In addition to a fridge full of various brands of cold beer, Chozom keeps a supply of home-made arra; this is a good place to try it.

Villagers come to town on holy days, which occur on the first, 10th and 15th of the Bhutanese month. They sell goods they have produced and buy manufactured goods to take home, then sample the local arra.

Getting There & Away

The local jeep drivers say that if you leave Trashigang at 3.30 am you can reach Thimphu at 8.30 pm, a total of 17 hours of gruelling driving later.

AROUND TRASHIGANG
Gom Kora

While Gom Kora is actually in Yangtse Dzongkhag, it is covered here for geographical convenience.

Gom Kora is a small temple to the east of the road 13km north of Chazam. Its correct name is Gomphu Kora. *Gomphu* is a sacred meditation site of Guru Rimpoche and *kora* means circumambulation. The Guru meditated here and left a body impression on a rock, similar to that in Kurjey Lhakhang in Bumthang.

The central figure in the goemba is Guru Rimpoche. To his left is Chenrezig in his 1000-arms aspect, Jampa and the protective angel of Guru Rimpoche. To the far right is a *jungshu*, a special kind of small chorten that is found only inside monasteries and dzongs. The paintings on the walls of the goemba are believed to be from the 15th century.

In small cubby-holes under the statue of Guru Rimpoche are numerous sacred objects that either miraculously appeared here or were brought by the Guru himself. The largest item is a dragon's egg, which is a very heavy, perfectly-shaped stone-like egg. There is also a hoof of Guru Rimpoche's horse and the footprint of a *khandroma*.

The old *thondrol* from Trashigang is stored here for safekeeping. It's unique because it is a painted thondrol, not appliqué. Gom Kora has its own thondrol, made in 1995 and displayed at the Gom Kora tsechu in spring (see boxed text 'Dances of the Tsechu' in the Facts about the Visitor chapter). People circumambulate the goemba and sacred rock throughout the night and *Kuensel* suggests that the evening's activities result in many marriages.

Behind the goemba is a large black rock with many fantastic aspects. As Guru Rimpoche was meditating in a small cave near the bottom of the rock, a demon appeared from the side of the river. The Guru, alarmed, stood up quickly and left the impression of his pointed hat at the top of the cave. The Guru then made an agreement with the demon to stay away until the end of his meditation. The contract was sealed with thumb prints, which are still visible on the rock.

A small sin-testing passageway leads from the cave to an exit below the rock. Only virtuous people can get through this passage. Visitors are welcome to try but you'll get dirty. There are two sharp bends along the way – one successful participant reported that you must move like a snake to get through the cave. There is a narrow crevice on the side of the rock in which water flows down on certain holy days.

Sherubtse College

Sherubtse College, Bhutan's only college, is 22km from Trashigang in the town of **Kanglung**. Father William Mackey, a Jesuit priest, was instrumental in setting up the college. It was first a junior high school, then became a high school and is now a college. India aided the construction of the school in 1964 as part of the construction of the road from Trashigang to the Indian border. From the road you can see the college with its clock tower and playing field.

Outside the gate are several small restaurants and an Indian snack bar which serves espresso. The small Zangto **Pelri Goemba** built in 1978 is on the opposite side of the road. Just beyond the college are numerous dormitories and student hostels, and a bit further is an assortment of shops that is the town proper. The region near Kanglung is quite heavily populated. If you look back down the valley from Kanglung you can see all the way back to Yadi and the long set of switchbacks leading down to Sherichhu.

Khaling

Khaling is a large village 54km (1½ hours) from Trashigang, 32km beyond Kanglung. The village is spread out in a large valley high above the Drangme Chhu. Several shops and small restaurants line the main street. Above the town is a narrow, unpaved road which leads downhill into the centre of the valley toward the elementary school and the school for the disabled. (See Trashigang to Samdrup Jongkhar later in this chapter for a description of the road from Trashigang to Khaling via Kanglung and Yonphula.)

In the centre of the valley below Khaling is a school for the blind. This is a very well-organised institution that tries to assimilate blind students from all over Bhutan into the local educational system by providing special resources and training. One of their accomplishments is the development of a Dzongkha version of Braille. The school was originally set up by missionaries 20 years ago and has been run by the government since 1987.

Handloom Development Project Three kilometres beyond Khaling is the Handloom Development Project operated by the National Women's Association of Bhutan (NWAB). They contract out weaving and provide cotton yarn on credit to villagers, who then return the finished product to be sold here or in Thimphu. They have samples of about 300 designs, though they don't have fabric from every design in stock. They will, however, take orders, and you can ask your guide to ensure that the order eventually gets delivered.

They are open from 10 am to 5 pm week-days, no appointment necessary.

They have samples of the natural dyes that they use and a have created a small display showing the various parts of plants that are used to produce each colour. They have a strict rule that prohibits photos of the workshops and of the design samples. Prices for a length of woven cloth vary from Nu 950 up to Nu 12,000. Most of the cotton is Indian, imported from Calcutta. NWAB has produced a book, *Bhutanese Weaving, a Source of Inspiration*, by Alet Kapma & Wouter Ton.

FAR EASTERN BHUTAN

An unpaved road heads downhill from Trashigang, then travels up the valley of the Gamri Chhu to Rangjung and Phongme.

There is a daily bus that plies this route, but it's a converted truck, and it's a very rough and dusty ride.

Trashigang to Rangjung
17km, ¾ hour

The road descends from Trashigang, weaving in and out of side valleys to the banks of the Gamri Chhu at 860m. A side road crosses the river here and leads 16km uphill to the town of Bartsam. The Rangjung road stays on the south side of the river, passing a large Tibetan-style chorten and the village of Lungtenzampa. The hydroelectric plant is up a stream just before the road makes a short climb to Rangjung at 1200m. An elaborate chorten sits in the centre of the town. Just above the town is the large **Rangjung Wodsel Chholing Monastery**, a large Nyingma goemba presided over by Garub Rimpoche.

Rangjung to Radi
9km, ½ hour

The road continues east, climbing through large rice terraces and fields of corn to Radi

(1630m). This region is a centre for weaving raw silk into fabric called *menzimatra* or *lungserma*. There are no shops or eating places in Radi; it is just a quiet cluster of houses and a primary school at a bend in the road.

Radi to Phongme
9km, ½ hour

Beyond Radi the road worsens and climbs through forests interspersed with barren hill-sides. This stretch of road is frequently closed by landslides and is usually impassable during the rainy season because it becomes a sea of deep mud. There is a tiny shop and a small goemba at Phongme (1800m).

The goemba is less than 150 years old and there is no monk body; the caretakers are elderly women. The central statue is of Chenrezig with 1000 arms and 11 heads; Sakyamuni is to the right. Many elaborate masks used in the small Phongme tsechu festival are stored on the rafters of the goemba's lower chapel.

The upstairs chapel has rough statues of Sakyamuni, the Shabdrung and Guru Rimpoche, and a wall painting depicts the life of Milarepa.

From Phongme a trail leads to the Brokpa minority villages of **Mera** and **Sakteng**. Tourists were permitted to make this three-day trek in the past, but the route is now closed to foreigners out of concern for the unique culture of the people living there. You can recognise the Brokpas by their sheepskin clothing and unusual yak hair hats with hanging spider-like legs that act as rain spouts.

Yangtse Dzongkhag

Previously a *drungkhag* (sub-district) of Trashigang, Yangtse became a fully fledged dzongkhag in 1995. It borders the Indian state of Arunachal Pradesh, and there is a bit of cross-border trade. The old trade route between east and west Bhutan used to go through Trashi Yangtse, over the mountains to Lhuentse and then over Rodang La (4200m) to Bumthang. This route is difficult and became neglected when the road from Trashigang to Bumthang via Mongar was completed. The district lies at the headwaters of the Kulong Chhu, and was earlier known as Kulong.

TRASHIGANG TO TRASHI YANGTSE

The drive from Trashigang to Trashi Yangtse is 53km and takes about 1¾ hours, but be sure to allow time to visit Gom Kora on the way. If you don't have time to drive all the way to Chorten Kora, do make the effort to make the short trip to Gom Kora.

Trashigang to Gom Kora
13km, ¼ hour

The road is level and you can move fairly quickly as it follows the east bank of the Drangme Chhu to Gom Kora. See the description of Gom Kora earlier.

Trashigang to Chazam
13km, ¼ hour

Follow the switchbacks down to the bridge at Chazam.

Gom Kora to Trashi Yangtse
28km, 1¼ hours

Two km from Gom Kora is the substantial village of **Duksum** (60m). There are many shops and small eating places here because it's the roadhead for many large villages higher in the valley, the largest of which is Tongmijangsa. You are likely to see women weaving cloth in particularly colourful patterns using back-strap looms.

Behind the village is an old, abandoned iron **chain-link bridge**. Despite its neglected condition, this bridge seems to be of some historical importance. It is believed that this is the last surviving bridge of those built by Thangtong Gyalpo (see the boxed text 'The Iron Bridge Builder' in the Western Bhutan chapter) in the 15th century. Nine wrought iron chains form the platform and hand rails. The bridge houses are a mess, but if you enter carefully, you can see how the chains

were securely held in place through several walls.

The road turns north-west and follows the Kulong Chhu valley towards Trashi Yangtse. The eastern fork of the river flows from India and is known as the Dawung Chhu.

Climbing high above the Kulong Chhu, the road passes the small settlement of Shali, then the intersection of an unpaved road which leads 13km to the town of **Tshenkarla** and the ruins of Tshenkarla dzong. The dzong was built in the first half of the 9th century by Tsangma, the eldest son of Tibetan King Trisong Detsen. Tsangma was banished from Tibet and established himself in eastern Bhutan. The old name of this town is Rangthang Woong.

There are many farms and houses along this stretch of road, but the habitation soon disappears as the valley becomes steeper and narrower. After traversing along a rocky cliff, a house-like building appears on a promontory where a side stream, the Dongdi Chhu, joins the valley. This is the original Trashi Yangtse Dzong and now houses a small monastery.

TRASHI YANGTSE

Though most maps and road signs place Trashi Yangtse at the site of the old dzong, the real town has always been at Chorten Kora, just to the north. The correct name of the town at Chorten Kora is Karmaling, but few people use that name. The old dzong is very small and is in a particularly inconvenient location; a new dzong has been built in Karmaling on a hill overlooking Chorten Kora.

In addition to Chorten Kora, the town is known for the excellent wooden containers, made here using water-driven and treadle lathes. You can find them for sale in small shops and local restaurants. The best bowls are those that are lined with silver to make drinking cups.

During the winter it is common to see black-necked cranes (see boxed text in the Facts about Bhutan chapter) feeding in the rice terraces near the town.

EASTERN BHUTAN

Orientation

It takes 10 minutes to visit the entire town. The road enters from the south near the large Chorten Kora. Just north of the chorten is a bazaar area with a few shops. A tall, elaborately decorated Bhutanese-style chorten sits beside a small stream, spanned by a concrete bridge, and doubles as the town's vegetable market. A few eating and drinking shops and a spartan guesthouse mark the end of the town. The road dead-ends 100m beyond at the archery ground and a footbridge that leads across the Kulong Chhu.

Two gravel roads lead from the town centre to the east. One goes to the new dzong, on a ridge 130m above the town, and the other to the primary school.

Rigney Institute

The Rigney Institute was opened in June 1997 in the buildings that used to be the subdistrict headquarters. The Trashi Yangtse school operates a slightly different curriculum from the Rigney school in Simtokha, where the emphasis is on religious literature and the development of Buddhist scholars.

Here the curriculum reflects Bhutan's efforts to provide opportunities for vocational training for those who, for one reason or another, do not continue in the system of higher education. The school strives to produce technically proficient craftspeople, while providing them with a basic educational foundation. The mornings are spent studying both spoken and written Dzongkha and English. After lunch the students learn crafts. The current curriculum includes wood carving, turning wooden bowls on a lathe, painting, embroidery and mask making. In the future, the plan is to include all of the 13 arts and crafts.

Trashi Yangtse Dzong

The original Trashi Yangtse Dzong was built by Pema Lingpa. It is on a hillock 3km south of Chorten Kora.

Because the old dzong was small and difficult to get to, a new dzong was built. This was inaugurated in 1997 and is high on the side of a ridge overlooking the valley. It's not as architecturally stunning as other dzongs and, being new, has little historical significance.

Places to Stay & Eat

If you have connections, you might be able to stay in the new *Royal Guest House*, which is just to the west of the dzong. The alternative is the *Thinley Dhendup Guest House*, which has five simple rooms that cost Nu 120, single or double. You can get the keys from the unnamed *restaurant* (☎ 04-81130) across the road.

A better solution may be to *camp* in the field at the north end of town, but don't place the tents between the two archery targets there.

Chorten Kora

Chorten Kora is large, but not nearly as large as the stupa of Boudhanath, after which it was patterned. A small goemba has been built next to it and several rows of prayer flags flutter in the wind in the cornfields at its front. It was constructed in 1740 by Lama Ngawang Loday, who had three purposes for the construction of this chorten.

The first was as a religious monument in loving memory of his late uncle, Jungshu Phesan. Secondly, the people of this valley were very religious and wanted to go to Nepal to see the Boudhanath Stupa. The lama went to Nepal himself and brought back a model of Boudhanath carved in a radish and had it copied here so that people could visit this place instead of making the trip to Nepal. The reason that Chorten Kora is not an exact copy of Boudhanath is because the radish shrunk during the trip and distorted the carving a bit. The third purpose of the chorten was to subdue the many evils and devils that were here in those days. The 13th Je Khenpo consecrated the site.

During the second month of the lunar calendar there is a big celebration here, which is known as *kora*, in which people gain merit by walking around the chorten. It is celebrated on two separate days, 15 days apart. The first day is for the people from the community behind the hill in Arunachal Pradesh, India. It is said that during the construction of this stupa an eight-year-old girl from Arunachal Pradesh sacrificed her life by entering the stupa. In her memory, one day is granted as the kora for the Arunachal Pradesh people. The second kora is for the Bhutanese, who come from all over eastern Bhutan.

Getting There & Away From Trashi Yangtse, it's a short 10 minute drive through forests into the large, open, heavily cultivated Karmaling valley. The large white monument of Chorten Kora is just to the east, below the road.

Bomdeling

Bomdeling is a one hour walk north of Chorten Kora. It is the roosting place of a flock of black-necked cranes (see boxed text in the Facts about Bhutan chapter). The flock, second only in size to that in Phobjikha, returns here year after year. The cranes fly south to Chorten Kora and feed in the rice fields during the day, then return to Bomdeling at night. Please do not disturb their roosting place. You can observe them during the day as they forage in the fields near Chorten Kora.

Samdrup Jongkhar Dzongkhag

There is almost nothing of interest to the traveller in south-eastern Bhutan. Unless you are a visiting professor at Sherubtse College in Khaling, the primary reason you would travel to Samdrup Jongkhar would be to exit from Bhutan after visiting Trashigang.

TRASHIGANG TO SAMDRUP JONGKHAR

It's a 180km drive from Trashigang to Samdrup Jongkhar on a winding road; the trip takes at least six hours.

Trashigang to Kanglung
22km, ¾ hour

Just 3km from Trashigang bazaar the southern road turns off the Mongar road near two motorcycle repair shops, then climbs past the petrol station, just a collection of oil drums and an ancient hand-cranked pump.

Climbing around a ridge and heading south the road passes the settlement of **Pam**, just a few houses and cornfields. The narrow unpaved road that leads uphill from here goes to the settlement of Rangshikhar.

Climb through the prosperous village of Rongthong, 17km from Trashigang, then to Kanglung, where you can see the extensive campus of the college below (see Kanglung in the Around Trashigang section earlier).

Kanglung to Khaling
32km, 1 hour

The road climbs through fields of corn and potatoes and past an agricultural project, then makes a switchback around a line of eight chortens. Above the road is the Yonphula army camp and further on is Yongphu Goemba. Hidden on a ridge above the road is Yonphula, Bhutan's second airstrip. There are hopes that this small airstrip will soon be served by domestic flights, which would make eastern Bhutan much more accessible.

The road crosses Yangphu La (2190m) and swoops along the top of the Bartsam valley, cuts across a ridge into another valley, then winds down again. A short climb leads the road over yet another ridge marked by chortens. It then descends to **Gumchu**, a collection of road workers' shacks and one Bhutanese-style house. Below, in a pretty valley, are several traditional houses surrounded by large, lush meadows.

Rounding a corner, the road enters the side valley of Khaling. A short distance beyond is the NWAB's handloom factory and showroom. See the Around Trashigang section for information about Khaling.

Khaling to Wamrong
27km, ¾ hour

Beyond Khaling the road traverses above scattered houses and cornfields. Leaving the cultivation and settlements behind, it climbs to the head of a rhododendron-filled valley, crossing a ridge at 2350m. There's a short descent through lots of loose rock, then another climb to a pass at 2430m.

Descending, the route passes a side road that leads east to Thrimshing, then a small private goemba that overlooks the valley and the town of **Wamrong** (2130m). The large building above the road is the administrative centre for this drungkhag. Several shops line one side of the main street. The local style *Dechen Wangdi* and *Yeshey* hotels can provide tea, biscuits and maybe a plate of rice. There is an immigration check post just below the town.

Wamrong to Pemagatshel Junction 20km, ¾ hour

The road descends from the village, passes the junior high school and makes its way down the ridge to **Riserboo**. The large hospital here is sponsored by the Danish agency Danida. There is a good view down the valley as the road stays fairly level, traversing in and out of side valleys past the hamlet of Moshi. Cross a ridge into another valley where the power lines go straight down and up again.

The road now follows a route that was blasted out of the side of a cliff and leads up to a pass between two valleys at 2180m. Cross the ridge to the east side and keep going up, then cross back to the original valley and cross a pass at 2510m and descend to the road junction to Pemagatshel. See the information about Pemagatshel Dzongkhag in the next section.

Pemagatshel Junction to Deothang 55km, 1¾ hours

The road descends into the upper part of the Bada River valley, passing a Shiva temple built into a cliff at the side of the road.

From the small village of **Narphung** the road climbs again to the Narphung La at 1698m. It follows a ridge that leads to the east, crossing from one side to the other and climbs to 1920m before beginning the final descent to the plains.

The road weaves down, reaching the PWD camp at **Morong** at an elevation of about 1600m. The workers here are probably responsible for the corny Indian-style homilies on road signs here: 'speed thrills but kills' and 'no hurry, no worry'.

The Chokey Gyantso Institute for Advanced Buddhist Philosophy marks the outskirts of **Deothang** at 850m. The old name for this town was Dewangiri, and it was the site of a major battle between the Bhutanese and the British in 1865. The town is dominated by a large Royal Bhutan Army (RBA) camp and the Royal Bhutan Polytechnic Institute. There is a small golf course behind the Dantak headquarters. A road winds its way east from Deothang to Bhangtar, another border town.

Deothang to Samdrup Jongkhar 18km, ½ hour

At a curve in the road there is finally a view of the plains. Drop to a stream and follow it along the valley bottom past the Chhoden Chemical Industries, which manufactures cement, carbide and ferro-silicon. In the jungle, well before Samdrup Jongkhar, is the police and immigration check post. You must have a valid permit in order to be allowed into the town.

SAMDRUP JONGKHAR

The road enters the town from the north, passing the Hifi Guest House and a road that leads west to the dzong. The Bank of Bhutan is on the east side of the road, then the road crosses a bridge. Turn south into the town itself. There are several hotels and many shops on this street and another parallel one to the west. If you go straight instead of turning south, you will pass the town's only petrol station and then cross the border to the Indian town of Darranga.

Places to Stay & Eat

The *Hifi Guest House* (☎ 04-51065) is in a tree-shaded compound at the north end of town. Other hotels are in the town centre. The *Peljorling Hotel* (☎ 04-51094) is the largest. It's an Indian-style establishment with a bar on the ground floor and the *Chopstix* restaurant upstairs. The *Hotel Shambala* (☎ 04-51222), just south of the Peljorling, also has a very Indian atmosphere.

Pemagatshel Dzongkhag

PEMAGATSHEL

The name Pemagatshel means 'Blissful Land of the Lotus'. This rural dzongkhag in the south-eastern part of the country is Bhutan's smallest district. Its headquarters, Pemagatshel, is reached via a side road that leads off the Samdrup Jongkhar to Trashigang road.

Chungkhar Goemba

NWAB operates a weaving centre here where about 40 women are trained annually in traditional weaving techniques and product design.

Yongla Goemba

Yongla Goemba is a few kilometres above the dzong in Pemagatshel. It is one of the holiest shrines in eastern Bhutan.

It was founded in the 18th century by Kheydup Jigme Kuenduel, who was advised by the great *terton* Rigzin Jigme Lingpa to establish a monastery on a mountain that looked like a *phurba* (three-bladed ritual dagger) that overlooked the vast plains of India. Later the goemba was used as a base for religious ceremonies by Trongsa penlop Jigme Namgyal during the great Duar War with the British in 1865.

East to West via India

It is a long, winding drive back to Thimphu from Eastern Bhutan. To avoid it, many Bhutanese travel into India, cross the plains and re-enter Bhutan at Phuentsholing. Tourists can use this route if they have made previous arrangements, or in the event of a road closure in Bhutan.

The journey from eastern to western Bhutan via India leads through parts of Assam that are under intense pressure from Indian separatist groups. The United Liberation Front of Assam (ULFA) is a militant political group seeking an independent Assamese state. The Bodo are an ethnic group also seeking their own homeland.

Travel here is severely discouraged by the Bhutanese because of the security problems. Be sure to check on the current situation in Assam and avoid travel here if conditions are not totally safe.

The route takes you through the duars, the area that the Bhutanese lost to British India during the Duar War in 1865. Once a deep jungle, the duars are now almost entirely covered with villages and rice paddies. There is a considerable amount of tea grown at the foot of the hills, near the border of Bhutan.

Darranga to Rangiya
48km, 1½ hours

There's no check post between Samdrup Jongkhar and the Indian town of Darranga, but there is an Indian immigration check post

---

Warning: Travel in Assam
There is a highly visible Indian army presence throughout the part of Assam adjoining Samdrup Jongkhar. Vehicles are conscientiously searched for weapons at several points, often under the direct aim of machine guns nestled in sandbagged embankments. If you choose (or are forced because of road blockage) to travel through this area, take these inspections very seriously. Army vehicles have been blown up and attacked by separatists, and the Indian army is very nervous and attentive here. This is not the time to make jokes or act difficult.

a few kilometres south of the border. You must have an Indian visa, and it is checked and endorsed here. The next 50km is along a narrow paved road similar to that in Bhutan where one (or both) vehicles must pull off to the side of the road in order to pass. Passing beautifully-manicured tea gardens and several army checkpoints, the road makes its way 14km to the village of Kumarikata.

It's another 15km to Tamulpur where the route turns west past a large army post. A short distance on is Rangiya, a crowded bazaar where your vehicle will have to make its way through hordes of horses, trucks, rickshaws, bicycles and people. There is a railway station here; several trains a day connect Rangiya to New Jalpaiguri in West Bengal. A road leads south from here to Guwahati (80km), then another 20km to the airport.

At Rangiya the road from Bhutan joins the major east-west trunk road which runs through the narrow Siliguri corridor linking the north-eastern region with the rest of India.

Rangiya to Howly
72km, 1½ hours
From Rangiya it's 22km to Barama on a two-lane road with heavy traffic including trucks. Another 50km of totally uninteresting driving leads to Howly.

Howly to Shrirampur
152km, 3½ hours
The road crosses the Manas river near the town of Barpeta Road a few kilometres beyond Howly. To the north is India's Manas Tiger reserve, which adjoins Bhutan's Royal Manas National Park.

The road traverses the duars with the hills of Bhutan sometimes visible to the north. Bongaigaon is a large industrial city with lots of truck traffic collecting petroleum products from the Assam oil refinery here.

The road surface in this part of Assam is dreadful with lots of potholes. At Shrirampur, on the border of the state of West Bengal, an octroi tax is collected on goods crossing the state line. There is usually a long line of trucks negotiating with various local agents and fixers that advertise their services alongside the road.

Shrirampur to Hasimara
66km, 1½ hours
If you are lucky, one of the highlights of this road trip may be lunch at a *dhaba* (basic roadside restaurant) where you can fill up on *chappatis* (unleavened bread), dal and spicy curries. More interesting is the improvement in the road once you enter West Bengal.

About 8km past Shrirampur is Borobisha, where a road leads north to the Bhutanese border town of Kalikhola. Along this stretch the road passes the southern border of the Buxa Tiger Reserve, which extends all the way to Phuentsholing.

Near the Indian Air Force base at Hasimara the road again gets close to the hills and the landscape is transformed by neatly manicured, shaded tea gardens stretching to the horizon.

Hasimara to Jaigaon
19km, ¾ hour
The route to Bhutan turns north at Hasimara bazaar. It's then 19km on a narrow road to Jaigaon. If you continue east from Hasimara you will reach Siliguri after 150km and the airport at Bagdogra 12km later.

The road between Hasimara and Jaigaon is lined with a continual array of tea gardens and shops. Jaigaon is a large noisy Indian town. See Phuentsholing in the Western Bhutan chapter for information about the border crossing.

EASTERN BHUTAN

Trekking

Towns, dzongs and temples are one aspect of Bhutan, but the majority of the country is still deep forests with a scattering of tiny settlements and high grazing lands. A trek provides the best opportunity to experience the real heart of Bhutan and get a unique insight into the rural culture of the kingdom through contact with people in remote villages and the staff accompanying you.

STYLE OF TRIP

Government rules dictate that all treks must be arranged as camping trips. This also happens to be the only practical solution because there are no lodges or hotels in the hills. The Tourist Authority of Bhutan (TAB) operates a guide training and registration programme and requires that a licensed guide accompany all trekking tourists. A Bhutanese crew also treks with you to set up camp, cook and serve meals. You carry a backpack with only a water bottle, camera and jacket.

Treks in Bhutan do not rely on porters. Instead, all your personal gear plus tents, kitchen and food is carried by pack horses or, at higher elevations, yaks. There are so few villages and facilities along trek routes that the people driving the pack animals carry their own food and camping gear and camp each night alongside you.

As you begin the trek, fresh vegetables and meat are available, and camp meals tend to be even better than those available in Thimphu. On a longer trek, the fresh food goes off after the first week or so, and you are largely reduced to tinned food. A skilled cook can still prepare reasonably good western-style food using a variety of Bhutanese and Indian tinned ingredients.

Because it's a camping trek, you will sleep in a two-person tent with foam pads placed on the floor to use as a mattress. All your gear goes into the tent with you at night. Having a tent gives you a reasonably private place and you have the freedom to go to bed when you

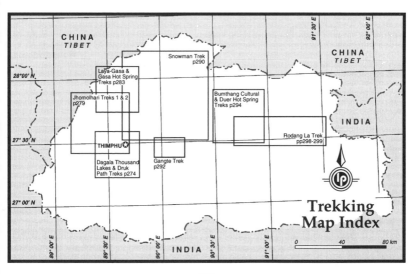

Trekking Map Index

Differences Between Treks in Nepal & Bhutan

People used to trekking in Nepal will find similar conditions in Bhutan with some differences, mostly dictated by geography. The hillsides in Bhutan tend toward the near vertical. This means that there are fewer farms and villages (less than 8% of the country's total land area is under cultivation) and fewer reasonable camp sites. Trekking parties (and you are not allowed to trek except with an organised group) are allowed to camp only at designated camp sites.

Because geographical considerations make the distance between these greater than the average distance between camps in Nepal, trekking days tend to be longer. Side-hill climbing on steep slopes also tends to mean that you do more up-and-down climbing to get around vertical cliffs, avalanche tracks and side canyons. The trails are generally good but in many places have been worn down, through centuries of use, to paths of scattered rounded rocks or to just plain mud.

You may not see other trekkers on the trail but, because camp sites are designated, you are likely to share your camp spot with one or more other parties. Generally speaking, the trekkers you see are older than your counterparts in Nepal. This, I assume, is because older, settled people are better able to afford the high cost of travel in Bhutan than young adventurers. Many of the camp sites have huts that can serve as kitchens for your crew or used as dining rooms if the weather is bad.

In my experience, trekkers meals in Bhutan compare well with restaurant meals. If you are used to Nepal's two hour-plus lunch breaks learn to adjust to a much shorter midday stop here. In Nepal, the crew takes time to cook a hot meal while the members nap. In Bhutan, they bring along a hot dish in an insulated container (with other goodies) for what amounts to a glorified trail lunch. The crew, incidentally, tends to be much smaller than those who serve you in Nepal. Three or four people do the work of five to seven or more. Maybe one reason for this is that there are no security problems in Bhutan and thus no need for extra people to guard the camp.

Horses and, at higher elevations, yaks carry tents and duffel bags. The animals of one district are not allowed to cross the border into the next district and thus have to be replaced by new ones at district borders. Anxious trekkers may worry about the possibility of being left at some windswept mountain pass abandoned by *all* animals. It happens, but rarely.

In most places in Nepal, the local people have become accustomed to trekkers but in Bhutan you are still a curiosity. People stare at you with open, friendly faces or greet you warmly as you pass – even come up to you and shake your hand. You become used to kids running to greet you, shouting 'bye bye!'. Some have not learned that it is no-no to ask for pens. Others startle you by bowing low and bidding 'good afternoon, sir!'.

Robert Peirce

choose. You can retire immediately after dinner to read or sleep, or you can sit up and watch the moon rise as you discuss the day's outing with your companions. Because there are also tents for the Bhutanese guides and the packers, you do not need to camp near villages and can trek comfortably to remote regions and high altitudes.

A Wilderness Experience

Most of Bhutan's landscape is covered with forests, and nowhere is this more obvious than on a trek. All treks climb up and down hills, passing through various biological zones, and there is a large variety of trees and other vegetation. As there is a lot of wildlife in the hills of Bhutan and most treks are in protected areas, there are good opportunities to see wildlife in its native habitat.

Once you step off the road to start the trek you are in true wilderness much of the time. Though there are established trails, there are no planes flying overhead, no roads and very few villages; instead there are views of snow-capped peaks and forested hillsides stretching to eternity.

Not a Climbing Trip

Throughout Bhutan's trekking regions there are ancient, well-developed trails through forests and across mountain passes. Even at high altitudes, trails lead to temporary shelters that are used during the summer by shepherds. You can easily walk on any trail without the aid of ropes or mountaineering skills. There are rare occasions when there is snow on the trail, and if snow blocks the high passes you either retreat, wait for yaks to clear a path, or wait for spring, so alpine techniques are almost never required on a trek. Anyone who has walked extensively in mountains has all the skills necessary for an extended trek in Bhutan.

A Bhutan trek will not allow you to fulfil any Himalayan mountaineering ambitions. Bhutan's regulations prohibit all mountaineering activity because of concerns expressed by local people for the sanctity of the mountain peaks, which they revere as the home of their deities.

Physical Fitness

A Bhutan trek is physically demanding because of its length and the almost unbelievable changes in elevation. If you add all the climbing in the 14-day Laya-Gasa trek, for example, it is more than 7000m of elevation gain and loss during many steep ascents and descents. On most treks, the daily gain is less than 500m in about 18km, though ascents of as much as 1000m are possible on some days. You can always take plenty of time during the day to cover this distance; the physical exertion, though quite strenuous at times, is not sustained. You can take time for rest, but the trek days in Bhutan are long, requiring seven to nine hours of walking.

Probably the only physical problem that may make a trek impossible is a history of knee problems on descents. Throughout the Himalaya the descents are long, steep and unrelenting. There is hardly a level stretch of trail in the entire country. If you are an experienced walker and often hike 20 to 25km a day with a pack, a trek should prove no difficulty. You will be pleasantly surprised at how easy the hiking can be if you carry only a light backpack and do not have to worry about setting up a camp, finding water and preparing meals.

Previous experience in hiking and living outdoors is, however, helpful as you plan your trek. The first night of a two-week trip is too late to discover that you do not like to sleep in a sleeping bag. Mountaineering skills are not necessary, but you must enjoy walking.

A Trek is Long

A short trek in Bhutan is three or four days long, an average trek is a week, and a trek of 23 days or more is possible. Every day you walk leads you one day further into the hills and you will have to walk that same distance to get back to a road. It's worth making proper preparations before you start so that you don't find three days into the trek that you are ill equipped, totally exhausted or unable to cope with the thought of walking all that distance back.

Trail Conditions

There are lots of steep, long climbs and descents on rocky trails. Bhutan is amazingly rocky and on many routes the trail traverses long stretches of round river rocks. It requires some agility to hop between these. The trail is often extremely muddy, sometimes requiring a diversion to keep your feet dry. It can be a tricky balancing act on stones and bits of wood to get across stretches that have been ground into sloppy mud by the hooves of passing horses. Another unpleasant aspect of a trek in Bhutan is attacks by leeches during the rainy season. Leeches are rare during the normal trekking seasons but, if you want to see the alpine flowers, you need to come during July and August when the rain and leeches make life more difficult.

High Altitude

Most treks in Bhutan reach altitudes that bring about symptoms of altitude sickness in many people. Be sure you understand the dangers and symptoms of altitude sickness before you begin a trek in Bhutan (see the boxed text on the following pages).

Acclimatisation & Altitude Illness

There are relatively few well-established trekking routes open to tourists in Bhutan, and to our knowledge, no trekker has died of altitude illness here. However, this may be a matter of luck and relatively small numbers of people at risk. The following information will help prevent you and your friends from becoming the first altitude illness victims in Bhutan.

Our bodies have the ability to adjust to higher altitudes if given enough time. This process of adaptation is called acclimatisation. If a person travels up to altitude more rapidly than his or her body can adjust, symptoms develop called acute mountain sickness (AMS). If ignored, the symptoms can occasionally progress to more severe forms of altitude illness described in the following paragraphs.

Your body adjusts to altitude initially by increasing the rate and depth of breathing. Studies have shown that people who adapt well to altitude automatically increase their breathing more than individuals who get altitude sickness easily. This sensitivity to a change in altitude appears to be genetic. Other adaptations include an increase in heart rate and a gradual increase in red blood cells. Once you have acclimatised to a given height for a few days, you are very unlikely to get mountain sickness at that height, but you can still get ill when you travel higher.

Altitude illness occurs as the result of failure to adapt to a higher altitude. Fluid accumulates in between the cells in the body and eventually collects where it can do the most harm: in the lungs and brain. As fluid collects in the lungs, you become breathless more easily while walking and eventually more breathless at rest. A cough begins, initially dry and irritative, but progressing to the production of pink, frothy sputum in its most severe form. The person ultimately drowns in this fluid if they don't descend. This syndrome is referred to as high-altitude pulmonary oedema (HAPE). When fluid collects in the brain, you develop a headache, loss of appetite, nausea and sometimes vomiting. You become increasingly tired and want to lie down and do nothing. As you progress, you develop a problem with your balance and coordination (ataxia). Eventually you lie down and slip into coma, and death is inevitable if you don't descend. This syndrome is called high-altitude cerebral oedema (HACE). HAPE and HACE can occur singly or in combination.

Since individual susceptibility to altitude illness varies widely and most people don't have prior experience with prolonged stays at high altitude, it is impossible to design itineraries that would completely prevent altitude illness symptoms in all people. Therefore, some individuals will get altitude illness, even on reasonable itineraries. The important thing is to react appropriately if symptoms do occur. To prevent altitude illness:

Rule One Learn to recognise the early symptoms of mountain sickness.

Early symptoms of altitude illness include headache, loss of appetite, nausea and fatigue. Once you are familiar with these symptoms, you must be willing to admit that you have them. Trekkers tend to be very goal-oriented and ambition can lead people to want to deny their symptoms. If you feel ill at altitude and you are not sure why, assume it is AMS and respond accordingly. Guessing wrong can have serious consequences.

Many cases of altitude sickness occur in trekking groups that have the problem of sticking to a group schedule. If a person fails to acclimatise on a given day they often have to be left behind. Since people don't want to be left behind on a 'trip of a lifetime', they will often hide or minimise their symptoms. Even if their symptoms become apparent, an inexperienced trek leader may choose to minimise the importance of the symptoms to avoid the logistical complications of having to split up the group. Adjusting the schedule to allow an extra day to acclimatise can be life saving.

Rule Two Never ascend to sleep at a new altitude if you have *any* symptoms of AMS.

Once you recognise that you have the early symptoms of AMS, it is imperative that you do not

STAN ARMINGTON

STAN ARMINGTON

STAN ARMINGTON

Trekking
Trekking is the ideal way to immerse yourself in the rural spirit of Bhutan. Whether you are camping beneath a majestic peak like Gangchenta (top left) or snaking through vast mountain passes like Nyile La (top right) you're sure to prick the curiosity of locals (above).

NICHOLAS REUSS

TONY WHEELER

NICHOLAS REUSS

Trekking
If you go trekking you may wish you'd brought a dictionary to help you describe your first glimpse of the kingdom's most sacred mountain, Jhomolhari (top); the sprinkling of ice covering the mountains across the Mo Chhu in Western Bhutan (right); and the feeling of being the first to cut a trail through dense forest as on the approach to Phephe La, Central Bhutan (left).

ascend to sleep at a higher altitude. Virtually all fatalities from altitude illness occur in people who persist in ascending despite symptoms that should have been recognised as AMS. You may find yourself in a situation where it is necessary to ascend in order to descend – for example, when crossing a pass. If your symptoms are still mild and you feel certain that you can get over the pass to a lower height by the end of the day, this may be all right. But it is a decision that requires some mountaineering judgement. However, if you climb to a higher altitude and spend the night, even the mildest symptom of AMS will become worse. This rule is the single most important point to prevent deaths from altitude illness.

Rule Three Descend immediately if your symptoms persist or are getting worse while resting at the same altitude.

If your symptoms persist or slowly become worse instead of better while resting at the same height, it is imperative that you descend to a lower altitude. Once the cycle of AMS symptoms starts to get progressively worse, it will not start to improve without descent. Most of the time it is necessary to get below the height at which the symptoms began; in any case you must descend until you feel that the symptoms are starting to get better. Once they start to improve, you can generally continue to rest at that altitude until recovery is complete.

Two symptoms deserve prime attention. People with the cerebral form of altitude illness, ie headache, nausea, vomiting and fatigue, must be checked for signs of uncoordination while walking, known medically as 'ataxia'. Have the person stand up and walk a straight line while putting the heel of the front foot on the toe of the back foot (the classic 'drunk test' administered to drivers by police who are looking for signs of alcohol intoxication). If the person steps off the imaginary line, or falls altogether, they have developed severe HACE and must descend immediately. Someone with moderately severe symptoms of AMS, but who can still walk the line without imbalance, should think about descending, but if it is night time, or if descent would be logistically difficult due to weather or terrain, they can be watched closely for a while. Anyone with signs of ataxia, however, should descend immediately, regardless of the time of day. They are only hours away from unconsciousness.

The other significant symptom to watch for is breathlessness at rest. HAPE can have an insidious onset, starting out as just feeling like you can't hike as fast you think you should. Later you find that you have to rest more and more often and don't recover your breathing rate at rest. No matter how hard you have to breathe while walking uphill at altitude, your breathing rate should return to normal after five to 10 minutes of rest. If you continue to feel breathless after 10 minutes at rest, you are developing HAPE, and you should immediately descend. The problem with HAPE is that exercise makes it worse and even exerting to descend can make things worse before the decrease in altitude starts to make things better. This can be a fine line to walk, so early recognition of breathlessness at rest is imperative.

Once you have recovered completely from altitude illness by descending, you have the option of re-ascending slowly, watching for relapse. Many people will have had enough by then, but determined people can try to go back to altitude if they have completely recovered from all their symptoms.

Treatment of AMS

The treatment of AMS is, first, not to ascend with symptoms; and, second, if symptoms persist or become more severe, to descend. Descent will always bring improvement and should not be delayed to try some other form of therapy in serious cases. In rare cases where descent is difficult or impossible, a portable pressure chamber is effective. The portable pressure chamber consists of a nylon tube hooked to a foot pump. The patient is zipped inside the bag and the pressure is increased, mimicking an instant descent of several thousand feet.

There are American, French and Australian versions of portable pressurisation bags. They range in price from US$1000 to US$2500, and may also be rented for specific trips. You should consider carrying a pressurisation bag if you are travelling into a remote high-altitude area where descent is difficult.

Drug treatments should never be used to avoid descent or to enable further ascent.

- *Acetazolamide (Diamox)* Diamox can prevent mild symptoms of AMS if taken prior to ascent. You should not routinely take Diamox for a trek in Bhutan, as most people will not need it for the gradual ascents that are usually associated with trekking. However, if you know from past experience that you do not acclimatise well, and your itinerary has an unavoidable sudden increase in altitude, taking Diamox before you ascend may prevent you from getting AMS symptoms. Diamox does not prevent the progression to severe symptoms of HAPE or HACE, so you must still watch closely for AMS symptoms and respond appropriately. Diamox prevents or improves AMS by increasing the respiratory rate and depth, mimicking the breathing of someone who is a good acclimatiser. Thus, if you feel better on Diamox, you actually are better; and Diamox does not mask the symptoms of AMS.

  Diamox is useful in treating the headache and nausea associated with mild AMS and it can also improve your sleep at altitude if you are being disturbed by the irregular breathing and breathlessness that can occur. It is recommended to carry Diamox with you to treat mild symptoms and use it prophylactically only if you have had experience before with AMS on a certain schedule. The usual dose is 125mg (half a tablet) every 12 hours as needed. Mild tingling of hands and feet is common after taking Diamox and is not an indication to stop its use. Diamox is a diuretic, so increased urine output can be expected when taking the drug. People with a known allergy to sulfa drugs should not take Diamox.

- *Dexamethasone (Decadron)* Dexamethasone is a potent steroid drug which improves the symptoms of HACE through an unknown mechanism, apparently without improving acclimatisation. It is an important drug to carry for emergency use, but should never be taken prophylactically to prevent AMS. People with a severe headache and loss of balance can be improved enough with this drug to allow them to avoid a nighttime descent or to convert them from a stretcher case to being able to walk. The improvement with dexamethasone is occasionally so dramatic that people might be tempted to continue upward while still taking the drug. However, since adaptation to altitude has not been improved, this could be dangerous. Once the drug is started, the person should refrain from going to a higher altitude while still taking it. If you are able to go off the drug for 24 hours and have no further symptoms, you may continue your ascent.

- *Nifedipine* Nifedipine is a drug that is ordinarily used to treat heart problems and high blood pressure. However, it has been shown to reduce pressure in the main artery in the lungs, dramatically improving severe HAPE. For this reason, nifedipine should be included in trekking first-aid kits. The initial dose is 10mg every eight hours. Treatment with nifedipine should be accompanied by immediate descent.

David Shlim, MD

PLANNING

There are a tremendous number of factors that can influence your plans for a trek in Bhutan, but the most important consideration is weather. Most trekkers come in the autumn; spring is the second most popular season.

When to Trek

Winter snows and summer rains limit the ideal trekking season in Bhutan to two brief periods. Late September to mid-November is generally recognised as the best time for trekking, and it's high tourist season during the time of best weather in the autumn. Flights and hotels are fully booked and you will meet other trekkers on the popular routes.

During autumn the nights are cold in the mountains, but the bright sun makes for pleasant daytime temperatures – in the high 20s, falling to 5°C at night, between 1000m and 3500m. At higher altitudes temperatures range from about 20°C down to -10°C. Mornings are usually clear with clouds building up after 1 pm, but they typically disappear at night to reveal spectacular starry skies. Most high passes are snowbound from late November until February and in some years the snow does not disappear until April or May.

Late March to mid-May affords warmer weather and blooming rhododendron, but there is a higher chance of rain if you trek during this time. Alpine wildflowers are in bloom during August and September, but the mud is deep and there are no mountain views. The ardent botanist (or the insane) might select July and August for a trek.

Schedule Changes

Despite all the pre-planning and the complicated advance arrangements, there are still numerous factors that can upset a trek schedule. Snow can block trails, horses can fail to appear on schedule or the horse drivers may consider the trail too dangerous for their animals. There is little recourse when the trek cannot proceed and you should always be prepared for possible disappointment.

TOPO MAPS

The entire country has been mapped by the Survey of India at one inch to a mile, but these maps are restricted and hard to obtain because large-scale topo maps are secret documents in India. There is a related series of topo maps produced by the Survey of Bhutan, but these are also restricted. The US Army Map Service produced a set of maps in the 1950s (Series U502 at 1:250,000, sheets NG45-4 and NH46-1) based on the Survey of India maps. They are outdated, the topography is extremely inaccurate and they, too, are hard to obtain. Another series is the 1:200,000 Russian Military Topographic set which takes ten sheets to cover Bhutan, but its text is in Russian.

In cooperation with an Austrian project, TAB is producing large-scale contour maps of the major trekking routes based on the Survey of Bhutan series. These are the best, though not entirely accurate, trekking references available.

MEDICAL ISSUES

For general advice on medical issues not specifically related to trekking see the Health & Safety section in the Facts for the Visitor chapter.

Medical Exam & Prescriptions

Although trekking is just walking around in the mountains, due to the altitude, strenuous terrain and isolation it is a good idea to make sure that you are as healthy as possible before starting out. It is worthwhile investigating little nagging problems or any unexplained recurrent symptoms before you go, because problems have a way of escalating under the stress of travel. If you take medications regularly for chronic problems, such as high blood pressure, make sure you stay on your medications for the trek and carry the medications with you when you fly, rather than carrying them in your luggage. If you have chronic medical problems or a history of something complicated that could flare up on a trip, carry a brief outline of your problem, possibly written by your physician, with you. This can be

Water Purification

As repugnant as it sounds, the germs that cause diarrhoea, typhoid fever and hepatitis are acquired mainly from eating someone else's stool. One of the major medical advances of western countries was developing a sure way of keeping stool out of the water supply. This problem has not been solved in Bhutan and all water must be viewed as being potentially contaminated. Obviously, some urban water may be extremely contaminated and some mountain water may be almost pure, but it is better to disinfect all water before drinking it. While there is no consensus on the best method of purifying water in all circumstances, the following sections examine the considerations.

Boiling All of the stool pathogens (disease producers) are killed by boiling water. Although there is some confusion as to the optimum length of time that water must be boiled to make it safe, a consensus paper by the Wilderness Medical Society in the USA has confirmed that *just bringing water to the boil* is sufficient to kill all potential disease-causing organisms, even at high altitude.

Iodine As an alternative to boiling, chemicals can be added to water to kill the germs. Iodine preparations and chlorine preparations are equally effective in killing the germs, but iodine is a bit more reliable in the field. There are three practical ways to carry iodine on a trek: as tetraglycine hydroperiodide tablets, Lugol's solution and iodine crystals.

Tetraglycine hydroperiodide tablets are not available in Bhutan and can deteriorate in as little as six months in their original containers. Purchase bottles before you travel. The tablets are convenient to use and not messy to carry. One bottle contains 50 tablets, enough to purify 50L of water.

Lugol's solution is a water-based iodine concentrate; four to eight drops per litre of water are sufficient to make the water drinkable within 20 to 30 minutes. It is not available in Bhutan and may be hard to find at home, but it's readily available in Kathmandu. It's best to carry the solution in a small bottle with an eyedropper.

Iodine crystals have the advantage of being able to purify an almost unlimited amount of water. Four or five grams of iodine crystals in a 30ml glass bottle will purify water for months. The crystals will only dissolve in water to a certain degree; once the water is saturated, it will not accept any more iodine. To make a saturated solution, fill the small bottle with water and wait 30 minutes. The resulting saturated solution may be added to your water bottle to purify the water for drinking: add 15 to 30ml of the solution to your one-litre water bottle and wait for 30 minutes before drinking. Refill the glass bottle at the same time and after 30 minutes it will be ready to use again as well. Be particularly careful not to ingest an iodine crystal, as this can be fatal.

Note: If your main objection to using iodine is the taste, this can be completely eliminated by adding a small quantity of vitamin C (ascorbic acid) after you have waited for the iodine to work. Approximately 50mg of vitamin C when crumbled into a litre of water and shaken for a few seconds will completely neutralise the iodine flavour in the water, making the water taste like pure spring water. Some people are concerned about possible health consequences of using iodine over long periods of time or during pregnancy. However, no evidence has been presented that using iodine to purify water, even for long periods of time, causes any harm.

Water Filters Filtering devices for field use have become popular in recent years. No filtering device can guarantee the elimination of viruses that cause diarrhoea or hepatitis, so iodine must also be used in addition to a filter in Bhutan. Some filters incorporate a pentaiodine resin which iodinates the water as it filters it. For the most part, water in Bhutan appears clear and has good taste, so filtering for sediment and taste is not usually necessary. If you plan to use a filter, make sure it has a pore size of 0.2 microns or less.

Note: Don't believe manufacturers' claims that filtering without also adding iodine will eliminate viruses from water.

David Shlim, MD

extremely useful in the event that you are forced to seek care from another physician while you are travelling.

People over 45 often worry about altitude and potential heart problems. There is no evidence that altitude is likely to bring on previously undiagnosed heart disease. If you are able to exercise to your maximum at sea level, you should not have an increased risk of heart attack while trekking at altitude. However, if you have known heart disease and your exercise is already limited by symptoms at low altitude, you may have trouble at altitude. If you have a history of heart disease, you should consult a doctor who has some knowledge of high altitude before committing yourself to a trek.

Physical Conditioning

Trekking in Bhutan involves long stretches of steep up-and-down terrain. This can prove physically tiring, especially as the altitude increases, and can put a lot of stress on your knees. The best training is to walk up and, in particular, down hills as much as possible. If you have a busy life, with little access to hiking on weekends, you should train with exercise machines (such as 'Stairmasters'), ride a bicycle or jog. Trekking puts most of the strain on the quadriceps muscles in the front of the thigh. If you have no hills to train on, try putting a pack on your back to increase the strength training associated with walking or jogging. Take stairs whenever possible in preference to a lift (elevator). Trekking in Bhutan is strenuous and the time you put into physical training before you go will definitely be rewarded.

Medical Problems

The following suggestions will be useful in handling some medical problems specific to trekking.

Snow Blindness This is a temporary, painful condition resulting from sunburn of the clear surface of the eye (the cornea). It comes from heavy exposure to ultraviolet radiation, almost exclusively in situations where someone is walking on snow without sunglasses.

Snow blindness is almost unheard of where there is no snow on the ground to reflect additional light rays into your eyes. In Bhutan it can affect a person who does not carry sunglasses, someone who has an accident on snow and loses their sunglasses, and trek crew, who generally don't own sunglasses or sell the ones they have been given. If you are in a party of trekkers attempting to cross a high pass that is covered with snow, try to make sure that everyone has something to protect their eyes.

The treatment is simply to try to relieve the pain. Cold cloths held against the outside of the eyelids help relieve the pain and swelling. Antibiotic eye drops are not necessary and anaesthetic drops should be avoided as they slow down the healing and make the eyes vulnerable to other injuries. The cornea will be completely repaired within a few days and there are no long-term consequences.

Trekker's Knee Trekking in Bhutan invariably involves multiple long ascents and descents. If your legs have not been gradually accustomed to walking uphill and downhill through training, there is a chance that you will develop some degree of knee soreness after a long descent. The pain generally comes from mild trauma repeated thousands of times on the descent. The two areas that are most involved are the outer side of the knee and the area under the kneecap. You may experience difficulty walking and have to rest for a few days before continuing. Anti-inflammatory pills are helpful, as are ski poles or a walking stick. The pain can take several weeks to go away completely, but there are no long-term consequences.

Blisters Blisters on your feet result from repeated rubbing of the skin against a hard surface (the inside of your shoe or boot). The superficial surface of the skin eventually gets lifted off its base and fluid collects in the resulting bubble. Blisters can usually be avoided by conscientious attention to your feet as you hike. Any sore spot on your foot while walking should be investigated immediately and some form of additional protection should be put over the area that is being rubbed. There are many commercial products on the market which protect your feet from blisters in specific areas. Moleskin is the most popular item, but adhesive tape can also work well. Newer products, utilising soft gels, have recently been added to the mix of products. Using a thin inner sock inside a thicker sock can provide a sliding layer that can reduce the friction on the foot. Try not to begin a trek in brand-new shoes or boots.

Blisters are not infected when they first form, but after the bubble breaks bacterial infection can develop. Try to wash the area and keep it clean. If swelling and redness develop, you will need to take oral antibiotics.

Mountain Rescue

If you find yourself ill or injured in the mountains, don't panic. If someone falls, take some time to assess the situation: suspected broken bones may only be bruises; and a dazed person may wake up and be quite all right in an hour or two. If the problem is severe diarrhoea, follow the guidelines under Diarrhoea in the Health & Safety section of the Facts for the Visitor chapter. If it is acute mountain sickness, descend with the victim; do not wait for help. If the illness is severe, but not diagnosable, evaluate your options. In most areas of Bhutan, some kind of animal, either horses or yaks, will be available to help transport a sick or injured trekker.

Sometimes either the seriousness of the injuries or the urgency of getting care will make land evacuation impractical. If this is the case, then the only alternative is to request a helicopter rescue flight. Fortunately, in Bhutan, this is a reasonably straightforward process, but remember that once you ask for a helicopter, you cannot cancel it later and you will be charged for the service. Prices start at US$1500 and can go much higher, especially if weather conditions are bad and the chopper has to make two or three attempts to rescue you.

Rescue helicopters are Indian units from the Air Force base in Hasimara or the army facility at Bagdogra airport. If there is need for an evacuation during a trek, the guide will send a message to the appropriate tour operator. The tour operator contacts TAB to request a rescue helicopter, TAB forwards the request to the Royal Bhutan Army and they then request the Indian Army to send the chopper. It's a well-organised and efficient chain of communication and a helicopter is usually dispatched within a day.

TREKKING ROUTES

In this chapter 12 of the 13 permitted trekking routes in Bhutan are described. The last one, the two-day Cheli La trek, is described briefly in the Paro section of the Western Bhutan chapter. Other trekking routes may be possible with prior negotiation between tour operators and TAB, but the major treks offer everything that a trekker could want, including what is described as the world's most difficult trek. There are numerous variations possible, even within the prescribed itineraries. Most of the routes can be trekked in the reverse direction, though this sometimes causes logistical problems because horses are not always available at the standard end points of the treks.

These descriptions will give you some insight into the type of country, wildlife and culture you may encounter on specific treks. They should also help you to choose the area you wish to visit because they give an indication of the difficulty of each trek and the number of days it will take to follow a particular route.

There is a general explanation of the lay of the land and cultural background, but these are not self-guiding trail descriptions. Though some treks follow old trade routes, local people don't use many of them today. Because there is usually no one around to ask for directions, you need to stay reasonably close to the guide or horsemen to ensure that you are on the correct path.

Many places feel so remote that you can imagine you are the first person ever to visit. As you sit contemplating this, read about the invading armies or royal processions that preceded you decades – or centuries – ago and you will be amazed at what these people accomplished.

Conventions
Bhutan is a maze of valleys and rivers that wind around in unexpected turns. It is, therefore, difficult to always define in which compass direction a river is flowing at a particular spot. Instead of referring to the north or south bank of rivers, the slightly technical term of 'river right' or 'river left' has been used in the route descriptions. This refers to the right or left side of the river as you face downstream, which is not necessarily the direction you are walking. In the route descriptions, right and left in reference to a river always refers to river right or river left.

Daily Stages The route descriptions are separated into daily stages. This helps to make them readable and gives a quick estimate of the number of days required for each trek. The stages are those defined by TAB as designated camping sites, and the rules state that you must camp at these places. This doesn't usually create any hardship, because in most cases the designated camping places are the only spots that have water and a space flat enough for making a camp.

Some Bhutanese trekking staff have a very relaxed approach to schedules and late morning starts are common. Because the daily stages are quite long, this often results in late arrivals to camp, sometimes after dark. Be sure to always carry a torch in your rucksack and bring plenty of spare batteries.

Time & Distance The route descriptions list approximate walking times. These are estimates based on personal experience and information produced by TAB. Any moderately fit trekker can accomplish the suggested daily stages in a single day.

The distances shown are those published by TAB. It is easy to judge distances from a

map, but a printed map is two-dimensional. With the many gains and losses of altitude – and all the turns and twists of the trail – a map measurement of the routes becomes virtually meaningless. The distances are estimates and have not been determined by any accurate method of measurement.

Rest Days The route descriptions here are based on the minimum number of days needed to complete the trek. You should add several days to each trek for rest, acclimatisation or exploration.

Trekking Maps in this Book
The maps included in this book are based on the best available maps of each region. As with everything else, they are reasonably accurate, but not perfect. To make them legible, only those villages and landmarks mentioned in the route descriptions are shown on the maps. The maps show elevations for peaks and passes only – other elevations, including for each camp, are given in the route descriptions. The trails and roads follow the general direction indicated on the maps, but maps this size obviously cannot show small switchbacks and twists in the trail.

Instead of contour lines, the maps depict only ridge lines. This is the line of the highest point on a ridge. If the trail crosses one of these lines, you must walk uphill. If the trail leads from a ridge line to a river, you must walk downhill. In the lowlands, where the hills are gentle, the location of ridge lines can be more arbitrary than when they cross the top of a high peak.

Altitude Measurements
The elevations shown in the route descriptions are composites, based on measurements with an altimeter or GPS and the best available maps. Except for specific elevations shown on maps produced by the Survey of Bhutan, all elevations are rounded to the nearest 10m. There is no definitive list of the elevations or names of the peaks or passes in Bhutan, and various maps and publications differ significantly. In most cases the peak elevations are those defined in the mountain

database produced by the Alpine Club in Britain.

This uncertainty over precise elevations will cause no problems during a trek. The primary reason that you need to know the elevation is to learn whether the trail ahead goes uphill or downhill and whether it is a long or short ascent (or descent). The elevations shown here fulfil that purpose.

Place Names & Terminology

The route descriptions list many mountains and places that do not correlate with names in other descriptions of the same route or with names on maps. The diversity occurs because most maps were made before the Dzongkha Development Commission produced their guidelines for Romanised Dzongkha. An effort has been made to use the new standards for all place names throughout Bhutan.

Many streams and landmarks remain nameless in the trail descriptions. Most trekking routes go through sparsely populated country, where there is less formality about place names. Though some places have official, historically accurate names, many camping places are in meadows or yak pastures. Local herders, or perhaps trekking guides, made up names for some of these places which now appear on official maps. Numerous small streams, valleys and other landmarks do not have any names at all or, if they do have local names, there is nobody living nearby to ask.

In some places there is a facility that the Bhutanese call a 'community hall'. This is a stone building that the staff can use for cooking and shelter and may be available for trekkers to use as a dining room.

TREKKING FOOD

You can rely entirely on the camp meals and not carry any food with you to Bhutan. You might carry a small supply of chocolate bars or trail mix for snacks, and possibly a few packets of seasoning to liven up soups, but it's not really necessary. The trekking company sends along an extensive assortment of supplies for the cook to work with, so you don't need to worry about food at all.

Your cook can look after any special dietary requirements if given notice.

Because there is almost no fresh food available on trek routes, the entire food supply must be carried from the start of the trek.

Meals usually include a rice dish, a potato dish or, frequently, both. Fresh meat and vegetables appear for the first week, then disappear and are replaced by tinned varieties. The cook prepares meals over stoves fuelled by bottled gas, and most Bhutanese trekking cooks are adept at producing a good variety of western-style meals. They often add interesting Bhutanese touches, such as cheese sauces, but know to avoid hot chillies unless you specifically request them.

The midday meal is often a packed lunch, carried by the cook, and may consist of fried rice or noodles, boiled potatoes or chappatis. It is normally accompanied by tea from a large thermos flask. Sometimes the cook loads a lunch horse with a gas cylinder and a basket of food and produces a hot lunch on the trail, but this is infrequent because on most trekking days there is not a good place to cook and eat at the right time.

TREKKING EQUIPMENT

There is no trekking gear available in Bhutan; you must bring all your equipment with you. You probably already have most of it if you hike much in cold weather. A trek is a good place to destroy clothing that is outdated or nearly worn out.

If you follow the suggestions you can have many happy hours planning the trek, sorting gear, packing and repacking. If you don't have lots of time to prepare, you can probably gather most of the items you need in a single visit to an outdoor equipment shop.

The equipment checklist is based on the experience of many trekkers in both Bhutan and Nepal. Everything on the list is useful, and most of it necessary, on a long trek. You can omit many items if your trek does not exceed three weeks in duration or ascend above 4000m. All of this gear (except perhaps the sleeping bag) will pack into a duffel bag weighing less than 15kg.

Personal Equipment Checklist

FOR ALL TREKS

Footwear
- [ ] trekking or running shoes
- [ ] camp shoes or thongs
- [ ] socks – polypropylene

Clothing
- [ ] down or fibre-filled jacket
- [ ] jumper or pile jacket
- [ ] hiking shorts (for men) or skirt (optional)
- [ ] waterproof jacket, poncho or umbrella
- [ ] hiking pants
- [ ] T-shirts or blouses
- [ ] underwear
- [ ] sun hat
- [ ] swimwear (optional)

Other Equipment
- [ ] rucksack
- [ ] sleeping bag
- [ ] water bottle
- [ ] torch (flashlight), batteries & bulbs

Miscellaneous Items
- [ ] toilet articles
- [ ] toilet paper & cigarette lighter
- [ ] small knife
- [ ] sunblock (SPF 15-plus)
- [ ] towel
- [ ] laundry soap
- [ ] medical & first-aid kit
- [ ] pre-moistened towelettes
- [ ] sewing kit
- [ ] bandanna

FOR TREKS GOING ABOVE 4000M

Footwear
- [ ] mountain trekking boots
- [ ] socks, wool, to wear with boots
- [ ] socks, light cotton, for under wool socks
- [ ] down booties (optional)

Clothing
- [ ] insulated pants
- [ ] nylon windbreaker
- [ ] nylon wind pants
- [ ] long underwear
- [ ] woollen hat (or balaclava)
- [ ] gloves
- [ ] long gaiters

Miscellaneous Items
- [ ] goggles or sunglasses
- [ ] sunblock for lips

OPTIONAL EQUIPMENT & TOYS

Photography Equipment
- [ ] camera & lenses
- [ ] lens cleaning equipment
- [ ] film (about 20 rolls)

Toys & Navigation Aids
- [ ] global positioning system (GPS)
- [ ] an altimeter is particularly useful
- [ ] thermometer
- [ ] compass

Miscellaneous Items
- [ ] binoculars
- [ ] books for reading while waiting for planes
- [ ] duffel bag with a padlock, some stuff sacks and lots of plastic bags
- [ ] A small duffel bag or suitcase to leave your city clothes in is also useful.

Some gear will not be necessary on your trek. You might be lucky enough to trek during a warm spell and never need a down jacket. It might be so cold and rainy that you never wear short pants. These are, however, unusual situations, and it is still important to be prepared for both extremes.

Make a special effort to reduce the weight of the baggage you bring on the trek. Each pack animal carries 30kg and it is expected that one animal will carry the luggage of two trekkers. Hence, any baggage over 15kg is a complication. Some trekkers, especially those following the equipment guidelines of large American adventure travel companies, haul huge duffel bags to Bhutan which complicates packing arrangements as much of the gear is unnecessary.

What is Provided

The trek operator will provide two-person tents with foam mattresses, eating utensils and kitchen equipment. TAB rules specify that the trek operator should also provide a first aid kit and a pressure bag for high altitude treks, but you should still carry your own supply of basic medical needs.

Most trek operators expect you to bring your own sleeping bag. There are no sleeping bags available for rent in Bhutan.

Footwear

Trekking or Running Shoes Proper footwear is the most important item. Your choice will depend on the length of the trek and the terrain. Tennis or running shoes are good, even for long treks, provided you won't be walking in snow.

There are numerous brands of lightweight trekking shoes that have stiffer lug soles and are available in both low and high-top models. High top shoes provide ankle protection, but low-cut shoes are cooler to walk in. Most trekking shoes are leather and nylon combination and many have Gore-Tex waterproofing, but they are expensive, ranging from US$60 to US$100.

Try out the shoes you plan to wear on the trek during several hikes (particularly up and down hills) before you come to Bhutan. Be sure your shoes provide enough room for your toes. There are many long and steep descents and short boots can painfully jam your toes (causing the loss of toenails).

Mountain Trekking Boots Wherever there is snow (likely anywhere above 4000m), proper waterproof boots can become an absolute necessity. Since animals are carrying all your gear, you have the luxury of carrying two sets of shoes and swapping them from time to time.

Camp Shoes Tennis shoes are comfortable to change into for the evening. They can also serve as trail shoes in an emergency.

Socks Nylon-wool blend socks are fine, but artificial fibre hiking socks (which cost astronomical prices) are the best. Several manufacturers, including Thorlo, Wigwam and Patagonia, make several varieties of hiking socks designed to prevent blisters by wicking moisture away from your feet. It's sometimes difficult to wash clothes on a trek in Bhutan so bring more socks than you think you will need.

Down Booties Many people consider these excess baggage, but they are great to have and not very heavy. If they have a thick sole, preferably with ensolite insulation, they can serve as camp shoes at high elevations. They're also good for midnight trips outside in the cold.

Clothing

Down-Filled or Fibre-Filled Jacket Down clothing has the advantage of being light and compressible. It will stuff into a small space when packed, yet bulk up when you wear it. You should bring a good jacket on a trek. Most ski jackets are not warm enough and most so-called expedition parkas are too heavy and bulky. The secret is to choose one that will be warm enough even at the coldest expected temperatures, but also comfortable when it is warmer. Don't bring both a heavy and light down jacket; choose one that will serve both purposes, preferably one with a hood.

Your down jacket can serve many functions on the trek. It will become a pillow at night and will protect fragile items in your backpack or duffel bag. If you are extremely cold at high altitude, wear your down jacket to bed inside your sleeping bag. You don't wear down gear for walking as it rarely gets that cold even at 5000m.

Artificial fibre jackets (filled with Polargard, Thinsulate or Fibrefill) are a good substitute for down and much less expensive.

Jumper or Pile Jacket Two light layers of clothing are better than a single heavy layer, and one of two light jumpers (sweaters), shirts or polypro layers are superior to a heavy jacket.

Pile jackets made of polyester fleece come in a variety of styles and thicknesses. They are light, warm (even when wet) and easy to clean. If possible, buy a jacket that uses fleece that is made from recycled plastic bottles.

Hiking Shorts or Skirt Most treks are at altitudes where it is cool, even during the day, so most people are comfortable in long pants. Pants, however, pull at the knees and are hot, so some prefer shorts. Either 'cutoffs' or fancy hiking shorts with big pockets are fine, but only for men. Skimpy track shorts are culturally unacceptable throughout Bhutan.

Women should wear a skirt, perhaps over a pair of shorts. Many women who have worn skirts on treks are enthusiastic about them. The most obvious reason is the ease in relieving yourself along the trail. There are long stretches where there is little chance to drop out of sight, and a skirt solves the problem. Skirts are also useful when the only place to wash is in a stream crowded with trekkers. A wrap-around skirt is easy to put on and take off in a tent. Long 'granny' skirts are not good because you will be walking through too much mud to make them practical.

Raingear It is almost certain to rain at some time during your trek. The condensation inside a waterproof jacket can make you even wetter than standing out in the rain. Fancy Gore-Tex jackets are supposed to keep you dry by allowing the jacket to breathe, but in Bhutan you sweat a lot on the steep hills and they don't always work as advertised.

One way to keep dry while hiking in the rain is to use a poncho – a large, often hooded, tarp with a hole in the centre for your head. The weather is likely to be warm, even while raining, and you can get air circulation with a poncho if you drape it over your rucksack. An inexpensive plastic poncho is often as good as more expensive coated nylon gear. The plastic one is completely waterproof at a fraction of the cost.

The most practical way of keeping dry is an umbrella. This is an excellent substitute for a poncho (except on windy days), and can serve as a sunshade, a walking stick, an emergency toilet shelter and a dog deter-

rent. Collapsible umbrellas are a good compromise.

Sun Hat Obviously, a hat with a wide brim affords greater protection. Fix a strap that fits under your chin to the hat so it does not blow away in a wind gust.

Swimwear The only reasonable places to bathe are in hot springs. Skinny dipping is taboo if you are more than 10 years old. Bring along swimwear or use shorts or a skirt when you go into the hot spring.

Clothing – High Altitude
Insulated Pants Some kind of insulated pants are a real asset on a trek that goes above 4000m. You can bring pile pants, ski warm-up pants or down pants and put them on over your hiking pants or under a skirt when you stop. You can also wear them to bed for extra warmth when the nights become particularly cold.

Often you will arrive at your camp or hotel at 3 pm and will not dine until 6 pm, so unless you choose to do some exploring, there will be about three hours of sitting around before dinner. In cold weather, insulated pants make these times much more comfortable.

Nylon Windbreaker Strong winds are rare in the places visited by most treks, but a windbreaker is helpful in light wind, light rain and drizzle, when a poncho is really not necessary. If you already have a waterproof jacket as your 'outer layer', you don't need another shell garment. Your windbreaker should breathe, otherwise perspiration cannot evaporate and you will become soaked. A windbreaker is more in the line of emergency gear. If there is a strong wind, you must have it, otherwise you will probably not use it. If you can afford it, or spend a lot of time in the outdoors, a Gore-Tex parka is a good investment.

Nylon Wind Pants The temperature will often be approaching 30°C and most people prefer to hike in shorts except in the early morning when it is chilly. Wind pants are popular because they provide the best of both worlds. Wear them over your shorts or under your skirt in the morning, then remove them to hike in lighter gear during the day. Most wind pants have special cuffs that allow you to remove them without taking off your shoes.

You can substitute ski warm-up pants, or even cotton jogging pants, for both wind pants and down-filled pants. The cost will be lower and there is hardly any sacrifice in versatility or comfort.

Hiking Pants Almost any long pants will do. Many women wear tights under their skirt in order to stay both warm and culturally inoffensive.

T-shirts or Blouses You'll spend a lot of time walking in short sleeves – what the equipment catalogues call the first layer. Cotton garments are fine, but if you can afford (and find) a synthetic T-shirt, you will be much more comfortable. You will perspire excessively, and a polypropylene (with brand names like Capilene and Thermax) shirt wicks the moisture away from your skin. This means that when you put your rucksack on after a rest stop your back is not cold and damp. The wicking effect also makes a Gore-Tex parka work better.

Long Underwear Long johns are a useful addition to your equipment. A complete set makes a good warm pair of pyjamas and is also useful during late-night emergency trips outside your tent. Unless the weather is especially horrible, you will not need them to walk in during the day. You can bring only the bottoms and use a woollen shirt for a pyjama top. Cotton underwear is OK, though wool or polyester is much warmer.

Woollen Hat or Balaclava A balaclava is ideal because it can serve as a warm hat or you can roll it down to cover most of your face and neck. You may even need to wear it to bed on cold nights. Because much of your

body heat is lost through your head, a warm hat helps keep your entire body warmer.

Gloves Warm ski gloves are suitable for a trek. You might consider taking along a pair of woollen mittens also, just in case your gloves get wet.

Gaiters There is an enormous amount of mud on the trails of Bhutan, and a pair of high gaiters is a must to help keep your boots and socks clean and dry.

Other Equipment
Rucksack A backpack should have a light internal frame to stiffen the bag and a padded waistband to keep it from bouncing around and to take some weight off your shoulders. There are many advantages to keeping your pack small. It will prevent you from trying to carry too much during the day, is handy to carry on a plane and will fit easily inside your tent at night.

Sleeping Bag Buy the best sleeping bag that you can afford, and be sure it is large enough. It is quite cold from November to March, even in the lowlands, so a warm sleeping bag is a very worthwhile investment. You cannot rent a sleeping bag in Bhutan; you must bring your own.

Water Bottle By day your bottle provides the only completely safe source of cold drinking water. If you use iodine, fill your water bottle from streams, add the iodine and have cold safe water half an hour later.

Torch (Flashlight) Almost any torch will do, though many people prefer a headlamp – which is particularly useful for reading or when finding a toilet. Spare batteries are almost impossible to find during a trek, so bring a supply with you. Larger batteries perform better in the cold than small penlight cells, but they are heavier.

Duffel Bag You will need a strong duffel bag to pack your gear. Several companies make good duffel bags with a zipper along the side for easy entry. This is not an item to economise on; get a bag that is durable and has a strong zipper. A duffel 35cm in diameter and about 75cm long is large enough to carry your gear and will usually meet the weight limit of pack animals and domestic flights – typically 15kg. Army surplus duffel bags are cheaper, but they are inconvenient because they only open from the end, although there is no zipper to jam or break. In Bhutan your duffel bag is placed inside a jute sack keep them from getting wrecked by the pack animals.

During the day, you will carry your camera, water bottle, extra clothing and a small first-aid kit in your backpack. Do not overload the backpack, especially on the first day of the trek.

Your duffel bag will sit on the back of a horse or yak all day; when it rains, it will get wet. Pack it in a way that important items stay dry during rainstorms. A waterproof duffel bag and waterproof nylon or plastic bags inside your bag are both necessary. Given the high likelihood of rain in Bhutan, it would not be unreasonable to pack your gear in a waterproof river bag.

Use a small padlock that will fit through the zipper pull and fasten to a ring sewn to the bag. The lock will protect the contents from pilferage during the flight to and from Bhutan and will help protect the contents on your trek.

Extra Duffel Bag or Suitcase When starting a trek, you will leave your city clothes and other items in the storeroom of your hotel or travel agent. Bring a small suitcase or extra duffel bag with a lock to use for this purpose.

Stuff Bags It is unlikely that you will be able to find a completely waterproof duffel bag or backpack. Using coated nylon stuff bags helps you to separate your gear, thereby lending an element of organisation to the daily chaos in your tent or hotel. Stuff sacks also provide additional protection in case of rain. If you get stuff bags with drawstrings, the addition of spring-loaded clamps

will save a lot of frustration trying to untie the knots you tied in too much haste in the morning. You can also use plastic garbage bags, but these are much more fragile. A plastic bag inside each stuff sack is a good bet during the rainy season.

Sunglasses or Goggles The sun reflects brilliantly off snow, making good goggles or sunglasses with side protection essential. At high altitude they are so essential that you should have an extra pair in case of breakage or loss. A pair of regular sunglasses can serve as a spare if you rig a side shield. The lenses should be as dark as possible. At 5000m, the sun is intense and ultraviolet rays can severely damage unprotected eyes. Store your goggles in a metal case as, even in your backpack, it is easy to crush them.

Sunblock During April and May and at high altitudes throughout the year, sunburn can be severe. Use a protective sunblock; those with more sensitive skin need a total sunblock such as zinc oxide cream. Snow glare at high altitude is a real hazard; you'll need a good sunblock, not just suntan lotion.

To protect your lips at high altitude you need a total sunblock such as Dermatone or Labiosan.

Additional Items There is not much to say about soap, scissors and the like, but a few ideas may help. If there are two people travelling, divide a lot of this material to save weight and bulk.

Indian laundry soap in bars is available in Bhutan. This avoids an explosion of liquid or powdered soap in your luggage.

Pre-moistened towelettes are great for a last-minute hand wash before dinner. You can avoid many stomach problems by washing frequently. If you bring a supply of these, check the way they are packaged. You can buy them in a plastic container and avoid leaving a trail of foil packets in your wake.

A pair of scissors on your pocket knife is useful. Also bring a sewing kit and some safety pins – lots of uses.

Put all your medicines and toiletries in plastic bottles with screw-on lids. If in doubt, reread the section on the treatment duffel bags receive.

Bring a cigarette lighter or matches so you can burn your used toilet paper. You might also bring a small shovel or trowel to dig a toilet hole when you get caught on the trail with no toilet nearby.

Be sure you have the wherewithal to deal with blisters, and carry this with you at all times. It's important to treat blisters as soon as you discover them.

Optional Equipment & Toys The equipment checklist suggests several items that you might bring on a trek. Do not carry all of them as you will overload your backpack.

Cameras Your camera can be anything from a tiny point-and-shoot to a heavy Hasselblad. While most trekkers do bring a camera, it is equally enjoyable to trek without one.

A trek is long, dusty and damp. Carry lens caps, lens tissue and a brush to clean the camera and lenses as frequently as possible.

Three lenses: a wide angle (28mm or 35mm), a standard lens (50mm or 55mm) and a telephoto lens (135mm or 200mm) are useful but heavy. Since you will probably carry them in your backpack day after day, you may want to limit your selection. If you must make a choice, you will find a telephoto (or zoom) lens is more useful than a wide angle, because it will allow you close-up pictures of wildlife, mountains and portraits of shy people. A polarising filter is a very useful accessory. Insure your camera equipment.

ON THE TREK
Pack Animals

There is a well-organised system for arranging pack animals in Bhutan. Contractors at the starting point of each trek arrange for horses to carry the loads. The owners of the horses accompany the trek to load the animals and see that they get where they are supposed to each day. The ancient *dolam* system in Bhutan defines specific grazing grounds allocated to each village. For this reason, pack animals are not allowed to cross district boundaries. Messages are sent ahead so that replacement animals are, hopefully, waiting at the boundary. At higher elevations yaks, not horses, carry the loads.

Food, tents and camp gear is packed in large rectangular, covered baskets called *zhim*, which are then lashed to a wooden pack saddle. Trekkers' duffel bags are usually placed inside a jute sack for protection and then tied onto the animals. The process of saddling and loading the animals in the morning is a slow and tedious chore. Each trek is supposed to be accompanied by a riding horse for emergency use.

You won't have much to do with your pack animals, except at camp, but you will probably pass them, and other pack animals, along the trail. You can just stand off to the side to let horses pass, but with yaks you must get as far as possible off to the side because they are much more skittish and won't pass if you are close to them. Be sure to stand on the uphill side of the trail so you don't get pushed off as the animals pass.

Because yaks do not do well below 2500m, horses are the mode of transport below the tree line. Yak herders like to keep their animals out of the roadside settlements such as Drukgyel Dzong near Paro because yaks are not used to crowds of people and most have never seen motorised vehicles. It's a real problem when the yaks bolt off into the brush, dragging the loads behind them.

Guides & Camp Staff

A small, but efficient, trek staff accompanies you. If you are trekking with a small group, the guide and cook will team up to handle the logistics. With a large group, the team will include a 'trek organiser' who will see that the loads are packed, tents set up and pack animals loaded on time. English names, not Dzongkha, are used for the various job titles. In addition to the cook and guide, there will be one or more 'waiters' who serve food and handle the kitchen chores.

Be sure you have the itinerary, including rest days, worked out in advance. Messages are sent ahead to arrange pack animals and,

Quick Reference Trek List

Trek	Start	End	Days	Maximum Elevation (m)
Dagala Thousand Lakes Trek	Chhuzom	Simtokha	7	4500
Druk Path	Paro	Thimphu	6	4210
Jhomolhari Trek 1	Drukgyel Dzong	Thimphu	9	4890
Jhomolhari Trek 2	Drukgyel Dzong	Drukgyel Dzong	8	4890
Laya-Gasa Trek	Drukgyel Dzong	Tashithang	14	5005
Gasa Hot Spring Trek	Tashithang	Tashithang	5	2430
Snowman Trek	Drukgyel Dzong	Sephu	23	5140
Gangte Trek	Phobjikha Valley	Tikke Zampa	3	3440
Bumthang Cultural Trek	Toktu Zampa	Mesitang	3	3360
Duer Hot Spring Trek	Toktu Zampa	Toktu Zampa	8	4700
Rodang La Trek	Toktu Zampa	Trashi Yangtse	10	4160
Samtengang Winter Trek	Punakha	Wangdue Phodrang	5	1500

if you don't meet them on the specified day, they might not wait for you. A trek is structured according to a prearranged itinerary and the Bhutanese guides expect to arrive at certain camp sites on schedule.

Most Bhutanese trekking guides are true professionals. They are all licensed by TAB and are accommodating as long as they understand what you want. If you don't wish to follow their daily routine, decide early in the trek. A routine, once established with the crew, is difficult to change.

How Far & How Difficult

As you discuss the following day's trek with a guide or horsemen, be aware of how they think. In their minds a 'hard' day is one that has a lot of walking and covers a long distance, and an 'easy' day does not. Most Bhutanese totally ignore the issue of elevation gain as they discuss the difficulty of a trail. Most westerners evaluate a walk in exactly the opposite way: a long, level walk is easy and a short, steep climb is difficult.

Routefinding

It isn't easy to get totally lost in the hills, but it has happened to some trekkers, and there are very few people around who can help you find the correct trail. If you are on a major trekking route, the trail is usually well defined and there is only one route, though there may be a few confusing short cuts. Watch for the lug sole footprints of other trekkers or for arrows carved into the trail and marked on rocks by guides with trekking parties. You can also use the footprints and dung of your pack animals to confirm that you are on the correct trail. If you find yourself going a long way down when the trail should be going up, if the trail vanishes, or if you suddenly find yourself alone, *stop and wait for the rest of your party to catch up*.

RESPONSIBLE TREKKING

Bhutan's trekking rules require that your staff carry a supply of fuel for cooking. Until the 1996 season the use of wood was allowed. The horsemen and yak drivers who live here sometimes violate the code and cook their own meals over wood. This is theoretically prohibited, but it's a hard rule to enforce.

Camp fires are prohibited, and you should decline the offer if your staff suggests one. It's sometimes a problem deciding what to do if the packers build a fire or if one appears as part of a 'cultural show' in a village.

Considerations for Responsible Trekking

Trekking places great pressure on wilderness areas and you must take special care when trekking to help preserve the ecology and beauty of Bhutan. The following tips are just good sense, but they are also mandated by TAB, and you, or your guide, could be fined for not observing them.

Rubbish

- Carry out all your rubbish. If you've carried it in you can carry it out. Don't overlook those easily forgotten items, such as silver paper, cigarette butts and plastic wrappers. Empty packaging weighs very little and should be stored in a dedicated rubbish bag. Make an effort to carry out rubbish left by others.
- Minimise the waste you must carry out by taking minimal packaging and taking no more than you will need. If you can't buy in bulk, unpack small-portion packages and combine their contents in one container before your trek. Take re-useable containers or stuff sacks.
- Don't rely on bought water in plastic bottles. Disposal of these bottles is creating a major problem, particularly in developing countries. Use iodine crystals or purification tablets instead.
- Sanitary napkins, tampons and condoms should also be carried out despite the inconvenience. They burn and decompose poorly.

Human Waste Disposal

- Contamination of water sources by human faeces can lead to the transmission of hepatitis, typhoid and intestinal parasites. It can cause severe health risks not only to members of your party, but also to local residents and wildlife.
- A toilet tent will be set up at each camp; please use it.
- Where there is none, bury your waste. Dig a small hole 15cm deep and at least 100m from any watercourse. Consider carrying a lightweight trowel for this purpose. Cover the waste with soil and a rock. Use toilet paper sparingly and bury it with the waste. In snow, dig down to the soil otherwise your waste will be exposed when the snow melts.

Washing

- Don't use detergents or toothpaste in or near watercourses, even if they are biodegradable. For personal washing, use biodegradable soap and a basin at least 50m away from the water-

Environmental Problems

The main reason for the destruction of forests throughout the Himalayan hill region is the pressure of a population that requires natural vegetation for food, fodder, fuel and even shelter. Because of Bhutan's low population and the steepness of the hills, much of the country has remained undeveloped and trees have been preserved, though pressures from logging are still a threat. Bhutan's extensive forestation has prevented the devastating landslides that are typical in the rest of the Himalayan foothills.

Near villages, however, firewood is har-

vested. The lack of infrastructure, combined with the lack of any local deposits of fossil fuels, allows no easy alternative. About 70% of Bhutan's total domestic energy consumption comes from wood. The inevitable result of the destruction of forests is an increase in erosion and extensive loss of topsoil.

What You Can Do to Help

Try to follow the guidelines in the boxed text. If your trek staff is not digging the pits for toilets deep enough, or not filling them in properly, the time to solve that problem is on the spot. It does no good to go home and

course. Widely disperse the wastewater to allow the soil to filter it fully before it finally makes it back to the watercourse.

Erosion
- Hillsides and mountain slopes, especially at high altitudes, are prone to erosion. It is important to stick to existing tracks and avoid short cuts that bypass a switchback. If you blaze a new trail straight down a slope it will turn into a watercourse with the next heavy rainfall and eventually cause soil loss and deep scarring.
- If a well-used track passes through a mud patch, walk through the mud: walking around the edge will increase the size of the patch.
- Avoid removing the plant life that keeps the topsoil in place.

Fires
- The use of wood fires by trekking groups is forbidden in Bhutan. The trekking outfitter is required to carry gas cylinders and stoves to prepare all meals for the trekkers and the staff.
- There is a tremendous amount of wood lying around, and guides might offer to make a campfire. Refuse this offer, because it defeats the entire purpose of carrying cooking gas in the first place. Be sure you have enough warm clothing and you won't need to stand around a fire.

Wildlife Conservation
- Don't buy items made from endangered species.
- Don't assume animals in huts to be nonindigenous vermin and attempt to exterminate them. In wild places they are likely to be protected native animals.
- Discourage the presence of wildlife in camp by not leaving food scraps behind you.
- Do not disturb or feed wildlife or do anything to destroy their natural habitat.

Cultural Conservation
- Respect the culture and traditions of local people, whether these are villagers, your own camp staff or your horse drivers.
- Do not give candy, money, medicines or gifts to local people, particularly children as this encourages begging.
- Do not buy local household items or religious artefacts from villagers.

write a letter complaining about something that could have been easily solved by some simple assistance and instructions from you.

Trash Fires Bhutanese trek staff usually dispose of trash properly and are concerned about preserving the landscape, but the horsemen or yak drivers often have a less sophisticated approach. Burning garbage can be offensive to deities, especially within sight of a sacred mountain such as Jhomolhari. Be aware of this cultural issue and try to arrange for trash to be packed out, burned or disposed of in a way that does not cause offence.

Trekking Disclaimer
Although the authors and publisher have done their utmost to ensure the accuracy of all information in this guide, they cannot accept responsibility for any loss, injury or inconvenience sustained by people using this book. They cannot guarantee that the routes described here have not become impassable for any reason in the interval between research and publication. The fact that a trek or area is described does not mean that it is safe for your trekking party. You are ultimately responsible for judging your own capabilities in the light of the conditions you encounter.

TREKKING

Dagala Thousand Lakes Trek

This is a short trek, near Thimphu, to a large number of lovely high altitude lakes. The trek is not difficult and most trekking days are short but there are some long steep climbs.

It is not a popular route, and you will probably encounter no other trekkers.

Season
The recommended times for this trek are April, September and October.

Access
It's a 29km drive from Thimphu to the junction of a rough, unpaved road leading to the starting point. If you are in a 4WD vehicle, you can drive 1.5km up a rough road to a BHU at Khoma (2850m), otherwise you can walk, making a gradual climb on the rough road. Villagers in this region collect and sell matsutake and chantarelle mushrooms.

Day 1: Khoma to Geynikha
14km, 4 hours
Start walking along the road, which soon becomes a trail across terraced paddy fields and through coniferous forest, to the settlement of Geynikha (2950m). The route then descends to a chorten that marks a camping place alongside a stream at 2800m.

Day 2: Geynikha to Gur
5km, 4 hours
Crossing a suspension bridge, the trail heads west for a while, then climbs steeply towards the south to a rock platform and a crest at 3200m. A further walk of about two hours leads to a camp in a forest clearing at 3350m.

Day 3: Gur to Labatamba
12km, 5 hours
A long stiff climb leads up the ridge and across meadows to a pass at 4240m for a spectacular view of the whole Dagala range. This is now yak country. You will pass several herders camps en route to the foot of the broad Labatamba valley at 4050m. Climb beside a stream to a camp at 4300m near Utsho lake, where plenty of golden trout flourish. The high altitude area near the lakes is a mass of wild alpine flowers in September.

You should schedule an extra day here to walk to the numerous lakes in the vicinity and perhaps do some trout fishing.

Day 4: Labatamba to Panka
8km, 4 hours
There are two possible routes and the pack animals will take the lower one. The trekking route is not well marked, and is more of a cross-country traverse. It climbs along the western side of the lake to a saddle at 4500m, where there are good mountain views. If you want a better view, you could scramble to the top of a 4700m peak to the east. From the pass there is a steep descent to another lake at 4350m. A short distance beyond the lake you rejoin the trail and follow it through meadows out of the valley to Panka at 4000m. Because

there is a water problem here during spring, it may be necessary to continue to an alternate camp 30 minutes beyond.

Day 6: Panka to Talakha
8km, 4 hours
The route leads north crossing a pass at 4000m, then climbs along the side of a ridge to a crest at 4270m. From here there is a view of the Dagala range and a view of Thimphu, far to the north. It is then a long descent through forests to the goemba and village of Talakha (3080m).

Day 7: Talakha to Simtokha
3km, 3 hours
You can arrange to have vehicles pick you up at Talakha or you can walk downhill on a steep, eroded trail to Simtokha. The trail descends steeply through mixed forest of rhododendron and bamboo, finally dropping through a maze of apple orchards to the roadhead above Simtokha Dzong.

Druk Path

Although this is a short trek, it still goes to high altitude, making it moderately strenuous.

It is possible to shorten this trek but you must be in good enough shape to walk for more than eight hours a day. With the shorter schedule you would camp at Jili La, Jimilang Tsho and Phajoding, arriving in Thimphu on the fourth day. Some agents modify the Druk Path into a four-day trek in the reverse direction, starting at Motithang and ending by hiking down from Jimilang Tsho to the roadhead at Tsaluna.

Season
This trek is usually possible from late February to June and from September to December, though snow sometimes closes the route in late autumn and early spring. Days are normally warm, but nights can be very cold at times and in winter there is often snow. Avoid the monsoon season of July and August.

Access

There are two possible starting points. Yours will depend on what arrangements have been made with the horse owners. Drive north from Paro town up the Do Chhu valley and cross the river. Most groups start walking from Dopshare, near the gravel pit on the eastern side of the river at 2300m but you can save some climbing if you continue up the road towards the National Museum (Ta Dzong) to a trailhead at 2510m.

Day 1: Dopshare to Jili Dzong
10km, 4 hours

Start with a short walk to Jili Dzong, which you can see atop a ridge above Paro. From Dopshare the trail crosses a brook and makes a long, gradual climb to a wooded crest. It's then a gentle walk along the ridge to a camp site in a yak pasture at 3450m. If you are coming from Ta Dzong, it is a one hour gentle walk to a fork in the trail. Take the left-hand trail and climb steeply to the camp. Above the camp is **Jili La** (3490m) and Jili Dzong, which is mostly in ruins, though there is a *lhakhang* with a statue of Sakyamuni. You can visit the courtyard, but there is no resident caretaker, and you probably cannot get into the building itself. If the weather is clear, the Paro valley can be seen with Jhomolhari and other snow-capped peaks in the distance.

Day 2: Jili Dzong to Jangchu Lakha
10km, 3-4 hours

After crossing the pass the route stays below the ridge, climbing through thick alpine forest and rhododendron to a saddle at 3590m. It then follows the ridge, making many ups and downs, staying just above the tree line. The trail goes from one side of the ridge to the other, following it north to a yak herders camp at Jangchu Lakha, 3780m. There are views of Jhomolhari and other snow peaks, and you are likely to see or hear some monal pheasants during the day.

Day 3: Jangchu Lakha to Jimilang Tsho
11km, 4 hours

The trail follows the ridge for about 1½ hours to a saddle at 4040m, then drops a bit and follows the ridge back to Jangchu La at 4180m. Descend to a camp at 3880m, close to the large Jimilang Tsho (Sand Ox Lake), named for a bull that emerged from the lake and joined the cattle of a family that uses the area as a summer grazing ground. The lake is also known for its giant trout (which some people believe were taken to Bhutan by early British visitors). There are good views of 6989m Jichu Drake, the peak representing the protective deity of Paro, to the west.

It is possible to cut the trek short by descending towards the east through a forest of blue pine to the road at Tsaluna, above Bjimena. This route passes Tsalu Ney, a 14th century lhakhang on the site of a cave where Guru Rimpoche meditated.

Day 4: Jimilang Tsho to Simkota Tsho
11km, 4 hours

The trail climbs through dwarf rhododendron to the lake of Janye Tsho, another yak herders camp. It's a short climb along the side of the ridge and then a short, steep descent to camp at 4040m, close to Simkota Tsho, where there is another chance to fish for trout.

Day 5: Simkota Tsho to Phajoding
10km, 3-4 hours

The day begins with a gradual climb to a saddle at 4180m. A short descent leads past another small lake, then the trail climbs to Phume La (4210m), where you are greeted by a vast array of prayer flags. Weather permitting, there are views of Gangkhar Puensum and other Himalayan peaks here. Below sprawls the entire Thimphu valley. The route then descends past Thujidrag Goemba, a meditation centre that hangs on the side of a precipitous rock face. The descent continues through juniper trees to a camp site beside a community hall near Phajoding Goemba, an important pilgrimage site at 3870m.

Day 6: Phajoding to Thimphu
4-5km, 3 hours

The trek is all downhill through forest. Follow a steep trail to the road near the old Motithang Hotel or stay on the ridge and meet your vehicles at the radio tower above Thimphu.

Jhomolhari Trek 1

There are two versions of this trek and TAB counts them as two separate treks. The shorter and easier version (Trek 2) is a three-day trek from Paro to the Jhomolhari Base Camp at Jangothang, returning to Paro via the same route or by an alternative trail. The longer version crosses two high passes from Jangothang and makes its way to Thimphu.

The views of 7314m Jhomolhari from Jangothang are spectacular. This trek also affords an excellent opportunity to see yaks.

Season

This trek is best from April to June and September to November. Days are normally warm, but nights can be very cold, especially above Jangothang. There is a lot of mud on this trek and it can be pretty miserable in the rain. Snow usually closes the high passes in mid to late November and they don't reopen until April.

Access

Drive up Paro valley to the end of the road at Drukgyel Dzong ruins, where the white peak of Jhomolhari beacons in the distance.

Day 1: Drukgyel Dzong to Sharna Zampa 17km 5-6 hours

The first three days of the trek follow the Paro Chhu valley, climbing gently with only a few short, steep climbs over side ridges.

The trek starts from Drukgyel Dzong at 2580m with a short downhill walk on a wide trail. After descending about 100m, you reach the river where a primitive stone bath has been carved into the bank. Look back and see how well positioned the dzong was to keep watch over this valley.

A short distance upriver is the small settlement of Chang Zampa. A bridge (*zam*) crosses to river left here. Don't cross it: the trek stays on the south bank (river right). The fields on this side of the river are planted with potatoes and wheat; on the opposite side of the river, it's rice.

A short walk takes you to the settlement of Mitshi Zampa, where there's a little hotel and shop. Just beyond the shop the route crosses to the left bank of the clear, fast-flowing Paro Chhu via a short suspension bridge.

The trail climbs very gently, traversing through well-maintained rice terraces and fields of millet. It's a well-worn trail with lots of round stones and irrigation water running down it. A short walk through a forest of blue pines leads to Sangatung, a pleasant farmhouse surrounded by fields near a small stream and a white chorten.

The route now enters an area of apple orchards and forests and the trail is littered with rocks sticking out of the mud. On some parts of the trail logs have been placed in washboard fashion. In other places it's necessary to leap from rock to rock to keep your feet dry. When it's not muddy, the trail is deep in dust. Don't cross the cantilever bridge that leads to the south; stay on river left, climbing gently to Chobiso, a single house at 2800m.

Soon the valley widens and you reach the army post of **Gunyitsawa** at 2810m. There is also a primary school and shops here. This is the last stop before Tibet; all army personnel and civilians are required to report to the checkpost. The trek permit that your tour operator arranged will be checked and endorsed here; wait for your guide so that the registration formalities can be completed. The large dormitory-style buildings across the river is quarters for enlisted men and their families.

Just below the shop at Gunyitsawa the trail crosses the Paro Chhu to river right on a wooden cantilever bridge. It then climbs a little to the rustic little village of Sharna Zampa. On the opposite side of the river you can see a helicopter pad and archery field. At 2870m, just beyond Sharna Zampa, are several good camping places in meadows surrounded by trees.

Day 2: Sharna Zampa to Thangthangka 22km, 6-7 hours

The trail continues its gradual climb alongside the Paro Chhu through conifers and rhododendron. In places it is quite close to the river; if the water is high you might have to climb over a few small hills to get around places where the water has flowed onto the trail. About 15 minutes beyond Sharna Zampa are the remnants of an old bridge with a house and a chorten on the other side. At this point the route enters Jigme Dorji National Park.

The trail makes a continuous, but gentle, climb on a rocky trail through oaks, rhododendron and ferns, crossing several small streams. About two hours from camp is Shing Karap, a stone house and a clearing at 3110m. This is where most guides choose to serve lunch. Some distance beyond is the route to the Tremo La, which is the stone-paved trail leading off to the left. This is the old invasion and trade route from Phari Dzong in Tibet. Don't take this inviting-looking trail: several trekkers have done so in the past and made a long, exhausting side trip to nowhere. Immediately after the trail junction is a wooden bridge over a substantial side stream.

Climb a short set of switchbacks over a little ridge, then descend and cross the Paro Chhu on a wooden cantilever bridge at 3230m to river left. The route up this side of the river goes up and down on a rocky trail through forests of birch and fir. There are numerous short climbs and descents, and one small slide area to cross. There is not much elevation gain, but the continual little 5-10m ups and downs add up to a fair amount of uphill during the day. Among the tree species along this part of the trail are blue pine, maple and larch.

Finally there's a bridge back to river right of the Paro Chhu at 3560m. The trail climbs to a place where you can see a white chorten on the opposite side of the river. There is a bridge here that leads back across the river, but don't cross it. Follow the trail on river right uphill over a small ridge as the Paro Chhu makes a noticeable bend. Fifteen minutes from the bridge is a lovely meadow with Jhomolhari looming at the head of the valley. This is Thangthangka, elevation 3630m. There is a small stone shelter and a Bhutanese-style house in a cedar grove at the edge of the meadow.

Day 3: Thangthangka to Jangothang
19km, 5-6 hours

This is not a long day, but there is a 450m elevation gain, and you will be comfortably worn out when you reach camp. Jhomolhari was probably covered with clouds when you arrived last night. Be sure to get up early for a view. As you climb beyond the camp, Jhomolhari disappears behind a ridge. Less than an hour from camp, at 3730m, is an army post with rough stone barracks and a small prayer wheel. It's amazing to see the number of trees they have felled here to keep the post going.

The trail crosses a wooden bridge over a fast-flowing stream a short distance beyond the army post. The hillside on the opposite side of the Paro Chhu is a near-vertical rock face with a few trees clinging to it. The trail along this stretch can be extremely muddy; there are lots of big stones that you can use to rock-hop along the trail. At 3770m, about an hour from camp, the trail turns sharply right at a whitewashed *mani* wall.

A short climb leads to a small chorten on a ridge. You are now entering yak country and you will see these huge beasts lumbering across the hillside and lazing about in meadows alongside the trail. One of the products made from yak milk is dried cheese called *chugo*. They string the cheese in a necklace of white blocks.

There are two trails, an upper and a lower route; both contour up the valley from the chorten and end up near the riverbank, following the bottom of the valley as it makes a sharp bend to the right. Parts of the hillside are covered with larch, which turns a light yellow in the autumn. Above the trail is the village of **Soe**. You cannot see it until you are beyond and above it, but you may meet people herding yaks near the river.

An hour beyond Soe is the settlement of **Takethang**, a cluster of stone houses on a plateau at 3940m. The villagers grow barley and a large succulent plant called kashaykoni that is fed to the yaks during the winter.

The trail follows straight across the plateau, quite high above the river. It then crosses a little stream on a bridge made of big stones laid on some logs. On the opposite side are a white chorten and the few houses of **Dangochang**. The people of this village grow potatoes, turnips and radishes and keep a few sheep. This area is snowbound from mid-November till the end of March; one resident said that the snow is so deep that they have to pee out of the second storey window, but this sounds like another Bhutanese myth.

It is slow going uphill beside a side stream to the camp at Jangothang, 4090m and a spectacular view of Jhomolhari. The ruins of a small fortress sit atop a rock in the middle of the side valley that leads north-west to Jhomolhari. A chain of snow peaks forms the eastern side of the Paro Chhu valley.

There's one small hut and a larger community hall with a kitchen and a large flat spot for camping. This is a popular trek route and Jangothang is one of the most spectacular camping places in the entire Himalaya. You are unlikely to have the camp to yourself.

The guidelines for pack animals require that you exchange your horses for yaks from

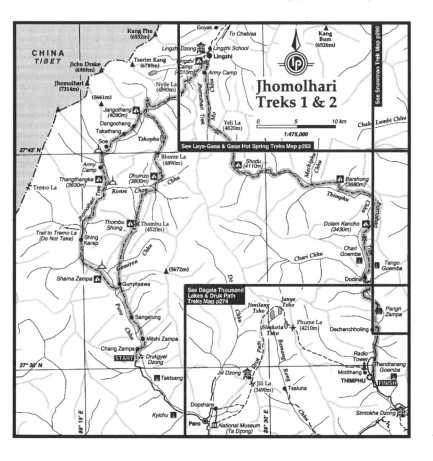

Soe. Don't be alarmed when your loads get dumped at the camp and the animals disappear down the valley, leaving you alone with a mountain of baggage. The yaks *will* show up on schedule when you are ready to leave.

Day 4: Acclimatisation & Exploration in Jangothang

If you are going on to Lingzhi, you should spend a day here for acclimatisation. If you are returning to Paro, a day in Jangothang is the highlight of the trek; the views don't get any better than here. There are lots of day hikes that you can make and a day here is very well spent.

There are four major possibilities for day hikes. The first is a three to four hour excursion up the ridge to the north of the camp. There's no trail, but it's a broad open slope and you can just scramble up it. The ridge is endless, but after an hour or so of climbing there is a good view of Jichu Drake (6989m), though the upper part of the ridge blocks the view of Jhomolhari.

A second alternative is to go up towards the head of the valley in the direction of Jhomolhari. There is a very rough overgrown trail that cuts across moraines and through brush that leads to the foot of the mountain. You can't get very far, but there are good views in the upper part of the valley.

A third hike, which can be combined with the walk up the ridge, is to trek up the main valley towards the last house, then continue up the valley towards Jichu Drake. You will see much of this country if you trek over Nyile La to Lingzhi.

The last alternative is a fishing expedition to Tshophu, a high-altitude lake. High on the opposite side of the river to the east is a bowl with a lake that has a good supply of spotted trout. To get to the fishing lake, follow the trail north to the last settlement in the valley. Below the houses you can spot a bridge and see the trail that heads up the opposite side of the valley. At the top is a big cirque and the lake. It takes about 1½ hours to get to the top of the ridge and then another half hour following a stream to the lake.

Typical fishing gear is a tin can with some line and a spinner. A fishing licence costs Nu 15 per day for Bhutanese, more for foreigners, but the game warden doesn't come by this lake very often. The desire for variety in meals often outweighs Buddhist sentiment and you may discover that one of your staff has gone on a fishing expedition and produced fresh fish for dinner.

Day 5: Jangothang to Lingzhi 18km, 5-6 hours

The remainder of this trek crosses two high passes. If you are having problems with the altitude at Jangothang, don't go on to Lingzhi.

Ten minutes beyond the camp are three stone houses inhabited by a few elderly people. This is the last settlement in the valley and it's an extremely isolated place. Near the houses the trail turns a corner and there's a spectacular view of Jichu Drake.

Descend a little and cross a log bridge to the left bank of the Paro Chhu, then start up a steep traverse that heads back downstream. The trail crests at the foot of a large side valley and follows the valley eastwards. Jichu Drake towers above the Paro Chhu valley and soon the top of Jhomolhari appears over the ridge above the camp at Jangothang. The third snow peak in the middle is a secondary summit of Jhomolhari.

At 4470m the trail traverses under the big rocks that were visible from the camp, leads to the left and enters a large east-west glacial valley with numerous moraines. The trees have been left far below; there are a few small gentians, but otherwise it's just grass, tundra and small juniper bushes.

There is a false summit with a cairn at 4680m. As the trail approaches the ridge you can see the snow peak of Tserim Kang, elevation 6789m, to the north. After a very short downhill stretch the trail climbs further up a moraine and offers spectacular views of the sharp ridge that juts out from Jichu Drake. You can see the prayer flags on the pass far above.

The final pull is up a slope of very small rocks called scree to **Nyile La** at 4890m, about four hours from the camp. If you're ambitious you can climb the ridge to the north-west and go even higher. On one side of the ridge you can see the peaks of Jhomolhari and Jichu Drake; on the other side is Tserim Kang. There is a view of Lingzhi village in the valley far below.

As the Nyile La is frequently very windy, you probably won't stay long on the pass. The descent is through more scree along the side of the hill. This makes it awkward and uncomfortable to walk because the trail slopes outward as it traverses the side of the hill.

It's a long descent to a stream on the floor of a side valley at 4450m. There is some vegetation here, mostly grass, juniper and cotoneaster. This is an excellent place to stop for lunch.

The trail now travels north, contouring along the side of the hill high above the floor of the main valley. The river that flows below is a tributary of the Mo Chhu, and is known locally as the Mo Chhu, flows northward before making a turn and joining the southward-flowing Mo Chhu south of Gasa. The opposite hillside is completely covered with rhododendron. It's a long traverse on a good trail with a couple of little ups, but mostly down and level. Eventually you can see an army camp in the valley that you will traverse tomorrow if you are following the Jhomolhari trek to Thimphu. Lingzhi Dzong is visible on the top of a ridge in the distance.

Walk along the side of the hill to a lookout at 4370m, then descend steeply into yet another side valley. There are a lot of switchbacks on the rocky trail as it makes its way down through heavy stands of rhododendron and oak to a yak pasture on the valley floor. Tserim Kang towers over the head of the valley and there are some remarkable examples of moraines in the lower part of the valley. Much of the rest of the trek is an outstanding lesson in physical geography, with several good examples of both terminal and lateral moraines.

The camp is at 4010m, near a large stone community hall that is used by both Bhutanese travellers and trekking groups. Higher up in the valley is a small monastery, but it's not visible from the trail.

If you take a spare day at Lingzhi, you can make an excursion to a lake near the base camp of Tserim Kang. During the hike you may encounter blue sheep and musk deer. If you are returning to Thimphu, be sure to schedule a rest day here. Lingzhi is worth visiting, and it's useful to rest up for the following strenuous trek day.

Day 6: Lingzhi to Shodu
22km, 8-9 hours

The Laya Gasa route leaves the Jhomolhari trek here and climbs the ridge opposite the camp towards the dzong. If you are following the route back to Thimphu, start early because this day is long and tiring.

The Jhomolhari Trek route climbs toward a small white chorten on a ridge above the camp, then turns south up the deep Mo Chhu valley. The trail stays on the west side of the largely treeless valley, climbing steadily a short distance above the Mo Chhu. It then crosses the river, which is now only a stream, and climbs steeply for two hours to **Yeli La** (4820m). There are two false summits and the long climb at the end of the day is tiring. Try to avoid walking with the yaks because near the pass the trail is carved into a rock cliff and is quite narrow. From the pass, on a clear day, you can see Jhomolhari, Gangchhenta, Tserim Kang and Masang Gang.

Descend alongside a stream to a shelter, then further downstream to a camp at Shodu (4110m), a meadow with a chorten.

Day 7: Shodu to Barshong
16km, 5-6 hours

The trail winds up and down gently, along the Thimphu Chhu through a steep-walled canyon with cliffs to the north and a cypress forest to the south. The route crosses the river six times on bridges built of huge logs, eventually ending up on the left bank. It makes a gradual climb for one hour to Barshong, where there is a community hall and the ruins of a small dzong. The designated camp is just below the ruins at 3680m, but it is in a swampy meadow and most groups elect to continue down to another meadow on a lower ridge.

Day 8: Barshong to Dolam Kencho
15km, 5-6 hours
The trail descends gently through a dense forest of rhododendron, birch and conifers, then drops steeply to meet the Thimphu Chhu. It stays on river left, climbing over ridges and descending to side streams. It traverses steep cliffs to Dolam Kencho, a camp among pasture land at 3430m.

Day 9: Dolam Kencho to Thimphu
8km, 3 hours
The trail goes in and out of side valleys above the Thimphu Chhu, making a long ascent through a forest of conifers and high altitude broadleaf species to a pass at 3510m. The trail then drops steeply to the river and follows it southward to the roadhead at Dodina, elevation 2600m, just opposite the bridge that leads to Chari Goemba.

Jhomolhari Trek 2

It's possible to return from Jangothang to Drukgyel Dzong by the same route and avoid high altitude. The following is an alternative route that is less strenuous than the classic Jhomolhari trek, but it still reaches an elevation that could cause altitude problems.

Days 1-4: Drukgyel Dzong to Jangothang
Follow Days 1-4 of the Jhomolhari Trek 1.

Day 5: Jangothang to Dhumzo
16km, 6-7 hours
The trail leads north to the last settlement in the valley and drops to the Paro Chhu, crossing it on a wooden bridge. Switchback up the side of the hill to a large cirque and the lake of Tshophu (4380m). Stay on the eastern side of the lake, passing a second lake as the trail gets steeper climbing to **Bhonte La** (4890m).

From the pass the route winds down a ridge with a lot of crisscrossing yak trails. It finally switchbacks down to a stream. Trek downstream to a bridge, cross to the south side of the stream and continue a short distance to a camp at 3800m.

Day 6: Dhumzo to Thombu Shong
11km, 4-5 hours
The trail climbs 100m over a ridge, then drops to another stream. Crossing that stream, the trail heads up the hillside, dropping into a small side valley before emerging onto a ridge. Here the route turns south, ascending past a few huts to **Thombu La** (4520m). A steep descent leads to Thombu Shong (4180m) with two small herders huts.

Day 7: Thombu Shong to Sharna Zampa
13km, 4-5 hours
Climb out of the valley to a crest at 4360m, then make a steep descent along the ridge, finally reaching the helipad at Gunyitsawa (2730m). Cross the river and go upstream to camp at the same place as trek Day 1.

Day 8: Sharna Zampa to Drukgyel Dzong
17km, 5-6 hours
Follow Day 1 of the Jhomolhari Trek 1 in reverse to Drukgyel Dzong.

Laya-Gasa Trek

This trek is an extension of the Jhomolhari trek and offers diverse flora and fauna, including a good opportunity to spot blue sheep. If you are lucky, you may also see takin and Bhutan's national flower, the blue poppy (see Flora & Fauna in the Facts about Bhutan chapter). It also introduces you to the unusual culture of the Layap people and offers a stop at a natural hot spring in Gasa.

Season
Snow can close the high passes on this trek, but it is generally open from April to June and mid-September to mid-November. The best trekking month in the Laya region is April.

Access
The trek begins in the Paro valley and follows the same route as the Jhomolhari trek as far as Lingzhi, then heads north into the high country.

Days 1-5: Drukgyel Dzong to Lingzhi
Follow days 1-5 of the Jhomolhari Trek 1.

Day 6: Lingzhi to Chebisa
10km, 5-6 hours
Cross the stream below the camp on a wooden bridge and climb up the opposite side to a chorten just below Lingzhi Dzong. In the valley to the east is a cluster of wood-shingled houses which is one part of Lingzhi village. If you look back at Tserim Kang you can see a very distinct rock pinnacle sticking up at the end of the east ridge.

There is a direct route that stays level and follows along the side of the hill, but you can take a short diversion and climb to **Lingzhi Dzong** to get a close look at it. From the chorten it is a short climb to the dzong, which sits at 4220m atop a ridge that separates the main valley from a side valley.

The name of Lingzhi's small dzong is Yugyel Dzong; it was built in the 17th century and played a role in controlling travel over Lingzhi La between Bhutan and Tibet. See the Western Bhutan chapter for more information about Lingzhi. From the dzong

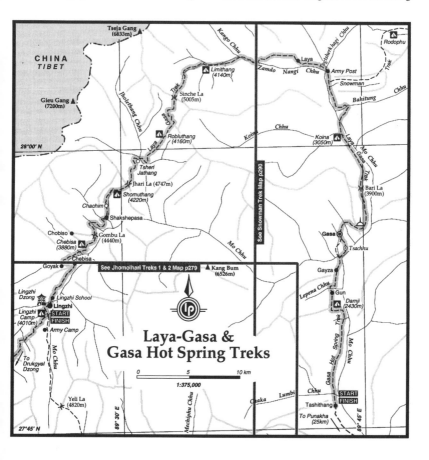

you can walk down the ridge and rejoin the lower trail.

The largest part of Lingzhi village is hidden in a valley formed by the ridge upon which the dzong was built. There are fields of wheat and barley in the upper part of the side valley. The trail crosses the lower part, where there are a few houses and at 4080m.

After a look around the village, you walk out of town on a level trail. It's a pleasant walk on a good trail along a hillside covered in flowers and juniper. Far to the north you can see the Jhari La and some of the sharp hills that you must cross to get to Laya.

The trail traverses high above the river, which flows in a valley that is so steep that there are very few houses. The path descends to cross a small stream, then continues along the side of the valley, climbing gently. This area is known for many plants of medicinal value and the entire hillside looks like a colourful herb garden.

About an hour from Lingzhi the trail reaches a cairn and prayer flags on a ridge at 4140m. The route turns into another side valley and makes a long gradual descent to the pleasant settlement of **Goyak** (3870m). In this compact village the stone houses are clustered together, unusual in Bhutan. Surrounding the village are large fields of barley.

Goyak is at the side of a stream with dramatic rock walls towering above. Leaving Goyak, the trail climbs then traverses for an hour to a chorten that overlooks another side valley. A short descent leads into the spectacular Chebisa valley, with a frozen waterfall at its head. The camp site is on a meadow just opposite Chebisa village (3880m). Just upstream of the camp is the twin village of Chobiso.

Day 7: Chebisa to Shomuthang
17km, 6-7 hours

The route climbs the ridge behind Chebisa, passing a few houses above the main part of the village, then makes a long, steep climb up a featureless slope. There are several large herds of blue sheep living in the rocks above which you are sure to spot along this part of the trail. Also watch for bearded vultures and

Himalayan griffons flying overhead. At about 4410m the trail levels out and traverses to Gombu La (4440m). It's not really a pass; it just crosses a ridge that leads off the top of the hill. From the ridge the trail descends into a side valley through a deep forest of rhododendron.

It's a long descent to a stream at 4170m, then the trail climbs again over a small ridge through a cedar forest, passing several places where the hillside burned. It's a long climb over the ridge, cresting at 4210m, then the trail descends on a muddy path into the main Jholethang Chhu valley in a deep forest of fir and birch. There's a little climb past some yak herders huts and then over the side of the valley and down to **Shakshepasa** at 3980m and a helipad, marked by a big H.

At the bottom there's a marsh and a fairly messy stream crossing with many little channels to jump across on hummocks of moss, muddy earth and rocks. On the opposite side is a good spot for lunch.

There are yak herders huts downstream, but otherwise the valley is uninhabited. The trail now goes quite steeply up the northern side of the valley. At about 4200m it levels and heads into a side valley, passing a couple of yak herders huts and traversing high above the valley floor on stream right to Chachim, a yak pasture at 4260m.

The camp is in a cluster of brush beside a stream at the bottom of the valley. There is a path that leads directly to the camp from the pasture at Chachim, but it's a steep, rough trail with a lot of bushwhacking. A longer, but better, route follows a larger trail which contours up the side of the valley past the camp. You can then drop down a side trail to Shomuthang (4220m).

This deserted spot is not a particularly good camp site but you get a head start on tomorrow's pass. If you're travelling in the opposite direction, you should camp down by the river at Shakshepasa.

Day 8: Shomuthang to Robluthang
18km, 6-7 hours

The trail climbs from the camp up the valley, starting on river right, crossing to river left and then crossing back again at 4360m. The white flowers are edelweiss and the snow peak visible to the south-east is Kang Bum (6526m).

The trail climbs out of the valley through pretty desolate country up to **Jhari La** (4747m), about two hours from camp. There are four cairns and some prayer flags here. In the distance to the north-east you can see Sinche La, the next obstacle on the route to Laya. The big snow peak to the north is 6840m Gangchhenta (Great Tiger Mountain; *ta* means tiger). Tserim Kang and the top of Jhomolhari are visible if the weather is clear.

On the north side of the pass the trail switchbacks down to a little stream at 4490m, then becomes a rough, rocky route through rhododendron on the stream's left. Soon the vegetation changes to big rhododendron, birch and firs and there are lots of little slippery loose rocks on the trail. There is a pleasant lunch spot at the bottom beside a log bridge and stream at 4050m.

Follow the stream gently downhill through bushes on stream left as it makes its way to the main valley. It's a gradual descent to a meadow by the Jholethang Chhu at 3990m. Hopefully the bridge that was not there at the time of research will have been rebuilt by the time you read this. If not, there is a small log bridge about 1km upstream, or you may be able to hitch a ride on one of your pack animals. It's also possible to wade the river, but it's cold and the river is quite fast and deep. There is a yak trail that leads up the valley towards Tibet.

The camp by the river is called **Tsheri Jathang**. Herds of takin migrate to this valley in summer and remain for about four months. Takin are very disturbed by the presence of other animals. The valley has been declared a special takin sanctuary, and yak herders have agreed not to graze their animals in the valley when the takin are here.

The trail climbs steeply on the northern side to a crest at about 4150m. It then traverses into a side valley past a tiny lake. There are good camping places in a rocky meadow named Robluthang at 4160m.

Day 9: Robluthang to Limithang
19km, 6-7 hours

This is a long, hard day, crossing Sinche La, the last and highest pass on the trek.

Over the hill, just above the camp, is a little stone house where a Laya woman lives. She'll be happy to sell you trinkets if you are in the mood for shopping; she is also the person responsible for the local arra that your guide was drinking last night. The trail climbs through the remnants of a burned forest and up the hillside through some boggy patches. It follows a set of steep switchbacks to a shelf at 4390m, then turns into another large glacial side valley. From here the pass looks a long way away – and it is.

Follow a stream for a while, crossing to stream right on an icy log bridge at 4470m, then climb onto a moraine and traverse past lots of marmot holes. You may be able to spot blue sheep high on the slopes to the north before the trail crosses back to stream left. Another climb through rocks leads to the foot of the pass at 4720m.

It's a tough climb from here to the pass because the high altitude will slow you down considerably. Passing a false summit with a cairn, the trail levels out a little before reaching some rock cairns and prayer flags on **Sinche La** (5005m), about five hours from camp. The snow-covered peak of Gangchhenta fills the horizon to the north.

The descent is on a rough, rocky trail that follows a moraine into another glacial valley. Lots of small rocks on the path keep sliding out and threatening to twist your ankle. Eventually you arrive at the Kango Chhu, a stream below a terminal moraine that forms the end of another valley to the west.

Cross the Kango Chhu to stream left on a small log bridge at 4470m. A short distance beyond the stream crossing is a yak pasture and camping spot next to a huge rock. It's best to continue to Limithang to camp; follow the valley northward, staying high as the stream falls away below you.

The valley from Gangchhenta enters from the north-west and provides more lessons in glaciology. There is a huge terminal moraine and a glacial lake at the foot of the valley. You can see classic examples of lateral moraines where the glacier has pushed rocks up on both sides of the valley.

Beyond an uninhabited stone house the trail starts a steep descent to the valley floor. It switchbacks down with the terminal moraine looming above, crossing the Kango Chhu on a bridge at 4260m. After a short climb through rhododendrons the trail levels out on a plateau above the Zamdo Nangi Chhu. It's then a short walk on a good trail through a cedar forest interspersed with small meadows to Limithang (4140m), a lovely camp site in a big meadow by the river. The peak of Gangchhenta towers over the campsite, even though it's quite a distance away.

Day 10: Limithang to Laya
10km, 4-5 hours

After 20 minutes of walking, the trail crosses to river left and enters a deep cedar forest, crossing many little, muddy side streams. After a while there is a stone herders hut with a sod roof; here the vegetation changes to fir trees draped with lichen.

A short but strenuous diversion is necessary to bypass a large stream that flows in from the north. Make a steep rocky descent down the side of the valley to the river at 3800m and cross to river right on a wooden cantilever bridge. A short distance later, cross back and make a stiff climb up.

It's a long walk through the heavily wooded, uninhabited valley. Descend, then cross a waterfall that flows across the trail then traverse with many small ups and downs. Near a point where you can see a single house on a ridgetop to the east, there is an inconspicuous trail junction. It's not important which one you choose: the upper one leads to the top of Laya, and the other leads to the lower part of the village.

If you take the upper trail you will cross a ridge and see the stone houses and wheat fields of Laya laid out below you with some abandoned houses and a *goemba* up above.

Gangchhenta dominates the skyline to the west of the village and from some

places you can get a glimpse of Masang Gang, 7165m. In the village centre is a community school, a hospital, archery field and the first shop since the Paro valley. You can camp in the fields below the school at 3840m. See the Central Bhutan chapter for a description of Laya and the strange cone-shaped bamboo hats Laya women wear.

Day 11: Laya to Koina
19km, 6-7 hours

Layaps are not noted for their reliability and punctuality, and the horses may arrive late. Below the village the trail drops back to the river. The trail exits the village through a *khonying* (arch chorten), then passes another chorten at Taje-kha as it descends on a muddy trail to a stream. There are a few houses near the trail, but it's mostly deep forest all the way to the river.

There is an alternative camping place on a plateau at 3590m, next to the large Togtserkhagi Chhu which flows in from the north-east. Cross the river on a wooden bridge and climb to the stone buildings of the **army camp** on the opposite side. At the army post is a wireless station and a check-post where the guide registers the names of the trekkers; you'll have to wait here until the formalities are completed. The peak of Masang Gang (7165m) is barely visible at the head of the side valley.

The route follows the Mo Chhu downstream all the way to Punakha. Beyond the army camp the trail goes uphill, crossing a few streams and making little ups and downs. About half an hour from the army post is an inconspicuous trail junction at 3340m. The route for the Snowman Trek leads uphill from here on a tiny path. The route to Gasa keeps going downstream on a muddy trail. After a while it turns a corner and goes into a side valley, goes a short distance up the valley and crosses the Bahitung Chhu at 3290m. This is the traditional lunch spot for this day of the trek.

The trail travels alongside the Mo Chhu to an overhanging rock that forms a cave, then crosses to river right at 3240m on a cantilever bridge. The canyon closes in and the trail must now make several major climbs over side ridges as it makes its way downstream. Beyond another cave formed by a large overhanging rock the first long steep climb starts, cresting at the top of a ridge at 3390m. It's a 150m descent to a clear side stream, then the trail wanders up and down near the river as it runs fast through some big cascades in a gorge. After some more ups and downs through bamboo about 100m above the river there is another serious climb to the Kohi Lapcha at 3300m. The muddy trail stays high for about half an hour until it reaches a stone staircase, where it turns into a side valley, traversing for a bit, then dropping to a large stream. Welcome to Koina (3050m), a muddy bog in the forest by the bridge. There is a single stone house with some muddy camping places scattered around. Because of the deep black mud that you must wade through and the damp, soft ground upon which you must pitch your tent, this is the worst camp on the whole trek and perhaps the most unpleasant camp in the Himalaya.

Day 12: Koina to Gasa
14km, 6-7 hours
You may think that because you are headed downstream this trek is finished, but there's another major ascent ahead to get over Bari La, which crosses a side ridge.

Cross the bridge at Koina and start up the hill. Parts of the trail are so muddy that logs have been placed on the trail to form little bridges. There are also places where the trail follows the side of a ridge and you walk gingerly across logs that dangle out into space. The muddy trail keeps going through a deep forest of firs in and out of side valleys for almost three hours to **Bari La** (3900m). There's a small rock cairn and a few prayer flags at the pass, then it's a reasonably level walk to another chorten. There are not many good places to stop along this part of the trail, so lunch today will probably be an impromptu event.

The route starts down again, sometimes steeply, through a bamboo forest to a stream. At 3080m it rounds a corner where you can

finally see Gasa Dzong on the opposite side of a large wooded side valley. The trail descends past an old chorten, then crosses a ridge into a big side valley below Gasa. It drops and crosses a large stream at 2780m, then traverses along the side of the valley to four chortens on the ridge at 2810m.

The chortens mark the southern boundary of Gasa village (2770m). The trail traverses above the Jigme Dorji National Park headquarters and the soccer and archery ground past several small tea shops. The trail leads intersects Gasa's main street, a stone-paved path that leads uphill to the dzong, school and a Basic Health Unit (BHU) and downhill to the bazaar which consists of about nine shops and a police checkpost. This bazaar is a favourite with trekkers because it is the first place on the trek where beer is available. The police post checks permits, providing a perfect excuse for a stop.

You can camp in a field near the town, or continue downhill for 1½ hours to the *tsachhu* (hot spring). Many trek itineraries schedule an extra day to laze around in the hot springs – a useful activity after the last two days of strenuous walking in the mud. See Day 2 of the Gasa Hot Spring Trek for details. If it is raining, the remainder of this trek is perfect country in which to meet leeches.

Day 13: Gasa to Damji
18km, 5-6 hours
Follow the trail generally south, passing a few houses and mani walls, as it descends to the primary branch of the Mo Chhu, which has flowed through the mountains from Lingzhi to join the other branch of the Mo Chhu that flows from Gasa. Look back for a good view of the dzong, sitting on the top of the hill. Be careful as you follow this trail: near a chorten there is a fork where a second trail leads steeply downhill to the hot spring. The trail towards Damji goes straight here.

After a long descent, cross the river at 2360m on a new cable suspension bridge high above the water. The trail starts climbing immediately on the opposite side. At 2510m there's a picnic table at a lookout, from where you can see down to the hot spring and back to a large part of yesterday's trail, although it's all in the forest. Gasa Dzong with its distinctive rounded front wall is visible behind you, glued to the valley wall and seeming to float in space.

There's a crest at 2330m where the trail turns south along the Mo Chhu (and from here downstream there is only one river known as the Mo Chhu) and then goes up and down on the side of the valley, high above the river. It descends through bamboo to a little stream, then starts climbing back again to a meadow at 2530m. Gasa Dzong and the snow peaks up towards Laya are still visible.

The trail stays high, crossing a meadow and descending a little to the small village of Gayza at 2500m. The trail then drops into a deep subtropical ravine filled with trees and ferns, crossing the Lepena Chhu on a spectacular suspension bridge high above a narrow wooded gorge at 2300m.

The trail climbs to another crest and traverses around the top of a side valley to the four houses of Gun at 2400m, then drops again and climbs back up to a chorten. Then it's a short walk to the large village of Damji (2430m), which lies in a huge side valley with an amphitheatre of rice terraces. Pass the school and traverse to the southern end of the village where there is a large cluster of houses and a little chorten at 2380m. A road from Tashithang to Damji is planned for completion in 2003.

Day 14: Damji to Tashithang
16km, 5 hours
There are a few more houses and many fields as the trail climbs to a chorten at the southern end of the village. The trail begins a long descent to the river, first winding down gently in the jungle past a few streams, then switchbacking steeply down on a rocky trail in the shadow of a huge rock. After a long descent you will cross a wooden bridge over a side stream at 1960m. There is an alternative camp site here near the banks of the river, about an hour below Damji.

The trail now makes small ups and downs close to the river, passing a big cave under a

rock. You may encounter rhesus monkeys playing alongside the river, and it is said that there are takin in this part of the valley. After a long walk you will cross a high suspension bridge over the Chaka Lumbi Chhu. Look upstream and see the monstrous boulders that this river has carried down from above. The main valley is still very closed in with sub-tropical vegetation such as wild banana trees, creepers and orchids. The trail climbs over a small ridge at 1880m, then makes a final short drop to an unfinished portion of the road at 1840m.

There is a lot of construction going on in connection with the road to Damji which may require a diversion along this stretch of trail. It should be a short walk along the roadbed to a stream. The road is already completed to a forestry office at Tashithang, a short distance south of the stream. If all goes well, vehicles will be waiting there to take you to Punakha. It's a total of 18km (a one hour drive) to Punakha Dzong; it's a good road, but the first 5km is unpaved.

Gasa Hot Spring Trek

This trek is the last part of the Laya Gasa trek in reverse. The hot springs are fun, but there is a lot of uphill climbing to get there.

Season
Being at a reasonably low elevation, this trek is possible from February to March and October to December. There are lots of leeches in the lower part of the trek, which make it particularly unpleasant during the rainy season.

Access
It's an 18km drive from Punakha to Tashithang, where the trek begins.

Day 1: Tashithang to Damji
16km, 5-6 hours
Follow Day 14 of the Laya-Gasa trek in reverse, walking up the Mo Chhu, then

Prayer Flags

You'll see prayer flags fluttering throughout Bhutan, reciting prayers as they fly in the wind (as below at Gogona Lhakhang, on the Gangte Trek). Blue, green, red, yellow and white represent the elements of water, wood, fire, earth and wood respectively. There are four different types of flag and, while they may look similar, each has a specific function (see the boxed text 'Prayer Flags' in the Eastern Bhutan chapter).

JULIA WILKINSON

Prayer Wheels

The turning of prayer wheels is a ubiquitous practice in Bhutan. The cylindrical wheels, which can be hand-held or huge powered versions, are filled with prayers which are 'said' each time the wheel is turned. Monks and devotees spin the wheels to gain additional merit and to concentrate the mind on the mantras and prayers they are reciting.

RICHARD I'ANSON

climbing steeply to the terraced rice fields of Damji (2430m).

Day 2: Damji to Gasa Tsachhu
16km, 4-5 hours

Follow Day 13 of the Laya-Gasa trek in reverse along the side of the valley, then drop to the large stream below Gasa. A trail leads north from here, following the stream directly to the hot spring at 2240m. The Jigme Dorji National Park administers the hot spring complex and offers various kinds of accommodation in a grove of large birch trees. There are some houses that can be rented, a few buildings that can be used as kitchens, a dormitory and numerous good camping places. It is a pleasant place to spend a day.

The hot springs are by the bank of the stream, below the hotel complex. There are five cement pools and a shower room, with more under construction. The water temperature is 40°C, which is comfortably warm, but not scalding.

You may encounter women selling souvenirs; it's mostly Tibetan-style jewellery made in Nepal.

Day 3: Day at Gasa Tsachhu

You can laze around in the hot springs or you can take a packed lunch and climb about two hours to Gasa village and the dzong.

Days 4-5: Gasa Tsachhu to Tashithang

Follow Days 13-14 of the Laya-Gasa Trek and drive back to Punakha or Thimphu.

Snowman Trek

The Snowman trek travels to the remote Lunana district and is said to be the most difficult trek in the world. The combination of distance, altitude, remoteness and weather makes this a tough journey. Fewer than half of the people who attempt this trek actually finish it, either because of problems with altitude or heavy snowfall on the high

passes. If you plan to take this trek be sure that you have emergency evacuation insurance (see Travel Insurance in the Facts for the Visitor chapter). If you get into Lunana and snow blocks the passes, the only way out is by helicopter, an expensive way to finish an already expensive trek. Another obstacle that often hampers this trek is bridges in remote regions that get washed away.

With the 1997 change in regulations which increased trekking fees to US$200 a night, the trek has seen a sharp decline in the number of trekkers that attempt it. Few people can afford a 23-day trek for US$4600.

Season

The Snowman trek is frequently closed because of snow, and is impossible during the winter. Because it's above the leech line, it is possible during summer. The season for this trek is generally considered to be from mid-June to mid-October.

Access

The classic snowman trek begins in Paro and follows the Jhomolhari and Laya-Gasa treks as far as Laya. You can save a few days of walking by starting in Punakha and trekking north up the Mo Chhu, following the Laya-Gasa trek in reverse.

Days 1-5: Drukgyel Dzong to Lingzhi

Follow Days 1-5 of the Jhomolhari Trek 1.

Days 6-10: Lingzhi to Laya

Follow Days 6-10 of the Laya-Gasa Trek.

Day 11: Rest Day in Laya

You should spend a day recuperating from the trek to Laya and preparing for the rest of this rigorous trek. The army post here has a radio; you will need to send a runner back here with a message in an emergency.

Day 12: Laya to Rodophu
19km, 6-7 hours

The trek leads gradually downhill to the Lunana trail junction, then makes a gradual climb to the camp through a forest of conifers, maple and rhododendron. The trail improves and becomes wider as you climb out of the river valley. The camp site is in a pasture near a small stream at an altitude of 4160m.

Day 13: Rodophu to Narethang
17km, 5-6 hours

The trail leads uphill through dwarf rhododendron bushes and a barren area with ups and downs across great boulders to **Tsomo La** (4780m). Descend through more boulders to a camp at Narethang, a yak pasture used by Laya people. It's at about 4500m on a small plateau beneath the 6395m peak of Gangla Karchung.

Day 14: Narethang to Tarina
18km, 5-6 hours

Climb to **Karchung La** (5120m), then down to glacial lakes that are the source of the Tang Chhu. Above the lakes tower the mighty peaks of Jejekangphu Gang (7300m) and Tsenda Kang (7100m). The trail descends a rough moraine, then makes a further steep descent into rhododendrons on a notoriously dreadful trail with lots of rhododendron

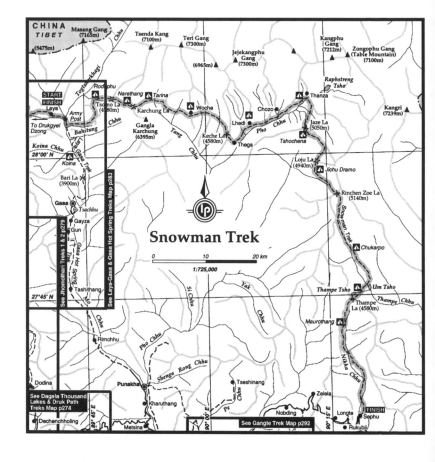

Snowman Trek

roots and slippery mud. Camp at Tarina, 4020m.

Day 15: Tarina to Woche
17km, 5 hours
The walk leads down through conifer forest, following the upper reaches of the Pho Chhu. The trail then climbs over a ridge and drops to Woche at 3940m, the first village since Gasa. The trek has now entered the Lunana region.

Day 16: Woche to Lhedi
17km, 5-6 hours
Make a gradual climb towards **Keche La** (4580m), then downhill to Thega village. The walk continues to Lhedi village (3700m), where there is another wireless station.

Day 17: Lhedi to Thanza
17km, 5-6 hours
The trail climb gradually following the main source of the Pho Chhu to Chozo village. At the small Chozo Dzong there are some lay monks. Above Chozo the valley opens as you approach Thanza village, near the foot of 7100m Zongophu Gang, which is also known as Table Mountain. Camp at Thanza, 4090m, the main village of Lunana district. At 4500m, two hours walk from Thanza, is a large glacial lake, Raphstreng Tsho, which is 105m deep. The moraine burst and created a flood that destroyed part of Punakha Dzong in 1969; it broke again in 1996. There are about 500 workers at work here using pumps and tractors to try to prevent a recurrence.

Most groups schedule a rest day at Thanza. This is as far as the Laya horses go, and it takes time to round up enough yaks for the rest of the trek.

Day 18: Thanza to Tshochena
20km, 7-8 hours
Today is a long trek. Yak drivers willing, you should start as early as possible. It's a long climb over three false summits to **Jaze La** (5050m). It's then less than an hour down to the camp site at the lake of Tshochena. You may see blue sheep during the hike. This is the first of three nights of camping above 4900m.

Day 19: Tshochena to Jichu Dramo
14km, 4-5 hours
The trail is gradual ups and downs between the snow-capped peaks and across **Loju La** (4940m). Camp at Jichu Dramo (4880m).

Day 20: Jichu Dramo to Chukarpo
18km, 5-6 hours
The trek is a climb of **Rinchen Zoe La** (5140m), the highest point on the trek. It is then a long downhill to Chukarpo, which is just above the tree line at 4950m.

Day 21: Chukarpo to Thampe Tsho
18km, 5-6 hours
It's a long, mostly downhill, walk along the river, then a climb back to Um Tsho at 4230m. In this lake Pema Lingpa found a number of religious treasures. A bit farther is a camp by the lake of Thampe Tsho.

Day 22: Thampe Tsho to Maurothang
14km, 5 hours
It's a two-hour walk to the base of **Thampe La** and then a steep climb to the pass at 4580m. The trek is then all downhill through rhododendron bushes to the yak pasture of Maurothang at 4000m. You will probably exchange your yaks for horses here to make the final walk to Sephu.

Day 23: Maurothang to Sephu
18km, 5-6 hours
The trail follows the Nikka Chhu through bamboo thickets and fields to the road at the village of Sephu at 2500m.

Gangte Trek

This is a short trek at relatively low elevations which visits several remote villages.

Season
This trek is recommended from March to May and September to November. It is especially beautiful in April, when rhododendrons are in bloom.

Access

You can start the trek from the valley floor below Gangte Goemba or from the Phuntsho Chholing Guest House at the eastern end of the Phobjikha valley.

Day 1: Gangte to Gogona
15km, 6-7 hours

The trek leaves the valley at 2830m and leads south, then west through meadows and fields. It then climbs through a mixed forest of juniper, bamboo, rhododendron and magnolia. The trail is rough and rocky and weaves through trees where pack animals have created deep muddy furrows. After crossing **Tsele La** (3440m) the trail crosses several meadows, then descends through forests to Gangak (3020m). It is then a short climb to the camp at Gogona (3100m), a beautiful hilltop site overlooking a long valley. Nearby is Gogona Lhakhang and dozens of poles with white prayer flags fluttering.

A 30 minute walk beyond Gogona is a hamlet where you may find homemade arra to buy. The women here weave blankets and speak a different dialect called *Bjop-kha* (language of the nomads).

Day 2: Gogona to Khothangkha
16km, 6-7 hours

The trail winds gently up above Gogona village, past flocks of sheep and ploughed fields. Climb into a forest of firs, oak, spruce, dwarf rhododendron, miniature azaleas, cypress and juniper. A large area of this forest was burned by a fire which was probably caused by lightning. Much of the undergrowth is daphne, the plant that is used for hand-made paper and may be identified by its yellow flowers.

A long but gradual climb leads to **Shobju La** (3410m). The trail down from the pass is rocky and muddy, weaving through the forest and criss-crossing a small stream. Above the trail is a small coal mine and the camp used by the miners. Eventually, at about 3000m, the trail meets a rough track used by tractors to collect wood from the forest. Follow the road, with a few short cuts through the woods, to a sawmill and woodcutters camp at Dolonga (2830m). Still heading down, the trail overlooks the broad Khothangkha valley and eventually reaches a clearing, Chorten Karpo, where there are four chortens dedicated to the four

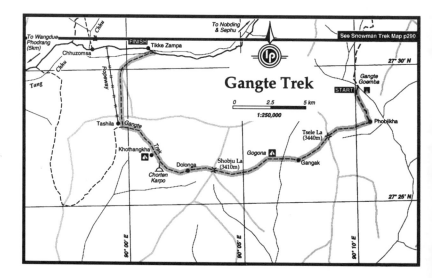

Je Khenpos who came from this area. Three of the chortens are square, in Bhutanese style, and the fourth is Nepali style.

The best camp is in this clearing at 2790m, beside a forest of large blue pines overlooking the valley and the village of Khothangkha, comprising about 60 rustic houses.

Day 3: Khothangkha to Tikke Zampa 12km, 5 hours

A short, steep climb along a well-worn path takes you to **Tashila** (2800m). This is the upper terminus of the 'cable car' that transports wood down to Chhuzomsa, 1300m below. If you send a message ahead, you can ride the cable car down, but note the warning: 'The passenger who travels by Tashila ropeway will be at their own risk'.

The walk down is through a beautiful forest, with the undergrowth changing from rhododendron and magnolia to ferns and dwarf bamboo. Experts claim that this stretch of trail is one of the finest bird-watching areas in Bhutan. Among the species found here are laughing thrush, shrike, magpie and woodpecker. The trail plunges down past steep terraced wheat fields to a cluster of houses at Wachay. The trail eventually meets the road near Tikke Zampa at 1500m. Keep your ears open for the whistles of loggers above you, which are to warn you to watch for the huge logs that they are sliding down the hillside.

A third alternative is to continue west, descending along a treeless ridge towards Wangdue Phodrang (Wangdi), crossing the Tang Chhu below the army camp east of town.

Bumthang Cultural Trek

This trek is named because the opportunities to visit villages and lhakhangs are greater than on most other treks in Bhutan. Though it is a short trek, the Bumthang trek is strenuous because it involves a 500m climb to Phephe La (3360m).

Season

This trek is usually possible from March to May and then again from September to November.

Access

It is a 3km drive up the unpaved road from Kurjey Lhakhang to Toktu Zampa at 2540m. With luck, the pack horses will be waiting and you can start walking with a minimum of delay.

Day 1: Toktu Zampa to Ngang Lhakhang 12km, 4-5 hours

It's two minutes down to a suspension bridge over a clear stream, the Duer Chhu. A carved Buddha on the rock beyond the bridge is protected by a little shrine. The trail is level as it follows the right bank of the Bumthang Chhu upstream through buckwheat fields to a government animal husbandry office. It's then a short distance to Thankabi Goemba with its distinctive yellow roof and the small village of Thankabi. See the brief description of this goemba in the Central Bhutan chapter.

The trail follows a broad ledge above the river past a 70m-long painted mani wall and a khonying with a mandala painted on the roof inside. Just beyond the archway is a trail junction. The trail to Ngang Lhakhang crosses the river on a new suspension bridge and traverses through pleasant meadows and forests of blue pine and scrub bamboo.

Follow the left bank of the Bumthang Chhu (known locally as the Chamkhar Chhu) to a small cluster of houses and turn uphill to a small old Tibetan-style chorten surrounded by prayer flags. The trail then makes a short, steep climb to a settlement of old-looking houses at 2800m. There are two water-driven prayer wheels; the water comes down an interesting sluiceway of carved wooden pipes. This is Ngang Lhakhang, the 'Swan Temple'. See the description of this interesting temple in the Bumthang section of the Central Bhutan chapter.

Alternative Route The camp at Ngang Lhakhang is small, and many guides prefer to camp at Damphay, near the Bumthang Chhu. This adds less than half an hour to the following day's walk, so it does not upset the trek schedule much. To get to Damphay, do not cross the large suspension bridge; stay on the right bank of the Bumthang Chhu. Follow the trail upstream through meadows to a second suspension bridge, just before the village of Sangsangma.

Just across that bridge you'll find a good camp next to a line of prayer flags in a meadow below a small cluster of houses. You can tell that this is a popular camping

place because of the village women selling yathra and trinkets at prices higher than in Thimphu.

This village is an excellent place to try the local Bumthang buckwheat delicacies of *khule* (pancakes) and *utta* (noodles). A small flock of black-necked cranes (see the boxed text in the Flora & Fauna section of the Facts about Bhutan chapter) winters in this area and you may see them foraging in the fields. Wild boar are common in the area and bears occasionally startle both locals and trekkers.

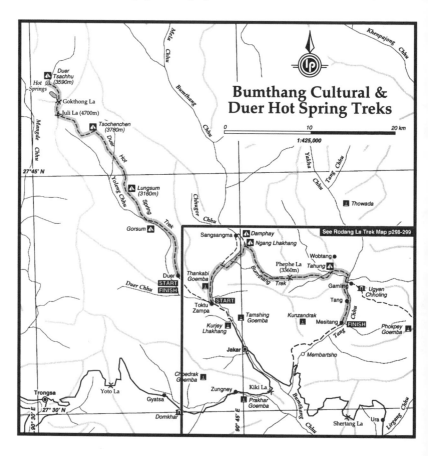

Bumthang Cultural & Duer Hot Spring Treks

Day 2: Ngang Lhakhang to Tahung
16km, 6 hours

The day's walk starts out across meadows, with a view to the valley below and several small hamlets in the hills. Fifteen minutes beyond Ngang Lhakhang the trail forks and you take the lower, smaller, more level one that leads to the right through a muddy area with rocks. There is a lot of dwarf bamboo and there are several little streams to cross.

The little trail cuts across the top of some fields, goes over a small hill and down to a stream. Soon you will be convinced that this cannot be the correct trail and you are hopelessly lost. Don't worry, but be sure that you stick with your guide or the horsemen through here because it is a narrow, indistinct trail through forests.

After crossing a stream the trail starts climbing, crossing back and forth across the stream on a series of slippery logs and stones. The forest is birch, sycamore, dwarf bamboo and lots of real bamboo, forming a cold, sunless forest. Spanish moss drapes from trunks and petrified trees, giving an eerie feel to the steep climb.

Finally the stream disappears and the climb continues in a dry gully to a rock cairn and a little stone shrine stuffed with offerings of branches and a few Nu 1 notes. Tattered prayer flags stretch across the path atop Phephe La (3360m). There is no view from the pass; it is a forested ridge with big birch and fir trees.

There is more deep forest on the opposite side; the trail leads down to a stream at 3200m, then into a side valley covered in dwarf bamboo, passing a small mani wall and a khonying chorten. Much of the walk is delightful, breaking out of the forest into broad meadows and pastures of grazing cows.

It continues through ploughed fields and wide meadows and then into a broad valley, surrounded by rounded treeless hills. Near a herder's hut the trail becomes indistinct as it crosses a meadow. To stay on track, just aim for the trees on the right side of the meadow.

The route keeps going downhill, crossing a stream to the right bank on a difficult temporary bridge formed by a small tree with some twigs sticking out. As the trail approaches the bottom of the valley, there are several side trails that lead to pastures and buckwheat fields. Take the most prominent trail, which leads downhill to a large stream and a substantial wooden bridge at 2790m.

There are several alternative camping places in this valley. Be sure you are with someone who knows where you are headed at this point. The most likely camp is uphill, behind the village of Tahung. There are other camping places on the flats beside the stream to the east of the village. There is a third possible camp on the banks of the Tang Chhu near Gamling, about 45 minutes downstream.

Day 3: Tahung to Mesitang
16km, 5-6 hours

Behind Tahung is the Australian-assisted Wobtang sheep development project. A rough road suitable only for tractors follows the right bank of the Tang Chhu from the project all the way down the valley to Tang village. The road improves between Tang and the National Highway below Membartsho. The trekking route leads downstream in meadows next to the river, sometimes on the road and sometimes on a footpath. It crosses the stream that you have been following on a road bridge and turns a corner into the main valley of the Tang Chhu at 2640m.

You can head straight back down the road from here to Mesitang, which is 2km south of Tang and 15km from the junction of the paved road near Membartsho. Vehicles will come to Mesitang to meet you. Alternatively, an interesting side trip leads to Ugyen Chholing, a 45 minute climb from the Tang Chhu valley at this point.

Side Trip to Ugyen Chholing Cross a muddy field on some logs, then across the Tang River to Gamling, a large, wealthy village noted for its yathra weaving. Walk downstream from Gamling to a stream, cross the stream and follow the trail around a farmyard. Soon it starts climbing onto a ridge, reaching four chortens and several large houses at 2760m. Ugyen Chholing Palace is on the top of the hill to the right. The complex is in the traditional Bhutanese palace design, with servants quarters to the left and right of the entrance gate and the palace itself occupying a massive building in the centre of the stone-paved courtyard. A large lhakhang forms the eastern side of the compound. There is more information about Ugyen Chholing in the Bumthang section of the Central Bhutan chapter.

It is about three hours from Ugyen Chholing to Mesitang.

Duer Hot Spring Trek

This trek is the old expedition route to Gangkhar Puensum and, with special permission, it might be possible to extend the trek to the base of the mountain itself, though this is a rough, difficult route. *Tsachhu* is dzongkha for hot spring.

Season
Snow covers the route during winter so the trek is considered open from March to April and from September to early November.

Access
To reach the starting point for this trek, drive to Kurjey Lhakhang and then 3km up an unpaved road to Toktu Zampa. It's then one more hour (5km) of rough driving to Duer village (3120m), where you start walking.

Day 1: Duer to Gorsum
18km, 6-7 hours
The route follows the valley of the Yoleng Chhu, which is famous for trout.

Day 2: Gorsum to Lungsum
12km, 5 hours
The route is through a forest of cyprus, juniper, spruce, hemlock and maple. This trail is muddy and climbs gradually to the camp site at 3160m.

Day 3: Lungsum to Tsochenchen
15km, 6-7 hours
Trek through more forest to the camp site, which is just above the tree line at 3780m.

Day 4: Tsochenchen to Duer Tsachhu
18km, 6-7 hours
The day's walk is all uphill, passing a small lake, until you finally reach Juli La (4700m), a rocky saddle with a few prayer flags and a good view of the surrounding mountains. After crossing the pass the trail descends to a lake, then climbs again to Gokthong La. The path then switchbacks steeply down through jungle to a camp near the Duer hot springs at 3590m. Along this part of the trail it may be possible to see musk deer, Himalayan bear and herds of blue sheep.

Day 5: Day at Duer Tsachhu
Take a rest day to relax in the tsachhu. There are several wooden tubs set into the ground inside a rough wooden shelter.

Day 6: Duer Tsachhu to Tsochenchen
18km, 6 hours
Return via the same route to Tsochenchen.

Day 7: Tsochenchen to Gorsum
27km, 9 hours
Follow the upward route back down the valley.

Day 8: Gorsum to Duer
18km, 6 hours
Return to the road and drive back to Jakar.

Rodang La Trek

The trek across the top of eastern Bhutan is tough and involves a tremendously long, steep descent. Though it was an important trade route before the National Highway was built, few people travel this way any more. The trek crosses the road near Lhuentse, which breaks up the continuity of the experience, but offers a chance to visit the remote dzong. The logistics are complicated and horses are often difficult to obtain for the final four days of the trek.

Season
Rodang La is subject to closure because of snow, and this trek is best planned in October and early November as well as late spring.

Access
Most people combine this trek with the Bumthang Cultural Trek and start from near Kurjey Lhakhang in the Choskhor valley. Alternatively, you can start the trek by driving up the Tang valley to Mesitang or on to Tang village itself, saving two days of walking.

Days 1-2: Toktu Zampa to Ugyen Chholing
Follow Days 1-2 of the Bumthang Cultural Trek to Ugyen Chholing (2760m).

Day 3: Ugyen Chholing to Phokpey
17km, 5-6 hours
The long climb to Rodang La takes two days. Above Ugyen Chholing the trail is rutted with the hoof prints of cattle. If it's wet, this is a very muddy, miserable, slippery climb. The trail levels out at about 2900m and meets a stream. At about 3000m the cow trails end and it becomes a small footpath through muddy fields and dwarf bamboo.

At 3400m the trail crosses a meadow with more dwarf bamboo. This is a meadow, and not a forest, because of a fire that burned a large part of the hillside. High on the opposite hill you can see the recently built Phokpey Goemba. Climb through the meadow and traverse through forest to another steep, high meadow, finally turning a corner into a side valley. The opposite side is all big firs.

The trail leads up a draw towards the head of the valley and the camp in a meadow at 3680m. This is a summer pasture and there is the frame for a house which herders cover with a plastic sheet to use as a shelter. The meadow is surrounded by forest and the ground is dotted with tiny blue alpine flowers. Once the sun goes down, the temperature plummets.

Day 4: Phokpey to Pemi
20km, 6-7 hours
The trail goes through a small notch and onto another ridge at 3700m. It traverses along the east side of the ridge, passing big rhododendrons with large leaves that curl up in the cold. Soon you will see the pass up ahead. After a long traverse at 3770m the trail begins the final climb to the pass up big stone slabs and a steep stone staircase. **Rodang La** (4160m) is about a two hour climb from camp. There's a small stone chorten here.

Once across the pass it's a steep descent of nearly 2500m to the valley floor. The descent starts on some rough rocks at the back of the ridge that the pass crosses. This is a steep descent on an unbelievably long and steep stone staircase which was built when this was the trade route between eastern and western Bhutan. This is the same near-vertical slope that the road descends on the eastern side of Thrumshing La, which is only 20km to the south.

The trail skirts just below the top of the ridge, then drops off the side on a good stone staircase. You can see the trail far below, snaking down the ridge to the east. This is a tough route for horses, and it is said that even the king walked downhill here.

Part of the route is along a vertical face and the trail is on wooden galleries that are fastened into the side of the cliff. There are a few small meadows as the trail winds its way down on a complex route through a region where sightings of ghosts and yetis have been reported. Leaving the pines and conifers, it makes a gentle descent through a forest of broad-leafed species along a ridge to the east to a big meadow called Pemi at about 3000m. After a short wander through some dwarf bamboo you reach the ruins of a house and a camp site at 2950m. This is not an ideal camping place because the water is 15 minutes down the side of a hill; go easy on the washing here. The ruined stone building was the grain store-house during the time of the first and second kings, when royal parties travelled regularly between Bumthang and Kurtoe.

Day 5: Pemi to Khaine Lhakhang
21km, 7-8 hours

From Pemi the trail tumbles into the valley of the Noyurgang Chhu. The route leads from the camp through more dwarf bamboo, then heads down a damp rock-filled gully with lots of leaves, moss and wet rocks to pick your way through.

At about 2600m the vegetation changes to ferns and rhododendrons and there is a long level stretch through the mud. It then goes down steeply again, working its way out towards the end of a side ridge and a meadow called Sang Sangbe (2300m), where a ghost is said to live. High on the hillside on the opposite side of the valley is Yamalung Goemba, hidden behind a bunch of very tall trees planted in a circle. The trail drops off the side of the ridge to a bridge over a stream at 1700m. The village of **Ungaar** is on a ledge just above the stream

and downstream is another small village named Zhobi. It's then a short walk across rice fields in the bottom of the valley to a suspension bridge over the Noyurgang Chhu at 1660m.

Cross to river left and start climbing away from the bridge through ferns and tropical jungle to the village of Bulay (1800m). It passes above the rice terraces of the village, turns a corner and climbs up a little draw. The valley below is covered with rice and little temporary shelters used by planters.

The trail makes a long climb as it heads along the valley, traversing in and out of several side valleys and passing numerous villages. Kulaypang (1930m) is a few rough houses and some corn fields. There's an inviting-looking trail that goes down and cuts across the next ridge but the correct trail, of course, goes up.

The trail passes below the settlement of Gomda (2040m). The language spoken in these villages is Kurtepa, which Dzongkha speakers cannot understand. After passing a chorten, the trail drops to cross a stream at 2000m, then climbs again to a mani wall at 2020m. Then it's a level walk past corn-

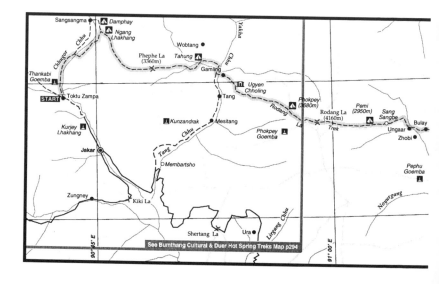

fields to the few houses of Gongdra and a Tibetan-style chorten.

Beyond Chanteme, a spread-out village with extensive corn fields, the trail crosses a stream and makes a climb to Khaine Lhakhang. Follow the cement irrigation canal for a while and then climb onto a little hillock, where the temple sits at 2010m. There are two tall cedars by this monastery and fields of soybeans surrounding it.

You can see a goemba and a village at the eastern end of the ridge on the opposite side of the river. Pephu Goemba is high above and the town below is Songme.

Day 6: Khaine Lhakhang to Tangmachu
18km, 6-7 hours

The trail goes down to a stream and back up to a BHU and community school in Gorsam. It then goes in and out of more side valleys and climbs to 2130m. It's level for about 15 minutes and then starts climbing gently through trees. You can see a glimpse of the road at the bottom of the Kuri Chhu valley.

The Tibetan-style Umling Mani at 2180m is at the corner between the Noyurgang Chhu and the Kuri Chhu valleys. It was built by a lama from Tibet and marks the boundary between the two *gewogs*. Here the route turns north up the Kuri Chhu.

The next stretch of trail traverses through four large side valleys, descending to a stream and climbing to the next ridge. The trail emerges from the first valley at Gumbar Gang (2120m). After a long, almost level, stretch the trail goes down and then up again to a chorten on Zerim La (1940m).

The route contours down to the head of a valley at 1840m, where there is a little chorten and a prayer wheel, then immediately starts climbing back up through chir pines to 1890m. It then traverses grassy slopes in the main valley to another ridge and several herders huts.

There's one more big side valley to traverse. Descend to a mani wall and pass the fields and houses of Menjabi, a pretty village with large white Bhutanese houses. Cross the stream at 1540m, then start a long, hot climb on a grassy slope to five chortens on **Tage La** (1760m). Just south-east of the pass is the

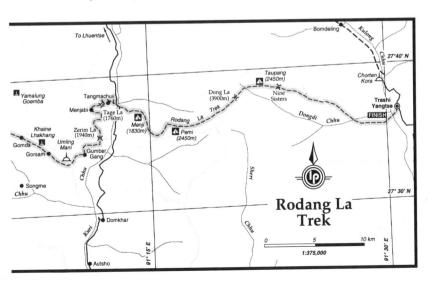

Khaine Lhakhang

Some people believe that the remote Khaine Lhakhang is one of the 108 temples built by King Songtsen Gampo in 659. Three small statues from here are said to have flown of their own accord to Kanchosum Lhakhang in Bumthang, which is said to have been built at the same time.

The primary statue is a 2.5m high Sakya-muni figure. A statue of Karmapa is on his right and Shabdrung Rimpoche is above him on the left. There are also smaller statues of Milarepa and Guru Rimpoche. The main protective deity is a ferocious god named *Taxan*, who is depicted riding on a horse. A two day festival is celebrated here in mid-November.

Tangmachu High School, where 400 students study on the top of this windswept ridge. It may be possible to camp near the school or, better yet, have vehicles waiting to drive you down to the valley.

It's 8km down the dirt road to the paved road, and 13km from the junction on the road along the Kuri Chhu to Lhuentse. The best way to arrange the logistics here is to arrange for a vehicle to meet you at Tangmachu, take you to Lhuentse to see the impressive dzong and then drop you off at the bottom of the hill to finish the last stage of the trek. The vehicle can then drive on to Trashi Yangtse to pick you up four days later.

Day 7: Tangmachu to Menji
16km, 4-5 hours

From the bridge at 1140m, below Tang-machu, the trek starts gradually up through rice terraces and corn fields to Chusa. It then becomes a steep haul up a treeless slope, though the path is beautifully scented with wild mint, lemon grass and artemisia. Camp is at 1830m near Menji village, beside the Darchu Pang Lhakhang. The lhakhang's well-kept garden is full of flowers – marigolds, geraniums, dahlias and nasturtiums – and has a vegetable patch of Indian tomatoes and huge cucumbers. There are banana trees, too, and dozens of long-tailed birds in the trees.

Day 8: Menji to Pemi
20km, 6-7 hours

Continue uphill through the thick, humid forest packed with dense foliage of ferns and creepers and a constant whistle of cicadas. The trail is narrow, steep and rutted. Climb steadily for two hours to a ridgetop meadow, then plunge back into the forest to reach the camp at Pemi (2450m) on a narrow ridgetop clearing with a view out to a forested gorge and mountains. There's not a village or house in view, though Menji villagers use this area as a summer pasture.

Day 9: Pemi to Taupang
21km, 7-8 hours

The trail stays in damp cold forest, with oc-casional summer pastures with bamboo herders shelters. The climb goes on and on, but the area is a botanist's delight, with shrubs of every kind, pungent with a sweet fermented smell, thick with humus. Continue up to **Dong La** (3900m), where there are good high mountain views and a few prayer flags on a pile of rocks.

On the opposite side of the pass the trail traverses nine passes, nicknamed the Nine Sisters of Dong La. Finally descend steeply through thick evergreen forests on a trail strewn with rocks, logs and slippery leaves to a ridgetop meadow. The last part of the trek starts easily enough, down through a pasture, but then becomes increasingly rocky and muddy as it nears the Dongdi Chhu. The only way across the river is on a tree trunk balanced on rocks.

The path on the other side is even mud-dier and rockier; parts of it are layered with a makeshift washboard-style log path. It's more like jungle than forest here, with ferns and creepers above and the river roaring nearby. The camp is at Taupang (2450m), a clearing in the forest with a cowherds wooden shelter.

Day 10: Taupang to Trashi Yangtse
24km, 8-9 hours

The path through the forest beside the river is damp and muddy. You will encounter huge ferns, red-berried palms and occasional leeches. The forest is alive with birds and monkeys. Two hours of sloshing through mud or springing from stone to log to stone brings you to the village of Shukshing, a cluster of bamboo huts on the hillside, surrounded by corn fields, banana trees and grazing cows.

The trail stays on the ridge on the northern side of the valley working its way gradually downhill to Yangtse. The dzong suddenly appears at the end of the valley on a hilltop above the river. The trek ends at the dzong; cross the Kulong Chhu and climb up to the road to meet the vehicles, or walk 3km into Chorten Kora.

Samtengang Winter Trek

This is a low-altitude trek north of Punakha. Like Dagala, this route sees few trekkers.

The following is a very brief description of the trek.

Season

Low elevation makes this trek possible throughout the winter.

Day 1: Punakha to Limukha
12km, 4 hours

Cross the footbridge over the Pho Chhu from Punakha Dzong and walk to Shengana. The trek begins with a gradual climb through a forest of chir pine to Limukha.

Day 2: Limukha to Chhungsakha
14km, 5 hours

The trail travels through rhododendron and oak forests to Chhungsakha.

Day 4: Chhungsakha to Samtengang
13km, 5 hours

Trek through the village of Sha to Samtengang.

Day 5: Samtengang to Chhuzomsa
15km, 5-6 hours

The trail leads downhill to the roadhead at Chhuzomsa to meet transport to Wangdue Phodrang.

Language

The official language of Bhutan is Dzongkha, which is similar to Tibetan, from which it is derived. It is, however, sufficiently different that Tibetans cannot understand it. Dzongkha is written in a slightly modified version of Tibetan script that was developed in the 1960s by the third king. English is the medium of instruction in schools, so most educated people speak it fluently.

There are English signboards, books and menus throughout the kingdom. Road signs and government documents are all written in both English and Dzongkha. The national newspaper, *Kuensel*, is published in three languages: English, Dzongkha and Nepali. In the monastic schools Choekey, the classical Tibetan language, is taught.

In the eastern part of Bhutan most people speak *Sharchop* (language of the east), which is totally different from Dzongkha. In the south of the kingdom, most people speak Nepali.

Because many parts of Bhutan are very isolated, there are numerous languages and dialects; some of these language varieties are so different that people from different parts of the country can't understand each other. *Bumthangkha* is a dialect of the Bumthang region, and most of the minority groups have their own language. Among the languages in Bhutan's tower of Babel are *Khengkha* from Zhemgang, *Kurtoep* from Lhuentse, *Mangdip* from Trongsa and *Bumthap* from Bumthang.

The Dzongkha Development Commission has established a system of transliterating Dzongkha script into Roman characters without the use of any accent marks. This does not duplicate the exact pronunciation, but provides a readable and uncomplicated system of transliteration.

There are numerous sounds in Dzongkha that have no English equivalent, and these can only be approximated in a Romanised system. Pronunciation guidelines for a few of these are listed below.

Pronunciation
Vowels
a	as in 'father'
e	as the 'ey' in 'hey'
i	as in 'hit'
o	as in 'go'
u	as in 'put'

Consonants
Most consonants in Dzongkha are pronounced as in English. The letter 'h' in the combinations **dh**, **gh**, **kh**, **ph** and **th** indicates that they are 'aspirated', ie released with a slight puff of air – listen to the two 'p' sounds in the word 'pip'; the initial 'p' is aspirated, the second is not. Don't worry too much if you have trouble pronouncing the aspirated consonants – you should still be understood if you treat them as though the 'h' were not there. Note that the **ch** and **sh** combinations are not aspirated.

ch(h)	as in 'church'
dh	as in 'dear'
gh	as in 'gear'
kh	as the 'c' in 'car'
ph	as in 'pin'
sh	as in 'ship'
th	aspirated 't' as in 'Thailand', never as in 'those'
tr	pronounced more or less as 't'
ng	as in 'sing'; practise using the 'ng' sound at the beginning of a word, eg *Ngawang* (a name)

Greetings & Civilities
Hello.	*kuzo zangpo la*
Goodbye.	*legzhembe joen* (person leaving)
	legzhembe zhug (person staying)
Good luck.	*trashi delek*
Thank you.	*kadinchhey*
Yes.	*ing, yoe*
No.	*me*
Maybe.	*im wong*

Small Talk

Hello, how are you?	*chhoe gadebe yoe?*
I'm fine.	*nga leshom bera yoe*
Where are you going?	*chhoe gati jou mo?*
What's your name?	*chhoe ming gachi mo?*
My name is ...	*ngi ming ... ing*
Where are you from?	*chhoe gatile mo?*
I'm from ...	*nga ... le ing*
I'm staying at ...	*nga ... doep ing*
It's cold today.	*dari jam me*
It's raining.	*chhaep chap de*
I know.	*nga she*
I don't know.	*nga mi she*
May I take your photo?	*chhoegi pachi tabgey me?*
That's OK.	*di tubay*

Directions

What time does the bus leave?	*bus chhutshoe gadem chikka jow mo?*
I want to stop here.	*nga na doegobe*
Is it near?	*bolokha ing na?*
Is it far?	*thag ring sa ing na?*
Go straight ahead.	*thrang de song*

left	*yoen*
right	*yae*
in front of	*donkha*
next to	*bolokha*
behind	*jabkha*
opposite	*dongo, dongte*
north	*jang*
south	*lho*
east	*sha*
west	*nub*

Around Town

The word *khang* means building; in many cases it's only necessary to add the kind of building.

Where is a ...	*... gati mo*
bank	*nguekhang*
book shop	*pekhang*
cinema	*lognyen*
hospital	*menkhang*
market	*throm*
monastery	*goenpa*

police station	*gagpai makhang*
post office	*dremkhang*
public telephone	*mimang juethrim*
shop	*tshongkhang*
temple	*lhakhang*
toilet	*chabsang*

Where is the toilet?	*chabsang gati ing na?*
How far is the ... ?	*... gaday chi thag ringsa mo?*
I want to see ...	*nga ... tagobe*
I'm looking for ...	*nga ... tau ing*
What time does it open?	*chhutshoe gadem chilu go chheu mo?*
What time does it close?	*chhutshoe gadem chilu godam mo?*
Is it still open?	*datoya chhidi ong ga?*
I want to change some money.	*Nga tiru sogobe*

Food Words & Phrases

Where is a ... ?	*... gati mo?*
local bar	*chhangkhang*
restaurant	*zakhang*

I don't eat meat.	*nga sha miza*
This is too spicy.	*di kha tsha du*
I don't like food with chillies.	*nga zhego emadang chikha miga*
Is the food good?	*zhego zhim mega?*
What is this?	*di gachi mo?*
This is delicious.	*di zhim mey*
Please give me a cup of tea.	*ngalu ja phop gang nang*
Do you have food now?	*chhoe dato to zawai gang ing na?*
It's enough.	*digi lam me*

beer (local)	*singchhang*
whisky (local)	*arra*
tea	*ja*
water	*chhu*
hot water	*chhu tshatom*
cold water	*chhu khoem*
boiled water	*chhu koekew*
hot (spicy)	*khatshalulu*
tasty	*zhimtoto*

cabbage	*bandakopi*
cauliflower	*metokopi*

chicken (meat)	*ja sha*
chilli	*ema*
cooked vegetable	*tshoem*
corn (maize)	*gedza*
egg	*gongdo*
food	*zshego, to*
meat	*sha*
mushroom	*shamu*
mustard	*peka*
potatoes	*kewa*
radish	*laphu*
rice (cooked)	*to*
turnips	*ando*
vegetable	*tshose*

Shopping

Bargaining is not a Bhutanese tradition, but if you are buying Bhutanese handicrafts at the weekend market, you might be able to lower the price a bit.

How much is it?	*dilu gadechi mo?*
That's too much.	*gong drape/gong bom me*
I'll give you no more than ...	*ngagi ... anim chile troe mitshug be*
What's your best price?	*chhoe ben gadechi labni mo?*

Trekking Words & Phrases

Which trail goes to ...?	*... jo sai lam gati mo?*
Is the trail steep?	*lam di zatra ing na?*
Where is my tent?	*ngi gu di gati ing na?*
What's the name of this village?	*Ani uegi ming gachi sew mo?*

house	*chhim*
steep uphill	*gyen gatra*
steep downhill	*gyen zatra*
tired	*wu dugchhi*
cold (weather)	*sitrag-tra*
warm (weather)	*drotogto*

Other Useful Words

cheap	*khe tog to*
expensive	*gong bom*
big	*boam*
small	*chhungku*
clean	*tshang tog to*

dirty	*kham log sisi*
good	*legzhim*
not good	*legzhim men du*
enough	*toobey, lame*
happy	*gatokto*
heavy	*gig*

this	*di*
that	*phi di*
mine	*ngi gi*
yours	*chhoe gi*
his, hers	*kho gi, mo gi*

here	*na, nalu*
there	*pha, phalu*
where	*gati*
which	*gadi*

Family

mother	*ama*
father	*apa*
daughter	*bum*
son	*bu*
elder sister	*azhim, au*
younger sister	*num, sim*
elder brother	*phogem, acho*
younger brother	*nuchu*
friend	*totshang, chharo*

In the Country

bird	*ja*
chicken	*bja*
cow	*ba*
dog	*rochi, chi*
horse	*ta*
pig	*phap*
water buffalo	*mahe*
yak (male/female)	*yak/bji*

barley	*na*
buckwheat	*gyare*
corn (maize)	*gyeza*
millet	*moemja*
field rice	*bja*
husked rice	*chhum*
wheat	*kaa*

alpine hut	*bjopai bja*
alpine pasture	*tsamjo*
bridge	*zam*

hills	ri
lake	tsho
mountain	gangri
mountain pass	la
mule track	ta lam
plain or meador	thang
prayer flag	dashi
prayer stone	do koe
river	chhu, tsangchhu
trail	lam, kanglam
village	yul

Time & Dates

What time is it (now)?	chhutshoe gademchi mo?
It's five o'clock.	chhutshoe nga
today	dari
tomorrow	nangpa
day after tomorrow	nangpa nangtshe
yesterday	khatsha
sometime	retshe kab
morning	droba
afternoon	cheru
day	nyim, za
night	numo

Days of the Week

Sunday	za dawa
Monday	za migma
Tuesday	za lhakpa
Wednesday	za phurbu
Thursday	za pasang
Friday	za penpa
Saturday	za nyim

Numbers

1	chi	11	chuchi
2	nyi	12	chunyi
3	sum	13	chusum
4	zshi	14	chuzshi
5	nga	15	chenga
6	dru	16	chudru
7	duen	17	chubduen
8	gye	18	chobgye
9	gu	19	chugu
10	chutham	20	nyishu khechi

25	nyishu tsanga
30	sumchu
40	zshipchu/khenyi
50	ngabchu
60	drugchu/khesum
70	duenchu
80	gyebchu
90	gubchu
100	chigja/khenga
1000	chigton/tongthra chi
10,000	thrichi
100,000	bumchi/bum
one million	sayachi

Health & Emergencies

I'm ill.	nga naw me
I feel nauseous.	nga chug ni zum beu me
I feel weak.	nga thang chhep me
I keep vomiting.	nga khale chugtirang doep me
I feel dizzy.	nga guyu khorme
I'm having trouble breathing.	nga bung tangni gi kangel yoe

LANGUAGE

Glossary

anim – Buddhist nun
anim goemba – nunnery
arra – home-made spirit distilled from barley, wheat or rice
ashi – title for a queen or lady of aristocracy

bangchung – round bamboo basket with a tight-fitting cover
bodhisattva – a being who has the capacity of gaining Buddhahood in this life but who refuses it in order to be reincarnated in the world to help other beings
Bon – ancient pre-Buddhist animistic religion of Tibet; its practitioners are called Bon-po
Brokpa – minority group in eastern Bhutan
bukhari – wood-burning stove
bumpa – vase, usually used to contain holy water in *goembas*

cairn – pile of stones marking a trail or pass
carom – a game similar to snooker or pool played on a small wooden board using checkers instead of billiard balls
cham – dance
chang – north
chappati – flat unleavened bread
chhang – beer made from rice, corn or millet, pronounced as 'chung'
chhu – river, also water
chilip – foreigner
chimi – member of National Assembly
Choekey – classical language of religion
chorten – round stone Buddhist monument, often containing relics
chugo – hard dried yak cheese

daal – lentil soup
dasho – honorary title conferred by the king
deb raja – British term for the *desi* during the period 1652-1907
desi – secular ruler of Bhutan
dharma – Buddhist teachings
dharma raja – British name for the Shabdrung during period from 1652 to 1907
dochey – inner courtyard of a *dzong*
doma – beetel nut, also known by its Indian name, paan
dorji – a stylised thunderbolt used in rituals; '*vajra*' in sanskrit
dratshang – central monk body
driglam chhoesum – code of etiquette
driglam namzha – traditional values and etiquette
drubda – meditation centre for monks
Druk Gyalpo – the King of Bhutan
Drukpa Kagyu – the official religion of Bhutan, a school of tantric Mahayana Buddhism
drungkhag – sub-district
dukhang – room for ceremonies and communal meals in a *goemba*
dungpa – head of a sub-district
dzong – fort-monastery
dzongda – district administrator
Dzongkha – national language of Bhutan

dzongkhag – district
dzongpen – old term for lord of the *dzong*

gakpa – police
gangri – snow mountain
gewog – block, the lowest administrative level
gho – traditional dress for men
global positioning system (GPS) – a device that calculates position and elevation by reading and decoding signals from satellites
goemba – a Mahayana Buddhist monastery
goenkhang – chapel devoted to protective and terrifying deities, usually *Mahakala*
gorikha – porch of a *lhakhang*, literally 'mouth of the door'
gup – elected leader of a village
Guru Rimpoche – the common name of Padmasambhava, the founder of *Mahayana* Buddhism
gyalpo – ruler or king

himal – Sanskrit word for mountain

Je Khenpo – Chief Abbot of Bhutan

kabney – scarf worn over the shoulder on formal occasions
khandroma – female celestial beings; '*dakini*' in Sanskrit
khonying – archway chorten
kora – circumambulation
Kuensel – Bhutan's national newspaper

la – mountain pass
lam – path or road
lama – Mahayana Buddhist teacher or priest
lha – god or deity
lhakhang – temple, literally 'god house'
lhentshog – commission
lho – south
losar – Bhutanese and Tibetan new year
lu – serpent deities, called naga in Sanskrit
lyonpo – minister

Mahakala – Yeshey Goenpo, the guardian god of Bhutan, who manifests himself as a raven
Mahayana – school of Buddhism, literally 'great vehicle'

Mandala – cosmic diagram; '*kyilkhor*' in *Dzongkha*
mani stone – stone carved with the Buddhist mantra '*om maani padme hum*'
mantra – prayer formula or chant
momos – steamed or fried dumplings
moraine – ridge of rocks that a glacier pushed up along its edges (a medial moraine) or at its foot (a terminal moraine)

naktshang – temple dedicated to warlord or protective deity, literally 'place of vows'
ngultrum – unit of Bhutanese currency
nup – west
Nyingma – lineage of Himalayan Buddhism; its practitioners are Nyingmapa

om maani padme hum – sacred Buddhist mantra, roughly translates as 'hail to the jewel in the lotus'
outreach clinic – health posts in remote villages

penlop – regional governor, literally lord-teacher
phajo – priest
prayer flag – long strips of cloth printed with prayers that are 'said' whenever the flag flaps in the wind
prayer wheel – cylindrical wheel inscribed with, and containing, prayers

rabdey – district monk body
rachu – shoulder cloth worn by women on formal occasions
rigney – name used for a school for traditional studies
rimpoche – reincarnate lama, usually the abbot of a *goemba*
river left – the left bank of a river when facing downstream
river right – the right bank of a river when facing downstream

Sakyamuni – another name for Gautama Buddha
Shabdrung – title of the reincarnations of the Shabdrung Ngawang Namgyal
shar – east
shedra – Buddhist college

shing – wood
shunglam – highway
sonam – good luck
stupa – hemispherical Buddhist structure from which the *chorten* evolved

terma – texts and artefacts hidden by *Guru Rimpoche*
terton – discoverer of *terma*
thang – plain
thangka – painted or embroidered religious picture
thondrol – huge *thangka* unfurled on special occasions, literally 'liberation on sight'
thos – a heap of stones representing the kings of the four directions
thukpa – noodles, often served in a soup
torma – ritual cake made of *tsampa*, butter and sugar
trulku – a reincarnation; the spiritual head of a *goemba*

Tsa-Wa-Sum – Government, Country and King
tsachhu – hot spring
tsampa – barley flour, a staple food in hill villages
tseri – the practice of shifting cultivation
tshamkhang – small meditation quarters
tsho – lake
Tshogdu – National Assembly

utse – the central tower that houses the *lhakhang* in a *dzong*

yak – main beast of burden and form of cattle above 3000m elevation
yathra – strips of woven woollen cloth
yeti – the abominable snowman

Zangto Pelri – the celestial abode or heaven of *Guru Rimpoche*

Index

MAPS

TEXT

Map references are in **bold** type.

BOXED TEXT

LONELY PLANET PHRASEBOOKS

Nepali phrasebook — Listen for the gems

Ethiopian Amharic phrasebook — Speak your own words

Latin American Spanish phrasebook — Ask your own questions

Ukrainian phrasebook — Master of your own image

Greek phrasebook

Vietnamese phrasebook

Building bridges,
Breaking barriers,
Beyond babble-on

- handy pocket-sized books
- easy to understand Pronunciation chapter
- clear and comprehensive Grammar chapter
- romanisation alongside script to allow ease of pronunciation
- script throughout so users can point to phrases
- extensive vocabulary sections, words and phrases for every situation
- full of cultural information and tips for the traveller

'...vital for a real DIY spirit and attitude in language learning' – Backpacker

'the phrasebooks have good cultural backgrounders and offer solid advice for challenging situations in remote locations' – San Francisco Examiner

'...they are unbeatable for their coverage of the world's more obscure languages' – The Geographical Magazine

---

Arabic (Egyptian)
Arabic (Moroccan)
Australia
  Australian English, Aboriginal and Torres Strait languages
Baltic States
  Estonian, Latvian, Lithuanian
Bengali
Brazilian
Burmese
Cantonese
Central Asia
Central Europe
  Czech, French, German, Hungarian, Italian and Slovak
Eastern Europe
  Bulgarian, Czech, Hungarian, Polish, Romanian and Slovak
Ethiopian (Amharic)
Fijian
French
German
Greek

Hindi/Urdu
Indonesian
Italian
Japanese
Korean
Lao
Latin American Spanish
Malay
Mandarin
Mediterranean Europe
  Albanian, Croatian, Greek, Italian, Macedonian, Maltese, Serbian and Slovene
Mongolian
Nepali
Papua New Guinea
Pilipino (Tagalog)
Quechua
Russian
Scandinavian Europe
  Danish, Finnish, Icelandic, Norwegian and Swedish

South-East Asia
  Burmese, Indonesian, Khmer, Lao, Malay, Tagalog (Pilipino), Thai and Vietnamese
Spanish (Castilian)
  Basque, Catalan and Galician
Sri Lanka
Swahili
Thai
Thai Hill Tribes
Tibetan
Turkish
Ukrainian
USA
  US English, Vernacular, Native American languages and Hawaiian
Vietnamese
Western Europe
  Basque, Catalan, Dutch, French, German, Irish, Italian, Portuguese, Scottish Gaelic, Spanish (Castilian) and Welsh

LONELY PLANET JOURNEYS

JOURNEYS is a unique collection of travel writing – published by the company that understands travel better than anyone else. It is a series for anyone who has ever experienced – or dreamed of – the magical moment when they encountered a strange culture or saw a place for the first time. They are tales to read while you're planning a trip, while you're on the road or while you're in an armchair, in front of a fire.

JOURNEYS books catch the spirit of a place, illuminate a culture, recount a crazy adventure, or introduce a fascinating way of life. They always entertain, and always enrich the experience of travel.

IN RAJASTHAN
Royina Grewal

Indian writer Royina Grewal's travels in Rajasthan take her from tribal villages to flamboyant palaces. Along the way she encounters a multitude of characters: snake charmers, holy men, nomads, astrologers, dispossessed princes, reformed bandits . . . And as she draws out the rarely told stories of farmers' wives, militant maharanis and ambitious schoolgirls, the author skilfully charts the changing place of women in contemporary India. The result is a splendidly evocative mosaic of life in India's most colourful state.

Royina Grewal lives on a farm in Rajasthan, where she and her husband are working to evolve minimal-impact methods of farming. Royina has published two monographs about the need for cultural conservation and development planning. She is also the author of *Sacred Virgin*, a travel narrative about her journey along the Narmada River, which was published to wide acclaim.

SHOPPING FOR BUDDHAS
Jeff Greenwald

Here in this distant, exotic land, we were compelled to raise the art of shopping to an experience that was, on the one hand, almost Zen – and, on the other hand, tinged with desperation like shopping at Macy's or Bloomingdale's during a one-day-only White Sale.

Shopping for Buddhas is Jeff Greenwald's story of his obsessive search for the perfect Buddha statue. In the backstreets of Kathmandu, he discovers more than he bargained for . . . and his souvenir-hunting turns into an ironic metaphor for the clash between spiritual riches and material greed. Politics, religion and serious shopping collide in this witty account of an enlightening visit to Nepal.

Jeff Greenwald is also the author of *Mister Raja's Neighborhood* and *The Size of the World*. His reflections on travel, science and the global community have appeared in the *Los Angeles Times*, the *Washington Post*, *Wired* and a range of other publications. Jeff lives in Oakland, California.

LONELY PLANET TRAVEL ATLASES

Lonely Planet has long been famous for the number and quality of its guidebook maps. Now we've gone one step further and produced a handy companion series: Lonely Planet travel atlases – maps of a country produced in book form.

Unlike other maps, which look good but lead travellers astray, our travel atlases have been researched on the road by Lonely Planet's experienced team of writers. All details are carefully checked to ensure the atlas corresponds with the equivalent Lonely Planet guidebook.

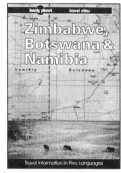

The handy atlas format means no holes, wrinkles, torn sections or constant folding and unfolding. These atlases can survive long periods on the road, unlike cumbersome fold-out maps. The comprehensive index ensures easy reference.

*   full-colour throughout
*   maps researched and checked by Lonely Planet authors
*   place names correspond with Lonely Planet guidebooks
    – no confusing spelling differences
*   legend and travelling information in English, French, German, Japanese and Spanish
*   size: 230 x 160 mm

Available now:
Chile & Easter Island • Egypt • India & Bangladesh • Israel & the Palestinian Territories •Jordan, Syria & Lebanon • Kenya • Laos • Portugal • South Africa, Lesotho & Swaziland • Thailand • Turkey • Vietnam • Zimbabwe, Botswana & Namibia

---

LONELY PLANET TV SERIES & VIDEOS

Lonely Planet travel guides have been brought to life on television screens around the world. Like our guides, the programmes are based on the joy of independent travel, and look honestly at some of the most exciting, picturesque and frustrating places in the world. Each show is presented by one of three travellers from Australia, England or the USA and combines an innovative mixture of video, Super-8 film, atmospheric soundscapes and original music.

Videos of each episode – containing additional footage not shown on television – are available from good book and video shops, but the availability of individual videos varies with regional screening schedules.

Video destinations include: Alaska • American Rockies • Australia – The South-East • Baja California & the Copper Canyon • Brazil • Central Asia • Chile & Easter Island • Corsica, Sicily & Sardinia – The Mediterranean Islands • East Africa (Tanzania & Zanzibar) • Ecuador & the Galapagos Islands • Greenland & Iceland • Indonesia • Israel & the Sinai Desert • Jamaica • Japan • La Ruta Maya • Morocco • New York • North India • Pacific Islands (Fiji, Solomon Islands & Vanuatu) • South India • South West China • Turkey • Vietnam • West Africa • Zimbabwe, Botswana & Namibia

The Lonely Planet TV series is produced by:
Pilot Productions
The Old Studio
18 Middle Row
London W10 5AT UK

For video availability and ordering information contact your nearest Lonely Planet office.

Music from the TV series is available on CD & cassette.

PLANET TALK

Lonely Planet's FREE quarterly newsletter

We love hearing from you and think you'd like to hear from us.

When...*is the right time to see reindeer in Finland?*
Where...*can you hear the best palm-wine music in Ghana?*
How...*do you get from Asunción to Areguá by steam train?*
What...*is the best way to see India?*

For the answer to these and many other questions read PLANET TALK.

Every issue is packed with up-to-date travel news and advice including:

* a letter from Lonely Planet co-founders Tony and Maureen Wheeler
* go behind the scenes on the road with a Lonely Planet author
* feature article on an important and topical travel issue
* a selection of recent letters from travellers
* details on forthcoming Lonely Planet promotions
* complete list of Lonely Planet products

To join our mailing list contact any Lonely Planet office.

Also available: Lonely Planet T-shirts. 100% heavyweight cotton.

LONELY PLANET ONLINE

Get the latest travel information before you leave or while you're on the road

Whether you've just begun planning your next trip, or you're chasing down specific info on currency regulations or visa requirements, check out Lonely Planet Online for up-to-the minute travel information.

As well as travel profiles of your favourite destinations (including maps and photos), you'll find current reports from our researchers and other travellers, updates on health and visas, travel advisories, and discussion of the ecological and political issues you need to be aware of as you travel.

There's also an online travellers' forum where you can share your experience of life on the road, meet travel companions and ask other travellers for their recommendations and advice. We also have plenty of links to other online sites useful to independent travellers.

And of course we have a complete and up-to-date list of all Lonely Planet travel products including guides, phrasebooks, atlases, Journeys and videos and a simple online ordering facility if you can't find the book you want elsewhere.

www.lonelyplanet.com
or
AOL keyword: lp

LONELY PLANET PRODUCTS

Lonely Planet is known worldwide for publishing practical, reliable and no-nonsense travel information in our guides and on our web site. The Lonely Planet list covers just about every accessible part of the world. Currently there are nine series: *travel guides, shoestring guides, walking guides, city guides, phrasebooks, audio packs, travel atlases, Journeys – a unique collection of travel writing and Pisces Books - diving and snorkeling guides.*

EUROPE

Amsterdam • Austria • Baltic States phrasebook • Berlin • Britain • Canary Islands• Central Europe on a shoestring • Central Europe phrasebook • Czech & Slovak Republics • Denmark • Dublin • Eastern Europe on a shoestring • Eastern Europe phrasebook • Estonia, Latvia & Lithuania • Finland • France • French phrasebook • Germany • German phrasebook • Greece • Greek phrasebook • Hungary • Iceland, Greenland & the Faroe Islands • Ireland • Italian phrasebook • Italy • Lisbon • London • Mediterranean Europe on a shoestring • Mediterranean Europe phrasebook • Paris • Poland • Portugal • Portugal travel atlas • Prague • Romania & Moldova • Russia, Ukraine & Belarus • Russian phrasebook • Scandinavian & Baltic Europe on a shoestring • Scandinavian Europe phrasebook • Slovenia • Spain • Spanish phrasebook • St Petersburg • Switzerland •Trekking in Spain • Ukrainian phrasebook • Vienna • Walking in Britain • Walking in Italy • Walking in Switzerland • Western Europe on a shoestring • Western Europe phrasebook

Travel Literature: The Olive Grove: Travels in Greece • On the Shores of the Mediterranean • Round Ireland in Low Gear

NORTH AMERICA

Alaska • Backpacking in Alaska • Baja California • California & Nevada • Canada • Chicago • Deep South• Florida • Hawaii • Honolulu • Los Angeles • Mexico • Mexico City • Miami • New England • New Orleans • New York City • New York, New Jersey & Pennsylvania • Pacific Northwest USA • Rocky Mountain States • San Francisco • Seattle • Southwest USA • USA phrasebook • Washington, DC & the Capital Region

Travel Literature: Drive thru America

CENTRAL AMERICA & THE CARIBBEAN

•Bahamas and Turks & Caicos •Bermuda •Central America on a shoestring • Costa Rica • Cuba •Eastern Caribbean •Guatemala, Belize & Yucatán: La Ruta Maya • Jamaica

Travel Literature Green Dreams: Travels in Central America

SOUTH AMERICA

Argentina, Uruguay & Paraguay • Bolivia • Brazil • Brazilian phrasebook • Buenos Aires • Chile & Easter Island • Chile & Easter Island travel atlas • Colombia Ecuador & the Galápagos Islands • Latin American Spanish phrasebook • Peru • Quechua phrasebook • Rio de Janeiro • South America on a shoestring • Trekking in the Patagonian Andes • Venezuela

Travel Literature: Full Circle: A South American Journey

ISLANDS OF THE INDIAN OCEAN

Madagascar & Comoros • Maldives• Mauritius, Réunion & Seychelles

AFRICA

Africa - the South • Africa on a shoestring • Arabic (Moroccan) phrasebook • Cairo • Cape Town • Central Africa • East Africa • Egypt • Egypt travel atlas• Ethiopian (Amharic) phrasebook • Kenya • Kenya travel atlas • Malawi, Mozambique & Zambia • Morocco • North Africa • South Africa, Lesotho & Swaziland • South Africa, Lesotho & Swaziland travel atlas • Swahili phrasebook • Tunisia • Trekking in East Africa • West Africa • Zimbabwe, Botswana & Namibia • Zimbabwe, Botswana & Namibia travel atlas

Travel Literature: Mali Blues • The Rainbird: A Central African Journey • Songs to an African Sunset: A Zimbabwean Story

MAIL ORDER

Lonely Planet products are distributed worldwide. They are also available by mail order from Lonely Planet, so if you have difficulty finding a title please write to us. North American and South American residents should write to 150 Linden St, Oakland CA 94607, USA; European and African residents should write to 10a Spring Place, London NW5 3BH; and residents of other countries to PO Box 617, Hawthorn, Victoria 3122, Australia.

NORTH-EAST ASIA

Beijing • Cantonese phrasebook • China • Hong Kong • Hong Kong, Macau & Guangzhou • Japan • Japanese phrasebook • Japanese audio pack • Korea • Korean phrasebook • Kyoto • Mandarin phrasebook • Mongolia • Mongolian phrasebook • North-East Asia on a shoestring • Seoul • Taiwan • Tibet • Tibet phrasebook • Tokyo
Travel Literature: Lost Japan

MIDDLE EAST & CENTRAL ASIA

Arab Gulf States • Arabic (Egyptian) phrasebook • Central Asia • Central Asia phrasebook • Iran • Israel & the Palestinian Territories • Israel & the Palestinian Territories travel atlas • Istanbul • Jerusalem • Jordan & Syria • Jordan, Syria & Lebanon travel atlas • Lebanon • Middle East • Turkey • Turkish phrasebook • Turkey travel atlas • Yemen
Travel Literature: The Gates of Damascus • Kingdom of the Film Stars: Journey into Jordan

ALSO AVAILABLE:

Brief Encounters • Travel with Children • Traveller's Tales

INDIAN SUBCONTINENT

Bangladesh • Bengali phrasebook • Bhutan • Delhi • Goa • Hindi/Urdu phrasebook • India • India & Bangladesh travel atlas • Indian Himalaya • Karakoram Highway • Nepal • Nepali phrasebook • Pakistan • Rajasthan • Sri Lanka • Sri Lanka phrasebook • Trekking in the Indian Himalaya • Trekking in the Karakoram & Hindukush • Trekking in the Nepal Himalaya
Travel Literature: In Rajasthan • Shopping for Buddhas • A Season in Heaven • A Short Walk in the Hindu Kush • Slowly Down the Ganges

SOUTH-EAST ASIA

Bali & Lombok • Bangkok • Burmese phrasebook • Cambodia • Ho Chi Minh City • Indonesia • Indonesian phrasebook • Indonesian audio pack • Indonesia's Eastern Islands • Jakarta • Java • Laos • Lao phrasebook • Laos travel atlas • Malay phrasebook • Malaysia, Singapore & Brunei • Myanmar (Burma) • Philippines • Pilipino phrasebook • Singapore • South-East Asia on a shoestring • South-East Asia phrasebook • South-West China • Thailand • Thailand's Islands & Beaches • Thailand travel atlas • Thai phrasebook • Thai audio pack • Thai Hill Tribes phrasebook • Vietnam • Vietnamese phrasebook • Vietnam travel atlas

AUSTRALIA & THE PACIFIC

Australia • Australian phrasebook • Bushwalking in Australia • Bushwalking in Papua New Guinea • Fiji • Fijian phrasebook • Islands of Australia's Great Barrier Reef • Melbourne • Micronesia • New Caledonia • New South Wales • New Zealand • Northern Territory • Outback Australia • Papua New Guinea • Papua New Guinea phrasebook • Queensland • Rarotonga & the Cook Islands • Samoa • Solomon Islands • South Australia • Sydney • Tahiti & French Polynesia • Tasmania • Tonga • Tramping in New Zealand • Vanuatu • Victoria • Western Australia
Travel Literature: Islands in the Clouds • Sean & David's Long Drive

ANTARCTICA

Antarctica

THE LONELY PLANET STORY

Lonely Planet published its first book in 1973 in response to the numerous 'How did you do it?' questions Maureen and Tony Wheeler were asked after driving, busing, hitching, sailing and railing their way from England to Australia.

Written at a kitchen table and hand collated, trimmed and stapled, *Across Asia on the Cheap* became an instant local bestseller, inspiring thoughts of another book.

Eighteen months in South-East Asia resulted in their second guide, *South-East Asia on a shoestring*, which they put together in a backstreet Chinese hotel in Singapore in 1975. The 'yellow bible', as it quickly became known to backpackers around the world, soon became *the* guide to the region. It has sold well over half a million copies and is now in its 9th edition, still retaining its familiar yellow cover.

Today there are over 350 titles, including travel guides, walking guides, language kits & phrasebooks, travel atlases and travel literature. The company is the largest independent travel publisher in the world. Although Lonely Planet initially specialised in guides to Asia, today there are few corners of the globe that have not been covered.

The emphasis continues to be on travel for independent travellers. Tony and Maureen still travel for several months of each year and play an active part in the writing, updating and quality control of Lonely Planet's guides.

They have been joined by over 80 authors and 200 staff at our offices in Melbourne (Australia), Oakland (USA), London (UK) and Paris (France). Travellers themselves also make a valuable contribution to the guides through the feedback we receive in thousands of letters each year and on our web site.

The people at Lonely Planet strongly believe that travellers can make a positive contribution to the countries they visit, both through their appreciation of the countries' culture, wildlife and natural features, and through the money they spend. In addition, the company makes a direct contribution to the countries and regions it covers. Since 1986 a percentage of the income from each book has been donated to ventures such as famine relief in Africa; aid projects in India; agricultural projects in Central America; Greenpeace's efforts to halt French nuclear testing in the Pacific; and Amnesty International.

'I hope we send people out with the right attitude about travel. You realise when you travel that there are so many different perspectives about the world, so we hope these books will make people more interested in what they see. Guidebooks can't really guide people. All you can do is point them in the right direction.'

– Tony Wheeler

LONELY PLANET PUBLICATIONS

Australia
PO Box 617, Hawthorn 3122, Victoria
tel: (03) 9819 1877 fax: (03) 9819 6459
e-mail: talk2us@lonelyplanet.com.au

USA
150 Linden St
Oakland, CA 94607
tel: (510) 893 8555 TOLL FREE: 800 275-8555
fax: (510) 893 8572
e-mail: info@lonelyplanet.com

UK
10a Spring Place,
London NW5 3BH
tel: (0171) 428 4800 fax: (0171) 428 4828
e-mail: go@lonelyplanet.co.uk

France:
71 bis rue du Cardinal Lemoine, 75005 Paris
tel: 01 44 32 06 20 fax: 01 46 34 72 55
e-mail: bip@lonelyplanet.fr

World Wide Web: http://www.lonelyplanet.com
or *AOL keyword: lp*